# Security–Aware Systems Applications and Software Development Methods

Khaled M. Khan
*Qatar University, Qatar*

| Managing Director: | Lindsay Johnston |
| Senior Editorial Director: | Heather A. Probst |
| Book Production Manager: | Sean Woznicki |
| Development Manager: | Joel Gamon |
| Acquisitions Editor: | Erika Gallagher |
| Typesetter: | Jennifer Romanchak |
| Cover Design: | Nick Newcomer, Lisandro Gonzalez |

Published in the United States of America by
Information Science Reference (an imprint of IGI Global)
701 E. Chocolate Avenue
Hershey PA 17033
Tel: 717-533-8845
Fax: 717-533-8661
E-mail: cust@igi-global.com
Web site: http://www.igi-global.com

Library of Congress Cataloging-in-Publication Data

Security-aware systems applications and software development methods / Khaled M. Khan, editor.
    p. cm.
 Includes bibliographical references and index.
 ISBN 978-1-4666-1580-9 (hardcover) -- ISBN 978-1-4666-1581-6 (ebook) -- ISBN 978-1-4666-1582-3 (print & perpetual access) 1. Computer networks--Security measures. 2. Computer software--Development. 3. Computer security. I. Khan, Khaled M., 1959-
 TK5105.59.S43924 2012
 005.8--dc23
                                    2012002105


British Cataloguing in Publication Data
A Cataloguing in Publication record for this book is available from the British Library.

The views expressed in this book are those of the authors, but not necessarily of the publisher.

# Editorial Advisory Board

# Associate Editors

# Table of Contents

**Section 3**
**Vulnerability Detection**

**Section 4**
**Protection Mechanisms**

**Section 5**
**Tools for Security-Aware Development**

**Section 6**
**Secure Software Education and Training**

# Detailed Table of Contents

## Section 1
## Secure Software Development Process

    *Torstein Nicolaysen, NTNU, Norway*
    *Richard Sassoon, NTNU, Norway*
    *Maria B. Line, SINTEF ICT, Norway*
    *Martin Gilje Jaatun, SINTEF ICT, Norway*

In this article, the authors contrast the results of a series of interviews with agile software development organizations with a case study of a distributed agile development effort, focusing on how information security is taken care of in an agile context. The interviews indicate that small and medium-sized agile software development organizations do not use any particular methodology to achieve security goals, even when their software is web-facing and potential targets of attack. This case study confirms that even in cases where security is an articulated requirement, and where security design is fed as input to the implementation team, there is no guarantee that the end result meets the security objectives. The authors contend that security must be built as an intrinsic software property and emphasize the need for security awareness throughout the whole software development lifecycle. This paper suggests two extensions to agile methodologies that may contribute to ensuring focus on security during the complete lifecycle.

    *Aderemi O. Adeniji, University of North Carolina at Charlotte, USA*
    *Seok-Won Lee, University of North Carolina at Charlotte, USA*

Software Assurance is the planned and systematic set of activities that ensures software processes and products conform to requirements while standards and procedures in a manner that builds trusted systems and secure software. While absolute security may not yet be possible, procedures and practices exist to promote assurance in the software lifecycle. In this paper, the authors present a framework and step-wise approach towards achieving and optimizing assurance by infusing security knowledge, techniques, and methodologies into each phase of the Software Development Lifecycle (SDLC).

## Chapter 3

*George O. M. Yee, Carleton University, Canada*

The growth of electronic services (e-services) has resulted in large amounts of personal information in the hands of service organizations like banks, insurance companies, and online retailers. This has led to the realization that such information must be protected, not only to comply with privacy regulations but also and more importantly, to attract clients. One important dimension of this goal is to design e-services that protect privacy. In this paper, the author proposes a design approach that incorporates privacy risk analysis of UML diagrams to minimize privacy risks in the final design. The approach iterates between the risk analysis and design modifications to eliminate the risks until a design is obtained that is close to being risk free.

## Section 2
## Security Requirements Analysis and Modeling

## Chapter 4

*Joseph Barjis, Delft University of Technology, The Netherlands*

Security requirements must be tackled early in software design and embedded in corresponding business process models. As a blueprint for software design, business process models complemented with security requirements will prevent many security breaches. To accomplish secure business process modeling, the underlying method must adhere to certain capabilities and capture actions, actor roles, and interactions. The resultant models should lend themselves to automatic analysis (simulation) to ensure captured security requirements are correctly aligned with the process flow. Thus, the tradeoff between the level of security and business performance can be studied before actual software design. Since unauthorized actions cause security breaches, the software the system's social setting could be a cradle for defining security requirements. Security requirements can be identified based on the roles, authorities, and obligations of the social actors using the system. This paper introduces a method for security embedded business process modeling. The proposed method draws on two well-tested theoretical foundations—enterprise ontology and organizational semiotics.

## Chapter 5

*Thuong Doan, University of Connecticut, USA*
*Steven Demurjian, University of Connecticut, USA*
*Laurent Michel, University of Connecticut, USA*
*Solomon Berhe, University of Connecticut, USA*

Access control models are often an orthogonal activity when designing, implementing, and deploying software applications. Role-based access control (RBAC) which targets privileges based on responsibilities within an application and mandatory access control (MAC) that emphasizes the protection of information via security tags are two dominant approaches in this regard. The integration of access control into software modeling and analysis is often loose and significantly lacking, particularly when security is such a high-priority concern in applications. This paper presents an approach to integrate RBAC and MAC into use-case, class, and sequence diagrams of the unified modeling language (UML), providing a cohesive approach to secure software modeling that elevates security to a first-class citizen in the process. To insure that a UML design with security does not violate RBAC or MAC requirements, design-time analysis checks security constraints whenever a new UML element is added or an existing UML element is modified, while post-design analysis checks security constraints across the entire design for conflicts and inconsistencies. These access control extensions and security analyses have been prototyped within a UML tool.

## Chapter 6

*Nancy R. Mead, Carnegie Mellon University, USA*

The premise of this paper is that pilot case studies in security requirements engineering provide both benefits and challenges to the underlying research, education, and technology transition effort. Over the past four years we have worked with seven development groups in five organizations in the process of refining and transitioning the Security Quality Requirements Engineering (SQUARE) and SQUARE-Lite methods into practice. These experiences have provided the opportunity to step back and assess the use of pilots in conjunction with student projects to support method refinement and technology transition. Although SQUARE and SQUARE-Lite are concerned with security requirements, the benefits and challenges that have been observed would apply to many security research and technology transition efforts. We itemize and justify these benefits and challenges and discuss their practical relevance and application to ensuring adequate information assurance protection.

## Chapter 7

*Armstrong Nhlabatsi, The Open University, UK*

*Bashar Nuseibeh, Lero, Ireland & The Open University, UK*

*Yijun Yu, The Open University, UK*

Long-lived software systems often undergo evolution over an extended period. Evolution of these systems is inevitable as they need to continue to satisfy changing business needs, new regulations and standards, and introduction of novel technologies. Such evolution may involve changes that add, remove, or modify features; or that migrate the system from one operating platform to another. These changes may result in requirements that were satisfied in a previous release of a system not being satisfied in subsequent versions. When evolutionary changes violate security requirements, a system may be left vulnerable to attacks. In this paper we review current approaches to security requirements engineering and conclude that they lack explicit support for managing the effects of software evolution. We then suggest that a cross fertilisation of the areas of software evolution and security engineering would address the problem of maintaining compliance to security requirements of software systems as they evolve.

## Section 3
## Vulnerability Detection

## Chapter 8

*Hossain Shahriar, Queen's University, Canada*

*Mohammad Zulkernine, Queen's University, Canada*

Buffer overflow (BOF) is a well-known, and one of the worst and oldest, vulnerabilities in programs. BOF attacks overwrite data buffers and introduce wide ranges of attacks like execution of arbitrary injected code. Many approaches are applied to mitigate buffer overflow vulnerabilities; however, mitigating BOF vulnerabilities is a perennial task as these vulnerabilities elude the mitigation efforts and appear in the operational programs at run-time. Monitoring is a popular approach for detecting BOF attacks during program execution, and it can prevent or send warnings to take actions for avoiding the consequences of the exploitations. Currently, there is no detailed classification of the proposed monitoring approaches to understand their common characteristics, objectives, and limitations. In this paper, the authors classify runtime BOF attack monitoring and prevention approaches based on seven major characteristics. Finally, these approaches are compared for attack detection coverage based on a set of BOF attack types. The classification will enable researchers and practitioners to select an appropriate BOF monitoring approach or provide guidelines to build a new one.

## Chapter 9

*Huning Dai, Columbia University, USA*

*Christian Murphy, Columbia University, USA*

*Gail Kaiser, Columbia University, USA*

Many software security vulnerabilities only reveal themselves under certain conditions, that is, particular configurations and inputs together with a certain runtime environment. One approach to detecting these vulnerabilities is fuzz testing. However, typical fuzz testing makes no guarantees regarding the syntactic and semantic validity of the input, or of how much of the input space will be explored. To address these problems, the authors present a new testing methodology called Configuration Fuzzing. Configuration Fuzzing is a technique whereby the configuration of the running application is mutated at certain execution points to check for vulnerabilities that only arise in certain conditions. As the application runs in the deployment environment, this testing technique continuously fuzzes the configuration and checks "security invariants" that, if violated, indicate vulnerability. This paper discusses the approach and introduces a prototype framework called ConFu (CONfiguration FUzzing testing framework) for implementation. Additionally, the results of case studies that demonstrate the approach's feasibility are presented along with performance evaluations.

## Section 4
## Protection Mechanisms

## Chapter 10

*San-Tsai Sun, University of British Columbia, Canada*

*Konstantin Beznosov, University of British Columbia, Canada*

This paper presents an approach for retrofitting existing Web applications with run-time protection against known, as well as unseen, SQL injection attacks (SQLIAs) without the involvement of application developers. The precision of the approach is also enhanced with a method for reducing the rate of false positives in the SQLIA detection logic, via runtime discovery of the developers' intention for individual SQL statements made by Web applications. The proposed approach is implemented in the form of protection mechanisms for J2EE, ASP.NET, and ASP applications. Named SQLPrevent, these mechanisms intercept HTTP requests and SQL statements, mark and track parameter values originating from HTTP requests, and perform SQLIA detection and prevention on the intercepted SQL statements.

The AMNESIA testbed is extended to contain false-positive testing traces, and is used to evaluate SQL-Prevent. In our experiments, SQLPrevent produced no false positives or false negatives, and imposed a maximum 3.6% performance overhead with 30 milliseconds response time for the tested applications.

Yves Younan, Katholieke Universiteit Leuven, Belgium
Wouter Joosen, Katholieke Universiteit Leuven, Belgium
Frank Piessens, Katholieke Universiteit Leuven, Belgium
Hans Van den Eynden, Katholieke Universiteit Leuven, Belgium

Memory managers are an important part of modern language and are used to dynamically allocate memory. Many managers exist; however, two major types can be identified: manual memory allocators and garbage collectors. In the case of manual memory allocators, the programmer must manually release memory back to the system when it is no longer needed. Problems can occur when a programmer forgets to release it, releases it twice or uses freed memory. These problems are solved in garbage collectors. However, both manual memory allocators and garbage collectors store management information. This paper describes several vulnerabilities for C and C++ and how these could be remedied by modifying the management information of a representative manual memory allocator and garbage collector. Additionally, the authors present an approach that, when applied to memory managers, will protect against these attack vectors.

Sergey Bratus, Dartmouth College, USA
James Oakley, Dartmouth College, USA
Ashwin Ramaswamy, Dartmouth College, USA
Sean W. Smith, Dartmouth College, USA
Michael E. Locasto, George Mason University, USA

The mechanics of hot patching (the process of upgrading a program while it executes) remain understudied, even though it offers capabilities that act as practical benefits for both consumer and mission-critical systems. A reliable hot patching procedure would serve particularly well by reducing the downtime necessary for critical functionality or security upgrades. However, hot patching also carries the risk—real or perceived—of leaving the system in an inconsistent state, which leads many owners to forgo its benefits as too risky; for systems where availability is critical, this decision may result in leaving systems un-patched and vulnerable. In this paper, the authors present a novel method for hot patching ELF binaries that supports synchronized global data and code updates, and reasoning about the results of applying the hot patch. In this regard, the Patch Object format was developed to encode patches as a special type of ELF re-locatable object file. The authors then built a tool, Katana, which automatically creates these patch objects as a by-product of the standard source build process. Katana also allows an end-user to apply the Patch Objects to a running process.

Yun Bai, University of Western Sydney, Australia

With the ever increasing demand for the Web-based applications over the Internet, the related security issue has become a great concern. Web document security has been studied by many researchers and various security mechanisms have been proposed. The aim of this paper is to investigate the security issue of the XML documents. We discuss a protection mechanism and investigate a formal approach to ensure the security of Web-based XML documents. Our approach starts by introducing a high level language to specify an XML document and its protection authorizations. We also discuss and investigate the syntax and semantics of the language. The flexible and powerful access control specification can effectively protect the documents from unauthorized attempts.

## Section 5
## Tools for Security-Aware Development

### Chapter 14

*Khaled M. Khan, Qatar University, Qatar*
*Jun Han, Swinburne University of Technology, Australia*

This paper presents a tool for the integration of security-aware services based applications that is constructed on the principles of security characterization of individual software services. The tool uses the technique of reasoning between the ensured security properties of the services and the security requirements of the user's system. Rather than reporting the research outcomes, in this paper the authors describe the architecture and capabilities of the tool for secure software integration. The main objective of this paper is to show that an automatic tool support could assist the process of security-aware service based software integration.

### Chapter 15

*Shamal Faily, University of Oxford, UK*
*Ivan Fléchais, University of Oxford, UK*

Understanding how to better elicit, specify, and manage requirements for secure and usable software systems is a key challenge in security software engineering, however, there lacks tool-support for specifying and managing the voluminous amounts of data the associated analysis yields. Without these tools, the subjectivity of analysis may increase as design activities progress. This paper describes CAIRIS (Computer Aided Integration of Requirements and Information Security), a step toward tool-support for usable secure requirements engineering. CAIRIS not only manages the elements associated with task, requirements, and risk analysis, it also supports subsequent analysis using novel approaches for analysing and visualising security and usability. The authors illustrate an application of CAIRIS by describing how it was used to support requirements analysis in a critical infrastructure case study.

## Section 6
## Secure Software Education and Training

### Chapter 16

*J. J. Simpson, System Concepts, LLC, USA*
*M. J. Simpson, System Concepts, LLC, USA*
*B. Endicott-Popovsky, University of Washington, USA*
*V. Popovsky, University of Idaho, USA*

This article establishes a context for secure information systems development as well as a set of models used to develop and apply a secure software production pedagogy. A generic system model is presented to support the system context development, and to provide a framework for discussing security relationships that exist between and among information systems and their applications. An asset protection model is tailored to provide a conceptual ontology for secure information system topics, and a stable logical framework that is independent of specific organizations, technologies, and their associated changes. This asset protection model provides a unique focus for each of the three primary professional communities associated with the development and operation of secure information systems. In this paper, a secure adaptive response model is discussed to provide an analytical tool to assess risk associated with the development and deployment of secure information systems, and to use as a security metric. A pedagogical model for information assurance curriculum development is then established in the context and terms of the developed secure information system models. The relevance of secure coding techniques to the production of secure systems, architectures, and organizational operations is also discussed.

**Chapter 17**

    *Nancy R. Mead, Carnegie Mellon University, USA*

    *Julia H. Allen, Carnegie Mellon University, USA*

    *Mark Ardis, Stevens Institute of Technology, USA*

    *Thomas B. Hilburn, Embry-Riddle Aeronautical University, USA*

    *Andrew J. Kornecki, Embry-Riddle Aeronautical University, USA*

    *Rick Linger, Carnegie Mellon University, USA*

    *James McDonald, Monmouth University, USA*

Modern society is deeply and irreversibly dependent on software systems of remarkable scope and complexity in areas that are essential for preserving this way of life. The security and correct functioning of these systems are vital. Recognizing these realities, the U. S. Department of Homeland Security (DHS) National Cyber Security Division (NCSD) enlisted the resources of the Software Engineering Institute at Carnegie Mellon University to develop a curriculum for a Master of Software Assurance degree program and define transition strategies for implementation. In this article, the authors present an overview of the Master of Software Assurance curriculum project, including its history, student prerequisites and outcomes, a core body of knowledge, and curriculum architecture from which to create such a degree program. The authors also provide suggestions for implementing a Master of Software Assurance program.

**Chapter 18**

    *Frédéric Girard, Henri Tudor Public Research Center, Luxembourg*

    *Bertrand Meunier, Henri Tudor Public Research Center, Luxembourg*

    *Duan Hua, Henri Tudor Public Research Center, Luxembourg*

    *Eric Dubois, Henri Tudor Public Research Center, Luxembourg*

In Luxembourg, like in many other countries, information security has become a central issue for private companies and public organizations. Today, information is the main asset of a company for its business and, at the same time, regulations are imposing more and more rules regarding its management. As a consequence, in Luxembourg, a clear need has emerged regarding the development of new learning trajectory fulfilling the requirements of the new job profile associated with a Chief Security Officer. This need was relayed by the national professional security association which asked for the development of a new education program targeting professional people engaged in a lifelong learning trajectory. The paper reports on the rigorous and scientific participatory approach for producing the adequate learning program meeting requirements elicited from the professional association members. The authors present the skills card that has been elaborated for capturing these requirements and the program, which has been built together with the University of Luxembourg for matching these requirements. This program proposes a holistic approach to information security management by including organization, human and technical security risks within the context of regulations and norms.

# Preface

## ISSUES AND CHALLENGES IN SECURITY-AWARE SOFTWARE DEVELOPMENT

### Introduction

This is the first collection of the *Advances in Engineering Secure Software* series. This book addresses the paradigm of security-aware software development which is increasingly becoming an important area of software engineering, and steadily gaining solid ground as the computing technologies evolve and new security threats emerge. The paradigm deals with the problem of development duality between constructing a functional software system, and at the same time creating a secure system; that is, security concerns are integrated with the analysis and design of the systems functionality during the software development process. In this practice, security is considered as an integral part in all phases of software development. The engineering of secure software systems emphasizes security from a software engineering perspective, and deals with technical, as well as managerial aspects of software security. The process includes all aspects of software security in the development, deployment, and management processes of software systems. The "Build Security In" initiative by Homeland Security essentially advocates for secure software engineering that would provide adequate practices, tools, guidelines, rules, principles, and other resources that software development stakeholder can use to build security into software (Homeland security).

In this book, we use *security-aware software development* and *secure software engineering* interchangeably. The process of security-aware software development has two distinct but related objectives: *software assurance* and *security assurance* of the software. Various definitions of these are available in literature. In the context of this book, the former focuses more on an operational software that is free from defects, reliable, and provides a level of confidence. Software assurance includes the development process that ensures reliable functions and execution of software products as expected. Whereas, security assurance guarantees that security requirements of the software are adequately met and software can withstand security attacks. These two objectives are claimed to be achieved only when software continues to be operational correctly even under attacks. To achieve these, we need to address security throughout the entire lifecycle of the software development process.

In an another view point (Goertzel et al., 2008), a secure software must exhibit three properties: dependability, trustworthiness, and survivability. Dependability refers to the notion of software assurance, that is, the software executes correctly under attack or even can run on a malicious host. Software is trustworthy if it contains little vulnerability, or no malicious logic. Survivability is the ability of software to recover as quickly as possible with negligible damage from attacks. In this perspective, secure software must provide justifiable confidence that it is free of vulnerabilities, executes as expected, does not compromise any of its required security properties, and can be trusted to continue executing under attacks.

Security-aware software development is not a single task that would produce secure software products; rather, it involves corporate policies, entire software life cycle, development culture of team members, budgeting, scheduling, etc. It may affect the way software is developed, the procedures are used, and the practices are adopted. It requires organizations to define or modify their existing development process in order to tailor towards security-aware development. Merely adopting security aspects into the traditional development process may not be very useful unless an evaluation and monitoring of the effectiveness of the new process is carried out.

## Focus Areas

The conventional approach of bolting-in security functions on the top of software product after the implementation of software is definitely not a good practice. It is often argued that security of software has two binary values, either secure or not secure; and a software could only be secure by implementing security functions such as cryptography, firewalls, access control mechanisms etc. However, this view of better access control and cryptographic protocols and firewalls would keep a software secure does not hold anymore. Security functions such as cryptography or firewalls alone cannot solve the problem of software security. In contrast, security vulnerabilities in the software cause most of the security problems, and vulnerabilities are only present in bad software. Security functions such as encryptions, access control cannot change bad software into a good one. It is stated rightly in (Viega & McGraw, 2001) that bad software is the main reason for every computer security problem and malicious attacks. Thus, the main goal of security-aware software development is how to design and build good software. This leads us to identify the following focus areas that security-aware software development should include:

- A software development process that is well defined, and integrates the security issues from the early phases of development.
- Sound requirements analysis and modeling techniques that support and address security requirements along with the functional requirements as opposed to modeling security in isolation
- Tools and techniques to detect vulnerabilities and monitor attacks at the systems functional level.
- Development of adequate protections against the identified vulnerabilities and attack scenarios
- Availability of supporting tools to aid the security requirements modeling, testing, and secure integration of software, and
- Establishment of adequate training and practices for security-aware software development.

We discuss each of these briefly in the following sections.

## Secure Software Development Process

In order to ensure good software production, there is a need for the establishment of a sound foundation of knowledge and capabilities in the software development process. We need a secure software development process that begins early with the analysis and modeling of functional and security requirements, identification of vulnerabilities, planning for protection, and finally designing the software for security.

The development process should include required activities, methods, tools, and procedures to ensure that the software product resulted of the process has necessary assurances in terms of operational and security objectives of the software.

Failing to recognize the importance of security aspects up front may cause many security problems and could be overlooked and left for post-development solutions. Secure software can be produced by integrating security strategies, designs, and procedures into each phase of the development lifecycle. Traditionally, security requirements in the software have often been considered as an afterthought, and as a consequence, security is delayed to the end of the development.

The idea of integrating security requirements and objectives from the early stages of the software development process began in late 1990s. In 2001, the US President's then special advisor for cyberspace security pointed out it clearly that members of IT Industry must build information security into their products at the point of development, and not treat security as an afterthought (Ghosh et al., 2001). The need for security-aware software was important and urgent that the concern was raised at the highest level of the US administration. By not addressing security along with the systems functionality at an earlier development stage, software engineers consequently may end up with bad software (Viega & McGraw, 2001). The Software Engineering Institute's (SEI) CERT program, and Team Software Process (TSP) (Humphrey, 2000) initiatives launched a joint effort called TSP-Secure to develop secure software. Main objective of this effort is to develop software that ensures quality and security. This process has typical tasks such as identifying security risks, eliciting and defining security requirements, secure design, secure code reviews, fuzz testing etc. The Office of Homeland Security also initiated the approach of "Build Security In" in mid 2000s. The International Secure Software Engineering Council (ISSECO), founded in 2008, focuses on the production of secure software, and its goal is to establish a secure computing. The challenge is how to fit the 'security aspects' into the 'functional aspects' of the software development process. Can the existing development methodologies be mixed with the rigid and formal processes associated with software security, and how?

## Security Requirements Analysis And Modeling

Security requirements engineering deals with the protection of assets from potential attacks that may cause the software dis-functional (Haley et al. 2008). The current approaches have limited capability for identifying and modeling security requirements of a software system at the beginning of the development process. Security requirements analysis after the completion of a software system has created a negative effect on ensuring a secure system. Security requirements need to be analyzed along with the systems functional requirements at the early stages of the development process. Security requirements cannot be analyzed in isolation from the functional requirements of the system. There is a need for a balance between the conventional way of doing security requirements analysis and the iteration-centric, feedback-driven systems functional requirements.

There are considerable research works done in this direction. To represent multilevel access control (MAC) and role based access control (RBAC), UML notations have been used in (Shin & Ahn, 2000) and (Ray et al., 2003) rather than extending the UML notations. In contrast, UMLsec proposed in (Jurjens, 2002) is an extension of UML. It allows software engineers to perform security analysis of the system and verify if the model satisfies security requirements of a functionality. It also focuses on MAC of message in sequence/state diagrams. Another work reported in (Alghathbar & Wijesekera, 2003) proposes a framework called AuthUML for addressing security in use cases. The main idea is that the software engineer can specify a list of functionalities, and the possible security issues of each of the functionalities.

Other approaches to analysing and modeling security requirements include KAOS (van Lamsweerde 2004), Secure Tropos (Mouratidis et al. 2003; Giorgini et al. 2005; Mouratidis et al. 2006), and Secure i*(Liu et al. 2003). KAOS is used for reasoning about confidentiality requirements of a software system (de Landtsheer and van Lamsweerde 2005). Secure Tropos is used to model security concerns of a system such as security constraints, trust issues, and delegation of permission. Secure i* analyses security requirements by analyzing the relationships between various system stakeholders and potential attackers. SecureUML proposed in (Lodderstedt et al. 2002), an another extension of UML, is used to model access control policies and how the policies could be integrated into the software development.

The approach to elicit, specify and analyze security requirements proposed in (Haley et al. 2008) addresses both systems requirements and security requirements in the development process. It uses functional requirements with security constraints in a security engineering perspective. The approach in abuse frames (Lin et al. 2003) is used to analyze security requirements to determine security vulnerabilities. It is based on the notion of an anti-requirement -the requirement of a malicious user that can subvert the systems security requirement.

The process of understanding and modeling threats and security concerns at the atomic functional level helps drive the analysis and design of the software towards more robust secure systems. This early analysis of security requirements helps find potential security holes at the design level rather than wait after the implementation is complete. This practice of identifying security design flaws from the start will not only ensure design for security, it will also safe significant resources typically needed for post development patching. Addressing the post-development security design flaws requires a major upgrade and patching effort to minimize the resulting security problems which are usually too expensive. This approach definitely calls for a concerted efforts from software engineers and security experts to work together during the development process. They should strive together to mitigate the identified security problems at the analysis and design level before coding.

## Detecting Vulnerabilities and Attacks

Another important issue in secure software development needs attention, that is, identifying as well as predicting attack vulnerabilities in software design. One of the pre requisite for secure software is the guarantee of absence of vulnerabilities in the software. Vulnerabilities can be introduced in the software at any point in the software development process. Vulnerabilities are exploited by any entity to launch attacks. Most common code-level vulnerabilities include buffer overflow, format string bugs, SQL injection, cross site scripting, and cross site request forgery. These vulnerabilities are directly exploitable by attackers. A vulnerable software can be exploited at runtime by providing specially crafted data to overflow the buffer of the program, or SQL injection attack.. Buffer overflow (BOF) is one of the worst and oldest vulnerabilities in software. It allows attackers to overflow data buffers in order to execute arbitrary code. A vulnerable program can be exploited by specially crafted inputs to overflow data buffers in order to execute malicious code or execute denial of service attacks by the attacker. In SQL injection attacks, a malicious entity may bypass systems authentication, change privileges, launch a denial-of-service attack, or run remote commands to install malicious software in the application. To address buffer overflow vulnerabilities, various approaches are proposed such as static analysis, testing, and fixing of vulnerable code. Static analysis is an approach to address this. It is the examination of code in order to identify patterns that indicate potential design errors and/or security problems. The technique is a very useful tool in detecting vulnerable code in programs. More severe form of buffer overflow vulnerability attacks might not be identified until the program is operational. One of the main objectives of security-aware software development is to reduce vulnerabilities as much as possible, and improve protections to potential attacks in the software.

## Software Protection

There is a need for "programmatic" protection techniques to address security problems related to software. These may include language based approach, better memory management, efficient, hot and static patching, or logic based reasoning techniques. Programmers could use secure coding practices such as avoiding coding errors, the awareness of bugs, guarding variables from exploitations etc. Developing supportive tools for secure integration and testing software is also essential to aid the protection of software. Defensive coding practices require training of developers and modification of the legacy applications to assure the correctness of validation routines and completeness of the coverage for all sources of input. Adequate training and good software security practices can help ensure that a software is secure.

## Education and Training

The awareness, caution, intention, and adherence are the important elements that need to be integrated in training and practices for secure software development. It is important that awareness of security is reflected in every phases of the process. There is a strong demand for skilled professionals who can build security from the ground up. The IEEE Computer Society (IEEE-CS) and Association for Computing Machinery (ACM) have recently recognized the Master of Software Assurance (MSwA) Reference Curriculum for a master's program in software assurance (http://www.cert.org/mswa/). This recognition sends signals to the educational community that software assurance is an important part in computing education.

## Challenges Ahead

To achieve the goals of security software development, several challenges need to be addressed.

- There is an urgent need for closed collaborations between security experts and software engineers during all phases of the development process. Security personnel should be integrated in the software development team. Calling in security experts only after the completion of software development would not bring much benefits. The practice of thinking security as a post development phase would not help secure software engineering much.
- We need a complete software development life cycle that integrates security aspects in all phases in the development process. It is difficult to identify how and which ways security could be dealt with in different phases of the development process. In other words, security requirements should be analyzed along with the functional units of the software.
- The development of a culture of "think security" in the development environment might be difficult to achieve. Changing the mindset of all team members of the software development team needs a different approach. The development projects should motivate their team members not to think security just as an afterthought. This paradigm calls for the change of corporate culture, and there is a chance that it may face resistance within the organization.

- The development of automatic tools that could aid the process of modeling, designing, and testing of security along with the functional requirements of the system. Without automatic or semi-automatic tool support, it would be difficult to achieve the objectives of secure software engineering. Development of new tools and languages need more research.
- There is a need for assurances that the process of security-aware development would not undermine other non-functional attributes of the process as well as the finished software products. In other words, a secure software, for example, would not degrade or ignore the usability of the system due to the inclusion of security as a necessary quality property of the software. The challenge is how to make a balance between security and other quality properties of the system.
- Enough care should be needed so that the process of secure software development does not become clumsy and too complicated for the stakeholder. Imposing an overly complex and unrealistic process would not be very beneficial for the achievement of the main goals of this new paradigm, rather, this may be counter-productive in software development.
- Controlling and monitoring budgets and schedules of secure software development project could be problematic if proper process is not adopted. There is a possibility for overblown budgets and delayed delivery schedules.
- Finally, convincing senior management in software development organizations could be difficult for some managers. This challenge is important because any changes to the development processes and practices involve resources, and these resources need to be approved by the top managerial body of the organization. This requires organizations to modify their organizational as well as management policies and activities.

## Organization of the Book

The materials of this book are selected around six related themes of secure software engineering process that have already been discussed earlier. This collection catalogues total eighteen chapters, and they are grouped into six parts corresponding to six broad themes:

- Section 1: Secure Software Development Process
  - Chapters 1, 2 and 3
- Section 2: Security Requirements Analysis and Modeling
  - 4, 5, 6 and 7
- Section 3: Vulnerability Detection
  - Chapters 8 and 9
- Section 4: Protection Mechanisms
  - Chapters 10, 11, 12, 13
- Section 5: Tools for Security-Aware Development
  - Chapter 14 and 15
- Section 6: Secure Software Education and Training
  - Chapters 16, 17, and 18.

## Chapter Abstracts

Chapter 1 focuses upon software security as the resistance against misuse and/or attacks. This chapter argues that secure code features are important, aiming at making the code un-exploitable, preventing attacks like buffer overflow. It presents an empirical study on how agile software developers include security in their software projects. The chapter also presents a case study showing that software development without a persistent focus on security results in software with a number of vulnerabilities. Finally, the chapter presents two possible extensions to agile methodologies, intended to increase developers' awareness of software security.

Chapter 2 presents a framework and step-wise approach towards achieving and optimizing assurance by infusing security knowledge, techniques, and methodologies into each phase of the Software Development Lifecycle (SDLC). This chapter outlines a progression of techniques and procedures that help promote and optimize security assurances. By infusing security into the SDLC from inception to implementation, security is proactively considered while preserving customer priorities and mitigating threat agent's opportunities to negatively impact those goals and assets. The detailed approaches provide a basis for understanding software assurance techniques and methodologies that could be used throughout the project development process.

Chapter 3 proposes a design approach that incorporates privacy risk analysis using UML diagrams to minimize privacy risks in the final design. The approach iterates between the risk analysis and design modifications to eliminate the risks until a design is risk free. The objective of this chapter is to propose an e-services design approach that incorporates privacy risk analysis to obtain designs that are more likely to preserve privacy. The final design is obtained as the culmination of a series of alternative designs where each alternative design is obtained by re-design to avoid or lessen privacy risks identified through a privacy risk analysis on the last design.

Chapter 4 introduces a method for security embedded business process modeling that captures security functions during the business process modeling phase. The proposed method draws on two well-tested theoretical foundations – enterprise ontology and organizational semiotics. The proposed method results in a security-embedded business process model that is completely based on formal semantics. That is, the models can be automatically analyzed or simulated to study the impact of the incorporated security requirements and whether the security requirements compromise business performance in any way. The resultant models can be straightforwardly simulated in order to observe how the security functions are executed.

Chapter 5 presents an approach to integrate RBAC and MAC into use-case, class, and sequence diagrams of the unified modeling language (UML), providing a cohesive approach to secure software modeling that elevates security to a first-class citizen in the process. This chapter details a practical approach that integrates RBAC and MAC into UML for secure software modeling and analysis with a two-fold emphasis. These access control extensions and security analyses have been prototyped within a UML tool.

Chapter 6 discusses the role of pilot case studies in security requirements engineering and their impact on method refinement, student projects, and technology transition. The chapter starts by providing some general background on the importance of requirements engineering and some specifics on the problems encountered in security requirements engineering. It then introduces the SQUARE and SQUARE-Lite methods, which were the research models used in the case studies. The chapter discusses both benefits and challenges to the underlying research, education, and technology transition effort.

Chapter 7 reviews current approaches to security requirements engineering and conclude that they lack explicit support for managing the effects of software evolution. It then suggests that a cross fertilization of the areas of software evolution and security engineering would address the problem of maintaining compliance to security requirements of software systems as they evolve. The chapter suggests that one approach to addressing this problem of preserving security properties is a cross fertilization of approaches to managing software evolution in security engineering

Chapter 8 classifies runtime Buffer overflow (BOF) attack monitoring and prevention approaches based on seven major characteristics. It then compares these approaches for attack detection coverage based on a set of BOF attack types. The classification is expected to enable researchers and practitioners to select an appropriate BOF monitoring approach or provide guidelines to build a new one.

Chapter 9 proposes a new testing methodology called Configuration Fuzzing. As the application runs in the deployment environment, this testing technique continuously fuzzes the configuration and checks "security invariants" that, if violated, indicates vulnerability. The chapter discusses the approach and introduces a prototype framework called ConFu (CONfiguration FUzzing testing framework) for implementation. It also presents the results of case studies that demonstrate the approach's feasibility and evaluate its performance.

Chapter 10 presents an approach for retrofitting existing web applications with run-time protection against known as well as unseen SQL injection attacks (SQLIAs) without the involvement of application developers. The precision of the approach in this chapter is also enhanced with a method for reducing the rate of false positives in the SQLIA detection logic, via runtime discovery of the developers' intention for individual SQL statements made by web applications. The proposed approach is implemented in the form of protection mechanisms for J2EE, ASP.NET, and ASP applications. The AMNESIA test bed is extended to contain false-positive testing traces, and is used to evaluate SQLPrevent.

Chapter 11 describes several vulnerabilities for C and C++, and how these could be remedied by modifying the management information of a representative manual memory allocator and garbage collector. The chapter examines the security of several memory allocators and discusses how they could be exploited.

Chapter 12 presents a method for hot patching executable and linkable format (ELF), formerly called Extensible Linking Format binaries that supports synchronized global data and code updates; and reasoning about the results of applying the hot patch. It develops a format, which is called Patch Object, for encoding patches as a special type of ELF relocatable object file. It then builds a tool called Katana that automatically creates these patch objects as a by-product of the standard source build process.

Chapter 13 primarily investigates security issues of the XML documents, and discusses a protection mechanism, and presents a formal approach to ensure the security of web-based XML documents. The proposed approach starts by introducing a high level language to specify an XML document and its protection authorizations. The chapter also examines the syntax and semantics of the language.

Chapter 14 presents a prototype tool for the integration of security-aware services based applications. The tool is constructed on the principles of security characterization of individual software services. It uses the technique of reasoning between the ensured security properties of the services and the security requirements of the user's system. Rather than reporting the research outcomes, this chapter describes the architecture and capabilities of the tool for secure software integration. It demonstrates the applicability of the tool with an example.

Chapter 15 details CAIRIS (Computer Aided Integration of Requirements and Information Security), a step towards tool-support for usable secure requirements engineering. The chapter claims CAIRIS not only manages the elements associated with task, requirements, and risk analysis, it also supports subsequent analysis using novel approaches for analysing and visualising security and usability. The chapter illustrates an application of CAIRIS by describing how it was used to support requirements analysis in a critical infrastructure case study.

Chapter 16 proposes a context as well as a set of models used to develop and apply a secure software production pedagogy. A secure adaptive response model is discussed in the chapter to provide an analytical tool to assess risk associated with the development and deployment of secure information systems. A pedagogical model for information assurance curriculum development is then established in the context of the developed secure information system models. The relevance of secure coding techniques to the production of secure systems, architectures and organizational operations is also discussed.

Chapter 17 presents an overview of the Master of Software Assurance curriculum project, including its history, student prerequisites, and outcomes, a core body of knowledge, and a curriculum architecture from which to create such a degree program. The chapter also provides recommendations for implementing a Master of Software Assurance program.

Chapter 18 reports on the rigorous and scientific participatory approach for producing the adequate learning program meeting requirements elicited from the professional association members. It presents the skills card that has been elaborated for capturing these requirements and the program, called Master in Information System Security Management, which has been built together with the University of Luxembourg for matching these requirements. This program proposes a holistic approach to information security management by including organization, human and technical security risks within the context of regulations and norms.

## CONCLUSION

As one can see from the above abstracts that all these chapters are timely in terms of their importance, coverage and new ideas. It is not an easy task to select chapters that are appropriate for various aspects of secure software engineering, and are in the correct sequence in terms of their focus. Carefully selected, these chapters reasonably cover major aspects of security-aware software development that have been discussed in this preface. I am sure that the selected chapters in this book address some of the challenges pointed out here. This collection of research work not only serves the hard technological aspects, but rather some of these also address other areas such as e-commerce and educational issues of secure software engineering. The contributing authors are drawn from different parts of the world ranging from Norway to Australia to Gulf and North America. This collection is a fine blending of various researchers with different focus and writing styles. I am very positive that our readers with different backgrounds will enjoy this collection.

*Khaled M. Khan*
*Qatar University, Qatar*

# REFERENCES

Alghathbar, K., & Wijesekera, D. (2003). AuthUML: A three-phased framework to model secure use cases. Proceedings of the Workshop on Formal Methods in Security Engineering: From Specifications to Code, pp. 77-87

de Landtsheer, R., & van Lamsweerde, A. (2005). Reasoning about confidentiality at requirements engineering time. In Proceedings of the 10th European software engineering conference, Lisbon, Portugal: ACM. pp. 41-49.

Ghosh, A., Howell, C., & Whittaker, J. (2002). Building software securely from the ground up. *IEEE Software, 19*(1), 14–16. doi:10.1109/MS.2002.976936

Goertzel, K. (2008). *Enhancing the Development Life Cycle to Produce Secure Software. A reference Guidebook on Software Assurance.* Department of Homeland Security.

Giorgini, P., Massacci, F., Mylopoulos, J., & Zannone, N. (2005). Modeling security requirements through ownership, permission and delegation. in Proceedings of 13th IEEE International Conference on Requirements Engineering, Paris, France, pp. 167-176

Haley, C. B., Laney, R., Moffett, J., & Nuseibeh, B. (2008). Security Requirements Engineering: A Framework for Representation and Analysis. *IEEE Transactions on Software Engineering, 34*(1), 133–153. doi:10.1109/TSE.2007.70754

Security, H. Build Security In – Setting a high standard for software assurance. https://buildsecurityin.us-cert.gov/bsi/home.html (Extracted on January 29, 2012)

Humphrey, W. (1990). *Introduction to the Team Software Process.* Addison Wesley.

Jurjens, J. (2002). UMLsec: extending UML for secure systems development. Proceedings of UML, Springer LNCS, Vol. 2460, pp. 1-9.

Lin, L., Nuseibeh, B., Ince, D., Jackson, M., & Moffett, J. (2003). Introducing abuse frames for analysing security requirements. in Proceedings of 11th IEEE International Requirements Engineering Conference, pp. 371-372

Liu, L., Yu, E., & Mylopoulos, J. (2003). Security and Privacy Requirements Analysis within a Social Setting, In Proceedings of the 11th International Requirements Engineering Conference, IEEE CS Press, pp. 151-161

Lodderstedt, T., et al. (2002). SecureUML: A UML-based modeling language for model-driven security. In Proceedings of UML, Springer LNCS, Vol. 2460, pp. 426-441.

Mouratidis, H., Giorgini, P., & Manson, G. (2003). Modelling secure multiagent systems. In Proceedings of the 2nd international joint conference on Autonomous agents and multiagent systems Melbourne, Australia:ACM, pp. 859-866.

Mouratidis, H., Jurjens, J., & Fox, J. (2006). Towards a Comprehensive Framework for Secure Systems Development. In Advanced Information Systems Engineering, pp. 48-62.

Ray, I., et al. (2003). Using parameterized UML to specify and compose access control models. Proceedings of the 6th IFIP Working Conference on Integrity and Internal Control in Information Systems, ACM Press, pp. 115-124.

Shin, M., & Ahn, G. (2000). UML-based representation of role-based access control. Proceedings of the 9th International Workshop on Enabling Technologies: Infrastructure for Collaborative Enterprises, IEEE Computer Society, pp. 195-200.

van Lamsweerde, A. (2004). Elaborating security requirements by construction of intentional anti-models. in 26th International Conference on Software Engineering, pp. 148-157

Viega, J., & McGraw, G. (2001). *Building Secure Software - How to avoid security problems the right way*. Addison-Wesley.

# Section 1
# Secure Software Development Process

# Chapter 1
# Agile Software Development:
## The Straight and Narrow Path
## to Secure Software?

**Torstein Nicolaysen**
*NTNU, Norway*

**Richard Sassoon**
*NTNU, Norway*

**Maria B. Line**
*SINTEF ICT, Norway*

**Martin Gilje Jaatun**
*SINTEF ICT, Norway*

## ABSTRACT

*In this article, the authors contrast the results of a series of interviews with agile software development organizations with a case study of a distributed agile development effort, focusing on how information security is taken care of in an agile context. The interviews indicate that small and medium-sized agile software development organizations do not use any particular methodology to achieve security goals, even when their software is web-facing and potential targets of attack. This case study confirms that even in cases where security is an articulated requirement, and where security design is fed as input to the implementation team, there is no guarantee that the end result meets the security objectives. The authors contend that security must be built as an intrinsic software property and emphasize the need for security awareness throughout the whole software development lifecycle. This paper suggests two extensions to agile methodologies that may contribute to ensuring focus on security during the complete lifecycle.*

## 1. INTRODUCTION

A decade or so ago, the waterfall model was the favored way of managing/building projects, resulting in a very formal approach where security was handled both implicitly and specifically. Due to the rigid and formal nature of the waterfall model, there was a place for security in specific parts of the process. This does not automatically mean that the waterfall model will make the software secure; it still requires skilled people and determination to create secure software.

DOI: 10.4018/978-1-4666-1580-9.ch001

Agile software development has become a buzzword, and most modern IT-companies brag about how they are using it. Scrum (Scrum Alliance, 2009) is a popular and widely used agile software development methodology, which contains no specific techniques or help for handling critical elements like security. As Scrum is more of a project management methodology, it might not be up to Scrum to handle all aspects of security, but it does define how the requirements are elicited and how to communicate with the customer. If done by the book, the customer has to request security and then prioritize it. If neither the customer nor the developers are concerned with security, it will most likely never end up in the product backlog, and therefore it will be neglected.

This article refers to software security as the resistance against misuse and/or attacks. Specific security features such as login functionality and encrypted communication are part of this, but even more important is *secure code* features, aiming at making the code unexploitable, preventing attacks like buffer overflow, XSS and similar.

The big question is how software security fits into software development projects where agile methodologies are used. Can agile methodologies be mixed with the rigid and formal processes associated with software security, and if so, how?

This article presents an empirical study of how agile software developers include security in their projects. It also presents a case study showing that software development without a persistent focus on security results in software with a number of vulnerabilities. Finally, the article presents two possible extensions to agile methodologies, intended to increase developers' awareness of software security.

## 2. BACKGROUND

Enabling information systems to communicate via open networks such as the Internet will always be associated with elements of risk. (Mavridis, Georgiadis, Pangalos, & Khair, 2001) correctly state that "Security risks cannot be entirely removed when transmitting information over the Internet". The European Parliamentary Technology Assessment (EPTA) network has made similar considerations and specifically expressed concerns that privacy is challenged by the increase in development of ICT applications for the healthcare sector (EPTA, 2006). Such concerns are also raised by others, such as (Ilioudis & Pangalos, 2001) and (van der Haak et al., 2003).

(Boström, Wäyrynen, Bodén, Beznosov, & Kruchten, 2006) detail an extension to the XP planning game that is intended to establish a balance between the conventional (document-centric and plan-driven) way of doing security engineering, and the iteration-centric, feedback-driven XP practices. This is relevant as they try to solve a problem closely related to ours. The main difference is that they are specific to the XP methodology and only try to integrate the security requirements engineering (software security) activity, where as our approach is more generic for Agile methods and not focusing on just one specific security activity.

(Beznosov & Kruchten, 2004) attempt to find the pain points between agile methods and *security assurance*, and suggest some means on how to alleviate them. They group the problems and evaluate how good they match up against activities from security assurance. They focus on a specific problem, like Boström et al.'s approach, and do not seek to solve a more general problem.

(Siponen, Baskerville, & Kuivalainen, 2005) provide an example on how to integrate some security activities into agile development methods. They focus on four key security elements: security-relevant subjects, security-relevant objects, security classification of objects and subjects, and risk management. In the provided example where they apply their technique, it becomes apparent that it requires a lot more effort than what can be expected from an average developer. We therefore consider this too heavy for general applications with agile software development. Their result gives us an indication of what makes a process too thorough.

(Keramati & Mirian-Hosseinabadi, 2008) provide a semi-formal way of evaluating the agility of an agile method. When adding software security activities to an existing agile method, their work can be used to calculate how much the activity reduces the *degree of agility*. They also introduce a parameter named agility reduction tolerance, which indicates how willing the organization is to accept heavyweight security activities about to be integrated with their agile methods.

# 3. EMPIRICAL STUDY

Six different software development companies in Trondheim, ranging from consulting firms, private enterprises and government-based organisations, were interviewed. The six companies were chosen due to their geographical location and their usage of agile methodologies. Each company was represented by a software developer, and half of them had some experience with software security. Only one of the companies had an extensive focus on software security, and many of their projects are subject to stricter security requirements than average. Examples include tax submission and insurance systems.

The interviews were carried out in order to confirm or falsify the following research hypothesis:

*Software security is not a specific concern in an agile software development setting.*

We expected the interviews to confirm that security is too often neglected during software development. However, we also hoped to uncover some new or existing techniques, as a "reality check" on how scientifically developed methods actually work in practice regarding how security can be ensured in agile projects.

In the following we present our findings from the interviews.

## 3.1. Functionality before Security

For most of the interviewed companies, functional requirements are more important than non-functional requirements. Only one of the companies had a somewhat clear method for software security. From a cynical business perspective, it is not difficult to understand why functionality is the priority, while security, performance, availability and the other quality attributes are neglected until they are needed.

It is difficult to calculate what is more cost-efficient when faced with the option between securing or not. Securing has a 100% certain price tag of <insert big number here>, while being hacked might be a calculated risk discounted down to <insert slightly smaller number here>. The accepted wisdom (Boehm & Basili, 2001) is that costs for fixing (security) bugs rise exponentially toward the end of the development process, so if the company is unwilling to focus on security early, it is not more likely to do it later. On the other hand, the company's reputation will be damaged, which is discussed in more detail later. This part is what makes it difficult to calculate the total cost. Money lost due to loss of customers might not be calculated into the initial risk analysis. Most of those interviewed were honestly concerned about this part, but some of the companies were in a dominant market position allowing them to take a punch from bad PR and loss of customers. This did not necessarily mean that they ignored security, but they did not have it as their top priority.

Running a business is about making money. Seen from a company's viewpoint, up-front securing a non-critical piece of software might not seem like a good return on investment right there and then. Functionality is what the customer ordered, and it is naturally the top priority, but it is still hard to comprehend that the non-functional requirements are so utterly neglected. Although the cases presented in the interviews might not seem like they needed security, there had rarely been conducted any formal security activities up front (or during the process for that matter), thus leaving a possibility for major security issues that never were considered.

## 3.2. Agile vs. Security

Of all the companies interviewed, only one had tried to combine software security and agile software development. The Norwegian Data Inspectorate enforces strict policies and regulations when operating with sensitive data, which makes it hard to work agile. A lot of documentation has to be written. Each project usually needs a specific permission to access e.g. tax databases, involving routines for setting up servers, authorizations and many other activities that slow down agile methods. It would be unfortunate if every Norwegian citizen's tax details, social security number and personal information were available to all developers on a project. However, the friction between such routines and agile methods is noticeable. None of the interview subjects had any ideas as how to make that kind of processes more streamlined. This said; none of them gave any examples of how they had tried to. On the other hand, some of the interview subjects were eager to discuss what agile methods and software security had to do with each other.

## 3.3. Securing with Infrastructure

Many companies secure the software they create by protecting it with infrastructure like private networks, firewalls and restricted access to resources. This results in a situation where we end up with "crunchy shell around a soft, chewy center" (Cheswick, 1990), which might be viewed as an acceptable short-time solution in cases where time-to-market is critical. Not many of our interviewees had thought about what would happen if the system were taken outside the intended environment: If a new group of system administrators decided to move one of the servers outside the private intranet, data might be exposed to the public.

Some servers containing files only meant for internal use are completely open because they are on a private intranet. Some use real data sets for testing. They often contain semi-sensitive information like addresses, phone numbers and such. If the test-database is not given the same security focus as the rest of the system, it is probably an easy target for someone who wants that information. These are issues that infrastructure and routines cannot easily protect against. It is important to note that while a secure infrastructure is vital, it should always be in addition to software security.

## 3.4. Lack of Formal Knowledge about Software Security

Few of the interviewees had any formal knowledge about software security. This is understandable as it is a relatively new concern, and not everyone had the possibility of taking a class during their education to learn about software security. One company has software security as their specialty, and it was important that all employees knew the core principles of software security. To assist the developers building secure software, the company had created a set of routines that they had to follow.

A reassuring thought is that some Norwegian agencies possessing security critical information have a security department with formal knowledge and experience. They assist the developers that are often without security expertise in implementing the correct security measures. This is often necessary to handle the legal problems involved.

The lack of knowledge indicates that many security problems might be undetected, and that in some applications, the only form of "security" is that which is acquired through obscurity.

## 3.5. Untreated Concern

Almost all companies were worried about how their reputation would suffer if a vulnerability in their software became wide known, but when asked if it was enough to put an extra effort into securing their software, the answers were vague and non-committing. It is difficult to put a price on how much the company will suffer, but it is guaranteed to have a negative impact.

## 3.6. Customers' Take on Security

Companies dealing with external customers experience that about half of them are concerned about security. This is an indication that there are customers who are aware of some of the dangers out there.

The general impression of customers of IT services is that they are somewhat passive and uneducated in the threats that lurk in their domain. Banking and finance is forced to consider software security when taking their services online. They have most certainly also learned from experience. Customers in other sectors, like the energy industry, are not too concerned with security, even though there are threats. Customers of software solutions will often opt out of security features if given a choice. One customer elegantly thwarted a security solution that one company forced into a product just because they did not like it.

## 3.7. The Weirdest Thing

Strangely, only a couple of the interview subjects had experienced concrete security breaches. The first critical idea was that the lack of audit trails, logging and intrusion detection systems (IDS) could have made it easy for a hacker to penetrate a system without being noticed. It is of course not something a company would want to advertise to the public, and it is quite possible that they take serious action to prevent such news from reaching the media. We suspect that security breaches are more prominent than given in the interviews, and that hackers easily can remove most of their traces.

## 3.8. Summary of Interview Findings

None of the companies had found or created any fully developed technique for integrating software security into agile software development. In our opinion it should have been an issue, but it would be naïve to think that companies would prioritize security over functionality without seeing it as a good return of investment. It is unknown whether upper management considers the potential loss if something is compromised.

The general opinion is that few developers are concerned with security, even fewer are formally trained. The organization is fully capable of sending their employees to courses, or encouraging learning software security in work hours.

The trend with securing with infrastructure alone seems to be recurring in most software solutions shipped. Many rely too heavily on the system administrators, assigning all responsibility for software security to them. The system administrators are often informed orally on how to protect the software. *Make sure it stays on the intranet* could be one such rule. If the system administrators all at once decided to leave, what would happen to these rules? The replacements might re-organize the infrastructure, and put a server on a public LAN, where it was never supposed to be.

As to how so many of the companies have managed to go without any remarkable break-ins or attacks, this is a mystery. As noted earlier, it might just be that they have not noticed them or that the media have not learned of them. Increased media focus on attacks that do happen may be what it takes for companies to be more concerned with software security. White-/gray-hat hackers might need to alert the media directly, as well as the company when they find vulnerabilities.

Unfortunately, such news is probably not interesting for the mainstream media, and therefore the effect might be lost.

# 4. CASE STUDY: A DISTRIBUTED DEVELOPMENT EFFORT

Our case study (Sassoon, Jaatun, & Jensen, 2010) is based on the results of a European research project developing a healthcare platform. Since the platform deals with sensitive health data, it should comply with ("Directive 95/94/EC of the European Parliament and of the Council of 24 October 1995 on the protection of individuals with regard to the processing of personal data and on the free movement of such data," 1995), which regulates the handling of private data for the member states of the EU. The Norwegian implementation of this directive was studied in order to define a set of security requirements to be included in the security design. As part of the evaluation, several components of the WS-* specifications were reviewed, in search of proper ways to deal with security for Web Services.

## 4.1. Project Characteristics

The case study project was funded by the European Commission's 6th Framework Programme, and thus had to satisfy a number of constraints. The project partners had to be diverse in geographical location and represent industry, academia and research institutions. EU research proposals all follow a set template, and it is implicitly assumed that the work will be organized in "Work Packages".

Although an agile Scrum approach was chosen for the project, the different work packages were established in a conventional manner, and developed independently. A separate security WP was a part of the plan, which should have been a good approach, since this would contribute to setting focus on the security aspects of the project.

Unfortunately, due to a serious lack of continuity of key members in the project, the security design was delayed for a long period and it had to be elaborated in parallel with the implementation, and thus the implementation of the security mechanisms started before the security design was finished.

Other early project decisions contributed to the delay of the security design and the resulting parallelism mentioned above: No threat modeling was employed and no security requirements were thought of. The latter had to be done, finally, when the security design document was being developed.

The development process followed a Scrum approach for the most part. The security design process, however, ended up having more in common with a traditional waterfall approach, which may have contributed to the security work falling out of synch with the rest. In line with the chosen Scrum approach, a backlog of functional requirements was maintained. Somehow, only the functional results of the security design made it out of the backlog (e.g., the authentication and token management services were implemented), leaving most non-functional security aspects alone in the dark.

## 4.2. Assessment Results

The assessment proved that the proof-of-concept application and the middleware platform are vulnerable to common attacks targeting web applications. Considering the *OWASP Top 10 web application vulnerabilities* ("Top 10 2007 - OWASP,"), seven of them are present in our case study system:

1. Cross Site Scripting (XSS)
2. Injection Flaws
3. Information Leakage and Improper Error Handling
4. Broken Authentication and Session Management
5. Insecure Cryptographic Storage

6. Insecure Communications
7. Failure to Restrict URL Access

Based on our observations, we can infer that SOA-based systems in general are expected to suffer from the same problems if security is not treated properly. While this is not surprising, the fact that an organization that is concerned with data confidentiality and integrity does not implement basic security mechanisms makes us wonder how many other similar cases might exist.

Even though we evaluated a healthcare system, we can extrapolate the results to other domains since the vulnerabilities found are not specific. Therefore, the findings presented are relevant when considering the development of secure applications, based on SOA or not.

## 5. SECURITY EXTENSIONS TO AGILE METHODS

Both the literature and our empirical study show that there is a need for methods that ensure security issues to be taken care of during agile software development processes. In the following two extensions are suggested, both fitting well into an agile setting; Security backlog and Security-oriented TDD.

### 5.1. Security Backlog

When adding items to the backlog with the customer, the developers should spot security touchpoints and add them to a (possibly) separate security backlog, where each of the items has a reference to the product backlog items for which it is relevant. Here a separate backlog item is useful because a many-to-many relation can exist. Each item should also contain one or more misuse stories to describe how a person with malicious intent could do harm. Each item is prioritized according to risk[1]. The customer should be a part of the risk analysis, i.e., assigning (based on experience and

intuition) H(igh), M(edium) or L(ow) to probability and consequence. Items with the highest risks are exposed to a more detailed and thorough process if the developers consider it necessary.

The intention of this method is to involve software security processes while not reducing the degree of agility (Keramati & Mirian-Hosseinabadi, 2008), thus its techniques should be lightweight. Exceptions are considered, and there should always be room for special cases on high-risk items. Consider using Microsoft Azure (Microsoft) when creating a new financial service on the web. At the time of writing, Azure is still considered new, and little is written on the security implications of having such services on a cloud platform. If the customer demands that the service should run on Azure, and none of the developers know enough about the security risks associated with cloud computing, then it should be considered an exception and extra effort should be put into making sure that the developers can secure it. This would probably involve having a spike[2] if using Scrum, and just learning as much as possible about the technology and security risks before proceeding. Of course, this reduces the degree of agility, but on high-risk items, security should outweigh functionality.

The following steps are based on how many Scrum projects are performed, and mainly contain extensions. Even though presented with focus on Scrum, the ideas are generic and agile enough to be used in other Agile methods.

### 5.1.1. Step 1: Requirements Gathering Phase

The customer and the developers are gathering requirements for a new system, and the customer provides various requirements, such as *The user must be able to log in*. This is a *security feature*. A developer points out a security threat he knows of, namely brute force attack. Stakeholders agree that this is a security issue, and the original requirement goes into the product backlog, while the newly identified security threats now go through a short detailing phase. Developers involve the customer in such a way that he/she understands the threat and is capable of evaluating at least the consequence of an exploit. The developers ask helpful questions like *"On a low/medium/high scale, how big is the consequence of a non-authenticated person gaining access to the system?"* and *"Are there competitors interested in the information within this system?"* The customer often knows the domain well, and is capable of giving an accurate consequence, and the developers know that the probability is linked to factors like competition, value of data inside the system etc. The customer and developers can now calculate the risk for the new security backlog item. Next step is to create at least one misuse story. Based on information from the customer, the developers are able to create an artifact like the one in Figure 1. Here it is important to note the artifacts are detailed as little as possible. They are to serve as reminders of what the concern was during the initial requirements phase. The technical details come in a later phase.

A special case worth mentioning is how to handle *secure code*. Another developer could have pointed out that the user input could be used to cause a *buffer overflow*, and that it is important to write secure code. It is on a higher level than a security feature, and it is something that often relates to all backlog items if the system is meant to be secure. We believe that this belongs in some sort of general policy that applies to the developers. The policy could specify rules as how to treat user input, and should be updated when issues are spotted during the various detailing phases.

## 5.1.2. Step 2: Iteration 0

In iteration 0 the project starts up, teams are assembled and an initial architecture is laid out. The architect goes through the list of items on the product backlog to get an overview of the system. The architect goes through the list of items on the security backlog, and tries to form a picture

of any architectural security features required. It is important that the chosen architecture does not impose restrictions on possible security features that might be needed later. For instance, the architect thinks it is a good idea to have a single access point in order to mitigate the brute force attack. This highlights the need for security patterns. All developers should evaluate the initial architecture together, as well as discussing how it holds up against the security requirements. There might be a need for discussing potential implementation issues. One developer might have spotted a problem with product backlog item n, which might interfere with security backlog item m. Discussing this in plenum ensures that every piece of combined knowledge is used, and many future problems can be avoided. An important feature of this method is the exception handling of high-risk items. If an item is marked as high risk, it should undergo an extra process where it is decided whether it should be thoroughly evaluated. This involves more rigorous security activities. Keep in mind that this might be needed to uncover everything about the item that is relevant in order to make sure it is properly secured when implemented. This requires that someone in the team has knowledge of a security process, or that someone is hired for this specific purpose.

## 5.1.3. Step 3: Sprint Planning (Each Iteration)

When the development cycle starts, developers pick the top prioritized backlog items and start detailing them in the beginning of each iteration. In a Scrum process, this is called a sprint-planning meeting. During this detailing-phase, the developers know there are items on the security backlog that is linked to the product backlog items they have picked. For example, one product backlog item may have a couple of security backlog items linked to it. This means that when creating more detailed user stories and acceptance criteria for the backlog items, they have to consider the se-

*Figure 1. Example of security backlog item artifact*

**#19 - Brute force attack against login functionality**
*2010-01-21*
Linked to backlog item(s): #12

Risk: M x L = L

*Misuse story #1:*
As a hacker hired by a competitor
I want to brute force the login
So that I can gain access to business data

*Misuse story #2:*
As a disgruntled employee
I want to brute force the login
So that I can steal business data

curity implications as well. A simple solution is to integrate the security backlog items into the sprint backlog items. When integrating, create an acceptance criterion that can be used to verify that the threat is mitigated, and one or more security focused user stories. The process of consciously thinking of software security means that the developers are more aware of the security aspects of the tasks. The misuse stories from the security backlog items should also extend the sprint backlog item. The detail level on all artifacts increases in this step, and elicitation of misuse stories must be more precise and detailed (Peeters, 2005).

The goal is to have a simple process with as few extra artifacts as possible. If the developers just become more aware of security, then there is already a gain from the process.

### 5.1.4. Step 4: Implementation

During the implementation of the items on the sprint backlog, developers now have a detailed description of user stories, misuse stories and acceptance criteria to help them correctly implement the item. What it comes down to now, is the developer's knowledge and experience when it comes to software development and software security. Testing should be used to verify that the acceptance criteria are achieved during this phase. Best practice would be to implement each item using TDD and ensure that each user story and misuse story are implemented. This is good agile practice as it forces loosely coupled design, which in time requires less maintenance, is more robust and flexible. The tests also serve as documentation in respect to how things have been implemented. The idea is that writing tests first forces the developer to learn about the security threat he tries to protect against. Of course, the test-code can be poorly written, and not actually test that the system is protected. Here the collective code ownership rule might help. When having code-reviews, poorly written tests should be detected, and team members with more security expertise might know a more effective test to confirm that a given threat has been mitigated.

### 5.1.5. Step 5: Verification

When the system is nearing completion, penetration testing should be used to verify that it resists attacks as intended. A rigorous and well-performed penetration test of the system can expose parts that are not secure enough. If the testing reveals vulnerabilities, one sprint must be held to fix all these. All the tests written previously should of course pass, and should in theory be proof that the security backlog items have been considered and implemented. It should be confirmed that each item on the security backlog has been included in the process. Use of static code analysis tools is encouraged, since it can uncover common programming mistakes and potential problems.

## 5.2. Security-Oriented TDD: Security Tests

Robert C. Martin (Martin, 2008) provides a short summary of the workflow in the three laws of TDD:

- You are not allowed to write any production code unless it is to make a failing unit test pass.
- You are not allowed to write any more of a unit test than is sufficient to fail [...].
- You are not allowed to write any more production code than is sufficient to pass the one failing unit test.

This workflow works very well for implementing functional requirements. Our goal is to adjust this workflow to suit testing of security features, and attempt to keep it applicable to most agile methodologies.

We assume that the planning phase has resulted in functional requirements and security requirements. In addition, all requirements are already detailed, and the security requirements (in form of misuse stories[3]) are placed in the security backlog (see section 5.1). All these items are required in order to write good tests. Here it is again impor-

tant to point out the difference between "security features" and "secure features"; that the former should be able to resist an attack might seem obvious, but it will require significantly more imagination and inspiration to describe misuse stories for "ordinary" features.

What follows is an example of a workflow: When a developer picks a task to work on, he should at the same time retrieve and review the related security backlog items. Not all tasks need have security requirements, but in our example they do. Usually, a developer would start working directly on the functional requirements, and writing tests before implementing production code. Depending on the type of feature that is to be secured, the developer must decide whether to write a unit test or a security test first. This is something the developer can decide by intuition with some training. The best thing would be to always write the security tests first, and then shape both implementation code and unit tests to support the security tests. Unfortunately, this is not always feasible. If developers were to follow the standard TDD, they would need to "break the rules" in order to make the test pass. It is not always possible to write a security test before there exists production code to secure.

A security test aimed at verifying that only authenticated users have access to the admin page will always pass if nothing has been implemented. If the test tries to load a non-existing page, the result could be an HTTP code 404 (Not Found), and the user by definition does not have access to the admin page. To mitigate this, the rules must be bent a bit. The sequence in which the developer writes unit and security tests must be adapted to the situation. It is important that the developer try to get back on *TDD-track* as soon as possible, and follow the recommended workflow. The problems only occur as the first tests for new functionality are written.

Developers should strive to verify that important security requirements are implemented and that the functional requirements are protected sufficiently. To ensure this, each functional requirement has one or more security tests. A security test attempts to verify that a specific security requirement is implemented and protects against an identified threat. This includes one or more test attempts to exploit parts of the systems for a vulnerability described in the security requirement. Where applicable, test-permutations (e.g., through use of fuzzing) should be used to uncover weird boundary conditions, possible overflows etc.

## 6. DISCUSSION

The core idea of having a security backlog is that security should become more of a concern for the developers than it is today. This is a lightweight method with very little overhead. The intention is that it will not scare off developers as some of the other humongous security processes might. There are few new things to learn, and the customer can easily be included. This method depends on having at least one person in the development team with software security competence, or having a budget that allows hiring in someone for the job. The efficiency of this method depends on how quickly developers uneducated in software security can pick up the new mindset, learn specific techniques to avoid security holes, learn where to look up known problems and learn how to learn from others. If developers are unwilling to change from their regular routine where programming is just a straightforward task of "making things work", then this approach will fail.

Security-oriented TDD, like security backlogs, is a way of getting developers more engaged in software security. Being aware that there are security touchpoints, and having defined threats to protect against, might very well give good results in practice. Developers can verify that misuse stories are countermeasured. These tests are readable for low-tech stakeholders, and they can verify that they agree on how the system is tested. Newcomers can quickly read the tests and see what is tested (and how it is tested).

There might not be a need for defining security specific tests, as (Boström et al., 2006) have shown that abuser stories can be translated into security-oriented user stories, which in theory should be testable. However, problems occur when following a strict TDD workflow. When there is no production code, writing tests to protect it might be useless. Therefore, the developer must choose his own way of solving the problem.

When it comes to the case study, we have to take into account that both the proof-of-concept application and the middleware platform were prototypes of an ongoing research project, and are still not ready for production. Even so, this is not an excuse for the apparent relaxed focus on security aspects, considering that the formal plans maintained a high security posture. Nevertheless, the costs for fixing the issues at this point in the project are certainly higher than if the assessment was performed earlier, or if security testing had been part of the secure development lifecycle (SDLC).

We can wonder about the project aspects that may have influenced the security achieved and perceived. Is Scrum the problem? Is it Waterfall? Or is it simply a communication problem? As the original project plan did not comprise testing, no problems could be discovered and associated to a particular moment in time.

Is the idea to implement a separate security work package a good one? Work packages are typically enough unto themselves, evolving on their own while ignoring other WPs. Is it better to include security in every work package? We have to consider that there are re-usable security "components", and these are probably best developed in a separate work package. Furthermore, a separate security WP gives security the proper attention, avoiding a project falling into the usual trap: *"We'll take care of security AFTER everything else works"*.

McGraw argues that security needs to be in focus from the beginning (McGraw, 2006), and that the focus should continue during the whole project. The fact that the security design was delayed and, therefore, other components were developed without considering the security work package, set the stage for a big hole in the platform. Communication problems among project members intensified the issues, by not bringing word about the integration of the results from the security WP and the consequences related to their (non-) use. According to (Lipner & Howard, 2005), there is a need for a *security push* in the whole organization, or project groups, in order to focus on security and identify problems.

Security requirements were not part of the project requirements. Partly using a Model-Driven Development (semi-agile) approach, the system design was based on models/diagrams, such as use cases, from which functional requirements were derived. The use cases in question did not cover security, and thus no security requirements were generated (we would have expected some obvious ones, such as confidentiality-protection of a doctor-patient message). Employing misuse cases would have been a good idea in this setting, but they were voted down early in the project.

Although agile methods make it difficult to comply with the stringent documentation requirements of, e.g., the Common Criteria (*Evaluation criteria for IT security Part 1: Introduction and general model* 2005)[4], several authors have argued that agility and security need not be inversely proportional measures. (Beznosov, 2003) opines that the agile XP methodology can provide "good enough" security, while (Wäyrynen, Boden, & Boström, 2004) claim that the solution to achieving security in an XP development is simply to add a security engineer to the team. (Siponen et al., 2005) advocate a solution that more or less can be summed up as "think about security in every phase".

(Poppendieck & Morsicato, 2002) argue that agile methods (specifically: XP) are just as suitable as traditional development methods for developing safety-critical applications. It may not follow immediately that "safe" software is also "secure", but the former is required to pass auditing procedures that should be customizable to suit requirements for the latter.

Throughout the conducted interviews, we noticed that many of the professionals within the field of software security use several terms in an ambiguous fashion. For instance, when some papers talk about Microsoft's STRIDE method, they refer to it as a risk analysis tool, even though Microsoft themselves refer to it as a threat modeling tool. There is also a lack of clear definitions, even for something as fundamental as "security requirements". For newcomers, this field gives an impression of being immature and disorganized. This problem has been recognized by academics and professional for quite some time, but they do not know how to fix it. We believe that the secure software engineering community must decide on a clearly defined terminology as a first step toward maturity.

Although it might be tempting to suggest that a project where security is vital should be performed using a formal top-down project methodology, we have to face the fact that software development is becoming more and more agile, and there should be a way of mitigating the security drawbacks of using agile methodologies. This might be projects where security is vital (e.g., military, finance, health), or projects where security is not a concern at first, but emerges as the software evolves.

An excellent example is Adobe Acrobat – a PDF-document editor/reader. The initial version was intended for creation and reading of PDF files, and not much else. Security was probably not a big concern, because who could exploit documents following the PDF-standard? However, in version 3.02 of Adobe Acrobat, JavaScript features were added to the application. This new functionality was soon exploited (Narraine, 2006), and was the first of many security problems with Adobe Acrobat. They have now added support for viewing

3D-objects, playing Flash files, viewing CAD-files and third-party plug-in support. CERT[5] reports 25 security vulnerabilities related to Adobe Acrobat per Feb 17th, 2010. This example supports the notion that all software should boast secure features, i.e., even code without specific security features should be un-exploitable.

Unfortunately, there is no silver bullet for making software secure - it is all about knowledge. There is no obvious way of ensuring that security is taken care of in agile software development, but an important fact many tend to neglect is that most agile methods require experienced developers for optimal performance. With sufficient experience combined with the concept of collective knowledge in agile methods, project participants might spot security issues as they occur if one or more of them have training in software security. Another important issue with agile software development is that few of the methods have practices for rigid testing of security. In the waterfall model, there is a dedicated phase named verification, which is used to verify that the software behaves as the customer wants. This includes various types of both automated and manual testing.

## 7. LIMITATIONS

Our empirical study was based on agile teams working closely together in one location, while the case study was a project performed by a distributed agile team. This difference makes it difficult to draw conclusions covering both cases.

It is also difficult to generalize from the case study as EU projects do not produce production-quality code. However, there were explicit security objectives in this project, and that is why it is still an interesting project for us to analyze.

The case study has been approached from a single viewpoint, and should ideally have been augmented with in-depth interviews of more project participants.

The suggested method extensions have not been tested and evaluated, which will be a natural part of further work in this area.

## 8. FURTHER WORK

There is a lack of empirical knowledge regarding the relative security benefits of agile development vs. conventional (e.g., waterfall) development practices. We would like to conduct a larger study, comparing the degree of software security resulting from different development methodologies. This would entail tackling several non-trivial problems, such as defining how to measure "software security" in a given piece of software, and how to compare software products that by necessity must be quite different.

In this project we have been studying organizations using the Scrum methodology. It would be interesting to study organizations using the agile components of the Microsoft Secure Development Lifecycle (Sullivan, 2008) to see whether this methodology changes developers' mindset and increases the focus on software security throughout the complete development cycle.

## 9. CONCLUSION

The interviews and case study presented in this article suggest that it is necessary that every person involved in a project is aware of the consequences of not thinking about, implementing and testing security from the beginning. Only then will it be possible to achieve more secure systems.

Combining software security with agile software development appears to be difficult to do in an elegant way without any compromises. Our suggested solution is to integrate parts of security activities into any suitable agile activities, while trying to figure out the pain threshold for when the reduction of agility becomes too large.

This article has suggested two possible extensions to the agile Scrum method. These extensions are an attempt to take the edge off some of the incongruence between secure software development and an agile mindset. Both Security backlog and Security-oriented TDD are lightweight methods that do not require much documentation and artifact production.

## ACKNOWLEDGMENT

Thanks to Jostein Jensen for his valuable input on earlier phases of this research.

## REFERENCES

Beznosov, K. (2003). *eXtreme Security Engineering: On Employing XP Practices to Achieve "Good Enough Security" without Defining It.* Paper presented at the First ACM Workshop on Business Driven Security Engineering (BizSec).

Beznosov, K., & Kruchten, P. (2004). *Towards Agile Security Assurance.* Paper presented at the New Security Paradigms Workshop, Nova Scotia, Canada.

Boehm, B., & Basili, V. R. (2001). Top 10 list *Computer, 34*(1), 135–137. doi:10.1109/2.962984

Boström, G., Wäyrynen, J., Bodén, M., Beznosov, K., & Kruchten, P. (2006). *Extending XP practices to support security requirements engineering.* Paper presented at the Proceedings of the 2006 international workshop on Software engineering for secure systems (SESS '06).

Cheswick, B. (1990). *The Design of a Secure Internet Gateway.* Paper presented at the USENIX Conference.

*Directive 95/94/EC of the European Parliament and of the Council of 24 October 1995 on the protection of individuals with regard to the processing of personal data and on the free movement of such data.* (1995). Retrieved October 6, 2008, from http://eur-lex.europa.eu/LexUriServ/LexUriServ.do?uri=CELEX:31995L0046:EN:HTML

EPTA. (2006). *ICT and Privacy in Europe, Experiences from technology assessment of ICT and Privacy in seven different European countries.* Retrieved September 23, 2008, from http://epub.oeaw.ac.at/ita/ita-projektberichte/e2-2a44.pdf

Ilioudis, C., & Pangalos, G. (2001). A framework for an institutional high level security policy for the processing of medical data and their transmission through the Internet. *Journal of Medical Internet Research, 3.*

ISO. (2005). *Evaluation criteria for IT security Part 1: Introduction and general model* (Tech. Rep. No. 15408-1). Geneva, Switzerland: ISO/IEC.

Keramati, H., & Mirian-Hosseinabadi, S. H. (2008). *Integrating software development security activities with agile methodologies.*

Lipner, S., & Howard, M. (2005). *The Trustworthy Computing Security Development Lifecycle.* Retrieved from http://msdn2.microsoft.com/en-us/library/ms995349.aspx

Martin, R. C. (Ed.). (2008). *Clean Code: A Handbook of Agile Software Craftsmanship.* Upper Saddle River, NJ: Prentice Hall.

Mavridis, I., Georgiadis, C., Pangalos, G., & Khair, M. (2001). Access Control based on Attribute Certificates for Medical Intranet Applications. *Journal of Medical Internet Research, 3*(1). doi:10.2196/jmir.3.1.e9

McGraw, G. (2006). *Software Security: Building Security.* Reading, MA: Addison-Wesley.

Microsoft. (n.d.). *Windows Azure Platform.* Retrieved February 19, 2010, from http://www.microsoft.com/windowsazure/

Narraine, R. (2006). *Hacker Discovers Adobe PDF Back Doors*. Retrieved from http://www.eweek. com/c/a/Security/Hacker-Discovers-Adobe-PDF-Back-Doors/

OWASP. (2007). *Top 10 2007*. Retrieved July 10, 2008, from http://www.owasp.org/index.php/ Top_10_2007

Peeters, J. (2005). *Agile Security Requirements Engineering*. Paper presented at the Symposium on Requirements Engineering for Information Security.

Poppendieck, M., & Morsicato, R. (2002, September). XP in a Safety-Critical Environment. *Cutter IT Journal, 15,* 12–16.

Sassoon, R., Jaatun, M. G., & Jensen, J. (2010). *The road to Hell is covered with good intentions: A story of (in)secure software engineering*. Paper presented at the 4th International Workshop of Secure Software Engineering (SecSE 2010).

Scrum Alliance, I. (2009). *What is Scrum?* Retrieved March 23, 2010, from http://www. scrumalliance.org/learn_about_scrum

Siponen, M., Baskerville, R., & Kuivalainen, T. (2005). *Integrating Security into Agile Development Methods*. Paper presented at the Hawaii International Conference on System Sciences, HI.

Sullivan, B. (2008). Agile SDL: Streamline Security Practices for Agile Development. *msdn Magazine*. Retrieved from http://msdn.microsoft. com/en-us/magazine/dd153756.aspx van der Haak, M., Wolff, A. C., Brandner, R., Drings, P., Wannenmacher, M., & Wetter, T. (2003). Data security and protection in cross-institutional electronic patient records. *International Journal of Medical Informatics, 70*(2/3), 117-130.

Wäyrynen, J., Boden, M., & Boström, G. (2004). Security engineering and eXtreme programming: An impossible marriage? In *Proceedings of the Extreme Programming and Agile Methods - Xp/ Agile Universe 2004* (Vol. 3134, pp. 117-128). Berlin: Springer Verlag.

## ENDNOTES

[1] Risk = Probability x Consequence
[2] A time-period set aside to experiment and learn something unknown in a user story.
[3] Similar to user stories, but consider them textual versions of misuse cases.
[4] Assurance level 4 and less can be verified for legacy systems not developed with CC evaluation in mind.
[5] www.kb.cert.org

*This work was previously published in International Journal of Secure Software Engineering, edited by Khaled M. Khan, pp. 71-85, Volume 1, Issue 3, copyright 2010 by IGI Publishing (an imprint of IGI Global).*

# Chapter 2
# Assimilating and Optimizing Software Assurance in the SDLC:
## A Framework and Step-Wise Approach

**Aderemi O. Adeniji**
*University of North Carolina at Charlotte, USA*

**Seok-Won Lee**
*University of North Carolina at Charlotte, USA*

## ABSTRACT

*Software Assurance is the planned and systematic set of activities that ensures software processes and products conform to requirements while standards and procedures in a manner that builds trusted systems and secure software. While absolute security may not yet be possible, procedures and practices exist to promote assurance in the software lifecycle. In this paper, the authors present a framework and step-wise approach towards achieving and optimizing assurance by infusing security knowledge, techniques, and methodologies into each phase of the Software Development Lifecycle (SDLC).*

## INTRODUCTION

Software Assurance is steadily gaining ground in the Information Technology industry. The notion of proving secure software while supporting organization and system priorities is appealing to developers and customers alike. Software assurance aims to provide *justifiable confidence* that software is trusted to behave as intended even amidst intentional and unintentional attacks (Goertzel et al., 2007; Sinclair, 2005).

Based on experiences and lessons learned from designing a graduate level software assurance curriculum, assurance optimization is aided by implementing techniques in each phase of the SDLC. The intent of this paper is to share a strategy for integrating software assurance throughout the lifecycle in a methodical manner, proving a secure

DOI: 10.4018/978-1-4666-1580-9.ch002

and trusted system. Several of the foundations, tools and methods used for optimization, shown on Figure 1, will be highlighted throughout the context.

## BACKGROUND

Software is the core component of modern products and services, supporting business operations for all sectors of life. With each software use, there are factors which contribute to increased mission risk including: project size and complexity, attack sophistication, and use of third-party vendors (Ellison, 2006; McGraw, 2005). Dependence on this software makes security a primary concern (Allen et al., 2010). Software Assurance is achieved by

understanding the mechanics of software built and/or acquired and incorporating validation tools and strategies into each phase of its lifecycle to build a trusted and secure product. Figure 2 diagrams this process, showing a step-wise approach for infusing assurance techniques into the SDLC by outlining approaches and artifacts produced. Knowledge gained from performing each step in a methodical and well-defined manner is carried forward, resulting in progressive learning. This is an iterative process, as education acquired from one phase will allow for more intelligent review in another. Assurance optimization can be achieved by mitigating common weaknesses in software throughout the aforementioned process. Peter G. Neumann identified nine sources of problems in computer systems (1994). A framework for

*Figure 1. Software assurance foundations, methods and tools*

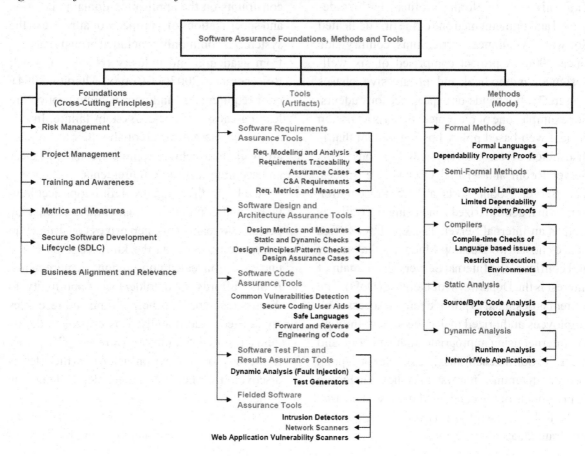

*Table 1. Sources of problems in computer systems and their corresponding software assurance phase*

| Neumann's Sources of Problems in Computer Systems | Assurance Phase(s) |
|---|---|
| 1. Requirements definitions, omissions and mistakes | Requirement & Operational, Design |
| 2. System design flaws | Design |
| 3. Hardware implementation flaws | Implementation/Code |
| 4. Software implementation errors (program bugs, compiler bugs, etc.) | Implementation/Code |
| 5. System use, operations error and inadvertent mistakes | Requirement & Operational |
| 6. Willful system misuse | Requirement & Operational, Design |
| 7. Hardware, communication, or other equipment malfunction | Implementation/Code |
| 8. Environmental problems, natural causes and acts of God | Requirement & Operational |
| 9. Evolution, maintenance, faulty upgrades and decompositions | Implementation/Code |

assurance in the SDLC has been developed and these vulnerability sources will be addressed in appropriate phases, shown in Table 1.

## Course Implementation

The University of North Carolina Charlotte designed and implemented one of the first dedicated Software Assurance curriculums countrywide since 2006. A project comprised of six well-designed, methodical and progressive phases (Figure 2) offer hands-on experience for students. For example, one of the project bases is a mission critical web-based policy hosting system that is distributed across two physical locations: 1) A Server Room and 2) End User Office Spaces. The Server Room hosts a Web Presentation Server in a demilitarized zone using firewalls, as well as an Internal Server. The End User Office Spaces hosts two Desktop Machines that access and configure the Internal Server. The domain of interest is the Department of Defense (DoD). The system is designed to provide remote access to all employees authorized to use the system through the Internet using appropriate authentication and identification mechanisms. The simple conceptual network diagram of the system is shown in Figure 3. Fragments of the completed work will be used in the following step-wise assurance approach to illustrate ideas and concepts.

## PHASE 1: REQUIREMENTS – SECURITY REQUIREMENTS IDENTIFICATION

Requirements are descriptions of how the system should behave. They provide information and constraints on the application domain/operation and specifications of a property or attribute in the system. As commonly concluded in many surveys from academia and industry (Neumann, 1994; Roisencrance, 2007; IT-Cortex; Altarum, 2004), poor requirements and poor communication are leading causes of project/system failure. In this assurance phase, several collaborative techniques are available to achieve complete, consistent, clear and accurate security requirements.

We begin this stage by defining project keywords and components. Semantics can vary by person and team. This step drives consistency in terminology, expands the knowledge base and uncovers concealed/non-obvious requirements. It also affords stakeholders an opportunity to discuss discrepancies before time and resources are wasted. Additionally, it is critical to define items deemed "common knowledge" as they frame the project. Any confusion with these terms discovered further in the lifecycle challenge the project's success.

The next step is to research and model the domain including perspectives from broad secu-

*Figure 2. Knowledge flow chart for software assurance in the SDLC*

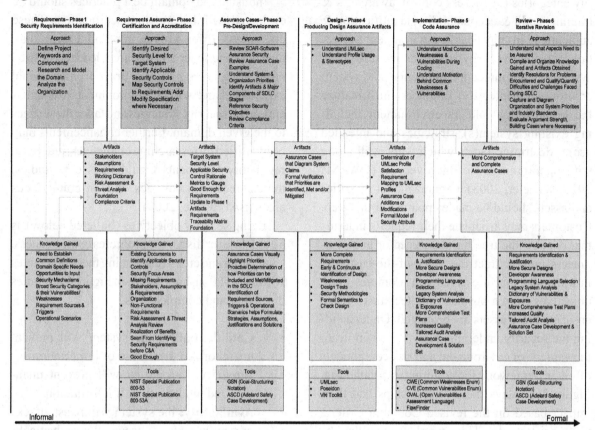

*Figure 3. Network diagram of a web-based policy hosting system*

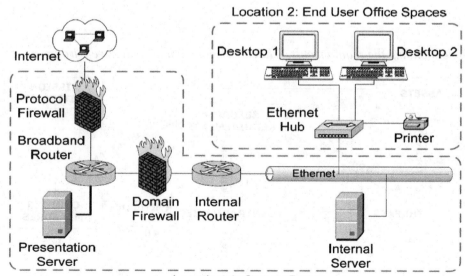

rity categories (i.e. access control, awareness & training, audit & accountability, identification & authentication, physical & environment protection, personnel security, risk assessment policies, system & communication protection, and system & information integrity). Engineers must analyze the organization and its environment including existing system(s), strategies and intended use to determine facets which work well along with opportunities for improvement (OWASP, 2010; Wheeler, 2003). Organizational priorities and assets should be made apparent in this step. Customers may articulate their requests in terms that conceal the true business need or goal. Engineers must extract the voice-of-the-customer in a manner that preserves and promotes these objectives from a business and technical stance ensuring these assets are protected. Understanding the security underpinnings of a system from the vantage of environment and risk components offers a framework for requirements gathering. Figure 4 displays these relationships and their impact based on the revised Common Criteria (2006) risk model. This knowledge can then be extrapolated and added as applicable requirements or assumptions to preserve their value.

Industry and domain best practices should be evaluated to further craft the specifications. These documents offer proven methodologies that, through experience and research, lead to a desired result. Engineers can also draw from personal experiences and working environments to enumerate known security strategies and tailor those specs to the given domain. Further enhancements may be identified by researching challenges, practices, regulatory documents & guidelines, case studies, trends, recent discoveries and on-going focus areas (SAFECode, 2008).

Using security objectives (bulleted below) as a guideline for discovery promotes completeness. Evaluating and cross-referencing these objectives with the relationships shown in Figure 4 promotes discovery and completeness.

- **Confidentiality:** the system will prevent unauthorized disclosure of information
- **Integrity:** the system will prevent unauthorized modification of information
- **Availability:** the system will resist attacks or rapidly return to usage after such attacks
- **Usage:** the system will prevent, detect and /or deter improper use

*Figure 4. Understanding the requirements, related risk components and the environment*

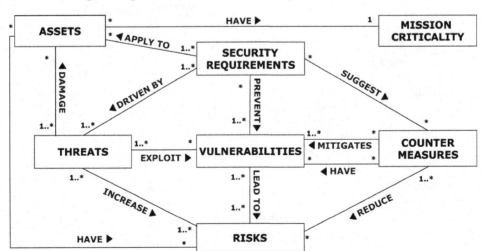

- **Authentication:** the system will ensure users are who they say they are
- **Audit:** the system will record events to allow for later tracking and analysis

Misuse and abuse cases are helpful in this phase as well (Hope, McGraw & Anton, 2004). They highlight requirements necessary to prevent, detect or deter attacks. This knowledge can then be communicated with the client for additional risk analysis. Another review of the components in Figure 4 is useful at this point to ensure all assets are protected and risk scenarios are mitigated.

Requirements should also undergo rigorous evaluation. With each discovery, verify requirements for secure software (broader, holistic view of security goal, i.e., validating user access) as well as requirements for security functionality (narrower, tailored focus on individual component i.e. user logon) are captured. Traceability must be performed as well to ensure elicited specifications address customer's need and system/environment security concerns. Operational scenarios for each security requirement should be analyzed as they may lead to additional assumptions and/or requirements.

Lastly, documentation must be complete, consistent, clear and accurate including all aspects which help achieve system and security goals (Pfleeger & Atlee, 2005). An approval process must be in place to manage changes and scope (Ellison, 2006). All assumptions must be recorded, capturing even items which seem insignificant to prevent confusion once the document is presented and agreed upon with the customer. The team should pinpoint business units and individuals, both internal and external that will be affected by the project, clearly identifying decision makers. Each requirement should be documented with requirement type, broad security category, source, trigger/rationale, operational scenario(s), criticality and compliance criteria or factors required to ensure the requirement is met. It is typically better to have many requirements than risk not having

enough in the initial stages, especially for less experienced requirement engineers. Identifying all relevant specifications promotes the discovery of non-actionable (non-functional) and actionable (functional) requirements without regard to the constraints or difficulty they may present to later stages.

## Knowledge Gained and Artifacts Produced

Collectively using the approaches discussed above allows for the realization of opportunities to input security mechanisms and achieve protection objectives. This assurance phase is beneficial as security is viewed in the context of the entire system and its environment (secure software) rather than just a specific feature (security functionality). Researching and modeling the domain from the stance of broad security categories also allows for concentration on vulnerabilities, weaknesses and threats that may be present or emerge in each area.

Artifacts produced in this phase include the identification of stakeholders, decision makers and resources directly impacted by the project team with clearly defined roles and responsibilities. An unbiased set of requirements which support security objectives and meet project/system goals are explicitly outlined. Each requirement is also classified by type, category, source, trigger, and operational scenarios. Engineers should assign criticality levels to each requirement to help prioritize threats/vulnerabilities and identify compliance criteria during this initial stage. Proactive determination of compliance criteria to ensure requirements have been or will be met helps build confidence and trust in the system and must be included with each specification. Compliance criteria will account for exception handling and outline attack deterrence and mitigation steps. Assumptions or statements necessary for success but outside of the project scope are also clearly stated and defined.

## PHASE 2: REQUIREMENTS ASSURANCE – CERTIFICATION AND ACCREDITATION

Certification is the process of accessing the security controls in the information system to determine whether they are implemented correctly, operating as intended and meet the system's security requirements (DoD, 1997; Welke, 2004). Accreditation offers risk acceptance and management, establishing the extent that a particular design and implementation meets a set of specified security requirements. The Designated Approval Authority (DAA) or other authorizing officials determine the risks to operations, assets, or individuals and their acceptability weighed against the business need and system mission. Certification & Accreditation (C&A) offers a formal authorization process to create more credible, complete, reliable and trustworthy information for authorizing officials to use as guidelines during accreditation. It was developed to achieve more secure information systems within the organization, provide information system controls for management, offer operational and technical safeguards (or countermeasures), and recommend severity levels for each control.

C&A provides discipline to the security process by formally requiring certification and accreditation of a system throughout the entire lifecycle, ensuring security remains forethought (Oar & Jackson, 1998). Figure 5 shows the DITSCAP C&A process, as an example, including components and types of items that will undergo review (Lee, Gandhi 2006). Several tools are available to assist with C&A. The National Institute of Standards and Technology (NIST) released publication 800-53, Recommended Security Controls for Federal Information Systems, providing guidelines for selecting security controls in support of federal government systems (NIST 2009). NIST Special Publication 800-53A, Guide for Assessing the Security Controls in Federal Information Systems (Ross et al., 2008) and Guide for Applying the Risk Management Framework to Federal Information Systems (Ross et al., 2010) also provide guidelines for building effective security assessment plans and a comprehensive set of procedures for assessing the effectiveness of security controls in support of federal government systems.

The first step in the C&A process is to determine the acceptable level of security needed for the system of interest, for example – low, moderate or high. Establishing a security baseline ensures that objectives necessary to achieve that goal are prioritized for inclusion. The next step is identifying valid checks. Security controls as provided in guiding documents (i.e. NIST Special Publication 800-53) should be referenced for applicability, sharing relevant controls and their necessity with the customer and project team. Lastly, requirements and assumption artifacts from phase 1 should be mapped to selected controls, adding and/or modifying statements and criticality assignments as necessary.

### Knowledge Gained and Artifacts Produced

The C&A process offers a means to achieve requirements assurance, evidence that the specification describes the characteristics of the system and its environment while meeting the desired security properties (Bishop & Davis, 2006). Phase 2 revealed guideline documents such as the NIST Special Publications which help identify common security focus areas and promote consistency. These documents provide families or target areas that may were possibly overlooked, ignored or taken for granted in phase 1. Mapping threats, vulnerabilities and weaknesses to artifacts previously acquired help validate completeness and consistency. The overall system security level is designated in this phase. This selection allows the project team and customer to evaluate the amount of associated risk and come to an amicable consensus on its acceptability or proposed mitigation strategies. Identifying this security level also ensures the C&A process can be performed

*Figure 5. DITSCAP (Department of Defence Information Technology Security Certification and Accreditation Process) C&A Process*

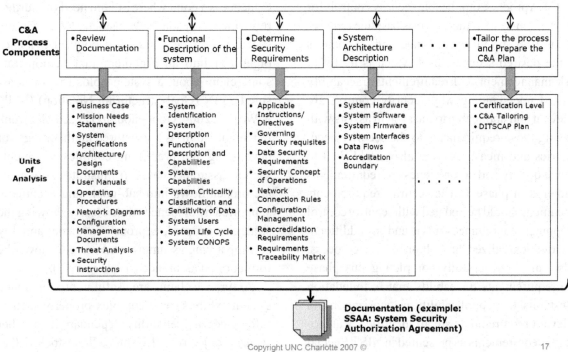

in a manner that guarantees baseline concerns are accounted for in the system. Given the various number of individuals, teams and organizations that may be involved with any system, it is essential to the success of the project that all are familiar with the desired security level and accompanying controls that need to be considered and met. Communicating in this manner also provides increased security awareness throughout the team and ensures all parties are working towards a common goal. Reviewing C&A tools in their entirety offers a universal sense of security controls, including non-technical disciplines such as environment considerations and user training/awareness. Understanding common target areas allows requirement engineers to analyze existing practices and policies & procedures for threats, vulnerabilities, and weaknesses that may have otherwise gone unnoticed. Additionally, measures and metrics can be established through the C&A

process to quantify and qualify how well the desired security level is met and supported by the requirements. For instance, numerical analysis can be performed on the amount of controls met or omitted to assess completeness. Also worth mentioning are the benefits in identifying security requirements in Phase 1 prior to performing C&A. While guideline and regulatory documents exist that provide baseline security controls, solely using these documents stymies the breadth of security thinking. There may be a number of requirements that are not specifically outlined in these regulatory documents and will remain undiscovered if they are solely relied upon. The security controls mentioned in these documents are not intended to provide an all-inclusive or exhaustive list of specifications. Rather, understanding these minimum controls stimulates discussion and thought around requirements that need to be added or modified in order to holistically secure the system and ensure proper functionality.

C&A produces applicable security controls for the domain/system that serve as baseline requirements. It also provides a rationale for these controls at the desired security level which is useful in risk management and requirements traceability tests. Understanding why security controls are relevant and applicable to the system assists with tracing those requirements to the security need. Metrics and measures were also established to gauge quality and completeness of requirements gathered in phase 1. The security requirements document should be updated with security control mappings, compliance criteria and any additional discoveries realized throughout the C&A process. Also, after successfully completing this phase the requirements traceability matrix foundation is established as applicability, categorization and relevant requirements are all identified. Categorizing requirements as presented in NIST Special Publication 800-53 enables proper classification and cataloging of specifications. Requirements can be easily grouped and assessed for redundancy or omissions. The document should be updated with realizations discovered throughout C&A.

## PHASE 3: ASSURANCE CASES – PRE-DEVELOPMENT

Diagrams and other visuals are often helpful in offering explanations, proving ideas and highlighting areas where opportunities for improvement exist. Carrying this notion over to assurance, offering a way to show both the customer and project team that system and organizational priorities are captured builds trust and confidence. Assurance cases consist of a structured set of arguments and corresponding body of evidence to demonstrate that a system satisfies specific claims to a reasonable degree of certainty (Goodenough et al., 2008). Claims embody what is to be shown, arguments tell why to believe a claim has been

met based upon sub-claims and evidence (i.e., results of tests, simulations, analysis, etc.) and evidence is a point where a claim needs no further refinement (Lipson & Weinstock, 2008). Simply stated, assurance cases are a body of evidence organized into an argument that demonstrate some claim about a system holds true or is assured. GSN (Goal-Structuring Notation) (Kelly & Weaver, 2004; Goodenough et al., 2008; Strunk & Knight, 2006) is a structured methodology for developing and presenting complex arguments such as assurance cases. It illustrates how goals are broken down into sub-goals and eventually supported by evidence while clearly showing the strategies adopted, approach rationale, and any accompanying assumptions. Figure 6 shows the format of an assurance case (Figure 6).

Assurance claims are useful in proving that a system exhibits some complex property such as safety, security, reliability, dependability or other security objectives (Lipson & Weinstock, 2008; Redwine, 2007; Bishop, Bloomfield, & Guerra, 2004). They offer formal verification that organizational and system priorities are achieved or that opportunities to meet those objectives still exist. Arguments are assessed by the validity of the claim. As a result, argument strength and soundness is a focal point in this stage. The State-of-the-Art Report (SOAR) (Goertzel et al., 2007) suggests strong arguments and useful claims are created by acquiring a solid knowledge of customer priorities, security objectives, and identifying artifacts and major components of each SDLC stage. It is important to determine which claims are important to stakeholders then conclusively show how these assertions are met and upheld. To be effective, claims must be relevant, accurate and factual. A few priorities of utmost importance to clients are: Money – spent vs. earned; Time – spent efficiently vs. lost; Ease of doing business; Resources – employees, equipment, facilities, and data; and Customer satisfaction and relationships. The challenge, which can be mitigated by practice and research, is creating arguments that incorpo-

*Figure 6. Assurance case diagram (adapted from Goodenough et al., 2008)*

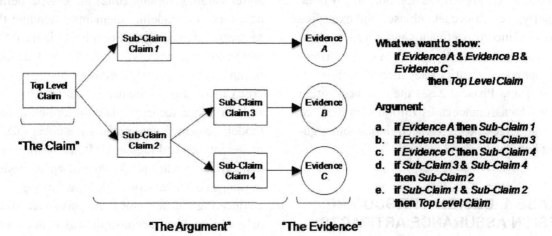

rate these objectives while carefully bridging the gap between business operations and technical solutions. Sub-claims and/or solutions can be created by utilizing the compliance criteria and security control areas documented in Phase 1 and refined in Phase 2. The updated requirements documentation and knowledge gained offer strategies and scenarios to prove prescribed notions. Claims such as no errors in the design or mission critical systems have 100% availability are useful to both the customer and project team. Proving these assertions builds trust that the system will meet these priorities and offer a framework with supporting results of how they were achieved. These cases also assist with quantifying claims with strategies corresponding to metrics and evidences corresponding to measures (Jarzombek et al., 2007).

## Knowledge Gained and Artifacts Produced

Assurance cases are the artifacts produced in this phase. The argument structure serves as a solid communication tool. These cases describe in layman's terms how priorities will be incorporated throughout the project and make it easier for customers to understand how those objectives were

accomplished. The project team can also review the diagram for easy identification of impacted lifecycle phases. Designers and developers can use these diagrams in their respective stages to brainstorm approaches, outline objectives and potentially trigger the discovery of additional creative solutions. Additionally, diagram review by experts from each stage of the SDLC before case delivery is essential in assuring the claims presented are accurate and the processes that lead to solutions are correct. Assurance cases offer a proactive approach to security. They magnify problem areas, highlight omitted requirements and ensure strategies are in place to meet objectives, priorities and claims. These illustrations allow for the early identification of specifications needed to alleviate or mitigate (sub)claims. Any weaknesses, unknown or less developed areas easily emerge in these visual aids allowing for research and refinements by appropriate members of the project team. Developing assurance cases after the requirements stage of the lifecycle is advantageous. It either proves that proposed technical solutions will achieve organization and system priorities or underscore opportunities for improvement before the design is created, allotting adequate time to mitigate risk and/or develop practical solutions. Another sizeable advantage to creating assurance cases is a comprehensive solution set. If done properly, we achieve an unbiased and extensive set of evidence to meet claims and assertions. Also noteworthy, documenting requirements with their corresponding security relevance as outlined in Phase 1 and Phase 2 eases the data acquisition process for assurance cases. Information captured in these stages was referenced throughout argument construction and review.

## PHASE 4: DESIGN – PRODUCING DESIGN ASSURANCE ARTIFACTS

The main objective of the design phase is to develop a product that satisfies the agreed upon requirements. Specifications created in phase 1, 2 and 3 determine the "what" and the design outlines the "how". The project transitions from problem identification to outlining the solution in this stage. The design document produced in this stage is the blueprint for implementation and any errors created here become expensive to correct in the future. Long term cost-saving strategies are needed to prove the design is error-free, clear, complete, and will behave as expected under (ab) normal conditions. Design assurance satisfies this need and creates evidence that security policy specifications are met. Static and dynamic tools such as secure design principles, threat modeling, and risk mitigation are used to combat attacks (Shabalin, 2004). Results from these techniques measure how well the design meets the requirements and provide justifiable confidence in security accuracy.

Formal and informal analysis techniques support claims about design completeness and accuracy (Sinclair, 2005). UML Security (Jürjens, 2004) is a formal semantic which mathematically verifies whether security constraints hold true in a given design. It is a light-weight extension of the Unified Modeling Language used for designing and modeling secure software systems. UMLsec is built on profiles containing stereotypes, tags and constraints (Jürjens, 2002). Stereotypes define new types of modeling elements extending the semantics of existing types or classes in the UML meta-model. Tagging values to a model element is one way of explicitly defining a security property. Constraints can be used to refine semantics and add more security related information to a model element. Requirements are encapsulated in stereotypes and tags in UMLsec profiles and managed by constraints. The use of such a modeling language makes it possible to perform security engineering and mechanical analysis, successfully determining whether constraints associated with stereotypes are fulfilled in the specification and design. Tools like Poseidon (GentleWare) are used to draw UMLsec diagrams and allow for modeling of security properties such as fair exchange, non-repudiation, secure information flow and secure communication link (Jürjens, 2002). These tools can be used in conjunction with kits like Viki Framework (Jürjens, 2003) which is an error-checking tool for UMLsec diagrams and evaluates whether security properties are satisfied or flawed.

## Knowledge Gained and Artifacts Produced

A solid UML foundation is essential to success in this phase. It aids the introduction to UMLsec which captures a number of important recurring security areas. It is critical to appreciate the importance and usage of each profile along with their accompanying stereotypes and constraints. Understanding how these security requirements relate to the organization's priorities allow the design to be constructed and assessed appropriately. Modeling security principles and their potential adversary behavior in designs helps reduce missing requirements or weaknesses in organizational practices and/or policies & procedures. Measures taken to mitigate adversarial situations are captured and validated against the specifications and customer practices. Another benefit is the early and continuous identification of design weaknesses. Designers can keep a constant pulse on their progress and success by tracking these vulnerabilities. This process also helps discern which components can be tweaked without compromising security principles and allow for adequate review of change implications which is extremely beneficial. Identifying which security cases need to be trapped allow for more tailored test cases as well. Scripts can be constructed to focus on specific security concerns. Testing is also enhanced by using tools to validate if stereotype constraints are fulfilled in a given specification or scenario. Methodologies like UMLsec, which encapsulate knowledge of common security concerns, help detect the existence of familiar security issues in design models. The major benefit of community learning tools like UMLsec is that designers without a strong security background can capitalize on the same knowledge without the steep learning curve. Additionally, formal semantics is advantageous because normal and adversary behavior can be modeled prior to implementation which has been challenging in the past. Designers are able to predict how a system will behave and react during execution but prior to implementation, allowing for proactive considerations independent of coding or deployment. This process traps potential errors and preserves time, resources and budget that would be created from any re-work or correction in later stages.

Artifacts produced from this stage include test and analysis results that UMLsec stereotypes are satisfied in the design. Formal, empirical results are often placed in higher regard because of their mathematical foundation. Formal models of security attributes are produced and positive results further strengthen arguments and claims. The requirements document may be updated, once properly approved, based on discoveries during this phase. Metrics and measures can be produced from reviewing the specifications and results produced during analysis. Lastly, assurance cases created in phase 3 are updated using

results and findings during this stage as well. Test results and new findings can be added to claims and solutions as appropriate.

## PHASE 5: IMPLEMENTATION – CODE ASSURANCE

Designs are translated into code during the implementation phase and an executable is created to satisfy the client's need and specifications. The type of programming language and platform used depend on the requirements and application in question. While each language has strengths and weaknesses, there are inherent coding concerns that must be addressed and properly mitigated to promote security. Code assurance provides evidence establishing the implementation is consistent with the requirements and design. It proves common vulnerabilities and weaknesses are eliminated or successfully mitigated in support of security requirements.

Assessing how well the implemented system meets specifications can be achieved through thorough testing and proof of correctness techniques, a methodology to quantify and qualify accuracy objectives. Another important technique is secure programming practices, including training and manual/automatic code inspection. This combination of techniques helps produce error-free code that withstands familiar attacks.

Several taxonomies are available to identify software security flaws, vulnerabilities and weaknesses. The Common Weaknesses Enumeration (CWE) (MITRE, 2010a) provides a unified, measurable set of software weaknesses which is used to more effectively select security tools to locate these weaknesses in source code (Kass, 2005). The Common Vulnerabilities and Exposures list (MITRE, 2010b) is a dictionary of publicly known information security vulnerabilities and exposures. Both the CWE and CVE lists are created and maintained by the Software Assurance community that includes individual researchers and representatives from participating organizations. Mitigation strategies are typically included with each list entry for added assistance. OVAL (Open Vulnerabilities and Assessment Language) (MITRE, 2010c) is an information security community standard promoting open and publicly available security content and standardized information transfer across the spectrum of security tools and services. Taxonomies of functions and techniques which detect or prevent flaws are also available. FlawFinder (Wheeler), a formal mechanism for uncovering security flaws, performs static analysis by examining source code and reporting possible security weaknesses or flaws by risk level. These tools quickly identify possible security concerns and are useful in trapping potential issues before a program is widely released to the public.

Requirements should be evaluated against community enumeration lists like CWE, CVW and OVAL. Doing so allows each specification to be evaluated for exploitation likeliness and a resulting priority can be established. Developers can use potential consequences identified in these lists to construct tests and validate solutions adequately combat those threats.

## Knowledge Gained and Artifacts Produced

Adhering to good engineering practices during development, testing and maintenance along with following industry and organization best practices are essential towards achieving code assurance. Understanding the most common and prevalent weaknesses and vulnerabilities created during the implementation stage is critical. Enumerations like CWE, CVE and OVAL should be reviewed allowing developers to understand all the potential risks associated with code. Researching the underpinnings and cornerstones of these risks offers a better understanding of what steps can be taken to prevent, detect and deter. The clear advantage is this review can take place in-house prior to deployment. Additionally many of these

documents offer the likelihood of exploitation, common consequences and potential mitigation strategies for various stages of the lifecycle, which assists the entire project team with strategizing. For instance, developers can use these findings to better communicate potential threats to requirement engineers. As a result, requirement engineers are better equipped to help customers assess risk and justify requirements. While their identification in this stage is certainly more expensive, mapping weaknesses and vulnerabilities to their affected requirements or lack thereof provides another opportunity to discover omissions. It is also helpful for designers to understand these threats to promote more accurate analysis and modeling during the design stage. Proactively educating designers reduces the amount of rework required during the implementation phase.

Security efforts as seen in these community lists serve to heighten developer awareness and spark research on spin-off attacks. As attackers develop and evolve, developers must do the same. Maintaining an awareness of relevant security concerns and breaches from a coding standpoint is important in devising creative yet durable solutions and/or appropriate patches. Also, these centralized lists are extremely useful for developers with a limited security background. They provide a means to use knowledge acquired by peers and specialists in lieu of individual security experience. In addition, proactive consideration of typical attacks and their target areas allows security features to be massaged throughout the code. These repositories also provide assistance in selecting a programming language by understanding common weaknesses in relation to language strength and vulnerabilities. Recognizing security concerns grow increasingly over time, it is highly likely that attacks which are common and powerful today were either not considered in legacy systems or have become more sophisticated. Understanding these issues allows for the review and inclusion of security in existing systems. Audit advantages are realized by performing specialized analysis when reviewing logs and/or monitoring real-time usage and educating auditors to identify suspicious activity as identified in the lists. Lastly, the collective knowledge obtained from understanding common weaknesses and vulnerabilities supports the development of more extensive assurance cases and their accompanying solution sets. It provides a means to assess how claims can be achieved through various phases of the lifecycle in light of an attacker's objectives and opportunities to attack when the system is deployed. Static tools like FlawFinder exist to evaluate source code and dynamic tools are also available to highlight vulnerabilities in the run-time environment. Reviewing these results alongside standard testing procedures like white-box and black-box techniques help uncover and resolve code weaknesses (Mancoridis, 2008)

The artifacts produced in this phase include the identification of relevant weaknesses, their likelihood of exploitation and the common consequences presented from each. Mitigation strategies are devised and shared with the project team for incorporation into each phase of the SDLC. Requirement completeness is again evaluated and measured by mapping relevant requirements to identified weaknesses and vulnerabilities. Any additions or modifications necessary to omit or mitigate these weaknesses should be sent through the change management process prior to product release. Assurance cases are be updated with tool results, measurements and findings acquired during this phase.

## PHASE 6: REVIEW – ITERATIVE REVISION

As time and resources permit, lifecycle and assurance case iterations should take place to further promote completeness, correctness, clarity and accuracy. Knowledge acquired from iterations should be shared with the project team for inclusion in their respective stage. The ability to prove

security arguments are both sound and stable rests with updating assurance cases after each stage along with validating organization and system claims are accurate.

Updates and additions to assurance cases should be made based on the knowledge gained and artifacts obtained from each phase. All activities that contribute to security evaluation should be included to ensure that the cases are comprehensive before product delivery, developing any weak areas appropriately. In an effort to build more complete arguments, difficulties and challenges faced in each phase should be quantified and qualified where possible. Workaround strategies employed as a result of difficulties and challenges must be captured and shown on the diagrams as well.

## Knowledge Gained and Artifacts Produced

Understanding how assurance is achieved in each phase of the SDLC allows for the development of more complete assurance cases. Recognizing the "holes" that existed while building assurance cases in Phase 3 promotes mitigation strategizing throughout the remaining phases and iterations. Identifying which claims are important to the system and organization takes practice. It is easy to identify major issues (i.e., free from errors) but the specific and granular objectives that must be assured to satisfy the overachieving claim need to be modeled to collectively build confidence.

Maintaining assurance cases throughout the SDLC allows for continuous improvements and enhancements as new learnings become available. Given the developing nature of systems, emergent properties can be accurately captured and diagrammed using this incessant approach. Updating assurance cases during design and development allows for security analysis of the system in its entirety which is advantageous. This holistic vantage point allows validation of components to be compared with validation of the system, identifying how weaknesses in one area impact the system as a whole.

Lastly, assurance artifacts from Figure 2 must be incorporated into arguments. This proves to both the customer and development team that proper procedures and analysis have been performed throughout the lifecycle, ultimately resulting in a trusted and secure system.

Knowledge gained throughout each stage is successfully communicated with the team and incorporated during these repetitions. Metrics and measures show positive results and meet established baselines to prove success. After the final iteration, the requirements document is complete and sound assurance cases are constructed.

## EXPERIENCES/LESSONS LEARNED

Evaluating security as a dependability requirement and emergent property in the overall behavior of system software serves as the motivation for software assurance. Software Assurance prescribes a methodology for building secure and trusted systems, appropriately addressing trustworthiness, predictable execution and conformance (Jarzombek, 2006). This paper presents a repeatable approach towards achieving and optimizing assurance by infusing security knowledge, techniques, procedures, and methodologies throughout the Software Development Lifecycle. The materials prescribed teach Software Assurance in a manner that bridges the gap between software engineering and information security/assurance. Objectives of the presented framework and approach include:

- Understanding of assurance features from the perspective of software development lifecycle
- Creation of phase-wise methodology that includes unique assurance methods
- Understanding of artifacts that were consumed, created and produced by each phase and its usage by the next phase

- Understanding of knowledge gained through each phase
- Suggestion of potential tools that fit to the purpose of each phase and its application

Working progressively and in methodical phases, a high level of certainty that the system is free from vulnerabilities and weaknesses is established. Each of the six phases explained, develop justifiable confidence that goals are met, priorities are maintained and security is enforced to successfully prevent, detect and/or deter vulnerabilities and weaknesses. Their concerns and values must be accounted for throughout development. The project team is responsible for understanding owner-threat agent associations as shown in Figure 4 and identifying how they may be compromised or promoted. The team must then apply that knowledge to each assurance phase as summarized below. Phase 1: Requirements – Security Requirements Identification, identified many of the owner's assets. Consideration is given to protect those assets from vulnerabilities, threats and risks. Challenges were seen when assessing "good enough" with regard to completeness and granularity of specifications. Though domain, environment and industry research offered assistance there is not yet a clear method to measure requirement accuracy and thoroughness. The desired security level is established in Phase 2: Requirements – Certification & Accreditation. Industry guidance such as the NIST 800-53 publication provides assistance in selecting security controls and assessing their effectiveness. This phase allows for the realization of impacts caused by people, process and technology. The C&A process helps elicit additional assets, vulnerabilities, risks and threats that may have been overlooked during Phase 1. It provides an opportunity to further enumerate countermeasures and mitigation strategies to help protect and/or alleviate those findings. Completing this stage helped settle a little of the uneasiness experienced in Phase 1 regarding the precision of requirements. Using industry security controls offered further assistance as to the level of detail required and the omissions made without the use of such guides. Arguments that postulate about features and facets that hold true in the system are presented in Phase 3: Assurance Cases – Pre-Development. The owner/ threat relationship (Figure 4) is again useful in creating claims and highlighting objectives and goals from both perspectives. The first two phases focus on informal methods to achieve assurance. Phase 3 moves into a more semi-formal method by utilizing a graphical language, Goal Structuring Notation (GSN). The sentiment of accuracy or lack thereof arises again in this phase resulting in uncertainty as to whether all possible claims and supporting notions have been captured. Phase 4: Design – Producing Design Assurance Artifacts introduces the use of formal methods to prove security and trust are included. UMLsec presents a number of profiles which allow for security requirements to be modeled as stereotypes. Tags or constraints are then added to these profiles to evaluate specifications for possible vulnerabilities and weaknesses. We move from informal to formal analysis in this stage by using UMLsec or like methodologies to ensure security requirements enforce a given security policy. The use of tools which offer automated results is extremely beneficial in evaluating progress. It also allows for insight to be proactively shared with the project team for use in latter stages and iterations. Phase 5:

Implementation – Code Assurance, allows for the discovery of community-created and maintained dictionaries. These glossaries present enumerations of weaknesses and vulnerabilities commonly found during implementation along with their foundation and potential countermeasures. Tools are available to check for the presence of such threats, offering another formal mechanism to build secure and trusted systems. Again, utilizing automated tools for dynamic/static code testing proves extremely beneficial. Coders can quickly identify and resolve programming vulnerabilities before deployment. Phase 6: Review – Iterative Revision prescribes time to revise arguments established in Phase 3. Assurance cases are updated based on the knowledge gained and artifacts obtained throughout the lifecycle. Though shown as a standalone stage to allot review time, assurance cases should be constantly updated in stages 3-5. Optimization is achieved by assuring each phase then using those learnings in a progressive and iterative manner. Figure 7 displays the necessary stage reliance.

Also noteworthy, there are many methods, tools and methodologies that deal with security engineering. While only a few are highlighted in this paper, it is more important to understand the fundamentals behind their use. Takeaways from such tools include appreciating the characteristics, embedded knowledge and applicability as it relates

*Figure 7. Design of a trusted system*

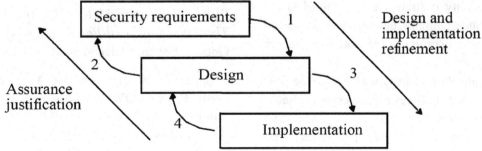

to goals and objectives in each phase of the engineering lifecycle.

## CONCLUSION

One impeding question throughout this process is how software assurance differs from verification and validation (V&V). After systematically completing the project, the distinctions became more evident. Verification asks the question, are we building the product "right"? Meaning, the software must conform to its specification. Validation asks the question, are we building the "right" product? The software must do what the user really requires. V&V seeks to discover defects in a system and assess whether the system is operationally useful and usable as they are needed by the users. However, it does not focus on the properties of secure and trusted systems, nor does it evaluate completeness, correctness and consistency.

Incorporating the knowledge gained through this step-wise approach to assurance allows the project team to realize the collective benefits in infusing security concepts. The project becomes more cohesive and a better understanding of the rationale behind functions and mechanisms is obtained. In years past, security has been an afterthought for a number of reasons. One of which is the lack of security experts on the project team and the other focuses on incorporating security functionality rather than working towards secure software as a whole, which are two fundamentally different aspects. Working in the succession suggested, security is strategically included in the system's underpinnings and iteratively reviewed for accuracy, optimizing the notion of secure software.

While absolute security may not yet be possible, this paper outlines a progression of techniques and procedures that help promote and optimize assurance. By infusing security into the SDLC from inception to implementation se-

curity is proactively considered while preserving customer priorities and mitigating threat agent's opportunities to negatively impact those goals and assets. The approaches detailed provide a basis for understanding software assurance techniques and massaging these methodologies throughout project development. It is our intent that the framework provided will promote continued exploration and advancement in academia and the industry alike.

## ACKNOWLEDGMENT

We would like to thank Robin Gandhi and Gail-Joon Ahn for their contributions in providing invaluable insights throughout the process of software assurance curriculum development and teaching at the UNC Charlotte.

## REFERENCES

Allen, J. H., Ellison, R. J., Mead, N. R., Barnum, S., & McGraw, G. (2010). *A Look at Software Security Engineering: A Guide for Project Managers*. CrossTalk Journal of Defense Software Engineering.

Altarum Institute. (2004). *Does Eveyrone Struggle As Much As We Do? The Role of the Integrated Acquisition Life Cycle in Program Success*. The Hidden Principles of Program Success.

Bishop, M., & Davis, U. C. (2006). *Foundations of Computer and Information Security – Requirements* (Lecture No. 26).

Bishop, P., Bloomfield, R., & Guerra, S. (2004). *The Future of Goal-Based Assurance Cases*. Ontario, Canada: Adelard and City University.

Chandra, P. (2010). Open Web Application Security Project (OWASP*). Software Assurance Maturity Model: A Guide to Building Security into Software Development v1*. Retrieved from http://www.opensamm.org/downloads/SAMM-1.0.pdf

Common Vulnerabilities and Exposures (CVE). (n.d.). *Community list. MITRE.* Retrieved http://cve.mitre.org/

Common Weakness Enumeration (CWE). (n.d.). *Community list. MITRE.* Retrieved http://cwe.mitre.org/

Department of Defense (DoD). (1997). *DoD Information Technology Security Certification and Accreditation Process (DITSCAP).* Washington, DC: DoD.

Ellison, R. J. (2006). *Security and Project Management.* Pittsburgh, PA: Carnegie Mellon University.

Failure Causes Statistics. (1995). *The Bull Survey (1998), KPMG Canada Survey (1997), and Chaos Report (1995).* Retrieved from http://www.it-cortex.com/Stat_Failure_Cause.htm

Goertzel, K., Winograd, T., McKinley, H. L., Oh, L., Colon, M., & McGibbon, T. (2007). *Software Security Assurance: A State-of-the-Art Report.* Fort Belvior, VA: DTIC-I.

Goodenough, J., Lipson, H., & Weinstock, C. (2008). *Arguing Security – Creating Security Assurance Cases.* Pittsburgh, PA: Carnegie Mellon University. Retrieved from https://buildsecurityin.us-cert.gov/daisy/bsi/articles/knowledge/assurance/643-BSI.html

Hope, P., McGraw, G., & Anton, A. (2004). Misuse and Abuse Cases: Getting Past the Positive. *IEEE Building Security in Security & Privacy Magazine, 2*(3), 32–34.

Jarzombek, J. (2006). A Strategic Initiative of the U.S. Department of Homeland Security to Promote Integrity, Security, and Reliability in Software. In *Considerations in Advancing the National Strategy to Secure Cyberspace.* Software Assurance.

Jarzombek, J. (2007). Software Assurance: A Strategic Initiative of the U.S. Department of Homeland Security to Promote Integrity, Security, and Reliability in Software. In *Proceedings of the Enabling Role and a Broader Perspective for Measurement.*

Joint Holders in Australia/New Zealand, Canada, France, Germany, Japan, Netherlands, Spain, United Kingdom and United States. (2006). *Common Criteria for Information Technology Security Evaluation, Version 3.1, Revision 1.*

Joint Task Force Transformation Initiative. (2009). *National Institute of Standards and Technology (NIST) Special Publication 800-53 revision 3.* Recommended Security Controls for Federal Information Systems and Organizations.

Jürjens, J. (2001). Towards Development of Secure Systems using UMLsec. In *Proceedings of the Fundamental Approaches to Software Engineering (FASE/ETAPS) 2001, International Conference.* Berlin: Springer Verlag.

Jürjens, J. (2002). UMLsec Presenting the Profile. In *Proceedings of the 6th Annual Workshop on Distributed Objects and Components Security (DOCsec2002),* Baltimore, MD.

Jürjens, J. (2003). Critical Systems Development with UML. In *Proceedings of the 21st IASTED International Multi-Conference Applied Informatics, International Conference on Software Engineering.*

Jürjens, J. (2004). *Secure Systems Development with UML.* Berlin: Springer Verlag.

Kass, M. (2005). A Taxonomy of Software Assurance Tools and the Security Bugs they Catch. In *Proceedings of the OWASP AppSec DC.*

Lee, S. W., & Gandhi, R. (2006). *Requirements as Enables for Software Assurance.* CrossTalk Journal of Defense Software Engineering.

Lipson, H., & Weinstock, C. (2008). *Evidence of Assurance: Laying the Foundation for a Credible Security Case*. Pittsburgh, PA: Carnegie Mellon University.

Mancoridis, S. (2008). *Software Vulnerabilities: Definition, Classification, and Prevention*. Philadelphia: Drexel University, Reverse Engineering Software Security Course Materials.

McGraw, G. E. (2005). *Risk Management Framework*. Cigital, Inc.

Neumann, P. G. (1994). *Computer-Related Risks*. Reading, MA: Addison-Wesley Professional.

Oar, G. L., & Jackson, R. H. (1998). *The Benefits of Applying the DoD Information Technology Security Certification and Accreditation Process to Commercial Systems and Applications*. Manassas, VA: SphereCom Enterprises Inc.

Open Vulnerability and Assessment Language (OVAL). (n.d.). *Community list. MITRE*. Retrieved from http://oval.mitre.org/

Pfleeger, S. L., & Atlee, J. (2005). *Software Engineering Theory and Practice* (3rd ed.). Upper Saddle River, NJ: Pearon Prentice Hall.

*Poseidon for UML by GentleWare*. (n.d.). Retrieved from http://www.gentleware.com/

Redwine, S. (2007). Introduction to Assurance Cases. In *Proceedings of the OMG Software Assurance Workshop*.

Rosencrance, L. (2007). *Survey: Poor Communication Causes Most IT Project Failures*. Computerworld Electronic Journal.

Ross, R., Katzke, S., Johnson, A., Katzke, S., Toth, P., Stoneburner, G., & Rogers, G. (2007). *NIST Special Publication 800-53A*. Guide for Assessing the Security Controls in Federal Information Systems.

Ross, R., Katzke, S., Johnson, A., Swanson, M., Stoneburner, M., & Rogers, G. (2004). *NIST Special Publication 800-37*. Guide for the Security Certification and Accreditation of Federal Information Systems.

SAFECode. (2008). *Software Assurance: An Overview of Current Industry Best Practices. Software Assurance Forum for Excellence in Code (SAFECode)*. Retrieved from http://www.safecode.org/publications/SAFECode_BestPractices0208.pdf

Shabalin, P. (2004). *Model Checking UMLsec*. München, Germany: University of München.

Sinclair, D. (2005). *Introduction to Assurance*. Dublin, Ireland: School of Computing.

Strunk, E. A., & Knight, J. C. (2006). *The Essential Synthesis of Problem Frames and Assurance Cases*. Charlottesville, VA: University of Virginia, Department of Computer Science.

Welke, S. (2004). *Security Certification & Accreditation: DITSCAP vs. DCID 6/3*. Herndon, VA: Trusted Computer Solutions, Inc.

Wheeler, D. (2003). *Secure Programmer: Developing Secure Programs*. Alexandria, VA: Institute for Defense Analyses.

Wheeler, D. (n.d.). *Flawfinder*. Retrieved from http://www.dwheeler.com/flawfinder/

*This work was previously published in International Journal of Secure Software Engineering, edited by Khaled M. Khan, pp. 62-80, Volume 1, Issue 4, copyright 2010 by IGI Publishing (an imprint of IGI Global).*

# Chapter 3
# Towards Designing E–Services that Protect Privacy

**George O. M. Yee**
*Carleton University, Canada*

## ABSTRACT

*The growth of electronic services (e-services) has resulted in large amounts of personal information in the hands of service organizations like banks, insurance companies, and online retailers. This has led to the realization that such information must be protected, not only to comply with privacy regulations but also and more importantly, to attract clients. One important dimension of this goal is to design e-services that protect privacy. In this paper, the author proposes a design approach that incorporates privacy risk analysis of UML diagrams to minimize privacy risks in the final design. The approach iterates between the risk analysis and design modifications to eliminate the risks until a design is obtained that is close to being risk free.*

## INTRODUCTION

Numerous electronic services (e-services) targeting consumers have accompanied the rapid growth of computerization. For example, e-services are available for banking, shopping, learning, healthcare, and Government Online. E-services include "web services" that are based on the service oriented architecture (SOA) (O'Neill et al., 2003). However, most of these services require a consumer's personal information in one form or another, leading to concerns over privacy.

Researchers have proposed various approaches to protect personal information, including data anonymization (Iyengar, 2002; Kobsa & Schreck, 2003) and pseudonym technology (Song et al., 2006). Other such proposals include treating privacy protection as an access problem and then bringing the tools of access control to bear for privacy control (Adams & Barbieri, 2006), treating privacy protection as a privacy rights management problem using the techniques of digital rights management (Kenny & Korba, 2002), and considering privacy protection as a privacy policy compliance

DOI: 10.4018/978-1-4666-1580-9.ch003

problem, verifying compliance with secure logs (Yee & Korba, 2004). However, most e-services today do not use the above approaches, preferring to rely instead on stating a privacy policy and then trying to follow that policy manually, without any of the above techniques or tools or any automated checks in place. As a result, the public is often the victim, as privacy leaks (e.g., credit card files stolen) are discovered and reported in the media. Thus, today's e-services do a poor job of protecting consumer privacy and new effective approaches for such protection are always needed. This is the motivation for this work.

The area of e-services has been chosen for this work because it probably holds the highest risk for the loss of privacy today, in terms of the amount of private information held and the growth of that information. Consider the following. E-services probably require the most consumer private information in order to function than any other type of application. This can be seen once one realizes that if an application requires consumer private information, it can probably be categorized as an e-service. E-services include e-health services where privacy is critical. E-services are growing very rapidly, along with the Internet.

The various approaches for protecting privacy described above all presume to know where and what protection is needed. They presume that some sort of analysis has been done that answers the question of "where" and "what" with respect to privacy risks. Without such answers, the effectiveness of the protection comes into question. For example, protection against house break-ins is totally ineffective if the owner only secures the front door without securing other vulnerable spots such as windows (the "where"). Of course, how the owner secures these spots is critical too ("what" protection). A more effective break-in risk analysis would have identified the windows as being vulnerable to break-ins as well, resulting in better protection against break-ins if the owner additionally secures the windows. In the same

way, privacy risk analysis of service systems, considering "where" and "what", is essential to effective privacy protection.

The objective of this paper is to propose an e-services design approach that incorporates privacy risk analysis to obtain designs that are more likely to preserve privacy than designs that did not use privacy risk analysis. The final design is obtained as the culmination of a series of alternative designs where each alternative design is obtained by re-design to avoid or lessen privacy risks identified through a privacy risk analysis on the last design. Each design is comprised of UML diagrams and the privacy risk analysis is done on a Personal Information Map (PIM, explained below) that is derived from UML diagrams. UML has been chosen for its widespread use among software developers. Basing this approach on UML will make it easier to adopt this approach in practice. Note that the approach does not guarantee that the system implemented from the final design is totally free of privacy risks. Such risks can arise due to implementation errors or the final design itself was not totally risk free (a totally risk free design may not have been feasible due to other constraints, e.g., tight financial budget).

This design approach is based on the principal that it is more effective to design privacy protection into a software system from the beginning, rather than to add it later after the system has been implemented. This is the same principal that it is more effective to design in security from the beginning rather than adding it after implementation, as described in McGraw (2002).

This paper is organized into the following sections: "Privacy and E-Services" defines privacy, privacy policies, privacy risks, and what they mean for e-services. "Approach for Designing E-Services that Protect Privacy" presents the proposed design approach. "Related Work", "Evaluation of Approach" and "Conclusions and Future Research" are as suggested by their names.

## PRIVACY AND E-SERVICES

As defined by Goldberg et al. (1997), privacy refers to the ability of individuals to *control* the collection, retention, and distribution of information about themselves. This leads to the following definitions for this work.

**Definition 1:** *Privacy* refers to the ability of individuals to *control* the collection, use, retention, and distribution of information about themselves.

**Definition 2:** A user's *privacy policy* is a statement that expresses the user's desired control over an e-service's collection, use, retention, and distribution of information about the user.

**Definition 3:** A *user privacy risk* of an e-service is the potential occurrence of any action or circumstance that will result in a violation of a user's privacy policy.

Definition 1 is the same as given by Goldberg et al. except that it also includes "use". To see that "use" is needed, consider, for example, that one may agree to give out one's email address for use by friends to send email but not for use by spammers to send spam. This definition also suggests that "personal information", "private information" or "private data" is any information that can be linked to a person; otherwise, the information would not be "about" the person. Thus, another term for private information is "personally identifiable information (PII)". These terms are used interchangeably in this paper. The linking can be explicit, e.g., the person's name is attached to the information, or implicit, e.g., the information is part of a transaction that can be linked to a specific person.

Definition 2 refers to a user's privacy policy. In this work, the e-service provider also has a privacy policy that details the control that the provider is willing to accept as specified in the user's privacy policy. User information can only be disclosed to the provider if both the user's policy and the provider's policy are in agreement with each other. Figure 1 (adapted from Yee and Korba (2005)) gives an example of user/provider privacy policies for an e-service that implements an online bookseller. This service is used below to illustrate the proposed design approach. *Policy Use* indicates the type of e-service for which the policy will be used. *Valid* holds the time period during which the policy is valid. The fields *collector*, *what*, *purposes*, *retention time*, and *disclose-to* are mandatory. They respectively indicate who is to receive the information, what is the information, for what purposes will the information be used, how long the provider can retain the information, and who outside the provider's organization can also receive the information. These fields derive from privacy principles that form the basis of the Canadian Standards Association Model Code for the Protection of Personal Information (CSA, n.d.). These principles reflect privacy legislation (e.g., United States' Health Insurance Portability and Accountability Act (HIPAA), n.d.) shared by many countries, including Canada, the United States, the European Union, and Australia (Yee et al., 2006).

The policies in Figure 1 are minimum privacy policies in the sense that for any information item, the fields *collector*, *what*, *purposes*, *retention time*, and *disclose-to* form the minimum set of fields required to satisfy privacy legislation. Each set of such fields is termed a *privacy rule* describing a particular information item.

In this work, a privacy risk analysis refers to an analysis of *user* privacy risk. This work considers only risks that involve potential violations of user privacy policies that have been derived from privacy legislation (Definition 3), i.e., violations of the fields *collector*, *what*, *purposes*, *retention time*, and *disclose-to*. The violations can be extended to other concerns should that be necessary.

This work assumes that an e-service and its user have certain requirements and obligations with respect to the user's personal information that is passed to the e-service, as follows:

*Figure 1. Example user (left) and provider (right) privacy policies*

| |
|---|
| *Policy Use:* Bookseller<br>*Owner:* Alice Buyer<br>*Valid:* unlimited |
| *Collector:* All Books Inc.<br>*What:* name, address,<br>book selection<br>*Purposes:* order placing<br>*Retention Time:* unlimited<br>*Disclose-To:* none<br><br>*Collector:* All Books Inc.<br>*What:* credit card details<br>*Purposes:* payment<br>*Retention Time:* 1 week<br>*Disclose-To:* none |

| |
|---|
| *Policy Use:* Bookseller<br>*Owner:* All Books Inc.<br>*Valid:* unlimited |
| *Collector:* Online Dept.<br>*What:* name, address,<br>book selection<br>*Purposes:* order placing<br>*Retention Time:* 1 year<br>*Disclose-To:* none<br><br>*Collector:* Online Dept.<br>*What:* credit card details<br>*Purposes:* payment<br>*Retention Time:* 3 days<br>*Disclose-To:* none |

A. The e-service requires the user's personal information in order to carry out its service to the user. For example, a bookseller e-service requires the user's address for shipping purposes.

B. The e-service and the user exchange privacy policies prior to the start of the service. These policies must agree and be accepted by both the e-service and the user before the service can begin. If there is disagreement, the e-service provider and the user can try to negotiate to a mutually acceptable privacy policy (Yee & Korba, 2003a; Yee & Korba, 2003b).

C. The e-service obtains the user's personal information after agreeing with the user's privacy policy, either before the service begins, during the course of the service, or both.

D. The e-service agrees that once it is in possession of the user's personal information, it will make every effort within its power to comply with the user's privacy policy in good faith, i.e., the e-service is not malicious. However, violations of the user's policy by malicious employees or other insiders of

the e-service are still possible and are not treated in this work.

E. Once the e-service is in possession of the user's personal information, the e-service may transmit the information (e.g., move it from one group to another within the e-service's organization), store the information (e.g., store the information in a data base), and make use of the information to provide the service (e.g., print out shipping labels with the user's address, use the information as input to a calculation, or combined with other data for display in a report).

## APPROACH FOR DESIGNING E-SERVICES THAT PROTECT PRIVACY

The approach for designing e-services that protect privacy consists of the following steps:

A. Perform a privacy risk analysis on the latest UML design (at the start of this approach, the latest design is the starting design). Are there any privacy risks? If yes, go to step

B. If no, the latest design becomes the final design that protects privacy.

B.    Can the latest design be modified to reduce the privacy risks found in A? If yes, make the modifications; the modified design becomes the latest design; go to step A. If no, the latest design becomes the final design that protects privacy.

These steps are illustrated by the flowchart in Figure 2. In this figure, the first decision diamond labeled "Privacy Risks?" refers to whether or not there are privacy risks in the latest UML design. The second decision diamond questions whether or not this design can be modified to reduce the privacy risks that were found.

## Step A: Privacy Risk Analysis

The method for privacy risk analysis is based on the notion that potential violations of the user's privacy policy arise from where the personal information is *located*. This idea is well recognized and applied by traditional non-electronic services. For example, sensitive personal information in paper documents may be protected by removing them from plain view on a desktop (an unprotected location) and placing them in a safe (a protected location). For an e-service, storing the user's personal information in an encrypted database with secure access controls is the equivalent of storing it in a safe, with corresponding minimal privacy risks. The privacy risk analysis, then, consists of a) determining from the UML design all the possible locations in the implemented system where the user's personal information could reside, i.e., looking at how personal information flows through the system, and b) evaluating at each of these locations the possible ways in which the user's privacy policy could be violated. Since a UML design consists of several types of diagrams, it is convenient to disassemble the parts of the diagrams that indicate personal information flows and reassemble them into a concise representation of the

flows called a Personal Information Map (PIM). The privacy risk analysis is done using the PIM.

The following description of how to do step A uses the example bookseller e-service from Section "Privacy and E-Services". This service requires the following personal information: name and address, book selection, and credit card details.

## Method for Privacy Risk Analysis of an UML Design

1.    Starting with the combined component/ deployment diagrams (CCDDs), begin drawing the PIM by drawing a circle to represent each component. Draw a square to represent each database or storage of information. Use a dashed rectangle to enclose circles or squares, corresponding to a unit of hardware in the CCDD in which the components (circles or squares) execute. Units of hardware allow the identification of risks for any data transmission between them. Label the circles and squares with letters. Each such label corresponds to a description of what the component does or a description of the type of storage and is identified in a legend. For example, consider the CCDD of the bookseller e-service given in Figure 3. The corresponding circles, squares, and dashed rectangles (partial PIM) are shown in Figure 5.

2.    The next step in drawing the PIM is to draw arrows between the circles and squares to represent the flow of data between the components in the CCDD. This is done using the sequence charts together with the object-to-component mapping. For each object-to-object data flow in a sequence diagram, draw an arrow between the corresponding circles or squares in the partial PIM where this correspondence is defined by the object-to-component mapping. In other words, an arrow emanates from a circle or square if the latter represents the CCDD

*Figure 2. Flowchart of design approach*

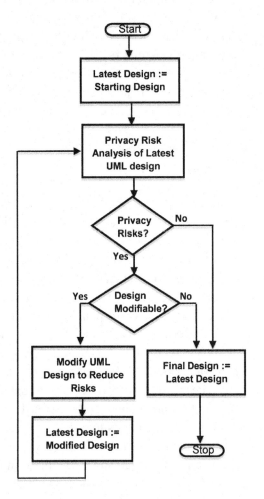

component that contains the object from which the data flow emanates in the sequence diagram. Similarly for an arrow termination. For example, consider the CCDD and sequence diagram for the bookseller service in Figures 3 and 4, respectively, together with its object-to-component mapping (Table 1). The sequence diagram shows an "order data" data flow from the "interface (order server)" object to the "database" object. Since the object-to-component mapping shows that the "interface (order server)" and "database" objects belong to the "order server interface" and "order server database" components, respectively, an arrow is drawn in the PIM,

from the circle labeled "A" (representing the "order server interface" component) to the square labeled "B" (representing the "database" component). In this manner, an arrow is drawn in the PIM for each data flow in the sequence diagram. Next, label each arrow with a number and describe the corresponding data item in the legend. Identify which arrows represent personal data flow by matching the data descriptions in the legend with the descriptions of personal data in the user's privacy policy as given in Figure 1. For example, "order data" consists of name, address, book selection, and credit card details (Figure 3).

3.    Since these data items all appear in the user's privacy policy (Figure 1), they are all personal. "Order data" itself is just a convenience label for all these personal data items. Once all personal data flows have been identified in this way, distinguish the 2 types of data flows, personal and non-personal, in the PIM by changing the non-personal flows to dashed arrows. Finally, combine arrows of the same type (personal data or non-personal data) that have the same origin and destination, and label them with the numbers of the component arrows. The resulting personal data arrows represent physical communication channels for personal information. Following the above procedure produces the completed PIM shown in Figure 6. For clarity, Figure 6 shows only the data flows for a successful order. The flows left out are all non-personal and will not impact the risk analysis.

4.    Inspect the PIM resulting from step 1, and for each location (arrow, square, and circle) and each personal information item, enumerate the possible ways in which a privacy rule may be violated in terms of violations of each of *collector*, *what*, *purposes*, *retention time*, and *disclose-to* in turn (see Section "Privacy and E-Services"). This may be achieved by

asking risk questions for each field, as suggested in Table 2, and drawing conclusions based on knowledge and experience with information security, privacy, and systems. The risk questions are "how" questions, based on the idea that a risk arises where there is some way (i.e. how) for a violation to occur. Record the results in a Privacy Risks Table containing two columns: the left column for records of the form "($PII_1$, $PII_2$, .../ locations)" and the right column containing the corresponding privacy risks. The Privacy Risks Table is the goal of Step A. If this table shows no privacy risks, then the latest design is the final design. Otherwise, it is necessary to proceed with Step B. Table 3 illustrates this step for the PIM in Figure 6.

Table 3 does contain privacy risks, so for the online bookseller example, it is necessary to proceed with Step B.

## Step B: Modify Design to Minimize Privacy Risks

The goal of this step is to come up with a new design that would eliminate or minimize the privacy risks, trying not to compromise other constraints that may exist for the design, such as performance or financial budget. This may be done using the following method.

## Method for Modifying the Design to Minimize Privacy Risks

1.  Examine the Privacy Risks Table from Step A and for each privacy risk, envision how the design can be changed to remove or mitigate the risk, based on knowledge and experience with information security, privacy, software engineering, and systems. The changes are listed in a third column on the Privacy Risks Table with column header "Privacy Risk Mitigation" and are numbered to correspond

with the risks. The resulting table is called a Privacy Risks and Mitigation Table (Table 4 for the online bookseller).

2.  Make modifications to the UML design to reflect the privacy risk mitigation changes in the Privacy Risks and Mitigation Table. For the online bookseller, the path reductions of change 1 (Table 4) can be implemented by combining the "shipping server interface" and the "payment server interface" into the "processing server interface" as one component. The latter interface would then call the "processing server print label" (renamed from "shipping server print label") and the "processing server bill credit card" (renamed from "payment server bill credit card") components as needed (see Figure 7). These 3 components can all run on one platform in order not to introduce additional inter-platform communication paths. Secure channels can be implemented using the Transport Layer Security (TLS) / Secure Sockets Layer (SSL) protocol (Wikipedia, n.d.). Change 2 can be done by adding functionality to the "order server interface" to check the user's privacy policy before requesting information. Change 3 can be carried out by protecting the database from SQL attacks and specifying that anti-malware utilities be used to protect the running system. Finally, change 4 can be implemented by adding functionality to the database to automatically delete PII that is past its retention time. It is assumed that the above changes do not violate any other design constraints. They therefore result in a new UML design with new CCDD (Figure 7) and new sequence diagram (Figure 8). Note that in Figures 7 and Figure 8, "1" has been appended to "Interface" and "Database" to reflect the added functionality for changes 2-4. Of course the above changes may necessitate changes to other UML diagrams as well, e.g., class diagram; these other diagrams are omitted here since they would add little to our discussion.

*Figure 3. CCDD for the bookseller service*

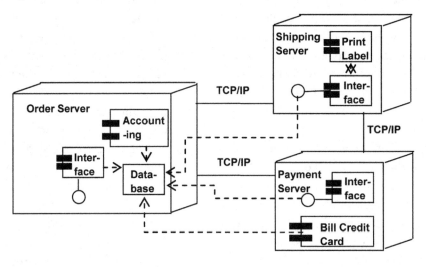

To complete the online bookseller example, Step A is re-entered once the new UML design is obtained, giving the PIM in Figure 9, where A' and B' represent A and B, respectively, with the above changes added. This PIM has one less personal data transmission path compared to the PIM in Figure 6. The ensuing privacy risk analysis of the new PIM shows that all previously identified privacy risks have been mitigated and that no new privacy risks have been introduced. In accordance with the proposed approach, the new design is the final design that protects user privacy, as specified in the user's privacy policy.

## Remarks on the Approach

The object-to-component mapping (Table 1) is not a standard artifact of UML. However, this mapping should be readily available from the software designers. In addition, the example Table 1 contains objects that are not in the sequence diagram, namely "label" and "billing". These objects do not provide any data flow information and can be ignored for drawing the PIM.

It is important to remember that the PIM is not a program logic flow diagram and one should not try to interpret it as such. It shows *where* personal information is located at any moment in time, consistent with the notion that potential violations of the user's privacy policy arise from where the personal information is *located*, mentioned at the start of Step A above.

It was assumed in Step B that for the online bookseller, the changes to mitigate the privacy risks do not violate any other design constraints. In the presence of such a violation, it would be necessary to carefully weigh the advantages and disadvantages of the change, and decide on the course of action (implement the change or not) that would be best for the system. This may not be straightforward (e.g., the risks may need to be quantified) and is part of future research. In the bookseller service, combining the shipping and billing interfaces into one order processing interface and having all order processing components run on one platform may violate a performance constraint. If performance would indeed be violated, it would be necessary to weigh the decrease in performance with the probability of risk realization and make a decision that would be best for the system. A possible alternative solution would be to not make this change and convert the

*Figure 4. Sequence diagram for the bookseller service (note: "order data" consists of name, address, book selection, and credit card details)*

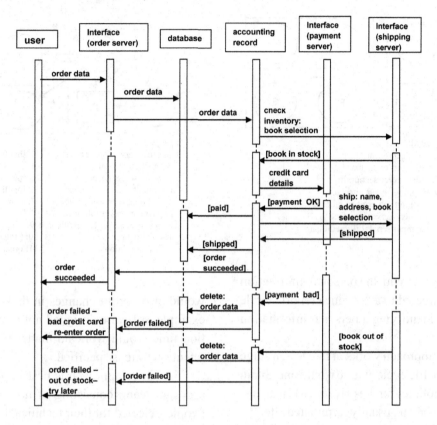

transmission path that would not be removed into a secure channel.

Keeping non-personal information flows in the PIM is important to identify potential unintended leakages of personal information. For example, personal information may be "anonymized" (any obvious links to the information owner removed) and placed in a report, together with non-personal information, for public distribution. The presence of the non-personal informa-

*Table 1. Object-to-component mapping for the bookseller service*

| Components | Objects Contained in Components |
|---|---|
| order server interface | interface (order server) |
| order server database | database |
| order server accounting | accounting record |
| shipping server interface | interface (shipping server) |
| shipping server print label | label |
| payment server interface | interface (payment server) |
| payment server bill credit card | billing |

*Table 2. Risk questions*

| Field | Risk Questions |
|---|---|
| collector | How can the PII be received by an unintended collector either in addition to or in place of the intended collector? |
| what | How can the user be asked for other PII, either intentionally or inadvertently? |
| purposes | How can the PII be used for other purposes? |
| retention time | How can the PII retention time be violated? |
| disclose-to | How can the PII be disclosed either intentionally or inadvertently to an unintended recipient? |

*Figure 5. Partial PIM for the bookseller*

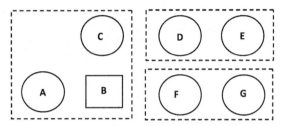

Legend:
A: order server interface
B: order server database
C: order server accounting
D: shipping server interface
E: shipping server print label
F: payment server interface
G: payment server bill credit card

*Figure 6. PIM for the bookseller (flows for a successful order only)*

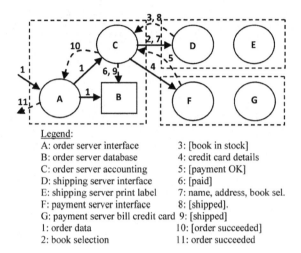

Legend:
A: order server interface
B: order server database
C: order server accounting
D: shipping server interface
E: shipping server print label
F: payment server interface
G: payment server bill credit card
1: order data
2: book selection

3: [book in stock]
4: credit card details
5: [payment OK]
6: [paid]
7: name, address, book sel.
8: [shipped].
9: [shipped]
10: [order succeeded]
11: order succeeded

tion flows together with the personal information flows, both directed to a "produce report" circle could lead to identifying a personal information leakage risk.

Since this approach works at the design stage of the software life cycle, where would one obtain user privacy policies for the privacy risk analysis, since user policies are usually formulated after the service is working? This can be solved by considering privacy policy content as part of software requirements gathering, which occurs before the design phase. As with functional requirements, service providers can meet with users or user groups to agree on common privacy requirements, such as those required by privacy legislation. Subsequent individual privacy policies can still differ from these common requirements but only in terms of detail, e.g., specific values of privacy rules like the values for retention time. Software designed for the common privacy requirements

would also permit changes in these details. For example, software designed not to violate retention time would work no matter what value of retention time is specified.

The above approach is best implemented by a design team, consisting of no more than six people, selected for their technical knowledge of the service design as well as information security and privacy. Good candidates for the team include the service's designers, testers, and at least one expert in information security and privacy, who should lead the team. A team can be more effective at discovering privacy risks by virtue of more people being involved in brainstorming the risks.

The approach can also be semi-automated. Derivation of the PIM from UML can be fully automated. The privacy risk analysis and risk mitigation portions can be semi-automated with the use of rules-based machine learning or expert

*Table 3. Privacy Risks Table for the PIM in Figure 6*

| (PIIs / locations) | Privacy Risks |
|---|---|
| (1/ path into A); (2, 7 / path into D); (4 / path into F) | 1. Man-in-the-middle attack steals data and violates *collector*, *purposes*, and *disclose-to*. 2. For the path into A, the user could be asked for personal information that violates *what*. |
| (1 / A, B, C); (2, 7 / D); (4 / F) | 3. Trojan horse, hacker, or SQL attack (for B) violates *collector*, *purposes*, and *disclose-to*. 4. For B, information could be kept past the *retention time*. |

*Figure 7. CCDD for the re-designed bookseller service*

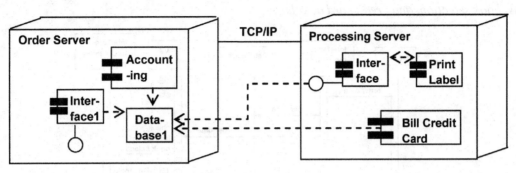

systems. In this case, the team would still be needed to verify and add to the results. Automation is seen as necessary for this approach to be practical and is part of future work.

## RELATED WORK

Related work falls into four categories. The first category concerns threat analysis and software engineering. Hong et al. (2004) proposed the use of privacy risk models to help designers design ubiquitous computing applications that have a reasonable level of privacy protection. Their privacy risk model consists of two parts: a privacy risk analysis part and a privacy risk management part. The risk analysis identifies the privacy risks while the risk management part is a cost-benefit analysis to prioritize the risks and design artifacts to man-

age the risks. Hong et al.'s privacy risk analysis is similar to a privacy impact analysis (Treasury Board of Canada, n.d.), consisting of a series of questions for the designer to answer that help to identify the privacy risks. They differ from this work in that they do not work with UML nor do they use graph-based methods for risk analysis, such as the PIM-based risk analysis described above. Xu and Nygard (2005) present a formal approach to threat-driven modeling and verification of secure software using aspect-oriented Petri nets. Using this language to model behaviors, threats, and mitigations as a whole, they verify properties between behaviors, threats, and the absence of threats. These authors differ from this work in that they focus on software verification rather than design. Further, they do not employ UML nor are they concerned specifically with privacy. Karger (2006) presents a privacy and security threat

*Table 4. Privacy Risks and Mitigation Table for the PIM in Figure 6*

| (PIIs / locations) | Privacy Risks | Privacy Risks Mitigation |
|---|---|---|
| (1/ path into A); (2, 7 / path into D); (4 / path into F) | 1. Man-in-the-middle attack steals data and violates *collector*, *purposes*, and *disclose-to*.<br>2. For the path into A, the user could be asked for personal information that violates *what*. | 1. Reduce the number of such paths where possible. Ensure that all such paths use data encryption and are secure channels.<br>2. Add functionality to ensure that the user is only asked for information allowed by his privacy policy. |
| (1/ A, B, C); (2, 7 / D); (4 / F) | 3. Trojan horse, hacker, or SQL attack (for B) violates *collector*, *purposes*, and *disclose-to*.<br>4. For B, information could be kept past the *retention time*. | 3. Screen for Trojans and add protection against SQL attacks.<br>4. Add functionality to ensure that information is not kept past the *retention time*. |

*Figure 8. Sequence diagram for the re-designed bookseller service (note: "order data" consists of name, address, book selection, and credit card details)*

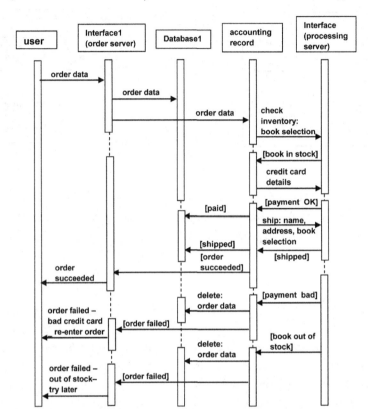

analysis of the American Federal Employee Personal Identity Verification Program based on the standard FIPS PUB 201 (Karger, 2006). However, the privacy threat analysis does not appear to be based on any published method but is done in an ad hoc fashion based on personal knowledge and thinking through scenarios. They differ from this work in that their analysis results are not directed to re-designing the system to avoid the threats. Microsoft (2007) provides a method and tool for threat analysis. Microsoft's method differs from this work in that it does not work for UML, and is concerned with security rather than privacy. McGraw (2005) proposes seven "touch points" or best practices for developing secure software. Touch Point 2 proposes risk analysis during the design phase as does this work. However, Touch Point 2 differs from this work in that there is no

method for the risk analysis and specifically no method for risk analysis of UML. Again, McGraw's touch points are focused on security rather than privacy. Other authors who have written on threat analysis include Rippon (2006) and Bauer (2002). Bauer (2002) is an older reference for basic threat analysis.

A second category of related work involves the use of UML for building secure systems. Jürjens (2005) presents an extensible framework for verifying security properties of UMLsec (Jürjens, 2002), the security extension of UML, relying on automated theorem provers for the verification. Jürjens' work differs from this work in that it concerns verification rather than design. Basin et al. (2006) focus on building secure access control by combining UML with a security modeling language for formalizing access control

*Figure 9. PIM for the bookseller's new design (flows for a successful order only)*

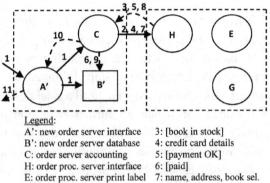

Legend:
A': new order server interface
B': new order server database
C: order server accounting
H: order proc. server interface
E: order proc. server print label
G: order proc. server bill
    credit card
1: order data
2: book selection

3: [book in stock]
4: credit card details
5: [payment OK]
6: [paid]
7: name, address, book sel.
8: [shipped].
9: [shipped]
10: [order succeeded]
11: order succeeded

requirements. They automatically generate access control infrastructures for server-based applications. Basin et al. differ from this work in that they focus on ensuring secure access rather than on design for privacy and are not concerned with privacy, although there is some overlap between secure access and privacy. For example, having secure access to a database of private information could mean that there are mechanisms in place to deter theft of the information and thereby protect privacy.

A third category of related work is the work on privacy impact analysis (PIA) (Treasury Board of Canada, n.d.), mentioned above, and the area of privacy audits (e.g., Enright, n.d.). PIA is a manual process, consisting of a series of questionnaires that are answered by the privacy analyst or a team of privacy analysts in order to identify "impacts" to privacy of a new service or a change to an existing service. Privacy audits strive to identify vulnerabilities or risks in managing private information in order to comply with privacy legislation. PIA and privacy audits are different from this work in that they do not focus on design for privacy, are not specifically designed for electronic services, and do not use the graphical techniques proposed here.

A fourth category of related work is the work on security threat analysis, e.g., Salter et al. (1998). Security threats are related to privacy risks because such threats can increase privacy risks. For example, a Trojan horse attack (security threat) can lead directly to the lost of privacy when private data is unwittingly disclosed to the attacker. Trojan attacks were identified above as a privacy risk for the bookseller example. This category differs from this work in that it is not about design for privacy but about how to do threat analysis. As such it provides some theory for the privacy risk analysis in this work.

Finally, this work is an evolution of Yee (2007) where this author first introduced the PIM notation for privacy risk analysis of web services. Yee (2007) focused on the use of the PIM for privacy risk analysis and input for drawing the PIM was taken from the analyst's knowledge and experience. This work focuses on *how* to design e-services that protect privacy and proposes a design approach to do so. The approach makes use of the risk analysis method given in Yee (2007), but input for drawing the PIM is taken directly from UML diagrams, which if automated would represent a significant advantage over manually drawing the PIM from the analyst's knowledge of the system.

## EVALUATION OF APPROACH

Some strengths of the approach include: a) it provides a structured way to design privacy preserving e-services based on privacy risk analysis of the UML design, b) it appears (but remains to be shown) that the graphical notation for the risk analysis is easy to use, c) input for drawing the PIM is taken directly from UML diagrams thereby not requiring the privacy analyst to have knowledge of how the software is put together, d) the risk analysis is based on an easily understood concept - focus on risks that arise based on the locations that hold the personal information, and

e) it appears (but remains to be shown) that the method is scalable, i.e., larger systems simply require more time in a linear fashion.

Some weaknesses of the approach are: a) filling out the Privacy Risks Table and adding the risk mitigations require expertise in security and privacy, b) the method is a manual process that is prone to error, c) the approach only removes risks that are clear violations of privacy policy – it does not, for example, remove risks associated with unforeseen privacy leaks, where privacy policy has not been violated, and d) the method can never produce services that are totally privacy risk free. Weakness a) is unavoidable as even expert systems must get their expertise from people. Weakness b) can be attenuated through automation as mentioned above in Subsection "Remarks on the approach". Weakness c) will have to stand until the privacy risk analysis can identify such risks, if feasible. In Subsection "Remarks on the approach", it was mentioned that the inclusion of non-personal information flows might help such identification. Nevertheless, unforeseen events are by definition unforeseen, making planning for such events next to impossible. Weakness d) may have to stand, as it is very difficult if not impossible to overcome. Some reasons for why this is so were mentioned in Section "Introduction", i.e. implementation error and conflicting design constraints, but it is also due to the nature of security, that no system can be completely secure.

The proposed approach can be applied to any e-service for end users (e.g., e-banking, e-learning, e-health, B2C e-commerce) and even software systems in general. However, the requirements for privacy are usually more stringent in e-services and this is why e-services were selected as the application area (see Section "Introduction"). The approach can also be easily adapted to B2B e-commerce provided that privacy policies are used to manage privacy at both ends of the transaction (adaptations may be needed to accommodate new types of privacy rules).

# CONCLUSION AND FUTURE RESEARCH

This work has proposed an approach for designing e-services that protect privacy based on privacy risk analysis of UML. The approach repeats a privacy risk determination step, followed by a privacy risk elimination step, until a final design is obtained for which no further reduction in privacy risks is feasible without violating design constraints. The approach has both strengths and weaknesses, as described in Section "Evaluation of Approach", and remains to be field-tested.

The proposed design approach is novel from at least three points of view, as far as this author can tell. First, it is the only approach for designing software specifically for protecting privacy. Second, it is the only design approach that focuses on preventing violations of privacy legislation. Third, it is the only design approach that permits privacy risk analysis of a design specified in UML. With regard to the first point of view, there are plenty of proposals for how to design secure software and we have mentioned some of them in Section "Related Work". However, security is not the same as privacy. With regard to the second point of view, it is highly beneficial that violations of privacy legislation be the focus since such violations can lead to heavy fines. As for the third point of view, the advantage of being able to do privacy risk analysis of UML cannot be overstated. The translation from UML to the PIM can easily be automated. In time, privacy risk analysis of the PIM and the derivation of risk mitigations can also be automated (requires further research). This means that the entire process of identifying privacy threats for UML designs and their associated mitigations will be automated. Since developers tend not to adopt a new approach unless it is easy or automated, automated threat identification of UML models and associated mitigations will be welcomed, and will lead to more software that protects consumer privacy. Moreover, this benefit will be increased many times since UML is a standard model that is widely used.

Future research includes: a) experimenting with the approach to determine its effectiveness by applying it to re-engineer existing e-services, b) determining what other information may be needed to facilitate deciding to proceed with a design modification or not, where the modification violates another design constraint, c) building tools for use in automating privacy risk analysis of UML (such a tool is currently in progress), and d) automating the derivation of risk mitigations.

# REFERENCES

Adams, C., & Barbieri, K. (2006). Privacy Enforcement in E-Services Environments. In Yee, G. (Ed.), *Privacy Protection for E-Services*. Hershey, PA: IGI Global.

Basin, D., Doser, J., & Lodderstedt, T. (2006). Model Driven Security: From UML Models to Access Control Infrastructures. *ACM Transactions on Software Engineering and Methodology, 15*(1), 39–91. doi:doi:10.1145/1125808.1125810

Bauer, M. (2002). Practical Threat Analysis and Risk Management. *Linux Journal, 9*(93).

*CSA*. (n.d.). *Principles in Summary. Canadian Standards Association*. Retrieved August 13, 2009, from http://www.csa.ca/cm?c=CSA_Content& childpagename=CSA%2FLayout&cid=123912 4803011&p=1239124810319&packedargs=loc ale%3D1238188967079&pagename=CSA%2F RenderPage

Enright, K. P. (n.d.). *Privacy Audit Checklist*. Retrieved May 6, 2006, from http://cyber.law. harvard.edu/clinical/privacyaudit.html

Goldberg, I., Wagner, D., & Brewer, E. (1997). Privacy-Enhancing Technologies for the Internet. In. *Proceedings of the IEEE COMPCON, 97*, 103–109.

HIPAA. (n.d.). *Health Insurance Portability and Accountability Act of 1996 (HIPAA) Privacy Rule*. Retrieved August 13, 2009, from http://www.hhs. gov/ocr/privacy/index.html

Hong, J. I., Ng, J. D., Lederer, S., & Landay, J. A. (2004). Privacy Risk Models for Designing Privacy-Sensitive Ubiquitous Computing Systems. In *Proceedings of the 2004 Conference on Designing Interactive Systems: Processes, Practices, Methods, and Techniques*, Cambridge, MA (pp. 91-100).

Iyengar, V. S. (2002). Transforming Data to Satisfy Privacy Constraints. In *Proceedings of SIGKDD '02*, Edmonton, Alberta.

Jürjens, J. (2002). UMLsec: Extending UML for Secure Systems Development. In *Proceedings of the 5th International Conference on the Unified Modeling Language* (LNCS 2460, pp. 412-425). Berlin: Springer Verlag.

Jürjens, J. (2005, May 15-21). *Sound Methods and Effective Tools for Model-based Security Engineering with UML*. Paper presented at the International Conference on Software Engineering (ICSE'05), St. Louis, MO.

Karger, P. A. (2006). Privacy and Security Threat Analysis of the Federal Employee Personal Identity Verification (PIV) Program. In *Proceedings of the Second Symposium on Usable Privacy and Security*, Pittsburgh, PA (pp. 114-121).

Kenny, S., & Korba, L. (2002). Adapting Digital Rights Management to Privacy Rights Management. *Computers & Security, 21*(7), 648–664. doi:doi:10.1016/S0167-4048(02)01117-3

Kobsa, A., & Schreck, J. (2003). Privacy Through Pseudonymity in User-Adaptive Systems. *ACM Transactions on Internet Technology, 3*(2), 149–183. doi:doi:10.1145/767193.767196

McGraw, G. (2002). Building Secure Software: Better than Protecting Bad Software. *IEEE Software*, *19*(6), 57–58. doi:doi:10.1109/MS.2002.1049391

McGraw, G. (2005). The 7 Touchpoints of Secure Software. *Dr. Dobb's*. Retrieved August 15, 2009, from http://www.ddj.com/security/184415391

Microsoft. (2007). *Microsoft Threat Analysis and Modeling v2.1.2*. Retrieved August 15, 2009, from http://www.microsoft.com/downloads/details.aspx?FamilyId=59888078-9DAF-4E96-B7D1-944703479451&displaylang=en

O'Neill, M., Hallam-Baker, P., MacCann, S., Shema, M., Simon, E., Watters, P. A., & White, A. (2003). *Web Services Security*. New York: McGraw-Hill/Osborne.

Rippon, W. J. (2006, April). Threat assessment of IP based voice systems. In *Proceedings of the 1ˢᵗ IEEE Workshop on VoIP Management and Security 2006*, Vancouver, B.C., Canada (pp. 19-28).

Salter, C., Saydjari, O. S., Schneier, B., & Wallner, J. (1998, September). Towards a Secure System Engineering Methodology. In *Proceedings of New Security Paradigms Workshop*.

Song, R., Korba, L., & Yee, G. (2006). Pseudonym Technology for E-Services. In Yee, G. (Ed.), *Privacy Protection for E-Services*. Hershey, PA: IGI Global.

Treasury Board of Canada. (n.d.). *The Privacy Impact Assessment Guidelines: A Framework to Manage Privacy Risk*. Retrieved May 6, 2006, from http://www.tbs-sct.gc.ca/pgol-pged/piatp-pfefvp/course1/mod2/mod2-5_e.asp

*Wikipedia*. (n.d.). Retrieved February 15, 2009, from http://en.wikipedia.org/wiki/Transport_Layer_Security

Xu, D., & Nygard, K. (2005, November 7-11). A Threat-Driven Approach to Modeling and Verifying Secure Software. In *Proceedings of the 20ᵗʰ IEEE/ACM International Conference on Automated Software Engineering (ASE '05)*, Long Beach, CA.

Yee, G. (2007, July 9-13). Visual Analysis of Privacy Risks in Web Services. In *Proceedings of the 2007 IEEE International Conference on Web Services (ICWS 2007)*, Salt Lake City, UT.

Yee, G., & Korba, L. (2003a, May 18-21). The Negotiation of Privacy Policies in Distance Education. In *Proceedings of the 14th IRMA International Conference*, Philadelphia, PA.

Yee, G., & Korba, L. (2003b, January 27-31). Bilateral E-services Negotiation Under Uncertainty. In *Proceedings of the 2003 International Symposium on Applications and the Internet (SAINT2003)*, Orlando, FL.

Yee, G., & Korba, L. (2004, July 6-9). Privacy Policy Compliance for Web Services. In *Proceedings of the 2004 IEEE International Conference on Web Services (ICWS 2004)*, San Diego, CA.

Yee, G., & Korba, L. (2005). Semi-Automatic Derivation and Use of Personal Privacy Policies in E-Business. *International Journal of E-Business Research*, *1*(1), 54–69.

Yee, G., Korba, L., & Song, R. (2006). Legislative Bases for Personal Privacy Policy Specification. In Yee, G. (Ed.), *Privacy Protection for E-Services*. Hershey, PA: IGI Global.

*This work was previously published in International Journal of Secure Software Engineering, edited by Khaled M. Khan, pp. 18-34, Volume 1, Issue 2, copyright 2010 by IGI Publishing (an imprint of IGI Global).*

# Section 2
# Security Requirements Analysis and Modeling

# Chapter 4
# Software Engineering Security Based on Business Process Modeling

**Joseph Barjis**
*Delft University of Technology, The Netherlands*

## ABSTRACT

*Security requirements must be tackled early in software design and embedded in corresponding business process models. As a blueprint for software design, business process models complemented with security requirements will prevent many security breaches. To accomplish secure business process modeling, the underlying method must adhere to certain capabilities and capture actions, actor roles, and interactions. The resultant models should lend themselves to automatic analysis (simulation) to ensure captured security requirements are correctly aligned with the process flow. Thus, the tradeoff between the level of security and business performance can be studied before actual software design. Since unauthorized actions cause security breaches, the software the system's social setting could be a cradle for defining security requirements. Security requirements can be identified based on the roles, authorities, and obligations of the social actors using the system. This paper introduces a method for security embedded business process modeling. The proposed method draws on two well-tested theoretical foundations—enterprise ontology and organizational semiotics.*

## 1 INTRODUCTION

Business process modeling plays a pivotal role in software system design (Barjis, 2008), which is often referred to as a software system blueprint (Nagaratnam et al., 2005). Due to this important role, business process models are becoming a natural focus for incorporation of security requirements that consequently should be passed to the software design and development phases. Business process modeling allows software designers to capture functional requirements better and more easily while automatically generating these requirements from the business process models (Basin et al., 2003). Especially with the prevailing process-centric approach in software design, business process models are the appropriate departure point for understanding the business

DOI: 10.4018/978-1-4666-1580-9.ch004

domain for which a software system is developed, and for understanding the social setting in which the software system will be used.

Failing to recognize this importance up front may cause many security requirements to be overlooked and left for end-of-pipe solutions. The lack of appropriate security requirements, such as authorized access control in the activities carried out by the actors, leaves the software system as well as the whole enterprise vulnerable to possible threats (D'Aubeterre et al., 2008). In regard to the social environment of a software system, identification and definition of behavioral rules serve as a valuable source of security requirements. Despite this obvious importance, software system design is mainly driven by functional requirements.

Systems requirements define the functional aspects of a system such as what a system is supposed to achieve, therefore often these functional requirements dominate the business requirements and constraints even if the latter are well defined (Khan et al., 2004). The fact that the business requirements and constraints are not captured in the corresponding conceptual models in any form for later usage, and most of them are not available for further consultation at the implementation stage, leaves the chance of omitting essential security constraints wide open. In order to avoid this pitfall, Khan et al. (2004) suggest (diagrammatically) incorporating security requirements into the model and making them part of the created artifact (model). In this manner, the security requirements identified at the business level will better make their way to the later phases of software systems design.

In this paper, we introduce a business process modeling method that captures security functions during the business process modeling phase. Actually, this approach has been discussed and tested in many past studies, where existing methods have been extended with the capability of capturing security requirements, for example Baskerville (1988), Herrmann and Pernul (1999), Backes et

al. (2003), Mana et al. (2003). A similar approach is also proposed in D'Aubeterre et al. (2008), where security requirements are incorporated into the business process model, or in the works that resulted in enriched Use Case (Siponen et al., 2006), where the UML Use Case diagram is extended to incorporate security requirements in the design phase. Actually, UML, as the *de facto* industry standard, has been widely favored by the proponents of secure business process modeling researchers (Lodderstedt et al., 2002; Firesmith, 2003; Jurjens, 2004; Basin et al., 2006).

Despite diligent efforts made by these researchers, security-driven business process modeling is still far from becoming a true departure point for secure software development and therefore it is not an adapted practice in companies (Neubauer et al., 2006). One of the dominant reasons the role of business process modeling in software engineering is not realized is that the existing methods suffice to address merely conceptual and semantic levels and, therefore, they present little pragmatic value for software designers. By using the existing methods, it is difficult to automatically analyze the models and, therefore, the embedded security functions are not possible to test and simulate.

The core contribution of this paper is introduction and discussion of a modeling method developed for secure business process modeling (secure BPM) that incorporates not only the related business transactions but also security functions with the resultant model being based on formal semantics. The starting point for the proposed modeling method is identification of business transactions, then the roles and interactions of the actors as they carry out the assigned operations, tasks, and actions.

In comparison to the existing methods for incorporation of security requirements in business process models, the method proposed in this paper offers certain advantages:

1.  The proposed method results in a security-embedded business process model that is completely based on formal semantics. That is, the models can be automatically analyzed or simulated to study the impact of the incorporated security requirements and whether the security requirements compromise business performance in any way.

2.  The proposed modeling method is based on the theoretical foundation laid out in the studies of enterprise ontology (Dietz, 2006), which is proven to achieve a complete ontological model (business process model). This, in turn, indicates that the likelihood of completeness of defined security functions is significantly improved.

3.  The security functions are defined and incorporated using the Norm Analysis Method (Stamper, 1994; Stamper, Liu, Hafkamp, & Ades, 2000). This method allows defining behavioral rules that lead to security functions. This method allows that all security functions be defined in a rigorous manner, which is done separately from the process modeling. This allows flexibility for the design as security functions can be always modified (removed or added) without changes in the process model. Second, the security functions are defined, but not in terms of conditions or true and false statements. Definitions are operationalized in terms of behavioral rules, which provide a rather rich picture for how to define security functions or measures.

4.  Finally, the strength of the proposed method is in capturing not only the actions, but also the roles of actors that are assigned for execution of each action. Thus, defining behavioral rules for each actor in relation to the actions they are authorized to perform capture the social dimension or environment, in which the intended software system will be deployed.

This paper is structured in the following manner: An introduction to the topic of this paper is provided in this section; a discussion of the proposed modeling framework for security embedded business process modeling is carried in the following section (section 2); discussion of theoretical foundations and methods that are the basis for the proposed method takes place in section 3; also an illustrative healthcare example is given in section 3 to illustrate secure business process modeling (Secure BPM); section 4 is devoted to a brief discussion of the related works; and the last section contains discussion and conclusion based on the contribution of this paper.

In this research, phrases such as security embedded business process modeling, security driven business process modeling, or secure business process modeling are used interchangeably. The same is true for security requirements, security functions, and security constraint, which are also used interchangeably. Also 'Secure BPM' stands for 'secure business process modeling' and 'secure business process model', which will be obvious from the context.

## 2. A FRAMEWORK FOR SECURE BPM

In this section, we discuss a framework and approach for developing a secure business process model, which represents actions as well as the roles, authorities, and responsibility of the related actors.

## 2.1. The Modeling Framework

The modeling framework, illustrated in Figure 1, visualizes the discussion we had in the introduction section. This framework illustrates that a secure business process model (Secure BPM) can serve as a blueprint for defining security requirements in a software system. This framework has two main components that need to be developed and integrated in order to create a secure business process model. The first component is the 'business transactions' that need to be identified based on a 'business domain' description that an analyst should obtain first. This component constitutes a business process model without security functions.

The second component is 'security functions' that is mainly defined based on the security policy of the related organization. This component contains the related security functions that are defined for each business transaction. These two components are developed in correlation with each other in a collaborative manner. It is assumed that an organization already has a well documented and defined security policy (determiners), or they will document them as new policies are adapted as a result of changes in the organization's internal and external environments. Together, the two components create a Secure BPM, as depicted by the dashed-line rectangle in Figure 1, which contribute to both functional requirements and security requirements during software engineering.

Security Policy (security determiners) – these are rules and procedures that an organization wants to have implemented with regard to processes and actors behavior. These determiners define the business transactions that carry security-sensitive actions, for example, any action on sensitive and personal records (read, delete, modify), or whether a transaction may be executed in the boundary of two organizations when transmitting credit card information, healthcare records, and so on.

Once the security functions are defined, business transactions are coupled with their corresponding security functions and every time a transaction is initiated these security functions might be also executed. Actually, security functions are not necessarily implemented for each business transaction. In fact, designers may consider a reasonable trade-off between the level of security and business performance. As security is only one of the design objectives, it certainly competes with other design objectives for software systems such as performance, functionality, and usability. Therefore, security aspects of a system

*Figure 1. Modeling framework for secure BPM*

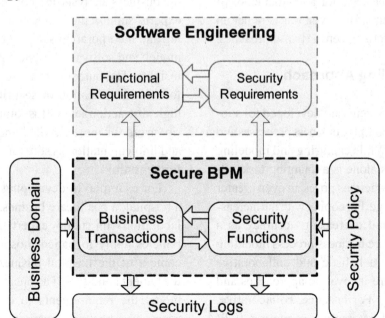

should aim at rather "good enough" to allow other competing demands to be met (Elahi & Yu, 2007). Here is when methods based on formal semantics demonstrate superiority as they allow simulation of the resultant models for performance analysis.

The 'security logs' component contains records of all business transactions that trigger the security functions. This contains the actor's identity and time stamp for business transactions along with the triggered security functions. This component will also allow monitoring and managing access and execution of sensitive transactions.

Before concluding, there are two aspects of the above framework that deserve to be highlighted. First, the modeling framework of Figure 1 should be seen from a process centric approach towards secure business process modeling, which is distinct from a road map for secure business process management as discussed in (Neubauer et al., 2006) or security reference models such as one discussed in (Matulevicius et al., 2008). Second, this modeling framework might marginally resemble the three criteria for determination of "adequate security requirements" discussed in (Haley et al., 2008). These three criteria are: definition of security requirements, incorporation of assumptions about behavior, and satisfaction of security requirements. However, this is rather an approximate parallel between the two approaches.

## 2.2. The Modeling Approach

Modern software systems are developed for supporting extremely complex business processes and user interactions. While capturing and modeling business processes alone is a daunting task, addition of security functions poses an even greater complexity challenge. For coping with the increasing complexity (and decreasing accuracy as a consequence), secure business process modeling definitely requires a holistic and collaborative approach. There are innovative approaches and methods emerging. For instance, collaborative, participative, and interactive modeling (CPI

Modeling) suggests a broader and inclusive participation of expertise in the modeling efforts (Barjis, 2009).

The approach we consider along with the mentioned framework is of collaboration of different areas of expertise which allows developing a secure BPM as specified in Figure 1. The inclusive participation of experts in the proposed modeling framework contributes towards more adequate security requirements based on the underling business transactions.

The overall proposition is that for secure BPM, close collaboration of different types of expertise is becoming more and more prevalent and crucial. This approach is illustrated through the secure business process modeling collaboration quadrant shown in Figure 2. As depicted in the collaboration quadrant, the 'business analyst' role is emphasized as a prominent and central role. Although the business modeling phase is led by business analysts, it is carried out in collaboration with domain experts (users), policy experts, and software designers. Each of these groups plays an essential role in developing secure models: 'business analyst' leads the whole work; 'domain experts' provide domain-specific knowledge to the business analysts and policy experts; 'policy experts' support the business analysts in identifying and incorporating security functions into the model; and software designers provide technical insights. The outcome of these collaborative efforts is identification of security functions at a high abstraction level. It is rather flagging security areas for more detailed and robust analysis and implementation as software design activities further unfold.

For example: In developing secure BPM for a hospital, a healthcare business analyst (in collaboration with a policy expert) determines which policies apply to patient hospitalization in the context of the hospital business processes and the patient condition. The business analyst might model the requirements to control authorized access to a healthcare activity or assets such as

*Figure 2. A collaboration quadrant for developing secure BPM*

medical records, and to ensure that the medical information flow is protected from unauthorized access thus ensuring confidentiality. The medical security requirements can be defined within the secure BPM. These models rather provide a reference that may be used by the hospital compliance officers, such as security auditors, to verify and monitor adherence to the hospital security and confidentiality policies.

Although the proposed modeling framework and modeling approach are fairly specific and cover detailed security functions, they are still abstract enough to allow developers and security experts to employ their implementation creativity, i.e., it is not a trespassing into the security experts authority, who are dealing with the development and implementation aspects.

In summary, in the suggested approach, business processes are described in terms of business transactions, where each transaction entails interaction of actors (human actors), business units, and artifacts (software components). Depending on the sensitivity of the carried activities, transactions are complemented with security functions.

Up to this point, we discussed a few things: the need for secure BPM to ensure better security functions in the envisioned software system; a modeling framework for conducting secure BPM; and a collaborative approach for secure BPM.

Basically, we set a stage for the main contribution this paper is making. What we do in the remainder of this paper is to introduce and discuss a modeling method that complies with the objectives we laid down so far – a business process modeling method that allows developing secure business process models, defining security functions and allowing to simulate the model. The starting point for the proposed modeling method is to look at the roles and interactions of the actors as they carry out the assigned tasks and actions for which they are responsible..

Since interaction of components (actors, artifacts, agents) is the center-point of our approach, the ontological business transaction concept is used as a theoretical basis for identifying business activities. The ontological transaction concept is a core constituent of the DEMO Methodology for organizational and enterprise modeling (Dietz, 2006). Next to the ontological transaction concept, Petri net is adapted for constructing the model diagrams. In fact, due to its formal semantics, models based on Petri net notations are formal and lend to automatic analysis. Each security function is defined using the Norm Analysis Method (Stamper, 1994) of the Organizational Semiotics (Stamper, 1997; Liu, 2000). The norm analysis method is adapted to define rules, norms, authorities, responsibilities, and exceptions for the execution of each transaction. Both the ontological transaction concept and the norm analysis method are discussed in the following section.

## 3. SECURE BPM

In order to develop secure business process models (secure BPM), as we discussed in the previously presented modeling framework, we need a modeling concept, modeling language, and a method for definition of security functions. In the following subsection, we introduce both a modeling concept and the modeling language (graphical notations) to implement it. Then, we discuss a method for definition of security functions. In fact, the subsections below are organized according to the modeling framework we discussed earlier. Each of the components of the modeling framework is carried out by first discussing a theoretical underpinning for it and then the application approach.

### 3.1. Secure BPM: Business Transactions

In the core of our modeling lies the concept of business transaction or ontological transaction. It should be clarified that by a business transaction, we always refer to an ontological transaction, which is introduced, defined, and discussed in Dietz (2006). There empirical studies have been conducted over the span of almost two decades during which a business process model was developed based on the concept of ontological transaction resulting in a complete model without leaving any ontological transaction out (Dietz, 2006). This is the superiority of the ontological transaction concept as a modeling concept, which is not the case with many existing modeling methods used in the current practice, including the well-known UML models. We will return to this assertion later in this paper and discuss the implications of this claim for software security functions.

Now, let us discuss what an ontological (business transaction) is and which theoretical and conceptual notions are underlying the concept of ontological or business transaction according to the Enterprise Ontology (Dietz, 2006):

- An ontological transaction is a platform and implementation-free atomic process that creates a unique fact (or result):
  ○ **For example:** the 'buy a new insurance policy' atomic process is an ontological transaction that creates a new insurance policy once executed
- An ontological transaction is carried out by two actor roles:
  ○ **For example:** the 'buy a new insurance policy' transaction involves a customer and an insurance company
- The roles in an ontological transaction are distinct:
  ○ **For example:** the 'buy a new insurance policy' transaction involves one initiator role (customer) and one executor role (insurance company)

An ontological transaction is a generic pattern consisting of both an 'action' and 'interactions'. An action is also referred to as 'productive act' that brings about a new result. An interaction is also referred to as 'communicative act' directed at negotiations and commitments by the actors.

Below we provide more examples of an ontological transaction:

- **Buy a plane ticket:** In this transaction the two roles played are a passenger and a carrier, and the new fact is the purchase of a ticket.
- **Conduct a medical examination:** In this transaction the two roles played are a patient and a physician, and the new fact created is examination results which suggest possible treatment given to the patient.

Examination results still need to be interpreted, so there's another step in there perhaps. But we will discuss a composite transaction or a transaction nesting further transactions later in the paper.

An ontological transaction is an atomic process, which is carried out in three phases. In these three phases, a productive act and communicative acts are taking place (read more about these notions in Dietz, 2006; Barjis, 2007; Barjis, 2008). The following is how these two types of acts evolve (refer to Figure 3a as reading the following):

- In order to buy a new insurance policy, the initiating actor should make such a request. The executing actor takes the request and sees whether the desired type of insurance and the stated conditions can be fulfilled. If it is possible, then the executing actor makes a promise of handling the request. For distinction, this part of an ontological transaction is referred to as Order phase and denoted through a capital 'O'.

- Once a commitment (promise) is made, the executing actor is now starting to produce the requested service by processing the request and submitted documents to issue a new policy. This part of the ontological transaction is referred to as Execution phase and denoted through a capital 'E'.

- When the result is ready (a new policy with all calculation and terms), it is presented by the executing actor toward the initiating actor, who eventually will accept it (we assume the successful path). This part of the ontological transaction is referred to as Result phase and denoted through a capital 'R'.

The phases of an ontological transaction and their corresponding acts can be explicit or implicit. Often the communicative acts, especially promise and accept, might be rather implicit. But we recognize that such an act might take place in the generic pattern that represents an ontological transaction. The above discussion is more directed at the principle and foundation of what is called an ontological transaction. For a more pragmatic purpose, it might be useful if we just illustrate an ontological transaction as a sequence of three phases (Figure 3b) distinguishing the start and end points by different circles.

## 3.2. Secure BPM: Security Functions

The method we adapted for definition of security functions is derived from the Organizational Semiotics (Stamper, 1997; Liu, 2000). Organizational semiotics consists of a set of methods including the Norm Analysis Method (Stamper, 1994) discussed in this section. The Norm Analysis Method

*Figure 3. Business transaction: a) detailed steps; b) simplified OER form*

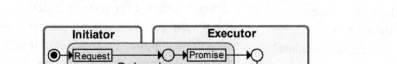

(NAM) is adapted for governing actors' (agents) actions and authorization for certain actions. Authorization of access to the organization assets (resources) represents essential importance to the security of the whole system as compromising access authorization may pose significant harm to the organization (Bai, 2008). In particular, authorization enforces certain security mechanisms which are in compliance with the rules and norms specified by the organization's security strategies. We find the NAM to be an adequate method and tool to reinforce such a security mechanism driven by rules and norms that govern actors' behavior and access to the organization assets. Authorization allows only the authorized actors to have the privilege of executing certain activities that may present adverse consequences such as modifying or revealing data.

While the transaction concept captures the business activities, the norm analysis method is used as a suitable complement to capture behavioral norms (for more reading on organizational semiotics, refer to Stamper, 1994; Stamper, 1997; Liu, 2000).

Understanding of the norms and patterns of actors' behavior within an organization provides a solid foundation for designing secure software system. According to the organizational semiotics framework, there are five types of norms that influence certain aspects of human behavior. They are 'perceptual norms', 'cognitive norms', 'evaluative norms', 'behavioral norms' and 'denotative norms' (Stamper, 1994). Each of these norms manifests either a mental state or a constraint on the behavior that one will adopt. Out of these five norms, behavioral norms are more observable and are the ones that affect and regulate humans' behavior in an organization.

In business, most rules and regulations fall into the category of behavioral norms. These norms prescribe what people must, may, and must not do, which are equivalent to three deontic operators "is obliged," "is permitted," and "is prohibited."

Therefore, particular attention is given to the behavioral norms since they are expressed as business rules, and have direct impacts on business operations and corresponding software security. Behavioral norms govern human behavior within regular patterns. The following format is considered suitable for specification of behavioral norms – a generic structure for all norms derived from Stamper (1994), but with a slight extension of 'alternative action' clause as an alternative course of actions needs to be defined if an action fails to meet security constraints:

In this generic structure of behavioral norms, the condition clause describes a matching situation where the norm is to be applied, and sometimes further specified with a state clause (this clause is optional). The actor clause specifies the responsible actor for the action. The actor can be a staff member, a customer, or a software component. As for the next clause, it quantifies a deontic state and usually expresses in one of the three operators - permitted, forbidden and obliged. For the next clause, it defines the consequence of the norm. The consequence possibly leads to an action or to the generation of information for others to act. The final clause is the alternative course of actions ('else') that may lead to a different action or a complex action that itself may contain a nested norm. We refer to this format as a generic structure for security functions.

For example: whenever a patient with prior appointment applies for treatment, if the patient has valid insurance policy, then the physician is obliged to provide proper healthcare, else, if the patient fails to present proof of insurance coverage but has an emergency case, the medical facility is still obliged to provide an adequate service. In practice, the alternative action clause 'else' can be

*Figure 4. Graphical representation of a generic security function with possible (dotted box) alternative course of action*

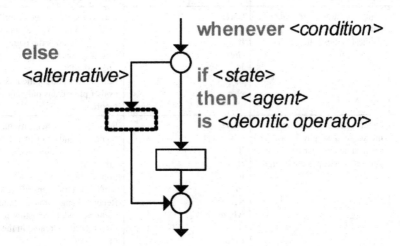

rather more complex, e.g., delivering the patient to a third-party provider should it be required.

These clauses can be also represented in a generic scheme, as illustrated in Figure 4. This is rather a simple scheme as it can be extended to a more detailed one by incorporating 'alternative action' in a more elaborated manner. For example, the alternative action could be freezing any further action, or it can be iteration until the security function is satisfied, or offering a limited access, etc. Here, we rather leave it as a simple structure assuming that this high level representation will allow better room for different implementation strategies. In any case, the reader should be cautious that the schema of Figure 4 is a step towards implementation of a rule while the above generic structure is more of a context, which represents a richer implementation space for the rules.

## 3.3. Secure BPM: A Healthcare Example

The example we use in this paper for illustration is just a simple medical treatment process. In this process, there are only three ontological transactions identified. These transactions are presented in Table 1. The process starts with a patient applying

for medical treatment. We denote this transaction as T1. However, this transaction seems to be a composite transaction as it nests at least two further transactions. For example, when the treatment starts, a nurse should conduct a complete general check up. We denote this second transaction as T2. Also the treatment process might require that the patient has to do some basic lab work (e.g., EKG) as part of the treatment while in the doctor's office. We denote this third transaction as T3.

In a similar manner, we identify security functions that should be defined for each ontological transaction. We identify security functions and then assign them the same number as the corresponding transaction number. We denote each security function through a capital 'S' and number them according to the corresponding transaction number. Since each transaction may have more than one security function, we use two orders of numbering, where the first number corresponds to the transaction number and the second number to the number of security function for that transaction. When defining security functions, not necessarily all the clauses should be included or defined. For example, some security functions may not include the 'state' clause ('if') or the 'alternative action' clause.

*Table 1. Ontological (or business) transactions and security functions*

| Ontological (or Business) Transactions | | Security Functions | |
|---|---|---|---|
| **T1:**<br>**Initiator**<br>**Executor**<br>**Fact** | apply for medical treatment<br>patient<br>medical center (physician)<br>patient is treated | **S1.1:**<br>**whenever**<br>**if**<br>**then**<br>**is**<br>**to**<br>**else** | Patient record update security function<br><a physician examines a patient ><br><the physician is the patient family doctor><br><the physician><br><permitted><br><update the patient medical records><br><other physicians only allowed make new records> |
| **T2:**<br>**Initiator**<br>**Executor**<br>**Fact** | conduct general checkup<br>medical center (physician)<br>medical center (nurse)<br>general checkup is conducted | **S2.1:**<br>**whenever**<br>**if**<br>**then**<br>**is**<br>**to**<br>**S2.2:**<br>**whenever**<br>**if**<br>**then**<br>**is**<br>**to** | Record creation security function<br><a nurse conducts general checkup><br><the nurse is authorized so><br><the nurse><br><obliged><br><enter all vital signs of the patient><br>Record change security function<br><a nurse updates existing records><br><the record is created in the past ><br><the nurse><br><prohibited><br>< make changes to existing records> |
| **T3:**<br>**Initiator**<br>**Executor**<br>**Fact** | perform lab test<br>medical center (physician)<br>medical center (lab technician)<br>lab tests are performed | **S3.1:**<br>**whenever**<br>**then**<br>**is**<br>**to** | Quality assurance<br><the accuracy of local lab results might be questioned><br><the lab technician><br><prohibited><br><conduct the lab tests locally> |

Now that we have identified the related ontological transactions and defined their corresponding security functions, we build a corresponding secure business process model. In Figure 5, all identified transactions are put in relation to each, which make up the patient treatment process. For example, T1 is a composite transaction. Its execution triggers at least two further transactions. Therefore, the T1 execution phase is split into sub-phases to incorporate the two nested transaction. The first nested transaction that should be completely carried out is T2 (general check up). Since this is a simple transaction and nests no further transactions, we represent T2 in a compact form (all the three phases are condensed into one box). The second nested transaction is T3 (lab works). However, this transaction is an optional transaction. This optionality is indicated by a diamond shape added to the box. An optional transaction is not always carried out as its initia-

tion depends on certain conditions. Thus, the execution phase (T1/E) of transaction T1 consists of three sub-phases denoted through a small 'e' and numbered accordingly (T1/e1, T1/e2, T1/e3).

The above model of the patient treatment process is based on fully formal semantics. The model is simulated and the effect of security functions can be studied. Construction of this model completes all the components of the modeling framework we discussed earlier in the modeling framework. This model includes all business transactions we identified while each business transaction is complemented by a set of security functions that are called when the business transaction is executed. This way, the presented model is a secure business process model according to the modeling framework we discussed. Although this model is just a simple illustrative example, a model of any size and complexity can be studied in the same manner. The interested

*Figure 5. Patient treatment process*

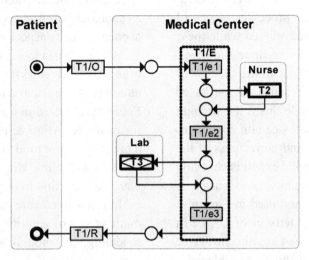

reader is referred to Barjis (2007) or Barjis (2008), where they will find a complete description of the modeling language and how complex models can be furnished by using compact and composite notations.

Due to space restriction in this paper, the simulation discussion is very limited.. It should suffice to mention that the model of Figure 5 is a direct input for simulation without any further modification, transformation or translation. Any discrete event simulation tool will allow for its simulation. Depending on the tool, it is required to enter the security functions we identified in Table 1 in the tool specific format.

## 4. RELATED WORK

Security-driven business process modeling attracted many researchers during the recent year, during which significant studies have been done in this regard. These researchers profoundly advocate the need for sliding security matters down the system design ladder to the business process modeling phase (Herrmann & Pernul, 1999; Mana et al., 2003; Backes et al., 2003; Neubauer et al., 2006; Herrmann & Herrmann, 2006; Rodríguez et al., 2006; Rodriguez & Guzman, 2007).

Incorporation of security requirements in business process modeling essentially improves secure software engineering. In Nagaratnam et al. (2005), the authors argue that business process modeling is an ideal time in the life cycle of software system development to begin capturing the business security requirements that address security concerns related to the business. This argument of incorporating security early into the business specifications has been consistently raised, supported, and advocated by security researchers and business analysts. Actually, secure business process modeling attracted researchers long before that within the information systems community and continues doing so (Baskerville, 1988; Backhouse & Dhillon, 1996; Lopez et al., 2005; Siponen et al., 2006).

One of the earliest works tackling security issues of information systems using existing methodologies is Backhouse and Dhillon (1996). In this work, the authors propose a concept for using the notions of authority and responsibility in order to ensure that activities are carried out by the authorized actors. The underlying concept of authority and responsibility in (Backhouse & Dhillon, 1996) is based on the works of Gibson (1977) and Stamper (1988), and is graphically represented using a semantic schema (ontology chart, an informal diagram). Although semantic schema is rich with information, it has two challenges. First, for complex processes, series of these schemas should be developed while these schemas are represented as separate segments. Second, the schemas and the whole process of capturing and model representation are based on informal approach. While this is the strength of semantic schema, it poses certain challenges to check the consistency and correctness of the schemas unless a well trained expert is checking the models (schemas) manually, i.e., visually.

The approach and method used in Firesmith (2003) is based on the extension of UML. In particular, the author proposes a method to derive security-use cases in order to model a problem domain for secure application development. Actually, due to its popularity as a requirements elicitation method, the security-use case approach has been researched and developed by many researchers (Jürjens, 2004; Sindre, 2007). Every modeling or security modeling effort based on UML diagrams inherits the same challenges that have been widely discussed and addressed in regard to UML modeling. First, this includes the difficulty of using UML modeling due to multiple diagrams and a huge set of notations. Second, UML diagrams are an informal graphical representation that often translates into other formal diagrams for model checking purposes.

Another popular and widely-used modeling language and method extended with security properties is BPMN (business process modeling notation). In Rodríguez et al. (2007), the authors integrate security requirements through business process modeling. In particular, they propose BPMN extension through business process diagrams. Although BPMN is almost a standard modeling method and tool, it is a modeling language lacking a theoretical underpinning that would allow studying complex socio-technical settings where envisioned software systems will be used and implemented.

There have been some studies on using Petri nets as a modeling language for security modeling.

For example Horvath and Dörges (2008) proposes an approach based on agents modeling taking into account security aspects as well and Mikolajczak and Gami (2008) look at security from an interorganizational workflow perspective. Similar attempts can be also found in earlier works, where Petri nets are used in modeling security aspects, for example (Atluri & Huang, 1996). However, a process-centric modeling approach using Petri net as a modeling language has received only marginal attention in the current literature.

In order to elevate the importance and pragmatic values of security-driven business process modeling, the models are required to possess certain qualities.

- First of all, the resultant model should be amenable to test and simulation in order to capture how and when security functions will be triggered and enacted. The best pragmatic quality a model can present from the analysis and design perspective is when the model's dynamic behavior can be captured and investigated. Actually, this is where one can see whether the embedded security functions make a difference and the design tradeoffs can be profoundly discussed.
- Secondly, the models should capture social roles, authorities, and responsibilities pertaining to each action. This will address many of the security concerns that stem from unauthorized access to informational assets.
- Thirdly, it is imperative that the models capture interactions between different entities (human actors, business units, applications) to identify the level of security sensitivity (e.g., access and modification of sensitive data or inter-organizational transactions may be of special security scrutiny). These qualities are the research motivations and drivers for this paper.

In this paper, we attempted to show that the proposed method for developing secure business processes yields the mentioned qualities to a certain extent, and the research findings reported here advance the existing experience from both the theoretical and applications perspective.

This paper attempted to further advance the study of security-driven business process modeling by introducing an innovative method and approach, and proposed a conceptual model for secure BPM based on collaborative modeling approach. The contribution of this paper is a distinguished method and approach that fills the gap or addresses the aspects which are overlooked or omitted in existing methods and approaches. In particular, proven theories are needed to underline security specification and identification; rigorous methods allowing sound security modeling need to be rooted in theory; analytical approaches (simulation) will allow systems to cope with complex models--not only ATM-like examples found in the literature; consideration of social setting as it reveals actors who do the work and make security a natural aspect of their daily activities. The main strength of the proposed method is to understand and capture security requirements in their organizational context, i.e., social setting. As such, the proposed method is geared to the very social interactions among the actors as they are enacting the business of an organization, which also encompasses access to the organization assets (including information).

The advantage of the proposed method is its underlying formal semantics, which allows the models to be automatically analyzed and simulated. In comparison to the existing methods and methodologies, the proposed approach and method allows visualization and automatic analysis of the enactment of security constraints through modeling and simulation, and while the model is executed it generates security logs.

Studies conducted within the enterprise ontology (e.g., Dietz, 2006; www.demo.nl) have established that using the ontological transac-

tion concept will lead to a complete ontological model of business processes. Taking this claim as a ground, we can state that one major advantage of the proposed modeling method is that it will better facilitate a more complete identification and definition of security functions as the underlying model is a complete ontological model.

## 5. DISCUSSION AND CONCLUSION

Achieving a good level of software security is a daunting task, especially if this task is left for later phases in the software development life cycle. Security constraints should be applied while software systems design is in its early stages such as the business process modeling phase. We studied that the current methods for secure business process modeling are predominantly based on the extension of existing methods with additional notations that implement secure access to read sensitive data, authorization to perform certain actions, or confidentiality when transforming data. For software designers, contribution of the existing methods is rather a conceptual insight and helps a semantic understanding of the domain. It is due to the fact that the existing methods build security components based on notations (Semantic Scheme, UML activity diagram or use case) that are semiformal or informal diagrams. Therefore the resulting secure BPMs are hard to test (simulate) in order to study the behavior of secure models and their performance.

In this paper, we have discussed secure business process modeling (Secure BPM) as a step for software engineering security. We proposed a method that allows constructing models based on Petri net's formal semantics. The resultant models can be straightforwardly simulated in order to observe how the security functions are executed. For example, if a nurse wants to modify existing medical records, this action will trigger a security function with which the nurse should be able to comply. However, we do not discuss the implementation aspects of how it can be implemented as this trespasses into the realm of other specialists.

Recognizing the fact that secure BPM is a considerable challenge, especially for complex software systems, the contribution of this paper goes beyond the proposition of a secure BPM method. In particular, the paper introduces and discusses a modeling framework for developing secure BPMs that can be generalized equally to many existing or new modeling methods. Although this framework may appear to be common sense, which can be found in many existing works, there are certain articulations and accents provided in this paper. Furthermore, in this paper, we recognize the importance of collaborative, participative, interactive modeling (CPI Modeling) emerging as a powerful approach for complex process modeling. The paper emphasized a collaborative approach in secure BPM as security-embedded modeling represents a multi-disciplinary task and requires a multi-perspective approach in developing accurate and secure BPMs.

Based on the discussion of software security and the role of secure BPMs we provided in this paper, here are some conclusions that can be drawn regarding the pitfalls of neglecting security issues early in the software development life cycle. Actually, a number of issues may arise if security requirements are overlooked during the business process analysis phase:

- Firstly, business analysts have first-hand access to the process domain, thus have a certain grasp on capturing security aspects along with the business processes. Business analysts work directly with domain users, and it is natural that users helping with business process description can also provide valuable input regarding security sensitivity and importance from the users' perspective. As the users provide the process domain knowledge, they also convey valuable information about rules, policies, and constraints related to their activities. There are some empirical studies carried out proving the ability of users to express vital security concerns and highlighting crucial aspects of an envisioned secure system. Skipping this opportunity may dramatically hinder the adequacy and completeness of security requirements at the later stages, especially in the implementation phase.

- Secondly, the models get more detailed and grow in complexity throughout the development life cycle. Over time, it becomes even more challenging to accurately identify security functions and the likelihood of overlooking certain security requirements increases.

- Thirdly, tackling security at a later stage leads to a number of compromises. Often software projects are under time pressure and resource constraints, and belated security fixes will obviously cause further delays to the project and increase the budget. This makes it even more likely that the final software system will contain a lot of security holes.

In line with these conclusions and thoughts, this research is definitely intended to be further developed into a number of directions. More specifically, one future research initiative is to develop a method and build model constructs where a secure business process model can be easily constructed using a predefined library of building blocks. In this regard, how reusable security requirements (Firesmith, 2004) can be specified and assembled into a library of reusable security functions should also be studied. Such an approach should allow fast building of both secure and regular business process models in order to study the model performance and security trade-offs.

# REFERENCES

Atluri, V., & Huang, W. (1996). An Extended Petri Net Model for Supporting Workflows in a Multilevel Secure Environment. In *Proceedings of DBSec 1996*, Como, Italy (pp. 240-258).

Backes, M., Pfitzmann, B., & Waidner, M. (2003). Security in Business Process Engineering. In *Proceedings of 2003 International Conference on Business Process Management* (LNCS 2678, pp. 168-183). New York: Springer.

Backhouse, J., & Dhillon, G. (1996). Structures of responsibility and security of information systems. *European Journal of Information Systems, 5*, 2–9. doi:10.1057/ejis.1996.7

Bai, Y. (2008). Reasoning for Incomplete Authorizations. *KES, 1*, 278–285.

Barjis, J. (2007). Automatic Business Process Analysis and Simulation Based on DEMO. *Journal of Enterprise Information Systems, 1*(4), 365–381. doi:10.1080/17517570701646590

Barjis, J. (2008). The Importance of Business Process Modeling in Software Systems Design. *Journal of the Science of Computer Programming, 71*(1), 73–87.

Barjis, J. (2009). Collaborative, Participative and Interactive Enterprise Modeling. In J. Filipe & J. (Eds.), *Enterprise Information Systems* (LNBIP 24). Berlin: Springer Verlag.

Basin, D. A., Doser, J., & Lodderstedt, T. (2003). Model driven security for process-oriented systems. In. *Proceedings of SACMAT, 2003*, 100–109.

Basin, D. A., Doser, J., & Lodderstedt, T. (2006). Model driven security: From UML models to access control infrastructures. *ACM Transactions on Software Engineering and Methodology, 15*(1), 39–91. doi:10.1145/1125808.1125810

Baskerville, R. (1988). *Designing Information Systems Security*. New York: John Wiley & Sons.

D'Aubeterre1, F., Singh, R., & Iyer, L. (2008). Secure activity resource coordination: empirical evidence of enhanced security awareness in designing secure business processes. *European Journal of Information Systems, 17*, 528-542.

Dietz, J. L. G. (2006). *Enterprise Ontology – Theory and Methodology*. New York: Springer.

Elahi, G., & Yu, E. (2007). A Goal Oriented Approach for Modeling and Analyzing Security Trade-Offs. In C. Parent, K.-D. Schewe, V. C. Storey, & B. Thalheim (Eds.), *Proceedings of ER 2007* (LNCS 4801, pp. 87-101). Berlin: Springer.

Firesmith, D. (2003). Security Use Case. *Journal of Object Technology, 2*(3), 53–64.

Firesmith, D. (2004). Specifying reusable security requirements. *Journal of Object Technology, 3*(1), 61–75.

Gibson, J. J. (1977). The Theory of Affordances. In Shaw, R., & Bransford, J. (Eds.), *Perceiving, Acting, and Knowing*.

Herrmann, G., & Pernul, G. (1999). Viewing business-process security from different perspectives. *International Journal of Electronic Commerce, 3*(3), 89–103.

Herrmann, P., & Herrmann, G. (2006). Security requirement analysis of business processes. *Electronic Commerce Research, 6*(3-4), 305–335. doi:10.1007/s10660-006-8677-7

Horvath, V., & Dörges, T. (2008). From security patterns to implementation using Petri nets. In. *Proceedings of SESS, 2008*, 17–24.

Jürjens, J. (2004). *Secure Systems Development With UML*. New York: Springer.

Khan, K. M., Kapurubandara, M., & Chadha, U. (2004). Incorporating Business Requirements and Constraints in Database Conceptual Model. In *Proceedings of APCCM* (pp. 59-64).

Liu, K. (2000). *Semiotics in Information Systems Engineering*. Cambridge, UK: Cambridge University Press. ISBN 0521 593352

Lodderstedt, T., Basin, D., & Doser, J. (2002). SecureUML: A UML-Based Modeling Language for Model-Driven Security. In *Proceedings of the UML 2002* (pp. 426-441).

Lopez, J., Montenegro, J. A., Vivas, J. L., Okamato, E., & Dawson, E. (2005). Specification and design of advanced authentication and authorization services. *Computer Standards & Interfaces*, *27*(5), 467–478. doi:10.1016/j.csi.2005.01.005

Mana, A., Montenegro, J. A., Rudolph, C., & Vivas, J. L. (2003). A business process-driven approach to security engineering. In *Proceedings of the 14th International Workshop on Database and Expert Systems Applications*, Prague (pp. 477-481).

Matulevicius, R., Mayer, N., Mouratidis, H., Dubois, E., Heymans, P., & Genon, N. (2008). Adapting Secure Tropos for Security Risk Management in the Early Phases of Information Systems Development. In *Proceedings of CAiSE*, *2008*, 541–555.

Mikolajczak, B., & Gami, N. (2008). Design and Verification of Loosely Coupled Inter-Organizational Workflows with Multi-Level Security. *JCP*, *3*(1), 63–78. doi:10.4304/jcp.3.1.63-78

Nagaratnam, N., Nadalin, A., Hondo, M., McIntosh, M., & Austel, P. (2005). Business-driven application security: From modeling to managing secure applications. *IBM Systems Journal*, *44*(4). doi:10.1147/sj.444.0847

Neubauer, T., Klemen, M., & Biffl, S. (2006). Secure business process management: a roadmap. In *Proceedings of the First International Conference on Availability, Reliability and Security (ARES 2006)* (pp. 457-464).

Rodríguez, A., & de Guzman, I. G.-R. (2007). Obtaining Use Case and Security Use Cases from Secure Business Process through the MDA Approach. In *Proceedings of WOSIS 2007*.

Rodríguez, A., Fernández-Medina, E., & Piattini, M. (2006). Towards a UML 2.0 Extension for the Modeling of Security Requirements in Business Processes. *Trust and Privacy in Digital Business* (LNCS 4083, pp. 51-61). Berlin: Springer.

Rodríguez, A., Fernández-Medina, E., & Piattini, M. (2007). A BPMN Extension for the Modeling of Security Requirements in Business Processes. *IEICE - Transactions on Information and Systems. E (Norwalk, Conn.)*, *90-D*(4), 745–752.

Sindre, G. (2007). Mal-activity Diagrams for Capturing Attacks on Business Processes. In P. Sawyer, B. Paech, & P. Heymans (Eds.), *Proceedings of REFSQ 2007* (LNCS 4542, pp. 355-366). Berlin: Springer.

Siponen, M. T., Baskerville, R., & Heikka, J. (2006). A design theory for secure information systems design methods. *Journal of the Association for Information Systems*, *7*(8), 568–592.

Stamper, R. K. (1994). Social Norms in Requirement Analysis – an outline of MEASUR. In Jirotka, M., & Gorguen, J. (Eds.), *Requirements Engineering: Social and Technical Issues*. London: Academic Press Ltd.

Stamper, R. K. (1997). Organizational Semiotics. In Mingers, J., & Stowell, F. (Eds.), *Information Systems: An Emerging Discipline*. London: McGraw Hill.

Stamper, R. K., Liu, K., Hafkamp, M., & Ades, Y. (2000). Understanding the Role of Signs and Norms in Organisations, - a semiotic approach to information systems design. *Journal of Behaviour and Information Technology*, *19*(1), 15–27. doi:10.1080/014492900118768

*This work was previously published in International Journal of Secure Software Engineering, edited by Khaled M. Khan, pp. 1-17, Volume 1, Issue 2, copyright 2010 by IGI Publishing (an imprint of IGI Global).*

# Chapter 5
# Integrating Access Control into UML for Secure Software Modeling and Analysis

**Thuong Doan**
*University of Connecticut, USA*

**Steven Demurjian**
*University of Connecticut, USA*

**Laurent Michel**
*University of Connecticut, USA*

**Solomon Berhe**
*University of Connecticut, USA*

## ABSTRACT

*Access control models are often an orthogonal activity when designing, implementing, and deploying software applications. Role-based access control (RBAC) which targets privileges based on responsibilities within an application and mandatory access control (MAC) that emphasizes the protection of information via security tags are two dominant approaches in this regard. The integration of access control into software modeling and analysis is often loose and significantly lacking, particularly when security is such a high-priority concern in applications. This paper presents an approach to integrate RBAC and MAC into use-case, class, and sequence diagrams of the unified modeling language (UML), providing a cohesive approach to secure software modeling that elevates security to a first-class citizen in the process. To insure that a UML design with security does not violate RBAC or MAC requirements, design-time analysis checks security constraints whenever a new UML element is added or an existing UML element is modified, while post-design analysis checks security constraints across the entire design for conflicts and inconsistencies. These access control extensions and security analyses have been prototyped within a UML tool.*

DOI: 10.4018/978-1-4666-1580-9.ch005

## INTRODUCTION

The inclusion of security in software design and development has often been an afterthought, delayed to near or post-deployment stages of the software development process or delegated to database administration. However, security has emerged as fundamental concern early and in all phases of the software process, prevalent in user interfaces (to control what each user can see), functional capabilities (to control what each user can do), and repositories (to control what data a user can access/modify). The specific focus of the paper is the integration of access control into the UML (Booch et al., 1999), to provide the means for software designers and engineers to jointly model their application's functional and security requirements and constraints, augmented with analyses that insures the access control model characteristics, capabilities, and constraints that are being utilized are not violated. Note that despite the existence of parallels between security and elements in UML, direct support for security specification is not provided (OMG).

For access control, we leverage: role-based access control (RBAC) that focuses on user responsibilities via roles (Sandhu et al., 1996; Ting, 1988) with constraints to restrict behavior (Ferraiolo et al., 2001); and, mandatory access control (MAC) that defines classifications for objects and clearances for subjects (Bell & La Padula, 1975) with access based on the relationship between subjects and objects (Biba, 1977; Osborn et al., 2000). For security, RBAC is a flexible approach to grant/revoke permissions to/from users via roles, while MAC controls information flow (read/write on objects) for highly secure systems. Both models are augmented in this approach with lifetime constraints that determine a temporal window of activity for privileges.

This paper details a practical approach that integrates RBAC and MAC into UML for secure software modeling and analysis with a two-fold emphasis. First, UML requirements definition (use case diagram) and design (class and sequence diagrams) are extended with visual and non-visual security capabilities and constraints for MAC, lifetime, and RBAC. Second, security modeling is augmented with analyses via the checking of security constraints. The *design-time analysis* checks these constraints as the application is created and changed as a result of every action taken by an engineering/designer. The *post-design analysis* (akin to a compile) checks these constraints across the entire application at a particular increment. Both the modeling and analysis capabilities have been programmatically integrated into Borland's UML design tool Together Architect (2009). The snapshots of the implementation illustrate the examples in the paper. This work goes beyond our prior efforts (Doan et al., 2004a; Doan et al., 2004b) by collectively bringing all of the security extensions to UML along with their respective analyses into one context that clearly demonstrates the capabilities and potential of the work in total.

The work presented herein contrasts with other efforts on security for UML. The work of Shin and Ahn (2000) and Ray et al. (2003) simply *uses* UML to represent MAC and/or RBAC systems, as opposed to explicitly *extending* UML with RBAC and MAC. UMLsec (Jurjens, 2002a, 2002b) focuses on multi-level security (MAC) of message in sequence/state diagrams and is similar to our work on MAC extension. SecureUML (Lodderstedt et al., 2002) introduces new meta-model components and authorization constraints expressed for RBAC that involve meta-model changes. Lastly, Alghathbar and Wijesekera (2003a) incorporate security into use cases, similar to our approach. The main difference between our approach and others is one of comprehensiveness; we are doing RBAC, MAC, constraints, and lifetimes for temporal access, which combines many features of the aforementioned work with other capabilities that they do not provide.

This remainder of this paper is organized as follows. Section 2 provides brief background on UML and access control models. Section 3 introduces security extensions to UML with a focus on changes to use case, class, and sequence diagrams, and support for security constraints. Section 4 presents the subsequent security analyses. Section 5, compares and contrasts our approach with other researchers' work. Finally, Section 6 concludes the paper and discusses ongoing research.

## BACKGROUND

Section 2.1 briefly reviews UML and introduces a survey management example used throughout the remainder of the paper. Section 2.2 examines role-based and mandatory access control. Section 2.3 details the prototyping effort and platform.

## The Unified Modeling Language (UML)

This section concentrates on use case, class, and sequence diagrams (available in versions 1.x and 2 of UML), since they are sufficient for our focused scope on security extensions and analyses of UML design (see Sections 3 and 4). A *use case diagram* is a collection of use cases and actors. A *use case* represents an encapsulation of behavior for a specific portion of an application. An *actor* is an external entity that interacts with software (use cases) at some level, to represent the simulation of possible events (business processes) in the system. To illustrate, consider a Survey Institution that performs and manages public surveys. Once raw data of the survey is collected, a senior staff actor will add a survey header into the database. Then, another staff (senior or junior) will add questions into that survey, and also have the ability to categorize questions and add a new question category if needed. However, special questions with more sensitive content are restricted to only senior staff. Figure 1 depicts a use case diagram for creating a new survey entry, where the actor *Staff* has two children *Junior Staff* and *Senior Staff* that are inherited for specialization.

The actor *Senior Staff* has two inherited children *Supervisor* and *Editor*. Only *Editor* can perform the use cases: *Add Survey Header* to include a new survey header entry, *Approve Question* to accept the question content, and *Verify Survey* to check the whole survey. The *Staff* actor can perform the use case *Add Question* that includes the *Categorize Question*, and can be extended to *Add Question Category* if a new category must be added to the database. But, only the *Senior Staff* actor can perform the use case *Add Special Question* to include special sensitive questions in a survey. Only *Supervisor* can perform use case *Survey Admin* to decide whether the survey is ready for publishing on the Internet by extending *Web Publish Survey* and *Activate/Deactivate Survey on Web*.

A *class* is an abstraction for a set of objects that have the same attributes and operations. An *operation* is called a method; its execution against an instance of the class is called a *message*. Figure 2 shows the (partial) class diagram of the survey management with classes: *Survey_Hdr_Add_Pg* for the interface page of adding a *survey_header*, *Survey_List* for maintaining a list of surveys, *Survey_Header* for storing the survey header information, *Question* for storing question text, *Special Question* for storing special sensitive question text, *Response* for storing response data of a question, and *Category* for storing the category names of a question. *Survey List* is a container of *Survey_Header*. *Survey_Header* is a container of *Question*. A *Question* is, in its own right a container of *Response*. A *Question* is associated with a *Category*. *Special_Question* inherits *Question* and adds some restriction information.

A *sequence diagram* represents dynamic interactions of objects via messages, as illustrated in Figure 3 for the use case *Add Survey Header*. To create a new survey header *Internet Usage*, the *Editor* enters data and then clicks the submit button in the *Server Header Add* interface page, implemented by *Survey_Hdr_Add_Pg*. This action

*Figure 1. A use case diagram for new survey entry*

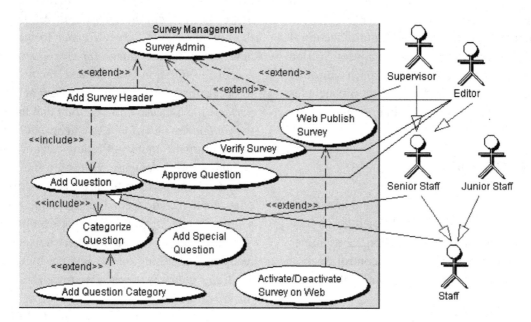

is modeled as the *Editor*'s sending message *on-Submit* to the interface *Survey_Hdr_Add_Pg*. On reception of the *onSubmit* message, the *Survey_Hdr_Add_Pg* object searches for the added survey title in the *Survey_Repository* (a *Survey_List*) by sending a message *Survey_Title_Search* to the

*Survey_Repository* object. If a survey title does not exist in the *Survey_Repository*, the *Survey_Hdr_Add_Pg* instance sends a new header data to *Survey_Repository* object via the *Add_Survey_Header* message. On reception of the *Add_Survey_Header* the *Survey_Repository* object

*Figure 2. A class diagram for survey management*

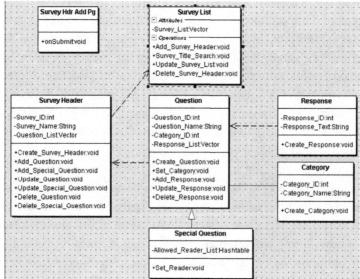

invokes *Create_Survey_Header* to instantiate a new survey header (*Internet_Usage*) of class *Survey_Header*. Lastly, a new item in survey list is created via the *Upd_S_List* message.

## Access Control Models

Our work utilizes role-based access control (RBAC) (Sandhu et al., 1996; Ting, 1988) and mandatory access control (MAC) (Bell & La Padula, 1979; Sandhu, 1993). The National Institute for Standards (NIST) RBAC model (Ferraiolo et al., 2001) lists four reference models to materialize RBAC in a secure system: $RBAC_0$, hierarchical $RBAC_1$, constrained $RBAC_2$, and symmetric $RBAC_3$. In RBAC, roles are assigned to users to specify named functions or responsibilities to be performed in the organization. Each role is then assigned a set of permissions (or privileges) that allows the role to perform specific operations on certain objects. In other words, there are many-to-many assignments of user vs. role and role vs. permission in a basic $RBAC_0$ model. An important feature of the reference model $RBAC_2$ is the assignments of different constraints. For instance, the separation of duty constraints (SoD) (Clark &

Wilson, 1987) serves to avoid the accumulation of too many privileges via assignment of multiple roles. Thus, the least privileges principle can be enforced.

MAC considers three abstract concepts: *subject (S)* which is an entity seeking to access some information; *object (O)* which is the information available to be provided to the subject; and, *sensitivity level (SL)* that refers to the extent of the confidentiality of the object or subject. The sensitivity levels in the generalized MAC form a lattice structure, but the most typical example is a linear ordering from least to most secure: Unclassified (U) < Confidential (C) < Secret (S) < Top Secret (TS). Each subject *s* is assigned a SL, called the *clearance (CLR)* that implies the capacity of *s* to access objects. Each object *o* is assigned a SL, called the *classification (CLS)* that specifies the protection degree for the security concern of the information provided by *o*. The permission of the subject *s* to read or write on the object *o* depends on the rules between the CLR of *s* (written CLR(*s*)) and the CLS of *o* (written CLS(*o*)) as defined by the following properties: Simple Security Property (read down - no read up) (Bell, 1975) where *s* can read *o* only if CLR(*s*)

*Figure 3. A sequence diagram for add survey header*

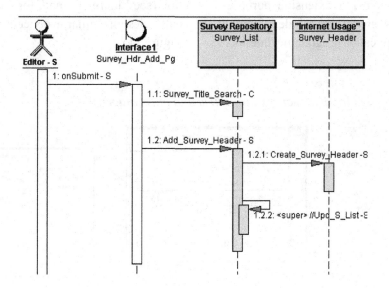

*Figure 4. Inspector windows to illustrate use-case extensions*

| Inspector: Staff | |
|---|---|
| **Security Properties** | |
| Description  HTMLdoc  Requirements | |
| Properties  Hyperlink  View | |
| **Name** | **Value** |
| Starting Date | 01/01/2005 |
| Ending Date | 12/31/2009 |
| Read Min Value | Unclassified |
| Read Max Value | Confidential |
| Write Min Value | Unclassified |
| Write Max Value | Confidential |
| Press Ctrl+Alt+I to finish editing and close Inspec... | |

| Inspector: Editor | |
|---|---|
| **Security Properties** | |
| Description  HTMLdoc  Requirements | |
| Properties  Hyperlink  View | |
| **Name** | **Value** |
| Starting Date | 01/01/2005 |
| Ending Date | 12/31/2009 |
| Read Min Value | Unclassified |
| Read Max Value | Top Secret |
| Write Min Value | Confidential |
| Write Max Value | Secret |

| Inspector: Add Question | |
|---|---|
| **Security Properties** | |
| Description  HTMLdoc  Requirements | |
| Properties  Hyperlink  View | |
| **Name** | **Value** |
| Starting Date | 01/01/2005 |
| Ending Date | 12/31/2010 |
| Read Min Value | Unclassified |
| Read Max Value | Confidential |
| Write Min Value | Unclassified |
| Write Max Value | Confidential |

$\geq$ CLS($o$) $o$; Strict *-Property (write equal) (Osborn, 2000) where $s$ can write $o$ only if CLR($s$) = CLS($o$); Liberal *-Property (write up - no write down) (Bell and La Padula, 1975; Osborn et al., 2000) where $s$ can write $o$ only if CLR($s$)$\leq$CLS($o$); and, Simple Integrity Property (write down - no write up) (Biba, 1977) where $s$ can write $o$ only if CLR($s$) $\geq$ CLS($o$).

## Prototyping Effort

For prototyping, we utilized Borland Together Architect, a Java-based product which allows the modeling of all standard UML 1.4 diagrams. The tool fully supports the synchronization of distributed diagrams, automatic code, and documentation generation. For extension purposes, the tool provides an integrated development toolkit via open application programmer interfaces

(APIs) and a modular plug-in structure that easily facilitates both modifications to existing UML diagrams and the inclusion of new custom code (including graphic user interfaces, displays, etc.). The latter allows us to provide our own custom Java code. Together Architect's structure in this regard allows us to easily include the security extensions that are changes to existing diagrams (see Sections 3.1, 3.2, and 3.4) and the creation of new information related to dependencies and constraints (see Sections 3.3 and 3.5). In addition, its GUI event handlers allow us to perform security analyses (see Section 4.3) in two situations: whenever an insertion or modification occurs on a UML diagram which prohibits the action and generates a message if there is a security violation (see Figure 10); and, for analysis across the entire design similar in concept to a compile (see Figure 11).

*Figure 5. The MAC and lifetime security properties in a class diagram*

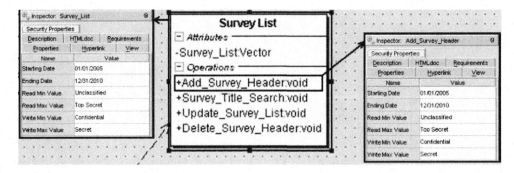

*Figure 6. Tracking use-case to class/method connections*

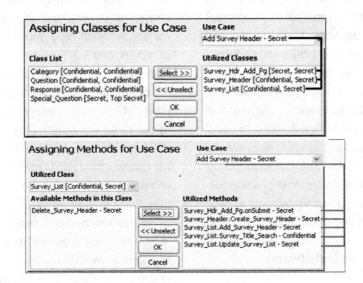

## SECURITY EXTENSIONS TO UML

We now review the UML security extensions for RBAC, MAC, and lifetimes, focusing on use case diagrams in Section 3.1, class diagrams in Section 3.2, and sequence diagrams in Section 3.4. Section 3.3 examines the extensions for disallowed usage and mutual exclusion constraints for $RBAC_2$, and details the UML extensions to capture dependencies between use case and class diagrams that are needed to support sequence diagram extensions and facilitate the security analysis presented in Section 4. We expect stakeholders to create use-case, class, and sequence diagrams with associated

*Figure 7. An extended sequence diagram for add survey header*

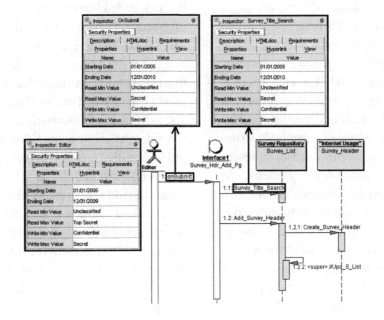

elements and connections as part of the design phase. These specifications provide access control (RBAC and MAC), associated constraints, and information on when access is allowed (referred to as lifetimes). To facilitate the analysis, we further assume that the connections in use case, class, and sequence diagrams are acyclic, and that multiple inheritance (in use case diagrams among use cases and actors and in class diagrams among classes) is not allowed. The analysis insures that all access control model characteristics, capabilities, and constraints are never violated as a UML application is created and modified.

## Use Case Diagram Extension

Use-case diagrams have been extended by: the alignment of actors to roles, the inclusion of MAC sensitivity levels (see Section 2.2) for use cases and actors, and the use of lifetimes to track temporal limits on privileges. First, by aligning actors to roles we establish a link from an actor to a role in NIST RBAC$_1$ (Ferraiolo et al., 2001), and we align actor inheritance with the comparable role inheritance of RBAC$_1$. From a security privilege perspective, each of the lines that connect an actor to a use case represents an assigned privilege. In Figure 1, Supervisor is assigned to the use cases Survey Admin and Web Publish Survey, and also inherits the privileges associated with the Senior Staff (parent) and Staff (grandparent); this acquisition is consistent with the NIST model. There is also the implicit assignment of other connected use cases, linked to directly assigned use case by include, extend, or inheritance. Collectively, all the directly or indirectly reachable use cases represent the assigned privileges on an actor-by-actor basis.

Second, we extend the use case diagram with MAC sensitivity levels and security properties (see Section 2.2). For each actor or use case in a use case diagram we define two clearances or classifications, respectively, as related to its read and write capabilities. Recall that security properties (Strict *, Simple Security, etc.) differentiate

between read and write access for SLs. To be consistent in realizing SLs in UML, we differentiate between read and write access for CLR of actors and CLS of use cases. In fact, since actors are connected to use cases, and use cases are connected to one another, assigning a single CLR or CLS is not feasible. Instead, for each actor or use case, we assign a read security capability (RSC) with a minimum value (RSC.min) and a maximum value (RSC.max), and a write security capability (WSC) with a minimum value (WSC.min) and a maximum value (WSC.max); each set of values represents a range of SLs. The RSC/WSC refers to the capability of the UML element to obtain or modify the application's information (stored in the attributes of some classes) via an interaction chain with other UML elements (via UML connections) requiring that the SL of the accessed information lies within the RSC/WSC of the accessing UML element. The minimum and maximum SLs of RSC/WSC are taken from a set, such as {Unclassified, Confidential, Secret, Top Secret}. Figure 4 is an illustration of the UML inspector window showing the RSC/WSC for the actors *Staff* and *Editor* corresponding to the use case diagram of Figure 1. These UML inspector windows from Borland's Together Architect have been extended (using available APIs) to include the Security Properties tab. In the Figure, the Read Min (Max) Value refers to RSC.min (RSC.max) and the Write Min (Max) Value refers to WSC.min (WSC.max). In Figure 4, actor *Staff* has RSC.min of Unclassified and RSC.max of Confidential and WSC.min of Unclassified and WSC.max of Confidential, while actor *Editor* has Read Values of Unclassified and Top Secret and Write Values of Confidential and Secret. The Read and Write values of Add Question are also shown.

The third addition is the concept of a *lifetime (LT),* a temporal range that indicates when the particular UML element is active from a security perspective. Outside of that period (before or after), the role is not available to be used within the application. As an abstract concept, a lifetime can be a continuous time interval, a repeating interval (e.g., one day per week), or any quantifiable collection of intervals. For simplicity, we assume a temporal interval of the form [starting time, ending time]. As shown in Figure 4, the Start and End Dates are given for the two actors and one use case. These are clearly coarse grained in this prototype (day-month-year); yet, from a modeling perspective, these can be very fine-grained. Further, we extend UML connections by adding an LT to the connection between actor and use case, and include/extend associations, to indicate when the interaction (from actor to use case or between use cases) is allowed. When a designer draws a connection from the actor *Staff* to the use case *Add Question* (see Figure 1 for the connection), the designer is prompted for its LT. We do not apply lifetimes to inheritance since this is a condition that always holds, i.e., it is not possible for an ancestor to exist only some of the time. One final note, the alignment of roles to actors, the linking of connections to direct and implicit privileges, the inclusion of MAC sensitivity levels, and lifetimes for allowable access time periods are leveraged so that when an addition or change is made to a diagram, it is automatically analyzed. For example, drawing a new connection between an actor and a use case may be disallowed if the sensitivity level of the actor does not appropriately dominate the sensitivity level of the use case. The security analysis will be discussed in Section 4.

## Class Diagram Extension

The extensions to class diagrams includes both the Read/Write Security Capacities (RSC/WSC) and a lifetime for every class and each method of a class, with LTs tracked for class association and class aggregation; we treat inheritance as a condition that always holds regardless of time since a class can't have an ancestor only some of the time. To illustrate, in Figure 5, we excerpt from the class diagram of Figure 2 to show the Survey

List class and two inspector windows. *Survey List* has RSC.min of Unclassified and RSC.max of Top Secret, WSC.min of Confidential and WSC.max of Secret, and LT of 01/01/2005 to 12/31/2010. The method *Add_Survey_Header* has RSC.min of Unclassified and RSC.max of Top Secret, WSC. min of Confidential and WSC.max of Secret, and LT of 01/01/2005 to 12/31/2010. Note that the RSC/WSC for the *Survey List* must subsume the RSC/WSC values for every one of its methods; once the class value is set, the RSC/WSC values of the methods are constrained when a designer creates a new method or modifies the RSC/WSC value of an existing method. This is also true for LTs, where a method can't have a LT outside the LT of its class. Further, the LT of a parent must subsume the LT of all of its descendants both direct and indirect. For inheritance, there is also a subsumption among RSC/WSC sensitivity levels. Lastly, whenever classes are connected by association or aggregation, lifetimes are tracked for those connections, and must be consistent with the source and destination classes being connected (not shown).

## Connections

UML does an excellent job of tracking associations in its structural and behavioral diagrams. However, there is no diagram that can show directly what structural elements (classes) should be used for realizing which behavior elements (use cases). Recall that when an actor is connected to a use cases (either directly or indirectly), the privileges of that actor/role are defined (see Section 3.1). Use cases are functional entities to be eventually implemented using classes (and their methods). For security consistency tracking, it is imperative to associate use cases to the classes and methods that realize them to create a chain where privileges can be traced from a role (actor) to its use cases and ultimately to classes and their methods. Thus, we introduce connections from a use case to a set of classes to be utilized

*Figure 8. Disallowed usage and mutual exclusion constraints*

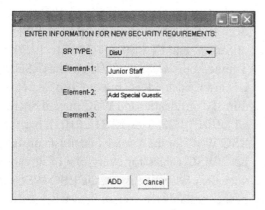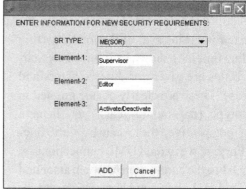

to realize the use case, and for each class in the set, to identify a subset of its methods. The first new connection, *Use Case-Class Utilization,* allows the designer to assign a subset of the set of classes to a use case, shown in the top of Figure 6 for the *Add_Survey_Header* use case. This is a new window that has been coded and included as part of Borland's Together Architect. For security analysis, the Use Case-Class Utilization case is checked on the RSC/WSC and lifetime properties of the use case and the class to guarantee the MAC and LT security requirements hold. The second connection, *Use Case-Method Utilization,* allows the designer to assign the methods of each

selected classes to be utilized in realizing the use case. As shown in the bottom of Figure 6, for a given use case, the Utilized Class can be selected, displaying all of its methods, from which a subset can be selected. For security analysis, the Use Case-Method Utilization is checked on the RSC/WSC and LT properties of the use case and the method to guarantee the MAC and LT security requirements hold.

## Sequence Diagram Extension

In a sequence diagram, the actors and methods already have the RSC/WSC and LTs. To rep-

*Figure 9. Tracking dependencies in UML via closures*

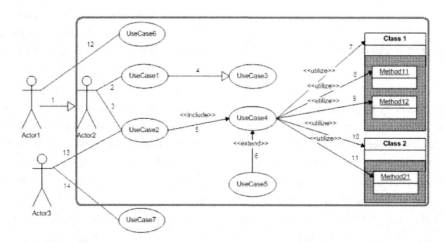

*Figure 10. Inter-element security property analysis*

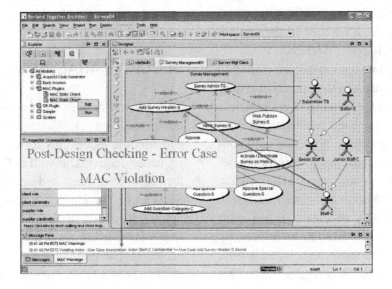

resent the message passing, the designer may draw: *Actor-Method Utilization* from an actor to a method (callee) and *Method-Method Calling* from a method (caller) to another method (callee); each of these two new connections is augmented with a LT to indicate the temporal condition that allows the actor or caller method to utilize the callee method. Figure 7 shows the MAC and

LTs of actor *Editor*, and methods *OnSubmit* and *Survey_Title_Search*. The designer must also provide LTs of the connection from actor *Editor* to method *OnSubmit* and from method *OnSubmit* to method *Survey_Title_Search* (not shown). Note that the LTs of the Actor-Method Utilization or Method-Method Calling limit the time span of usage from a security perspective.

*Figure 11. Post-design analysis*

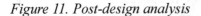

## RBAC Constraints

To complete our extensions to UML, we discuss the inclusion of RBAC constraints that are realized as part of the NIST RBAC standard (Ferraiolo et al., 2001). RBAC constraints can be defined in different ways. First, *disallowed usage constraints* are utilized to identify essentially negative privileges, defining what use cases, classes, and methods that an actor (role) is prohibited from using. Second, *mutual exclusion constraints* restrict the role-permission assignment to define the conditions under which one role uses multiple UML elements (use case, classes, and methods) at the same time or two or more roles are allowed to access (or not) the same UML element. A *disallowed usage constraint* is a negative permission, and is specified to explicitly prohibit an actor (role) from using some non-actor UML element (use case, class, or method). A disallowed usage as a negative permission is necessary to explicitly prevent the indirect (positive) permission of an actor (for instance, via the inheritance of its parent actor) to utilize some non-actor element. Continuing with the example from Section 2, suppose that the security policy required by the customer states that the actor Junior Staff must not utilize the use case *Add Special Question* which is intended for other role(s). The designer specifies disallowed usage (DisU) as shown on the left side of Figure 8 via a new window that extends Borland's Together Architect.

The remaining two constraints are related to mutual exclusion as a mean for separation of duty that helps to enforce the least privileges principle by limiting the accumulated privileges via multiple user-role assignments. Note, we only consider the static mutual exclusion constraints between actors (roles) and non-actor UML elements. First, for a *static object-roles mutual exclusion constraint* (ME(SOR)), an object (a non-actor UML element) is not allowed to be utilized by multiple actors at the same time based on the enterprise's separation of duty requirements. This means that two or more actors are prohibited from using the same use case, class, or method at the same time; there can be multiple ME(SOR) constraints. For example, if the security policy required by the customer states that the actors *Supervisor* and *Editor* must not utilize the use case *Activate/Deactivate Survey on Web* at the same time. The designer specifies a ME(SOR) as shown in the right side of Figure 8.

Conversely, a *static role-objects mutual exclusion constraint* (ME/SRO)) prohibits an actor from using multiple non-actor UML elements at the same time based on the enterprise's separation of duty requirements. In other words, to support the "check and balance" principle or to avoid the conflict of interest, the security officer may create a ME(SRO) constraint to disallow an actor to utilize a set of non-actor UML elements at the same time. For example, suppose that the security policy required by the customer states that the Junior Staff actor must not utilize both the *Add Question* and *Approve Question* use cases (not shown). Both types of static mutual exclusion constraints are defined at design time and enforced at runtime. As before, the definition of disallowed usage and static mutual exclusion introduces another area for analysis to make sure that these definitions and other security and non-security features are conflict-free as the design is created and modified.

## SECURITY ANALYSES

This section defines the conditions for secure design analyses in UML involving RBAC, MAC, and lifetime extensions to use-case, class, and sequence diagrams, as well as RBAC constraints for disallowed usage and mutual exclusion (see Section 3). Section 4.1, discusses the underlying mechanism that facilitates analysis, which involves the treatment of a UML design as a connected acyclic graph and the computation of the closure(s) of a UML element (or connection) to determine sub-graphs of reachable elements (or connections). Then, Section 4.2 enumerates all of the available analyses including: MAC sensitivity level analyses both within and between UML elements, lifetime analyses; and, RBAC constraint analyses for disallowed usage and mutual exclusion. Section 4.3 then discusses when the analyses can occur: *design-time analysis* institutes checks whenever a designer creates a new UML element/connection or modifies an existing element/connection; and, *post-design analysis,* akin to a "compile", institutes a complete analysis of the entire design at a design increment or milestone.

## Mechanism for Facilitating Analysis

A UML design that has been created with security as described in Section 3, is essentially a directed acyclic graph with connections from actors (roles) all the way through to methods. The connections in a UML design include: actor-to-actor inheritance; use case inheritance, include, and extend; actor-to-use-case utilization; use-case-to-class and use-case-to-method realization (via new use-case to class and method connections discussed in Section 3.3 and shown in Figure 6); class inheritance, aggregation, and association; and method-to-method linkage (once there is code that implements each method). These connections are shown in Figure 9: *Actor1* inherits from *Actor2* which utilizes *UseCase1* and *UseCase2*; *UseCase1* inherits from *UseCase3*; *UseCase2* includes *UseCase4* which is extended with *UseCase5*; *UseCase4* utilizes *Class1* and *Class2* for its realization, including two methods from *Class1* (*Method11* and *Method12*) and one from *Class2* (*Method21*); and, Actor1 interacts directly with *UseCase6*. Using this diagram, it is possible to compute a *forward closure of elements (FCE)* to identify all directly or indirectly reachable UML elements (actors, use cases, classes, methods) connected to a given UML element: FCE(*Actor1*) = {*Actor1, Actor2, UseCase3, UseCase5, UseCase6, UseCase7,*

*Class1, Class2, Method11, Method12, Method21*}. Note that we have not included method-to-method connections, but if available, these would be part of the closure. A *forward closure of connections (FCC)* can be computed: FCC(*Actor1*)= {*Conn1 ... Conn12*} with *Conn13* and *Conn14* are not included. A *backward closure of elements (BCE)* is the set of all UML elements that are connected directly or indirectly via incoming connections: BCE(*UseCase5*) = {*Actor1, Actor2, Actor3, UseCase2, UseCase4*}. All of these closures are important for the analysis, since they provide the means to identify from a given UML element, all other linked elements and their connections. The consistency analysis for the lifetimes (discussed in Section 4.2) requires both the FCE and BCE in order to examine their overlap (intersection).

## Enumerating Security Analysis Capabilities

Security analysis involves the checking of consistency of UML elements and connections in regards to MAC sensitivity levels (read and write SLs) and associated properties (e.g., Simple Security, Simple Integrity, Liberal-*, etc., in Section 2.2), lifetimes, and RBAC constraints on disallowed usage (UML elements a role cannot access) and mutual exclusion (multiple roles against the same UML element or one role against multiple elements). This section reviews each of these three types of checks in turn. To begin, recall that LTs are assigned to each UML element, and to the connections between each element (see Section 3 and Figures 4, 5, and 6). Conceptually, when two UML elements are connected with one another (e.g., an actor to a use case) which are also not connected to any other UML element, the intersection of the LTs at the source and destination of the connection are checked for overlap; if so, the connection is allowed. In general, the *lifetime analysis* operates as follows:

- **Upon the insertion of a new UML connection:** For a UML source element *se* and destination element *de* of the connection *c*, calculate the closure set CS = {BCE(se), FCE(se), FCE(de), FCC(c)}. This determines all reachable elements and involved connections. The intersection of all lifetimes for all elements in CS is calculated and if there is a non-null overlap, then the connection is allowed; otherwise, the connection is prohibited.
- **Upon the updating of the lifetime of an existing UML element or connection:** For a given UML element *e*, calculate CS = {BCE(e), FCE(e), FCC(c)} and check the intersection; if non-null, allow the lifetime change, otherwise do not.

In practice, as a designer creates a UML model over time, adding elements and connections, the analysis of LTs constantly occurs, so this design time analysis is very easy, often involving just the source and destination (since the elements in the closure have already been checked during earlier connections). However, as discussed in Section 4.3, a designer can turn off the automatic analysis and then analyze the entire design at a particular increment or milestone (much like a compiler). In this case, the closure sets must be calculated in total for each UML element to analyze the lifetimes across the entire design at once (rather than one connection at a time).

The second security analysis involves MAC with respect to sensitivity levels (SLs) and properties of UML elements. There are two types of analyses. First, *intra-element SL analysis* involves a limited examination of the read and write security capabilities (RSC/WSC – see Section 3.2) for each UML element to make sure that the RSC.min ≤ RSC.max and WSC.min ≤ WSC.max, meaning that the minimum clearance (or classification) cannot exceed the maximum. Intra-SL analysis is performed when a designer creates a New UML Element (so that the RCS/WSC min and max are

defined) or updates an Existing UML Element's min or max. Next, *inter-element security property analysis* involves the checking of the read and write, min and max, between two elements, based on the security properties that have been chosen. Recall from Section 2.2 the four properties Simple Security (read down - no read up), Strict *- (write equal), Liberal *-, and Simple Integrity (write down - no write up), which involved comparing sensitivity levels (Unclassified, Confidential, Secret, and Top Secret) with one another (e.g., for Simple Security, $CLR(s) \geq CLS(o)$, and for Liberal *- $CLR(s) \leq CLS(o)$). For the SLs of two UML elements, based on the chosen security properties (one for read and one for write), the RSC/WSC mins and maxes of the source and destination must be compared. Again, there are two cases for *inter-element security property analysis*:

- **Upon the insertion of a new UML connection *c*:** Calculate the closure set CS = {FCC(c)} and for each connection (*se,de*) in CS check se.RSC.min against de.RSC.min, se.RSC.max against de.RSC.max, se.WSC.min against de.WSC.min, and se.WSC.max against de.WSC.max. Compare the sensitivity levels according to the defined read (e.g., Simple Security) and write (e.g., Liberal-*) properties. All four comparisons must succeed for all connections in CS, for the connection to be allowed.
- **Upon updating the sensitivity level of an existing UML element *c*:** Calculate CS = {FCC(c)} and compare RSC/WSC min/max for source/destination based on chosen read/write security properties.

For design-time analysis, the *inter-element security property analysis* is quick, since only the single connection or directly connected elements must be checked (earlier connections or changes must have previously been checked); for post-design analysis, the computation of CS for each connection across the entire design is required, with the comparison of SLs/properties as described previously.

The final security analysis involves RBAC constraints for disallowed usage and mutual exclusion. Recall that disallowed usage (see Section 3.5 and left side of Figure 8) allows a designer to identify, for each actor (role), a list of prohibited use cases, classes, and/or methods, which results in the creation of the *disallowed usage set (DUS)* for each actor (which may be null). For a given actor *ac*, the *disallowed usage analysis* calculates $\{FCE(ac)\} \cap DUS(ac)$; a non-null result means there is a conflict between disallowed privileges and assigned privileges. For mutual exclusion, recall that there are two cases: *static object-roles mutual exclusion constraint (ME(SOR))* which prohibits two or more actors (roles) from using the same UML element at the same time; and, *static role-objects mutual exclusion constraint (ME(SRO))* which prohibits an actor (role) from using two or more UML elements at the same time. For the *ME(SOR) analysis*, a *prohibited actors set (PAS)* is maintained for each UML element. For any given element *e* (use case, class, or method), the analysis calculates $\{BCE(e)\} \cap PAS(e)$; if the intersection is not empty, there is a conflict. For the *ME(SRO) analysis*, a *prohibited elements set (PES)* is maintained for each actor. For any given actor *ac*, the analysis calculates $\{FCE(ac)\} \cap PES(ac)$; if the intersection is not empty, there is a conflict. The check for all RBAC constraints is performed when an existing actor is connected to a use case (or a parent actor), a new connection that impacts the actor is added, a new disallowed usage element is added to the actor, or a mutual exclusion constraint involving the actor is modified.

## Design-Time and Post-Design Analyses

The six security analyses (lifetime analysis, intra-element SL analysis, inter-element security property analysis, disallowed usage analysis, ME(SOR) analysis, and ME(SRO) analysis) are utilized in two different ways. First, *design-time analysis* occurs throughout the design process, with the analyses embedded into the UML tool (Borland Together Architect) so that whenever an action is performed (e.g., create a UML element, connect two existing elements, update an existing element, modify an RBAC constraint, etc.), the appropriate check occurs as detailed in Section 4.2. Second, we recognize that attempting to keep a complex design in a security consistent state during the design activity may be impossible; there are different class diagrams (some partial) being developed by different individuals and when users starts connecting them to one another (bring together the design components), the potential for conflicts is extremely high. As a result, designers can turn-off design-time analysis in the UML tool, and create a design with security extensions (MAC, lifetimes, RBAC constraints, etc.). At any design milestone, *post-design analysis*, akin to a compile, can be performed to analyze the entire design (all UML elements and connections) and report a list of errors. Both analyses are discussed below.

*Design-time analysis* runs in the background as the designer creates or alters UML diagrams for an application; the six analyses of Section 4.2 are always "ready-to-run" with hooks inserted into the UML tool to automatically trigger the appropriate analysis based on the user's action. Figure 10 illustrates this process where the designer attempts to connect the use case *Add Survey Header* with the Actor *Staff*, MAC inter-element security property analysis determines a conflict in the clearance (CLR) of the source (actor *Staff* has as sensitivity level of C) with the classification (CLS) of the destination (use case *Add Survey Header* has a sensitivity level of Secret). This conflict may result from the read or write security capability, and therefore the connection is not allowed to occur. Design-time analysis can be considered as taking the state of a UML diagram, evaluating a potential future state (with the change), and allowing a transition to a new state if there is no conflict. From a security perspective, there is a series of states based on the action taken by the designer, with security analysis performed based on the type of action as discussed in Section 4.2. In this way, the system always maintains a consistent security state. Note that we presented and proved a theorem that guarantees that, as long as the design-time analysis runs at all time, a user will produce design revisions that are always consistent (Doan, 2008).

*Post-design analysis* is utilized when a design becomes sufficiently large (containing numerous UML elements, connections, and RBAC constraints) and complex (bringing together different design components/diagrams) that design-time analysis would always find conflicts, effectively stalling the design process. Consequently, we provided in the prototype integrated into Borland's Together Architect the ability to turn off the design-time analysis. Once off, the designer can create a UML design with elements, connections, security features, etc., without continuous analyses. At regular milestones, the post-design analysis can be executed to produce an overall check (all six of the analyses in Section 4.2) of the design by iterating through all elements and all connections; this is shown in Figure 11. Since a connected UML design is an acyclic graph, the complexity of post-design time analysis is based on the number of UML elements (nodes) and connections (edges), coupled with the number of RBAC disallowed usage and mutual exclusion constraints. In the worst case, this is $O(m^3)$ where $m$ is the maximum of the number of nodes, edges, or RBAC constraints.

## RELATED WORK

In this section, we compare and contrast our work with the approach of others. In Epstein and Sandhu (1999), a proposed Framework for Network Enterprise utilizes UML notations to describe a role-based access control model, employing UML as a language to represent RBAC requirements. However, the representation is too general to incorporate subtle properties of RBAC such as separation of duty constraints (Ferraiolo et al., 2001) for different types of RBAC constraints. Shin and Ahn (2000) proposed an alternative technique to utilize UML notations to describe RBAC modeling and processing. With a more general approach, Lodderstedt et al. (2002) proposed SecureUML as an UML-based modeling language for RBAC. Their work introduced new meta-model components (e.g., User, Role, Permission, ActionType, ResourceType etc.) based on the UML stereotype definition (for the abstract level). These meta-model stereotypes express, for instance, the RBAC requirements among users, roles, permissions, types of actions that the permission can perform, and the resources that are affected by the action, etc. Note that their effort has been extended in (Basin et al., 2006) using model-driven architectures to assist in the security definition process via model transformation. The common objective of all of these efforts was to focus on the way that UML elements can be used to model roles rather than taking a larger view of examining secure software design with state tracking and constraint checking, which has been our focus.

In an effort similar to our work, Jurjens (2002a, 2002b) proposed UMLsec with extended UML features to accommodate security requirements. Their effort utilizes a mathematical Abstract State Machine model to formalize UML elements (no use cases) and extend several stereotypes to accommodate their proposed security framework towards theoretical security verification with UML. This is in contrast with our approach to extend properties of essential UML elements (use cases, actors, classes, and methods) and keep track of the evolving design state using functional representation in order to directly apply security models for secure software design.

In another effort, Alghathbar and Wijesekera (2003b), introduced a framework called AuthUML for incorporating security into use cases, with the assumption that the designer can specify a list of conceptual operations and their affected objects in each use-case. The authors indicate that their work is an application of the Flexible Authorization Framework (Jajodia et al., 2001) using Prolog-like predicates to represent RBAC constraints. The predicates are built in a special order to be shaped into a stratified logic program (for obtaining a stable model). Their approach is different from ours in terms of computational representation.

Our approach extends the UML with a RBAC model that is roughly at the constrained RBAC level in the NIST RBAC model (Ferraiolo et al., 2001). The symmetric RBAC model is not taken into account in our RBAC UML extension since the UML model does not consider specific users; UML only deals with actors as roles in RBAC. On the aspect of temporal security, Bertino et al. (2000) proposed a hierarchical temporal authorization model where the time span can be represented as periodic intervals. In a security model for distributed component-based environment, Phillips et al., 2002a; Phillips et al., 2002b) represented the lifetimes as the fixed intervals with the format of starting time/date and ending time/date. Our lifetime representation is more general since it is built on the concept of lattice and a partial order relation, and can represent many kinds of lifetime such as fixed intervals. Overall, we believe that these and other efforts were helpful resources for our research goal that targets the integration of two access control models into UML.

Finally, there have been efforts related to security analysis. UMLsec as discussed above has been extended with security analysis in Juergens et al. (2008) in which their UML security specification is translated into Prolog and an automated theorem prover analyzes it for correctness. Both their and our effort performs static analysis at design time. The recent work of Basin et al. (2009) extends

their SecureUML work (see above) so that modeled security properties can be evaluated against hypothetical run-time instances; this includes static analysis regarding users and permissions to roles which is similar to our work, but goes beyond our effort to consider the implications at runtime. Another effort of note in Sohr et al. (2008) works towards systematically verifying and validating non-temporal and history-based authorization constraints via UML's Object Constraint Language (OCL), which are then verified using a theorem prover. Such an approach could be utilized to underlie our current analysis for RBAC disallowed usage and mutual exclusion constraints.

## CONCLUSION

This paper has presented the integration of role-based access control (RBAC), mandatory access control (MAC), lifetime, and RBAC constraints into UML to provide a security model and associated security analyses. Our approach and the checking mechanism have been integrated into a UML tool to check and maintain design states as an application's design is created and modified over time. Section 2 presented background material on UML and RBAC and MAC. Using this as a basis, Section 3 presented the proposed extensions to UML, including: the treatment of actors as roles and their connections to use cases as positive privileges (Section 3.1); extensions to class and sequence diagrams for sensitivity levels and lifetimes (Sections 3.2 and 3.4); the introduction of new connections for use cases to classes and methods (Section 3.3); and, disallowed usage and mutual exclusion constraints (Section 3.5). For all, a common example was expanded upon, with screen shots that illustrated the changes and additions to the Borland UML Tool Together Architect. This naturally set the context for the analysis capabilities in Section 4, which included the concept of a closure for UML elements and connections (Section 4.1), the six different analyses for lifetimes, MAC, and RBAC constraints (Section 4.2), and design-time and post-design analyses (Section 4.3).

In terms of ongoing and potential future work, the areas include: integration of the lifetime into the RBAC constraints; optimization of security analysis algorithms; extension to include discretionary access control (Sandhu & Munawer, 1998); expansion to consider other UML diagrams; and, transitioning to implementation via secure code generation. Of particular note is the last item on that list, which may allow us to align with other research on extending UML for secure software engineering (Pavlich et al., 2008). In this complementary effort, the focus has been on proposing new security UML diagrams for capturing privileges based for users, roles, and delegation of authority (discretionary access control), which is then coupled with the automatic generation of aspect-oriented security enforcement code. The motivation for separate diagrams is to collect security that is distributed across the design into named diagrams; this complements our motivation to add security into UML with a limited impact by tweaking existing diagrams and their properties. There is a natural fit between the two efforts, since the definition of security in our model (Section 3) can be used to generate the new security UML diagrams of their work (and vice versa), which would allow our design extensions to automatically transition into enforcement code.

## REFERENCES

Alghathbar, K., & Wijesekera, D. (2003a). AuthUML: A three-phased framework to model secure use cases. In *Proceedings of the Workshop on Formal Methods in Security Engineering: From Specifications to Code* (pp. 77-87).

Alghathbar, K., & Wijesekera, D. (2003b). Consistent and complete access control policies in use cases. In *"UML" 2003 - The Unified Modeling Language* (LNCS 2863, pp. 373-387).

Basin, D. (2006). Model driven security: From UML models to access control infrastructures. *ACM Transactions on Software Engineering and Methodology*, *15*(1), 39–91. doi:10.1145/1125808.1125810

Basin, D. (2009). Automated analysis of security-design models. *Journal of Information and Software Technology*, *51*(5), 815–831. doi:10.1016/j.infsof.2008.05.011

Bell, D., & La Padula, L. (1975). *Secure computer systems: mathematical foundations model* (Tech. Rep. M74-244). Bedford, MA: Mitre.

Bertino, E. (2000). Temporal authorization bases: From specification to integration. *Journal of Computer Security*, *8*(4), 309–353.

Biba, K. (1977). *Integrity considerations for secure computer systems* (Tech. Rep. TR-3153). Bedford, MA: Mitre.

Booch, G., et al. (1999). *The Unified Modeling Language user guide*. Reading, MA: Addison Wesley Professional.

Borland. (2009). *Borland Together Architect*. Retrieved from http://www.borland.com/us/products/together/index.html

Clark, D., & Wilson, D. (1987). A comparison of commercial and military computer security policies. In *Proceedings of IEEE Symposium on Security and Privacy* (pp. 184-194).

Demurjian, S., et al. (2001). A user role-based security model for a distributed environment. In B. Thuraisingham, R. van de Riet, K. Dittrich, & Z. Tari (Eds.), *Data and applications security: Developments and directions* (LNCS 73, pp. 259-270).

Demurjian, S., et al. (2004). Concepts and capabilities of middleware security. In Q. Mohammed (Ed.), *Middleware for communications* (pp. 211-236). New York: John-Wiley & Sons.

Doan, T. (2008). *A framework for software security in UML with assurance*. Unpublished doctoral dissertation, Department of Computer Science and Engineering, University of Connecticut.

Doan, T., et al. (2004a). RBAC/MAC security for UML. In C. Farkas & P. Samarati (Eds.), *Research directions in data and applications security XVIII* (LNCS 144, pp. 189-204).

Doan, T., et al. (2004b). MAC and UML for secure software design. In *Specifications to Code: Proceedings of the 2nd ACM Workshop on Formal Methods in Security Engineering* (pp. 75-85). ACM Publishing.

Epstein, P., & Sandhu, R. (1999). Towards a UML based approach to role engineering. In *Proceedings of the 4th ACM workshop on Role-based Access Control* (pp. 75-85). ACM Publishing.

Ferraiolo, D. F. (2001). Proposed NIST standard for role-based access control. *ACM Transactions on Information and System Security, 4*(3), 224–274. doi:10.1145/501978.501980

Jajodia, S. (2001). Flexible support for multiple access control policies. *ACM Transactions on Database Systems, 26*(2), 214–260. doi:10.1145/383891.383894

Juergens, J., et al. (2008). Automated analysis of permission-based security using UMLsec. In *Fundamental approaches to software engineering* (LNCS 4961, pp. 292-295).

Jurjens, J. (2002a). *Principles for secure systems design*. Unpublished doctoral dissertation, Oxford University Computing Laboratory, Oxford University.

Jurjens, J. (2002b). UMLsec: Extending UML for secure systems development. *Proceedings of UML* (LNCS 2460, pp. 1-9).

Lodderstedt, T., et al. (2002). SecureUML: A UML-based modeling language for model-driven security. In *Proceedings of UML* (LNCS 2460, pp. 426-441).

OMG. (2009). *Superstructure, V2.1.2*. Retrieved from http://www.omg.org/spec/UML/2.1.2/Superstructure/PDF

Osborn, S. (2000). Configuring role-based access control to enforce mandatory and discretionary access control policies. *ACM Transactions on Information and System Security, 3*(2), 85–106. doi:10.1145/354876.354878

Pavlich-Mariscal, J. A., et al. (2008). A framework for component-based enforcement for access control. In *Proceedings of the XXVII International Conference of Chilean Computer Science Society* (pp. 13-22). Washington, DC: IEEE Computer Society.

Phillips, C., et al. (2002a). Security engineering for roles and resources in a distributed environment. In *Proceedings of 3rd ISSEA Conference*. Kluwer Academic Publishers.

Phillips, C., et al. (2002b). Towards information assurance in dynamic coalitions. In *Proceedings of the 2002 IEEE Information Assurance Workshop*. Washington, DC: IEEE Computer Society.

Ray, I., et al. (2003). Using parameterized UML to specify and compose access control models. In *Proceedings of the 6th IFIP Working Conference on Integrity and Internal Control in Information Systems* (pp. 115-124). ACM Publishing.

Sandhu, R. (1996). Role-based access control models. *IEEE Computer, 29*(2), 38–47.

Sandhu, R., & Munawer, Q. (1998). How to do discretionary access control using roles. In *Proceedings of the Third ACM Workshop on Role-Based Access Control* (pp. 47-54). ACM Publishing.

Shin, M., & Ahn, G. (2000). UML-based representation of role-based access control. In *Proceedings of the 9th International Workshop on Enabling Technologies: Infrastructure for Collaborative Enterprises* (pp. 195-200). Washington, DC: IEEE Computer Society.

Smith, G. W. (1991). Modeling security relevant data semantics. *IEEE Transactions on Software Engineering, 17*(11), 1195–1203. doi:10.1109/32.106974

Sohr, K. (2008). Analyzing and managing role-based access control policies. *IEEE Transactions on Knowledge and Data Engineering, 20*(7), 924–939. doi:10.1109/TKDE.2008.28

Ting, T. C. (1988). A user-role based data security approach. In C. Landwehr (Ed.), *Database security: Status and prospects* (pp. 187-208). Amsterdam: North-Holland.

*This work was previously published in International Journal of Secure Software Engineering, edited by Khaled M. Khan, pp. 1-19, Volume 1, Issue 1, copyright 2010 by IGI Publishing (an imprint of IGI Global).*

# Chapter 6
# Benefits and Challenges in the Use of Case Studies for Security Requirements Engineering Methods

**Nancy R. Mead**
*Carnegie Mellon University, USA*

## ABSTRACT

*The premise of this paper is that pilot case studies in security requirements engineering provide both benefits and challenges to the underlying research, education, and technology transition effort. Over the past four years we have worked with seven development groups in five organizations in the process of refining and transitioning the Security Quality Requirements Engineering (SQUARE) and SQUARE-Lite methods into practice. These experiences have provided the opportunity to step back and assess the use of pilots in conjunction with student projects to support method refinement and technology transition. Although SQUARE and SQUARE-Lite are concerned with security requirements, the benefits and challenges that have been observed would apply to many security research and technology transition efforts. We itemize and justify these benefits and challenges and discuss their practical relevance and application to ensuring adequate information assurance protection.*

## INTRODUCTION

In this paper we discuss the role of pilot case studies in security requirements engineering and their impact on method refinement, student projects, and technology transition. We start by providing some general background on the importance of requirements engineering and some specifics on the problems encountered in security requirements engineering. We then introduce the SQUARE and SQUARE-Lite methods, which were the research models used in our case studies. Next we discuss

DOI: 10.4018/978-1-4666-1580-9.ch006

the case studies, their organizations, and general case study results. We provide detailed results for one of the case studies. We go on to illustrate

- The use of the case studies in refining the SQUARE and SQUARE-Lite methods. We found that the case studies allowed us to identify issues in both methods, resulting in revision of the methods.
- The use of research projects as the basis for student projects. Benefits included the opportunity to work on real client projects, and to provide feedback to both the clients and the research project. Challenges included the need to limit the case studies to a single semester, and to help the students deal with the uncertainties of working on new research.
- The benefits and challenges associated with technology transition of new methods such as SQUARE. Benefits included the opportunity to impact organizational software processes and to provide projects with new insights into security requirements engineering. Challenges included the difficulty of getting busy staff members to work with us and the uphill battle to effect change in security requirements engineering practice, in the absence of larger organizational change.

Although none of these is unique, we seldom look at these three aspects in a unified way, and we almost never discuss the difficulties, since we are generally motivated to discuss our successes.

## BACKGROUND

It comes as no surprise that requirements engineering is critical to the success of any major development project (Mead, 2008b). Some studies have shown that requirements engineering

defects cost 10 to 200 times as much to correct once fielded than if they were detected during requirements development (Boehm & Papaccio, 1988; McConnell, 2001). Other studies have shown that reworking requirements, design, and code defects on most software development projects costs 40 to 50% of total project effort (Jones, 1986), and the percentage of defects originating during requirements engineering is estimated at more than 50%. The total percentage of project budget due to requirements defects is 25 to 40% (Wiegers, 2003).

A prior study found that the return on investment when security analysis and secure engineering practices are introduced early in the development cycle ranges from 12 to 21%, with the highest rate of return occurring when the analysis is performed during application design (Berinato, 2002). The National Institute of Standards and Technology (NIST) reports that software that is faulty in security and reliability costs the economy $59.5 billion annually in breakdowns and repairs (National Institute of Standards and Technology, 2002). The costs of poor security requirements show that even a small improvement in this area would provide a high value. By the time that an application is fielded and in its operational environment, it is very difficult and expensive to significantly improve its security.

Requirements problems are among the top causes (Charette, 2005) of why

- Projects are significantly over budget
- Projects are past schedule
- Projects have significantly reduced scope or are cancelled
- Development teams deliver poor-quality applications
- Products are not significantly used once delivered

Security requirements are often identified during the system life cycle. However, the requirements tend to be general specifications of the functions required, such as password protection, firewalls, and virus detection tools. Often the security requirements are developed independently of the rest of the requirements engineering activity and hence are not integrated into the mainstream of the requirements activities. As a result, security requirements that are specific to the system and that provide for protection of essential services and assets are often neglected.

Much of the study of requirements engineering research and practice has addressed the capabilities that the system will provide. So a lot of attention is given to the functionality of the system, from the user's perspective, but little attention is given to what the system should *not* do. In one discussion on requirements prioritization for a specific large system, ease of use was assigned a higher priority than security requirements. Security requirements were in the lower half of the prioritized requirements. This occurred in part because the only security requirements that were considered had to do with access control.

Current research recognizes that security requirements are negative requirements. Therefore, general security requirements, such as "The system shall not allow successful attacks," are generally not feasible because there is no consensus on ways to validate them other than to apply formal methods to the entire system, including COTS components. We are able to validate that mechanisms such as access control, levels of security, backups, replication, and policy are implemented and enforced. We can also validate that the system will properly handle specific threats identified by a threat model and correctly respond to intrusion scenarios.

If security requirements are not effectively defined, the resulting system cannot be effectively evaluated for success or failure prior to implementation. In addition to employing applicable software engineering techniques, the organization must understand how to incorporate the techniques

into its existing software development processes (Linger, Mead, & Lipson, 1998).

## SQUARE OVERVIEW

Security Quality Requirements Engineering (SQUARE) is a process model developed at Carnegie Mellon University (Mead, Hough, & Stehney, 2005).[1] This process provides a means for eliciting, categorizing, and prioritizing security requirements for information technology systems and applications. (Note that in this section we discuss security requirements, regardless of whether the term "security" is specifically used as a qualifier.) The focus of the method is to build security concepts into the early stages of the development life cycle. It can also be used for documenting and analyzing the security aspects of fielded systems and for steering future improvements and modifications to those systems.

Subsequent to initial development, SQUARE was applied in a series of client case studies (Chen et al., 2004; Gordon, Stehney, Wattas, Yu, & Mead, 2005; Chung, Hung, Hough, & Ojoko-Adams, 2006). The draft process shown in Table 1 was revised and baselined after the case studies were completed. The baselined process is shown in Table 2. Brief descriptions of each step follow; a detailed discussion of the method can be found in Mead et al. (2005).

**Step 1:** *Agree on definitions:* Is needed as a prerequisite to security requirements engineering. On a given project, team members tend to have definitions in mind, based on their prior experience, but those definitions often differ. For example, for some government organizations, security has to do with access based on security clearance levels, whereas for others security may have to do with physical security or cyber security. Sources such as the Institute for Electrical and Elec-

*Table 1. The original SQUARE process*

| **Step 1: Agree on definitions** |
| --- |
| **Input**: Candidate definitions from IEEE and other standards<br>**Technique**: Structured interviews, focus group<br>**Participant**: Stakeholders, requirements team<br>**Output**: Agreed-to definitions |
| **Step 2: Identify security goals** |
| **Input**: Definitions, candidate goals, business drivers, policies and procedures, examples<br>**Technique**: Facilitated work session, surveys, interviews<br>**Participant**: Stakeholders, requirements engineer<br>**Output**: Goals |
| **Step 3: Select elicitation techniques** |
| **Input**: Goals, definitions, candidate techniques, expertise of stakeholders, organizational style, culture, level of security needed, cost/benefit analysis, etc.<br>**Technique**: Work session<br>**Participant**: Requirements engineer<br>**Output**: Selected elicitation techniques |
| **Step 4: Develop artifacts to support security requirements definition** |
| **Input**: Potential artifacts (e.g., scenarios, misuse cases, templates, forms)<br>**Technique**: Work session<br>**Participant**: Requirements engineer<br>**Output**: Needed artifacts: scenarios, misuse cases, models, templates, forms |
| **Step 5: Elicit security requirements** |
| **Input**: Artifacts, risk assessment results, selected techniques<br>**Technique**: Joint Application Development (JAD), interviews, surveys, model-based analysis, checklists, lists of reusable requirements types, document reviews<br>**Participant**: Stakeholders facilitated by requirements engineer<br>**Output**: Initial cut at security requirements |
| **Step 6: Categorize requirements as to level (system, software, etc.) and whether they are requirements or other kinds of constraints** |
| **Input**: Artifacts, risk assessment results, selected techniques<br>**Technique**: Joint Application Development (JAD), interviews, surveys, model-based analysis, checklists, lists of reusable requirements types, document reviews<br>**Participant**: Stakeholders facilitated by requirements engineer<br>**Output**: Initial cut at security requirements |
| **Step 7: Perform risk assessment** |
| **Input**: Misuse cases, scenarios, security goals<br>**Technique**: Risk assessment method, analysis of anticipated risk against organizational risk tolerance, including threat analysis<br>**Participant**: Requirements engineer, risk expert, stakeholders<br>**Output**: Risk assessment results |
| **Step 8: Prioritize requirements** |
| **Input**: Categorized requirements and risk assessment results<br>**Technique**: Prioritization methods such as Triage, Win-Win<br>**Participant**: Stakeholders facilitated by requirements engineer<br>**Output**: Prioritized requirements |
| **Step 9: Inspect requirements** |
| **Input**: Prioritized requirements, candidate formal inspection technique<br>**Technique**: Inspection method such as Fagan, peer reviews<br>**Participant**: Inspection team<br>**Output**: Initial selected requirements, documentation of decision making process and rationale |

*Table 2. The Baselined SQUARE Process*

| Step 1: Agree on definitions |
|---|
| **Input**: Candidate definitions from IEEE and other standards<br>**Technique**: Structured interviews, focus group<br>**Participant**: Stakeholders, requirements team<br>**Output**: Agreed-to definitions |
| **Step 2: Identify assets and security goals** |
| **Input**: Definitions, candidate goals, business drivers, policies and procedures, examples<br>**Technique**: Facilitated work session, surveys, interviews<br>**Participant**: Stakeholders, requirements engineer<br>**Output**: Assets and goals |
| **Step 3: Develop artifacts to support security requirements definition** |
| **Input**: Potential artifacts (e.g., scenarios, misuse cases, templates, forms)<br>**Technique**: Work session<br>**Participant**: Requirements engineer<br>**Output**: Needed artifacts: scenarios, misuse cases, models, templates, forms |
| **Step 4: Perform risk assessment** |
| **Input**: Misuse cases, scenarios, security goals<br>**Technique**: Risk assessment method, analysis of anticipated risk against organizational risk tolerance, including threat analysis<br>**Participant**: Requirements engineer, risk expert, stakeholders<br>**Output**: Risk assessment results |
| **Step 5: Select elicitation techniques** |
| **Input**: Goals, definitions, candidate techniques, expertise of stakeholders, organizational style, culture, level of security needed, cost/benefit analysis, etc.<br>**Technique**: Work session<br>**Participant**: Requirements engineer<br>**Output**: Selected elicitation techniques |
| **Step 6: Elicit security requirements** |
| **Input**: Artifacts, risk assessment results, selected techniques<br>**Technique**: Joint Application Development (JAD), interviews, surveys, model-based analysis, checklists, lists of reusable requirements types, document reviews<br>**Participant**: Stakeholders facilitated by requirements engineer<br>**Output**: Initial cut at security requirements |
| **Step 7: Categorize requirements as to level (system, software, etc.) and whether they are requirements or other kinds of constraints** |
| **Input**: Initial requirements, architecture<br>**Technique**: Work session using a standard set of categories<br>**Participant**: Requirements engineer, other specialists as needed<br>**Output**: Categorized requirements |
| **Step 8: Prioritize requirements** |
| **Input**: Categorized requirements and risk assessment results<br>**Technique**: Prioritization methods such as Triage, Win-Win<br>**Participant**: Stakeholders facilitated by requirements engineer<br>**Output**: Prioritized requirements |
| **Step 9: Inspect requirements** |
| **Input**: Prioritized requirements, candidate formal inspection technique<br>**Technique**: Inspection method such as Fagan, peer reviews<br>**Participant**: Inspection team<br>**Output**: Initial selected requirements, documentation of decision making process and rationale |

tronics Engineers (IEEE) and the Software Engineering Body of Knowledge (SWE-BOK) provide a range of definitions to select from or tailor. A focus group meeting with the interested parties most likely enables the selection of a consistent set of definitions for the security requirements activity.

**Step 2:** *Identify assets and security goals:* Should be done at the organizational level and is needed to support software development in the project at hand. This provides a consistency check with the organization's policies and operational security environment. Different stakeholders usually have different goals. For example, a stakeholder in human resources may be concerned about maintaining the confidentiality of personnel records, so from their point of view the personnel records are an asset, whereas a stakeholder in a financial area may be concerned with ensuring that financial data is not accessed or modified without authorization, so they will feel that financial data are an asset. Once the assets and goals of the various stakeholders have been identified, they need to be prioritized.

**Step 3:** *Develop artifacts:* Is necessary to support all subsequent security requirements engineering activities. It is often the case that organizations do not have a documented concept of operations for a project, succinctly stated project goals, documented normal usage and threat scenarios, misuse or abuse cases, and other documents needed to support requirements definition. This means that either the entire requirements process is built on unstated assumptions or a lot of time is spent backtracking to try to obtain such documentation.

**Step 4:** *Perform risk assessment:* Requires an expert in risk assessment methods, the support of the stakeholders, and the support of a security requirements engineer. There are a number of risk assessment methods

to select from. The risk assessment expert can recommend a specific method based on the needs of the organization. The artifacts from Step 3 provide the input to the risk assessment process. The outcomes of the risk assessment can help in identifying the high-priority security exposures.

**Step 5:** *Select elicitation techniques:* Becomes important when there are diverse stakeholders. A more formal elicitation technique, such as the Accelerated Requirements Method (Hubbard, Mead, & Schroeder, 2000), Joint Application Design (Wood & Silver 1995), or structured interviews can be effective in overcoming communication issues when there are stakeholders with different cultural backgrounds. In other cases, elicitation may simply consist of sitting down with a primary stakeholder to try to understand that stakeholder's security requirements needs.

**Step 6:** *Elicit security requirements:* Is the actual elicitation process using the selected technique. Most elicitation techniques provide detailed guidance on how to perform elicitation. This step builds on the artifacts that were developed in earlier steps, such as misuse and abuse cases, attack trees, threats, and scenarios.

**Step 7:** *Categorize requirements:* Allows the security requirements engineer to distinguish among essential requirements, goals (desired requirements), and architectural constraints that may be present. Requirements that are actually constraints typically occur when a specific system architecture has been chosen prior to the requirements process. This categorization also helps in the prioritization activity that follows.

**Step 8:** *Prioritize requirements:* Depends not only on the prior step but may also involve performing a cost/benefit analysis to determine which security requirements have a high payoff relative to their cost. Of course prioritization may also depend on other consequences of security breaches, such as loss of life, loss of reputation, and loss of consumer confidence.

**Step 9:** *Inspect requirements:* Can be done at varying levels of formality, from Fagan inspections (a highly structured and proven technique for requirements inspection) (Fagan, 1999) to peer reviews. Once inspection is complete, the project team should have an initial set of prioritized security requirements. Finally, the project team should understand which areas are dependent on specific architectures and implementations and should plan to revisit those as well.

## SQUARE-Lite Overview

After our initial work on the SQUARE case studies, we realized that it had taken three student teams over a period of three semesters to do a thorough job of going through each SQUARE step, including the subsequent reflection on the method. As a result, it became clear to us that some organizations would not have the time or resources to adopt the entire SQUARE process. Therefore, we came up with the idea of a lightweight version of SQUARE, which we called SQUARE-Lite. SQUARE-Lite could be used in organizations that already had a requirements engineering process and therefore did not want to start over again with a whole new process specifically for security requirements. Our rationale for the initial version of SQUARE-Lite was as follows: We felt that Step 1, Agree on definitions, was still needed, because lack of agreed-to definitions of terms can cause many inconsistencies and errors in security requirements. As an example, one group of stakeholders had diverse ideas of the meaning of the term "availability" and as a consequence different stakeholders gave availability differing priorities. Step 2, Identify assets and security goals, is clearly needed as a framework for the subsequent requirements. We thought that we could eliminate Steps 3 through 5, Develop artifacts, Perform risk assessment, and

Select elicitation techniques. Clearly Step 6, Elicit security requirements, was needed. We would bypass Step 7, Categorize requirements, and go directly to Step 8, Prioritize requirements. Finally, we assumed that Step 9, Inspect requirements, would be handled the same as other requirements inspection or review on the project. As a consequence of this analysis, we arrived at the four-step SQUARE-Lite process shown in Table 3.

Subsequent to initial development, SQUARE-Lite was applied in a single client case study (Gayash, Viswanathan, Padmanabhan, & Mead, 2008). As a consequence of this case study, revisions were made to SQUARE-Lite, which are shown in Table 4 and explained later in this paper.

## OUR CASE STUDY CLIENTS AND GENERAL RESULTS

During the period from 2003 to 2008, we worked with seven development groups in five organizations to pilot and transition the SQUARE and SQUARE-Lite methods. These case studies allowed us to evaluate the effectiveness of SQUARE and SQUARE-Lite and to modify them as needed. Since all of the case studies included student involvement, we were able to observe the benefits and challenges of designing pilot case studies that were appropriate for students and often had to fit into one-semester project constraints. The case studies also provided an opportunity to observe firsthand the difficulties of transitioning new requirements engineering methods from theory into practice.

Although some of these aspects have been discussed in earlier publications (Chen et al., 2004; Gordon et al., 2005; Chung et al., 2006; Mead, 2008c), they have not been summarized and analyzed in their entirety. The case study reports (Chen et al., 2004; Gordon et al., 2005; Xie et al., 2004; Gayash et al., 2008) were developed in isolation, without considering the total effect of all the case studies on the research.

*Table 3. The Initial SQUARE-Lite Process*

| Step 1: Agree on definitions |
|---|
| **Input**: Candidate definitions from IEEE and other standards<br>**Technique**: Structured interviews, focus group<br>**Participant**: Stakeholders, requirements team<br>**Output**: Agreed-to definitions |
| **Step 2: Identify assets and security goals** |
| **Input**: Definitions, candidate goals, business drivers, policies and procedures, examples<br>**Technique**: Facilitated work session, surveys, interviews<br>**Participant**: Stakeholders, requirements engineer<br>**Output**: Assets and goals |
| **Step 3: Elicit security requirements** |
| **Input**: Artifacts, risk assessment results, selected techniques<br>**Technique**: Joint Application Development (JAD), interviews, surveys, model-based analysis, checklists, lists of reusable requirements types, document reviews<br>**Participant**: Stakeholders facilitated by requirements engineer<br>**Output**: Initial cut at security requirements |
| **Step 4: Prioritize requirements** |
| **Input**: Categorized requirements and risk assessment results<br>**Technique**: Prioritization methods such as Triage, Win-Win<br>**Participant**: Stakeholders facilitated by requirements engineer<br>**Output**: Prioritized requirements |

*Table 4. The Revised SQUARE-Lite Process*

| Step 1: Agree on definitions |
|---|
| **Input**: Candidate definitions from IEEE and other standards<br>**Technique**: Structured interviews, focus group<br>**Participant**: Stakeholders, requirements team<br>**Output**: Agreed-to definitions |
| **Step 2: Identify assets and security goals** |
| **Input**: Definitions, candidate goals, business drivers, policies and procedures, examples<br>**Technique**: Facilitated work session, surveys, interviews<br>**Participant**: Stakeholders, requirements engineer<br>**Output**: Assets and goals |
| **Step 3: Perform risk assessment** |
| **Input**: Misuse cases, scenarios, security<br>**Technique**: Risk assessment method, analysis of anticipated risk against organizational risk tolerance, including threat analysis<br>**Participant**: Requirements engineer, risk expert, stakeholders<br>**Output**: Risk assessment results |
| **Step 4: Elicit security requirements** |
| **Input**: Artifacts, risk assessment results, selected techniques<br>**Technique**: Joint Application Development (JAD), interviews, surveys, model-based analysis, checklists, lists of reusable requirements types, document reviews<br>**Participant**: Stakeholders facilitated by requirements engineer<br>**Output**: Initial cut at security requirements |
| **Step 5: Prioritize requirements** |
| **Input**: Categorized requirements and risk assessment results<br>**Technique**: Prioritization methods such as Triage, Win-Win<br>**Participant**: Stakeholders facilitated by requirements engineer<br>**Output**: Prioritized requirements |

We worked with Organization 1 on three student projects, spanning three semesters. Organization 1, a small IT firm based in Pennsylvania, had a medium-sized software product that was undergoing major revision. The product was a corporate asset management system that was sold as a commercial product. Initially it was installed in client organizations on stand-alone workstations that were not connected to the internet.

In the first two projects we worked through the SQUARE steps, and in the third project we revisited some of our recommendations to Organization 1 and improved on them. It was clear to us that the organization's staff would not have had the time to learn SQUARE and apply it themselves, but they were interested and cooperative, and they applied our recommendations to their product. The requirements were developed jointly by the organization's staff and the student team. Our primary contact point was one of the members of Organization 1's small development team, whose responsibility was in the area of user interface. Our most complete case study results were for Organization 1. Over the course of the three semesters that we worked with them, with their support we were able to produce documented outputs for all the SQUARE steps (Chen et al., 2004; Gordon et al., 2005; Chung et al., 2006; Xie et al., 2004). This included a complete set of use cases, misuse cases, attack trees, risks, security requirements, cost/benefit studies, and architectural and policy recommendations. They were able to prioritize the requirements and implement them over time. In addition, we used these results to help refine our prototype tools and to support some further student independent studies (Caulkins, Hough, Mead, & Osman, 2007).

Organization 2, a project team at a U.S. federal government research institute, was in the early project planning stages of developing a large database that contained sensitive data. The database would be accessed by various external groups. Each group had varying privileges as to the data they were permitted to view. The developers realized that security was a concern, and everyone on the team was motivated to learn and use SQUARE. Our primary contact point was the project manager. Organization 2 (Chung et al., 2006) probably helped us to produce the best set of security requirements, since the participants had a lot of expertise, but we did not produce all of the artifacts that came out of the case studies with Organization 1.

Organization 3, a small contract team, was in the development stage of a large web-based project for a department of the U.S. federal government. The biggest concern was with intruders defacing the website, changing information to be incorrect, and so on. The project team had already identified the security requirements, although the security requirements were not documented in closed form. Organization 3 clearly had the background to understand what we were trying to do, but since many of the critical security decisions had already been made, there wasn't much motivation to try something new or invest the time in the SQUARE process. Our primary contact point was the website development manager. Organization 3 (Chung et al., 2006) was a little too far along in the process to benefit from SQUARE.

Organization 4, a medium-sized commercial company based in Pennsylvania, had a large project that was in development. The project database included sensitive financial data and private client information. Many security mechanisms has been implemented, but formal identification and analysis of security requirements had not taken place. Although interested, the developers had an overriding concern with completing the work, as it was already behind schedule and had undergone some staffing and management changes. Therefore, the requirements were developed by the student team, with the project developers providing review. We worked with Organization 4 using student intern help and applying the SQUARE-Lite process. Our primary contact point was responsible for quality factors and software development process. About the time that we completed the case study, our primary contact point left the organization. Although the other contact points at the company appreciated the report that we provided them at the end of the case study, it is unknown whether our recommendations were implemented. Our work with Organization 4 (Gayash et al., 2008) allowed us to pilot SQUARE-Lite. The lack of organizational maturity made it difficult to achieve the desired results, although we were still able to make valuable recommendations to them and suggest useful directions.

Organization 5, a large multinational company, had a number of projects in process and a well-defined software engineering process. We worked with them to try to modify their software engineering process to focus more attention on security requirements, and also to identify a candidate pilot project. Our primary contact point was one of their in-house security experts. With Organization 5, we were able to suggest changes to their standard requirements engineering processes to incorporate SQUARE elements. It remains to be seen whether these changes will be supported in-house.

Organizations 1, 2, and 3 provided opportunities for direct pilots of the SQUARE process. Organization 4 provided the opportunity to pilot SQUARE-Lite. With Organization 5, we were less concerned with piloting SQUARE per se than with using SQUARE to improve their existing security requirements engineering process.

In all cases, we had interested and motivated points of contact. It was often the case that the contact point was in a staff function rather than a line function. For example, it might be someone who was responsible for security, process, or QA, rather than someone responsible for management of the development project. However, in other cases, the primary contact point was the development manager. What we found, not surprisingly, was that having good contact points was essential for the student projects to be successful. These contact points also provided valuable feedback that helped in refining the methods. However, the contact points were necessary but not sufficient for successful technology transition. Many other factors came into play.

## DETAILED CASE STUDY RESULTS

In this section we provide example results from one of our case studies, the Asset Management System (AMS) of Organization 1 (Allen, Barnum, Ellison, McGraw, & Mead, 2008).

**Step 1:** *Agree on definitions:* We worked with the client to agree on a common set of security definitions to create a common base of understanding. These are two examples of the definitions that were agreed on:

- **Access control:** Ensures that resources are granted only to those users who are entitled to them.
- **Access control list:** A table that tells a computer operating system which access rights or explicit denials each user has to a particular system object, such as a file directory or individual file.

The full set of definitions was drawn from resources such as IEEE, Carnegie Mellon University, industry, and dictionaries.

**Step 2:** *Identify assets and security goals:* We worked with the client to flesh out security goals that mapped to the company's overall business goals. This is one example set of goals:

- **Business goal of AMS:** To provide an application that supports asset management and planning.
- **Security goals:** Three high-level security goals were derived for the system:

- Management shall exercise effective control over the system's configuration and use
- The confidentiality, accuracy, and integrity of the AMS shall be maintained
- The AMS shall be available for use when needed

**Step 3:** *Develop artifacts.* Architectural diagrams, use cases, misuse cases, abuse case diagrams, attack trees, and essential assets and services were documented in this step. For instance, an attack scenario was documented in the following way:

System administrator accesses confidential information

1. By being recruited OR
   By being bribed OR
   By being threatened OR
   Through social engineering OR
2. By purposefully abusing rights

This step creates needed documentation that serves as input into the steps that follow.

**Step 4:** *Perform risk assessment:* The risk assessment techniques that were field tested were selected after completing a literature review. This review examined the usefulness and applicability of eight risk assessment techniques:

- General Accounting Office Model (U.S. General Accounting Office, 1999)
- National Institute of Standards and Technology (NIST) Model (Stoneburner, Goguen, & Feringa, 2002)
- NSA's INFOSEC Assessment Methodology (National Security Agency, 2004)
- Shawn Butler's Security Attribute Evaluation Method (Butler, 2002)
- Carnegie Mellon's Vendor Risk Assessment and Threat Evaluation (Lipson, Mead, & Moore, 2001)

- Yacov Haimes's Risk Filtering, Ranking, and Management Model (Haimes, 2004)
- Carnegie Mellon's Survivable Systems Analysis Method (Mead, Ellison, Linger, Longstaff, & McHugh, 2002)
- Martin Feather's Defect Detection and Prevention Model (Cornford, Feather, & Hicks, 2001)

Each method was ranked in four categories: (1) suitability for small companies, (2) feasibility of completion in the time allotted, (3) lack of dependence on historical threat data, and (4) suitability in addressing requirements.

After we averaged scores from the four categories, we selected NIST's and Haimes's models as useful techniques for the risk assessment step. Brainstorming, attack tree, and misuse case documentation were used to identify potential threat scenarios. The two independent risk assessment analyses produced a useful risk profile for the company's system. The two most meaningful findings were that insider threat posed the highest impact risk to the AMS and that because of weak controls, it was easy for an insider or unauthorized user to defeat authentication. In this particular case study, we also identified a set of essential services and assets as part of the artifact generation. This is not part of the standard SQUARE process but nevertheless can be a beneficial exercise if enough architectural information already exists to support it. All findings from the risk assessment, along with the findings from the essential services and asset identification process, were used to determine the priority level associated with each of the nine requirements.

**Step 5:** *Select elicitation techniques:* The students considered the following techniques:

○ Misuse cases (Sindre & Opdahl, 2000)

○ Soft Systems Methodology (SSM) (Checkland, 1990)

○ Quality Function Deployment (QFD) (QFD Institute, 2005)

○ Controlled Requirements Expression (CORE) (Christel & Kang, 1992)

○ Issue-based information systems (IBIS) (Kunz & Rittel, 1970)

○ Joint Application Development (JAD) (Wood & Silver, 1995)

○ Feature-oriented domain analysis (FODA) (Kang, Cohen, Hess, Novak, & Peterson, 1990)

○ Critical discourse analysis (CDA) (Schiffrin, 1994)

○ Accelerated Requirements Method (ARM) (Hubbard, Mead, & Schroeder, 2000)

They then developed a set of evaluation criteria, which are described in more detail in the case study report, and used a tabular approach to decide which methods looked promising. The results of this exercise are shown in Table 5. IBIS, JAD, and ARM were used for requirements elicitation. The best results were achieved with ARM, which has been used on several projects since then. We then worked with the client to categorize, prioritize, and rewrite the requirements.

**Steps 6 and 7:** *Elicit and Categorize security requirements:* Nine security requirements were identified and then organized to map to the three high-level security goals (see Step 2). Some of the requirements were

○ **Req 1:** The system is required to have strong authentication measures in place at all system gateways and entrance points (maps to Goals 1 and 2).

○ **Req 2:** The system is required to have sufficient process-centric and logical means to govern which system elements (data, functionality, etc.) users can view, modify, and/or interact with (maps to Goals 1 and 2).

○ **Req 3:** A continuity of operations plan (COOP) is required to assure system availability (maps to Goal 3).

○ **Req 6:** It is required that the system's network communications be protected from unauthorized information gathering and/or eavesdropping (maps to Goals 1 and 2).

*Table 5. Comparison of Elicitation Methods*

|  | Misuse Cases | SSM | QFD | CORE | IBIS | JAD | FODA | CDA | ARM |
|---|---|---|---|---|---|---|---|---|---|
| Adaptability | 3 | 1 | 3 | 2 | 2 | 3 | 2 | 1 | 2 |
| CASE tool | 1 | 2 | 1 | 1 | 3 | 2 | 1 | 1 | 1 |
| Stakeholder acceptance | 2 | 2 | 2 | 2 | 3 | 2 | 1 | 3 | 3 |
| Easy implementation | 2 | 2 | 1 | 2 | 3 | 2 | 1 | 1 | 2 |
| Graphical output | 2 | 2 | 1 | 1 | 2 | 1 | 2 | 2 | 3 |
| Quick implementation | 2 | 2 | 1 | 1 | 2 | 1 | 2 | 2 | 3 |
| Shallow learning curve | 3 | 1 | 2 | 1 | 3 | 2 | 1 | 1 | 1 |
| High maturity | 2 | 3 | 3 | 3 | 2 | 3 | 2 | 2 | 1 |
| Scalability | 1 | 3 | 3 | 3 | 2 | 3 | 2 | 1 | 2 |
| Total score | 18 | 18 | 17 | 16 | 22 | 19 | 14 | 14 | 18 |

*Note.* 3 = Very Good, 2 = Fair, 1 = Poor.

The nine security requirements were central to the security requirements document that was ultimately delivered to the client.

**Step 8:** *Prioritize requirements:* The nine security requirements were prioritized based on the following qualitative rankings:

- **Essential:** Product will be unacceptable if this requirement is absent.
- **Conditional:** Requirement enhances security, but the product is acceptable if this requirement is absent.
- **Optional:** Requirement is clearly of lower priority than Essential and Conditional requirements.

Req 1 from Steps 6 and 7, which dealt with authentication at borders and gateways, was deemed essential because of its importance in protecting against the high-impact, authentication-related risks identified in the risk assessment. Req 3, dealing with continuity of operations planning, was still seen as an important element and worth considering, but it was found to be an optional requirement relative to the other eight requirements. That is, though COOP plans are valuable, the risk assessment phase found that greater threats to the system resulted from unauthorized disclosure of information than from availability attacks.

We also used the Analytical Hierarchy Process (AHP) methodology to prioritize requirements and found it to be successful both in client acceptance and in its ability to handle security requirements (Karlsson & Ryan, 1997).

**Step 9:** *Inspect requirements:* We experimented with different inspection techniques and had varying levels of success with each. None of the inspection techniques were sufficiently effective in identifying defects in the security requirements. Instead, we recommend the Fagan inspection technique.

In one case study instance, each team member played a role in inspecting the quality of the team's work and deliverables. A peer review log was created to document what had been reviewed and was used to maintain a log of all problems, defects, and concerns. Each entry in the log was numbered and dated, addressing the date, origin, defect type, description, severity, owner, reviewer, and status. Each entry was assigned to an owner, who was responsible for making sure that defects were fixed. This step was used as a sanity check to ensure that the system met quality goals and expectations.

## USE OF THE CASE STUDIES IN REFINING THE SQUARE AND SQUARE-LITE METHODS

As a result of the case studies, a number of revisions were made to the SQUARE and SQUARE-Lite models. In the case studies the students were asked to provide two reports. One report went to the client, and included our recommendations for security requirements. The other report went to me, and included feedback on the SQUARE method. In all cases, the students suggested the changes to the method, which I then reviewed and considered. In the initial version of SQUARE, the steps were in a slightly different order, as shown in Table 1. After the second case study with Organization 1 (Gordon et al., 2005), it became clear that the order of the steps was not ideal. We felt that risk assessment needed to be done earlier, as it provided valuable input that was needed in eliciting security requirements. In fact, in the case study the risk assessment results caused us to go back and rethink the requirements. Therefore, risk assessment was moved from Step 7 up to Step 4, as noted in Table 2. Development of artifacts became Step 3, and selecting an elicitation technique was a more natural fit as Step 5, immediately prior to actually eliciting the requirements. The students also recommended combining Steps 5, 6, and 7 (eliciting, categorizing, and prioritizing requirements), so that the main requirements engineering activities would be in one step, but the recommended consolidation would have changed the granularity and combined some of the key requirements engineering steps, so this recommendation was not adopted. In the new order, after moving risk assessment to Step 4 and selecting an elicitation process to Step 5, the old Steps 5 through 7 became Steps 6 through 8.

In the initial version of SQUARE-Lite, we envisioned only four steps, as shown in Table 3. In our work with Organization 4 (Gayash et al., 2008), we found that the organization had done an assessment of the management risks, such as cost and schedule, but had not assessed technical risks, let alone security risks. The absence of a technical risk assessment made it impossible for us to generate an adequate set of security requirements. We had to perform a security risk assessment ourselves in order to have confidence in our recommendations. Therefore we felt compelled to add SQUARE Step 4, Perform risk assessment, back into the SQUARE-Lite process, thus making it a five-step process. The resultant process is shown in Table 4.

## CASE STUDY EDUCATIONAL ASPECTS

The use of case studies in security engineering education has been discussed in more detail in earlier publications (Hough & Mead, 2006; Mead & Shoemaker, 2008). Using the SQUARE and SQUARE-Lite methodologies, the students were able to understand the importance of security requirements in software systems, as well as to improve the security foundation of the client projects with which they worked. In each study, the students were graduate students at Carnegie Mellon University. All were enrolled in an information security oriented curriculum, although their primary focus varied between security technology and information security policy.

We have already briefly discussed the organizations that we worked with. Some of the educational considerations in project selection were (1) the ability to get access to key stakeholders in the organization, (2) projects that were a reasonable size for a one-semester project for a team of three to five students, (3) projects that were either new or major upgrades, although we did do some retrogressive analysis of existing projects, and (4) projects with a significant software development component. Note that clients were often concerned about the amount of time this would take, so we needed to be very sensitive to the need to manage meeting time and other client interactions. We also worked with a single point of contact on the client end so that we were not perceived as making constant demands on the time of large groups of staff members. We typically started with an overview briefing of the SQUARE process, identified key client participants, and then limited our interactions to only those participants until we were ready to report results.

## THE BENEFITS AND CHALLENGES ASSOCIATED WITH TECHNOLOGY TRANSITION OF NEW METHODS SUCH AS SQUARE

An earlier paper describes transitioning requirements engineering methods from theory into practice (Kaindl et al., 2002). That paper summarized a number of challenges faced when attempting to transition requirements engineering theory into practice. The experiences described in the paper suggest that many organizations don't have the needed infrastructure to support requirements engineering technology transition.

In reflecting on the more recent case studies, some additional common elements and challenges were observed. We will describe those here and discuss the impact that they have on the success of transitioning security requirements engineering methods from theory to practice.

In Organization 1, we had a motivated POC and cooperative staff in software development, marketing, and database development. This POC was able to get answers and set up meetings as needed. However, we found that some of the needed documents were out of date, and some had to be created by the team with help from the client organization. As noted above, we did three case studies with this organization.

In Organization 2, we had a motivated POC, who was the development manager, and a group of knowledgeable engineers. They were very enthusiastic about trying a new approach and could see the benefits right away. As noted above, they were in the early stages of the project and thus were able to benefit fully from trying a new approach.

In Organization 3, the product was near completion, so the case study was more of an academic exercise. Although the staff was interested, the project was too far along for our work to make much of a difference.

In Organization 4, we had a motivated POC. However, the POC was in a staff role and had some difficulty getting the developers involved. This was in part because they were in the midst of development, trying to meet delivery schedules, and we were revisiting the requirements in retrospect. This organization also had a hodge-podge of

processes. We found that many documents were out of date and incomplete

In Organization 5, we had a motivated POC. There was a defined process that included requirements engineering and even made mention of security requirements. However, the size of the organization meant that a lot of people needed to agree in order for something to change.

Table 6 summarizes the posture of the organizations when looking at the point of contact, existing process, cooperation of developers, cooperation of stakeholders, development phase, staffing, and the criticality of security. It might be possible to substitute any other quality factor for security and get similar results, although this was not our objective.

## TECHNOLOGY TRANSFER RESULTS

In the organizations with motivated but limited development staff, it became clear that they were interested in our recommendations and used them, but they did not have sufficient staff to undertake security requirements engineering on their own. Under such circumstances, the best outcome is that the organization will recognize the shortfall and either bring in additional staff or hire outside

*Table 6. Organizational Factors That Impact Adoption of New Security RE Methods*

|  | Motivated POC | Existing development process | Cooperative developers | Cooperative stakeholders | Development stage | Adequate staff | Importance of security | Result |
|---|---|---|---|---|---|---|---|---|
| Org 1 | Yes | Some | Yes | Yes | Planning/ major upgrade | Not enough | Low | Used recommendations |
| Org 2 | Yes | Some | Yes | Yes | Planning | Adequate | Moderate | Used recommendations |
| Org 3 | No | Yes | Yes | Yes | Development complete | Adequate | Moderate | Ignored recommendations |
| Org 4 | Yes | None | Somewhat | Yes | Under development | Stretched | High | May use recommendations |
| Org 5 | Yes | Yes | Somewhat | Yes | Varied by project | Adequate | Varied by project | Considering global process change |

consultants. On the plus side, because they were small, they did not have many layers of management to convince. If just a few people saw the benefit of a new approach, it could be implemented.

In the organizations with low motivation, poor processes, and/or limited staff, we did not obtain good enough documents to make more than the most general recommendations. In one organization the project missed its projected delivery date several times, and it became clear that our recommendations would be looked at only as time permitted.

It became clear that a number of factors had to be lined up perfectly in order to successfully transition a new security requirements engineering method. We needed a motivated POC, an existing defined process, cooperative developers and stakeholders, adequate staff, and, in our case, recognition of the importance of security requirements. We believe that our experiences shed some light on why transition of new security requirements engineering methods into practice is so hard.

We have completed our pilot study with Organization 4 on their project. It seems unlikely that they will be in a position to adopt the full SQUARE process anytime soon, as they are still working to define basic software engineering processes. The work with Organization 5 shows the most promise, and we will continue to work with our POC to try to effect changes to their standard development processes.

Since these case studies were completed, we have been in touch with several organizations that have the potential to adopt a new method, and it remains to be seen whether they will be able to work with us. With the renewed focus on cyber security, we feel that it is just a matter of time before SQUARE or other security requirements engineering approaches are adopted in the field.

## CONCLUSION AND FUTURE PLANS

Case studies can be used effectively for research, education, and technology transition. Typically, in our published work we focus on the benefits in just one of these areas (research, education, or technology transition), not all three. It is also the case that we seldom discuss in a systematic way the challenges that must be overcome. Although we tend to deal with these challenges as they occur, we are likely to focus on the benefits in our published work, and we seldom take the time to step back and look at the challenges.

In our case studies, at first we were concerned with whether SQUARE was a good approach for security requirements engineering. Then we were concerned about whether the case studies could be effectively completed when they were constrained to one-semester projects. Then we worried about whether we had a motivated contact point within the organization who was willing to work with us to help transition our methods into practice.

As researchers, we tend to be concerned with the quality of our research products. We also need to be concerned with the educational aspects of our research projects and the ability of our students to effectively support them, as well as the ability of practitioner organizations to successfully adopt our approaches.

We continue to use case studies and student assistants to support our research, but we are also looking for larger pilot and technology transition opportunities. In addition, we are working on extending the SQUARE method to encompass privacy (Miyazaki, Mead, & Zhan, 2008) and acquisition. Finally, we are in the process of developing robust tools to replace the prototype tools that were available when the initial case studies took place. Security requirements engineering is a very active research area, and it is our hope that methods such as SQUARE will improve the overall quality of security requirements in the future.

# REFERENCES

Allen, J. H., Barnum, S., Ellison, R. J., McGraw, G., & Mead, N. R. (2008). *Software security engineering: A guide for project managers* (1st ed.). Boston: Addison-Wesley Professional.

Berinato, S. (2002, April 8). Finally, a real return on security spending. *CIO*. Retrieved June 23, 2009, from http://www.cio.com.au/index.php/id;557330171;fp;fpid;pf;1

Boehm, B., & Papaccio, P. N. (1988). Understanding and controlling software costs. *IEEE Transactions on Software Engineering, 14*(10), 1462–1477. doi:10.1109/32.6191

Butler, S. (2002, May). *Security attribute evaluation method: A cost-benefit approach.* Paper presented at the 24th International Conference on Software Engineering, Orlando, FL.

Caulkins, J., Hough, E., Mead, N. R., & Osman, H. (2007). Optimizing investments in security countermeasures: A practical tool for fixed budgets. *IEEE Security & Privacy, 5*(5), 24–27. doi:10.1109/MSP.2007.117

Charrette, R. N. (2005). Why software fails. *IEEE Spectrum, 42*(9). doi:doi:10.1109/MSPEC.2005.1502528

Checkland, P. (1990). *Soft system methodology in action*. Toronto, Ontario, Canada: John Wiley & Sons.

Chen, P., Dean, M., Ojoko-Adams, D., Osman, H., Lopez, L., & Xie, N. (2004). *Systems Quality Requirements Engineering (SQUARE) methodology: Case study on asset management system (Special Rep. No. CMU/SEI-2004-SR-015)*. Pittsburgh, PA: Carnegie Mellon University, Software Engineering Institute.

Christel, M. G., & Kang, K. C. (1992). *Issues in requirements elicitation* (Tech. Rep. No. CMU/SEI-92-TR-012). Pittsburgh, PA: Carnegie Mellon University, Software Engineering Institute.

Chung, L., Hung, F., Hough, E., & Ojoko-Adams, D. (2006). *Security Quality Requirements Engineering (SQUARE): Case study phase III (Special Rep. No. CMU/SEI-2006-SR-003)*. Pittsburgh, PA: Carnegie Mellon University, Software Engineering Institute.

Cornford, S. L., Feather, M. S., & Hicks, K. A. (2001). *DDP – a tool for life-cycle risk management*. Retrieved June 23, 2009, from http://ddptool.jpl.nasa.gov/docs/f344d-slc.pdf

Fagan, M. E. (1999). Design and code inspections to reduce errors in program development. *IBM Systems Journal, 38*(2-3).

Gayash, A., Viswanathan, V., Padmanabhan, D., & Mead, N. R. (2008). *SQUARE-Lite: Case study on VADSoft project (Special Rep. No. CMU/SEI-2008-SR-017)*. Pittsburgh, PA: Carnegie Mellon University, Software Engineering Institute.

Gordon, D., Stehney, T., Wattas, N., Yu, E., & Mead, N. R. (2005). *System Quality Requirements Engineering (SQUARE): Case study on asset management system, phase II (Special Rep. No. CMU/SEI-2005-SR-005)*. Pittsburgh, PA: Carnegie Mellon University, Software Engineering Institute.

Haimes, Y. Y. (2004). *Risk modeling, assessment, and management* (2nd ed.). Hoboken, NJ: John Wiley and Sons, Inc.

Hough, E., & Mead, N. R. (2006). *Security requirements engineering for software systems: Case studies in support of software engineering education.* Paper presented at the 19th Conference on Software Engineering Education & Training, Turtle Bay, Hawaii.

Hubbard, R., Mead, N. R., & Schroeder, C. (2000). *An assessment of the relative efficiency of a facilitator-driven requirements collection process with respect to the conventional interview method.* Paper presented at the International Conference on Requirements Engineering.

Institute, Q. F. D. (2005). *Frequently asked questions about QFD.* Retrieved June 23, 2009, from http://www.qfdi.org/what_is_qfd/faqs_about_qfd.htm

Jones, C. (Ed.). (1986). *Tutorial: Programming productivity: Issues for the eighties* (2nd ed.). Los Angeles: IEEE Computer Society Press.

Kaindl, H., Brinkkemper, S., Bubenko, J. Jr, Farbey, B., Greenspan, S., & Heitmeyer, C. (2002). Requirements engineering and technology transfer: Obstacles, incentives and improvement agenda. *Requirements Engineering Journal, 7*(3), 113–123. doi:10.1007/s007660200008

Kang, K., Cohen, S., Hess, J., Novak, W., & Peterson, A. S. (1990). *Feature-Oriented Domain Analysis (FODA) feasibility study* (Tech. Rep. No. CMU/SEI-90-TR-021). Pittsburgh, PA: Carnegie Mellon University, Software Engineering Institute.

Karlsson, J., & Ryan, K. (1997). A cost-value approach for prioritizing requirements. *IEEE Software, 14*(5). doi:10.1109/52.605933

Kunz, W., & Rittel, H. (1970). *Issues as elements of information systems* (Working Paper No. 131). Berkeley, CA: University of California, Institute of Urban & Regional Development.

Linger, R. C., Mead, N. R., & Lipson, H. F. (1998). *Requirements definition for survivable systems.* Paper presented at the Third International Conference on Requirements Engineering.

Lipson, H. F., Mead, N. R., & Moore, A. P. (2001). *A risk-management approach to the design of survivable COTS-based systems.* Pittsburgh, PA: Software Engineering Institute.

McConnell, S. (2001). From the editor - an ounce of prevention. *IEEE Software, 18*(3), 5–7. doi:10.1109/MS.2001.922718

Mead, N. R. (2008a). Requirements elicitation case studies using IBIS, JAD, and ARM. *Build Security In.* Retrieved June 23, 2009, from https://buildsecurityin.us-cert.gov/daisy/bsi/articles/best-practices/requirements/532-BSI.html

Mead, N. R. (2008b). Security requirements engineering. *Build Security In.* Retrieved June 23, 2009, from https://buildsecurityin.us-cert.gov/daisy/bsi/articles/best-practices/requirements/243-BSI.html

Mead, N. R. (2008c). *SQUARE: Requirements engineering for improved system security.* Retrieved June 23, 2009, from http://www.cert.org/sse/square.html

Mead, N. R., Ellison, R. J., Linger, R. C., Longstaff, T., & McHugh, J. (2000). *Survivable systems analysis method* (Tech. Rep. No. CMU/SEI-2000-TR-013). Pittsburgh, PA: Carnegie Mellon University, Software Engineering Institute.

Mead, N. R., Hough, E. D., & Stehney, T., II. (2005). *Security quality requirements engineering* (Tech. Rep. No. CMU/SEI-2005-TR-009). Pittsburgh, PA: Carnegie Mellon University, Software Engineering Institute.

Mead, N. R., & Shoemaker, D. (2008). Novel methods of incorporating security requirements engineering into software engineering courses and curricula. In Ellis, H. J. C., Demurjian, S. A., & Naveda, J. F. (Eds.), *Software engineering: Effective teaching and learning approaches and practices* (pp. 98–113). Hershey, PA: IGI Global.

Miyazaki, S., Mead, N. R., & Zhan, J. (2008, December). *Computer-aided privacy requirements elicitation technique.* Paper presented at the 2008 IEEE Asia-Pacific Services Computing Conference.

National Institute of Standards and Technology. (2002). *Software errors cost U.S. economy $59.5 billion annually* (Rep. No. NIST 2002-10). Retrieved June 23, 2009, from http://www.nist.gov/public_affairs/releases/n02-10.htm

National Security Agency. (2004). *INFOSEC assessment methodology.* Retrieved June 19, 2009, from http://www.iatrp.com/iam.cfm

Schiffrin, D. (1994). *Approaches to discourse.* Oxford, UK: Blackwell.

Sindre, G., & Opdahl, A. L. (2000). *Eliciting security requirements by misuse cases.* Paper presented at the 37th International Conference on Technology of Object-Oriented Languages (Tools 37–Pacific 2000).

Stoneburner, G., Goguen, A., & Feringa, A. (2002). *Risk management guide for information technology systems (Special Publication 800-30).* Gaithersburg, MD: National Institute of Standards and Technology.

U. S. General Accounting Office. (1999). *Information security risk assessment: Practices of leading organizations - a supplement to GAO's May 1998 executive guide on information security management.* Washington, DC: Author.

Wiegers, K. E. (2003). *Software requirements.* Redmond, WA: Microsoft Press.

Wood, J., & Silver, D. (1995). *Joint application development* (2nd ed.). New York: John Wiley & Sons.

Xie, N. N., Mead, N. R., Chen, P., Dean, M., Lopez, L., & Ojoko-Adams, D. (2004). *SQUARE project: Cost/benefit analysis framework for information security improvement projects in small companies (Tech. Note No. CMU/SEI-2004-TN-045).* Pittsburgh, PA: Carnegie Mellon University, Software Engineering Institute.

## ENDNOTE

[1] The SQUARE work is supported by the Army Research Office through grant number DAAD19-02-1-0389 ("Perpetually Available and Secure Information Systems") to Carnegie Mellon University's CyLab.

*This work was previously published in International Journal of Secure Software Engineering, edited by Khaled M. Khan, pp. 74-91, Volume 1, Issue 1, copyright 2010 by IGI Publishing (an imprint of IGI Global).*

# Chapter 7
# Security Requirements Engineering for Evolving Software Systems:
## A Survey

**Armstrong Nhlabatsi**
*The Open University, UK*

**Bashar Nuseibeh**
*Lero, Ireland & The Open University, UK*

**Yijun Yu**
*The Open University, UK*

## ABSTRACT

*Long-lived software systems often undergo evolution over an extended period. Evolution of these systems is inevitable as they need to continue to satisfy changing business needs, new regulations and standards, and introduction of novel technologies. Such evolution may involve changes that add, remove, or modify features; or that migrate the system from one operating platform to another. These changes may result in requirements that were satisfied in a previous release of a system not being satisfied in subsequent versions. When evolutionary changes violate security requirements, a system may be left vulnerable to attacks. In this paper we review current approaches to security requirements engineering and conclude that they lack explicit support for managing the effects of software evolution. We then suggest that a cross fertilisation of the areas of software evolution and security engineering would address the problem of maintaining compliance to security requirements of software systems as they evolve.*

## INTRODUCTION

Software evolution refers to the process of continually updating software systems in response to changes in their operating environment and their requirements (Lehman and Ramil, 2001; Lehman and Ramil, 2003)2003). These changes are often driven by business needs, regulations, and standards which a software application is required to continue to satisfy (Lam and Loomes, 1998; Breaux and Anton, 2008). The changes may involve adding new features, removing or modifying existing features (Keck and Kuehn, 1998; Calder *et al.*, 2003), redesigning the system for migration to a new platform, or integration with other applications. Such changes may result

DOI: 10.4018/978-1-4666-1580-9.ch007

in requirements that were satisfied in a previous release of an application being violated in its updated version (Ghose, 1999; Ghose, 2000).

Security requirements engineering deals with the protection of assets from potential threats that may lead to harm (Haley *et al.*, 2008). This paper observes that current approaches to security requirements engineering have limited capability for preserving security properties that may be violated as a result of software evolution. In supporting this argument we review the state-of-the-art in both literatures of software evolution and security engineering.

In illustrating the need for security requirements engineering approaches to support software evolution, we consider how the introduction of a government regulation that only employees with valid work permits are allowed to work may affect a standalone payroll system. One way to enforce this regulation could be introducing a feature that allows a central immigration control system to access employee database records in the payroll system. Such a change, however, may require migrating the payroll system to a platform that supports public network access (such as the Internet) where it can communicate with remote applications. Allowing the immigration control application access to the payroll implies that immigration officers now have access to private employee data which were only available with the consent from the individual employees previously. Such evolution of the payroll system has violated confidentiality (a subclass of security) requirements of employees.

We suggest that one way to address the problem of violating security requirements as a result of evolution is a cross fertilisation of approaches to managing software evolution with security requirements engineering. As a first step towards achieving this cross fertilisation we propose to use Jackson and Zave's entailment relation (Zave and Jackson, 1997), which relates requirements, machine specifications and the environment, as a tool for reasoning about both software evolution

and security requirements engineering. We envisage two benefits of using the entailment relation. Firstly, it is based on a framework of requirements engineering that allows one to analyse software evolution at a holistic but finer level of granularity than other approaches in the literature (Lehman and Ramil, 2001; Lehman and Ramil, 2003). Secondly, by making context explicit, it allows one to elicit systematically security vulnerabilities associated with context, which are very often critical (Haley *et al.*, 2008).

We hope that the cross fertilisation leads to an ideal approach to *security requirements engineering for evolving systems*. However, we anticipate that such cross fertilisation is non-trivial as it has to strike a balance between security and evolution. The theme of these challenges is how to design software systems so that they are both secure and evolvable. Current research in software evolution does not explicitly address security issues and approaches to security requirements engineering do not provide systematic means to addressing software evolution concerns. Meeting these challenges is made harder by the fact that achieving software systems that are both evolvable and secure can be conflicting goals (Nhlabatsi *et al.*, 2008). One of the key characteristics of software evolution is that in response to new requirements, new features may be added to existing systems. This mandates composition of the existing feature set with new features. However, feature composition is non-monotonic (Velthuijsen, 1995); that is, properties that were true of an existing system before combination with a new feature, are not guaranteed to hold after the addition of new functionality.

This paper is structured as follows. In Section 2 we summarise the state of the art on approaches to understanding and managing requirements evolution. Section 3 reviews approaches to eliciting and analysing security requirements and presents a comparative evaluation of the extent to which security requirements engineering approaches support software evolution. The main objective of this paper is to identify research challenges that need to be addressed and to present a research agenda in order to make security requirements engineering for evolving systems possible. Section 4 discusses these challenges and where possible identifies promising approaches that could be leveraged to address them, from both software evolution and security requirements engineering perspectives. Since the context of our work is security requirements engineering, one of the research challenges we identify concerns what software evolution might mean from a requirements engineering perspective. In addressing these challenges we propose framing security evolution research within a requirements engineering framework. We conclude the paper in Section 5.

## APPROACHES TO SOFTWARE EVOLUTION

Software evolution refers to the process of developing a software system, and continually updating it due to change in its stakeholder needs and its operating environment (Lehman and Ramil, 2001; Lehman *et al.*, 2002; Lehman and Ramil, 2003). Over time software systems tend to increase in size and complexity. As a result of this increase their maintenance and adaptation becomes more challenging (Cook *et al.*, 2006). Approaches to the study of software evolution can broadly be classified into two categories: *explanatory* and *management* (Cook *et al.*, 2005). *Explanatory* approaches take a scientific view and are concerned with understanding the nature of software evolution. They often study evolution histories of an application in order to understand how it changed over time (Kemerer and Slaughter, 1999; Anton and Potts, 2003; Mens *et al.*, 2004; LaMantia *et al.*, 2008). In contrast *management* approaches take an engineering perspective and study the development of better methods and tools that can be used for managing the effects of software

evolution. We summarise both categories of approaches in the next two subsections.

## Explanatory Approaches

We classify explanatory approaches into two categories based on the type of data they use. The first category use historical data such as changes in source code over a period of time. Anton and Potts (Antón and Potts, 2001; Anton and Potts, 2003) proposed, *functional palaeontology*, the study of the functions offered by a system over its lifetime as a basis for understanding or predicting its evolutionary characteristics. The approach is similar to other approaches that study evolution histories (His and Potts, 2000; Ramil, 2002; Ramil and Smith, 2002; German, 2004; Gîrba and Ducasse, 2006; Barry *et al.*, 2007; Kozlov *et al.*, 2008). Girba and Ducasse (Gîrba and Ducasse, 2006) proposed Hlsmo – a metamodel in which functional evolution history is modelled as an explicit entity. Hlsmo was motivated by the lack of an explicit meta-model for software evolution analysis. Gall et al. (Gall *et al.*, 1999), Rysselberghe and Demeyer (Rysselberghe and Demeyer, 2004), Wu *et al.* (Wu *et al.*, 2004) proposed visualisation approaches for understanding software release histories. These approaches analyse evolution at the source code level (Greevy *et al.*, 2006). Using source code analysis to understand evolution is necessary but not sufficient in understanding evolution at the requirements level.

The second category study software evolution by using software trails and functional dependencies. German (German, 2004) proposed a method to recovering and analysing the evolution of a system using software trails. Software trails refers to information left behind by contributors to the development process of a software product such as software releases, documentation, version control logs, and websites. German's approach takes the software trails as input and reconstructs the evolution of an application. Fischer and Gall's (Fischer and Gall, 2004) approach to analysing feature evolution examines hidden dependencies between structurally unrelated features, which over time become coupled. The authors claim that such hidden feature dependencies must be identified as they may be an indication of architectural erosion. Architectural erosion refers to any detrimental deviation, with time, of a system's architecture from its original design conception (O'Reilly *et al.*, 2003).

## Management Approaches

Zave proposed *feature engineering* and *component architectures* as prescriptions for making systems modular and evolvable (Zave, 2003). Feature engineering involves describing features independently, composing features, detecting, and resolving feature interactions (Turner *et al.*, 1999; Zave, 2003). Component architecture supports feature engineering by providing structural bases on which new features can be added (Turner, 1997; Jackson and Zave, 1998; Bond *et al.*, 2004). One approach to modularisation for evolution is splitting a software system repository into smaller parts (Glorie *et al.*, 2009). The other is viewing an evolutionary system as being a software product line (Pena *et al.*, 2007) with each successive version being a product.

Over time software architecture ages and this weakens the system's ability to incorporate new features. *Continuous architecture evaluation* (Del Rosso, 2006) is one approach to ensuring that the architecture continues to satisfy its requirements. Capabilities (Ravichandar *et al.*, 2008) have been proposed as a tool for *minimizing and accommodating change*. Capabilities are change-tolerant functional abstractions that are foundational to system functionality and are based on the notion that the basic need for a software solution remains the same even though the solution may progressively become more refined over time.

Analysing and understanding the *impact of change* is one of the key problems at the forefront of software evolution management research

(Soffer, 2005; Lin *et al.*, 2009). Soffer's (Soffer, 2005) *scope analysis* approach determines the extent to which changes to one business process affects other business processes. However, this approach does not offer a practical method for tracking the impact of changes to the software systems that support the business process. In addressing this limitation, Lin *et al.* (Lin *et al.*, 2009) proposed capturing requirements changes as a series of atomic changes in specifications and using algorithms to relate changes in requirements to corresponding changes in specifications.

## APPROACHES TO SECURITY REQUIREMENTS ENGINEERING

Security is increasingly considered as a fundamental part of the software development lifecycle and as a result current research trends suggest that security engineering should be an integral part of software engineering (Mouratidis *et al.*, 2005; Mouratidis and Giorgini, 2006). This is motivated by the notion that an ad hoc integration of security into a software system that has already been developed has a negative effect on its maintainability and security. In this section we review approaches to security requirements engineering. We classify these approaches according to the constructs that they are founded on, namely: goals-based (3.1), model-based (3.2), problem-based (3.3), and process-oriented (3.4) approaches. Our classification is partly based on previous surveys by Tondel et al. (Tondel *et al.*, 2008), Villarroel et al (Villarroel *et al.*, 2005), and Mouratidis and Giorgini (Mouratidis and Giorgini, 2006) and partly by our own understanding of the literature in this area.

## Goal-Based Approaches

Goal-oriented approaches to security engineering focus on identifying threats to satisfaction of goals as the basis for identifying system vulnerabilities.

In comparison to low-level requirements, the high-level abstraction of goals implies that they are more stable than low-level requirements. This makes goals less likely to change compared to low-level requirements. However, a limitation resulting from this benefit is that goals may be insufficient for analysing low level security concerns.

Examples of goal-oriented approaches include: KAOS, Secure Tropos, and Secure i*. *KAOS* (van Lamsweerde, 2004) is an approach to modelling, specifying, and analysing security requirements. The approach extends an earlier framework on eliciting goals and identifying potential obstacles to satisfying goals (van Lamsweerde *et al.*, 1998). Recently KAOS has been extended to reasoning about confidentiality requirements (de Landtsheer and van Lamsweerde, 2005). *Secure Tropos* extends the Tropos (Mouratidis *et al.*, 2003; Giorgini *et al.*, 2005; Mouratidis *et al.*, 2006) software development methodology with the ability to explicitly model security concerns such as: security constraints; secure entities such as trust of permission; and delegation of permission. *Secure i** (Liu *et al.*, 2003) is based on the agent-oriented requirements modelling language i* and analyses security and privacy requirements by studying the relationships between system stakeholders, potential attackers, and agents acting on behalf of either attackers or stakeholders.

## Model-Based Approaches

Model-Based approaches are based on the notion that models help requirements analysts in understanding complex software problems and identifying potential solutions through abstraction (Fernández-Medina *et al.*, 2009). In this section we review two model-based approaches (UMLsec and SecureUML). While there may be other model-based approaches aimed at addressing security concerns in the literature, our focus on these two is purely on a representational basis.

*UMLsec* (Jurjens, 2004) is an extension of UML which allows an application developer to embed security-related functionality into a system design and perform security analysis on a model of the system to verify that it satisfies particular security requirements. *SecureUML* (Lodderstedt *et al.*, 2002) (another security extension of UML) is focused on modelling access control policies and how these (policies) can be integrated into a model-driven software development process using role-based access control (RBAC) as a metamodel for specifying and enforcing security.

## Problem-Oriented Approaches

Problem-oriented approaches (Jackson, 1995; Hall *et al.*, 2007; Hall *et al.*, 2008) provide intellectual tools for analysing, structuring, and understanding software development problems. In this section we review three problem-oriented approaches, namely: security requirements and trust assumptions (Haley *et al.*, 2004; Haley *et al.*, 2008), abuse frames (Lin *et al.*, 2003; Lin *et al.*, 2004), and misuse cases (Alexander, 2002; Alexander, 2003).

Haley *et al.*'s (Haley *et al.*, 2008) approach to eliciting, specifying and analysing security requirements combines concepts from requirements engineering and securing engineering. From a requirements engineering perspective it uses the concept of functional goals which can be refined into functional requirements with relevant constraints and from a security engineering perspective, it takes the idea that security is about protecting assets from harm assets.

*Abuse frames* (Lin *et al.*, 2003; Lin *et al.*, 2004) extends problem frames (Jackson, 2001) to analysing security problems in order to determine security vulnerabilities. While problem frames are aimed at analysing the requirements to be satisfied, in contrast, abuse frames are based on the notion of an anti-requirement - the requirement of a malicious user that can subvert an existing requirement.

Similar to abuse frames, *misuse cases* are a negative form of use cases (Jacobson, 1992) and thus are use cases from the point of view of an actor hostile to the system (Alexander, 2002; Alexander, 2003). They are used for documenting and analysing scenarios in which a system may be attacked.

## Process-Oriented Approaches

Process-oriented approaches focus on the steps for analysing security requirements. The steps may involve risk analysis for identifying security vulnerabilities and exploration of countermeasures for addressing identified weaknesses. The *Security Quality Requirement Engineering* (SQUARE) (Mead and Stehney, 2005) method is used for eliciting, analysing, categorising, prioritising, and documenting security requirements. Similar to other approaches, the motivation of this method is to enable requirements analysts to identify security requirements as part of the requirements engineering process rather than as an afterthought. In Georg *et al.* (Georg *et al.*, 2009) an *aspect-oriented* approach to designing secure applications is proposed. The approach models security mechanisms and attack models as aspects and involves risk analysis, misuse model generation, composed system misuse model generation, and alternative solution analysis.

## Evaluation of Support for Evolution in Security Requirements Engineering

Security engineering and software evolution, although often conflicting, are intertwined in the sense that a change in one may affect the other. For example a violation of security goals may result in new security requirements as countermeasures which in turn lead to an evolution of system functionality. Likewise, the inevitable evolution of a system may lead to the addition of new functionality which violates security properties.

In this subsection we make a comparative evaluation of the main characteristics of the security requirements engineering approaches discussed above. Our evaluation is based on a comparison criterion that examines support for software evolution in security engineering approaches. Our claim is that security engineering approaches lack support for software evolution. In order to substantiate this claim we examined the extent to which current approaches to security requirements engineering support software evolution. In the rest of this subsection we present our evaluation criteria and results.

## Evaluation Criteria

Based on the discussion on software evolution approaches in section 2, we identified five dimensions for evaluating support of software evolution in security requirements engineering approaches. These are modularity, component-based architecture, change propagation, and change impact analysis. We selected the dimensions in the evaluation criteria based on the notion that change is at the core of software evolution. Our analysis in section 2 seems to suggest that these dimensions are central to software evolution management (Zave, 2003). Thus, we consider them useful criteria for reasoning about secure software evolution.

Modularisation is a mechanism for enforcing separation of concerns - making it possible to develop software components independently. Constructs such as features, classes, objects, components, and aspects are all means to modularisation.

Component-based architectures provide an infrastructure where software modules can be added and removed with ease (Parsons *et al.*, 2006) by offering mechanisms for component interoperability and integration which make it possible to extend systems with third party components and hence provide support for evolution.

When a feature A is dependent on another feature B by way of B providing services to A, then a change in B may affect A. If B changes while A does not change accordingly, then some assumptions A make about B may be invalid. A *Change Propagation* process keeps track of such changes, and help in guaranteeing that the changes are correctly propagated and that no inconsistent dependency is left unresolved.

While change propagation is concerned with recording and assessing the ripple effect of changes, *change impact analysis* determines what would be affected by a change to a particular artefact (Bohner, 2002; Hassine *et al.*, 2005). This involves identifying the artefact to be changed and how other artefacts that depend on it should be changed. The ripple effects resulting from changing dependent features are often undesirable as they make it harder to manage change during evolution.

*Localisation of change* is a mechanism for minimising the resulting ripple effects by ensuring that the propagation of changes is kept to a minimum and changes in one part of an application do not affect other parts unnecessarily. In this respect, localisation of change is very similar to modularisation. As a result, our evaluation treated them as closely related concepts and deemed it sufficient to show the evaluation results of modularisation only.

## Evaluation Results

Table 3 presents a comparative evaluation of the security requirements engineering approaches discussed earlier using the evaluation criterion above. The evaluation of each approach is based on analysing the characteristics of its core representation, security specific representation, vulnerability identification technique, and countermeasure techniques to accommodating change. We evaluate each approach by assigning an integer value in the range 0 to 3. At the lower end, the value 0 implies that an approach offers little or no support for a particular aspect of software evolution. On the higher end of the scale, the value 3 implies that an approach fully supports the given aspect of evolution. The text next to evaluation value explains the rationale behind the rating.

Each column in Table 3 shows the extent to which each security approach supports a given evolution dimension. It is worth noting, that some approaches to security requirements engineering approaches discussed seem to provide some limited support for software evolution. For example KAOS provide good support for change propagation because it is based on goal models which show explicitly relationships between goals and their dependencies. However, it is very poor in supporting component architectures. Similarly, although Secure Tropos provides a systematic methodology for eliciting and analysing security requirements, it does not provide means for propagating changes between the different models. For instance, if there is a change in a trust of permission model there is no systematic way of relaying such changes to a delegation of permission model, security constraint model, or security entities model. A clear interaction relationship between the models would provide a systematic way of propagating changes between the different models and hence support compliance to security requirements as systems evolve.

Overall, our evaluation shows that none of the approaches discussed provide sufficient support for software evolution. By sufficient support we mean addressing all aspects of the dimensions of software evolution dimensions we have discussed in the evaluation criteria. As a first step towards addressing this limitation, in the next section, we propose a way of reasoning about software evolution and security concerns and present a research agenda for security requirements engineering for evolving systems.

## A RESEARCH AGENDA FOR SECURITY REQUIREMENTS ENGINEERING FOR EVOLVING SYSTEMS

In this section we suggest some open research issues and present a research agenda in security requirements engineering for evolving systems.

*Table 1. Evaluation of support for software evolution in security requirements engineering approaches*

| Conceptual Classification | Security Approach | Security Evolution Support | | | |
|---|---|---|---|---|---|
| | | Modularisation | Component Architectures | Change Propagation | Change Impact Analysis |
| Goal-Based | KAOS(van Lamsweerde, 2004) | 2: The decomposition of a system into goals supports modularity. | 0: There is no explicit support for component architectures. | 3: A goal model shows the relationship between goals and hence their dependencies. | 1: There is no explicit support for change impact analysis as the focuss is one identifying threats to existing goals (rather the effect of adding new goals) |
| | De Landtsheer and van Lamsweed (de Landtsheer and van Lamsweerde, 2005) | 1: Goals are used as a construct for modularity | 0: There is no explicit consideration for component infrastructures. | 3: Dependencies between goals are modelled in a goal model. | 1: There is no explicit support. Focussed on identifying violation of confidentiality by existing goals. |
| | Secure Tropos | 1: Although agents are used for identifying attackers, goals are the main unit of modularity. | 0: Component infrastructures are not explicitly supported. | 1: It requires extension to the analysis of dependency relationships between agents. | 1: There is no explicit support for analysing the impact of adding new goals. |
| | Secure i* | 1: same as for SecureTropos. | 0: There is no explicit support for component architectures. | 3: Achieved by modelling dependencies between stakeholders. | 2: Although there is support for analysing the security impact of existing goals, there is no explicit support on how the impact of adding new goals is analysed. |
| Model-Based | UMLsec (Jurjens, 2002) | 2: Support dependents on the OO nature of UML design models. | 2: Although UMLSec does not prescribe architectures, this can be extended from UML. | 2: Support for change propagation also depends on the underlying UML | 3: Model-Checking and Theorem proving techniques are used to verify the impact of change. |
| | SecureUML (Lodderstedt et al., 2002) | 2: Support depends on the component nature of UML. | 2: This is provided by UML. | 2: Same as for UMLsec | 1: There is no explicit support, although new functionality can be verified against authorisation constraints. |
| Problem-Oriented | Haley et al. (Haley et al., 2008) | 2: Modules are represented as problem descriptions. | 1: Focus is on eliciting security requirement rather how problem can be composed. | 1: There is no explicit modelling for dependencies between functions | 3: Argument satisfaction is used as a way of verifying that a specification satisfies a requirement in a given context. |
| | Abuse Frames (Lin et al., 2003) | 2: Modules are represented as problem descriptions. | 1: There is no explicit support for this. Depends on the structure of the system analysed. | 1: There is no explicit support for change propagation. | 1: Although there is no explicit support, change impact analysis can be achieved through problem analysis when new security problems are identified. |
| | Misuse Cases (Alexander, 2003) | 2: Modules are use cases. | 1: There is no explicit support for component architectures. | 0: Focus is on identifying potential system abuses than interaction between functions | 1: This is not explicit but this can be extended from the fact that misuse cases can be identified from corresponding use cases. |

*continued on following page*

*Table 1. Continued*

| Conceptual Classification | Security Approach | Security Evolution Support | | | |
|---|---|---|---|---|---|
| | | Modularisation | Component Architectures | Change Propagation | Change Impact Analysis |
| Process-Oriented | SQUARE (Mead and Stehney, 2005) | 0: There is no support for modularity. Focus is on risk analysis. | 0: The approach is focussed on steps for risk analysis independent of the underlying structure of the systems analysed. | 3: Risk analysis identifies dependencies, however, not necessary for change propagation. | 3: Although, the steps in the approach are 'water model' like rather than iterative, the approach can be used for impact analysis. |
| | Georg *et al.* (Georg *et al.*, 2009) | 2: The aspect is the construct for modularity. | 1: Aspect weaving techniques provide a way to compose aspects. | 3: Aspects encapsulate cross-cutting concerns, hence show dependency between components. | 1: Focus is on encapsulating security concerns in aspects. There is no explicit support for change impact analysis. |

We frame these issues around challenges in both software evolution and security requirements engineering, and where possible, highlight some promising ideas on how the issues arising from the integration of evolution and security engineering may be addressed. Some of our discussion of the challenges is based on previous works (Mens *et al.*, 2005; Mouratidis and Giorgini, 2006). While these works focussed on software evolution and security engineering, respectively, the theme of our discussion is how to maintain satisfaction of security requirements while supporting continuous evolution of software systems.

## Software Evolution from a Requirements Engineering Perspective

A majority of the approaches to software evolution discussed in section 2 are focussed on studying evolution at the source code level. The stringent nature of security concerns demands a broader but precise approach to studying secure evolution which enables comprehensive identification of security vulnerabilities. For this reason we propose an evaluation of the generic concepts of software evolution from a requirements engineering perspective. More specifically, we examine

what software evolution means in terms of Jackson and Zave's entailment relation (Zave and Jackson, 1997) which describes software in terms of *requirements*, *specification*, and *context*. In the evaluation we propose to classify approaches to software evolution according to whether they view evolution as change in requirements, specification, or context. In doing so we hope to clarify what secure software evolution means in requirements engineering. More importantly, the entailment relation allows us to reason about both security and software evolution at a finer level of granularity. Thus we propose it as a tool for cross-fertilising the areas of software evolution and security engineering and to reason about security engineering for evolving security systems.

- **Jackson and Zave's Entailment Relation:** The entailment relation relates three sets of descriptions: *requirements* (R), *domain assumptions* (W), and *specifications* (S). It states that a specification satisfies a requirement given that some assumptions about the behaviour of the context hold (formally, $S, W \mid\!- R$, where "$\mid\!-$" denotes entailment). A requirement describes a condition or capability that must be met or possessed by a system.

Requirements are optative descriptions in that they described how the world would be once the envisioned system is in place. For an electronic stability programme (ESP) feature in a car this could be: '*avoid vehicle skidding when brakes are applied*'. Domain assumptions describe facts about the behaviour of the environment where a system will be deployed. In this paper we use the term *context* to refer to the environment described in domain assumptions. In contrast to requirements, domain descriptions are indicative in that they describe the objective truth about the context. In the ESP example this could be: '*applying brakes continuously cause tires to lock*', '*tires are mounted on the vehicle's chassis*', and '*locked tires lead to vehicle skidding*'. Specifications then describe how the system should behave in order to satisfy the conditions described in R, given that the assumptions described in W hold. The specification for the ESP could be: '*if tire lock occurs during braking, apply and release braking pressure at short discrete periodic intervals*'.

- **Evolution as change in context:** The operating environment or context of an application plays an important role in its evolution as the design of a software system makes assumptions about the environment in which it will operate (Del Rosso, 2006; Gerdes, 2009). This is especially true for embedded systems (Chung and Subramanian, 2003). Examples of contextual changes include government regulations (Breaux and Anton, 2008), business process models (Soffer, 2005; Ibrahim *et al.*, 2008), platforms (Gerdes, 2009), anomalies observed in the operation of an application resulting from incompleteness of requirements and hardware failures or limitations which were not considered initially (Lutz and Mikulski, 2003) and software bugs (Wang *et al.*, 2006), and inconsistencies between requirements (Russo *et al.*, 1998; van Lamsweerde *et al.*, 1998; Nuseibeh *et al.*, 2000; Felty and Namjoshi, 2003). Changes in context may lead to software evolution and such contextual changes are translated into new requirements that an application has to satisfy in order to remain relevant and effective in its environment (Lam and Loomes, 1998). Therefore evolutionary changes in context may eventually be translated into new requirements and hence 'evolution as change in context' results in requirements evolution. It is worth noting that an application does not only evolve to satisfy new requirements imposed by changes in context but may also evolve to take advantage of new features available in the context. For example, windows applications have introduced new functionality in response to availability of novel features as the Windows operating system evolved (Hsi and Potts, 2000).

- **Evolution as change in specifications:** Research in software evolution has traditionally focussed on changes in source code (Mens *et al.*, 2002; German, 2004; Zenger, 2005; Ren *et al.*, 2006; Antonellis *et al.*, 2009) and software architecture (Chung and Subramanian, 2003; Roshandel *et al.*, 2004; Del Rosso, 2006; LaMantia *et al.*, 2008) as prime variables of system evolution. This has led to techniques such as program refactoring (Kosker *et al.*, ; Smith and McComb, 2008; da Silva *et al.*, 2009) and architectural configuration management systems (Roshandel *et al.*, 2004). In this paper we consider software architectures and code as solutions that are designed to satisfy requirements of an application. Hence we classify them as specifications. While changes in context may lead to new requirements or to changes in existing requirements, in contrast, evolution of speci-

117

fications is driven by changes in requirements (Ghose, 1999) and as such does not always lead to evolution in requirements. An illustration of this point is code refactoring – where the structure of program code may be changed without changing business logic. On the other hand, a change in a requirement often results in a change in business logic (Zowghi and Offen, 1997; Russo *et al.*, 1999; Fabbrini *et al.*, 2007).

- **Evolution as change in requirements:** In recent years, researchers in software evolution have turned their attention to changes in stakeholder needs (expressed as requirements) as one of the drivers of software evolution (Zowghi and Offen, 1997; d'Avila Garcez *et al.*, 2003; Seybold *et al.*, 2004; Hassine *et al.*, 2005). Several approaches have been proposed for supporting requirements evolution. Zowgi and Offen (Zowghi and Offen, 1997) proposed modelling and reasoning about the evolution of requirements using meta level logic for formally capturing intuitive aspects of managing changes to requirements models. Russo *et al.*'s (Russo *et al.*, 1999) proposed restructuring requirements to facilitate inconsistency detection and change management. While, Garcez *et al.*'s (d'Avila Garcez *et al.*, 2003) approach combines abductive reasoning and inductive learning for evolving requirements specifications. Other notable approaches include Fabrinni *et al.*'s (Fabbrini *et al.*, 2007) approach to controlling requirements evolution using formal concept analysis; Ghose's (Ghose, 1999) framework formal approach for addressing the problem of requirements inconsistencies resulting from evolution; Lam and Loomes (Lam and Loomes, 1998) meta and a process model approach; and Brier *et al.*'s (Brier *et al.*, 2006) approach to capturing, analysing, and understanding

how software systems adapt to changing requirements in an organisational context.

- **A secure evolution framework:** Software systems evolve with changing user needs and changes in their environment. Changes in the context of a system may lead to new requirements or modification of existing requirements. One the other hand, evolution in specifications does not always result in a corresponding evolution in requirements. This is due to the notion that requirements state stakeholder needs or the problems to be solved, while specifications describe the behaviour of software solutions that could satisfy the requirements. As a result the abstract problem stated as a requirement may remain the same even though its solutions may get progressively refined due to changes in context such as introduction of novel technologies. We envisage that the observations from our discussion may have important implications for research in secure software evolution. The main implication concerns approaches to secure change impact analysis. For example, the observation that changing requirements may lead to changing specifications could lead to a framework for understanding the impact of changes and traceability of the changes through artefacts in both requirements and specifications.

Similarly, such a change impact analysis framework could also be useful for analysing what impact changes in context may have on requirements and specifications. The change impact framework can be validated by doing more research on what the interaction is between the changes in the three elements of the entailment relation as illustrated in Figure 1. The arrows labelled *a* and *b* represents how changes in requirements impact context and how context evolution impact requirements evolution, respectively. Similarly, the arrows labelled *c* and *d* represent the impact of requirements evolution on specification evolution and impact of specification evolution on requirements, respectively. Arrow *e* represent the impact of changes in specification on context, meanwhile arrow *f* represents the impact of changes in context on specifications.

## Designing Change Tolerant Software Systems

Changing user needs induce new requirements and technological advances may require a change in the context of an application. Evolution of an application is inevitable and software systems often break due to changes resulting from evolution. There is need for an approach to designing software systems in such a way that they can tolerate change, that is, they are evolvable and their evolution does not lead to failure.

Promising approaches to designing change tolerant systems include: Ravichandar et al.'s (Ravichandar *et al.*, 2008) capabilities-based approach to designing change tolerant systems; Zave's (Zave, 2001) feature-based and component-centric architecture approach to evolving software systems; Zowghi (Zowghi and Offen,

1997) approach to modelling and reasoning about requirements evolution; and Garcez *et al.* (d'Avila Garcez *et al.*, 2003) to evolving specifications. Another promising approach is described in Shin and Gomaa (Shin and Gomaa, 2007). The approach models the evolution of non-secure applications into secure applications in terms of the software requirements model and software architecture model. Security requirements are captured separately from functional requirements and it is claimed that this separation makes possible to achieve the evolution from a non-secure application to a secure application with less impact on the application.

## Non-Monotonicity of Software Evolution

Achieving systems that are secure and evolvable is a hard goal because software evolution and security are conflicting goals (Nhlabatsi *et al.*, 2008). One of the key characteristics of software evolution is that in response to new requirements, new features may be added to legacy systems. This mandates composition of the existing feature set with new features. However, feature composition

*Figure 1. Software evolution through entailment relation*

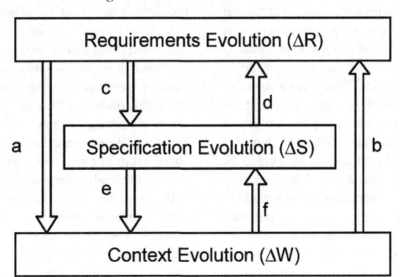

is non-monotonic (Velthuijsen, 1995) due to the feature interactions problem (Keck and Kuehn, 1998). A system is said to be Non-monotonic if it does not guarantee that properties that held prior to addition of new functionality will continue to hold after the functionality has been added (Hall, 2000).

Since software evolution involves the composition of existing features with new features, and feature composition is non-monotonic, then software evolution is intrinsically a non-monotonic activity. Therefore, one of the important challenges for security engineering for evolving systems is how to balance between the inevitable need for supporting continuous software evolution and the goal of designing systems which ensure that security requirements that held initially (and need to continue holding) are not violated by the addition of new functionality. This challenge can be summarised as follows: can continuous software evolution co-exist with stringent security requirements and how can this be achieved through sound design principles, methods, languages, and tools? How can vulnerabilities resulting from the addition of new features be minimized?

Garcez et al. (d'Avila Garcez *et al.*, 2003) approach of analysis and change holds some promise as it makes it possible for systems to be evolved in such a manner that allows the satisfaction of desirable requirements to be checked at the end of an evolution cycle. At its present state, this approach allows for the violation of security properties and then evolving the specification to remove the violation. This is not a desirable characteristic especially in cases where the effects of the violation of a security requirement cannot be reversed. An interesting challenge is how this approach (other similar approaches) could be modified such that evolutionary changes are only permitted only if the implication of any resulting violation to security requirements is minimal. This may involve taking into account the physical context of operation. This could be achieved by combining a analysis and revision approaches with

problem-oriented approaches security requirements engineering (such as those proposed by Haley *et al.* (Haley *et al.*, 2008) and Salifu *et al.* (Salifu *et al.*, 2007), and incorporating promising results from secure software composition (Focardi and Gorrieri, 1997; Mantel, 2001; Mantel, 2002; Francesco and Lettieri, 2003; Bartoletti *et al.*, 2005; Bartoletti *et al.*, 2008).

## Security for Evolving Adaptive Software

Adaptive applications have to maintain satisfaction of requirements despite changes in their operating conditions (Salifu *et al.*, 2007). Designing adaptive systems involves analysing possible variations in their context of operation and specifying behaviours in advance that would enable the system to maintain satisfaction of its requirements despite changes in context. Besides the repository of behaviours corresponding to different contexts, adaptive systems are also equipped with mechanisms for monitoring their context and switch between behaviours in response to contextual changes. Evolutionary changes in a context-ware application are often driven by the introduction of a new context of operation that had not been considered initially. This makes it necessary to specify new behaviours to enable the application to continue to operate in the new context and a specification of variables to be monitored in the new context.

Research in context-ware systems is relatively new. As a result current approaches to managing software evolution are focussed on systems that do not need to change their behaviour with changes in context. We envisage that the adaptive and dynamic nature of context-ware applications brings to fore additional concerns and challenges for both software evolution and security engineering. In software evolution one of the important research issues is whether the approaches proposed for managing evolution in none context-ware systems can be applied to context aware systems. There are at least two perspectives from which software evolution in an adaptive environment can studied. One concern involves evolution of system behaviour with changing context. The other relates to evolution in terms of new behaviour introduced to an application due to new context that was not considered initially. It is worth investigating the interaction between these perspectives of evolution and the security concerns they may raise.

An even harder challenge of security and evolution in adaptive systems is online software evolution (Wang *et al.*, 2006), which is a kind of software evolution that updates running programs without interruption of their execution. Evolution for such systems is dynamic and often has to be completed in relatively short time limits. This timing constraint raises at least two concerns. (1) How can the correctness of evolved software be verified? Current approaches to verification are based on model checking and theorem proofing (Felty and Namjoshi, 2003; Giannakopoulou and Magee, 2003; Letier *et al.*, 2005; Calder and Miller, 2006). Both of these verification techniques are resource intensive operations and often take long to complete. (2) If the event that the online evolution fails, can the evolution be rolled back? What are the implications of such roll back on security properties?

## CONCLUSION

Software systems evolve in response to changes in their operating environment and requirements. Such evolution often violates security requirements. We have reviewed the state-of-the-art in security engineering and concluded that current approaches to security engineering do not address the problem of preserving security properties that may be violated as a result of software evolution.

This paper suggested that one approach to addressing this problem of preserving security properties is a cross fertilisation of approaches to managing software evolution in security

engineering. We termed this as *security requirements engineering for evolving systems*. We have identified and discussed open research issues and challenges that may need to be addressed in order to achieve the goal of security engineering for evolving software systems. One of the main challenges we have identified is the need for an approach for reasoning about both software evolution and security engineering. To this end, we suggested Jackson and Zave's entailment relation as a basis for analysing secure system evolution at a finer level of granularity.

Other challenges we identified are designing change tolerant software systems, non-monotonicity of evolving software systems and secure evolution for adaptive software. In some cases we have discussed promising research directions on how the identified open issues could be addressed. We hope that the research agenda we have set will pave the way for investigating key research problems in security requirements engineering for evolving software systems.

## REFERENCES

Alexander, I. (2002). Initial industrial experience of misuse cases in trade-off analysis. In *Proceedings of IEEE Joint International Conference on Requirements Engineering*.

Alexander, I. (2003). Misuse cases: Use cases with hostile intent. *IEEE Software, 20*(1), 58–66. doi:10.1109/MS.2003.1159030

Antón, A. I., & Potts, C. (2001). Functional paleontology: System evolution as the user sees it. In *Proceedings of the 23rd International Conference on Software Engineering* (ICSE'01).

Anton, A. I., & Potts, C. (2003). Functional paleontology: The evolution of user-visible system services. *IEEE Transactions on Software Engineering, 29*(2), 151–166. doi:10.1109/TSE.2003.1178053

Antonellis, P., Antoniou, D., Kanellopoulos, Y., Makris, C., Theodoridis, E., Tjortjis, C., & Tsirakis, N. (2009). Clustering for monitoring software systems maintainability evolution. *Electronic Notes in Theoretical Computer Science, 233,* 43–57. doi:10.1016/j.entcs.2009.02.060

Barry, E. J., Kemerer, C. F., & Slaughter, S. A. (2007). How software process automation affects software evolution: a longitudinal empirical analysis. J*ournal of Software Maintenance and Evolution. Research and Practice, 19*(1), 1–31.

Bartoletti, M., Degano, P., & Ferrari, G. L. (2005). Enforcing secure service composition. In *Proceedings of the 18th IEEE Workshop Computer Security Foundations.*

Bartoletti, M., Degano, P., Ferrari, G. L., & Zunino, R. (2008). Semantics-Based design for secure Web services. *IEEE Transactions on Software Engineering, 34*(1), 33–49. doi:10.1109/TSE.2007.70740

Bohner, S. A. (2002). Software change impacts-an evolving perspective. In *Proceedings of International Conference on Software Maintenance.*

Bond, G. W., Cheung, E., Purdy, K. H., Zave, P., & Ramming, C. (2004). An open architecture for next-generation telecommunication services. *ACM Transactions on Internet Technology, 4*(1), 83–123. doi:10.1145/967030.967034

Breaux, T. D., & Anton, A. I. (2008). Analyzing regulatory rules for privacy and security requirements. *IEEE Transactions on Software Engineering, 34*(1), 5–20. doi:10.1109/TSE.2007.70746

Brier, J., Rapanotti, L., & Hall, J. G. (2006). Problem-based analysis of organisational change: A real-world example. In *Proceedings of the 2006 International Workshop on Advances and Applications of Problem Frames,* Shanghai, China, ACM.

Calder, M., Kolberg, M., Magill, E., & Reiff-Marganiec, S. (2003). Feature interaction: A critical review and considered forecast. *Computer Networks, 41*(1), 115–141. doi:10.1016/S1389-1286(02)00352-3

Calder, M., & Miller, A. (2006). Feature interaction detection by pairwise analysis of LTL properties: a case study. *Formal Methods in System Design, 28*(3), 213–261. doi:10.1007/s10703-006-0002-5

Chung, L., & Subramanian, N. (2003). Architecture-based semantic evolution of embedded remotely controlled systems. *Journal of Software Maintenance and Evolution: Research and Practice, 15*(3), 145–190. doi:10.1002/smr.273

Cook, S., Harrison, R., Lehman, M. M., & Wernick, P. (2005). Evolution in software systems: foundations of the SPE classification scheme. *Journal of Software Maintenance and Evolution: Research and Practice, 18*(1), 1–35. doi:10.1002/smr.314

Cook, S., Harrison, R., Lehman, M. M., & Wernick, P. (2006). Evolution in software systems: foundations of the SPE classification scheme. *Journal of Software Maintenance and Evolution: Research and Practice, 18*(1), 1–35. doi:10.1002/smr.314

d'Avila Garcez, A. S., Russo, A., Nuseibeh, B., & Kramer, J. (2003). Combining abductive reasoning and inductive learning to evolve requirements specifications. *IEEE Proceedings Software, 150*(1), 25–38. doi:10.1049/ip-sen:20030207

da Silva, B. C., Figueiredo, E., Garcia, A., & Nunes, D. (2009). Refactoring of crosscutting concerns with metaphor-based heuristics. *Electronic Notes in Theoretical Computer Science, 233,* 105–125. doi:10.1016/j.entcs.2009.02.064

de Landtsheer, R., & van Lamsweerde, A. (2005). Reasoning about confidentiality at requirements engineering time. Proceedings of the 10th European Software Engineering Conference, (pp. 41-49), Lisbon, Portugal, ACM.

Del Rosso, C. (2006). Continuous evolution through software architecture evaluation: a case study. *Journal of Software Maintenance and Evolution: Research and Practice, 18*(5), 351–383. doi:10.1002/smr.337

Fabbrini, F., Fusani, M., Gnesi, S., & Lami, G. (2007). Controlling requirements evolution: A formal concept analysis-based approach. *International Conference on Software Engineering Advances*.

Felty, A. P., & Namjoshi, K. S. (2003). Feature specification and automated conflict detection. *ACM Transactions on Software Engineering and Methodology, 12*(1), 3–27. doi:10.1145/839268.839270

Fernández-Medina, E., Jurjens, J., Trujillo, J., & Jajodia, S. (2009). Model-driven development for secure information systems. *Information and Software Technology, 51*(5), 809–814. doi:10.1016/j.infsof.2008.05.010

Fischer, M., & Gall, H. (2004). Visualizing feature evolution of large-scale software based on problem and modification report data. *Journal of Software Maintenance and Evolution: Research and Practice, 16*(6), 385–403. doi:10.1002/smr.302

Focardi, R., & Gorrieri, R. (1997). The compositional security checker: A tool for the verification of information flow security properties. *IEEE Transactions on Software Engineering, 23*(9), 550–571. doi:10.1109/32.629493

Francesco, N. D., & Lettieri, G. (2003). Checking security properties by model checking. *Software Testing, Verification and Reliability, 13*(3), 181–196. doi:10.1002/stvr.272

Gall, H., Jazayeri, M., & Riva, C. (1999). Visualizing software release histories: The use of color and third dimension. In *Proceedings of the IEEE International Conference on Software Maintenance*, IEEE Computer Society Washington, DC, USA.

Georg, G., Ray, I., Anastasakis, K., Bordbar, B., Toahchoodee, M., & Houmb, S. H. (2009). An aspect-oriented methodology for designing secure applications. *Information and Software Technology, 51*(5), 846–864. doi:10.1016/j.infsof.2008.05.004

Gerdes, J. (2009). User interface migration of Microsoft Windows applications. *Journal of Software Maintenance and Evolution: Research and Practice*.

German, D. M. (2004). Using software trails to reconstruct the evolution of software. *Journal of Software Maintenance and Evolution: Research and Practice, 16*(6), 367–384. doi:10.1002/smr.301

Ghose, A. K. (1999). A formal basis for consistency, evolution and rationale management in requirements engineering. In *Proceedings of the 11th IEEE International Conference on Tools with Artificial Intelligence*.

Ghose, A. K. (2000). Formal tools for managing inconsistency and change in RE. In *Proceedings of the 10th International Workshop on Software Specification and Design*.

Giannakopoulou, D., & Magee, J. (2003). Fluent model checking for event-based systems. In *Proceedings of the 9th European Software Engineering Conference*, (pp. 257-266) Helsinki, Finland: ACM Press.

Giorgini, P., Massacci, F., Mylopoulos, J., & Zannone, N. (2005). Modeling security requirements through ownership, permission and delegation. In *Proceedings of 13th IEEE International Conference on Requirements Engineering*, Paris, France.

Gîrba, T., & Ducasse, S. (2006). Modeling history to analyze software evolution. *Journal of Software Maintenance and Evolution: Research and Practice, 18*(3), 207–236. doi:10.1002/smr.325

Glorie, M., Zaidman, A., Deursen, A. v., & Hofland, L. (2009). Splitting a large software repository for easing future software evolution - an industrial experience report. *Journal of Software Maintenance and Evolution: Research and Practice, 21*(2), 113–141. doi:10.1002/smr.401

Greevy, O., & Ducasse, S. and Tudor Gîrba. (2006). Analyzing software evolution through feature views. *Journal of Software Maintenance and Evolution: Research and Practice, 18*(6), 425–456. doi:10.1002/smr.340

Haley, C. B., Laney, R., Moffett, J. D., & Nuseibeh, B. (2008). Security requirements engineering: A framework for representation and analysis. *IEEE Transactions on Software Engineering, 34*(1), 133–153. doi:10.1109/TSE.2007.70754

Haley, C. B., Laney, R. C., Moffett, J. D., & Nuseibeh, B. (2004). The effect of trust assumptions on the elaboration of security requirements. In *Proceedings of the 12th IEEE International Requirements Engineering Conference.*

Hall, J. G., Rapanotti, L., & Jackson, M. (2007). Problem oriented software engineering: A design-theoretic framework for software engineering. In *Proceedings of the 5th IEEE International Conference on Software Engineering and Formal Methods.*

Hall, J. G., Rapanotti, L., & Jackson, M. A. (2008). Problem oriented software engineering: Solving the package router control problem. *IEEE Transactions on Software Engineering, 34*(2), 226–241. doi:10.1109/TSE.2007.70769

Hall, R. J. (2000). Feature combination and interaction detection via foreground/background models. *Journal of Computer Networks, 32*(4), 449–469. doi:10.1016/S1389-1286(00)00010-4

Hassine, J., Rilling, J., Hewitt, J., & Dssouli, R. (2005). Change impact analysis for requirement evolution using use case maps. In *Proceedings of the 8th International Workshop on Principles of Software Evolution.*

His, I., & Potts, C. (2000). Studying the Evolution and enhancement of software features. In *Proceedings of the International Conference on Software Maintenance*, (p. 143), IEEE Computer Society.

Hsi, I., & Potts, C. (2000). Studying the evolution and enhancement of software features. In *Proceedings of the 16th IEEE International Conference on Software Maintenance* (ICSM'00), San Jose, California, USA.

Ibrahim, N., Wan Kadir, W. M. N., & Deris, S. (2008). Comparative evaluation of change propagation approaches towards resilient software evolution. In *Proceedings of the 3rd International Conference on Software Engineering Advances.*

Jackson, M. (1995). *Software requirements and specifications: A lexicon of practice, principles and prejudices.* London: Addison-Wesley.

Jackson, M. (2001). *Problem frames: Analysing and structuring software development problems.* Harlow: Addison-Wesley.

Jackson, M., & Zave, P. (1998). Distributed feature composition: A Virtual architecture for telecommunications services. *IEEE Transactions on Software Engineering, 24*(10), 831–847. doi:10.1109/32.729683

Jacobson, I. (1992). *Object oriented software engineering: A use case driven approach.* Addison-Wesley Professional.

Jurjens, J. (2002). UMLsec: Extending UML for Secure systems development. In *Proceedings of the 5th International Conference on The Unified Modeling Language*, Springer-Verlag.

Jurjens, J. (2004). *Secure systems development with UML.* Heidelberg, Germany: Springer-Verlag.

Keck, D. O., & Kuehn, P. J. (1998). The feature and service interaction problem in telecommunications systems: A survey. *IEEE Transactions on Software Engineering, 24*(10), 779–796. doi:10.1109/32.729680

Kemerer, C. F., & Slaughter, S. (1999). An empirical approach to studying software evolution. *IEEE Transactions on Software Engineering, 25*(4), 493–509. doi:10.1109/32.799945

Kosker, Y., Turhan, B., & Bener, A. (in press). Corrected Proof). An expert system for determining candidate software classes for refactoring. *Expert Systems with Applications.*

Kozlov, D., Koskinen, J., Sakkinen, M., & Markkula, J. (2008). Assessing maintainability change over multiple software releases. *Journal of Software Maintenance and Evolution: Research and Practice, 20*(1), 31–58. doi:10.1002/smr.361

Lam, W., & Loomes, M. (1998). Requirements evolution in the midst of environmental change: A managed approach. In *Proceedings of the 2nd Euromicro Conference on Software Maintenance and Reengineering.*

LaMantia, M. J., Cai, Y., MacCormack, A., & Rusnak, J. (2008). Analyzing the evolution of large-scale software systems using design structure matrices and design rule theory: Two exploratory cases. In *Proceedings of the Seventh Working IEEE/IFIP Conference on Software Architecture* (WICSA 2008), IEEE Computer Society, (pp. 83-92).

Lehman, M. M., Kahen, G., & Ramil, J. F. (2002). Behavioural modelling of long-lived evolution processes - Some issues and an example. *Journal of Software Maintenance and Evolution: Research and Practice, 14*(5), 335–351. doi:10.1002/smr.259

Lehman, M. M., & Ramil, J. F. (2001). Evolution in software and related areas. In *Proceedings of the 4th International Workshop on Principles of Software Evolution*, (pp. 1-16), Vienna, Austria. ACM.

Lehman, M. M., & Ramil, J. F. (2003). Software evolution: background, theory, practice. *Information Processing Letters, 88*(1-2), 33–44. doi:10.1016/S0020-0190(03)00382-X

Letier, E., Kramer, J., Magee, J., & Uchitel, S. (2005). Fluent temporal logic for discrete-time event-based models. S*IGSOFT Softw. Eng. Notes, 30*(5), 70–79. doi:10.1145/1095430.1081719

Lin, L., Nuseibeh, B., Ince, D., & Jackson, M. (2004). Using abuse frames to bound the scope of security problems. In *Proceedings of 12th IEEE International Requirements Engineering Conference.*

Lin, L., Nuseibeh, B., Ince, D., Jackson, M., & Moffett, J. (2003). Introducing abuse frames for analysing security requirements. In *Proceedings of 11th IEEE International Requirements Engineering Conference.*

Lin, L., Prowell, S. J., & Poore, J. H. (2009). The impact of requirements changes on specifications and state machines. *Software, Practice & Experience, 39*(6), 573–610. doi:10.1002/spe.907

Liu, L., Yu, E., & Mylopoulos, J. (2003). Security and privacy requirements analysis within a social setting. In *Proceedings of the 11th IEEE International Requirements Engineering Conference.*

Lodderstedt, T., Basin, D., & Doser, J. (2002). SecureUML: A UML-Based modeling language for model-driven security. *Lecture Notes in Computer Science*, (2460): 426–441. doi:10.1007/3-540-45800-X_33

Lutz, R. R., & Mikulski, I. C. (2003). Operational anomalies as a cause of safety-critical requirements evolution. *Journal of Systems and Software, 65*(2), 155–161.

Mantel, H. (2001). Preserving information flow properties under refinement. *IEEE Symposium on Security and Privacy.*

Mantel, H. (2002). On the composition of secure systems. *IEEE Symposium on Security and Privacy.*

Mead, N. R., & Stehney, T. (2005). Security quality requirements engineering (SQUARE) methodology. *SIGSOFT Software Engineering Notes, 30*(4), 1–7. doi:10.1145/1082983.1083214

Mens, K., Mens, T., & Wermelinger, M. (2002). Supporting software evolution with intentional software views. In *Proceedings of the International Workshop on Principles of Software Evolution,* (pp. 138-142), Orlando, Florida, ACM.

Mens, T., Ramil, J. F., & Godfrey, M. W. (2004). Analyzing the evolution of large-scale software. *Journal of Software Maintenance and Evolution: Research and Practice, 16*(6), 363–365. doi:10.1002/smr.300

Mens, T., Wermelinger, M., Ducasse, S., Demeyer, S., Hirschfeld, R., & Jazayeri, M. (2005). Challenges in software evolution. In *Proceedings of the 8th International Workshop on Principles of Software Evolution.*

Mouratidis, H., & Giorgini, P. (2006). *Integrating security and software engineering: Advances and future visions.* London: Idea Group Publishing.

Mouratidis, H., Giorgini, P., & Manson, G. (2003). Modelling secure multiagent systems. In *Proceedings of the 2nd international joint conference on Autonomous agents and multiagent systems,* (pp. 859-866), Melbourne, Australia, ACM.

Mouratidis, H., Giorgini, P., & Manson, G. (2005). When security meets software engineering: A case of modelling secure information systems. *Information Systems, 30*(8), 609–629. doi:10.1016/j.is.2004.06.002

Mouratidis, H., J. Jurjens and J. Fox (2006). Towards a comprehensive framework for secure systems development. *Advanced Information Systems Engineering*, 48-62.

Nhlabatsi, A., R. Laney and B. Nuseibeh (2008). Feature interaction: The security threat from within software systems. *Progress in Informatics* (5), 75-89.

Nuseibeh, B., Easterbrook, S., & Russo, A. (2000). Leveraging Inconsistency in software development. *Computer, 33*(4), 24–29. doi:10.1109/2.839317

O'Reilly, C., Morrow, P., & Bustard, D. (2003). Lightweight prevention of architectural erosion. In *Proceedings of 6th International Workshop on Principles of Software Evolution.*

Parsons, D., Rashid, A., Telea, A., & Speck, A. (2006). An architectural pattern for designing component-based application frameworks. *Software, Practice & Experience, 36*(2), 157–190. doi:10.1002/spe.694

Pena, J., Hinchey, M. G., Resinas, M., Sterritt, R., & Rash, J. L. (2007). Designing and managing evolving systems using a MAS product line approach. *Science of Computer Programming, 66*(1), 71–86. doi:10.1016/j.scico.2006.10.007

Ramil, J. F. (2002). *Laws of software evolution and their empirical support.* International Conference on Software Maintenance.

Ramil, J. F., & Smith, N. (2002). Qualitative simulation of models of software evolution. *Software Process Improvement and Practice, 7*(3-4), 95–112. doi:10.1002/spip.158

Ravichandar, R., Arthur, J. D., Bohner, S. A., & Tegarden, D. P. (2008). Improving change tolerance through Capabilities-based design: an empirical analysis. *Journal of Software Maintenance and Evolution: Research and Practice, 20*(2), 135–170. doi:10.1002/smr.367

Ren, X., Chesley, O. C., & Ryder, B. G. (2006). Identifying failure causes in Java programs: An application of change impact analysis. *IEEE Transactions on Software Engineering, 32*(9), 718–732. doi:10.1109/TSE.2006.90

Roshandel, R., Hoek, A. V. D., Mikic-Rakic, M., & Medvidovic, N. (2004). Mae - A system model and environment for managing architectural evolution. *ACM Transactions on Software Engineering and Methodology, 13*(2), 240–276. doi:10.1145/1018210.1018213

Russo, A., Nuseibeh, B., & Kramer, J. (1998). Restructuring requirements specifications for managing inconsistency and change: A case study. In *Proc. of 3ʳᵈ International Conference on Requirements Engineering* (ICRE `98), Colorado Springs, USA.

Russo, A., Nuseibeh, B., & Kramer, J. (1999). Restructuring requirements specifications. *IEEE Proceedings Software, 146*(1), 44–53. doi:10.1049/ip-sen:19990156

Rysselberghe, F. V., & Demeyer, S. (2004). Studying Software evolution information by visualizing the change history. In *Proceedings of the 20ᵗʰ IEEE International Conference on Software Maintenance* (ICSM'04).

Salifu, M., Yu, Y., & Nuseibeh, B. (2007). Specifying monitoring and switching problems in context. In *Proceedings of the 15ᵗʰ IEEE International Conference in Requirements Engineering* (RE '07), New Delhi, India.

Seybold, C., Meier, S., & Glinz, M. (2004). Evolution of requirements models by simulation. In *Proceedings of 7ᵗʰ International Workshop on Principles of Software Evolution.*

Shin, M. E., & Gomaa, H. (2007). Software requirements and architecture modeling for evolving non-secure applications into secure applications. *Science of Computer Programming, 66*(1), 60–70. doi:10.1016/j.scico.2006.10.009

Smith, G., & McComb, T. (2008). Refactoring real-time specifications. *Electronic Notes in Theoretical Computer Science, 214*, 359–380. doi:10.1016/j.entcs.2008.06.016

Soffer, P. (2005). Scope analysis: identifying the impact of changes in business process models. *Software Process Improvement and Practice, 10*(4), 393–402. doi:10.1002/spip.242

Tondel, I. A., Jaatun, M. G., & Meland, P. H. (2008). Security requirements for the rest of us: A survey. *IEEE Software, 25*(1), 20–27. doi:10.1109/MS.2008.19

Turner, C. R., Fuggetta, A., Lavazza, L., & Wolf, A. L. (1999). A conceptual basis for feature engineering. *Journal of Systems and Software, 49*(1), 3–15. doi:10.1016/S0164-1212(99)00062-X

Turner, K. J. (1997). An architectural foundation for relating features. In *Proc. Feature Interactions in Telecommunication Networks IV*. Amsterdam: IOS Press.

van Lamsweerde, A. (2004). Elaborating security requirements by construction of intentional anti-models. In *Proceedings of the 26ᵗʰ International Conference on Software Engineering.*

van Lamsweerde, A., Darimont, R., & Letier, E. (1998). Managing conflicts in goal-driven requirements engineering. *IEEE Transactions on Software Engineering, 24*(11), 908–926. doi:10.1109/32.730542

Velthuijsen, H. (1995). Issues of non-monotonicity in feature interaction detection. In Cheng, K. E., & Ohta, T. (Eds.), *Feature Interactions in Telecommunication Systems III* (pp. 31–42). Amsterdam: IOS Press.

Villarroel, R., Fernández-Medina, E., & Piattini, M. (2005). Secure information systems development - A survey and comparison. *Computers & Security*, *24*(4), 308–321. doi:10.1016/j.cose.2004.09.011

Wang, Q., Shen, J., Wang, X., & Mei, H. (2006). A component-based approach to online software evolution. *Journal of Software Maintenance and Evolution: Research and Practice*, *18*(3), 181–205. doi:10.1002/smr.324

Wu, J., Holt, R. C., & Hassan, A. E. (2004). Exploring software evolution using spectrographs. In *Proceedings of the 11th Working Conference on Reverse Engineering* (WCRE'04), 80-89.

Zave, P. (2001). Requirements for evolving systems: A telecommunications perspective. In *Proceedings of 5th IEEE International Symposium on Requirements Engineering* (RE'01), Toronto, Canada, IEEE Computer Society.

Zave, P. (2003). An experiment in feature engineering. *Programming methodology: Monographs In Computer Science*, (pp. 353 - 377).

Zave, P., & Jackson, M. (1997). Four dark corners of requirements engineering. *ACM Transactions on Software Engineering and Methodology*, *6*(1), 1–30. doi:10.1145/237432.237434

Zenger, M. (2005). KERIS: evolving software with extensible modules. *Journal of Software Maintenance and Evolution: Research and Practice*, *17*(5), 333–362. doi:10.1002/smr.320

Zowghi, D., & Offen, R. *(1997). A logical framework for modeling and reasoning about the evolution of requirements. In* Proceedings of the 3rd IEEE International Symposium on Requirements Engineering.

*This work was previously published in International Journal of Secure Software Engineering, edited by Khaled M. Khan, pp. 54-73, Volume 1, Issue 1, copyright 2010 by IGI Publishing (an imprint of IGI Global).*

# Section 3
# Vulnerability Detection

# Chapter 8
# Monitoring Buffer Overflow Attacks:
## A Perennial Task

**Hossain Shahriar**
*Queen's University, Canada*

**Mohammad Zulkernine**
*Queen's University, Canada*

## ABSTRACT

*Buffer overflow (BOF) is a well-known, and one of the worst and oldest, vulnerabilities in programs. BOF attacks overwrite data buffers and introduce wide ranges of attacks like execution of arbitrary injected code. Many approaches are applied to mitigate buffer overflow vulnerabilities; however, mitigating BOF vulnerabilities is a perennial task as these vulnerabilities elude the mitigation efforts and appear in the operational programs at run-time. Monitoring is a popular approach for detecting BOF attacks during program execution, and it can prevent or send warnings to take actions for avoiding the consequences of the exploitations. Currently, there is no detailed classification of the proposed monitoring approaches to understand their common characteristics, objectives, and limitations. In this paper, the authors classify runtime BOF attack monitoring and prevention approaches based on seven major characteristics. Finally, these approaches are compared for attack detection coverage based on a set of BOF attack types. The classification will enable researchers and practitioners to select an appropriate BOF monitoring approach or provide guidelines to build a new one.*

## INTRODUCTION

A vulnerable program can be exploited at runtime by providing specially crafted inputs. Buffer overflow (BOF) is a well known and one of the worst and oldest vulnerabilities in programs (Aleph One, 1996). It allows attackers to overflow data buffers that might be exploited to execute arbitrary code. Several mitigation techniques are widely used to mitigate BOF vulnerabilities. These include static analysis (e.g., Hackett et al., 2006), testing (e.g., Xu et al., 2008), and fixing of vulnerable code (e.g., Dahn et al., 2003). However, BOF vulnerabilities are widely discovered in programs (e.g.,

DOI: 10.4018/978-1-4666-1580-9.ch008

CVE, 2010). Moreover, some BOF vulnerability exploitations (or attacks) might not appear until a program is operational. Thus, BOF attack detection is a perennial task.

Monitoring is a widely used technique that can detect BOF attacks at an early stage and mitigate some of the consequences at runtime. In a monitoring approach, vulnerability exploitation symptoms are checked by comparing the current state of a program with a known state under attack. When there is a match (or mismatch) between the two states, a successful exploitation of a particular vulnerability occurs. A program might be stopped for further execution. A monitor remains silent as long as a program is not under an attack at the cost of additional memories and execution time (e.g., Jones et al., 1997). Nevertheless, a program monitor is accurate in detecting attacks compared to other complementary mitigation techniques such as static analysis. This unique feature makes it a useful prevention mechanism in a deployed program.

Although many monitoring approaches have been introduced in the literature to detect the exploitations of BOF vulnerabilities (or attacks) (e.g., Berger et al., 2006; Chiueh et al., 2001), there is no classification to understand the common characteristics, objectives, and limitations of these approaches. Moreover, the lack of a comprehensive comparative study provides little or no direction on choosing the appropriate monitoring techniques for particular needs.

In this paper, we perform an extensive survey on the state of the art runtime monitoring approaches that detect BOF attacks[1]. We classify the monitoring approaches based on seven most common characteristics: *monitoring objective, program state utilization, implementation mechanism, environmental change, attack response, monitor security,* and *overhead.* Moreover, for each of the characteristics, we further classify the current work to identify fine grained features that might be present in BOF monitoring techniques. We then perform a comparative analysis of existing

approaches for BOF attack detection coverage. We identify BOF attack types based on both vulnerable program code (operation, data type, overflow among object members, and pointer arithmetic) and runtime state (BOF location, BOF magnitude). The survey will help secure software developers, researchers, and practitioners to select a tool from the existing monitoring approaches by highlighting the BOF attack type detection capabilities. Moreover, it will provide a guideline to build a new monitoring technique based on their particular application needs.

This paper is organized as follows: the next section provides an overview of program monitor and BOF attack. Then we discuss the classification of the monitoring works followed by comparison of the works based on BOF attack types. We then review other similar efforts on comparing BOF attack monitoring approaches. Finally, we draw conclusions.

## OVERVIEW

### Program Monitor

In general, a program takes inputs, processes them with or without the help of runtime environment (e.g., API calls), and generates outputs as shown in Figure 1(a). A program monitor is deployed in a post-release stage. It provides an additional layer between a program and its execution environment (Figure 1(b)). A monitor passively checks runtime program states for the occurrence of attacks. The underlying assumption is that attack symptoms can be captured by program states. Program states are entities involved in program execution such as program memories containing modified (or unmodified) inputs and outputs, registers, opcode, and attribute of inputs (e.g., sizes). While executing, program states are captured at specific execution points (e.g., beginning of a function call, return from a function) and matched with known states under attacks. Any match (or mismatch) might

*Figure 1. (a) A program without a monitor, (b) program execution after monitoring*

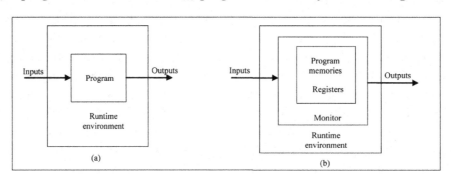

*Figure 2. C code snippet vulnerable to BOF*

```
1.  void foo (char *src) {
2.    int i;
3.    char buf [16];
4.    for (i=0; i<strlen(src); i++)
5.      buf[i] = src[i];
      ...
    }
```

indicate the occurrence of a successful attack. A monitor might have access to various elements of programs (e.g., source code) and environments (e.g., stack, code, data, inputs, APIs, processors).

## Buffer Overflow

A buffer overflow (BOF) vulnerability allows overflowing a data buffer in a program. The overwriting might corrupt sensitive neighboring variables of the buffer such as the return address of a function or the stack frame pointer. A BOF can occur due to vulnerable ANSI C library function calls, lack of null characters at the end of buffers, accessing buffer through pointers and aliases, logic errors (off by one), and insufficient checks before accessing buffers (Kratkiewicz et al., 2005).

We provide an example of BOF in a C code snippet as shown in Figure 2. The buffer declared at Line 3 (*buf*) is located in the stack region and has 16 bytes of memories for reading and writing

operations. The valid location of this buffer is between *buf[0]* and *buf[15]*. Line 4-5 copy the *src* into *buf* using a for loop. However, the code is vulnerable as there is no checking on destination buffer length. Thus, the loop allows copying more than the capacity of *buf*. A snapshot of the stack of *foo* function is shown in Figure 3 (Aleph One, 1996). The stack stores the argument of *foo* (*src*), the return address (*ret*), the saved frame pointer (*sfp*), and declared variables (*i* and *buf*), followed by the loop counter (*i*). Note that the direction of stack growth and buffer copy is opposite to each other. We assume that both *ret* and *sfp* occupy four bytes, whereas *i* occupies two bytes.

A BOF might occur during reading or writing operations. Writing past the *buf* by at least one byte corrupts the value of *i* (assuming no padding performed by a compiler) and results in unexpected behaviors. An attacker might clobber the return address (ret) with the location of the buffer and supply shell code as a payload of the buffer. When the function returns, the next instruction address is fetched from the buffer. Thus, an attacker can execute arbitrary code supplied in the buffer and exploit the vulnerability. This is known as "return address clobbering" or "direct code injection" attack (Erlingsson, 2007).

Many BOF attacks execute injected code based on "indirect code injection" which might circumvent partial mitigations implemented in program code. For example, a program might not allow an overflow long enough to modify the return address. An attacker can execute arbitrary code by overwriting the *sfp* to point to the location of the buffer (Younan et al., 2004). The *sfp* stores the address of stack top of the caller function of *foo*. As a result, the first four bytes of the buffer is considered as a newly saved frame pointer and the next four bytes is considered as the return address for the caller of *foo*. The content of the new return address now points to the location of the buffer containing injected code. The *foo* function returns to its caller as usual. However, when the caller returns, the injected code is executed.

BOF exploits can execute injected code by overwriting neighboring pointers (Younan, 2004). A dynamically allocated buffer might have a neighboring data pointer (e.g., a character pointer for storing a file name) which stores the address of a data variable. An attack can modify the pointer with an arbitrary address which might point an attacker injected input (e.g., argv[1]). The modified pointer is subsequently used by a program (e.g., opening a system file supplied through argv[1] instead of a non-malicious file pointed by the data pointer) and results in the modification of

sensitive information (Chien et al., 2002). A BOF might overwrite a function pointer. This results in unexpected behaviors when a function is invoked. Sophisticated heap-based attacks execute injected code which might reside in overflowed heap buffers. These attacks leverage the working mechanism of memory allocators and free functions (e.g., dlmalloc of Leah, 2000).

## COMPARISON OF BOF MONITORING APPROACHES

In this section, we compare monitoring approaches that detect BOF attacks based on seven major characteristics: *monitoring objective, program state utilization, implementation mechanism, environmental change, attack response, monitor security,* and *overhead.* We describe these characteristics in the next seven subsections. We provide a brief summary of these works in Table 1. A summary of the comparison is provided in Table 2.

### Monitoring Objective

This characteristic indicates what program properties are monitored to detect attacks during runtime. We divide monitoring objectives into seven categories as shown in the second column of Table 2. They are memory operation (e.g., Berger et al., 2006), code execution flow (e.g., Dalton et al., 2007), code origin (e.g., Tan et al., 2005), code structure (e.g., Gaurav et al., 2003), value integrity (e.g., Chiueh et al., 2001; Cowan et al., 1998), input validation (e.g., Lhee et al., 2002),

*Figure 3. Stack layout of foo function*

| buf [0] … | … buf [15] | i | sfp | ret | src |
|---|---|---|---|---|---|
| <------ [ | ][ | ][ | ][ | ][ | ] |
| top of stack | | | | | bottom of stack |

and fingerprinting (e.g., Han et al., 2007). Some approaches apply multiple monitoring objectives (e.g., memory operation, code execution flow, and code origin) (e.g., Clause et al., 2007).

1. **Memory operation:** In this case, an approach monitors whether memory read and write operations are performed on valid address space of a program or not. For example, memory bytes can be checked for allowable tagging information before performing read and write operations (Hastings et al., 1992). A variation of the objective is to allow accidental or intentional memory operations outside valid address spaces for the sake of program execution continuation during attacks (e.g., Rinard et al., 2004). In other words, programs become attack tolerant. Berger et al. (2006) develop a runtime memory manager which randomizes the location of objects into heap region and increases the size of allocated objects at least twice. Thus, successive objects are located at a wider gap, and the chance of BOF attacks is reduced.

2. **Code execution flow:** It monitors allowable and unallowable control flows. The objective is useful for detecting BOF attacks that change program control flows. Dynamic information flow tracking is a popular approach to check unintended execution flow (e.g., Suh et al., 2006). Input data sources (e.g., data from file or network) are marked as tainted and their propagations are tracked. If any value generated from a tainted value is used in either code execution flow (e.g., jump location) or as code (e.g., instructions and pointers), programs are halted.

3. **Code origin:** It is checked whether program code is loaded from known valid locations or not (e.g., Tan et al., 2005). Code origin violation might represent BOF attacks. For example, an attack might result in loading opcode from stack segments.

4. **Code structure:** This objective monitors if an executable code conforms to a desired syntactic structure that is valid and recognized by processors. The objective allows detecting injected code that might be provided through inputs. The programmer implemented source code is randomized initially. After including user inputs, the code is de-randomized before being executed by processors. As a result, an attacker supplied code becomes meaningless to a processor and only the implemented code is executed. For example, Gaurav et al. (2003) randomize machine code instructions by first identifying the relationship between actual instruction code (or opcode) and instruction set supported by a processor. Each opcode is XORed with a unique key. Before loading the code by a processor (i.e., CPU), the code is decoded with the same key. Therefore, any decoded injected code results in invalid opcode and a CPU throws runtime exceptions.

5. **Value integrity:** This objective monitors sensitive program or environment values which might be modified during attacks. Values include return addresses of functions (identified during function prologue) and sensitive variables (e.g., function pointers located adjacent to buffers) (e.g., Cowan et al., 1998). To prevent guessing of sensitive values by attackers, several approaches store encrypted values (e.g., Pyo et al., 2004).

6. **Input validation:** In this objective, user supplied data is examined and checked for the presence of any attribute that is unwanted. For example, the size of an input might be checked before performing read and write operations through library function calls (Lhee et al., 2002).

7. **Fingerprinting:** It requires executing programs with a set of normal (non attack) inputs (i.e., profiling) and identify constant properties which are not altered at runtime. A monitor identifies any deviation from the

learned profiles during an actual program run. Han et al. (2007) identify API invocation fingerprints. They obtain a set of legitimate API invocation sequences and compare API invocation sequences generated at runtime to identify BOF attacks.

## Program State Utilization

To detect an attack at runtime, a program state needs to be compared with a known program state under attack. These known states are derived from programs through information extraction, addition, or modification. We denote such derivation as *program state utilization*. We divide program state utilization into three categories: *extraction*, *addition*, and *modification* of information. The third column of Table 2 shows *program state utilization* for each of the work along with particular information.

1. **Information extraction:** Program code can be analyzed to extract useful information to detect attacks during runtime. For example, Han et al. (2007) obtain a set of legitimate API invocation sequences and stack size and return address for each API.

2. **Information addition:** Information can be added in current program state, which is retrieved later and compared with a future program state to detect attack. For example, function's return addresses and pointers adjacent to buffers can be added to safe locations (e.g., Chiueh et al., 2001). Several approaches add information in executable code or environment. These include variables (e.g., a canary or guard value before return address of a function) (Cowan et al., 1998), data structures containing allocated buffer size information (e.g., Fetzer et al., 2001), non-executable memory locations such as pages (PaX, 2003) and stack segments (Tan et al., 2005), and taint information of sensitive

variables (e.g., Clause et al., 2007; Dalton et al., 2007). Policies can be added to monitor allowable control transfers in executables as ways of detecting unwanted execution program flows during BOF attacks. In this case, a policy maps program instructions with allowable sources and destinations (Kiriansky et al., 2002).

3. **Information modification:** Some approaches modify current program states (e.g., code, stack) for detecting attacks. Memory objects can be allocated at random locations and two successive objects can be located far apart from each other to reduce BOF attacks (Berger et al., 2006). Program variables can be reorganized. For example, sensitive variables located after a buffer can be placed before the buffer to avoid their corruption during BOF attacks (Etoh, 2005). Moreover, program environments can be reorganized to alter program behaviors during BOF attacks. For example, the growth direction of two stack segments might be set opposite for two versions of a program (Salamat et al., 2008). This helps to detect BOF attacks based on different behaviors (outputs) of two programs.

## Implementation Mechanism

We identify seven mechanisms that implement monitoring objective as shown in the fourth column of Table 2. These include *spatial rearrangement* of memories, *compiler modification*, *code instrumentation*, *API hooking*, *modified processor*, *binary rewriting*, and *dynamic code optimizer extension*. We briefly describe them in the following.

1. **Spatial rearrangement:** In this technique, memory blocks (or objects) are allocated at random locations, and the objects are located apart to reduce BOF (Berger et al.,

*Table 1. A brief summary of BOF attack monitoring works*

| Work | Brief description |
| --- | --- |
| Jones et al., 1997 | Develop an object table to track allocated memories and sizes to detect arbitrary dereferences through pointer arithmetic. |
| Berger et al., 2006 | Randomize the location of memory objects, allocate at least twice the amount of memories than requested, and place two successive objects far apart to reduce the chance of BOF attacks. |
| Chiueh et al., 2001 | Create safe areas to store the return address of function to avoid their corruptions due to BOF attacks. |
| Etoh, 2005 | Place buffer variables after pointer variables to avoid the corruption of sensitive pointer values. |
| Fetzer et al., 2001 | Intercept C library function calls and perform boundary checking during memory write operations. |
| Cowan et al., 1998 | Save the sensitive return addresses before function calls and retrieve these addresses after function executions. |
| Ruwase et al., 2004 | Improve the approach of Jones (1997) by allowing out of bound pointers in pointer arithmetic operations. |
| Gupta et al., 2006 | Modify function prologue and epilogue to avoid arbitrary code executions by corrupting return addresses. |
| Gaurav et al., 2003 | Randomize machine code and modify interpreters to de-randomize instructions before executing programs to prevent injection attacks. |
| Han et al., 2007 | Profile legitimate pattern of API calls and compare runtime calls with these patterns to identify BOF attacks. |
| StackShield, 2001 | Protect programs from BOF attacks that might corrupt function return addresses and function pointers. |
| Lhee et al., 2002 | Add data structures in programs to include buffer types, names, and sizes, and build a table to track buffers names and sizes allocated in heap to detect BOF attacks. |
| Aggarwal et al., 2006 | Detect BOF attacks by saving a copy of the return address through an embedded monitor agent and compare a function's return address with the saved return address in an epilogue. |
| Hastings et al., 1992 | Develop a bit table to track allocated and free memories, and mark bytes for allowable read and write operations to detect and prevent arbitrary memory accesses. |
| Prasad et al., 2003 | Save a backup copy of return address in a function's prologue and check the integrity of the current return address in an epilogue. |
| Madan et al., 2005 | Save an encrypted return address, followed by a comparison of the current return address (encrypted) with the saved address to detect BOF attacks. |
| Kiriansky et al., 2002 | Apply program sheperding where allowable control flow transfers are monitored through a policy with legitimate instructions, sources, and destinations. |
| Newsome et al., 2005 | Apply dynamic tainted information flow tracking with binary rewriting of program code to detect BOF attacks. |
| Pyo et al., 2004 | Save the encrypted return address in a prologue and compare the current return address with the saved address in an epilogue. |
| Rinard et al., 2004 | Generate additional code to check out of buffer memory accesses and save excess inputs in hash tables. |
| Salamat et al., 2008 | Run two versions of the same code with opposite stack growth directions and compare end results to detect BOF attacks. |
| Dalton et al., 2007 | Apply dynamic information flow tracking to monitor, if untrusted inputs are used in sensitive operations such as pointer dereferences. |
| Suh et al., 2006 | Apply dynamic information flow tracking to generate exceptions, if spurious values are used as code execution and pointers. |
| Zhou et al., 2004 | Identify the relationship between instructions and accessed memory objects, and check whether any instruction accessing memory objects is violating the relationship or not. |
| Zhu et al., 2004 | Encrypt function pointers and decrypt them before reading from memories to avoid BOF exploits such as arbitrary function calls. |
| Clause et al., 2007 | Apply dynamic taint analysis with the provision to mention tainted sources, sinks, and propagation policies to detect BOF attacks. |
| PaX, 2003 | Transform stack and data pages to non-executable, and terminate a program, if it executes instructions from non executable pages. |
| Tan et al., 2005 | Make the stack segment non-executable by modifying code segment limit. |

2006). The mechanism requires developing customized memory managers. An approach might randomize the entire process memory for each instance of a program to make it difficult to guess sensitive memory location such as stack addresses and registers (PaX, 2003). Moreover, specific memory blocks (*e.g.*, stack, data) might be marked as non-executable to prevent execution of injected attack code.

2. **Compiler modification:** The technique patches compilers so that necessary monitoring code is automatically injected into programs automatically. For example, moni-

toring of BOF attacks requires saving return addresses to safe locations before function calls and comparing current return addresses with saved addresses after function calls. This can be done by adding necessary code in a function prologue and epilogue (Chiueh et al., 2001). A compiler can be modified to store rich data structure for tracking all pointers and save out of bound data in hash tables (Rinard et al., 2004). Moreover, prologue and epilogue can be modified to emulate a stack having an opposite growth direction (Salamat et al., 2008).

3.  **Code instrumentation:** In this technique, program code can be added with monitoring or prevention code (e.g., Gupta et al., 2006; Hastings et al., 1992). Additional code can be injected in the binary (Aggarwal et al., 2006) or in the object code generated by a compiler (Hastings et al., 1992). Binary code can be instrumented to add checks (e.g., taint a basic block before passing to a processor) (Clause et al., 2007; Newsome et al., 2005). Moreover, a kernel can be modified to save registers during context switches that contain tainted information of program data and control (Dalton et al., 2007). Note that "compiler modification" is different from "code instrumentation". In a compiler modification, monitoring code is embedded in the object code through a compiler. However, in a code instrumentation technique, additional code is injected in object, executable, or kernel source code.

4.  **API hooking:** In this technique, interesting library function calls are intercepted to detect or prevent attacks. For example, vulnerable function calls can be replaced with non vulnerable function calls which perform bound checking (Fetzer et al., 2001). Sometimes, buffer sizes and function calls are stored to detect attacks at later stages (Han et al., 2007). Operating system specific APIs are intercepted to modify behaviors such as ob-

taining initial stack region of a user program and relocating to non-executable memory regions (Tan et al., 2005).

5.  **Modified processor:** Processors execute opcode (or instruction sets) provided the instruction sets are supported by CPUs. This technique is applied for code randomization with a secret key, where randomized code must be de-randomized before passing to processors (Gaurav et al., 2003). The modification includes adding decryption mechanism before loading to processors.

6.  **Binary rewriting:** The technique adds or modifies different section of executable programs such as adding entries to symbol tables and hash tables in new sections to store data. Sometimes, monitoring code is implemented in a new section (Prasad et al., 2003).

7.  **Dynamic code optimizer extension:** Dynamic code optimization framework allows analyzing program code execution at different granular levels (e.g., statement, block). This technique leverages such framework to monitor programs to add checks such as allowing or disallowing control flow between two blocks (Kiriansky et al., 2002).

## Environmental Change

This characteristic indicates how an approach introduces program execution environment changes. A program execution environment change might include the modification of dynamically linked libraries, compilers, memories, operating system kernels, etc. Program object code can be modified to perform environment changes. The fifth column of Table 2 shows that the environment can be changed due to *implementation mechanism*, *program state utilization*, and *performance*. We describe them in the following.

1.  **Implementation mechanism:** Most of the approaches modify environments due to

*Table 2. Classification of BOF attack monitoring works*

| Work | Monitoring objective | Program state utilization | Implementation mechanism | Environmental change | Attack response | Monitor security | Overhead |
|------|---------------------|---------------------------|--------------------------|---------------------|-----------------|------------------|----------|
| Jones et al., 1997 | Memory operation (memory read and write) | Information addition (store base and size of memory objects) | Compiler modification (compare a pointer generated address with its intended base and size) | Implementation mechanism (DLL modification) | Runtime exception | N/A | Instrumentation (all pointers), integration |
| Berger et al., 2006 | Memory operation (memory read and write) | Information modification (memory object location) | Spatial rearrangement of memories (allocate objects at random locations) | Implementation mechanism (DLL modification) | Program termination | Resiliency | Increased memory (heap) |
| Chiueh et al., 2001 | Value integrity (return address) | Information addition (return address) | Compiler modification (save return addresses in prologues and compare them in epilogues) | Implementation mechanism (kernel system call patches) | Program termination | Safe repository (read only memory) | Store and lookup (return addresses) |
| Etoh, 2005 | Value integrity (canary) | Information modification (pointer variables before buffer variables) | Spatial rearrangement, compiler modification (add canary values in prologues and compare them in epilogues) | Program state utilization (frame pointer and return address location changes) | Program termination | Randomization (canary value) | Store and lookup (canary values) |
| Fetzer et al., 2001 | Memory operation (memory allocation) | Information addition (memory block sizes) | API hook (track the start and end location of each heap buffer) | Implementation mechanism (DLL modifications) | Error message and program termination | Randomization (Magic number) | Memory consumption |
| Cowan et al., 1998 | Value integrity (return address) | Information addition (canary values) | Compiler modification (add canary values in prologues and compare them in epilogues) | Program state utilization (prologue and epilogue) | Attack handler function execution | Randomization (canary value) | Store and lookup (canary values) |
| Ruwase et al., 2004 | Memory operation (memory read and write) | Information addition (store base and size of objects) | Compiler modification (compare a pointer generated address with its intended base and size) | Implementation mechanism (add object and hash table) | Runtime exception | N/A | Instrumentation (all pointers), memory consumption |
| Gupta et al., 2006 | Value integrity (return address) | Information addition (return address and stack frame) | Code instrumentation (save return addresses in prologues and compare them in epilogues followed by stack recovery) | Program state utilization (parallel stack frame) | Program state recovery | Inaccessible repository (separate stack) | Store and lookup (return address) |
| Gaurav et al., 2003 | Code structure (x86 opcode) | Information modification (encrypted opcode) | Modified processor (encode each opcode with a key and decode before loading to a processor) | Implementation mechanism (jump to even addresses) | Runtime exception | Randomization (encryption key) | Integration |
| Han et al., 2007 | Fingerprinting (legitimate API function call sequences) | Information addition and extraction (function name, stack size, etc.) | API hook (extract valid API call sequences and compare them at runtime) | Implementation mechanism (add DLL functions in programs) | Program termination | Safe process (BOF detection code) | Integration (profile database) |
| Stack-Shield, 2001 | Value integrity (return addresses) | Information addition (return addresses in global variables) | Compiler modification (save return addresses in prologues and compare them in epilogues) | Program state utilization (modify DATA section) | Program termination | Inaccessible repository (global variable) | Store and lookup (function address in text region) |
| Lhee et al., 2002 | Input validation (large sized inputs) | Information addition (table to store buffer variable names and sizes) | Compiler modification (Emit enhanced data structures for buffers in preprocessed code) | Program state utilization (a type table is added in object code) | Program termination | Inaccessible repository (static variable) | Store and lookup (type table) |
| Aggarwal et al., 2006 | Value integrity (return address, setjmp, longjmp) | Information addition (return address in a monitoring agent) | Code instrumentation (save return addresses and compare them later after function return from a parent process) | Implementation mechanism (a program runs under an agent) | Attack handler function execution | Safe process (message passing) | Integration (monitoring code execution) |

*continued on following page*

*Table 2. Continued*

| Work | Monitoring objective | Program state utilization | Implementation mechanism | Environmental change | Attack response | Monitor security | Overhead |
|---|---|---|---|---|---|---|---|
| Hastings et al., 1992 | Memory operation (memory read and write) | Information addition (a bit table to track readable and writable status of memories) | Code instrumentation (insert monitoring code to manage bit tables) | Program state utilization (a bit table is added in object code) | Attack handler function execution | N/A | Instrumentation (all memory accesses), memory consumption |
| Prasad et al., 2003 | Value integrity (return address) | Information addition (return addresses in prologues) | Binary rewriting (save return addresses in prologues and compare them in epilogues) | Program state utilization (return address repository) | Program termination | Safe repository (read only memory) | Instrumentation (RAD [5] in each function) |
| Madan et al., 2005 | Value integrity (return address) | Information addition (encrypted return address) | Compiler modification (save encrypted return addresses in prologues and compare them in epilogues in decrypted form) | Program state utilization (prologue and epilogue) | Program termination | Inaccessible repository, randomization (encryption key) | Store and lookup (return addresses) |
| Kiriansky et al., 2002 | Code execution flow, code origin | Information addition (policies to specify valid code origins and legitimate control flows) | Dynamic code optimizer extension (add checks for valid origin when a dynamic compiler copies a basic block into cache, and save blocks due to indirect branching within traces) | Performance (fast lookup of indirect branches by saving code blocks in cache memory) | Attack handler function execution | Restricted privilege | Integration (policy formulation) |
| Newsome et al., 2005 | Memory operation (memory write) | Information addition (taint information of data sources) | Code instrumentation (add taint analysis code in basic blocks before sending to processors) | Performance (save instrumented code blocks in cache memories) | Attack handler function execution | N/A | Instrumentation, memory consumption |
| Pyo et al., 2004 | Value integrity (return address) | Information storage (encrypted return address) | Compiler modification (save encrypted return addresses in prologues and compare them in epilogues in decrypted form) | Program state utilization (prologue and epilogue) | Attack handler function execution | Randomization | Store and lookup (return addresses) |
| Rinard et al., 2004 | Memory operation (memory write) | Information addition (a hash table to store out of bound data) | Compiler modification (insert code to check out of bound array writing) | Performance (Cache memory to store hash table) | Program execution continuation | Resiliency | Memory consumption |
| Salamat et al., 2008 | Value integrity (similar output in two programs) | Information modification (a duplicate stack) | Code instrumentation (develop a parent process which monitors execution of child programs) | Implementation mechanism (system call synchronizations) | Program termination | Resiliency | Memory consumption, checkpointing |
| Dalton et al., 2007 | Memory operation, code execution flow, code origin | Information addition (tainted values to program memories and input data sources) | Code instrumentation (modify Linux kernel to save registers containing tainted information during context switches) | Program state utilization (save registers, caches, and memories in context switch) | Attack handler function execution | Restricted privilege | Memory consumption |
| Suh et al., 2006 | Code execution flow | Information addition (tag for untrusted input values) | Code instrumentation (add software module to stop usage tainted data by a processor) | Program state utilization (propagation control registers) | Program termination | Inaccessible repository | Memory consumption |
| Zhou et al., 2004 | Fingerprinting (Instruction sets accessing memories) | Information extraction (Instruction sets accessing memories) | Compiler modification (monitors memory objects and return addresses based on inserted requests) | Performance (Check Look aside Buffer to store most recently accessed objects) | Warning message | N/A | Instrumentation (all memory objects) |
| Zhu et al., 2004 | Value integrity (function pointer) | Information storage (encrypted function pointers in memories) | Compiler modification (save encrypted function pointers and compare them during invocations) | Implementation mechanism (compiler generated code modification) | Warning message | Randomization (encryption key) | Store and lookup (function pointer) |

*continued on following page*

*Table 2. Continued*

| Work | Monitoring objective | Program state utilization | Implementation mechanism | Environmental change | Attack response | Monitor security | Overhead |
|------|---------------------|--------------------------|--------------------------|---------------------|-----------------|------------------|----------|
| Clause et al., 2007 | Memory operation, code execution flow | Information addition (tainted tag to program variables) | Code instrumentation (write customized APIs to add and maintain tainted information of program data and control flow) | Program state utilization (a bit vector) | Attack handler function execution | N/A | Memory consumption |
| PaX, 2003 | Code execution flow, code origin | Information addition (mark non-executable pages) and modification (address space randomization) | Spatial rearrangement of memories (randomize process memories) | Implementation mechanism (intercept page exceptions and distinguish between code execution and data access) | Runtime exception (thrown by processors) | Restricted privilege (non-executable memory regions) | Memory consumption (splits process memory into half) |
| Tan et al., 2005 | Code origin | Information addition (set effective code segment limit based on initial stack segment) | API hook (operating system services) | Program state utilization (relocating stack segment in upper address region of code segment) | Runtime exception (thrown by processors) | Restricted privilege (non-executable memory regions) | Integration (implement kernel interfaces to shift user mode stack) |

implementation techniques. For example, dynamically linked library calls are modified or injected (e.g., memory allocation and free) as part of attack detection (e.g., Berger et al., 2006). Spatial rearrangement of memories requires modifying memory managers to shift the base address of dynamically linked library code (PaX, 2003). Execution of multiple programs might be controlled through system call synchronizations to allow changing of program states due to inputs and outputs (Salamat et al., 2008) from environments. Kernel system calls can be patched or modified to detect unintended memory accesses (e.g., read only memory access) (Chiueh et al., 2001).

2. **Program state utilization:** Program states are utilized to detect attacks at runtime. However, program states are often added or modified with information. These result in changes of program execution environments. For example, information can be added in registers, cache memories, or the extended address space of programs (e.g., Pyo et al., 2004). Moreover, information can be added in the object code (e.g., Lhee et al., 2002;

StackShield, 2001). Kernel system calls are modified to add information such tainted information of memory locations (Dalton et al., 2007; Suh et al., 2006), data structures (Ruwase et al., 2004), and new stack regions (Tan et al., 2005). A duplicate stack frame can be created in an execution environment to save sensitive information (Gupta et al., 2006). Furthermore, information can be saved in the environment in the form of a bit vector table which saves the readable and the writable status of memory bytes (Hastings et al., 1992).

3. **Performance:** Several approaches try to reduce monitoring overheads by storing information in program environments. Many approaches use faster memory blocks such as cache, hash, and look aside buffer as ways of modifying environments. Cache memories are used to store the most recent program instructions that access memories (Zhou et al., 2004). Hash tables can be used to store out of bound data during BOF attacks (Rinard et al., 2004). Moreover, instrumented code blocks can be saved in cache memories to avoid re-instrumenting in future (Kiriansky et al., 2002).

## Response

It indicates how approaches respond to attack occurrences. From the sixth column of Table 2, we notice that most approaches terminate programs and generate error messages. We classify the response mechanisms into four types: attack handler function execution, program termination, exception throwing, and recovery.

1.  **Attack handler function execution:** Program execution control can be transferred to a dedicated attack handler module. It performs further actions such as stopping program executions (e.g., Clause et al., 2007; Cowan et al., 1998), logging alarms or error messages, and notifying users for further actions (e.g., Aggarwal et al., 2006).
2.  **Program termination:** A program can be terminated in response to a BOF attack (e.g., Berger et al., 2006; Etoh, 2005). For example, any attempt to read only location results in a core dump (Chiueh et al., 2001).
3.  **Exception throwing:** This technique leverages exceptions thrown by operating systems or processors (e.g., Gaurav et al., 2003; PaX, 2003).
4.  **Recovery:** A program can be recovered from a corrupted state to its corresponding normal state to allow further continuation after a BOF attack (Gupta et al., 2006).

## Monitor Security

It might be possible to circumvent monitoring approaches and perform successful BOF attacks. In particular, attackers might alter sensitive program state information saved by monitors. Thus, many approaches take steps to secure sensitive information to nullify attacks on programs guarded by monitors. In other words, steps are taken to make sure that sensitive program state information cannot be tampered easily at runtime. We denote such explicit steps as monitor security. We

classify these steps into five types as shown in Table 2: *inaccessible repository*, *randomization*, *safe process*, *restricted privilege*, and *resiliency*.

1.  **Inaccessible repository:** The idea is to make the location of repository where sensitive information is saved as inaccessible to avoid tampering. Sensitive program states can be saved in global or static variables (Lhee et al., 2002; StackShield, 2001). Thus, a BOF in a stack region cannot corrupt those variables located in a bss or data region. An approach might store sensitive program states in memory locations that exist only at runtime. For example, Gupta et al. (2006) store return addresses in separate stacks that reside in the same process space of programs. However, the stack is inaccessible from program code. Madan et al. (2005) store an encryption key in a special register (EBP) of the CPU that cannot be accessed from a user program. The approach of Suh et al. (2006) requires storing tainted tag information of user program memory locations into separate memory locations that cannot be accessed from user programs (i.e., a trusted kernel mode can modify the memories).
2.  **Randomization:** In this approach, program states are altered using some random techniques before saving into memories to be used later for detecting attacks. The randomization makes it difficult to guess the sensitive program states. For example, a canary can be set to a random value based on the CPU clock at runtime (Cowan et al., 1998; Etoh, 2005). Program code can be randomized with keys whose values are set at runtime (Gaurav et al., 2003). The key can be obtained from runtime values stored in special registers such as a base pointer register (EBP) (Madan et al., 2005). Fetzer et al. (2001) employ magic numbers to store the base address and size of heap objects. A magic number is unlikely to be present

in user data and marks the beginning of a memory block.

Randomization can be complex by combining several logical operations. For example, a four byte return address can be prepended with a two bit sensor followed by rotating a specific number of bits to make the sensor location guessing difficult (Pyo et al., 2004). Zhu et al. (2004) encrypt function pointers by XORing with keys. In this case, a key is constructed by performing an AND operation between the address of a function pointer and a random number.

3. **Safe process:** A user program is deployed as a protected process (same as kernel) so that any unwanted modification of code results in exceptions thrown by a kernel (Han et al., 2007). Moreover, monitoring techniques can be deployed as server processes where actual programs to be monitored are run as child processes (Aggarwal et al., 2006). In this case, sensitive information (e.g., return addresses) of child processes are passed to server processes through inter-process communication (IPC) or message passing technique. User programs cannot modify queues related to IPC or message passing techniques.

4. **Restricted privilege:** This technique restricts read and write operations on specific process memory locations where sensitive program states are saved. For example, return addresses can be saved in locations which can be set as read only for user programs. As a result, any attempt to modify a state through BOF attacks is thwarted (Chiueh et al., 2001; Prasad et al., 2003). Sensitive policy information such as legitimate control flow instructions and locations are stored in non-writable memory locations of programs (Kiriansky et al., 2002). It is common to prohibit a user program to access special registers for reading and writing that contains

tainted tag information of memory locations (Dalton et al., 2007). Moreover, memory regions can be set as non-executable by default to avoid execution of injected opcode (or shell code) (PaX, 2003; Tan et al., 2005).

5. **Resiliency:** Several approaches are based on the idea of program resiliency which means that a program is allowed to execute in presence of BOF attacks (e.g., Berger et al., 2006). The underlying technique disallows corruption of sensitive information by storing additional data supplied as part of BOF attacks in benign locations (e.g., heap memory).

Multi variant program execution approach itself makes it difficult for an attacker to avoid the detection of BOF attacks (Salamat et al., 2008). In this case, an attacker requires devising two sets of attack signatures to generate similar program behaviors. An attacker might discover two attack inputs to circumvent the approach. However, a program accepts only one input which disallows to perform attacks with two inputs simultaneously.

We also notice that several approaches (e.g., Jones et al., 1997; Ruwase et al., 2004) have not addressed the monitor security feature explicitly (marked as N/A in Table 2).

## Overhead

Every monitoring approach imposes overhead. Thus, practitioners need to know what might cause overheads. We divide overhead contributors into five categories: *memory consumption, instrumentation, store and lookup, integration,* and *checkpointing.*

1. **Memory consumption:** Increased amount of memories might pose a bottleneck for programs which are supposed to execute within limited amount of memories (e.g., embedded programs). A variety of sources contribute additional memory requirements.

For example, meta-information related to pointers containing base and size of allocated objects might need to be saved throughout the execution of programs (Fetzer et al., 2001). Out of bound objects for all out of bound pointer dereferences need to be saved present in a program (Ruwase et al., 2004). These objects are used later for computing new addresses through pointer arithmetic. An approach might reserve additional memories to detect attacks which may result in increased memory consumption. For example, additional bytes are reserved before and after each buffer declared or allocated in a program. These bytes are marked as non-readable and non-writable to prevent BOF attacks (Hastings et al., 1992).

Tainted data flow techniques require additional memories to store tainted tags of variables (e.g., Suh et al., 2006). Employing fine grained level of tainting might impose significant memory overhead in a monitoring approach. For example, an approach might save tainted data in four bytes for each byte of program data (e.g., Newsome et al., 2005).

Approaches that are intended to be attack tolerant demand more memories due to the nature of their defenses. This might include allocating more memories than requested (Berger et al., 2006), saving data written to out of bound memories of buffers (Rinard, 2004), and spawning additional programs (Salamat et al., 2008).

The lack of hardware support might result in the decrement of a program's memory space. For example, the presence of no execute (NX) bit in a processor results in dividing the process memory into two halves in the SEGMEXEC mode (PaX, 2003). The mode emulates the NX bit in a CPU that executes the x86 opcode. One half is used to store data, and the other half is dedicated for storing code. This allows the separation of data accesses from legitimate instruction fetches. However, it forces a program to access at most half of its normal address space for the data.

2. **Instrumentation:** To add monitoring code in programs, most approaches mandate practitioners to learn and tweak compilers and code optimization frameworks. This might pose a significant threat against the application of a monitoring technique smoothly. Moreover, instrumentation effort increases significantly, if monitoring needs to be performed at a very fine grained level of program operations. For example, interesting data types (e.g., pointer) need to be instrumented to check whether they are pointing valid memory addresses or not (e.g., Jones et al., 1997). All 'move' and 'arithmetic' operations are required to be instrumented to propagate tainted information (e.g., Newsome et al., 2005). Moreover, all declared memory objects need to be tracked to identify which instructions or statements access them (Zhou et al., 2004).

Instrumentation might not be easy for programs in executable code format. The impreciseness of disassembly tools makes it challenging to identify prologues and epilogues of functions (Prasad et al., 2003).

3. **Store and lookup:** Overhead may be added due to the execution of additional instructions at prologues and epilogues of functions. Common cases include storing and looking up of memory locations (Chiueh et al., 2001), canary values (Etoh, 2005), and return addresses (e.g., Cowan et al., 1998; Gupta et al., 2006) to detect BOF attacks. Function addresses can be checked to be within the code (or text) region of a process memory (StackShield, 2001). Moreover, the retrieval of table information containing buffer names and sizes takes times. In this case, additional code needs to be executed to check buffer

sizes while invoking vulnerable ANSI C library function calls (Lhee et al., 2002). Dereferencing every function pointers present in a program in decrypted forms might introduce overhead (Zhu et al., 2004).

4. **Integration:** The integration of monitoring framework with programs might pose burden. An approach might require additional effort for integrating library functions such as re-implementing vulnerable library functions (e.g., memcpy and strcpy) (Jones et al., 1997). Randomizing inaccessible program code such as shared libraries can pose overhead (Gaurav et al., 2003). Moreover, kernel interfaces might need to be implemented for preventing BOF attacks (e.g., shifting user stack region to non-executable address space) (Tan et al., 2005).

Some approaches require a great deal of work in profiling programs to identify patterns of function calls containing function names, stack sizes, and return addresses (Han et al., 2007). A program might need to run as a child process of a monitor which introduces programming overhead to coordinate the two processes (Aggarwal et al., 2006). Moreover, fine grained policies need to be developed to identify legitimate control flows and code origins as part of integrating target programs with monitors (Kiriansky et al., 2002).

5. **Checkpointing:** Multiple program execution is monitored by checkpointing program states which need to be implemented flawlessly. A program execution might be stopped if another variant of that program has not reached that execution point yet. For example, a program might request input data reading from a file, whereas another variant of that program has not issued the request yet. In this case, the earlier program needs to be stopped to synchronize with the latter program (Salamat et al., 2008).

# COMPARISON OF APPROACHES BASED ON BOF ATTACK TYPES

In this section, we first identify types of BOF attacks followed by analyzing the related works for attack detection coverage.

## BOF Attack Type

We first categorize attack types based on the following: program operation, BOF location, attack data type, object spatiality, magnitude, and pointer arithmetic.

- **Program operation:** It implies whether a BOF attack can be detected during a reading or a writing operation by an approach.
- **BOF location:** BOF attacks can be performed on four different regions of process memories such as stack, heap, block started by symbol (or bss), and data section. Here, bss section contains all global and static buffers that are not initialized. The data section contains all global and static buffers that are initialized.
- **Data type:** This feature indicates neighboring objects of buffers that are overwritten. Usually BOF attacks overflow character buffers. However, the overwritten objects vary based on data types supported in programming languages. These include data pointers (returned by memory allocation function), jump buffers, and function pointers.
- **Object spatiality:** This feature is applicable for complex data type or object (e.g., structure) having buffers as member variables. In this case, an overflow might corrupt either the neighboring members of a structure or another neighboring structure. We classify two types of overflow: intra object and inter object. We provide examples of these overflows in the left and right columns of Table 3, respectively. In

an intra object overflow, a buffer (e.g., buf2) might overflow another member (e.g., buf1) of the same object (i.e., structure) without overflowing the boundary of the structure (i.e., str1). Here, str1 is located in the stack region. In an inter-object overflow, a member of an object (e.g., str2. buf2) might overflow its neighboring variable (e.g., str1). Here, both the str1 and str2 are located in the stack region.

- **Magnitude:** Approaches can be classified based on detection capability of magnitude of overflows. For simplicity, we consider two types of BOF: one byte and multiple bytes.
- **Pointer arithmetic:** Pointer arithmetic operations (e.g., increment, decrement of a pointer variable) are intended to generated memory addresses which might be out of bound or invalid addresses.

BOF location and magnitude are considered as runtime state related features as their existence can be found at runtime only. However, program operation, data type, object spatiality, and pointer arithmetic are considered as program artifacts as they are visible from the source code. Thus, one can combine 12 possible program artifacts with eight different runtime state features to cover different attack types. Ideally, these six features allow us to represent 96 types of attacks.

Note that we are aware of two taxonomies of BOF attacks (Wilander et al., 2003; Zhivich et al., 2005). Wilander et al. (2003) propose a taxonomy of generating BOF attacks by combining buffer locations (e.g., stack, heap), data types (e.g., buffer, function pointer, jump buffer), and attack targets (e.g., return address, base pointer). Zhivich et al. (2005) classify BOF attacks in terms of buffer access modes (e.g., buffer index, pointer), overflow magnitudes (e.g., one byte), and buffer data types (e.g., character, integer). In contrast, we classify BOF attack types by combining responsible elements of program code and

runtime features. Nevertheless, one can think of our attack classification as a subset of Zhivich et al. (2005) and Wilander et al. (2003) taxonomies.

## Comparison of BOF Monitoring Approaches

Table 4 summarizes our evaluation of monitoring approaches for each of the works which are grouped based on monitoring objectives. For each attack type, we identify whether an approach can constituent attack features ("Y") or not ("N"). If an approach does not explicitly claim detecting a particular feature, we mark it as "N". We now describe our observation based on the six features in the following.

- **Operation:** All the approaches detect BOF attacks due to writing in buffer variables. Surprisingly, most approaches do not detect BOF attacks due to reading operation from buffer variables (e.g., Cowan et al., 1998).
- **Location:** Most approaches focus on detecting BOF attacks which smash stack memory locations (e.g., Jones et al., 1997; Ruwase et al., 2004). Several approaches can detect BOF in heap regions (e.g., Lhee et al., 2002). However, there is little effort on detecting BOF for bss and data regions explicitly (e.g., Jones et al., 1997). Very few approaches can detect attacks in all re-

*Table 3. Example of object spatial BOF attacks*

| Intra object | Inter object |
|---|---|
| struct {<br>char buf1 [12];<br>char buf2 [12];<br>}str1;<br>....<br>str1.buf2 [13] = 'x';<br>//overflows buf1<br>... | struct {<br>char buf1 [12];<br>}str1;<br>struct {<br>char buf2 [12];<br>}str2;<br>...<br>str2.buf2 [13] = 'x';<br>//overflows str1.buf1<br>... |

*Table 4. Comparison of approaches for BOF attack detection coverage*

| Monitoring objective | Work | Operation | | Location | | | | Data type | | | Object spatiality | | Magnitude | | Pointer arithmetic |
|---|---|---|---|---|---|---|---|---|---|---|---|---|---|---|---|
| | | Read | Write | Stack | Heap | bss | Data | Data pointer | Jump buffer | Function pointer | intra | inter | one | multiple | |
| **Memory operation** | Jones et al., 1997 | Y | Y | Y | Y | Y | Y | Y | N | N | N | Y | Y | Y | Y |
| | Berger et al., 2006 | N | Y | N | Y | N | N | N | N | N | N | N | N | Y | N |
| | Fetzer et al., 2001 | N | Y | N | Y | N | N | Y | Y | N | N | Y | N | Y | N |
| | Ruwase et al., 2004 | Y | Y | Y | Y | Y | Y | Y | N | N | N | Y | Y | Y | Y |
| | Hastings et al., 1992 | Y | Y | Y | Y | Y | Y | Y | N | N | N | Y | Y | Y | Y |
| | Rinard et al., 2004 | N | Y | Y | Y | N | N | Y | N | N | N | Y | Y | Y | Y |
| | Newsome et al., 2005 | N | Y | Y | N | N | N | Y | N | Y | N | Y | N | Y | N |
| **Value integrity** | Chieuh et al., 2001 | N | Y | Y | N | N | N | N | N | N | N | Y | N | Y | N |
| | Etoh, 2005 | N | Y | Y | N | N | N | N | N | Y | N | Y | N | Y | N |
| | Cowan et al., 1998 | N | Y | Y | N | N | N | Y | N | N | N | Y | N | Y | N |
| | Gupta et al., 2006 | N | Y | Y | N | N | N | N | N | N | N | Y | N | Y | N |
| | StackShield, 2001 | N | Y | Y | N | N | N | N | N | Y | N | Y | N | Y | N |
| | Aggarwal et al., 2006 | N | Y | Y | N | N | N | N | Y | N | N | Y | N | Y | N |
| | Prasad et al., 2003 | N | Y | Y | N | N | N | N | N | N | N | Y | N | Y | N |
| | Madan et al., 2005 | N | Y | Y | N | N | N | N | N | N | N | Y | N | Y | N |
| | Pyo et al., 2004 | N | Y | Y | N | N | N | N | N | N | N | Y | N | Y | N |
| | Salamat et al., 2008 | N | Y | Y | N | N | N | N | N | N | N | Y | N | Y | N |
| | Zhu et al., 2004 | N | Y | Y | N | N | N | N | N | Y | N | N | N | Y | N |
| **Code execution flow** | Kiriansky et al., 2002 | Y | Y | Y | Y | N | N | Y | Y | Y | N | Y | N | Y | N |
| | Suh et al., 2006 | N | Y | Y | Y | Y | Y | Y | Y | Y | N | Y | N | Y | N |
| | Dalton et al., 2007 | N | Y | Y | Y | Y | Y | Y | N | N | N | Y | N | Y | N |
| | Clause et al., 2007 | N | Y | Y | N | N | N | Y | Y | Y | N | Y | N | Y | N |
| **Code origin** | PaX, 2003 | Y | Y | Y | N | N | Y | N | N | N | N | Y | N | Y | N |
| | Tan et al., 2005 | N | Y | Y | N | N | N | N | N | N | N | Y | N | Y | N |
| | Dalton et al., 2007 | N | Y | Y | Y | Y | Y | Y | N | N | N | Y | N | Y | N |
| | Clause et al., 2007 | N | Y | Y | N | N | N | Y | Y | Y | N | Y | N | Y | N |
| **Code structure** | Gaurav et al., 2003 | N | Y | Y | N | N | N | N | N | N | N | N | N | Y | N |
| **Fingerprinting** | Han et al., 2007 | N | Y | Y | N | N | N | Y | N | N | N | Y | N | Y | N |
| | Zhou et al., 2004 | N | Y | Y | Y | N | N | Y | N | N | N | Y | N | Y | N |
| **Input validation** | Lhee et al., 2002 | N | Y | Y | Y | N | N | Y | N | N | N | Y | Y | Y | N |

gions (e.g., Dalton et al., 2007; Hastings et al., 1992; Suh et al., 2006).

- **Data type:** From Table 4, we note that most approaches can detect or prevent overwriting the data pointers through BOF attacks. Few approaches detect attacks overwriting jump buffers (e.g., Aggarwal et al., 2006) and function pointers (e.g., StackShield, 2001).
- **Object spatiality:** Many approaches can detect BOF attacks that result in corrupting neighboring objects (i.e., inter-object BOF) (e.g., Jones et al., 1997). However, none of the approach detects intra-object BOF attacks.
- **Magnitude:** Although a multiple byte BOF attack can be detected by all of the approaches, one byte overflow is detected by very few approaches (e.g., Ruwase et al., 2004).
- **Pointer arithmetic:** We notice that very few approaches are able to detect BOF attacks caused by pointer arithmetic operations (e.g., Rinard et al., 2004).

## OTHER EFFORTS ON COMPARING BOF MONITORING TOOLS AND TECHNIQUES

Wilander et al. (2003) develop a benchmark program suite to evaluate four dynamic BOF attack detection tools namely StackGuard (Cowan et al., 1998), StackShield (2001), ProPolice (Etoh et al., 2005), and Libsafe (Tsai et al., 2002). Libsafe is a library patch for replacing vulnerable function calls to non-vulnerable function calls and the approach fits well to a safe programming technique for developers. Thus, we do not discuss Libsafe in our analysis. Moreover, they construct test cases that overflow buffers located in stack, heap, bss, and data segments. The test cases modify program controls by making the overflow sufficient to reach

target locations such as return addresses, jump buffers (e.g., longjmp), and function pointers.

Zhivich et al. (2005) evaluate seven tools to identify BOF attack detection effectiveness that include both commercial (Chaperon and Insure++ from Parasoft, 2010) and open source tools (Bellard, 2003; Etoh, 2005; Necula et al., 2002; Ruwase et al., 2004; Valgrind, 2009). Their test suite contains BOF attacks of various magnitudes, data types, and locations. We do not discuss commercial tools in our analysis. CCured (Necula et al., 2002) and TinyCC (Bellard, 2003) suit well for program transformation related approaches which motivated us to exclude them in the analysis. Valgrind is mainly a debugging tool. Thus, we do not include it in the discussion.

Younan et al. (2004) study runtime BOF detection approaches through compiler patches (e.g., Cowan et al., 1998), library modifications (e.g., Tsai et al., 2002), and operating systems (e.g., Gaurav et al., 2003). Their survey focuses on limitation of techniques (e.g., mandatory availability of source code), attack responses (e.g., program termination), and overhead information (e.g., memory consumption). In contrast, we classify approaches from monitoring tool development point of view such as monitoring objective, program state utilization, and implementation mechanism.

Glaume et al. (2002) study the protection (or detection) capability of BOF attacks and related overheads for PaX (2003), Libsafe (Tsai et al., 2002), and StackShield (2001). They apply several small scale programs to evaluate these tools. In contrast, we compare a detailed set of approaches from monitor development point of view and analyze BOF attack detection capabilities of these approaches.

## CONCLUSION

Our analysis indicates that most monitoring approaches detect BOF attacks due to memory write operations. Thus, more attention is required to detect BOF attacks due to memory read operations. Moreover, none of the monitoring objective can detect all possible BOF attacks. Thus, one can combine the objectives to develop a new monitor for increased attack detection. We observe that many approaches monitor fine grained level of operations (e.g., accessing memory bytes). These approaches have higher overhead as they need to maintain more information for aiding monitoring. Moreover, many approaches do not include security of sensitive program state information which must not be corrupted to detect attacks. It is also evident that current approaches have limited attack detection coverage with respect to both vulnerable program code (e.g., data type and pointer arithmetic) and runtime state (e.g., magnitude and location). We note that off by one BOF attack is less addressed and many state of the art tools fail to detect those attacks. BOF attacks in all memory regions are not widely addressed among current approaches. Thus, another improvement can be to increase attack detection coverage based on both program code and runtime state. Moreover, a monitoring approach should modify program execution environments as less as possible to reduce both overhead and unwanted side effects during normal program operations.

## ACKNOWLEDGMENT

This work is partially supported by the Natural Sciences and Engineering Research Council of Canada (NSERC) and the Ontario Graduate Scholarship (OGS). We thank to the anonymous reviewers for their comments to improve this paper.

## REFERENCES

Aggarwal, A., & Jalote, P. (2006). Monitoring the Security Health of Software Systems. In *Proceedings of the 17ᵗʰ International Symposium on Software Reliability Engineering*, NC (pp. 146-158).

Bellard, F. (2003). *TCC: Tiny C Compiler*. Retrieved March 16, 2010, from www.tinycc.org

Berger, E., & Zorn, B. (2006). DieHard: Probabilistic Memory Safety for Unsafe Languages. In *Proceedings of the Conference on Programming Language Design and Implementation*, Ottawa, Canada (pp. 158-168).

Chien, E., & Szor, P. (2002). Blended Attacks Exploits, Vulnerabilities, and Buffer Overflow Techniques in Computer Viruses. In *Proceedings of the Virus Bulletin Conference*, New Orleans, LA.

Chiueh, T., & Hsu, F. (2006). RAD: A Compile-Time Solution to Buffer Overflow Attacks. In *Proceedings of the 21ˢᵗ International Conference on Distributed Computing Systems*, AZ (pp. 409-417).

Clause, J., Li, W., & Orso, A. (2007). Dytan: A Generic Dynamic Taint Analysis Framework. In *Proceedings of the International Symposium on Software Testing and Analysis*, London (pp. 196-206).

*Common Vulnerabilities and Exposures (CVE)*. (n.d.). Retrieved March 16, 2010, from http://cve.mitre.org

Cowan, C., Pu, C., Maier, D., Hinton, H., Walpole, J., Bakke, P., et al. (1998). Automatic Adaptive Detection and Prevention of Buffer Overflow Attacks. In *Proceedings of the 7ᵗʰ USENIX Security Conference*, San Antonio, TX.

Dahn, C., & Mancoridis, S. (2003). Using Program Transformation to Secure C Programs Against Buffer Overflows. In *Proceedings of the 10th Working Conference on Reverse Engineering*, Canada (pp. 323-332).

Dalton, M., Kannan, H., & Kozyrakis, C. (2007). Raksha: A Flexible Information Flow Architecture for Software Security. In *Proceedings of the 34th Annual International Symposium on Computer Architecture*, San Diego, CA (pp. 482-493).

Erlingsson, U. (2007). *Low-level Software Security: Attacks and Defenses* (Tech. Rep. MSR-TR-07-153). Microsoft Research, Redmond, WA.

Etoh, H. (2005). *GCC Extension for Protecting Applications from Stack-smashing Attacks*. Retrieved March 16, 2010, from http://www.trl. ibm.com/projects/security/ssp

Fetzer, C., & Xiao, Z. (2001). Detecting Heap Smashing Attacks through Fault Containment Wrappers. In *Proceedings of the 20th Symposium on Reliable Distributed Systems*, New Orleans, LA (pp. 80-89).

Glaume, V., & Fayolle, P. (2002). *A Buffer Overflow Study: Attacks & Defenses (Tech. Rep.)*. Talence, France: ENSEIRB, Network and Distributed Systems.

Gupta, S., Pratap, P., Saran, H., & Kumar, A. (2006). Dynamic Code Instrumentation to Detect and Recover from Return Address Corruption. In *Proceedings of the International Workshop on Dynamic Systems Analysis*, Shanghai, China (pp. 65-72).

Hackett, B., Das, M., Wang, D., & Yang, Z. (2006). Modular Checking for Buffer Overflows in the Large. In *Proceedings of the 28th International Conference on Software Engineering*, Shanghai, China (pp. 232-241).

Hastings, R., & Joyce, B. (1992). Purify: Fast Detection of Memory Leaks and Access Errors. In *Proceedings of the USENIX Winter Conference*, San Francisco, CA (pp. 125-138).

Jones, R., & Kelly, P. (1997). Backwards-compatible Bounds Checking for Arrays and Pointers in C Programs. In *Proceedings of Automated and Algorithmic Debugging*, Linköping, Sweden (pp. 13-26).

Kc, G., Keromytis, A., & Prevelakis, V. (2003). Countering Code-injection Attacks with Instruction-set Randomization. In *Proceedings of the 10th ACM Conference on Computer and Communications Security*, Washington, DC (pp. 272-280).

Kiriansky, V., Bruening, D., & Amarasinghe, S. (2002). Secure Execution via Program Shepherding. In *Proceedings of the 11th USENIX Security Symposium*, San Francisco, CA (pp. 191-206).

Kratkiewicz, K., & Lippmann, R. (2005). Using a Diagnostic Corpus of C Programs to Evaluate Buffer Overflow Detection by Static Analysis Tools. In *Proceedings of the Workshop on the Evaluation of Software Defect Detection Tools*, Chicago.

Leah, D. (2000). *A Memory Allocator*. Retrieved March 16, 2010, from http://g.oswego.edu/dl/html/malloc.html

Lhee, K., & Chapin, S. (2002). Type-Assisted Dynamic Buffer Overflow Detection. In *Proceedings of the 11th USENIX Security Symposium*, San Francisco, CA (pp. 81-88).

Madan, B., Phoha, S., & Trivedi, K. (2005). StackOFFence: A Technique for Defending Against Buffer Overflow Attacks. In *Proceedings of the International Conference on Information Technology: Coding and Computing*, Las Vegas, NV (pp. 656-661).

Necula, G., McPeak, S., & Weimer, W. (2002). CCured: Type-safe Retrofitting of Legacy Code. In *Proceedings of the Symposium on Princliples of Programming Languages*, Portland, OR (pp. 128-139).

Newsome, J., & Song, D. (2005). Dynamic Taint Analysis for Automatic Detection, Analysis, and Signature Generation of Exploits on Commodity Software. In *Proceedings of the Network and Distributed System Security Symposium*, San Diego, CA.

One, A. (1996). Smashing the Stack for Fun and Profit. *Phrack Magazine, 7*(49). Retrieved March 16, 2010, from insecure.org/stf/smashstack.html

*Parasoft*. (n.d.). Retrieved March 16, 2010, from www.parasoft.com/jsp/home.jsp

*PaX Project*. (2003). Retrieved March 16, 2010, from http://pax.grsecurity.net/docs/pax.txt

Prasad, M., & Chiueh, T. (2003). A Binary Rewriting Defense against Stack based Buffer Overflow Attacks. In *Proceedings of USENIX Annual Conference*, TX (pp. 211-224).

Pyo, C., Bae, B., Kim, T., & Lee, G. (2004). Runtime Detection of Buffer Overflow Attacks without Explicit Sensor Data Objects. In *Proceedings of the International Conference on Information Technology: Coding and Computing* (pp. 50). Nevada, USA.

Rinard, M., Cadar, C., Dumitran, D., Roy, D., & Leu, T. (2004). A Dynamic Technique for Eliminating Buffer Overflow Vulnerabilities (and Other Memory Errors). In *Proceedings of the 20th Annual Computer Security Applications Conference*, Tucson, AZ (pp. 82-90).

Ruwase, O., & Lam, M. (2004). A Practical Dynamic Buffer Overflow Detector. In *Proceedings of Network and Distributed System Security Symposium*, San Diego, CA (pp. 159-169).

Salamat, B., Gal, A., Jackson, T., Manivannan, K., Wagner, G., & Franz, M. (2008). Multi-variant Program Execution: Using Multi-core Systems to Defuse Buffer-Overflow Vulnerabilities. In *Proceedings of the International Conference on Complex, Intelligent and Software Intensive Systems*, Barcelona, Spain (pp. 843-848).

Shahriar, H., & Zulkernine, M. (2010). Classification of Buffer Overflow Vulnerability Monitors. In *Proceedings of the 4th International Workshop on Secure Software Engineering*, Krakow, Poland (pp. 519-524).

Stack Shield. (2001). *A "stack smashing" technique protection tool for Linux*. Retrieved March 16, 2010, from www.angelfire.com/sk/stackshield

Suh, G., Lee, J., Zhang, D., & Devadas, S. (2006). Secure Program Execution via Dynamic Information Flow Tracking. In *Proceedings of the 11th International Conference on Architectural Support for Programming Languages and Operating Systems*, CA (pp. 85-96).

Tan, Y., Zheng, J., Cao, Y., & Zhang, X. (2005). Buffer Overflow Protection Based on Adjusting Code Segment Limit. In *Proceedings of the IEEE International Symposium on Communications and Information Technology*, Beijing, China (pp. 947-950).

Tsai, T., & Singh, N. (2002). Libsafe: Transparent System-wide Protection Against Buffer Overflow Attacks. In *Proceedings of the International Conference on Dependable Systems and Networks*, Bethesda, MD (pp. 541-541).

*Valgrind*. (2009). Retrieved March 16, 2010, from http://valgrind.org/docs

Wilander, J., & Kamkar, M. (2003). A Comparison of Publicly Available Tools for Dynamic Buffer Overflow Prevention. In *Proceedings of the 10th Network and Distributed System Security Symposium*, San Diego, CA (pp. 149-162).

Xu, R., Godefroid, P., & Majumdar, R. (2008). Testing for Buffer Overflows with Length Abstraction. In *Proceedings of the International Symposium on Software Testing and Analysis*, Seattle, WA (pp. 27-38).

Younan, Y., Joosen, W., & Piessens, F. (2004). *Code Injection in C and C++: A Survey of Vulnerabilities and Countermeasures (Tech. Rep. No. CW 386)*. Leuven, Belgium: Katholiek Universiteit Leuven.

Zhivich, M., Leek, T., & Lippmann, R. (2005). Dynamic Buffer Overflow Detection. In *Proceedings of the Workshop on the Evaluation of Software Defect Detection Tools*, Chicago.

Zhou, P., Liu, W., Fei, L., Lu, S., Qin, F., Zhou, Y., et al. (2004). AccMon: Automatically Detecting Memory-related Bugs via Program Counter-based Invariants. In *Proceedings of 37th International Symposium on Microarchitecture*, OR (pp. 269-280).

Zhu, G., & Tyagi, A. (2004). Protection against Indirect Overflow Attacks on Pointers. In *Proceedings of the 2nd International Information Assurance Workshop*, NC (pp. 97-106).

## ENDNOTE

[1] An earlier version of this work has been published in Shahriar et al., 2010.

*This work was previously published in International Journal of Secure Software Engineering, edited by Khaled M. Khan, pp. 18-40, Volume 1, Issue 3, copyright 2010 by IGI Publishing (an imprint of IGI Global).*

# Chapter 9
# CONFU:
## Configuration Fuzzing Testing Framework for Software Vulnerability Detection

**Huning Dai**
*Columbia University, USA*

**Christian Murphy**
*Columbia University, USA*

**Gail Kaiser**
*Columbia University, USA*

## ABSTRACT

*Many software security vulnerabilities only reveal themselves under certain conditions, that is, particular configurations and inputs together with a certain runtime environment. One approach to detecting these vulnerabilities is fuzz testing. However, typical fuzz testing makes no guarantees regarding the syntactic and semantic validity of the input, or of how much of the input space will be explored. To address these problems, the authors present a new testing methodology called Configuration Fuzzing. Configuration Fuzzing is a technique whereby the configuration of the running application is mutated at certain execution points to check for vulnerabilities that only arise in certain conditions. As the application runs in the deployment environment, this testing technique continuously fuzzes the configuration and checks "security invariants" that, if violated, indicate vulnerability. This paper discusses the approach and introduces a prototype framework called ConFu (CONfiguration FUzzing testing framework) for implementation. Additionally, the results of case studies that demonstrate the approach's feasibility are presented along with performance evaluations.*

## INTRODUCTION

As the Internet has grown in popularity, security testing is undoubtedly becoming a crucial part of the development process for commercial software, especially for server applications. However, it is impossible in terms of time and cost to test all configurations or to simulate all system environments before releasing the software into the field, not to mention the fact that software distributors may later add more configuration options. The configuration of a software system is a set of

DOI: 10.4018/978-1-4666-1580-9.ch009

options that are responsible for a user's preferences and the choice of hardware, functionality, etc. Sophisticated software systems always have a large number of possible configurations, e.g., a recent version of Firefox has more than $2^{30}$ possible configurations, and testing all of them is infeasible before the release. Fuzz testing as a form of black-box testing was introduced to address this problem (Sutton et al., 2007), and empirical studies (Jurani, 2006) have proven its effectiveness in revealing vulnerabilities in software systems. Yet, typical fuzz testing has been inefficient in two aspects. First, it is poor at exposing certain errors, as most generated inputs fail to satisfy syntactic or semantic constraints and therefore cannot exercise deeper code. Second, given the immensity of the input space, there are no guarantees as to how much of it will be explored (Clarke, 2009).

To address these limitations, this paper presents a new testing methodology called *Configuration Fuzzing*, and a prototype framework called *ConFu* (CONfiguration FUzzing framework). Instead of generating random inputs that may be semantically invalid, ConFu mutates the application configuration in a way that helps valid inputs exercise the deeper components of the software-under-test and check for violations of program-specific "security invariants" (Biskup, 2009). These invariants represent rules that, if broken, indicate the existence of a vulnerability. Examples of security invariants may include: avoiding memory leakage that may lead to denial of service; a user should never gain access to files that do not belong to him; critical data should never be transmitted over the Internet; only certain sequences of function calls should be allowed, etc. ConFu mutates the configuration using the incremental covering array approach (Fouche et al., 2009), therefore guaranteeing considerable coverage of the configuration space in the lifetime of a certain release of the software.

Configuration Fuzzing works as follows: Given an application to test, the testers annotate the variables to be fuzzed in the configuration file and choose the functions to test. If needed, they can write additional surveillance functions for specific security invariants other than the built-in ones provided by our default implementation. The framework then generates the actual code for a fuzzer that mutates the values of the chosen configuration variables, as well as the test functions for each chosen function. Next, the framework creates instrumentation such that whenever a chosen function is called, the corresponding test function is executed in a sandbox with the mutated configuration and the security invariants are checked. Violations of these security invariants are logged and sent back to the developer.

Configuration Fuzzing is based on the observation that most vulnerabilities occur under specific configurations with certain inputs (Ramakrishnan & Sekar, 2002), i.e., an application running with one configuration may prevent the user from doing something bad, while another might not. Configuration Fuzzing occurs within software as it runs in the deployment environment. This allows it to conduct tests in application states and environments that may not have been conceived in the lab. In addition, the effectiveness of ConFu is increased by using real-world user inputs rather than randomly generated ones. However, the fuzzing of the configuration occurs in an isolated "sandbox" that is created as a clone of the original process, so that it does not affect the end user of the program. When a vulnerability is detected, detailed information is collected and sent back to a server for later analysis.

The rest of this paper is organized as follows. The problem statement, and identifies requirements that a solution must meet is formalized. The next section discusses the background, proposes the Configuration Fuzzing approach, and provides the architecture of the framework called ConFu. The results of our case studies and performance evaluation are then examined. Related work is then discussed. The paper ends with limitations and a conclusion.

## PROBLEM AND REQUIREMENTS

### Problem Statement

We have observed that configurations together with user input are the major factors of vulnerability exploitation. However, it is generally infeasible to test all functionality with all possible configurations in terms of time and cost before releasing the software into the field. For example, the Apache HTTP server has more than 50 options that generate over $2^{50}$ possible settings, and certain vulnerabilities[1,2] will only reveal themselves under specific configurations with specific user inputs. The effectiveness and efficiency of detecting such vulnerabilities in the testing process are greatly hampered due to the immensity of both the configuration and input space. Another issue of security testing resides in the difficulty of detecting vulnerabilities when the characteristics of the vulnerabilities are not deterministic and vary greatly among different vulnerabilities. A "test oracle" (Weyuker, 1982) alone is only sufficient in evaluating the correctness of a software but not its security. Furthermore, most configuration testing approaches such as Skoll (Memon et al., 2004) or MSET (Gross et al., 2006) provide little feedback beyond "pass/fail" and thus not addressing security issues.

### Requirements

A solution to this problem would need to address not only the issue of the immensity of the configuration and the input space, but also consider the effectiveness and efficiency of characterizing vulnerabilities and providing detailed information regarding detected vulnerabilities. Such a solution should meet the following requirements:

- **Guarantee a considerable degree of coverage of the configuration space.** In a limited amount of time, the solution has to guarantee sufficient coverage of the configuration space. Because some options have to match the external environment, it might be impossible to provide full-coverage testing. However, the solution must at least have covered the most common configurations.

- **Support representative user inputs with which to test.** The solution has to optimize the number of possible user inputs for a given configuration. The validity of the user inputs is crucial and these inputs should satisfy syntactic or semantic constraints and therefore exercise the deeper components of the software. "Maximum" coverage of the input space is desired, but with "minimum" actual test cases.

- **Be able to detect the most common vulnerabilities and provide an easy-to-use API to add rules for detecting other vulnerabilities.** The solution should provide an effective mechanism to detect common kinds of security issues such as directory traversal, denial of service, insufficient access control, etc. Also, it must be easy to add an additional rule if a new vulnerability or exploit arises, without having to change the existing framework.

- **Be capable of reporting vulnerabilities back to the software developers.** If a test fails and a vulnerability is discovered, the framework must allow for feedback to be sent to the software developers so that the failure can be analyzed and, ideally, fixed. In addition to sending a notification of a discovered vulnerability, the framework should also send back useful information about the system state so that the vulnerability can be reproduced.

- **Have low performance impact.** The user of a system that is conducting tests on itself during execution should not observe any noticeable performance degradation. The tests must be unobtrusive to the end user, both in terms of functionality and any configuration or setup, in addition to performance.

## APPROACH

### Background

Configuration Fuzzing is designed as an extension to the In Vivo Testing approach (Murphy et al., 2009), which was originally introduced to detect behavioral bugs that reside in software products. In Vivo Testing was principally inspired by the notion of "perpetual testing"(Osterweil, 1996; Rubenstein et al., 1997), which suggests that latent defects still reside in many (if not all) software products and these defects may reveal themselves when the application executes in states that were unanticipated and/or untested in the development environment. Therefore, testing of software should continue throughout the entire lifetime of the application. In Vivo Testing approaches this problem by executing tests at specified points in the context of the running program after the software is released.

In Vivo Testing conducts tests and checks properties of the software in a duplicated process of the original; this ensures that, although the tests themselves may alter the state of the application, these changes happen in the duplicated process, so that any changes to the state are not seen by the user. This duplicated process can simply be created using a "fork" system call, though this only creates a copy of the in-process memory. If the test needs to modify any local files, In Vivo tests can use a "process domain" (Osman et al., 2002) to create a more robust "sandbox" that includes a copy-on-write view of the file system. This layered file system allows different processes to have their own view of the file system, sharing any read only files but writing into their own private copies of files and directories.

In previous research into In Vivo Testing, the approach of continuing to test these applications even after deployment was proven to be both effective and efficient in finding remaining misbehavior flaws related to functional correctness (Chu et al., 2008; Murphy et al., 2009), but not necessarily

security defects. In this work, we modify the In Vivo Testing approach to specifically look for security vulnerabilities.

Extending the In Vivo Testing approach to Configuration Fuzzing is motivated by three reasons.

First, many security-related bugs only reveal themselves under certain conditions, which is the configuration of the software together with its runtime environment. For instance, the FTP server wu-ftpd 2.4.2 assigns a particular user ID to the FTP client in certain configurations such that authentication can succeed even though no password entry is available for a user, thus allowing remote attackers to gain privileges[3]. As another example, certain versions of the FTP server vsftpd, when under heavy load, may allow attackers to cause a denial of service (crash) via a SIGCHLD signal during a malloc or free call[4], depending on the software's configuration. Because In Vivo tests execute within the current environment of the program, rather than by creating a clean slate, it follows that Configuration Fuzzing increases the possibility of detecting such vulnerabilities that only appear under certain conditions.

Second, the "perpetual testing" foundation of In Vivo Testing ensures that testing can be carried out after the software is released. Continued testing improves the amount of the configuration space that can be explored through fuzzing; therefore it is more likely that an instance will find vulnerabilities under their error-prone configurations.

Third, In Vivo Testing uses real-world user inputs, which may be more likely to trigger vulnerabilities. Due to the impossibility of full coverage of the input space (Zhu et al., 1997), using real-world user inputs has a higher probability of detecting vulnerabilities over contrived lab inputs.

### Model

When an instrumented function is called, Configuration Fuzzing mutates the application configuration under predefined configuration constraints of the software-under-test to look for potential vulnerabilities. By extending the In Vivo Testing approach, Configuration Fuzzing tests are executed in the field, after deployment, and will provide representative real-world user inputs to test with and reveal vulnerabilities that are dependent on the application state. Furthermore, surveillance functions using security invariants are executed throughout the test in order to detect violations of security rules, which indicate the occurrence of a vulnerability if broken.

The model of Configuration Fuzzing Testing is shown in Figure 1. Given a function named *f* with input *x* to test, we create a sandbox (illustrated by fork() in Figure 1) before *f* actually gets called. The sandbox is a replica of the original process with the same system state. The original function *f* will be executed in the original process as normal while Configuration Fuzzing tests take place in the sandbox. Configuration Fuzzing tests are composed of three parts. First, configuration variables are mutated. However, since Configuration Fuzzing tests take place in a replica of the original process, the configuration variables stay unchanged in the original process. Second, the original function *f* is executed with the mutated configuration trying to exploit potential vulnerabilities. Last, a surveillance function that checks for violation of security invariants is called so as

to detect any vulnerability exploitation and send reports to the system administrator or developers if found. After this, the test process is terminated while the original process continues.

## Architecture

Here we introduce the architecture of a framework called ConFu (Configuration Fuzzing framework for vulnerability detection). ConFu mutates the configuration of an application with a covering array algorithm (Hartman, 2005) and checks for vulnerabilities using surveillance functions that monitor violations of security invariants. This framework allows the application to be tested as it runs in the field, using real input data. As described above, multiple invocations of the instrumented functions are run; however, the additional invocations must not affect the user and must run in a separate sandbox. The steps that software testers would take when using ConFu are as follows:

**Step 1:** *Identifying the configuration/setting variables.* Most software applications use external configuration, such as .config or .ini files, and/or internal configuration, namely global variables. Given an application to be tested, the tester first locates these con-

*Figure 1. The model of configuration fuzzing testing*

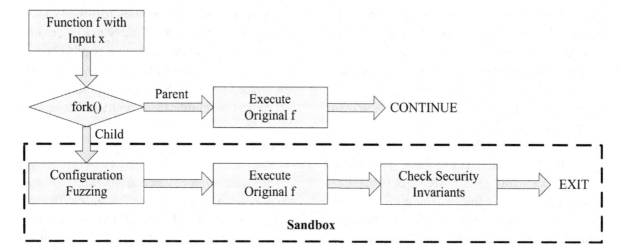

figuration parameters that can be mutated. We assume that the tester can annotate the configuration files in such a way that each field is followed by the corresponding variable from the source code and the range of possible values of that variable. A sample annotated configuration file is shown in Figure 2, with the corresponding variables and their values in braces. The examples listed are taken from our empirical study using OpenSSH[5], a secure shell server.

Our method mainly fuzzes those configuration variables that are responsible for changing modes or enabling options. These variables often have a binary value of 1/0 or y/n, or sometimes a sequence of numbers representing different modes. Not all configuration variables are modifiable in the sense of revealing vulnerabilities, e.g., fuzzing the host IP address of an FTP server will only lead to unable-to-connect errors. Also, configuration variables that rely on external limitations, such as hardware compatibility, should not be fuzzed. For instance, changing the variable representing the number of CPUs to four when the actual host only has two might cause vulnerabilities instead of detecting them. On the other hand, a considerable number of vulnerabilities are triggered under certain mode/option combinations in network-related applications. For example, WinFTP FTP Server 2.3.0, in passive mode, allows remote authenticated users to cause a denial of service via a sequence of FTP sessions[6]. Also, some early versions of Apache Tomcat allow remote

authenticated users to read arbitrary files via a WebDAV write request under certain configurations[7]. By only fuzzing the configuration variables representing modes and options, the size of the configuration space that our approach is fuzzing decreases considerably; however, even with such a decrease, the configuration space may still be too large to test prior to deployment, and thus an In Vivo Testing approach such as Configuration Fuzzing is still useful.

**Step 2:** *Generating fuzzing code.* Given the variables to fuzz and their corresponding possible values (as specified in the configuration file), a pre-processor produces a function that is used to fuzz the configuration, as shown in Figure 3. The fuzz_config() function uses a covering array algorithm (Hartman, 2005) to ensure a certain degree of coverage when exhaustive exploration of the configuration space is impossible in the lifetime of the software.

Consider $k$ as the number of variables a configuration needs to specify and $v$ as the number of possible values each of the $k$ variables can be. We define the level of coverage in terms of a parameter $t$, which if equal to $k$ will produce full coverage, and produce no coverage when equal to zero. The set of configurations generated is called a $t$-way covering array. Take a simple program that uses three ($k=3$) binary ($v=2$) variables as an example. A 3-way covering array will include all $2^3$ configurations, therefore guaranteeing full

*Figure 2. Part of the annotated configuration file for OpenSSH*

| | | |
|---|---|---|
| X11Forwarding | yes | #[options.x11_forwarding]@{0,1} |
| TCPKeepAlive | yes | #[options.tcp_keep_alive]@{0,1} |
| UseLogin | no | #[options.use_login]@{0,1} |
| Protocol | 1 | #[options.protocol]@{1,2,3} |

*Figure 3. An example fuzzer for OpenSSH*

```
typedef struct {
    int x11_forward;
    int tcp_keep_alive;
    ...
} result;

void fuzz_config()
{
  /* generate a set of options */
    result  r=covering_array();
    options.x11_forward = r.x11_forward;
    options.tcp_keep_alive = r.tcp_keep_alive;

    ...
}
```

coverage. A 2-way covering array will look like Figure 4; we notice that whichever two columns out of the three columns are chosen, all possible pairs of values appear. Specifically, the pairs 00, 01, 10 and 11 all appear in the rows when we look at the columns of AB only, AC only and BC only. This property is called "2-coverage", and corresponds to $t=2$. A notion called CAN($t$, $k$, $v$) represents the number of configurations in the smallest (optimal) set that holds the "$t$-coverage" property for a configuration space of size $k^v$. When using the covering array algorithm, our approach will start mutating the configuration variables with a CAN(2, $k$, $v$) covering array and increase $t$ afterwards if time permits. Ideally it would be possible to take $t=k$, but that might lead to too many configurations to test. Empirical studies (Hayhurst et al., 2001) show that for most software $t$ need not be more than 6 to find all errors. The covering_array() function is implemented using Jenny[8], an open sourced covering array generator.

**Step3:** *Identifying functions to test.* The tester then chooses the functions that are to be the instrumentation points for Configuration Fuzzing. These can conceivably be all of the functions in the program, but would generally be the points at which vulnerabilities would most likely be revealed, or the functions that are related to the configuration variables being fuzzed. Future work could investigate a general approach to determine which functions to test. The chosen functions are annotated with a special tag in the source code.

**Step4:** *Generating test code.* As an example, given an original function named do_child() in the program OpenSSH, a pre-processor first renames it to ConFu_do_child(), then generates a skeleton for a test function named ConFu_test_do_child(), which is an instance of a Configuration Fuzzing test. In the test function, the configuration fuzzer (as described above) is first called, and then the original function ConFu_do_child() is invoked.

*Figure 4. A 2-way covering array*

| A | B | C |
|---|---|---|
| 0 | 0 | 0 |
| 0 | 1 | 1 |
| 1 | 0 | 1 |
| 1 | 1 | 0 |

Based on the properties of the program being tested, different security invariants are predefined by the tester in order to check for violations. The tester writes a surveillance function called check_invariants() according to these security invariants. For example, the function could use the substring function strstr(current_directory, legal_directory) to check that the user's current directory has a specified legal directory as its root; if this function indicates otherwise, it may indicate that the user has performed an illegal directory traversal. As another example, the check_invariants() function may simply wait to see if the original function ConFu_do_child() returns at all; if it does not, the process may have been killed or be hanging as a result of a potential vulnerability. These surveillance functions run throughout the testing process, and log every security invariant violation with the fault-revealing configuration into a log file that could be sent to a server for later analysis. Figure 5 shows the test function for function do_child(). By default, ConFu has three built-in security invariants that check for denial of service, unauthorized directory traversal and insufficient privilege control.

**Step 5:** *Executing tests.* In the last step, a wrapper function with the name do_child() is created. As in the In Vivo Testing approach, when the function do_child() is called, it first forks to create a new process that is a replica of the original. The child process (or the "test process") calls the ConFu_test_do_child()

function, which performs the Configuration Fuzzing and then exits. Because the Configuration Fuzzing occurs in a separate process from the original, the user will not see its output. Meanwhile, the original function ConFu_do_child() is invoked in the original process (as seen by the user) and continues as normal. The wrapper function for function do_child() is shown in Figure 6.

## EVALUATION

### Setup

In order to demonstrate the feasibility of using Configuration Fuzzing to detect vulnerabilities, we reproduced certain known vulnerabilities and used ConFu to find them. Due to space limitations, we present only one example vulnerability. The vulnerability we chose is that early versions of OpenSSH do not properly drop privileges when the UseLogin option is enabled, which allows local users to execute arbitrary commands by providing the command to the ssh daemon[9]. The *CVSS Severity*[10] of this vulnerability was 10 (the highest) and we believe it was mainly caused by insufficient testing of the configurations of OpenSSH. We chose this vulnerability not only because of its high severity but also because insufficient privilege control is one of the most common vulnerabilities besides denial of service and unauthorized directory traversal. The following lists the details of each step in using ConFu to detect the vulnerability.

### Identifying the Configuration Variables

The sshd server OpenSSH 2.1.0 was used as the program-under-test in our feasibility study. From the configuration file (sshd_config) we found that there are a total of 15 modifiable (fuzzable) configuration variables: permit_root_login, ig-

*Figure 5. Test function for do_child()*

```
void ConFu_test_do_child(…)
{
    fuzz_config(); /*Fuzz configuration*/
    ConFu_do_child(…);  /*Call the
                    original function*/
    check_invariants();
}
```

nore_ rhosts, ignore_user_known_hosts, strict_ modes, x11_forwarding, print_motd, keepalives, rhosts_authentication, password_authentication, permit_empty_passwd, kerberos_authen tication, kerberos_or_local_passwd, kerberos_ticket_ cleanup, use_login, and check_mail. We annotated these variables with the possible values in the configuration file.

## Generating Fuzzing Code

After recognizing these configuration variables, ConFu generated the fuzz_config() function which mutates the configuration.

## Identifying Functions to Test

We picked the do_child() function as the function to test. The reason we picked this function in the role of software testers is that do_child() is responsible for creating a session and authenticating the user's identity when a ssh client tries to access the sshd server, and it is one of the functions most vulnerable to insufficient privilege control. Note that a wider range of functions can also be tested, including the main() function.

## Generating Test Code

The original function do_child() was renamed by a preprocessor to ConFu_do_child() and the test function ConFu_test_do_child() was generated with the fuzz_config() function and the check_in-variants() function. Several security invariants were checked in our experiment, including the security invariant for privilege control, which is that a user should never be able to use other users' identities. An initial surveillance function that checks this security invariant is shown in Figure 7, which checks whether the user identification has changed.

## Executing Tests

Last, ConFu generated a wrapper function with the name do_child() which forks a child process to execute the ConFu_test_do_child() function and runs the original function ConFu_do_child() in the parent process, as shown in Figure 6.

## Results

To facilitate the exploitation, we simulated both valid and invalid combinations of username and password as user inputs in the real-world for the

*Figure 6. Wrapper function for do_child()*

```
void do_child(...)
{
    int pid = fork();  /*Create new process*/
    if(pid == 0) {    /*Test function*/
        ConFu_test_do_child(...);
        exit(0);
    }
    return ConFu_do_child(); /*Originalfunction*/
}
```

instrumented sshd server. If the vulnerability is exploited, the server program records the exploitation with its corresponding configuration in a log file. We ran the program 10,000 times which took roughly ten minutes. A fragment of the log file is shown in Figure 8. By analyzing the log file, we were able to find the mapping between the UseLogin option and insufficient privilege control. It is also worth pointing out that the number of detections in the log file was identical to the number of tests where UseLogin was enabled (with valid input). We have not yet managed to detect new vulnerabilities, however, this study demonstrates the functional feasibility of the Configuration Fuzzing approach. Performance feasibility is discussed below.

## Performance

The performance impact of ConFu is crucial because Configuration Fuzzing tests are executed while the program-under-test is running. We evaluated our approach's performance by applying it to the OpenSSH server with the steps stated above. do_child() is chosen as the function to test and 15 configuration variables are fuzzed. All experiments were conducted on an Intel Core2Quad Q6600 server with a 2.40GHz CPU and 2GB of RAM running Ubuntu 8.04.3.

For both the original code (without instrumentation) and the instrumented code, we simulated user inputs (both valid and invalid) for the do_child() function and recorded the function's execution time. The OpenSSH service was provided on the test machine, and the do_child() function sent requests to IP address 127.0.0.1 rather than to other servers to eliminate any overhead from network traffic. We ran tests in which the function was called 100, 1000, 10000 and 100000 times in order to estimate the overhead caused by our approach.

Figure 9 shows the results we collected from the experiments. The first column shows the number of tests that were carried out, i.e., the number of times the do_child() function was called. The second and third columns are the overhead in seconds for the fuzz_config() function and the ConFu_do_child() function, respectively. The total average additional time (in seconds) per instrumented test is listed in the last column. From the results we can see that the average additional cost per test stayed around 45ms and did not increase when the number of tests grew. Thus, a single client of a server running OpenSSH with ConFu is unlikely to notice any performance slowdown. It is worth mentioning that most of the performance overhead comes from the cost of generating the covering arrays

*Figure 7. Surveillance function for ConFu_test_do_child()*

```
void check_invariants(Session *s)
{

    if(geteuid() != s.uid || getuid() != s.uid)
        /* Log the detection */
        log("Insufficient privilege control");
        /* Check for other security invariants */
        ...

}
```

in fuzz_config(), and this cost is only affected by the number of variables being fuzzed.

To obtain better performance, software testers could, in principle, pre-calculate the covering arrays for the chosen configuration variables before the software is shipped. However, since many configuration options are enabled or disabled at build time and later hotfixes might add more configuration options, it is more secure to calculate the covering array during the runtime of the software.

## RELATED WORK

### Security Testing

One approach to detecting security vulnerabilities is environment permutation with fault injection (Hsueh et al., 1997), which perturbs the application external environment during the test and checks for symptoms of security violations. Most implementations of this approach view the security testing problem as the problem of testing the fault-tolerance properties of a software system (Du & Mathur, 2000; Thompson et al., 2002). They consider each environment perturbation as a fault and the resulting security compromise a failure in the toleration of such faults. However,

as the errors being injected are independent of the software, most of these errors might not occur in real-world usage. Therefore, fault injection testing may raise false positives.

Instead of injecting faults, ConFu mutates the configuration under predefined configuration constraints of the software-under-test to produce potential vulnerabilities, which relies on the internal properties of the software. Hence it would decrease the occurrence of false positives considerably. The two approaches, however, could certainly be used in conjunction with each other; we leave this as future work.

Another security testing approach used to detect vulnerabilities is anomaly detection (Hangal & Lam, 2002; Krügel et al., 2002). Anomaly detection first establishes a model of normal behavior then detects data sets that cause the program to not conform to the model. Anomaly detection is potentially capable of detecting zero day attacks; however, it is always difficult to define normal behavior. Thus, these approaches depend on the validity of the normal behavior model being used. Anomaly detection may suffer severely from false positives.

ConFu treats the violations of security invariants as vulnerability exploits, and these security invariants are defined based on the consequences of known abnormal behaviors. In a sense, ConFu

*Figure 8. Log file of the OpenSSH server*

```
permit_root_login option is:0
…
…
UseLogin option is:1
Check_mail option is: 0
Insufficient privilege control

permit_root_login option is:1
…
…
UseLogin option is:1
Check_mail option is: 0
Insufficient privilege control
```

uses a model of abnormal behaviors that is much easier to obtain than a model of normal behaviors. Hence ConFu would be expected to have fewer false positives and false negatives; however, further empirical studies are needed to compare the effectiveness and efficiency between these two approaches.

Another popular approach is fuzz testing (Sutton et al., 2007). Typical fuzz testing is scalable, automatable and does not require access to the source code. It simply feeds malformed inputs to a software application and monitors its failures. The notion behind this technique is that the randomly generated inputs often exercise overlooked corner cases in the parsing component and error checking code. This technique has been shown to be effective in uncovering errors (Jurani, 2006), and is used heavily by security researchers (Clarke, 2009). Yet it also suffers from several problems: a single unsigned int value can vary from 0 to 65535; adding another int value to the input domain causes the input space to grow exponentially,

which can hardly be covered with limited time and cost. Furthermore, by only changing the input, a fuzzer may not put the application into a state in which the vulnerability will appear. White-box fuzzing (Ganesh et al., 2009) was introduced to help generate well formed inputs instead of random ones and therefore increases their probability of exercising code deep within the semantic core of the computation. It analyzes the source code for semantic constraints and then produces inputs based on them or modifies valid inputs. White-box fuzzing improves the effectiveness of fuzz testing; however, it overlooks the enormous size of the input space and also suffers from severe overhead (Godefroid et al., 2008).

ConFu deals with this problem by mutating the configuration rather than randomly generating inputs of the program-under-test. The space of the former is considerably smaller than the latter and is more relevant in triggering potential illegal states. In addition, extending the testing phase into

*Figure 9. Overhead of instrumented do_child()(in seconds) with varying number of tests*

| # of tests | Overhead introduced by fuzz_config() | Overhead introduced by ConFu_do_child() | Overhead introduced by check_invariants() | Total Avg. additional time per test |
|---|---|---|---|---|
| 100 | 3.446 | 0.271 | 0.001 | 0.037 |
| 1000 | 42.23 | 2.434 | 0.014 | 0.045 |
| 10000 | 378.2 | 29.92 | 0.157 | 0.041 |
| 100000 | 3694 | 236.8 | 1.628 | 0.039 |

deployed environments ensures representative real-world user inputs with which to test.

## Configuration Testing

Configuration testing plays an irreplaceable role in security testing. The importance of configuration testing has increased as more and more vulnerabilities are discovered to be caused by inappropriate configuration. However, most of these popular configuration testing approaches were not designed to reveal security defects. One approach named Rachet (Yoon et al., 2008), is designed to test the compatibility of a software with mutated configuration in the development process. Rachet models the entire configuration space for software systems and uses the model to generate test plans to sample a portion of the space, and later uses these test plans to test the compatibility during the compile time of the software.

Another approach called Skoll (Memon et al., 2004) is composed of software quality assurance (QA) processes that leverage the extensive computing resources of volunteer communities to improve software quality. Skoll takes a QA process' configuration space to build a formal model which captures all valid configurations for QA subtasks, and uses this model to generate test cases for each machine in the community. Skoll collects the pass/fail results of all the tests to provide feedback to the developers.

Both of these approaches are able to detect functionality errors when the program-under-test fails. However, vulnerabilities such as security defects are more difficult to find since most of them will not lead the program to failure. ConFu deals with this problem by checking the violations of security invariants with surveillance functions. Whereas vulnerabilities such as directory traversal and denial of service can easily hide themselves from being detected by Rachet or Skoll, ConFu can still catch these vulnerabilities when they alter the values checked by the security invariants.

## LIMITATIONS

The most critical limitation of the current implementation is that testers' intervention is required to identify the functions to test. In principal, one can always choose the main() function, but it might be less efficient and increase the overhead. A better way to determine the function-under-test might be integrating Configuration Fuzzing with a run-time injection approach such as the one proposed by Antoni et al. (2003), or picking the most frequently called functions according to real world usage. We leave this as future work.

ConFu relies on surveillance functions that check for violations of security invariants to detect vulnerabilities. Therefore, software testers need a priori knowledge of the potential exploitation behavior in order to design specific surveillance functions. ConFu's built-in surveillance functions check for common security invariants and are capable of detecting most well-known exploits, e.g., denial of service, directory traversal, etc. However, they might not be as effective in detecting zero day vulnerabilities.

Because each configuration is only tested with relatively few inputs, the chance of detecting a vulnerability that would only be revealed under one specific configuration with one particular input is relatively low using the current ConFu implementation. A distributed version of ConFu would increase the efficiency of detecting such vulnerabilities, in which the testing assignments are split amongst applications running in a homogenous "application community" (Locasto et al., 2006). We have developed a distributed In Vivo Testing framework(Chu et al., 2008) and we leave it as future work to develop a global coordinator that is in charge of allocating test cases for each deployed configuration across the user community, and collecting and analyzing the results for ConFu.

## CONCLUSION

In this paper, we explored an approach for software vulnerability detection in the domain of security testing and developed a framework called ConFu based on our approach. Vulnerability detection is difficult to achieve not only because the characteristics of vulnerabilities are hard to define but also because of the immensity of the input and configuration space. Our proposed approach, Configuration Fuzzing, deals with these problems by extending the testing phase into the deployment environment while ensuring a considerable degree of coverage configuration space and representative samples of the input space. Surveillance functions that check for violations of security invariants are executed during Configuration Fuzzing in order to detect vulnerabilities. Configuration Fuzzing tests

happen in a duplicated copy of the original process, so that they do not affect the state of the running application. As future work, we are planning to develop a distributed version of ConFu with a full-fledged sandbox, which will significantly further its potential in detecting software vulnerabilities. We believe that ConFu can help developers build more secure software and improve the security of existing software systems.

## ACKNOWLEDGMENT

The authors are members of the Programming Systems Lab, funded in part by NSF CNS-0905246, CNS-0717544, CNS-0627473 and CNS-0426623, and NIH 1 U54 CA121852-01A1.

## REFERENCES

Antoni, L., Leveugle, R., & Feher, B. (2003). Using run-time reconfiguration for fault injection applications. *IEEE Transactions on Instrumentation and Measurement, 52*(5). doi:10.1109/TIM.2003.817144

Biskup, J. (2009). *Security in computing systems challenges, approaches, and solutions*. New York: Springer-Verlag.

Chu, M., Murphy, C., & Kaiser, G. (2008). Distributed in vivo testing of software applications. In *Proceedings of the First International Conference on Software Testing, Verification and Validation* (pp. 509-512).

Clarke, T. (2009). *Fuzzing for software vulnerability discovery* (Tech. Rep. No. RHUL-MA-2009-4). London: University of London, Department of Mathematics.

Du, W., & Mathur, A. P. (2000). Testing for software vulnerability using environment perturbation. In *Proceedings of the International Conference on Dependable Systems and Networks* (p. 603).

Fouché, S., Cohen, M. B., & Porter, A. (2009). Incremental covering array failure characterization in large configuration spaces. In *Proceedings of the Eighteenth International Symposium on Software Testing and Analysis (ISSTA '09)* (pp. 177-188). New York: ACM.

Ganesh, V., Leek, T., & Rinard, M. (2009). Taint-based directed whitebox fuzzing. In *Proceedings of the 2009 IEEE 31st International Conference on Software Engineering (ICSE '09)* (pp. 474-484). Washington, DC: IEEE Computer Society.

Godefroid, P., Levin, M. Y., & Molnar, D. A. (2008). Automated whitebox fuzz testing. In *Proceedings of the Network Distributed Security Symposium (NDSS)*.

Gross, K. C., Urmanov, A., Votta, L. G., McMaster, S., & Porter, A. (2006). Towards dependability in everyday software using software telemetry. In *Proceedings of the Third IEEE International Workshop on Engineering of Autonomic & Autonomous Systems (EASE '06)* (pp. 9-18). Washington, DC: IEEE Computer Society.

Hangal, S., & Lam, M. S. (2002). Tracking down software bugs using automatic anomaly detection. In *Proceedings of the 2002 International Conference on Software Engineering* (pp. 291-301).

Hartman, A. (2005). *Graph Theory, Combinatorics and Algorithms* (*Vol. 34*, pp. 237–266). New York: Springer.

Hayhurst, K. J., Veerhusen, D. S., Chilenski, J. J., & Rierson, L. K. (2001). *A practical tutorial on modified condition/decision coverage* (Tech. Rep. No. NASA/TM-2001-210876). Houston, TX: NASA.

Hsueh, M.-C., Tsai, T. K., & Iyer, R. K. (1997). Fault injection techniques and tools. *Computer*, *30*(4), 75–82. doi:10.1109/2.585157

Jurani, L. (2006). *Using fuzzing to detect security vulnerabilities* (Tech. Rep. NO. INFIGO-TD-01-04-2006). Richmond, BC, Canada: INFIGO.

Krügel, C., Toth, T., & Kirda, E. (2002). Service specific anomaly detection for network intrusion detection. In *Proceedings of the 2002 ACM Symposium on Applied Computing (SAC '02)* (pp. 201-208). New York: ACM.

Locasto, M. E., Sidiroglou, S., & Keromytis, A. D. (2006). Software self-healing using collaborative application communities. In *Proceedings of the Internet Society (ISOC) Symposium on Network and Distributed Systems Security (NDSS 2006)* (pp. 95-106).

Memon, A., et al. (2004). Skoll: distributed continuous quality assurance. In *Proceedings of the 26th International Conference on Software Engineering (ICSE)* (pp. 459-468).

Murphy, C., Kaiser, G., Vo, I., & Chu, M. (2009). Quality assurance of software applications using the in vivo testing approach. In *Proceedings of the Second IEEE International Conference on Software Testing, Verification and Validation (ICST)* (pp. 111-120).

Osman, S., Subhraveti, D., Su, G., & Nieh, J. (2002). The design and implementation of Zap: A system for migrating computing environments. In *Proceedings of the Fifth Symposium on Operating Systems Design and Implementation (OSDI)* (pp. 361-376).

Osterweil, L. (1996). Perpetually testing software. In *Proceedings of the Ninth International Software Quality Week*.

Ramakrishnan, C., & Sekar, R. (2002). Model-based analysis of configuration vulnerabilities. *Journal of Computer Security, 10*, 189–209.

Rubenstein, D., Osterweil, L., & Zilberstein, S. (1997). An anytime approach to analyzing software systems. In *Proceedings of the 10th FLAIRS* (pp. 386-391).

Sutton, M., Greene, A., & Amini, P. (2007). *Fuzzing: Brute Force Vulnerability Discovery* (1st ed.). Reading, MA: Addison-Wesley.

Thompson, H. H., Whittaker, J. A., & Mottay, F. E. (2002). Software security vulnerability testing in hostile environments. In *Proceedings of the 2002 ACM Symposium on Applied Computing* (pp. 260-264). New York: ACM.

Weyuker, E. J. (1982). On testing non-testable programs. *The Computer Journal, 25*(4), 465–470.

Yoon, I.-C., Sussman, A., Memon, A., & Porter, A. (2008). Effective and scalable software compatibility testing. In *Proceedings of the 2008 International Symposium on Software Testing and Analysis (ISSTA '08)* (pp. 63-74). New York: ACM.

Zhu, H., Hall, P. A. V., & May, J. H. R. (1997). Software unit test coverage and adequacy. *ACM Computing Surveys, 29*(4), 366–427. doi:10.1145/267580.267590

## ENDNOTES

[1]   http://web.nvd.nist.gov/view/vuln/detail?vulnId=CVE-2007-5461

[2]   http://web.nvd.nist.gov/view/vuln/detail?vulnId=CVE-2007-1742

[3]   http://web.nvd.nist.gov/view/vuln/detail?vulnId=CVE-2008-1668

[4]   http://web.nvd.nist.gov/view/vuln/detail?vulnId=CVE-2004-2259

[5]   http://www.openssh.com/

[6]   http://web.nvd.nist.gov/view/vuln/detail?vulnId=CVE-2008-5666

[7]   http://web.nvd.nist.gov/view/vuln/detail?vulnId=CVE-2007-5461

[8]   http://burtleburtle.net/bob/math/jenny.html

[9]   http://web.nvd.nist.gov/view/vuln/detail?vulnId=CVE-CVE-2000-0525

[10]  http://www.oracle.com/technology/deploy/security/cpu/cvssscoringsystem.htm

*This work was previously published in International Journal of Secure Software Engineering, edited by Khaled M. Khan, pp. 41-55, Volume 1, Issue 3, copyright 2010 by IGI Publishing (an imprint of IGI Global).*

# Section 4
# Protection Mechanisms

# Chapter 10

# Retrofitting Existing Web Applications with Effective Dynamic Protection Against SQL Injection Attacks

**San-Tsai Sun**
*University of British Columbia, Canada*

**Konstantin Beznosov**
*University of British Columbia, Canada*

## ABSTRACT

*This paper presents an approach for retrofitting existing Web applications with run-time protection against known, as well as unseen, SQL injection attacks (SQLIAs) without the involvement of application developers. The precision of the approach is also enhanced with a method for reducing the rate of false positives in the SQLIA detection logic, via runtime discovery of the developers' intention for individual SQL statements made by Web applications. The proposed approach is implemented in the form of protection mechanisms for J2EE, ASP.NET, and ASP applications. Named SQLPrevent, these mechanisms intercept HTTP requests and SQL statements, mark and track parameter values originating from HTTP requests, and perform SQLIA detection and prevention on the intercepted SQL statements. The AMNESIA testbed is extended to contain false-positive testing traces, and is used to evaluate SQLPrevent. In our experiments, SQLPrevent produced no false positives or false negatives, and imposed a maximum 3.6% performance overhead with 30 milliseconds response time for the tested applications.*

## INTRODUCTION

SQL injection attacks *(SQLIAs)* are one of the foremost threats to Web applications (Halfond, Viegas, & Orso, 2006). According to the WASP Foundation, injection flaws, particularly SQL injection, were the second most serious type of Web application vulnerability in 2008 (OWASP, 2008). The threats posed by SQLIAs go beyond simple data manipulation. Through SQLIAs, an attacker may also bypass authentication, escalate privileges, execute a denial-of-service attack, or execute remote commands to transfer and install malicious software. As a consequence of SQLIAs,

DOI: 10.4018/978-1-4666-1580-9.ch010

parts of entire organizational IT infrastructures can be compromised. As a case in point, SQLIAs were apparently employed by Ehud Tenenbaum, who has been arrested on charges of stealing $1.5M from Canadian and at least $10M from U.S. banks (Zetter, 2009). An effective and easy to employ method for protecting numerous existing Web applications from SQLIAs is crucial for the security of today's organizations.

State-of-the-practice SQLIA countermeasures are far from effective (Anley, 2002) and many Web applications deployed today are still vulnerable to SQLIAs (OWASP, 2008). SQLIAs are performed through HTTP traffic, sometimes over SSL, thereby making network firewalls ineffective. Defensive coding practices require training of developers and modification of the legacy applications to assure the correctness of validation routines and completeness of the coverage for all sources of input. Sound security practices—such as the enforcement of the principle of least privilege or attack surface reduction—can mitigate the risks to a certain degree, but they are prone to human error, and it is hard to guarantee their effectiveness and completeness. Signature-based Web application firewalls—which act as proxy servers filtering inputs before they reach Web applications—and other network-level intrusion detection methods may not be able to detect SQLIAs that employ evasion techniques (Maor & Shulman, 2005).

Detection or prevention of SQLIAs is a topic of active research in industry and academia. An accuracy of 100% is claimed by recently published techniques that use static and/or dynamic analysis (Halfond & Orso, 2005; Buehrer, Weide, & Sivilotti, 2005; Su & Wassermann, 2006; Bandhakavi, Bisht, Madhusudan, & Venkatakrishnan, 2007), dynamic taint analysis (Nguyen-Tuong, Guarnieri, Greene, Shirley, & Evans, 2005; Pietraszek & Berghe, 2005), or machine learning methods (Valeur, Mutz, & Vigna, 2005). However, the requirements for analysis and/or instrumentation of the application source code (Halfond & Orso, 2005; Buehrer et al., 2005; Su & Wassermann, 2006; Bandhakavi

et al., 2007), runtime environment modification (Nguyen-Tuong et al., 2005; Pietraszek & Berghe, 2005), or acquisition of training data (Valeur et al., 2005) limit the adoption of these techniques in some real-world settings. Moreover, a common deficiency of existing SQLIA approaches based on analyzing dynamic SQL statements is in defining SQLIAs too restrictively, which leads to a higher than necessary percentage of false positives (FPs). False positives could have significant negative impact on the utility of detection and protection mechanisms, because investigating them takes time and resources (Julisch & Darcier, 2002; Werlinger, Hawkey, Muldner, Jaferian, & Beznosov, 2008). Even worse, if the rate of FPs is high, security practitioners might become conditioned to ignore them.

In this paper, we propose an approach for retrofitting existing Web applications with runtime protection against known as well as unseen SQL injection attacks (SQLIAs) without the involvement of application developers. Our work is mainly driven by the practical requirement of Web-application owners that a protection mechanism should be similar to a software-based security appliance that can be "dropped" into an application server at any time, with low administration and operating costs. This "drop-and-use" property is vital to the protection of Web applications where source code, qualified developers, or security development processes might not be available or practical.

To detect SQLIAs, our approach combines two heuristics. The first heuristic (labeled as "token type conformity") triggers an alarm if the parameter content of the corresponding HTTP request is used in non-literal tokens (e.g., identifiers or operators) of the SQL statement. While efficient, this heuristic leaves room for false positives when the application developer (intentionally or accidentally) includes tainted SQL keywords or operators in a dynamic SQL statement. This case would trigger an SQLIA alarm, even though the query does not result in an SQLIA. For instance, as a common case of result-set sorting, a developer could *intentionally* include a predefined parameter value in an HTTP request to form an "ORDER BY" clause in an SQL statement. As we explain later in the paper, the existing approaches and the detection logic based solely on the first heuristic would trigger an SQLIA alarm because the keywords "ORDER" and "BY" are tainted, even though the intercepted SQL statement is indeed benign. In this case, the user is supplying input intended by the programmer; she is not injecting SQL.

When a potential SQLIA is detected by the first heuristic, our approach employs the second heuristic (labeled as "conformity to intention") to eliminate the above type of false positives. We put forward a new view of an SQLIA: an attack occurs when the SQL statement produced by the application at runtime does not conform to the syntactical structure intended by the application developer. Intention conformity enables runtime discovery of the developers' intention for individual SQL statements made by Web applications. Defined more precisely later in the paper, such a view of an SQLIA requires "reverse engineering" of the developer's intention. Our approach not only "discovers" the intention but does so at runtime, which is critical for those applications that are provided without source code. To discover the intended syntactical structures, our approach performs dynamic taintness tracking at runtime and encodes the intended syntactical structure of a dynamic query in the form of SQL grammar, which we term *intention grammar*. Our detection algorithm triggers an alarm if the intercepted SQL statement does not conform to the corresponding intention grammar.

To evaluate our approach, we developed SQLPrevent. It is a software-based security appliance that (1) intercepts HTTP requests and SQL statements at runtime, (2) marks parameter values in HTTP requests as tainted, (3) tracks taint propagation during string manipulations, and (4) performs analysis of the intercepted SQL statements based on our heuristics. To evaluate SQLPrevent, we employed the AMNESIA (Halfond & Orso, 2005) testbed, which has been used for evaluating several other research systems. We extended the AMNESIA testbed to contain requests with new false positives, and added another set of obfuscated attack inputs per application. In our experiments, SQLPrevent produced no false positives or false negatives, and imposed little performance overhead (maximum 3.6%, standard deviation 1.4%), with 30 milliseconds response time for the tested applications.

The rest of the paper is organized as follows. In the next section, we explain how SQL injection attacks and typical countermeasures work. Then we review existing work and compare it with the proposed approach. We then describe our approach in detail for detecting and preventing SQL injection attacks. Next, we discuss the implementation of SQLPrevent in J2EE, ASP. NET, and ASP, followed by a description of the evaluation methodology and results. Finally, we discuss the implications of the results and the strengths and limitations of our approach before summarizing the paper and outlining future work

## BACKGROUND

In this section, we explain how SQLIAs work, why false positives are possible, and what countermeasures are currently available. Readers familiar with the subject can proceed directly to the next section.

## How SQL Injection Attacks Work

For the purpose of discussing SQLIAs, a Web application can be thought of as a black box that accepts HTTP requests as inputs and generates SQL statements as outputs, as illustrated in Figure 1. Web applications commonly use parameter values from HTTP requests to form SQL statements. SQLIAs may occur when data in an HTTP request is directly used to construct SQL statements without sufficient validation or sanitization. For instance, when S="SELECT * FROM product WHERE id="+req.getParameter("product_id") is executed in the Web application, the value of the HTTP request parameter product_id is used in the SQL statement without any validation. By taking advantage of this vulnerability, an attacker can launch various types of attacks by posting HTTP requests that contain arbitrary SQL statements. Below is an example of a malicious HTTP request:

```
POST /prodcut.jsp HTTP/1.1
product_id=2; exec master..xp_cmd-
shell 'net user hacker 1234 /add'
```

In the case of the above attack, the SQL statement constructed by the programming logic would be the following:

```
SELECT * FROM product WHERE id=2; _
exec master..xp_cmdshell 'net user
hacker 1234 /add'
```

If the injected code is executed by the database server, this attack would add a new user account named "hacker" with a password "1234" to the underlying Windows operating system. More malicious attacks, such as file upload and remote command execution, are also possible with similar attack techniques (Anley, 2002).

To confuse signature-based detection systems, attackers may also apply evasion techniques that obfuscate attack strings. Below is an obfuscated version of the above privilege-escalation attack.

```
POST /prodcut.jsp HTTP/1.1
product_id=2; /* */declare/* */@x/*
*/as/**/varchar(4000)
/* */set/* */@x=convert(varchar(4000)
,0x6578656320206D6173
7465722E2E78705F636D6473
68656C6C20276E65 742075736572206861
636B6572202F616464202/**/exec/* */
(@x)
```

The above obfuscation utilizes hexadecimal encoding, dropping white space, and inline comment techniques. For a sample of evasion techniques employed by SQLIAs, see (Maor & Shulman, 2005).

## False Positives

Web application developers typically use string manipulation functions to dynamically compose SQL statements by concatenating pre-defined constant strings with parameter values from HTTP requests. In these cases, programmers can freely incorporate user inputs to form dynamic SQL statements. Without taking developers' SQL-grammatical intentions into account, false posi-

*Figure 1. How SQL injection attacks work*

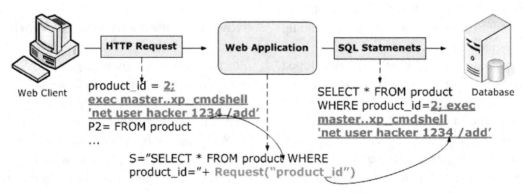

tives are possible in all existing dynamic SQLIA approaches. We illustrate this false-positive problem through a running example.

**Example 1:** Assume there is an HTML drop-down list named "order_by", which consists of three entries—"without order", "by id", "by name". Each entry and its corresponding value is shown in the following HTML code:

```
<select name='order_by'>
<option value=''>without order</op-
tion>
<option value='ORDER BY id'>by id</
option>
<option value='ORDER BY name'>by
name</option>
</select>
```

Assume a programmer intentionally uses the value of the parameter "order_by" to form an SQL query, as illustrated in the following Java code fragment:

```
S="SELECT c1 FROM t1" + request.
getParameter("order_by");
```

Based on a user's selection at runtime (assume the second entry is selected), the SQL statement constructed by the above programming logic would be "SELECT c1 FROM t1 ORDER BY id", where underlined labels indicate the data originated from an HTTP request.

Obviously, the above Java code fragment is vulnerable. An attacker can launch an arbitrary attack by simply appending an attack string to the legitimate input "order_by=ORDER BY id". However, during normal operations, the dynamically constructed SQL statements are indeed benign and harmless.

## Existing Countermeasures

Because SQLIAs are carried out through HTTP traffic, sometimes protected by SSL, most tradi-

tional intrusion-prevention mechanisms, such as firewalls or signature-based intrusion detection systems (IDSs), are not capable of detecting SQLIAs. Three types of countermeasures are commonly used to prevent SQLIAs: Web application firewalls, defensive coding practices, and service lock-down.

Web application firewalls such as WebKnight (AQTRONIX, 2007), ModSecurity (Breach Security Inc., 2007) and Security Gateway (Scott & Sharp, 2002) are easy to deploy and operate. They are commonly implemented as proxy servers that intercept and filter HTTP requests before requests are processed by Web applications. However, due to the limitation of signature databases or policy rules, they may not effectively detect unseen patterns or obfuscated attacks that employ evasion techniques. Also, false positives might occur if signatures or filter policy rules are too restrictive.

Defensive coding practices are the most intuitive ways to prevent SQLIAs, by validating input types, limiting input length, or checking user input for single quotes, SQL keywords, special characters, and other known malicious patterns. Using a parameterized query API (e.g., PrepareStatement in Java and SQLParameter in.NET) is another compelling solution for mitigating SQLIAs directly in code, as parameterized queries syntactically separate the intended structure of SQL statements and data literals.

Service lock-downs are procedures employed to limit the damage resulting from SQLIAs. System administrators can create least-privileged database accounts to be used by Web applications, configure different accounts for different tasks and reduce un-used system procedures. However, similar to defensive coding practices, these countermeasures are prone to human error, and it is difficult to assure their correctness and/or completeness.

Having discussed the state of the practice, in the next section we provide an overview of the state of the art.

## RELATED WORK

Existing research related to SQLIA detection or prevention can be broadly categorized based on the type of data analyzed or modified by the proposed techniques: (1) runtime HTTP requests, (2) design-time Web application source code, and (3) runtime dynamically generated SQL statements. Below, we discuss related work using this categorization, briefly summarize the advantages and limitations of existing approaches, and demonstrate why false positives are possible in some approaches. For a more detailed discussion, we refer the reader to a classification of SQLIA prevention techniques in Halfond et al. (2006) and our technical report (Sun & Beznosov, 2009).

**Web application source code analysis and hardening:** WebSSARI (Huang et al., 2004), and approaches proposed by Livshits and Lam (2005), Jovanovic, Kruegel, and Kirda (2006), and Xie and Aiken (2006) use information-flow-based static analysis techniques to detect SQLIA vulnerabilities in Web applications. Once detected, these vulnerabilities can be fixed by the developers. They have the advantages of no runtime overhead and the ability to detect errors before deployment; however, they need access to the application source code, and the analysis has to be repeated each time an application is modified. Such access is sometimes unrealistic, and repeated analysis increases the overhead of change management.

**Runtime analysis of SQL statements for anomalies:** Valeur et al. (2005) propose an SQLIA detection technique based on machine learning methods. However, the fundamental limitation of this and other approaches based on machine learning techniques is that their effectiveness depends on the quality of training data used. Training data acquisition is an expensive process and its quality cannot be guaranteed. Non-perfect training data causes such techniques to produce false positives and false negatives.

**Static analysis with runtime protection:** SQLrand (Boyd & Keromytis, 2004) modifies SQL statements in the source code by appending a randomized integer to every SQL keyword during design-time; an intermediate proxy intercepts SQL statements at runtime and removes the inserted integers before submitting the statements to the back-end database. For our running Example 1 of false positive, the intercepted SQL statement in SQLrand would read as "SELECT$^{key}$ c1 FROM$^{key}$ t1 ORDER BY id", where "key" represents the random key. The intercepted SQL statement would cause a false positive, since the keywords "ORDER" and "BY" are not appended with the random key.

SQLGuard (Buehrer et al., 2005) provides programmers with a Java library to manually bracket the placeholders of user input in SQL statements. During runtime, SQLGuard compares two parse trees of the dynamically created SQL statement with and without input values respectively. In the case of Example 1, SQLGuard will compare parse trees of (1) "SELECT c1 FROM t1 *key*ORDER BY id*key*", and (2) "SELECT c1 FROM t1 *keykey*", where the first query contains input value and the second does not. SQLGuard would trigger an alarm for this query since neither augmented query is a valid SQL statement.

AMNESIA (W. G. Halfond & Orso, 2005) builds legitimate SQL statement models using static analysis based on information flow. At runtime, SQL statements that do not conform to the corresponding pre-built model are rejected and treated as SQLIAs. Since the automaton of the model "SELECT $\rightarrow$ c1 $\rightarrow$ FROM $\rightarrow$ t1 $\rightarrow$ $\beta$" would not accept the example dynamic SQL (corresponding $\beta$ must be string or numeric constant), the SQL query from Example 1 would be an instance of false positive in AMNESIA.

WASP (Halfond, Orso, & Manolios, 2006) prevents SQLIAs by checking whether all SQL keywords and operators in an SQL statement are marked as trusted. To track trusted sources, WASP uses Java byte-code instrumentation techniques to mark all hard-coded and implicitly created strings in the source code, and strings from external sources (e.g., file, trusted network connection, database) as trusted. In the case of Example 1, WASP would view the intercepted SQL statement as "SELECT c1 FROM t1 ORDER BY id", where underlined labels indicate the data are trusted. Since the keywords "ORDER" and "BY" are not marked as trusted, the query would be rejected as an instance of false positive.

SQLCheck (Su & Wassermann, 2006) detects SQLIAs by observing the syntactic structure of generated SQL queries at runtime, and checking whether this syntactic structure conforms to an augmented grammar. The main limitation of SQLCheck is that it requires each parameter value to be augmented with the meta-characters in order to determine the source of substrings in the constructed SQL statement. This approach requires manual intervention of the developer to identify and annotate untrusted sources of input, which introduces incompleteness problems and may lead to false negatives. In addition, wrapping meta-characters around each parameter value might cause unexpected side-effects. For instance, if the programming logic in a Web application performs string comparison using the augmented parameter value, the result would be different than in the case of no meta-characters, which would cause unexpected results in business logic (e.g., math operations of two user inputs). In addition, the generated SQL statement for Example 1 would read as "SELECT c1 FROM t1 <ORDER BY id>", where < and > are special meta-characters added by SQLCheck. This query would be treated as an injection attack if the augmented grammar does not state user inputs are permitted in "ORDER" and "BY" keywords.

CANDID (Bandhakavi et al., 2007) transforms a Java Web application by adding a benign candidate variable $v_c$ for each string variable $v$. When $v$ is initialized from the user-input, $v_c$ is initialized with a benign candidate value that is the same length as $v$. If $v$ is initialized by the program, $v_c$ is also initialized with the same value. CANDID then compares the real and candidate parse trees at runtime. Using Example 1, the real and the corresponding candidate SQL statement would be "SELECT c1 FROM t1 ORDER BY id", and "SELECT c1 FROM t1 aaaaaaaaaaa", respectively. The intercepted SQL statement would be treated as an attack, since the parse trees derived from the two queries differ.

**Runtime analysis of HTTP requests and SQL statements:** Approaches employing dynamic taint analysis have been proposed by Nguyen-Tuong et al. (2005) and Pietraszek and Berghe (2005). Taint information refers to data that come from un-sanitized or un-validated sources, such as HTTP requests. Both approaches modify the PHP interpreter to mark tainted data as they enter the application and flow around. If tainted data have been used to create SQL keywords and/or operators in the query, the call is rejected. For the running example, the intercepted SQL statement would be viewed as "SELECT c1 FROM t1 ORDER BY id", where underlined labels indicate the data are tainted. Since the keywords "ORDER" and "BY" are marked as tainted, the query would be rejected—which is an instance of false positive. Sekar (2009) proposed a black-box taint-inference technique that infers tainted data in the intercepted SQL statements, and then employs syntax and taint-aware policies for detecting unintended use of tainted data. His technique achieves taint-tracking without intrusive instrumentation on target applications or modification to the run-time environment. However, false positives and false negatives are possible due to sub-optimal accuracy of the taint-inference algorithm and taint-awareness policies.

## APPROACH

Our approach enables retrofitting existing Web applications with run-time protection against known as well as unseen SQLIAs. The core of the approach is a software-based security appliance, SQLPrevent, which can be "plugged" into a Web server without any modifications to the hosted Web applications. As illustrated in Figure 2, SQLPrevent consists of HTTP Interceptor, Taint Tracker, SQL Interceptor, SQL Lexer, Intention Validator, and SQLIA Detector modules. When SQLPrevent is deployed in a Web server, the original data flow (HTTP request → Web application → database driver → database) is altered. First, the reference to the program object representing an incoming HTTP request is intercepted by HTTP Interceptor, and data in the request are marked as tainted. Second, propagation of tainted data is tracked by Taint Tracker. Finally, the SQL statements issued by Web applications are intercepted by the SQL Interceptor and passed to the SQLIA Detector. The SQLIA Detector module performs detection based on the two heuristics (token type conformity and conformity to intention) to detect an attack. Token type conformity determines whether an HTTP request is benign or potentially malicious by checking whether tainted data are used only as string or numeric literals in the intercepted SQL statement. SQL Lexer is used by SQLIA Detector module to tokenize SQL statements. Normally, most dynamically constructed SQL

statements are benign. When a potential SQLIA is detected (i.e., any non-literal token contains tainted characters), SQLIA Detector passes a tainted SQL statement to Intention Validator to confirm whether tainted non-literal tokens have been intentionally constructed by developers. If the intercepted SQL statement does not conform to the intended syntactical structure, SQLIA Detector, depending on the configuration, either triggers an alarm or prevents the malformed SQL statement from being submitted to the database. Note that any HTTP request that violates toke type conformity will be flagged as a potential vulnerability. Whereas the SQLPrevent architecture is based on a standard approach of implementing a security subsystem in the form of interceptors, our approach is distinguished by its detection logic. The following subsections describe each of the detection heuristics in detail.

## Token Type Conformity

The core of the token type conformity heuristic is based on the observation that SQLIAs always cause a parameter value, or its portion, to be interpreted by the back-end database as something other than an SQL string or numeric literal, thus

*Figure 2. Main elements of SQLPrevent architecture are shown in light grey. The data flow is depicted with sequence numbers and arrow labels. Underlined labels indicate that the data are accompanied by the tainted meta-data. Depending on whether an SQL statement is benign or potentially malicious, data may flow to the Intention Validator conditionally.*

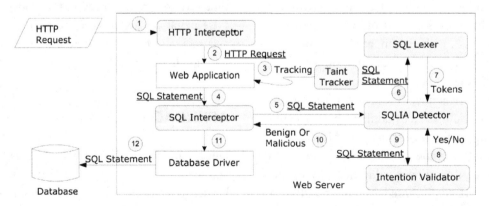

altering the intended syntactical structure of the dynamically generated SQL statement. In order to retain statements' intended syntactical structure, however, parameter values from HTTP requests should be used only as SQL string or numeric literals.

## Tracking of Tainted Data

Tainted data refers to data that originates from an untrusted source, such as an HTTP request. An SQLIA occurs when tainted data are used to construct an SQL statement in a way that alters the intended syntactical structure of the SQL statement. To trace the source of each character in an SQL statement for Web applications, we designed per-character taint propagation using a custom implementation of Java's string-related classes. Our design (1) contains an additional data structure—referred as *taint meta-data*—for tracking the taint status of each character in a string, and (2) implements public methods for setting/getting the taint meta-data. This meta-data is propagated during string manipulations, such as concatenation, extraction, or conversion.

## Lexical Analysis of SQL Statements

SQLPrevent performs lexical analysis of SQL statements at run-time in order to identify non-literal tokens in the SQL statements. Lexical analysis is the process of generating a stream of tokens from the sequence of input characters comprising the SQL statement. The goal of lexical analysis in our approach is to generate two sets of tokens: LITERALS and NON-LITERALS. The LITERALS set contains string and number tokens, and the NON-LITERALS set has tokens of all other types. The exact types of tokens in the NON-LITERAL set are irrelevant for the purpose of our detection logic. This simplified design of the lexical analyzer makes our approach efficient and more portable among databases. For instance, during the experiments, our implementation of

SQL lexer worked with MySQL without any modification, even though the lexer was originally designed for Microsoft SQL Server.

## Detecting SQLIAs

Applying our heuristic that parameter values should only be used as string or numeric literals in the dynamic SQL statements, the mechanisms of taint tracking, and SQL lexical analysis, we developed an algorithm for SQLIA detection using token type conformity. Shown in Algorithm 1 (Figure 3), the algorithm takes an SQL statement *s* and taint information about the characters in *s* as a implicit parameter. If tainted character(s) appears in any non-literal token (e.g., identifier, delimiter, or operator) of *s*, the algorithm returns true, otherwise false. For each token of an intercepted SQL statement, if the type of token is not a literal (i.e., not a string or number), and the token is tainted, then the intercepted SQL statement is potentially malicious.

The "token type conformity" heuristic was originally inspired by Perl taint mode (Wall, 2007). When in taint mode, the Perl runtime explicitly marks data originating from outside of a program as tainted. Tainted data are prevented from being used in any security-sensitive functions such as shell commands, or database queries. To "untaint" an untrusted input, the tainted data must be passed through a sanitizer function written in regular expressions. However, developers have to manually untaint user input data, and sanitizer functions might not catch all malicious inputs, especially when evasion techniques are employed. Nguyen-Tuong et al. (2005) and Pietraszek and Berghe (2005) modified PHP interpreter to support taint tracking. The main limitation of their approach is that they require modifications to the PHP runtime environment and database access functions, which may not be viable for other runtime environments such as Java, ASP.NET, or ASP.

The effectiveness of our approach depends on the precision of taint tracking. However, the traces

*Figure 3. Algorithm 1*

---

**Algorithm 1**: Token type conformity SQLIA detection algorithm

---

**Input**: An intercepted SQL statement string $s$

**Output**: A boolean value indicates whether $s$ is malicious or not

$\triangle \leftarrow$ set of tokens in $s$;

**for** every token $t$ in $\triangle$ **do**

   **if** typeOf($t$) $\neq$ string or number literal **and** isTainted(t)  **then**

      **return** true;

   **end if**

**end for**

**return** false;

---

of taint meta-data might be lost due to certain limitations in the tainting implementation. For instance, in Java, string-related classes export character-based functions (e.g., toCharArray) for retrieving internal characters of a string. The taint tracking module is unable to propagate taint meta-data to primitive types unless a modified version of JVM is employed. Thus, the taint information would be lost if an application constructs a new instance of string based on the internal characters of another string. Nevertheless, based on the experimental results and to the best of our knowledge, retrieving internal buffer of a string to construct an SQL statement is a rare case, and it is common coding practice that a programmer should validate any binary data retrieved from an unsafe buffer (Howard & LeBlanc, 2003).

## Conformity to Intention

To protect the integrity of SQL statements, our token type conformity heuristic, and some existing approaches, use pre-defined taint policies, implicitly or explicitly, to specify where in an SQL statement the untrusted data are allowed, and then check at runtime whether an intercepted SQL statement conforms to those policies. Based on the pre-defined taint policies, these approaches employ various mechanisms to track tainted data, and distinguish them in a dynamic query. However,

while these approaches are effective, by using static taint policies and not taking developers' intentions into account, false positives are possible (as we demonstrated in Example.

Instead of using pre-defined taint policies, we take the issue of explicit information-flow one step further, and treat SQLIA as a problem of detecting whether a given SQL query conforms to the original intention of the application developer. Our second heuristic, which we labeled as "conformity to intention", allows discovery of the intended syntactical structure of a dynamic SQL statement at runtime, and performing validation on the SQL statement against the dynamically identified intention. To the best of our knowledge, there is no dynamic SQLIA detection and prevention technique that employs a concept similar to "conformity to intention".

### Intention Statement

Web application developers typically specify the intended syntactical structure of an SQL statement using *placeholders* directly in code. For instance, the following Java code constructs a dynamic SQL statement by embedding parameter values from an HTTP request (each parameter might also pass through a sanitizer function):

**Example 2:** Typical Java code for constructing an SQL statement with the use of an HTTP request object:

```
statement= "SELECT book_name," + re-
quest.getParameter("p1")
+ " FROM " + request.
getParameter("p2")
+ " WHERE book_id='" + request.
getParameter("p3") + "' "
+ request.getParameter("p4");
```

The intended syntactical structure of the SQL statement in the above example can be expressed as shown in code Fragment 1, where an underlined question mark is used to indicate a placeholder:

```
"SELECT book_name,? FROM ? WHERE
book_id=? ? " (1)
```

We refer to such a parameterized SQL statement as an *intention statement*. Our approach relies on per-character taint tracking for deriving intention statements during runtime. When an SQL statement is intercepted, our taint tracker marks every character in a token as tainted when the token contains one or more tainted characters. Our approach constructs an intention statement by replacing each consecutive tainted substring in a dynamically constructed SQL statement with a special meta-character. Thus, when the SQL statement "SELECT book_name,price FROM book WHERE book_id='SQLIA' ORDER BY price" is intercepted, our approach substitutes each tainted substring with the placeholder meta-character (?) to form an intention statement, as shown in code Fragment 1. Note that even when a statement containing an SQLIA, such as "SELECT book_name,price FROM book WHERE book_id='SQLIA' ORDER BY price; UPDATE users SET password=null" is intercepted, the derived intention statement is the same as the one in code Fragment 1.

A placeholder in an intention statement represents an expanding point, where each expansion must conform to the corresponding grammatical rule intended by the developer. We denote a placeholder's corresponding grammar rule as an *intention rule*, which regulates the instantiation of a placeholder at runtime. Each intention rule maps to an existing nonterminal symbol (e.g., SELECT list) or terminal symbol (e.g., string literal or identifier) of a given SQL grammar. The collection of intention rules of an SQL statement serves as the intended syntactical structure, and can be discovered by using an SQL parse tree.

## Intention Tree and Intention Grammar

An intention statement is a string without explicit structure. To identify the intention rules of an intention statement, we use an SQL parse tree. Our approach constructs a parse tree (referred to in this paper as an *intention tree*) from an intention statement to represent the explicit syntactical structure of an intention statement. Figure 5 illustrates an intention tree for the intention statement in Fragment 1, based on the simplified SQL SELECT statement sample grammar shown in Figure 4. The sample grammar consists of a set of production rules, each of the form $\alpha ::= \omega$, where $\alpha$ is a single *nonterminal* symbol, and $\omega$ is any sequence of *terminals* and/or *nonterminals*. In the example from Figure 4, the select_statement is the start symbol. A parse tree represents the sequence of rule invocations used to match an input stream, and can be constructed by deriving an SQL statement from the start symbol of the given SQL grammar. For each grammar rule $\alpha ::= \omega$ matched during the derivation process, the matched rule forms a branch in the parse tree, where $\alpha$ is the parent node, and $\omega$ represents a set of child nodes of $\alpha$. A nonterminal symbol $\beta$ in $\omega$ would be replaced by another grammar rule that matches the nonterminal symbol $\beta$, which in turn forms another branch originated from $\beta$. During construction of an intention tree, the placeholder meta-character represents a special type of token that can match any nonterminal and terminal symbols during derivation. In addition, lookahead on input data corresponding to a placeholder are used to distinguish alternatives. The derivation process continues recursively until all input tokens are exhausted.

In Figure 5, oval boxes represent nonterminal symbols, square boxes are terminal symbols, and dash-lined boxes contain placeholders. In an intention tree, a placeholder is an expanding node. The branch expanded from a placeholder must follow the placeholder's intention rule. Given an intention tree, our approach uses the grammar rule of each placeholder's parent node as the intention rule for each placeholder. For the intention tree depicted in Figure 5, the intention rules of the three placeholders are as follows: (from left to right) two identifier lists (id_list), a string literal (STRING_LIT), and an ORDER BY clause (order_clause), respectively.

In addition to intention rules, the intended structure of a dynamic SQL statement includes constant symbols that are specified by developers at design-time. The intended constant symbols of an SQL statement can be represented by leaf nodes of an intention tree, excluding placeholder nodes. By walking through all leaf nodes of an intention tree, and replacing each placeholder with its intention rule, a new grammar rule can be derived for that specific dynamic SQL statement. We refer to the grammar rule derived from an intention tree as an *intention grammar*. For instance, code Fragment 2 shows the intention grammar derived from the intention tree in Figure 5, where double-quoted strings represent constant terminal symbols (e.g., "SELECT book_name,"), and id_list, STRING_LIT, and order_clause are existing grammar rules.

```
"SELECT book_name" id_list " FROM "
id_list
"WHERE book_id='" STRING_LIT " '" or-
der_clause (2)
```

## Detection of SQLIAs

Once an intention grammar is derived, an SQLIA can be detected by parsing the dynamic SQL statement using its intention grammar. If the dynamic SQL statement can be recognized by its intention grammar, then it is a benign statement; otherwise, it is malicious. For instance, while statements in both code Fragments 3 and 4 yield the same intention grammar (as shown in code Fragment 2), only the statement in Fragment 4 is malicious, as it does not conform to the intention grammar.

```
SELECT book_name,price FROM book
WHERE book_id='SQLIA' ORDER BY price
(3)
SELECT book_name,price FROM book
WHERE book_id='SQLIA'
ORDER BY price; UPDATE user set
password=null (4)
```

Our algorithm for SQLIA detection (Algorithm 2) employs taint tracking and intention grammar derivation. The algorithm takes an SQL statement $s$, the taint information $t$ about $s$, and an SQL grammar $G$ as arguments, and then returns a boolean to indicate whether the tainted SQL statement is malicious or not. The algorithm first constructs an intention statement $s^i$ from an SQL statement $s$ by replacing each consecutive tainted string in $s$ with a meta-character. The algorithm then parses $s^i$ using an SQL grammar $G$ to construct an intention tree Y. Once the intention tree is constructed, the algorithm derives an intention grammar $G^i$ by traversing through the leaf nodes of Y. If $s$ can be parsed by $G^i$, the algorithm returns false; otherwise, it returns true to indicate that the intercepted SQL statement is malicious.

Intention discovery reduces the rate of false positive in the SQL detection logic. However, the intended structure expressed by a developer might allow an SQLIA to pass through. To prevent SQLIAs from a programmer's permissive intention, our "conformity to intention" heuristic

*Figure 4. A simplified SQL SELECT statement grammar written in Backus-Naur Form (BNF).*

```
select_statement ::= ``SELECT'' select_list from_clause [where_clause]
                     [order_clause]
select_list       ::= ``*'' | id_list
id_list           ::= ID | ID ``,'' id_list
from_cause        ::= ``FROM'' id_list
where_clause      ::= ``WHERE'' cond { ( ``AND'' | ``OR'' ) cond }
cond              ::= value OPERATOR value
value             ::= ID | STRING | NUMBER
order_clause      ::= ``ORDER BY'' id_list
```

employ a baseline policy to restrict where in an SQL statement the untrusted data are allowed. In our design, in addition to literal tokens, only identifier tokens (e.g., table name, column name) and order by, group by, and having clauses are permitted to contain tainted data.

As with all existing SQLIA detection techniques that rely on SQL grammar parsing (e.g., SQLGuard, SQLCheck, CANDID), grammatical differences between the detection engine and the back-end database could potentially cause false positives. Nevertheless, for "token type conformity", the SQL lexical analyzer in our approach is required only to be able to distinguish between literals and non-literals. Even though most database vendors develop proprietary SQL dialects (e.g., Microsoft TSQL, Oracle PL-SQL, MySQL)

in addition to supporting standard ANSI SQL, the lexical analyzer required for our approach can simply treat all non-literal tokens equally and disregard the syntactical differences among SQL dialects due to different non-literal tokens supported. For instance, we used SQLPrevent with MySQL without any modification to the SQL lexer, even though the lexer was originally designed for Microsoft SQL Server. For intention discovery, we used ANSI SQL grammar during evaluation. Our implementation of SQLIA detection module can be configured to use different SQL dialects, and we are currently evaluating SQLPrevent with a real-world Web application that uses Oracle as a back-end database.

Due to space limitations, we only summarize the complexity-analysis results of proposed detec-

*Figure 5. The intention tree of the intention statement from Fragment 1. Oval boxes represent nonterminal symbols, square boxes represent terminal symbols, and dash-lined boxes are placeholders. The grammar rules for each placeholder are (from left to right) two id_lists, a STRING_LIT, and an order_clause.*

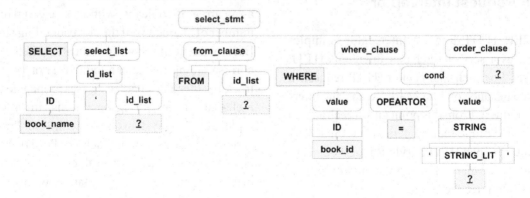

*Figure 6. Algorithm 2*

---
**Algorithm 2**: IsMaliciousSQL
---
> **Input**: SQL statement $s$
> **Input**: $s$ taint information $t$
> **Input**: SQL grammar $G$
> **Output**: A boolean value indicate whether $s$ is malicious or not
> intention statement: $s^i \leftarrow$ construct$(s, t)$;
> intention tree: $Y \leftarrow$ parse$(s^i, G)$;
> intention grammar: $G^i \leftarrow$ derive$(Y)$;
> **if** parse$(s, G^i)$ failed **then**
> > **return** true;
>
> **else**
> > **return** false;
>
> **end if**
---

tion logic here. For Algorithm 1, the computational complexity is $O(N)$, where $N$ is the length of the SQL statement in characters. For Algorithm 2, the computational complexity is the same as the worst-case complexity for constructing a parse tree, which is as follows:

$$\begin{cases} O(N) \cdots if \cdots G \cdots is \quad LALR \\ O(N^2) \cdots if \cdots G \cdots is \, not \, LALR \, but \, det \, er \min istic \\ O(N^3) \cdots if \cdots G \cdots is \, non\text{-}det \, er \min istic \end{cases}$$

## IMPLEMENTATION

In this section, we explain the implementation of SQLPrevent in J2EE, ASP.NET, and ASP. Our description is organized around the SQLPrevent architecture depicted in Figure 2.

## HTTP Request Interceptor

For J2EE, HTTP Request Interceptor is implemented as a servlet filter that intercepts HTTP requests. For each intercepted HTTP request, a separate instance of TaintMark 'wraps' the intercepted request. From this point on, on each access to the value of the request parameter, TaintMark calls the wrapped HTTPServletRequest object to get the value, marks it as tainted and only then returns it to the caller.

## Taint Tracker

The purpose of Taint Tracker is to mark the source of each character as either tainted or not, in an intercepted SQL statement. For J2EE, the Taint Tracker module is implemented as a set of *taint-enabled* classes, one for each string-related system class—such as String, StringBuffer, and StringBuilder. Taint Tracker provides dynamic per-character tracking of taint propagation in J2EE web applications. Each taint-enabled class has exactly the same class name and implements the same interfaces as the corresponding Java class—in fact, they are identical from a Web application point of view. In order to specify the taintness of each character in a string, each taint-enabled class has an additional data structure referred to as taint meta-data, and a set of functions for manipulating this structure. In Taint Tracker for J2EE, taint meta-data is implemented as an array of booleans, with its size equal to the number of characters of the corresponding string. Each element in the array indicates whether the corresponding character is tainted or not. For taint tracking, the taint-enabled classes propagate taint meta-data during string operations. In order to replace existing system classes with Taint Tracker at runtime, a Java Virtual Machine (JVM) needs to be instructed to load taint-enabled classes instead of the original ones. For instance, we used the

-Xbootclasspath/p:<path to taint tracker> option to configure Sun JVM to prepend the taint tracker library in front of the bootstrap class path.

## SQL Interceptor

SQL Interceptor for J2EE extends P6Spy (Martin, Goke, Arvesen, & Quatro, 2003), a JDBC proxy that intercepts and logs SQL statements issued by Web application programming logic before they reach the JDBC driver. JDBC is a standard database access interface for Java, and has been part of Java Standard Edition since the release of SDK 1.1. We have extended P6Spy to invoke the SQLIA Detector when SQL statements are intercepted.

## SQL Lexer, Intention Validator and SQLIA Detector

The SQL Lexer module is implemented as an SQL lexical analyzer. This module converts a sequence of characters into a sequence of tokens based on a set of lexical rules, and determines the type of each token during scanning. SQLIA Detector takes an intercepted SQL statement as input, passes the intercepted SQL statement to the SQL Lexer for tokenization, and then performs detection according to Algorithm 1. When a potential SQLIA is detected, SQLIA Detector passes the intercepted SQL statement to Intention Validator to check whether the query conforms to the intended syntactical structure of the designer, based on Algorithm 2. If an SQLIA is identified, the detector throws a necessary security exception to the Web application, instead of letting the SQL statement through.

## Design Details Specific to ASP and ASP.NET

SQLPrevent was originally implemented in J2EE, and subsequently ported to ASP.NET and ASP in order to assess the degree to which our approach is

generalizable and portable. In addition, we wanted to offer to the community a means of protecting legacy ASP applications. While the implementations of SQL Lexer, Intention Validator, and SQLIA Detector are identical among platforms (except the languages used), the design of HTTP Request Interceptor, Taint Tracker, and SQL Interceptor is specific to each execution environment. In particular, we used .NET profiling API (Pietrek, 2001) and Microsoft Intermediate Language rewriting techniques (Mikunov, 2003) to intercept SQL statements in ASP.NET. For ASP, we utilized a technique known as universal delegator (Brown, 1999) to intercept SQL statements generated from ActiveX Data Object. Due to space limitation, the design details of SQLPrevent for ASP.NET and ASP is presented in (Sun & Beznosov, 2009).

## EVALUATION

We evaluated SQLPrevent using the testbed suite from project AMNESIA (Halfond & Orso, 2005). We chose this testbed because it allowed us to have a common point of reference with other approaches that have used it for evaluation (Halfond & Orso, 2005; Su & Wassermann, 2006; Halfond et al., 2006; Bandhakavi et al., 2007; Sekar, 2009).

### Experimental Setup

The experimental set up is illustrated in Figure 7. The testbed suite consisted of an automatic testing script in Perl and five Web applications (Bookstore, Employee Directory, Classifieds, Events, and Portal), all included in the AMNESIA testbed. Each Web application came with the AT-TACK list of about 3,000 malformed inputs and the LEGIT list of over 600 legitimate inputs. In addition to the original ATTACK list, we produced another set of obfuscated attacks by obscuring the attack inputs that came with AMNESIA using hexadecimal encoding, dropping white space, and inline comments evasion techniques to validate the ability of SQLPrevent to detect obfuscated SQLIAs. To test whether the intention-validator module is capable of performing SQLIA detection without causing false positives, we modified each JSP in the testbed to intentionally include user inputs to form "ORDER BY" clauses in each dynamic SQL statement when an additional HTTP parameter named "orderby" is presented. We then modified the ATTACK and LEGIT lists by appending the additional parameter for each testing trace. To test whether the SQL lexer module is capable of performing lexical analysis in a database-independent way, we configured Microsoft SQL Server and MySQL as back-end databases. SQLPrevent was tested with each of the five applications, and each of the two databases resulting in 10 runs.

## Effectiveness

In our experiments, we subjected SQLPrevent to a total of 3,824 benign and 15,876 malicious HTTP requests. We also obfuscated the requests carrying SQLIAs and tested SQLPrevent against them, which resulted in doubling the number of malicious requests. We then repeated the experiments using an alternative back-end database. In total, we tested SQLPrevent with over 70,000 HTTP requests. None of these requests resulted in SQLPrevent producing a false positive or false negative.

## Efficiency

We measured the performance overhead of SQL-Prevent for two modes of operation: when the Web application receives one request at a time, and when it is accessed concurrently by multiple Web clients. First we describe the experimental setup common to both modes, and then discuss specifics of experiments for each mode and the results.

To make sure the performance measurements were not skewed by hardware, we performed them on both low-end and high-end equipment. For the low-end configuration, the Web applications and databases were installed on a machine with a 1.8 GHz Intel Pentium 4 processor and 512 MB RAM, running Windows XP SP2. The automatic test script was executed on a host with a 350 MHz Pentium II processor and 256 MB of memory, running Windows 2003 SP2. These two machines were connected over a local area network with 100 Mbps Ethernet adapters. Round-trip latency, while pinging the server from the client machine, was less than 1 millisecond on average. For the high-end configuration, the testing script and Web applications were installed on two identical machines, each equipped with eight Intel Xeon 2.33 GHz processors and 8 GB of memory, running Fedora Linux 2.6.24.3. Round-trip latency was less than 0.1 millisecond on average in this configuration.

**Sequential Access is used t**o measure the performance characteristics of SQLPrevent, we used nanosecond API in J2SE 1.5 and employed two sets of evaluation data. The first set was used for measuring *detection overhead*, which is the time delay imposed by SQLPrevent for each benign HTTP request. To calculate detection overhead, we measured the round-trip response time with SQLPrevent for each benign HTTP request, as shown in Figure 8, and applied the following formula: *Detection Overhead* $=(t_r+t_s)/t_b$, where $t_r$ and $t_s$ are the time delays for the request interceptor and SQLIA detector, respectively, and $t_b$ is the round-trip (from A to C in Figure 8) response time when a benign SQL statement is detected.

The second set of data was for measuring *prevention overhead*, which is the overhead imposed by SQLPrevent when a malicious SQL statement is detected and blocked. Prevention overhead shows how fast SQLPrevent can detect and prevent an SQLIA. If either overhead is too high, the system could be vulnerable to denial-of-service attacks that aim for resource over-consumption. To ensure that SQLPrevent would not impose high overhead when blocking SQLIAs,

*Figure 7. Design of the evaluation testbed*

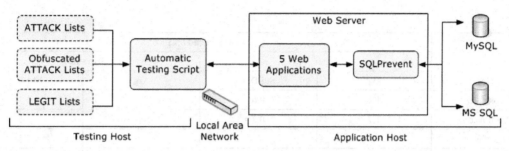

we conducted another performance experiment and used the following formula to

calculate prevention overhead: *Prevention Overhead* $=(t_r+t_s)/t_m$, where $t_r$ and $t_s$ are the time delays for request interceptor and SQLIA detector, respectively, and $t_m$ is the round-trip (from A to B) response time when a malicious SQL statement is detected and blocked.

For each Web application, Table 1 shows the average *detection overhead* and *prevention overhead* each with its corresponding standard deviation. When averaged for the five tested applications, the maximum performance overhead imposed by SQLPrevent was 3.6% (with standard deviation of 1.4%). This overhead was with respect to an average 30 milliseconds response time observed by the Web client.

**Concurrent Access is used t**o test SQLPrevent performance overhead under a high volume of simultaneous accesses, we used JMeter (Apache Software Foundation, 2007), a Web application benchmarking tool from Apache Software Foun-

dation. For each application, we chose one servlet and configured 100 concurrent threads with five loops for each thread. Each thread simulated one Web client. We then measured the average response time with SQLPrevent and applied the *prevention overhead* formula to calculate the overhead. During stress testing, SQLPrevent imposed an average 6.9% (standard deviation 1.3%) performance overhead, with respect to an average of 115 milliseconds response time for all five applications and both databases.

## DISCUSSION

In our evaluation, SQLPrevent produced no false positives or false negatives, and imposed low runtime overhead on the testbed applications. In addition to high detection accuracy and low performance overhead, the advantages of our technique are in its automatic adaptability to

*Figure 8. Detection and prevention performance evaluation. $t_b$ and $t_m$ are round-trip response time with SQLPrevent deployed, measured using benign and malicious requests, respectively*

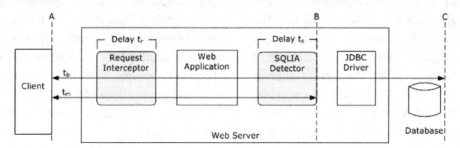

*Table 1. SQLPrevent overheads for cases of benign ("detection") and malicious ("prevention") HTTP requests*

| Subject | Overhead (%) | | | |
|---|---|---|---|---|
| | Detection | | Prevention | |
| | Avg | Std Dev | Avg | Std Dev |
| Bookstore | 1.2 | 0.6 | 3.4 | 1.1 |
| Employee | 1.7 | 0.7 | 4.3 | 1.5 |
| Classifieds | 1.5 | 0.7 | 3.6 | 1.5 |
| Events | 3.3 | 1.4 | 4.2 | 2.3 |
| Portal | 1.9 | 0.9 | 2.5 | 0.5 |
| **Average** | **1.9** | **0.9** | **3.6** | **1.4** |

developer's intentions, and its ease of integration with existing Web applications.

SQLPrevent can be easily integrated with existing Web applications. For instance, in order to protect a J2EE application with SQLPrevent, the administrator needs to (1) deploy the SQLPrevent Java library into the J2EE application server, (2) configure the HTTP Request Interceptor filter entry in the web.xml, (3) replace the class name of the real JDBC driver with the class name of SQL Interceptor in the configuration settings, and (4) configure the JVM to prepend the Taint Tracker library in front of the bootstrap class path. For ASP.NET and ASP, deploying SQLPrevent is a matter of copying and registering the binary components.

We ported SQLIntention to ASP.NET and ASP to assess the generalizability of our approach, and to offer protection for legacy Web applications. Legacy Web applications are natural targets of SQLIAs, since most vulnerabilities are known by attackers, and the resources for prevention and protection required from development or administration might have been re-allocated to other projects. To the best of our knowledge, none of the existing dynamic SQLIA detection techniques have been ported to ASP. The lack of support for ASP is mainly due to the lack of a standard mechanism for intercepting SQL statements in ASP. Furthermore, the ASP runtime environment

cannot be modified. ASP Web applications have been the target of waves of massive SQLIAs from October 2007 to April 2008 (Keizer, 2008). As a consequence of these attacks, more than half a million Web pages have been infected with malicious JavaScript code that redirects the visitors of compromised Web sites to download malware from malicious hosts (Provos, Mavrommatis, Rajab, & Monrose, 2008). Our approach can be integrated into an existing Web application with a few configuration setting changes. Security protection without additional effort from developers and administrators is vital to the protection of legacy Web applications.

The approach proposed in this paper is not a replacement for all other defenses against SQLIAs; it offers an alternative point in the trade-off space. Open-source and some other applications—source code for which can be analyzed and, if necessary, modified by the application owners—make those approaches that employ static analysis and/or alteration of the source code viable. For applications where an additional overhead of 2-5% is unacceptable, static detection and elimination of SQLIA vulnerability identification, or even the use of parameterized query APIs, would be more appropriate. Our approach offers the ability to protect existing applications effectively, efficiently, and without having to depend on application vendors or developers.

The concept of token type conformity and conformity to intention can be applied to other types of Web application security problem such as cross-site scripting (XSS) and remote command injection, for which taintness of tokens can be analyzed and the intended syntactical structures can be dynamically discovered. For instance, a Web application can check whether tainted data is used to construct script elements in the Document Object Model (DOM) of a dynamically generated HTML page to prevent XSS attacks.

## CONCLUSION

SQL injection vulnerabilities are ubiquitous and dangerous, yet many Web applications deployed today are still vulnerable to SQLIAs. Although recent research on SQLIA detection and prevention has successfully addressed the shortcomings of existing SQLIA countermeasures, the possibilities of false positive, the effort needed from Web developers—such as application source code analysis/modification, acquisition of the training traces, or modification of the runtime environment—has limited adoption of these countermeasures in some real world settings. In this paper, we presented a novel approach to runtime SQLIA protection, as well as a tool (SQLPrevent) that implements our approach. Our experience and evaluation of SQLIntention indicate that it is effective, efficient, easy to deploy without the involvement of Web developers, and does not require access to the application source code.

For future work, we plan to apply dynamic intention discovery to prevent other types of Web application attacks, and to port our approach to PHP in order to provide protection to Web applications developed in this popular platform. To obtain more realistic data on the practical possibility of false positives and false negatives, we plan to evaluate SQLPrevent on real-world Web applications, and make SQLPrevent an open source project. We also plan to apply SQLPrevent to dynamic discovery of SQLIA vulnerabilities.

## ACKNOWLEDGMENT

We thank William Halfond and Alex Orso for providing AMNESIA (Halfond & Orso, 2005) testbed applications and sample attacks for use in our evaluation, and Craig Wilson for improving the readability of the paper. Members of the Laboratory for Education and Research in Secure Systems Engineering (LERSSE) supplied valuable feedback on the earlier drafts of this paper. Special thanks go to Kirstie Hawkey and Kasia Muldner for their detailed suggestions on improving this paper.

## REFERENCES

Anley, C. (2002). *Advanced SQL injection in SQL server application* (Tech. Rep., NGSSoftware Insight Security Research). Retrieved from http://www.nextgenss.com/papers/advanced_sql_injection.pdf

Apache Software Foundation. (2007). *Apache JMeter*. Retrieved from http://jakarta.apache.org/jmeter/

AQTRONIX. (2007). *WebKnight*. Retrieved from http://www.aqtronix.com/?PageID=99

Bandhakavi, S., Bisht, P., Madhusudan, P., & Venkatakrishnan, V. N. (2007, October). CANDID: Preventing SQL injection attacks using dynamic candidate evaluations. In *Proceedings of the 14th ACM Conference on Computer and Communications Security (CCS)* (pp. 12–24). Alexandria, Virginia, USA.

Boyd, S. W., & Keromytis, A. D. (2004, June). SQLrand: Preventing SQL injection attacks. In *Proceedings of the second International Conference On Applied Cryptography And Network Security (ACNS)* (pp. 292–302).

Breach Security Inc. (2007). *ModSecurity*. Available from: http://www.modsecurity.org/.

Brown, K. (1999, January). Building a lightweight COM interception framework part 1: The universal delegator. *Microsoft Systems Journal*.

Buehrer, G. T., Weide, B. W., & Sivilotti, P. A. G. (2005, September). SQLGuard: Using parse tree validation to prevent SQL injection attacks. In *Proceedings of the 5th International Workshop on Software Engineering and Middleware* (pp. 106–113). Lisbon, Portugal.

Halfond, W. G., & Orso, A. (2005). AMNESIA: Analysis and monitoring for neutralizing SQL injection attacks. In *Proceedings of the 20th IEEE/ ACM international conference on automated software engineering* (pp. 174–183). Long Beach, CA, USA.

Halfond, W. G., Viegas, J., & Orso, A. (2006). A classification of SQL injection attacks and countermeasures. In *IEEE International Symposium On Secure Software Engineering*.

Halfond, W. G. J., Orso, A., & Manolios, P. (2006). Using positive tainting and syntax-aware evaluation to counter SQL injection attacks. In *Proceedings of the 14th ACM SIGSOFT International Symposium on Foundations of Software Engineering* (pp. 175–185). Portland, Oregon, USA.

Howard, M., & LeBlanc, D. (2003). *Writing secure code* (2nd Ed.). Redmond, Washington: Microsoft Press.

Huang, Y.-W., Yu, F., Hang, C., Tsai, C.-H., Lee, D. T., & Kuo, S.-Y. (2004). Securing Web application code by static analysis and runtime protection. In *Proceedings of the 13th International Conference on World Wide Web* (pp. 40–52).

Jovanovic, N., Kruegel, C., & Kirda, E. (2006, May). Pixy: A static analysis tool for detecting Web application vulnerabilities (short paper). In *Proceedings of the 2006 IEEE Symposium on Security and Privacy*.

Julisch, K., & Darcier, M. (2002). Mining intrusion detection alarms for actionable knowledge. In *Proceedings of the 8th ACM International Conference on Knowledge Discovery and Data Mining* (pp. 366-375).

Keizer, G. (2008, April). Huge Web hack attack infects 500,000 pages. *Computerworld*. Retrieved from http://www.computerworld.com/action/ article.do?command=viewArticleBasic &articleId=9080580

Livshits, V. B., & Lam, M. S. (2005, August). Finding security vulnerabilities in Java applications with static analysis. In *Proceedings of the 14th USENIX Security Symposium* (pp. 271-286).

Maor, O., & Shulman, A. (2005). *SQL injection signatures evasion*. Retrieved from http://www. imperva.com/application_defense_center/white_ papers/ sql_injection_signatures_evasion.html.

Martin, A., Goke, J., Arvesen, A., & Quatro, F. (2003). *P6Spy open source software*. Retrieved from http://www.p6spy.com/

Mikunov, A. (2003, September). Rewrite MSIL code on the fly with the. NET framework profiling API. *Microsoft MSDN Magazine*. Retrieved from http://msdn.microsoft.com/en-us/magazine/ cc188743.aspx

Nguyen-Tuong, A., Guarnieri, S., Greene, D., Shirley, J., & Evans, D. (2005, May 30-June 1). Automatically hardening Web applications using precise tainting. In *Proceedings of the 20th IFIP International Information Security Conference*, Chiba, Japan (pp. 296-307).

OWASP. (2008). *Open Web application security project (OWASP) top ten project*. Retrieved from http://www.owasp.org/index.php/ Category:OWASP_Top_Ten_Project

Pietraszek, T., & Berghe, C. V. (2005). Defending against injection attacks through context-sensitive string evaluation. In *Proceedings of the 8th International Symposium on Recent Advances in Intrusion Detection* (pp. 124-145).

Pietrek, M. (2001, December). The .NET profiling API and the DNProfiler tool. *Microsoft MSDN Magazine*. Retrieved from http://msdn.microsoft.com/en-us/magazine/cc301725.aspx

Provos, N., Mavrommatis, P., Rajab, M. A., & Monrose, F. (2008, June 22-27). *All your iFRAMEs point to us*. Paper presented at the 17th USENIX Security Symposium, Boston.

Scott, D., & Sharp, R. (2002, May). Abstracting application-level Web security. In *Proceedings of the 11th International Conference on the World Wide Web*, Honolulu, Hawaii (pp. 396-407).

Sekar, R. (2009, February 8-11). *An efficient black-box technique for defeating Web application attacks*. Paper presented at the 16th Annual Network and Distributed System Security Symposium NDSS'09, San Diego, CA.

Su, Z., & Wassermann, G. (2006, January). The essence of command injection attacks in Web applications. In *Proceedings of the 33rd Annual ACM SIGPLAN - SIGACT Symposium on Principles of Programming Languages*, Charleston, SC (pp. 372-382).

Sun, S.-T., & Beznosov, K. (2009, March 30). *SQLPrevent: Effective dynamic detection and prevention of SQL injection* (Tech. Rep. No. LERSSE-TR-2009-032). Vancouver, British Columbia, Canada: Laboratory for Education and Research in Secure Systems Engineering, University of British Columbia. Retrieved from http://lersse-dl.ece.ubc.ca

Valeur, F., Mutz, D., & Vigna, G. (2005). A learning-based approach to the detection of SQL attacks. In *Proceedings of the Conference on Detection of Intrusions and Malware & Vulnerability Assessment (DIMVA 2005)* (pp. 123-140).

Wall, L. (2007). *perlsec - perl security* (Library No. v.5.10). Retrieved from http://perldoc.perl.org/perlsec.html

Werlinger, R., Hawkey, K., Muldner, K., Jaferian, P., & Beznosov, K. (2008, July 23-25). The challenges of using an intrusion detection system: Is it worth the effort? In *Proceedings of the 4th Symposium on Usable Privacy and Security (SOUPS)*, Pittsburgh, PA (pp. 107-116).

Xie, Y., & Aiken, A. (2006, August). Static detection of security vulnerabilities in scripting languages. In *Proceedings of the 15th USENIX Security Symposium* (pp. 179-192).

Zetter, K. (2009, March 24). 'The analyzer' hack probe widens; $10 million allegedly stolen from U.S. banks. *Wired Magazine*. Retrieved from http://blog.wired.com/27bstroke6/2009/03/the-analyzer-ha.html

*This work was previously published in International Journal of Secure Software Engineering, edited by Khaled M. Khan, pp. 20-40, Volume 1, Issue 1, copyright 2010 by IGI Publishing (an imprint of IGI Global).*

# Chapter 11
# Improving Memory Management Security for C and C++

**Yves Younan**
*Katholieke Universiteit Leuven, Belgium*

**Wouter Joosen**
*Katholieke Universiteit Leuven, Belgium*

**Frank Piessens**
*Katholieke Universiteit Leuven, Belgium*

**Hans Van den Eynden**
*Katholieke Universiteit Leuven, Belgium*

## ABSTRACT

*Memory managers are an important part of modern language and are used to dynamically allocate memory. Many managers exist; however, two major types can be identified: manual memory allocators and garbage collectors. In the case of manual memory allocators, the programmer must manually release memory back to the system when it is no longer needed. Problems can occur when a programmer forgets to release it, releases it twice or uses freed memory. These problems are solved in garbage collectors. However, both manual memory allocators and garbage collectors store management information. This paper describes several vulnerabilities for C and C++ and how these could be remedied by modifying the management information of a representative manual memory allocator and garbage collector. Additionally, the authors present an approach that, when applied to memory managers, will protect against these attack vectors.*

## INTRODUCTION

Security has become an important concern for all computer users. Worms and hackers are a part of everyday internet life. A particularly dangerous attack is the code injection attack, where attackers are able to insert code into the program's address space and can subsequently execute it. Programs written in C are particularly vulnerable to such attacks. Attackers can use a range of vulnerabilities to inject code. The most well known and most exploited is of course the standard buffer overflow: attackers write past the boundaries of a stack-based buffer and overwrite the return address of a func-

DOI: 10.4018/978-1-4666-1580-9.ch011

tion and point it to their injected code. When the function subsequently returns, the code injected by the attackers is executed (Aleph One, 1996).

These are not the only kind of code injection attacks though: a buffer overflow can also exist on the heap, allowing an attacker to overwrite heap-stored data. As pointers are not always available in normal heap-allocated memory, attackers often overwrite the management information that the memory manager relies upon to function correctly. A double free vulnerability, where a particular part of heap-allocated memory is de-allocated twice could also be used by an attacker to inject code.

Many countermeasures have been devised that try to prevent code injection attacks (Younan, Joosen, & Piessens, 2004). However most have focused on preventing stack-based buffer overflows and only few have concentrated on protecting the heap or memory allocators from attack.

In this paper we evaluate a commonly used memory allocator and a garbage collector for C and C++ with respect to their resilience against code injection attacks and present a significant improvement for memory managers in order to increase robustness against code injection attacks. Our prototype implementation (which we call *dnmalloc*) comes at a very modest cost in both performance and memory usage overhead.

This paper is an extended version of work described in (Younan, Joosen, & Piessens, 2006) which was presented in December 2006 at the Eighth International Conference on Information and Communication Security. The paper is structured as follows: section explains which vulnerabilities can exist for heap-allocated memory. Section describes how both a popular memory allocator and a garbage collector can be exploited by an attacker using one of the vulnerabilities of section to perform code injection attacks. Section describes our new more robust approach to handling the management information associated with chunks of memory. Section contains the results of tests in which we compare our memory allocator

to the original allocator in terms of performance overhead and memory usage. In section related work in improving security for memory allocators is discussed. Finally, section discusses possible future enhancements and presents our conclusion.

## HEAP-BASED VULNERABILITIES FOR CODE INJECTION ATTACKS

There are a number of vulnerabilities that occur frequently and as such have become a favorite for attackers to use to perform code injection. We will examine how different memory allocators might be misused by using one of three common vulnerabilities: "heap-based buffer overflows", "off by one errors" and "dangling pointer references". In this section we will describe what these vulnerabilities are and how they could lead to a code injection attack.

### Heap-Based Buffer Overflow

Heap memory is dynamically allocated at run-time by the application. Buffer overflow, which are usually exploited on the stack, are also possible in this kind of memory. Exploitation of such heap-based buffer overflows usually relies on finding either function pointers or by performing an indirect pointer attack (Bulba & Kil3r, 2000) on data pointers in this memory area. However, these pointers are not always present in the data stored by the program in this memory. As such, most attackers overwrite the memory management information that the memory allocator stores in or around memory chunks it manages. By modifying this information, attackers can perform an indirect pointer overwrite. This allows attackers to overwrite arbitrary memory locations, which could lead to a code injection attack (anonymous, 2001; Younan, 2003). In the following sections we will describe how an attacker could use specific memory managers to perform this kind of attack.

## Off by One Errors

An off by one error is a special case of the buffer overflow. When an off by one occurs, the adjacent memory location is overwritten by exactly one byte. This often happens when a programmer loops through an array but typically ends at the array's size rather than stopping at the preceding element (because arrays start at 0). In some cases these errors can also be exploitable by an attacker (anonymous, 2001; Younan, 2003). A more generally exploitable version of the off by one for memory allocators is an off by five, while these do not occur as often in the wild, they demonstrate that it is possible to cause a code injection attack when little memory is available. These errors are usually only exploitable on little endian machines because the least significant byte of an integer is stored before the most significant byte in memory.

## Dangling Pointer References

Dangling pointers are pointers to memory locations that are no longer allocated. In most cases dereferencing a dangling pointer will lead to a program crash. However in heap memory, it could also lead to a double free vulnerability, where a memory location is freed twice. Such a double free vulnerability could be misused by an attacker to modify the management information associated with a memory chunk and as a result could lead to a code injection attack (Dobrovitski, 2003). This kind of vulnerability is not present in all memory managers, as some will check if a chunk is free or not before freeing it a second time. It may also be possible to write to memory which has already been reused, while the program think it is still writing to the original object. This can also lead to vulnerabilities. These last kind of vulnerabilities are, however, much harder to exploit in general programs than a double free. The possibility of exploiting these vulnerabilities will most likely rely on the way the program uses the memory rather than by using the memory manager to the attacker's advantage.

In the following sections we will describe a specific memory allocator could be exploited using dangling pointer references and more specifically, double free vulnerabilities. More information about these attacks can be found in (Dobrovitski, 2003; Younan, 2003; Younan, Joosen, Piessens, & Eynden, 2005).

## MEMORY MANAGERS

In this section we will examine a representative memory allocator and a garbage collector for C and C++. We have chosen Doug Lea's memory allocator on which the Linux memory allocator is based, because this allocator is in wide use and illustrates typical vulnerabilities that are encountered in other memory allocators. A discussion of how other memory allocators can be exploited by attackers can be found in (Younan et al., 2005). Boehm's garbage collector was chosen to determine whether a representative garbage collecting memory manager for C/C++ would be more resilient against attack.

We will describe how these memory managers work in normal circumstances and then will explain how a heap-vulnerability that can overwrite the management information of these memory managers could be used by an attacker to cause a code injection attack. We will use the same structure to describe both memory managers: first we describe how the manager works and afterwards we examine if and how an attacker could exploit it to perform code injection attacks (given one of the aforementioned vulnerabilities exists).

## Doug Lea's Memory Allocator

Doug Lea's memory allocator (Lea & Gloger, n.d.) (commonly referred to as *dlmalloc*) was designed as a general-purpose memory allocator that could be used by any kind of program. *Dlmalloc* is used as the basis for *ptmalloc* (Gloger, n.d.), which is the allocator used in the GNU/Linux operating system. *Ptmalloc* mainly differs from dlmalloc in that it offers better support for multithreading, however this has no direct impact on the way an attacker can abuse the memory allocator's management information to perform code injection attacks. The description of *dlmalloc* in this section is based on version 2.7.2.

## Description

The memory allocator divides the heap memory at its disposal into contiguous chunks[1], which vary in size as the various allocation routines (*malloc, free, realloc, ...*) are called. An invariant is that a free chunk never borders another free chunk when one of these routines has completed: if two free chunks had bordered, they would have been coalesced into one larger free chunk. These free chunks are kept in a doubly linked list, sorted by size. When the memory allocator at a later time requests a chunk of the same size as one of these free chunks, the first chunk of appropriate size will be removed from the list and made available for use in the program (i.e., it will turn into an allocated chunk).

## Chunk Structure

Memory management information associated with a chunk is stored in-band. Figure 1 illustrates what a heap of used and unused chunks could look like. *Chunk1* is an allocated chunk containing information about the size of the chunk stored before it and its own size[2]. The rest of the chunk is available for the program to write data in. *Chunk3* is a free chunk that is allocated adjacent to *chunk1*. *Chunk2* and *chunk4* are free chunks located in arbitrary locations on the heap.

*Chunk3* is located in a doubly linked list together with *chunk2* and *chunk4*. *Chunk2* is the first chunk in the chain: its forward pointer points to *chunk3* and its backward pointer points to a previous chunk in the list. *Chunk3*'s forward pointer points to *chunk4* and its backward pointer points to *chunk2*. *Chunk4* is the last chunk in our example: its forward pointer points to a next chunk in the list and its backward pointer points to *chunk3*.

- **Exploitation:** Dlmalloc is vulnerable to all three of the previously described vulnerabilities (Anonymous, 2001; Kaempf, 2001; Solar Designer, 2000; Dobrovitski, 2003). Here we will describe how these vulnerabilities may lead to a code injection attack.

*Figure 1. Heap containing used and free chunks*

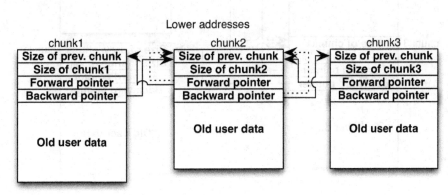

## Overwriting Memory Management Information

Figure 2 shows what could happen if an array that is located in *chunk1* is overflowed: an attacker has overwritten the management information of *chunk3*. The size fields are left unchanged (although these could be modified if needed). The forward pointer has been changed to point to 12 bytes before the return address and the backward pointer has been changed to point to code that will jump over the next few bytes. When *chunk1* is subsequently freed, it will be coalesced together with *chunk3* into a larger chunk. As *chunk3* will no longer be a separate chunk after the coalescing it must first be removed from the list of free chunks.

The *unlink* macro takes care of this: internally a free chunk is represented by a struct containing the following unsigned long integer fields (in this order): *prev_size*, *size*, *fd* and *bk*. A chunk is unlinked as follows:

```
chunk2->fd->bk = chunk2->bk
chunk2->bk->fd = chunk2->fd
```

Which is the same as (based on the struct used to represent malloc chunks):

```
*(chunk2->fd+12) = chunk2->bk
*(chunk2->bk+8) = chunk2->fd
```

As a result, the value of the memory location that is twelve bytes after the location that *fd* points to will be overwritten with the value of *bk*, and the value of the memory location eight bytes after the location that *bk* points to will be overwritten with the value of *fd*. So in the example in Figure 2, the return address would be overwritten with a pointer to injected code. However, since the eight bytes after the memory that *bk* points to will be overwritten with a pointer to *fd* (illustrated as dummy in Figure 2), the attacker needs to insert code to jump over the first twelve bytes into the

*Figure 2. Heap-based buffer overflow in dlmalloc*

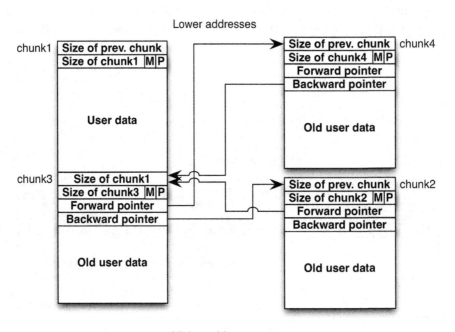

first eight bytes of his injected code. Using this technique an attacker could overwrite arbitrary memory locations (anonymous, 2001; Kaempf, 2001; Solar Designer, 2000).

## Off by One Error

An off by one error could also be exploited in the Doug Lea's memory allocator (anonymous, 2001). If the chunk is located immediately next to the next chunk (i.e., not padded to be a multiple of eight), then an off by one can be exploited: if the chunk is in use, the prev_size field of the next chunk will be used for data and by writing a single byte out of the bounds of the chunk, the least significant byte of the size field of the next chunk will be overwritten. As the least significant byte contains the prev_inuse bit, the attacker can make the allocator think the chunk is free and will coalesce it when the second chunk is freed. Figure 3 depicts the exploit: the attacker creates a fake chunk in the *chunk1* and sets the prev_size field accordingly and overwrites the least significant byte of *chunk2*'s size field to mark the current chunk as free. The same technique using the forward and backward pointers (in the fake chunk) that was used in section can now be used to overwrite arbitrary memory locations.

## Double Free

Dlmalloc can be used for a code injection attack if a double free exists in the program (Dobrovitski, 2003). Figure 4 illustrates what happens when a double free occurs. The full lines in this figure are an example of what the list of free chunks of memory might look like when using this allocator.

*Chunk1* is larger than *chunk2* and *chunk3* (which are both the same size), meaning that *chunk2* is the first chunk in the list of free chunks of equal size. When a new chunk of the same size as *chunk2* is freed, it is placed at the beginning of this list of chunks of the same size by modifying the backward pointer of *chunk1* and the forward pointer of *chunk2*.

*Figure 3. Off by one error in dlmalloc*

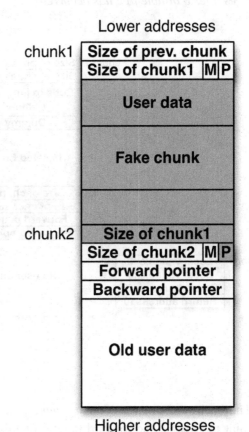

When a chunk is freed twice it will overwrite the forward and backward pointers and could allow an attacker to overwrite arbitrary memory locations at some later point in the program. As mentioned in the previous section: if a new chunk of the same size as *chunk2* is freed it will be placed before *chunk2* in the list. The following pseudo code demonstrates this (modified from the original version found in dlmalloc):

```
BK = front_of_list_of_same_size_
chunks
FD = BK->FD
new_chunk->bk = BK
new_chunk->fd = FD
FD->bk = BK->fd = new_chunk
```

*Figure 4. List of free chunks in dlmalloc: full lines show a normal list of chunks, dotted lines show the changes after a double free has occurred*

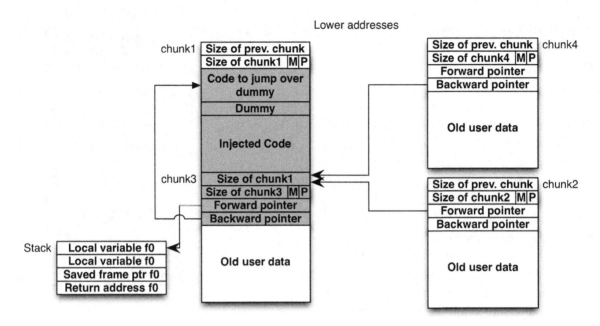

The backward pointer of *new_chunk* is set to point to *chunk2*, the forward pointer of this backward pointer (i.e., chunk2->fd = chunk1) will be set as the forward pointer for *new_chunk*. The backward pointer of the forward pointer (i.e., chunk1->bk) will be set to *new_chunk* and the forward pointer of the backward pointer (chunk2->fd) will be set to *new_chunk*.

If chunk2 would be freed twice in succession, the following would happen (substitutions made on the code listed above):

```
BK = chunk2
FD = chunk2->fd
chunk2->bk = chunk2
chunk2->fd = chunk2->fd
chunk2->fd->bk = chunk2->fd = chunk2
```

The forward and backward pointers of *chunk2* both point to itself. The dotted lines in Figure 4 illustrate what the list of free chunks looks like after a second free of *chunk2*.

```
chunk2->fd->bk = chunk2->bk
chunk2->bk->fd = chunk2->fd
```

But since both chunk2->fd and chunk2->bk point to *chunk2*, it will again point to itself and will not really be unlinked. However the allocator assumes it has and the program is now free to use the user data part (everything below 'size of chunk' in Figure 4) of the chunk for its own use.

Attackers can now use the same technique that we previously discussed to exploit the heap-based overflow (see Figure 2): they set the forward pointer to point 12 bytes before the return address and change the value of the backward pointer to point to code that will jump over the bytes that will be overwritten. When the program tries to allocate a chunk of the same size again, it will again try to unlink *chunk2*, which will overwrite the return address with the value of *chunk2's* backward pointer.

## Boehm Garbage Collector

The Boehm garbage collector (Boehm & Weiser, 1988; Boehm, n.d.) is a conservative garbage collector [3] for C and C++ that can be used instead of *malloc* or *new*. Programmers can request memory without having to explicitly free it when they no longer need it. The garbage collector will automatically release memory to the system when it is no longer needed. If the programmer does not interfere with memory that is managed by the garbage collector (explicit de-allocation is still possible), dangling pointer references are made impossible.

- **Description:** Memory is allocated by the programmer by a call to *GC_malloc* with a request for a number of bytes to allocate. The programmer can also explicitly free memory using *GC_free* or can resize the chunk by using *GC_realloc*, these two calls could however lead to dangling pointer references.

## Memory Structure

The collector makes a difference between large and small chunks. Large chunks are larger than half of the value of HBLKSIZE[4]. These large chunks are rounded up to the next multiple of HBLKSIZE and allocated. When a small chunk is requested and none are free, the allocator will request HBLKSIZE memory from the system and divide it in small chunks of the requested size.

There is no special structure for an allocated chunk, it only contains data. A free chunk contains a pointer at the beginning of the chunk that points to the next free chunk to form a linked list of free chunks of a particular size.

## Collection Modes

The garbage collector has two modes: incremental and non-incremental modes. In incremental mode, the heap will be increased in size whenever insufficient space is available to fulfill an allocation request. Garbage collection only starts when a certain threshold of heap size is reached. In non-incremental mode whenever a memory allocation would fail without resizing the heap the garbage collector decides (based on a threshold value) whether or not to start collecting.

## Collection

Collection is done using a mark and sweep algorithm. This algorithm works in three steps. First all objects are marked as being unreachable (i.e., candidates to be freed). The allocator then starts at the roots (registers, stack, static data) and iterates over every pointer that is reachable starting from one of these objects. When an object is reachable it is marked accordingly. Afterwards the removal phase starts: large unreachable chunks are placed in a linked list and large adjacent chunks are coalesced. Pages containing small chunks are also examined: if all of the chunks on the page are unreachable, the entire page is placed in the list of large chunks. If it is not free, the small chunks are placed in a linked list of small chunks of the same size.

- **Exploitation:** Although the garbage collector removes vulnerabilities like dangling pointer references, it is still vulnerable to buffer overflows. It is also vulnerable to a double free vulnerability if the programmer explicitly frees memory.

## Overwriting Memory Management Information

During the removal phase, objects are placed in a linked list of free chunks of the same size that is stored at the start of the chunk. If attackers can write out of the boundaries of a chunk, they can overwrite the pointer to the next chunk in the linked list and make it refer to the target memory location. When the allocator tries to reallocate a chunk of the same size it will return the memory location as a chunk and as a result will allow the attacker to overwrite the target memory location.

## Off by Five

The garbage collector will automatically add padding to an object to ensure that the property of C/C++ which allows a pointer to point to one element past an array is recognized as pointing to the object rather than the next. This padding forces an attacker to overwrite the padding (4 bytes on IA32). He can then overwrite the first four bytes of the next chunk with an off by eight attack. If the target memory location is located close to a chunk and only the least significant byte of the pointer needs to be modified then an off by five might suffice.

## Double Free

Dangling pointer references cannot exist if the programmer does not interfere with the garbage collector. However if the programmer explicitly frees memory, a double free can occur and could be exploitable.

Figures 5 and 6 illustrate how this vulnerability can be exploited: *chunk1* was the last chunk freed and was added to the start of the linked list and points to *chunk2*. If *chunk2* is freed a second time it will be placed at the beginning of the list,

but *chunk1* will still point to it. When *chunk2* is subsequently reallocated, it will be writable and still be located in the list of free chunks. The attacker can now modify the pointer and if more chunks of the same size are allocated eventually the chunk to which *chunk2* points will be returned as a valid chunk, allowing the attacker to overwrite arbitrary memory locations.

## SUMMARY

The memory allocator we presented in this section is representative for the many memory allocators that are in common use today. There are many others like the memory allocator used by Windows, the allocator used in the Solaris and IRIX operating systems or the allocator used in FreeBSD that are also vulnerable to similar attacks (Koziol et al., 2004; anonymous, 2001; BBP, 2003).

Very few garbage collectors exist for C and C++, in the previous section we also discussed how a garbage collector can be vulnerable to the same attacks that are often performed on memory allocators.

## A MORE SECURE MEMORY ALLOCATOR

As can be noted from the previous sections many memory managers are vulnerable to code injection attacks if an attacker can modify its management information. In this section we describe a new approach to handling the management information that is more robust against these kind of attacks. This new approach could be applied to the managers discussed above and we also describe a prototype implementation (called *dnmalloc*) where we modified *dlmalloc* to incorporate the changes we described.

*Figure 5. Linked list of free chunks in Boehm's garbage collector*

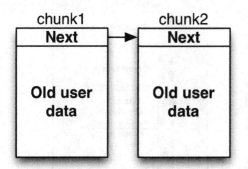

*Figure 6. Double free of chunk2 in Boehm's garbage collector*

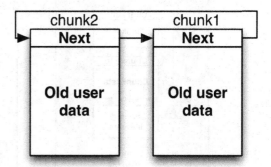

## Countermeasure Design

The main principle used to design this countermeasure is to separate management information (*chunkinfo*) from the data stored by the user (*chunkdata*). This management information is then stored in separate contiguous memory regions that only contain other management information. To protect these regions from being overwritten by overflows in other memory mapped areas, they are protected by guard pages. This simple design essentially makes overwriting the *chunkinfo* by using a heap-based buffer overflow impossible. Figure 7 depicts the typical memory layout of a program that uses a general memory allocator (on the left) and one that uses our modified design (on the right)

Most memory allocators will allocate memory in the datasegment that could be increased (or decreased) as necessary using the *brk* systemcall (Stevens, 1993). However, when larger chunks are requested, it can also allocate memory in the shared memory area [5] using the *mmap* [6] systemcall to allocate memory for the chunk. In Figure 7, we have depicted this behavior: there are chunks allocated in both the heap and in the shared memory area. Note that a program can also map files and devices into this region itself, we have de-

picted this in Figure 7 in the boxes labeled *'Program mapped memory'*.

In this section we describe the structures needed to perform this separation in a memory allocator efficiently. In the next paragraph we describe the structures that are used to retrieve the *chunkinfo* when presented with a pointer to *chunkdata*. In the paragraph that follows the next, we discuss the management of the region where these *chunkinfos* are stored.

- **Lookup table and lookup function:** To perform the separation of the management information from the actual *chunkdata*, we use a *lookup table*. The entries in the *lookup table* contain pointers to the *chunkinfo* for a particular *chunkdata*. When given such a *chunkdata* address, a lookup function is used to find the correct entry in the *lookup table*.

The table is stored in a map of contiguous memory that is big enough to hold the maximum size of the *lookup table*. This map can be large on 32-bit systems, however it will only use virtual address space rather than physical memory. Physical memory will only be allocated by the operating system when the specific page is written

199

*Figure 7. Original (left) and modified (right) process memory layout*

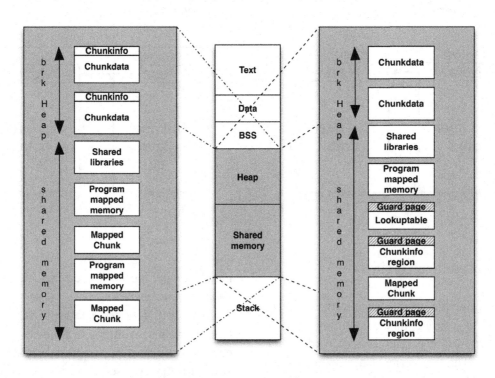

to. To protect this memory from buffer overflows in other memory in the shared memory region, a guard page is placed before it. At the right hand side of Figure 7 we illustrate what the layout looks like in a typical program that uses this design.

- **Chunkinfo regions:** *Chunkinfos* are also stored in a particular contiguous region of memory (called a *chunkinfo region*), which is protected from other memory by a guard page. This region also needs to be managed, several options are available for doing this. We will discuss the advantages and disadvantages of each.

Our preferred design, which is also the one used in our implementation and the one depicted in Figure 7, is to map a region of memory large enough to hold a predetermined amount of *chunkinfos*. To protect its contents, we place a guard page at the top of the region. When the region is full, a new

region, with its own guard page, is mapped and added to a linked list of *chunkinfo regions*. This region then becomes the active region, meaning that all requests for new *chunkinfos* that cannot be satisfied by existing *chunkinfos*, will be allocated in this region. The disadvantage of this technique is that a separate guard page is needed for every *chunkinfo region*, because the allocator or program may have stored data in the same region (as depicted in Figure 7). Although such a guard page does not need actual memory (it will only use virtual memory), setting the correct permissions for it is an expensive system call (requiring the system to perform several time-consuming actions to execute).

When a *chunkdata* disappears, either because the associated memory is released back to the system or because two *chunkdatas* are coalesced into one, the *chunkinfo* is stored in a linked list of free *chunkinfos*. In this design, we have a separate list of free *chunkinfos* for every region. This list is contained in one of the fields of the *chunkinfo* that is unused because it is no longer associated with a *chunkdata*. When a new *chunkinfo* is needed, the allocator returns one of these free *chunkinfos*: it goes over the lists of free *chunkinfos* of all existing *chunkinfo regions* (starting at the currently active region) to attempt to find one. If none can be found, it allocates a new *chunkinfo* from the active region. If all *chunkinfos* for a region have been added to its list of free *chunkinfos*, the entire region is released back to the system.

An alternative design is to map a single *chunkinfo region* into memory large enough to hold a specific amount of *chunkinfos*. When the map is full, it can be extended as needed. The advantage is that there is one large region, and as such, not much management is required on the region, except growing and shrinking it as needed. This also means that we only need a single guard page at the top of the region to protect the entire region. However, a major disadvantage of this technique is that, if the virtual address space behind the region is not free, extension means moving it somewhere else in the address space. While the move operation is not expensive because of the paging system used in modern operating systems, it invalidates the pointers in the *lookup table*. Going over the entire *lookup table* and modifying the pointers is prohibitively expensive. A possible solution to this is to store offsets in the *lookup table* and to calculate the actual address of the *chunkinfo* based on the base address of the *chunkinfo region*.

A third design is to store the *chunkinfo region* directly below the maximum size the stack can grow to (if the stack has such a fixed maximum size), and make the *chunkinfo region* grow down toward the heap. This eliminates the problem of invalidation as well, and does not require extra calculations to find a *chunkinfo*, given an entry in the *lookup table*. To protect this region from being overwritten by data stored on the heap, a guard page has to be placed at the top of the region, and has to be moved every time the region is

extended. A major disadvantage of this technique is that it can be hard to determine the start of the stack region on systems that use address space layout randomization (The PaX Team,). It is also incompatible with programs that do not have a fixed maximum stack size.

These last two designs only need a single, but sorted, list of free *chunkinfos*. When a new *chunkinfo* is needed, it can return, respectively, the lowest or highest address from this list. When the free list reaches a predetermined size, the region can be shrunk and the active *chunkinfos* in the shrunk area are copied to free space in the remaining *chunkinfo region*.

## PROTOTYPE IMPLEMENTATION

*Dnmalloc* was implemented by modifying *dlmalloc 2.7.2* to incorporate the changes described in Section. The ideas used to build this implementation, however, could also be applied to other memory allocators. *Dlmalloc* was chosen because it is very widely used (in its *ptmalloc* incarnation) and is representative for this type of memory allocators. *Dlmalloc* was chosen over *ptmalloc* because it is less complex to modify and because the modifications done to *dlmalloc* to achieve *ptmalloc* do not have a direct impact on the way the memory allocator can be abused by an attacker.

- **Lookup table and lookup function:** The *lookup table* is in fact a lightweight hashtable: to implement it, we divide every page in 256 possible chunks of 16 bytes (the minimum chunk size), which is the maximum amount of chunks that can be stored on a single page in the heap. These 256 possible chunks are then further divided into 32 groups of 8 elements. For every such group we have 1 entry in the *lookup table* that contains a pointer to a linked list of these elements (which has a maximum size of 8 elements). As a result we have a maximum of 32 entries for every page. The *lookup table* is allocated using the memory mapping function, mmap. This allows us to reserve virtual address space for the maximum size that the *lookup table* can become without using physical memory. Whenever a new page in the *lookup table* is accessed, the operating system will allocate physical memory for it.

We find an entry in the table for a particular group from a *chunkdata*'s address in two steps:

1.  We subtract the address of the start of the heap from the *chunkdata*'s address.
2.  Then we shift the resulting value 7 bits to the right. This will give us the entry of the chunk's group in the *lookup table*.

To find the *chunkinfo* associated with a chunk we now have to go over a linked list that contains a maximum of 8 entries and compare the *chunkdata*'s address with the pointer to the *chunkdata* that is stored in the *chunkinfo*. This linked list is stored in the hashnext field of the *chunkinfo* (illustrated in Figure 8).

*   **Chunkinfo:** A *chunkinfo* contains all the information that is available in *dlmalloc*, and adds several extra fields to correctly maintain the state. The layout of a *chunkinfo* is illustrated in Figure 8: the *prev_size*, *size*, *forward* and *backward* pointers serve the same purpose as they do in *dlmalloc*, the *hashnext* field contains the linked list that we mentioned in the previous section and the *chunkdata* field contains a pointer to the actual allocated memory.

*Figure 8. Lookup table and chunkinfo layout*

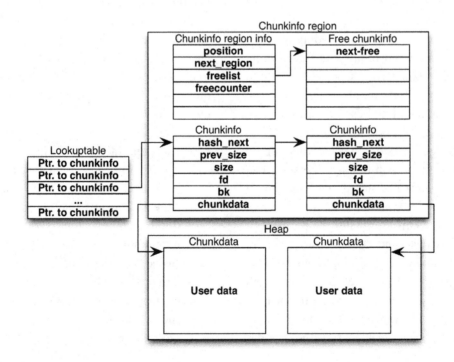

## Managing Chunk Information

The chunk information itself is stored in a fixed map that is big enough to hold a predetermined amount of *chunkinfos*. Before this area a guard page is mapped, to prevent the heap from overflowing into this memory region. Whenever a new *chunkinfo* is needed, we simply allocate the next 24 bytes in the map for the *chunkinfo*. When we run out of space, a new region is mapped together with a guard page.

One *chunkinfo* in the region is used to store the meta-data associated with a region. This metadata (illustrated in Figure 8, by the *chunkinfo region info* structure) contains a pointer to the start of the list of free chunks in the freelist field. It also holds a counter to determine the current amount of free *chunkinfos* in the region. When this number reaches the maximum amount of chunks that can be allocated in the region, it will be deallocated. The *chunkinfo region info* structure also contains a position field that determines where in the region to allocate the next *chunkinfo*. Finally, the next_region field contains a pointer to the next *chunkinfo* region.

## EVALUATION

The realization of these extra modifications comes at a cost: both in terms of performance and in terms of memory overhead. To evaluate how high the performance overhead of *dnmalloc* is compared to the original *dlmalloc*, we ran the full SPEC<<:$^{\textregistered}$:>> CPU2000 Integer reportable benchmark (Henning, 2000), which gives us an idea of the overhead associated with general-purpose programs. We also evaluated the implementation using a suite of allocator-intensive benchmarks, which have been widely used to evaluate the performance of memory managers (Grunwald, Zorn, & Henderson, 1993; Johnstone & Wilson, 1998; Berger, Zorn, & McKinley, 2001, 2002). While these two suites of benchmarks

make up the macrobenchmarks of this section, we also performed microbenchmarks to get a better understanding of which allocator functions are faster or slower when using *dnmalloc*.

Table 1 holds a description of the programs that were used in both the macro- and the microbenchmarks. For all the benchmarked applications we have also included the number of times they call the most important memory allocation functions: *malloc*, *realloc*, *calloc*[7] and *free* (the SPEC<<:$^{\textregistered}$:>> benchmark calls programs multiple times with different inputs for a single run; for these we have taken the average number of calls).

The results of the performance evaluation can be found in Section. Both macrobenchmarks and the microbenchmarks were also used to measure the memory overhead of our prototype implementation compared to *dlmalloc*. In Section we discuss these results. Finally, we also performed an evaluation of the security of *dnmalloc* in Section by running a set of exploits against real world programs using both *dlmalloc* and *dnmalloc*.

*Dnmalloc* and all files needed to reproduce these benchmarks are available publicly (Younan, 2005).

## Performance

This section evaluates our countermeasure in terms of performance overhead. All benchmarks were run on 10 identical machines (Pentium 4 2.80 Ghz, 512MB RAM, no hyperthreading, Redhat 6.2, kernel 2.6.8.1).

*Macrobenchmarks:* To perform these benchmarks, the SPEC<<:$^{\textregistered}$:>> benchmark was run 10 times on these PCs for a total of 100 runs for each allocator. The allocator-intensive benchmarks were run 50 times on the 10 PCs for a total of 500 runs for each allocator.

Table 2 contains the average runtime, including standard error, of the programs in seconds. The results show that the runtime overhead of our allocator are mostly negligible both for general

*Table 1. Programs used in the evaluations of dnmalloc*

| SPEC CPU2000 Integer benchmark programs | | | | | |
|---|---|---|---|---|---|
| Program | Description | malloc | realloc | calloc | free |
| 164.gzip | Data compression utility | 87,241 | 0 | 0 | 87,237 |
| 175.vpr | FPGA placement routing | 53,774 | 9 | 48 | 51,711 |
| 176.gcc | C compiler | 22,056 | 2 | 0 | 18,799 |
| 181.mcf | Network flow solver | 2 | 0 | 3 | 5 |
| 186.crafty | Chess program | 39 | 0 | 0 | 2 |
| 197.parser | Natural language processing | 147 | 0 | 0 | 145 |
| 252.eon | Ray tracing | 1,753 | 0 | 0 | 1,373 |
| 253.perlbmk | Perl | 4,412,493 | 195,074 | 0 | 4,317,092 |
| 254.gap | Computational group theory | 66 | 0 | 1 | 66 |
| 255.vortex | Object Oriented Database | 6 | 0 | 1,540,780 | 1,467,029 |
| 256.bzip2 | Data compression utility | 12 | 0 | 0 | 2 |
| 300.twolf | Place and route simulator | 561,505 | 4 | 13,062 | 492,727 |
| Allocator-intensive benchmarks | | | | | |
| Program | Description | malloc | realloc | calloc | free |
| boxed-sim | Balls-in-box simulator | 3,328,299 | 63 | 0 | 3,312,113 |
| cfrac | Factors numbers | 581,336,282 | 0 | 0 | 581,336,281 |
| espresso | Optimizer for PLAs | 5,084,290 | 59,238 | 0 | 5,084,225 |
| lindsay | Hypercube simulator | 19,257,147 | 0 | 0 | 19,257,147 |

programs as for allocator-intensive programs. However, for *perlbmk* and *cfrac* the performance overhead is slightly higher: 4% and 6%. These show that even for such programs the overhead for the added security is extremely low. In some cases (*vortex* and *twolf*) the allocator even improves performance. This is mainly because of improved locality of management information in our approach: in general all the management information for several chunks will be on the same page, which results in more cache hits (Grunwald et al., 1993). When running the same tests on a similar system with L1 and L2 cache[8] disabled, the performance benefit for *vortex* went down from 10% to 4.5%.

*Microbenchmarks:* We have included two microbenchmarks. In the first microbenchmark, the time that the program takes to perform 100,000 *mallocs* of random[9] chunk sizes ranging between

16 and 4096 bytes was measured. Afterwards the time was measured for the same program to *realloc* these chunks to different random size (also ranging between 16 and 4096 bytes). We then measured how long it took the program to *free* those chunks and finally to *calloc* 100,000 new chunks of random sizes. The second benchmark does essentially the same but also performs a *memset*[10] on the memory it allocates (using *malloc*, *realloc* and *calloc*). The microbenchmarks were each run 100 times on a single PC (the same configuration as was used for the macrobenchmarks) for each allocator.

The average of the results (in seconds) of these benchmarks, including the standard error, for *dlmalloc* and *dnmalloc* can be found in Table 3. Although it may seem from the results of the *loop* program that the *malloc* call has an enormous speed benefit when using *dnmalloc*, this is mainly

*Table 2. Average macrobenchmark runtime results for dlmalloc and dnmalloc*

| SPEC CPU2000 Integer benchmark programs | | | |
|---|---|---|---|
| Program | Dlmalloc r/t (s) | Dnmalloc r/t (s) | R/t overhead |
| 164.gzip | $253 \pm 0$ | $253 \pm 0$ | 0% |
| 175.vpr | $361 \pm 0.15$ | $361.2 \pm 0.14$ | 0.05% |
| 176.gcc | $153.9 \pm 0.05$ | $154.1 \pm 0.04$ | 0.13% |
| 181.mcf | $287.3 \pm 0.07$ | $290.1 \pm 0.07$ | 1% |
| 186.crafty | $253 \pm 0$ | $252.9 \pm 0.03$ | -0.06% |
| 197.parser | $347 \pm 0.01$ | $347 \pm 0.01$ | 0% |
| 252.eon | $770.3 \pm 0.17$ | $782.6 \pm 0.1$ | 1.6% |
| 253.perlbmk | $243.2 \pm 0.04$ | $255 \pm 0.01$ | 4.86% |
| 254.gap | $184.1 \pm 0.03$ | $184 \pm 0$ | -0.04% |
| 255.vortex | $250.2 \pm 0.04$ | $223.6 \pm 0.05$ | -10.61% |
| 256.bzip2 | $361.7 \pm 0.05$ | $363 \pm 0.01$ | 0.35% |
| 300.twolf | $522.9 \pm 0.44$ | $511.9 \pm 0.55$ | -2.11% |
| **Allocator-intensive benchmarks** | | | |
| Program | Dlmalloc r/t (s) | Dnmalloc r/t (s) | R/t overhead |
| boxed-sim | $230.6 \pm 0.08$ | $232.2 \pm 0.12$ | 0.73% |
| cfrac | $552.9 \pm 0.05$ | $587.9 \pm 0.01$ | 6.34% |
| espresso | $60 \pm 0.02$ | $60.3 \pm 0.01$ | 0.52% |
| lindsay | $239.1 \pm 0.02$ | $242.3 \pm 0.02$ | 1.33% |

because our implementation does not access the memory it requests from the system. This means that on systems that use optimistic memory allocation (which is the default behavior on Linux) our allocator will only use memory when the program accesses it.

To measure the actual overhead of our allocator when the memory is accessed by the application, we also performed the same benchmark in the program *loop2*, but in this case always set all bytes in the acquired memory to a specific value. Again there are some caveats in the measured result: while it may seem that the *calloc* function is much faster, in fact it has the same overhead as the *malloc* function followed by a call to *memset* (because *calloc* will call *malloc* and then set all bytes in the memory to 0). However, the place where it is called in the program is of importance here: it was called after a significant amount of

chunks were freed and as a result this call will reuse existing free chunks. Calling *malloc* in this case would have produced similar results.

The main conclusion we can draw from these microbenchmarks is that the performance of our implementation is very close to that of *dlmalloc*: it is faster for some operations, but slower for others.

## Memory Overhead

Our implementation also has an overhead when it comes to memory usage: the original allocator has an overhead of approximately 8 bytes per chunk. Our implementation has an overhead of approximately 24 bytes to store the chunk information and for every 8 chunks, a *lookup table* entry will be used (4 bytes). Depending on whether the chunks that the program uses are large or small, our overhead could be low or high. To test the memory

*Table 3. Average microbenchmark runtime results for dlmalloc and dnmalloc*

| Microbenchmarks | | | |
|---|---|---|---|
| Program | DL r/t | DL r/t | R/t Overh. |
| loop: malloc | 0.28721 ± 0.00108 | 0.06488 ± 0.00007 | -77.41% |
| loop: realloc | 1.99831 ± 0.00055 | 1.4608 ± 0.00135 | -26.9% |
| loop: free | 0.06737 ± 0.00001 | 0.03691 ± 0.00001 | -45.21% |
| loop: calloc | 0.32744 ± 0.00096 | 0.2142 ± 0.00009 | -34.58% |
| loop2: malloc | 0.32283 ± 0.00085 | 0.39401 ± 0.00112 | 22.05% |
| loop2: realloc | 2.11842 ± 0.00076 | 1.26672 ± 0.00105 | -40.2% |
| loop2: free | 0.06754 ± 0.00001 | 0.03719 ± 0.00005 | -44.94% |
| loop2: calloc | 0.36083 ± 0.00111 | 0.1999 ± 0.00004 | -44.6% |

overhead on real world programs, we measured the memory overhead for the benchmarks we used to test performance, the results (in megabytes) can be found in Table 4. They contain the complete overhead of all extra memory the countermeasure uses compared to *dlmalloc*.

In general, the relative memory overhead of our countermeasure is fairly low (generally below 20%), but in some cases the relative overhead can be very high, this is the case for *twolf*, *boxed-sim* and *cfrac*. These applications use many very small chunks, so while the relative overhead may seem high, if we examine the absolute overhead it is fairly low (ranging from 120 KB to 2.8 MB). Applications that use larger chunks have a much smaller relative memory overhead.

## Security Evaluation

In this section we present experimental results when using our memory allocator to protect applications with known vulnerabilities against existing exploits.

Table 5 contains the results of running several exploits against known vulnerabilities when these programs were compiled using *dlmalloc* and *dnmalloc* respectively. When running the exploits against *dlmalloc*, we were able to execute a code injection attack in all cases. However, when attempting to exploit *dnmalloc*, the overflow would write into adjacent chunks, but would not overwrite the management information, as a result, the programs kept running.

These kinds of security evaluations can only prove that a particular attack works, but it cannot disprove that no variation of this attack exists that does work. Because of the fragility of exploits, a simple modification in which an extra field is added to the memory management information for the program would cause many exploits to fail. While this is useful against automated attacks, it does not provide any real protection from a determined attacker. Testing exploits against a security solution can only be used to prove that it can be bypassed. As such, we provide these evaluations to demonstrate how our countermeasure performs when confronted with a real world attack, but we do not make any claims as to how accurately they evaluate the security benefit of *dnmalloc*.

However, the design in itself of the allocator gives strong security guarantees against buffer overflows, since none of the memory management information is stored with user data. We contend that it is impossible to overwrite it using a heap-based buffer overflow. If such an overflow occurs, an attacker will start at a chunk and will be able to overwrite any data that is behind it. Since such an buffer overflow is contiguous, the attacker will not be able to overwrite the manage-

*Table 4. Average memory usage for dlmalloc and dnmalloc*

| SPEC CPU2000 Integer benchmark programs | | | |
|---|---|---|---|
| Program | dlmalloc mem. use (MB) | our mem. use (MB) | Overhead |
| 164.gzip | 180.37 | 180.37 | 0% |
| 175.vpr | 20.07 | 20.82 | 3.7% |
| 176.gcc | 81.02 | 81.14 | 0.16% |
| 181.mcf | 94.92 | 94.92 | 0% |
| 186.crafty | 0.84 | 0.84 | 0.12% |
| 197.parser | 30.08 | 30.08 | 0% |
| 252.eon | 0.33 | 0.34 | 4.23% |
| 253.perlbmk | 53.80 | 63.37 | 17.8% |
| 254.gap | 192.07 | 192.07 | 0% |
| 255.vortex | 60.17 | 63.65 | 5.78% |
| 256.bzip2 | 184.92 | 184.92 | 0% |
| 300.twolf | 3.22 | 5.96 | 84.93% |
| **Allocator-intensive benchmarks** | | | |
| Program | dlmalloc mem. use (MB) | our mem. use (MB) | Overhead |
| boxed-sim | 0.78 | 1.16 | 49.31% |
| cfrac | 2.14 | 3.41 | 59.13% |
| espresso | 5.11 | 5.88 | 15.1% |
| lindsay | 1.52 | 1.57 | 2.86% |
| **Microbenchmarks** | | | |
| loop/loop2 | 213.72 | 217.06 | 1.56% |

ment information. If an attacker is able to write until the management information, it will be protected by the guard page. An attacker could use a pointer stored in heap memory to overwrite the management information, but this would be a fairly useless operation: the management information is only used to be able to modify a more interesting memory location. If attackers already control a pointer they could overwrite the target memory location directly instead of going through an extra level of indirection.

Our approach does not *detect* when a buffer overflow has occurred. It is, however, possible to easily and efficiently add such detection as an extension to dnmalloc. A technique similar to the one used in (Robertson, Kruegel, Mutz, & Valeur, 2003; Krennmair, 2003) could be added to the allocator by placing a random number at the top of

*Table 5. Results of exploits against vulnerable programs protected with dnmalloc*

| Exploit for | Dlmalloc | Dnmalloc |
|---|---|---|
| Wu-ftpd 2.6.1 (Zen-parse,) | Shell | Continues |
| Sudo 1.6.1 (M. M. Kaempf,) | Shell | Crash |
| Sample heap-based buffer overflow | Shell | Continues |
| Sample double free | Shell | Continues |

a chunk (where the old management information used to be) and by mirroring that number in the management information. Before performing any heap operation (i.e., malloc, free, coalesce, etc) on a chunk, the numbers would be compared and if changed, it could report the attempted exploitation of a buffer overflow. This of course only detects overflows which try to exploit the original problem that (Robertson et al., 2003; Krennmair, 2003) and we address: overwriting of the management information. If an overflow overwrites a pointer in another chunk and no heap operations are called, then the overflow will go undetected.

A major advantage of this approach over (Robertson et al., 2003) is that it does not rely on a global secret value, but can use a per-chunk secret value. While this approach would improve detection of possible attacks, it does not constitute the underlying security principle, meaning that the security does not rely on keeping values in memory secret.

Finally, our countermeasure (as well as other existing ones (Free Software Foundation, n.d.; Robertson et al., 2003)) focuses on protecting this memory management information, it does not provide strong protection to pointers stored by the program itself in the heap. There are no efficient mechanisms yet to transparently protect these pointers from modification through all possible kinds of heap-based buffer overflows. In order to achieve reasonable performance, countermeasure designers have focused on protecting the most targeted pointers. Extending the protection to more pointers without incurring a substantial performance penalty remains a challenging topic for future research.

## RELATED WORK

Many countermeasures for code injection attacks exist. In this section, we briefly describe the different approaches that could be applicable to protecting against heap-based buffer overflows,

but will focus more on the countermeasures which are designed specifically to protect memory allocators from heap-based buffer overflows.

## Protection from Attacks on Heap-Based Vulnerabilities

There are two types of allocators that try to detect or prevent heap overflow vulnerabilities: debugging allocators and runtime allocators. Debugging allocators are allocators that are meant to be used by the programmer. They can perform extra checks before using the management information stored in the chunks or ensure that the chunk is allocated in such a way that it will cause an error if it is overflowed or freed twice. Runtime allocators are meant to be used in final programs and try to protect memory allocators by performing light-weight checks to ensure that chunk information has not been modified by an attacker.

- **Debugging memory allocators:** *Dlmalloc* has a debugging mode that will detect modification of the memory management information. When run in debug mode the allocator will check to make sure that the next pointer of the previous chunk equals the current chunk and that the previous pointer of the next chunk equals the current chunk. To exploit a heap overflow or a double free vulnerability, the pointers to the previous chunk and the next chunk must be changed.

Electric fence (Perens,) is a debugging library that will detect both underflows and overflows on heap-allocated memory. It operates by placing each chunk in a separate page and by either placing the chunk at the top of the page and placing a guard page before the chunk (underflow) or by placing the chunk at the end of the page and placing a guard page after the chunk (overflow). This is an effective debugging library but it is not realistic to use in a production environment because of the large amount of memory it uses (every chunk is at least as large as a page, which is 4kb on IA32) and because of the large performance overhead associated with creating a guard page for every chunk. To detect dangling pointer references, it can be set to never release memory back to the system. Instead, Electric fence will mark it as inaccessible, this will however result in an even higher memory overhead.

- **Runtime allocators:** Robertson et al. (2003) designed a countermeasure that attempts to protect against attacks on the dlmalloc library management information. This is done by changing the layout of both allocated and unallocated memory chunks. To protect the management information a checksum and padding (as chunks must be of double word length) is added to every chunk. The checksum is a checksum of the management information encrypted (XOR) with a global read-only random value, to prevent attackers from generating their own checksum. When a chunk is allocated the checksum is added and when it is freed the checksum is verified. Thus if an attacker overwrites this management information with a buffer overflow a subsequent free of this chunk will abort the program because the checksum is invalid. However, this countermeasure can be bypassed if an information leak exists in the program that would allow the attacker to print out the encryption key. The attacker can then modify the chunk information and calculate the correct value of the checksum. The allocator would then be unable to detect that the chunk information has been changed by an attacker.

*Dlmalloc* 2.8.x also contains extra checks to prevent the allocator from writing into memory that lies below the heap (this however does not stop it from writing into memory that lies above the heap, such as the stack). It also offers a slightly modified version of the Robertson countermeasure as a compile-time option.

ContraPolice (Krennmair, 2003) also attempts to protect memory allocated on the heap from buffer overflows that would overwrite memory management information associated with a chunk of allocated memory. It uses the same technique as proposed by StackGuard (Cowan et al., 1998), i.e., canaries, to protect these memory regions. It places a randomly generated canary both before and after the memory region that it protects. Before exiting from a string or memory copying function, a check is done to ensure that, if the destination region was on the heap, the canary stored before the region matches the canary stored after the region. If it does not, the program is aborted. While this does protect the contents of other chunks from being overwritten using one of these functions, it provides no protection for other buffer overflows. It also does not protect a buffer from overwriting a pointer stored in the same chunk. This countermeasure can also be bypassed if the canary value can be read: the attacker could write past the canary and make sure to replace the canary with the same value it held before.

Although no performance measurements were done by the author, it is reasonable to assume that the performance overhead would be fairly low.

Recent versions of glibc (Free Software Foundation,) have added an extra sanity check to its allocator: before removing a chunk from the doubly linked list of free chunks, the allocator checks if the backward pointer of the chunk that the unlinking chunk's forward pointer points to is equal to the unlinking chunk. The same is done for the forward pointer of the chunk's backward pointer. It also adds extra sanity checks that make it harder for an attacker to use the previously described technique of attacking the memory allocator. However, recently, several attacks on this countermeasure were published (Phantasmagoria,). Although no data is available on the performance impact of adding these lightweight checks, it is reasonable to assume that no performance loss is incurred by performing them.

DieHard (Berger & Zorn, 2006) in standalone mode is a memory allocator that will add protection against accidental overflows of buffers by randomizing allocations. The allocator will separate memory management information from the data in the heap. It will also try to protect the contents of a chunk by allocating chunks of a specific chunk size into a region at random positions in the region. This will make it harder for an application to accidentally overwrite the contents of a chunk, however a determined attacker could still exploit it by replicating the modified contents over the entire region. Performance for this countermeasure is very good for some programs (it improves performance for some) while relatively high for others.

## Alternative Approaches

Other approaches that protect against the more general problem of buffer overflows also protect against heap-based buffer overflows. In this section, we give a brief overview of this work. A more extensive survey can be found in (Younan et al., 2004).

- **Safe languages:** Safe languages are languages where it is generally not possible for any known code injection vulnerability to exist as the language constructs prevent them from occurring. A number of safe languages are available that will prevent these kinds of implementation vulnerabilities entirely. Examples of such languages include Java and ML but these are not in the

scope of our discussion. However there are safe languages (Jim et al., 2002; Grossman et al., 2002; Necula, McPeak, & Weimer, 2002; Larus et al., 2004; Dhurjati, Kowshik, Adve, & Lattner, 2003; Kowshik, Dhurjati, & Adve, 2002) that remain as close to C or C++ as possible, these are generally referred to as safe dialects of C. While some safe languages (Condit, Harren, McPeak, Necula, & Weimer, 2003) try to stay more compatible with existing C programs, use of these languages may not always be practical for existing applications.

- **Compiler-based countermeasures:** Bounds checking (Austin, Breach, & Sohi, 1994; Jones & Kelly, 1997; Ruwase & Lam, 2004; Xu, DuVarney, & Sekar, 2004) is the ideal solution for buffer overflows, however performing bounds checking in C can have a severe impact on performance or may cause existing object code to become incompatible with bounds checked object code.

Protection of all pointers as provided by Point-Guard (Cowan, Beattie, Johansen, & Wagle, 2003) is an efficient implementation of a countermeasure that will encrypt (using XOR) all pointers stored in memory with a randomly generated key and decrypts the pointer before loading it into a register. To protect the key, it is stored in a register upon generation and is never stored in memory. However attackers could guess the decryption key if they were able to view several different encrypted pointers. Another attack, described in (Alexander, 2005) describes how an attacker could bypass PointGuard by overwriting a particular byte of the pointer. By modifying one byte, the pointer value has changed but the three remaining bytes will still decrypt correctly because of the weakness of XOR encryption. This significantly reduces the randomness (if only one byte needs to be overwritten, an attacker has a 1 in 256 chance of guessing the correct one, if two bytes are overwritten the chances are 1 in 65536, which is still significantly less than 1 in $2^{32}$.

Another countermeasure that protects all pointers is the Security Enforcement Tool (Yong & Horwitz, 2003) where runtime protection is performed by keeping a status bit for every byte in memory, that determines if writing to a specific memory region via an unsafe pointer is allowed or not.

- **Operating system-based countermeasures:** Non-executable memory (The PaX Team, n.d.; Solar Designer, n.d.) tries to prevent code injection attacks by ensuring that the operating system does not allow execution of code that is not stored in the text segment of the program. This type of countermeasure can however be bypassed by a return-into-libc attack (Wojtczuk, 1998) where an attacker executes existing code (possibly with different parameters).

Randomized instruction sets (Barrantes et al., 2003; Kc, Keromytis, & Prevelakis, 2003) also try to prevent an attacker from executing injected code by encrypting instructions on a per process basis while they are in memory and decrypting them when they are needed for execution. However, software based implementations of this countermeasure incur large performance costs, while a hardware implementation is not immediately practical. Determined attackers may also be able to guess the encryption key and, as such, be able to inject code (Sovarel, Evans, & Paul, 2005).

Address randomization (The PaX Team, n.d.; Bhatkar, DuVarney, & Sekar, 2003) is a technique that attempts to provide security by modifying the locations of objects in memory for different runs of a program, however the randomization is limited in 32-bit systems (usually to 16 bits for the heap) and as a result may be inadequate for a determined attacker (Shacham et al., 2004).

- **Library-based countermeasures:** LibsafePlus (Avijit, Gupta, & Gupta, 2004) protects programs from all types of buffer overflows that occur when using unsafe C library functions (e.g., *strcpy*). It extracts the sizes of the buffers from the debugging information of a program and as such does not require a recompile of the program if the symbols are available. If the symbols are not available, it will fall back to less accurate bounds checking as provided by the original Libsafe (Baratloo, Singh, & Tsai, 2000) (but extended beyond the stack). The performance of the countermeasure ranges from acceptable for most benchmarks provided to very high for one specific program used in the benchmarks.
- **Execution monitoring:** In this section we describe two countermeasures that will monitor the execution of a program and will prevent transferring control-flow which could be unsafe.

Program shepherding (Kiriansky, Bruening, & Amarasinghe, 2002) is a technique that will monitor the execution of a program and will disallow control-flow transfers[11] that are not considered safe. An example of a use for shepherding is to enforce return instructions to only return to the instruction after the call site. The proposed implementation of this countermeasure is done using a runtime binary interpreter, as a result the performance impact of this countermeasure is significant for some programs, but acceptable for others.

Control-flow integrity (Abadi, Budiu, Erlingsson, & Ligatti, 2005) determines a program's control flow graph beforehand and ensures that the program adheres to it. It does this by assigning a unique ID to each possible control flow destination of a control flow transfer. Before transferring control flow to such a destination, the ID of the destination is compared to the expected ID, and if they are equal, the program proceeds as normal. Performance overhead may be acceptable for some applications, but may be prohibitive for others.

## CONCLUSION

In this paper we examined the security of several memory allocators. We discussed how they could be exploited and showed that most memory allocators are vulnerable to code injection attacks.

Afterwards, we presented a redesign for existing memory allocators that is more resilient to these attacks than existing allocator implementations. We implemented this design by modifying an existing memory allocator. This implementation has been made publicly available. We demonstrated that it has a negligible, sometimes even beneficial, impact on performance. The overhead in terms of memory usage is very acceptable. Although our approach is straightforward, surprisingly, it offers stronger security than comparable countermeasures with similar performance overhead because it does not rely on the secrecy of random numbers stored in memory.

## REFERENCES

Abadi, M., Budiu, M., Erlingsson, U., & Ligatti, J. (2005, November). Control-flow integrity. In *Proceedings of the 12th acm conference on computer and communications security*, Alexandria, VA (p. 340-353).

Aleph One. (1996). Smashing the stack for fun and profit. *Phrack, 49.*

Alexander, S. (2005, June). Defeating compiler-level buffer overflow protection. *;login: The USENIX Magazine, 30*(3). anonymous. (2001). Once upon a free. *Phrack, 57.*

Austin, T. M., Breach, S. E., & Sohi, G. S. (1994, June). Efficient detection of all pointer and array access errors. In *Proceedings of the acm sigplan '94 conference on programming language design and implementation*, Orlando, FL (pp. 290-301).

Avijit, K., Gupta, P., & Gupta, D. (2004, August). Tied, libsafeplus: Tools for runtime buffer overflow protection. In *Proceedings of the 13th usenix security symposium,* San Diego, CA.

Baratloo, A., Singh, N., & Tsai, T. (2000, June). Transparent run-time defense against stack smashing attacks. In *Usenix 2000 annual technical conference proceedings*, San Diego, CA (pp. 251-262).

Barrantes, E. G., Ackley, D. H., Forrest, S., Palmer, T. S., Stefanović, D., & Zovi, D. D. (2003, October). Randomized instruction set emulation to disrupt binary code injection attacks. In *Proceedings of the 10th acm conference on computer and communications security (ccs2003)*, Washington, DC (pp. 281-289).

BBP. (2003, May). *BSD heap smashing.* Retrieved from http://www.security-protocols.com/modules.php?name=News&file=article&sid=1586.

Berger, E. D., & Zorn, B. G. (2006, June). Probabilistic memory safety for unsafe languages. In *Acm sigplan 2006 conference on programming language design and implementation (pldi 2006).* Ottawa, Canada: Diehard.

Berger, E. D., Zorn, B. G., & McKinley, K. S. (2001, June). Composing high-performance memory allocators. In *Proceedings of the acm sigplan 2001 conference on programming language design and implementation (pldi)*, Snowbird, UT (pp. 114-124).

Berger, E. D., Zorn, B. G., & McKinley, K. S. (2002, Nov). Reconsidering custom memory allocation. In *Proceedings of the 2002 acm sigplan conference on object-oriented programming systems, languages and applications (oopsla)*, Seattle, WA (pp. 1-12). New York: ACM Press.

Bhatkar, S., DuVarney, D. C., & Sekar, R. (2003, August). Address obfuscation: An efficient approach to combat a broad range of memory error exploits. In *Proceedings of the 12th usenix security symposium*, Washington, DC (pp. 105-120).

Boehm, H. (n. d.). *Conservative gc algroithmic overview*. Retrieved from http://www.hpl.hp.com/personal/Hans_Boehm/gc/gcdescr.html

Boehm, H. (n. d.). *A garbage collector for c and c++*. Retrieved from http://www.hpl.hp.com/personal/Hans_Boehm/gc/

Boehm, H., & Weiser, M. (1988, September). Garbage collection in an uncooperative environment. *Software, Practice & Experience*, *18*(9), 807–820. doi:10.1002/spe.4380180902

Bulba, & Kil3r. (2000). Bypassing Stackguard and stackshield. *Phrack, 56*.

Condit, J., Harren, M., McPeak, S., Necula, G. C., & Weimer, W. (2003). CCured in the real world. In *Proceedings of the acm sigplan 2003 conference on programming language design and implementation*, San Diego, CA (pp. 232-244).

Cowan, C., Beattie, S., Johansen, J., & Wagle, P. (2003, Aug). PointGuard: protecting pointers from buffer overflow vulnerabilities. In *Proceedings of the 12th usenix security symposium*, Washington, DC (pp. 91-104).

Cowan, C., Pu, C., Maier, D., Hinton, H., Walpole, J., & Bakke, P. (1998, January). StackGuard: Automatic adaptive detection and prevention of buffer-overflow attacks. In *Proceedings of the 7th usenix security symposium*, San Antonio, TX (pp. 63-78).

Dhurjati, D., Kowshik, S., Adve, V., & Lattner, C. (2003, June). Memory safety without runtime checks or garbage collection. In *Proceedings of the 2003 acm sigplan conference on language, compiler, and tool support for embedded systems*, San Diego, CA (pp. 69-80).

Dobrovitski, I. (2003, February). *Exploit for CVS double free() for linux pserver*. Retrieved from http://seclists.org/lists/bugtraq/2003/Feb/0042.html

Free Software Foundation. (n. d.). *The gnu c library*. Retrieved from http://http://www.gnu.org/software/libc.

Gloger, W. (n. d.). *ptmalloc*. Retrieved from http://www.malloc.de/en/.

Grossman, D., Morrisett, G., Jim, T., Hicks, M., Wang, Y., & Cheney, J. (2002, June). Region-based memory management in cyclone. In *Proceedings of the 2002 acm sigplan conference on programming language design and implementation*, Berlin (pp. 282-293).

Grunwald, D., Zorn, B., & Henderson, R. (1993, June). Improving the cache locality of memory allocation. In *Proceedings of the acm sigplan 1993 conference on programming language design and implementation (pldi)*, New York (pp. 177-186).

Henning, J. L. (2000, July). Spec cpu2000: Measuring cpu performance in the new millennium. *Computer*, *33*(7), 28–35. doi:10.1109/2.869367

Jim, T., Morrisett, G., Grossman, D., Hicks, M., Cheney, J., & Wang, Y. (2002, June). A safe dialect of C. In *Usenix annual technical conference* (pp. 275–288). Monterey, CA: Cyclone.

Johnstone, M. S., & Wilson, P. R. (1998, Oct). The memory fragmentation problem: Solved? In *Proceedings of the 1st acm sigplan international symposium on memory management*, Vancouver, Canada (pp. 26-36). New York: ACM.

Jones, R. W. M., & Kelly, P. H. J. (1997). Backwards-compatible bounds checking for arrays and pointers in C programs. In *Proceedings of the 3rd international workshop on automatic debugging* (pp. 13-26). Linköping, Sweden: Linköping University Electronic Press.

Kaempf, M. (2001). Vudo - an object superstitiously believed to embody magical powers. *Phrack, 57*.

Kaempf, M. M. (n. d.). *Sudo < 1.6.3p7-2 exploit.* Retrieved from http://packetstormsecurity.org/0211-exploits/hudo.c

Kc, G. S., Keromytis, A. D., & Prevelakis, V. (2003, October). Countering code-injection attacks with instruction-set randomization. In *Proceedings of the 10th acm conference on computer and communications security (ccs2003),* Washington, DC (pp. 272-280).

Kiriansky, V., Bruening, D., & Amarasinghe, S. (2002, August). Secure execution via program shepherding. In *Proceedings of the 11th usenix security symposium*, San Francisco, CA.

Kowshik, S., Dhurjati, D., & Adve, V. (2002, October). Ensuring code safety without runtime checks for real-time control systems. In *Proceedings of the international conference on compilers architecture and synthesis for embedded systems*, Grenoble, France (pp. 288-297). Retrieved from http://llvm.cs.uiuc.edu/pubs/2002-08-08-CAS-ES02-ControlC.html

Koziol, J., Litchfield, D., Aitel, D., Anley, C., Eren, S., & Mehta, N. (2004). *The shellcoder's handbook: Discovering and exploiting security holes.* New York: John Wiley & Sons.

Krennmair, A. (2003, November). *ContraPolice: a libc extension for protecting applications from heap-smashing attacks.* Retrieved from http://www.synflood.at/contrapolice/.

Larus, J. R., Ball, T., Das, M., DeLine, R., Fähndrich, M., & Pincus, J. (2004, May/Jun). Righting software. *IEEE Software, 21*(3), 92–100. doi:10.1109/MS.2004.1293079

Lea, D., & Gloger, W. (n. d.). *malloc-2.7.2.c. Comments in source code.* Retrieved from http://gee.cs.oswego.edu/dl/html/malloc.html

Lea, D., & Gloger, W. (n. d.). *A memory allocator.* Retrieved from http://gee.cs.oswego.edu/dl/html/malloc.html

Necula, G., McPeak, S., & Weimer, W. (2002, January). CCured: Type-safe retrofitting of legacy code. In *Proceedings of the Conference record of popl 2002: The 29th sigplan-sigact symposium on principles of programming languages*, Portland, OR (pp. 128-139).

Perens, B. (n. d.). *Electric fence 2.0.5.* Retrieved from http://perens.com/FreeSoftware/

Phantasmagoria, P. (n. d.). *The malloc maleficarum.* Retrieved from http://lists.grok.org.uk/pipermail/full-disclosure/2005-October/037905.html

Robertson, W., Kruegel, C., Mutz, D., & Valeur, F. (2003, October). Run-time detection of heap-based overflows. In *Proceedings of the 17th large installation systems administrators conference*, San Diego, CA (pp. 51-60).

Ruwase, O., & Lam, M. S. (2004, February). A practical dynamic buffer overflow detector. In *Proceedings of the 11th annual network and distributed system security symposium*, San Diego, CA.

Shacham, H., Page, M., Pfaff, B., Goh, E. J., Modadugu, N., & Boneh, D. (2004, October). On the Effectiveness of Address-Space Randomization. In *Proceedings of the 11th acm conference on computer and communications security*, Washington, DC (p. 298-307). New York: ACM Press.

Solar Designer. (2000, July). *JPEG COM marker processing vulnerability in netscape browsers.* Retrieved from http://www.openwall.com/advisories/OW-002-netscape-jpeg.txt.

Solar Designer. (n. d.). *Non-executable stack patch.* Retrieved from http://www.openwall.com

Sovarel, N., Evans, D., & Paul, N. (2005, August). Where's the FEEB? the effectiveness of instruction set randomization. In *Proceedings of the 14th usenix security symposium*, Baltimore, MD.

Stevens, W. R. (1993). *Advanced programming in the unix enironment*. Reading, MA: Addison-Wesley.

The PaX Team. (n. d.). *Documentation for the PaX project*. Retrieved from http://pageexec.virtualave.net/docs/

van der Pas, R. (2002, November). *Memory hierarchy in cache-based systems* (Tech. Rep. No. 817-0742-10). Santa Clara, CA: Sun Microsystems.

Wojtczuk, R. (1998). *Defeating Solar Designer's Non-executable Stack Patch*. Retrieved from http://www.insecure.org/sploits/non-executable.stack.problems.html

Xu, W., DuVarney, D. C., & Sekar, R. (2004, October-November). An Efficient and Backwards-Compatible Transformation to Ensure Memory Safety of C Programs. In *Proceedings of the 12th acm sigsoft international symposium on foundations of software engineering*, Newport Beach, CA (pp. 117-126). New York: ACM Press.

Yong, S. H., & Horwitz, S. (2003, September). Protecting C programs from attacks via invalid pointer dereferences. In *Proceedings of the 9th european software engineering conference held jointly with 10th acm sigsoft international symposium on foundations of software engineering* (pp. 307-316). New York: ACM Press.

Younan, Y. (2003). *An overview of common programming security vulnerabilities and possible solutions*. Unpublished master's thesis, Vrije Universiteit Brussel.

Younan, Y. (2005). *Dnmalloc 1.0*. Retrieved from http://www.fort-knox.org

Younan, Y., Joosen, W., & Piessens, F. (2004, July). *Code injection in C and C++: A survey of vulnerabilities and countermeasures* (Tech. Rep. No. CW386). Leuven, Belgium: Departement Computerwetenschappen, Katholieke Universiteit Leuven.

Younan, Y., Joosen, W., & Piessens, F. (2006, December). Efficient protection against heap-based buffer overflows without resorting to magic. In *Proceedings of the international conference on information and communication security (icics 2006)*, Raleigh, NC.

Younan, Y., Joosen, W., Piessens, F., & den Eynden, H. V. (2005, July). *Security of memory allocators for C and C++* (Tech. Rep. No. CW419). Leuven, Belgium: Departement Computerwetenschappen, Katholieke Universiteit Leuven.

Zen-parse. (n. d.). *Wu-ftpd 2.6.1 exploit*. Retrieved from http://www.derkeiler.com/Mailing-Lists/securityfocus/vuln-dev/2001-12/0160.html

## ENDNOTES

[1] A chunk is a block of memory that is allocated by the allocator, it can be larger than what a programmer requested because it usually reserves space for management information.

[2] The size of allocated chunks is always a multiple of eight, so the three least significant bits of the size field are used for management information: a bit to indicate if the previous chunk is in use (P) or not and one to indicate if the memory is mapped or not (M). The third bit is currently unused. The "previous chunk in use"-bit can be modified by an attacker to force coalescing of chunks. How this coalescing can be abused is explained later.

3   A conservative collector assumes that each memory location is a pointer to another object if it contains a value that is equal to the address of an allocated chunk of memory. This can result in false negatives where some memory is incorrectly identified as still being allocated.

4   HBLKSIZE is equal to page size on IA32.

5   Note that memory in this area is not necessarily shared among applications, it has been allocated by using *mmap*

6   mmap is used to map files or devices into memory. However, when passing it the *MAP_ANON* flag or mapping the */dev/zero* file, it can be used to allocate a specific region of contiguous memory for use by the application (however, the granularity is restricted to page size) (Stevens, 1993).

7   This memory allocator call will allocate memory and will then clear it by ensuring that all memory is set to 0

8   These are caches that are faster than the actual memory in a computer and are used to reduce the cost of accessing general memory (Pas, 2002).

9   Although a fixed seed was set so two runs of the program return the same results

10   This call will fill a particular range in memory with a particular byte.

11   Such a control flow transfer occurs when e.g. a *call* or *ret* instruction is executed.

*This work was previously published in International Journal of Secure Software Engineering, edited by Khaled M. Khan, pp. 57-82, Volume 1, Issue 2, copyright 2010 by IGI Publishing (an imprint of IGI Global).*

# Chapter 12

# Katana:
## Towards Patching as a Runtime Part of the Compiler–Linker–Loader Toolchain

**Sergey Bratus**
*Dartmouth College, USA*

**Ashwin Ramaswamy**
*Dartmouth College, USA*

**James Oakley**
*Dartmouth College, USA*

**Sean W. Smith**
*Dartmouth College, USA*

**Michael E. Locasto**
*George Mason University, USA*

## ABSTRACT

*The mechanics of hot patching (the process of upgrading a program while it executes) remain understudied, even though it offers capabilities that act as practical benefits for both consumer and mission-critical systems. A reliable hot patching procedure would serve particularly well by reducing the downtime necessary for critical functionality or security upgrades. However, hot patching also carries the risk—real or perceived—of leaving the system in an inconsistent state, which leads many owners to forgo its benefits as too risky; for systems where availability is critical, this decision may result in leaving systems un-patched and vulnerable. In this paper, the authors present a novel method for hot patching ELF binaries that supports synchronized global data and code updates, and reasoning about the results of applying the hot patch. In this regard, the Patch Object format was developed to encode patches as a special type of ELF re-locatable object file. The authors then built a tool, Katana, which automatically creates these patch objects as a by-product of the standard source build process. Katana also allows an end-user to apply the Patch Objects to a running process.*

## 1. INTRODUCTION

It is somewhat ironic that users and organizations hesitate to apply patches — whose stated purpose is to support availability or reliability — precisely *because* the process of doing so can lead to downtime (both from the patching process itself as well as unanticipated issues with the patch). Periodic reboots in desktop systems — irrespective of the vendor — are at best annoying. Reboots in enterprise environments (e.g., trading, e-commerce, core network systems), even for a few minutes,

DOI: 10.4018/978-1-4666-1580-9.ch012

imply large revenue loss — or require an extensive backup and failover infrastructure with rolling updates to mitigate such loss.

We question whether this *de facto* acceptance of significant downtime and redundant infrastructure should not be abandoned in favor of a reliable hot patching process.

Software, the product of an inherently human process, remains a flawed and incomplete artifact. This reality leads to the uncomfortable inevitability of future fixes, upgrades, and enhancements. Given the way such fixes are currently applied (i.e., patch and reboot), developers accept downtime as a foregone conclusion even as the software is released — and deployers who resist downtime resist the patches.

While patches themselves are a necessity, we believe that the process of *applying* them remains rather crude. First, the target process is terminated; the new binary and corresponding libraries (if any) are then written over the older versions; the system is restarted if necessary; and finally the upgraded application begins execution. Besides the appreciable loss in uptime, all context held by the application is also lost, unless the application had saved its state to persistent storage (Candea & Fox, 2003; Brown & Patterson, 2002) and later restored it (which is expensive to design for, implement, and execute). In the case of mission-critical services, even after a major flaw is unveiled and a patch subsequently created, administrators must choose between security (applying a patch) and availability. This conundrum serves as our motivation for *hot patching,* without restarting the program and losing state and time. We focus on systems, such as those found in the cyber infrastructure for the power grid, which require high availability and which store significant state (that would be lost on a restart).

## Challenges of Patching

Requiring and encouraging the adoption of the latest security patches is a matter of common wisdom and prudent policy. It appears, however, that this wisdom is routinely ignored in practice. This disconnect suggests that we should look for the reasons underlying users' hesitancy to apply patches, as these reasons might be due to fundamental technical challenges that are not yet recognized as such. We believe that the current mechanics of applying patches prove to be just such a stumbling block, and we contend that the underlying challenges need to and can be addressed in a fundamental manner *by extending the core elements of the ABI and the executable file format.*

Mission-critical systems seem hardest to patch. They can ill afford downtime, and the owner may be reluctant to patch due to the real or perceived risk of the patch breaking essential functionality. For example, patching a component of a distributed system might lead to a loss or corruption of state for the entire system. An administrator might also suspect that the patch is incompatible with some legacy parts of the system. Even so, the patch may target a latent vulnerability in a software feature that is not now in active use, but also cannot be easily made unreachable via configuration or module unloading. The administrator is forced to accept a particularly thorny choice: inaction holds as much risk as a proactive "responsible" approach. Since the risks of patching must be weighed against those of staying un-patched, we seek to *shift the balance of this decision toward hot patching by making it not only possible, but also less risky in a broad range of circumstances.* We contend that this can only be done through good engineering and making patching a part of the standard toolchain.

Our key observation is that current binary patches, whether "hot" or static, are almost entirely opaque and do not support any form of reasoning about the impact of the patch (short of reverse engineering both the patch and the targeted binary). In particular, it is hard for the software owner to find out whether and how a patch would affect any particular subsystem in any other way than applying the patch on a test system and trying it out, somehow finding a way to faithfully replicate the conditions of the production environment.

Given these circumstances, our tool Katana and our Patch Object format not only seek to make possible the mechanics of hot patching, but also enable administrators to reduce the risk of applying a particular fix by providing them with enough information to support examination of the patch structure, to reason[1] about its interaction with the rest of the system, and to understand the tradeoffs involved in applying it.

## Patching in the Toolchain

Hot patching should not be thought of as a bizarre operation, done crudely and infrequently. We argue that it is one of the fundamental transformations in the life cycle of any program, along with compilation, linking, dynamic linking, and (in unfortunate cases) dumping core. We note that each of these fundamental operations has its own type of ELF object devoted to it (re-locatable objects, executables, dynamic libraries, core dumps respectively) and a corresponding tool in the toolchain for performing each transformation or working with its output. *We contend that patching is very much like linking or dynamic linking.* Like those operations, it combines (or replaces) parts of programs and must generate, modify, and apply relocation information. The section types defined for the ELF format contain nearly all of the information necessary to describe a patch. Once we take the position that patching is like linking, it follows that a patch needs to store the same type of symbol and relocation information as does any re-locatable ELF object.

What the base ELF specification lacks is a way to describe types. Symbol information gives us only a location and a length, but there is no way to describe the internal layout of a piece of data. The DWARF format,[3] already heavily used with ELF for debugging and exception-handling purposes, provides exactly what is needed here as it provides a means to recursively describe types and variables, as well as a set of instructions originally designed for restoring register states

and examining the call stack but rich in possible applications.

Through the use of formats already employed in the binary tool chain, we hope to promote easy examination of patches, interoperability, and to show that patching fits comfortably into the rest of the toolchain. We therefore propose that the standard software life cycle now be as shown in Figure 1. Before hot patching, only the Development and Runtime stages of the figure were generally accepted.

## Why Not Just Employ Redundancy?

Redundant infrastructure, containing replicas of nodes and service paths, often helps an organization bridge the service disruption stemming from patches. We believe, however, that redundancy isn't always the best approach for ensuring availability during an upgrade or security-critical patching process. Rather than an established best practice, we invite the reader to see redundancy as an extreme measure that needlessly duplicates hardware, networking, and software of the original system. We suggest that redundancy is:

1. **Expensive:** In medium-sized enterprises, the cost of a single server, gateway, or switch is high enough to outweigh the benefits of redundancy.

2. **Wasteful:** Redundant systems are typically passive bystanders, lying in wait for an active machine to initiate a failover.

3. **Dependent upon complicated logic:** Transferring application state (even across multiple homogenous systems) is non-trivial, especially when the state transfer occurs within hardware (such as for call trunks).

4. **Specialized:** The process of building system redundancy is not easily generalizable across heterogenous systems and requires full knowledge of the underlying protocol and application state in order to provide faithful failover and failback.

*Figure 1. Revised software life cycle. Before hot patching, only the Development and Runtime portions existed*

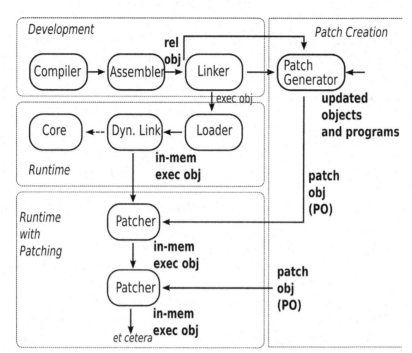

It should be noted that the last two items apply even for virtualized redundant systems, which often do not have the traditional overhead of redundant hardware. We do not claim that redundancy does not have its place, but redundancy does not provide the easy, ubiquitous solution to high-availability stateful applications that we hope to provide through patching.

## 2. KATANA DESIGN

In our prototype, a patch is may be generated as follows. The source directory corresponding to the target to be patched is replicated, and the source code is patched to the version desired. The modified source tree is then built and compared with the original source tree at the object (.o) level. Those object files that have changed between the modified and original source trees are added to the list of objects that must be examined for

type and code transformations (Figure 2). (Future work will include use of the *inotify* mechanism to avoid potentially expensive recursive directory comparison and provide more precise notification of changed files.)

To dynamically update the running application, Katana needs to patch both the code and the data within the process. It first creates a *patch object* (PO): an ELF file with sections that indicate the type of patch (code or data), the patch offsets and lengths within the process address space, patch data, function and data names, etc. The patch object may then be applied to the target at any time.

## 3. AUTOMATED PATCHING

In this section, we describe our data and code patching methods. We note that, compared to previous work, our PO data structures allow rea-

*Figure 2. An Example Code Base. From the top: each source file creates a corresponding object file; multiple object files are combined into intermediate compilation units (CU); and multiple CUs are merged to form the executable. All shaded blocks indicate modified files.*

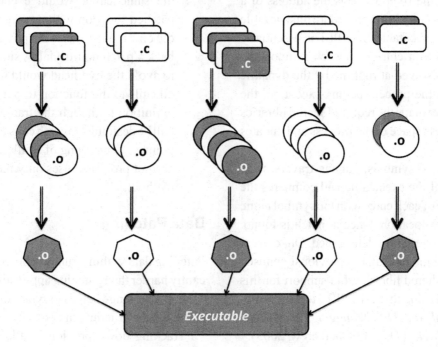

soning about the scope, extent, and impact of the patch (e.g., whether it affects particular subsystems within the process).

## Code Patching

This process involves several stages:

1.  **Code Identification:** Katana first needs to identify the section(s) of text that need to be modified within the running process. To do this, we consider the list of all modified object files from our tracking step and identify all functions (both static and global) within these files from their symbol table. Functions that differ between the original and modified versions of an object file are copied into the PO and marked as code.

2.  **Symbol Resolution:** After identifying all functions that require a patch, we need to resolve outstanding symbol references within each function. Typically, symbol resolution for an application happens at both the linking stage (called *static linking* when the symbol is present within another object file or archive), and the execution stage (or *dynamic linking*, when the symbol is present within a shared library). All code relocations are identified in the ELF sections .rel.text and .rela.text, within the object files and the final executable. Each relocation entry contains, among other information, the code offset that requires relocation and the outstanding symbol that provides this fix-up.

For each relocation entry, Katana copies the corresponding symbol into the PO. The actual value of the symbol is not necessary in the PO unless the target to be patched will be stripped, as the value of the symbol can be retrieved from the running target while performing the patching. This is key in allowing executables that have already been patched to be patched again. If the symbol was dynamic (i.e., present in a shared library such as libc), then the fixup value is the address of a corresponding entry in the procedure linkage table (*PLT*) of the executable. The PLT is essentially a jump table with entries for each symbol that needs to be resolved at runtime by the dynamic linker. When the process begins execution, the dynamic linker maps the required shared libraries into the address space of the process and updates each PLT entry.

For dynamic symbols, Katana traverses the PLT entries of the executable and compares the symbol name of each entry with the symbol name that requires relocation. Once a match is found, the symbol value can be determined. Our current prototype cannot add calls to previously unused functions in shared libraries, but support for this will be added using the "ALTPLT" technique described in *Embedded Elf Debugging: The Middle Head of Cerberus* (The ELF shell crew, 2005).

Finally, if the outstanding symbol's definition was not found within the replicated executable (either within the symbol table or within the PLT), then it was newly added by the patch; it is marked as such and added to the PO.

3. **Patch Application:** Applying a code patch is simple enough and has been researched in other systems (Ikebe & Kawarasaki, 2006; kai, 2004; Arnold & Kaashoek, 2009; Amato & Abe, 2009). We map the new function in memory and insert a trampoline jmp instruction at the beginning of the old function within the process memory image. This interposition allows the caller to execute our new function instead of the previous one at the cost of an extra jump. It is possible to avoid the overhead (from branch mis-prediction) of the jmp instruction by adding into the old function code that traces up the stack and modifies the caller's call instruction operand to point to the new address instead

of the old one. Although this optimization would ensure that all subsequent calls from the same caller would execute the new patched function without stepping into the old one, it does makes the process of rolling back a patch non-trivial. A simpler method to avoid the overhead would be to relocate all calls to the function to point to its new definition (although the trampoline would still be desirable, to catch calls from function pointers or anything of similar nature). The current prototype uses only the trampoline method.

## Data Patching

Patching data within a running process is significantly harder than patching application code. The primary challenge here is to synchronize the code and the data structures it acts on.

Tracking down previously allocated data is nontrivial (one of the reasons why garbage collectors are interwoven with the language implementation). Even after identifying the allocated chunks of memory, in the absence of some kind of type specification, the *internal structure* of memory remains opaque. We also need a method for extracting only the modified data variables from the patch and a means to discover the actual modifications that were performed. Our system solves both of these problems.

We first note that any code that acts on patch-modified data is already taken care of by Katana's code patching process because we rely on make to build the object files that correspond to all modified sources. We resolve the previously identified problems towards patching data by leveraging DWARF debugging information within the application executable. This requires the object files to be compiled with debugging support, but we do not see this as a limitation. Since we need DWARF information only while building the PO, all debugging symbols could be stripped from the executable during application deployment, if desired (this would require storing symbol values in the PO, however).

We now recall the representation of types in the DWARF format and then detail the various steps in Katana's data patching process.

## DWARF Type Information

The DWARF structure is laid out as a tree of DIEs (*Debugging Information Entries*) within the executable file. Each DIE has an associated tag and a set of attributes. The DIE that defines type information has the tag as one of DW_TAG_base_type, DW_TAG_structure_type or DW_TAG_union_type. Typedefs and other type modifiers (such as const, volatile, pointer etc.) are referenced by the DIE that defines the type. In case of structures or unions, each member is contained as a separate DIE within the parent DIE that identifies the struct/union. It is important to note that DWARF annotates types of *all* visibilities from the program sources - local, global and static.

Katana's data patching process contains a number of steps:

1. **Type Discovery:** We set out to discover all newly created or modified data types – those that are primarily user-defined (such as structures and unions in C). Katana traverses the type information (as identified by the above DWARF tags) from the newly created executable, and for each encountered type, it searches for the corresponding type-name within the *replicated* executable (from before the patch). If so found, the full types (i.e., the number, type and position of all member variables contained within) are compared to determine if they are identical. If not identical, a transformation between the old and new versions is generated, along with DWARF information identifying the type to insert into the PO as soon as a variable is found making use of the altered type. Else,

if the type name itself was not found within the replicated executable, then the current type was created by the patch, and is added as such to the PO.

2. **Data Traversal:** The next step is to traverse all variables defined within the new application, and for each one encountered, we first determine its lexical scope. If the scope is local, then we ensure that the corresponding function (the one that defines this variable) does not have an activation frame on the program stack while applying the patch. Else, the variable has been defined as either global or static. We first check whether the replicated executable defines the same variable. If not, then this variable has been created by the patch and we need not worry about it and may leave the symbol resolution up to the compiler (as only *new* code can use this variable). Otherwise, we verify whether the variable's type is one of the modified types identified during *type discovery*. If it is, then we add the variable along with its *original* address from the replicated executable, its *new* address from the patch, and its type information to the PO. At the end of this stage, Katana would have identified all newly created or modified variables from the patch.

3. **Patch Application:** Applying a data patch consists of first tracking down the relevant symbols in program memory. Katana reads in the PO, and for each data variable encountered, it checks whether the variable is a pointer or not. If it is, then the current validity of the pointer is verified (by bounds-checking the pointer value to within heap boundaries). If the pointer is found to be invalid, no further action is taken. If the pointer is valid, then memory for the new type(s) is allocated, the older structure is copied into the new one taking into account the difference in structure definition, the old memory is then freed, and the pointer is modified to point to the new

segment (in case of structures such as lists, trees, since we have the type specification, we can repeat this process recursively for each node on the list or tree). Else if the variable is not a pointer, then Katana modifies all its references in the program text to the updated memory location from the patch. Katana supports default values in the sense that if the variable has an initializer in the new version of the program text, that initializer will be used for any member variables within structures or array elements that did not previously exist in the executing target. Initializers from the new version are used for all const global variables. Eventually Katana it will support default values and programmer-written custom initializers.

## Challenges

Data patching, as described above, is not an easy task, even with DWARF type information. C, as well as many other directly compiled languages, does not have a strong type system, and is not designed to allow reflection. Structures are relatively straightforward to patch, because they contain a detailed specification. Unions and arrays, on the other hand, are generally quite opaque. If substantial changes have been made to one of the types in a union, Katana cannot do anything automatically, as there is no automatic way to determine which unioned type to act on. If an array changes size, Katana will assume that it is growing or shrinking at the end and will copy old data accordingly, but it will also issue a warning that this may not be the desired behavior. Pointers are handled, of course, but with some limitations currently. Unfortunately for our purposes, memory management is not part of the ABI. Further, there is no standard way to determine what block a given pointer is part of. Our current implementation correctly handles only memory management with malloc and only pointers to the beginning of blocks. Improvement of this is a major area of

future work. Multiple pointers to the same address are handled by keeping track of which addresses have been relocated. void* also poses a problem, as there is generally no way to determine the "real" type of the pointer. The general solution to all of these type problems is to ask the programmer for routines which perform the application-specific work. Minimizing programmer work is of foremost importance, because greater human interaction adds greater possibility for human error, thus possibly decreasing the reliability of the patch, but it is not avoidable in all situations.

Hot patching still faces a number of other challenges, including dealing with multithreaded programs and address space randomization (which slight changes to the OS loader can help us overcome). There is nothing inherent in our design which will not work with multithreading, but dealing with it through ptrace takes considerable work which we have not yet done. More importantly, deadlock avoidance work — required to ensure that we do at some point pause all threads but that we never pause a thread that another thread may be waiting on in order to reach a safe state (see below) — is nontrivial. We plan to address this in the future.

## 4. DISCUSSION

### When to Apply the Patch

Dynamically updating a running application requires diligence and patience. One cannot update the target application without any knowledge of the program's execution state, by which we mean the program stack, processor registers, etc. Even after possessing this information, the application has to be in what we call a "safe state" for Katana to apply the patch. We characterize a program state as a *safe state* if the following two conditions hold:

- All activation frames in the program stack belong to functions that *do not* get updated during code patching. It is easy to verify this by comparing each function on the stack with the list of upgradeable functions contained within the PO.

- All activation frames in the program stack belong to functions that do not access any global/static symbols identified during *Data Traversal* and that do not define any local variables of the modified types identified during *Type Discovery*. Again, since we maintain type and variable definitions within the PO, verifying this condition is easy.

Given the patch object, Katana uses Linux's ptrace interface to temporarily halt the execution of the target process, query the current execution stack, and determine whether the application is currently in a safe state. If so, then Katana applies the code patch followed by the data patch. We note that it is not possible to apply the code and data patches at different times since new code likely uses the new data, and hence postponing data patching to when only the second condition is satisfied is impractical and unsafe.

Let us adopt the following notation. For frames $X$ and $Y$ on the stack, where on the time scale $X$ precedes $Y$, let $(X:Y)$ denote all frames between $X$ and $Y$ on the stack, inclusive. Further, let $(1:Y)$ refer to all frames between the first (bottom) frame on the stack and frame $Y$. Let $A$ denote the current activation frame on the program stack, so $(1:A)$ refers to the current stack. Now, in case we determine $(1:A)$ to be an unsafe state, we could repeatedly keep querying the stack until the application reaches some safe state. However, this is highly inefficient and cumbersome.

Instead, when we determine the program to be in an unsafe state, we traverse up the stack from $A$, and for each preceding frame (say $A'$), we determine if $(1:A')$ is a safe state. This takes into consideration only $A'$ and all other frames preceding it. If $(1:A')$ is a safe state, then we insert a breakpoint on the return instruction pointer (EIP)

pointed to by the successive frame: $(A'+1)$. What this guarantees us is that when this breakpoint is hit, the state of the program stack will be $(1:A')$. Since we just determined this to be a safe state, we can reliably conduct the patching procedure. If however, no such frames preceding $A$ satisfy a safe state, then it means that the application cannot be patched successfully in its current execution since there will always be a function that violates our safety condition.

Finally we note that even after inserting a breakpoint, the problem of determining *when* the breakpoint will be hit is essentially a hard one, and so in such cases, Katana can provide no time-bounding guarantees. Still, this is a cleaner and more efficient approach than just naïvely retrying the full update procedure, which is both an expensive and an incomplete solution. In cases where the timely (or even eventual) application of a patch seems unlikely, it would be possible to add support for programmers to manually specify safe places for patching to occur. For programs built around a central loop (the vast majority of long-running programs), the likelihood of safe patching can be expedited by isolating the main loop into a simple routine unlikely ever to need patching. While safety determination is implemented in our prototype, we do not yet have enough real data about the likelihood of applications' failing to reach a safe state.

## Address Space Randomization

*Load-time address randomization* has become a stable and popular way of raising the bar for attackers, and so we must discuss how it interacts with our patching scheme. The gist of randomization schemes is invalidating various default assumptions regarding the locations of code and data elements that might facilitate exploitation. In particular, the virtual addresses of loadable segments are displaced by random[4] offsets by the loader, which *relocates* them (using their accompanying relocation sections).

Patching relocated code with our PO files requires knowledge of the displacements introduced at loading-and-relocation time. While there is no common ABI standard for saving this information, conceptually it is no different from saving virtual addresses of other files' loaded symbols in the *Global Offset Table* (GOT). We note that the names of the constituent object files themselves are customarily included in the symbol tables and that the symbol table entry format can be easily adopted for storing virtual addresses of the relocated objects.

Thus, at the cost of small modifications to the OS loader and the dynamic linker, we can make the information on the layout of the "randomly" relocated executable and libraries available to our patching process driven by our POs.[5]

## Future Work

Katana is a work in progress. We have demonstrated code patching (including dynamically linked functions), the use of our patch object format (discussed in detail in Section 5 below), and data patching including complex structures and variable addition. The remainder of the system is still under development. In the future we must address several important engineering issues, such as the interaction of patched code with dynamically loaded libraries (including the *dlopen* mechanism) and assuring that accumulation of administered patches does not lead to unacceptable performance degradation. We must also address the broader issue of describing and detecting software designs not amenable to runtime patching, and we must steer programmers to avoid them if possible.

## 5. PATCH OBJECT FORMAT

## Reasons and Needs

We have developed a Patch Object format for which the following holds:

- A PO is a valid ELF file.
- A PO utilizes DWARF information to describe types, variables, and functions requiring patching.
- A PO allows type transformations to be specified using a language defined by the DWARF standard.

Through the use of existing standards and well-structured ELF files utilizing a simple expression language for data patching, we aim to create patches that are easily examined (or modified) with existing tools. This easy compatibility with the existing binary tools and standards brings us to a very good point: why should patching not be a part of the ABI and of the standard toolchain? This does not necessarily have to be the precise format we use for Katana. Any such format that would become a standard, whether an actual standard or a *de facto* standard, should be well vetted by the community, but we argue that something like this should be included in the standard object types, along with re-locatable objects, executable objects, shared libraries, and core dumps. Consider the situation. Re-locatable objects containing new code and data which may be inserted at runtime are nothing new. This is the entire premise of the dynamic library. User-written functions which may have to run upon this code injection (in the case of patching data where the desired actions cannot be determined automatically) already exist as the .init and .fini sections. Because of this similarity between some of the functionality needed by patching and the functionality offered by dynamic libraries, some previous systems have performed patching by creating patches as dynamic libraries that contain not only the code and data to be patched but also the mechanism to perform the patching (Neamtiu et al., 2006; Chen et al., 2007). We argue that this is an unnecessary mixing of data and logic and, further, that a patch that contains merely the information necessary to fix a running process and not the code to do so is more desirable. The code to apply the patch should live in one place on any given system, as most other executable content does. We do not embed Emacs within our text files, after all. Dynamic libraries and other re-locatable, linkable objects do not contain code and data intended to overwrite data in an existing executable or process. Consider, however, that redefining certain symbols is only a slight twist on ordinary linker behaviour. Ordinary linker behaviour for global symbols is to fail if a symbol is defined more than once. Ordinary behaviour for weak symbols is to use a global definition if available or the weak symbol otherwise. When performing dynamic linking, generally the first appropriate symbol encountered in the chain of symbol tables is used. It is not a far difference to define the linkage rule that the symbol definition from the most recent patch takes precedence. Therefore, applying a patch consists of the following steps

1.  Injecting appropriate sections of the patch into memory. This includes putting their contents into memory and performing relocations on these sections (but not on the rest of the in-memory process) so that they fit into their environment
2.  Copying existing data to the appropriate regions of the newly mapped-in patch
3.  Performing relocation on the entire in-memory process such that the symbols defined by the patch take precedence.

These steps are all such fundamental operations that they should become universally supported by the ABI and the toolchain.

On the other hand, note that the specification of a general patch format does not completely prescribe the patch application. From a standard patch format, a patcher is still free to make decisions such as when to patch safely and whether to patch functions by inserting trampolines in the old versions of the functions or by relocating all references to the function (we currently do the former in Katana, but may later transition to doing the latter).

## Our Patch Object Format

Our Patch Object (PO) format is an ELF-based format. Figure 3 shows the sections contained in a simple patch..text.new and.rodata.new are of course the new code and supporting constants to inject..rela.text.new allows.text.new to be properly relocated after it is adjusted. While System V based systems use only relocation sections of type SHT_REL, we chose to use SHT_RELA in our patch objects because they make addends much easier to keep track of as we relocate from patched binary to patch object to patched process in memory. This is all really nothing new; storing ELF sections to be injected in-memory has been done before in other systems (Vanegue et al., 2009). What is new in our patch object is the inclusion of DWARF sections. The.debug_info section in an ordinary executable program contains a tree of DIEs (Debugging Information Entities) with information about every type, variable, and procedure in each compilation unit in the program. In a patch object, we store information only about the procedures and variables which have changed. This of course includes storing the type information for changed variables. An example of the DWARF DIE information contained in a patch can be seen in Figure 4.

*Figure 3. Headers for the PO*

```
Section Headers:
  [Nr] Name               Type
  [ 0]                    NULL
  [ 1] .strtab            STRTAB
  [ 2] .symtab            SYMTAB
  [ 3] .text.new          PROGBITS
  [ 4] .unsafe_functions  LOUSER+1
  [ 5] .rodata.new        PROGBITS
  [ 6] .rela.text.new     RELA
  [ 7] .debug_info        PROGBITS
  [ 8] .debug_abbrev      PROGBITS
  [ 9] .debug_frame       PROGBITS
  [10] .rel.debug_info    REL
  [11] .rel.debug_frame   REL
```

*Figure 4. DWARF DIEs in the PO*

```
.debug_info

COMPILE_UNIT<header overall offset = 0>:
<0><   11> DW_TAG_compile_unit
    DW_AT_name                  main.c

LOCAL_SYMBOLS:
<1><   19> DW_TAG_subprogram
    DW_AT_name                  printThings
    DW_AT_low_pc                0x0
    DW_AT_high_pc               0x70
<1><   40> DW_TAG_structure_type
    DW_AT_name                  _Foo
    DW_AT_byte_size             16
    DW_AT_MIPS_fde              16
    DW_AT_sibling               <93>
<2><   55> DW_TAG_member
    DW_AT_name                  field1
<2><   63> DW_TAG_member
    DW_AT_name                  field_extra
<2><   76> DW_TAG_member
    DW_AT_name                  field2
<2><   84> DW_TAG_member
    DW_AT_name                  field3
<1><   93> DW_TAG_base_type
    DW_AT_name                  int
    DW_AT_byte_size             4
<1><   99> DW_TAG_variable
    DW_AT_name                  bar
    DW_AT_type                  <40>
```

Note that we store considerably less information about each entity than is typically contained. This is so because we read most of the information from the DWARF and symbol table information of the executing process (unless it will have been stripped; then more information must be stored in the patch). This allows the patch to be more flexible as it does not require that all variables and procedures be located at exactly the addresses they were expected to be at when the patch was generated. This flexibility allows a single patch between versions *va* and *vb* to patch both an executable that was originally compiled to *va* and an executable that was patched from earlier versions to be equivalent to *va*. Ksplice, one of the few other patchers that operate solely at the binary level, does not have this capability (Arnold & Kaashoek, 2009). We will provide a mechanism for composing patches such that a patch from version *va* to *vb* may be composed with a patch from *vb* to *vc* to produce a patch from *va* to *vb*.

Note that patch versioning is currently a work in progress and not fully implemented.

Most of the information in the DIE tree is concerned only with names or how to locate code within the patch object (high and low pc). Of special interest, however, is the fde attribute of the DW_TAG_structure_type. This attribute specifies an offset in the .debug_frame section of an FDE (Frame Description Entity). DWARF FDEs are designed for use in transforming one call frame into the previous call frame, and thereby walking up a call stack for either debugging purposes or exception-handling purposes (using the .eh_frame section). Transforming one call frame to another, however, is not such a different operation from transforming one structure to another version of the same structure. We have aided this use with an implementation of the DWARF virtual machine that defines several special register types (exploiting the fact that for the purposes of generality, DWARF registers are specified as LEB128 numbers, giving an unlimited number of registers). The DWARF register instructions contained in the FDE referenced in Figure 4 for copying field1, field2, and field3 from the original version of a structure _Foo to a new version of _Foo that has gained the extra member field_extra in the middle of the existing fields would be represented as in Figure 5.

CURR_TARG_NEW and CURR_TARG_OLD are special symbolic values defined by the virtual machine. If we are patching the variable bar, then the CURR_TARG_OLD will be the old address of bar (its value in the symbol table), and CURR_TARG_NEW will be the new address bar is being relocated to. Our registers take advantage of the LEB128 encoding to hold a considerable amount of information in the register identifier. In the case seen above, the first byte identifies the class of the register (CURR_TARG_NEW or CURR_TARG_OLD in this example), the following word specifies the size of the storage addressed (this is included so that register assignments may copy an arbitrary number of bytes), and the final word specifies an offset from the address referred to by CURR_TARG_(NEW—OLD).

## 6. RELATED WORK

There are several hot-patching systems preceding Katana. One of the most well-known is probably Ginseng (Neamtiu et al., 2006). Ginseng — and systems drawing inspiration from it such as Polus (Chen et al., 2007) — have successfully demonstrated patching of such important software as apache and sshd. These systems perform analysis of the differences between the original and the patched versions at the source code level. This introduces considerable (and we argue unnecessary) complexity and inability to deal well with some optimizations such as inlining and hand-written assembly. The complexity of analyzing the source code ties these systems to generally a single language (C in the case of both Ginseng and Polus). By contrast, Katana is language agnostic as it works at the level of the binary ABI, and although we have not yet demonstrated its doing so, it should eventually be able to patch binaries compiled from any language, providing that the necessary symbol and relocation information is supplied. Ginseng also requires significant programmer interaction in annotating the code (Neamtiu, 2009) and requires compiling the code to use type-wrappers, allowing the patching of data types but at the cost of indirect access to them. The more programmer effort involved in generating a patch, the more likely the patch is to be incomplete or incorrect.

Motivated by many of the points in the above paragraph, the successful Ksplice system (Arnold & Kaashoek, 2009) patches at the binary level, as we do. We claim the following differences from and improvements over Ksplice.

*Figure 5. FDE instructions for data patching*

```
DW_CFA_register {CURR_TARG_NEW,0x4 bytes,0x0 off}
{CURR_TARG_OLD,0x4 bytes,0x0 off}
DW_CFA_register {CURR_TARG_NEW,0x4 bytes,0x8 off}
{CURR_TARG_OLD,0x4 bytes,0x4 off}
DW_CFA_register {CURR_TARG_NEW,0x4 bytes,0xc off}
{CURR_TARG_OLD,0x4 bytes,0x8 off}
```

- Ksplice operates on the kernel. As their paper states, most of their technique is not specific to the kernel, but there is no evidence that it has been implemented to function on userland programs. Katana operates on userland.

- Ksplice makes no attempt to patch data, relying entirely on programmer-written transformation functions when data types do change

- Ksplice patches are created as kernel modules. Ksplice does not provide a mechanism to perform operations, such as composition, on these patches.

To the best of our knowledge, Katana is the first system to utilize DWARF type information in patching.

Maintaining continuous availability, even in the absence of disruptive events like patches, is both a challenging technical exercise and the driving need for research on dependability, reliability, and fault tolereance (Zhou et al., 2007). Our work follows work focusing on enabling a software application to continue providing service or survive significant events like errors, exploits, and patches. This body of work includes research on dynamic kernel updates, software survivability, and software self-healing. However, other research areas also addressed the challenge of enabling software to adapt at runtime, e.g., the area of software evolution (e.g., Stefano et al., 2004).

The concept of crash-only software (Candea & Fox, 2003) advocates microrebooting: the procedure of retrofitting each component of a system with the ability to crash and reboot safely as the default mode of operation. Despite its appeal as a design principle, such an approach would be difficult to retrofit to legacy software. Although restarting a particular service or application is disruptive enough, rebooting the operating system itself multiplies this disruption. The need to avoid that kind of downtime helped drive the creation of frameworks like Loadable Kernel Modules for Linux, which allow for extending the kernel during runtime without a reboot. The ability to update the running kernel (as opposed to adding or removing modules) without rebooting was achieved at least ten years ago (Cesare, 1998) and recently rediscovered, albeit mostly for research, rather than commodity, kernels (sd & devik, 2001; Baumann et al., 2007; oules et al., 2003). Even so, dynamic updates of the kernel during runtime that don't require a reboot are difficult to apply to a commodity OS, although several efforts have been successful for the K42 experimental system (Soules et al., 2003; Baumann et al., 2005).

Software self-healing aims at ensuring continuous or increased availability for systems subjected to exploited vulnerabilities, either by automatically generating patches (Weimer et al., 2009; Sidiroglou et al., 2005) to gradually harden the application or by seeking to avoid a restart altogether by modifying certain runtime aspects (e.g., the memory subsystem (Rinard et al., 2004), properties of the execution environment (Qin et al., 2005), or selected control paths (Smirnov & Chiueh, 2005; Locasto et al., 2007) of the system in response to attacks. One major risk of employing self-healing in production environments is that the semantics of follow-on execution remains largely uncontrolled, although recent work in automatically correcting memory errors (Novark et al., 2008) seems to achieve fairly reliable results. Both automated responses and traditional patches can make it difficult for an administrator to understand the implications of a particular fix (Rinard, 2008).

## 7. CONCLUSION

We introduce a method for hot patching: a technique we believe to be a promising alternative to redundancy, ad hoc self–healing techniques, "patch and pray," or other approaches to dynamic software updates. Hot patching has the potential for aligning actual practices with acknowledged "best practices" relating to critical security or functionality updates. We hold that one major impediment to hot patching is the opaque nature of most patches (be it proprietary or open software), and our method of patching, along with the PO file format, is a first attempt at providing a basis for informed reasoning about the structure and implications of a patch.

We present a reasoned approach to making patching a part of the standard tool chain. We demonstrate a working binary userland patcher operating completely at the object level. Our system is, to our knowledge, the first to utilize DWARF type information to automate the transformation between old and new versions of a type. There yet remains much work to be done, and our future work involves support for patching multithreaded targets, better support for handling opaque types such as void*, and further development of patch versioning and the ability to perform operations on patch objects.

## ACKNOWLEDGMENT

Supported in part by the National Science Foundation, under grant CNS-0524695. The views and conclusions do not necessarily represent those of the sponsors. Supported in part by grant 2006-CS-001-000001 from the U.S. Department of Homeland Security under the auspices of the I3P research program. The I3P is managed by Dartmouth College. The opinions expressed in this paper should not be taken as the view of the authors' institutions, the DHS, or the I3P.

## REFERENCES

Arnold, J., & Kaashoek, M. F. (2009). Automatic Rebootless Kernel Updates. In *Proceedings of EuroSys*. Ksplice.

Baumann, A., Appavoo, J., Wisniewski, R. W., Silva, D. D., Krieger, O., & Heiser, G. (2007). Reboots Are for Hardware: Challenges and Solutions to Updating an Operating System on the Fly. In *Proceedings of the USENIX Annual Technical Conference*.

Baumann, A., Heiser, G., Appovoo, J., Silva, D. D., Krieger, O., Wisniewski, R., & Kerr, J. (2005). Providing Dynamic Update in an Operating System. In *Proceedings of the USENIX Annual Technical Conference* (pp. 279-291).

Brown, A., & Patterson, D. A. (2002). Rewind, Repair, Replay: Three R's to dependability. In *Proceedings of the ACM SIGOPS European Workshop*, Saint-Emilion, France.

Candea, G., & Fox, A. (2003). Crash-Only Software. In *Proceedings of the Workshop on Hot Topics in Operating Systems (HOTOS-IX)*.

Cesare, S. (1998). *Runtime Kernel kmem Patching*. Retrieved from http://vx.netlux.org/lib/vsc07.html

Chen, H., Yu, J., Chen, R., Zang, B., & Yew, P.-C. (2007). Polus: A powerful live updating system. In *Proceedings of the 29th international conference on Software Engineering (ICSE '07)* (pp. 271-281). Washington, DC: IEEE Computer Society.

Ikebe, T., & Kawarasaki, Y. (2006). Retrieved from http://pannus.sourceforge.net/

Locasto, M. E., Stavrou, A., Cretu, G. F., & Keromytis, A. D. (2007). From STEM to SEAD: Speculative Execution for Automatic Defense. In *Proceedings of the USENIX Annual Technical Conference* (pp. 219-232).

Neamtiu, I. (2009). *Ginseng user's guide*. Retrieved from http://www.cs.umd.edu/projects/PL/dsu/software.shtml

Neamtiu, I., Hicks, M., & Stoyle, G. (2006). Practical dynamic software updating for c. In *Proceedings of the ACM Conference on Programming Languages Design and Implementation* (pp. 72-83).

Novark, G., Berger, E. D., & Zorn, B. G. (2008). Exterminator: Automatically correcting memory errors with high probability. *Communications of the ACM, 51*(12), 87–95. doi:10.1145/1409360.1409382

Qin, F., Tucek, J., Sundaresan, J., & Zhou, Y. (2005). Rx: Treating Bugs as Allergies – A Safe Method to Survive Software Failures. In *Proceedings of the Symposium on Systems and Operating Systems Principles (SOSP)*.

Rinard, M., Cadar, C., Dumitran, D., Roy, D., Leu, T., & Beebee, W. J. (2004). Enhancing Server Availability and Security Through Failure-Oblivious Computing. In *Proceedings Symposium on Operating Systems Design and Implementation (OSDI)*. sd and devik (2001). *Linux on-the-fly Kernel Patching Without LKM*. Retrieved from http://doc.bughunter.net/rootkit-backdoor/kernel-patching.html

Rinard, M. C. (2008). Technical perspective patching program errors. *Communications of the ACM, 51*(12), 86–86. doi:10.1145/1409360.1409381

Sidiroglou, S., Locasto, M. E., Boyd, S. W., & Keromytis, A. D. (2005). Building a Reactive Immune System for Software Services. In *Proceedings of the USENIX Annual Technical Conference* (pp. 149-161).

Smirnov, A., & Chiueh, T. (2005). DIRA: Automatic Detection, Identification, and Repair of Control-Hijacking Attacks. In *Proceedings of the Symposium on Network and Distributed System Security (NDSS)*.

Soules, C. A. N., Appavoo, J., Hui, K., Wisniewski, R. W., da Silva, D., Ganger, G. R., et al. (2003). System Support for Online Reconfiguration. In *Proceedings of the USENIX Annual Technical Conference* (pp. 141-154).

Stefano, A. D., Pappalardo, G., & Tramontana, E. (2004). An infrastructure for runtime evolution of software systems. In. *Proceedings of the IEEE Symposium on Computers and Communications, 2*, 1129–1135.

The ELF shell crew. (2005). Embedded elf debugging: the middle head of cerberus. *Phrack Magazine, 11*(63).

Ukai, F. (2004). Retrieved from http://ukai.jp/Software/livepatch/

Vanegue, J., de Medeiros, J. A., Bisolfati, E., Desnos, A., Figueredo, T., Garnier, T., et al. (2009). *The eresi reverse engineering software interface*. Retrieved from http://www.eresi-project.org/

Weimer, W., Nguyen, T., Goues, C. L., & Forrest, S. (2009). Automatically Finding Patches Using Genetic Programming. In *Proceedings of the International Conference on Software Engineering (ICSE)*.

Yamato, K., & Abe, T. (2009). A Runtime Code Modification Method for Application Programs. In *Proceedings of the Ottawa Linux Symposium*.

Zhou, Y., Marinov, D., Sanders, W., Zilles, C., d'Amorim, M., Lauterburg, S., et al. (2007). Delta Execution for Software Reliability. In *Proceedings of the Third Workshop on Hot Topics in System Dependability (HotDep '07)*.

## ENDNOTES

[1] By which we mean manual, human-level reasoning, although applying automated reasoning methods is an interesting (and open) avenue of research.

2. For example, consider adding a new member to a C struct definition and an additional clause to the logic that processes it.
3. http://dwarfstd.org
4. In reality, the choice of offset is still limited by the platform's alignment requirements.
5. We note that saving this information about the post-relocation layout of the process does not weaken "randomization," for the latter does not assume the attacker's ability to arbitrarily read process memory (in which case the address of required symbols are easily found by scanning it for their code or data patterns), but rather breaks hard-coding of these symbols' expected addresses.

*This work was previously published in International Journal of Secure Software Engineering, edited by Khaled M. Khan, pp. 1-17, Volume 1, Issue 3, copyright 2010 by IGI Publishing (an imprint of IGI Global).*

# Chapter 13
# A Formal Approach for Securing XML Document

**Yun Bai**
*University of Western Sydney, Australia*

## ABSTRACT

*With the ever increasing demand for the Web-based applications over the Internet, the related security issue has become a great concern. Web document security has been studied by many researchers and various security mechanisms have been proposed. The aim of this paper is to investigate the security issue of the XML documents. We discuss a protection mechanism and investigate a formal approach to ensure the security of Web-based XML documents. Our approach starts by introducing a high level language to specify an XML document and its protection authorizations. We also discuss and investigate the syntax and semantics of the language. The flexible and powerful access control specification can effectively protect the documents from unauthorized attempts.*

## INTRODUCTION

The extensible markup language (XML) is used over the Internet for information exchange. With the increasing demand for the Web-based applications over the Internet by government, financial institution, business and trading, secure Web documents is becoming an essential issue. Web based document security has become a great concern, and has been studied by many researchers. Various security mechanisms have been proposed and investigated since then.

HTML was the initial language used for Web-based information processing. However HTML does not provide a clear structure and semantics, and often its design is just limited for a specific browser. XML was proposed by the World Wide Web Consortium (W3C) to overcome these limitations. XML improves HTML by providing a clear semantics without losing the initial HTML functions and capabilities. With XML, different applications can define and declare their own tags and attributes freely. XML is now widely accepted as a universal language for Web-based information exchange and processing.

DOI: 10.4018/978-1-4666-1580-9.ch013

Since XML is becoming the favourable format for information exchange over the Internet, XML document security has been increasingly studied and has become an active research area. Fine grained access control for XML documents has been investigated by some researchers. Murata et al. (2003) proposed a static analysis for XML access control. Given an access control policy and an access query, they use a static analysis to decide if to grant or deny such an access request. In this way, run-time evaluation is only needed when the static analysis is unable to make such decision. This pre-execution analysis improves the performance of the system response to a query. Damiani et al. (2002) presented a language for specification of access control by exploiting the characteristics of XML to define and enforce access control directly on the structure and content of the document. They provide a flexible security mechanism for protecting XML documents. An authentication approach for XML documents is proposed in (Devanbu, Gertz, Kwong, Martel, Nuckolls, & Stubblebine 2001). The proposal uses signature techniques to ensure the authenticity of the XML documents by having a server processing queries and certifying answers using a digital signature with an on-line private key. This approach allows un-trusted servers to answer certain type of path queries over the Internet without the need for a trusted on-line signing key. It provides the security of XML documents over the Internet by using a signature based document authentication.

Access control or authorization specifications have long been an important issue in computer system security. A variety of authorization specification approaches such as access matrix (Dacier & Deswarte 1994; Denning 1976); role-based access control (Crampton, & Khambhammettu, 2008); access control in database systems (Bertino, Jajodia, & Samarati 1996; Fernandez, Gudes, & Song 1989; Meadows, 1991), authorization delegation (Murray & Grove, 2008); procedural and logical specifications (Bai & Varadharajan, 1997; Bertino, Buccafurri, Ferrari, & Rullo, 2000) have

been investigated. Some of the works emphasize on the specification of the access control policies and their functions; others on the access control for specific application areas and their delegations in the mechanism.

Since logic based specification has a clear and precise semantics and powerful expressiveness as stated in (Fagin, Halpern, Moses, & Vardi, 1995), a variety of logic authorization specification approaches have been proposed. A logic language (Jajodia, Samarati, Sapino, & Subrahmanian, 2001) has been proposed for expressing authorizations. They used predicates and rules to specify the authorizations; their work mainly emphasizes the representation and evaluation of authorizations. A formal approach using default logic to represent and evaluate authorizations has also been reported in (Woo & Lam, 1992). However, the constraints of the access control of the system are not considered in their work. Hence it is not clear how to judge whether a policy base is legitimate or not with respect to the system restriction. This approach is not suitable for XML documents security specification since it is hard to capture the hierarchical structure and the constraints of the documents.

A general framework (Bertino, Catania, Ferrari, & Perlasca 2003) on a logic formalism was proposed to model discretionary, mandatory access control and role-based access control models. The syntax and the semantics of the framework are given and also some example applications are presented. This work is mainly used for the analysis and the comparison of some existing access control models and their decidability. Whether this general framework can be used to model access control in XML documents scenario is not clear. The proposed rule-based security policy framework (Bettini, Jajodia, Wang, & Wijesekera, 2002) includes provisions and obligations. It investigated a reasoning mechanism within this framework in a general database scenario. This work investigates authorization policy with a logic framework from management point of view.

The aim of this paper is to address high level authorization specifications in XML documents scenario. The works so far regarding XML document security generally lack a formal semantics to characterize different types of inheritance properties of authorization policies among the semi-structured elements of the document. This work investigates formal methods on XML document security. Based on the initial work of (Bai, 2007, 2008), this paper investigates XML document security comprehensively from a formal logic point of view. In this paper, we propose a high level formal logic language with a precise and declarative semantics to capture the properties of the XML documents and their security features. The flexible and powerful access control specification can effectively protect the documents from unauthorized attempts.

The paper is organized as follows. In section 2, we investigate and discuss the features of the XML document and specify the document by a formal, high level logic language, we explore the syntax and semantics of the language. In section 3, we analyse the security features of the document, and extend the language by incorporating access control rules into the XML document specification to provide the protection of the document. We also discuss the syntax and semantics of the extended language. In section 4, we discuss the reasoning about authorizations on the relationships of the elements of the XML document and investigate certain authorization inheritance properties. A case study is also presented. Finally section 5 concludes the paper with remarks and discussions of the future work.

## XML DOCUMENT SPECIFICATION: SYNTAX AND SEMANTICS

An XML document contains a sequence of nested elements. Each element is represented by a pair of begin and end delimiter tags such as <record> and </record>. An element has a set of attributes associated with it. The elements within a document form a tree structure. Here is an example of XML document frame (Figure 1) and its corresponding tree structure.

This XML frame represents a tree structured document as shown in Figure 2

In the tree structure, we use rectangle node for the element and oval node for the attribute of the element. "Mary is an admin staff, her duty is to assist the dean" is an instance of such a document frame. From the structure we observe that the elements of the document reside in a hierarchy of a tree structure and have inheritance properties. For instance, an *acad* staff has the general attributes (*name, salary*) a staff has, which are inherited from its parent element *staff*. Apart from the general inherited properties, it has its specific properties of *research* and *teaching*. Now we propose a logic language L to formally specify the XML document.

## Syntax of Language L

The vocabulary of language L consists of:

1. A finite set of *element variables* $EV = \{e, e_1, e_2, \ldots\}$ and a finite set of *element constants* $EC = \{E, E_1, E_2, \ldots\}$. We will simply name $E = EV \cup EC$ as *element set*.
2. Binary symbols $<$, $<<$ and $\in$.
3. Auxiliary symbol $\Rightarrow$.

For simplicity, we do not separate the element and its attributes. We use A|B to indicate the attribute B of an element A. Together they are viewed as an object to be accessed by a user or an application. We call such user or application **subject**.

We use $<$ and $<<$ to denote the hierarchy relationship between two elements. $E_1 < E_2$ indicates that $E_1$ is an immediate child of $E_2$; $E_1 << E_2$ indicates that $E_1$ is at a lower but not immediate hierarchy of $E_2$. The different hierarchy definitions $<$ and $<<$ are used to solve conflicts of inherited

*Figure 1. An XML document frame*

```
<record>
      <staff>
            <name type="char">
            </name>
            <salary type="int">
            </salary>
            <acad>
                  <teaching type="char">
                  </teaching>
                  <research type="char">
                  </research>
            </acad>
            <admin>
                  <duty type="char">
                  </duty>
            </admin>
      </staff>
</record>
```

authorizations. We also use ∈ to represent membership relationship. For instance, "Mary ∈ *admin*" represents that Mary is a member of *admin* staff. The symbol ⇒ is used to map an element to its associated attributes.

The basic building blocks of an XML document are **elements** nested in the hierarchical file structure; the **relationships** among these elements indicate how they are related; and the **restric-**

**tions** on the elements to satisfy certain document requirements. Logic language L has a simple yet flexible syntax. It can be suitably used to formalize various features of the XML documents. In the language, the set of element *constant* represents element instances of the document and the set of element *variables* represents a general framework of elements in the document.

An *element proposition* is an expression of the form

$$E \Rightarrow \Pi_1,$$

$$\dots,$$

$$\Rightarrow \Pi_m. \tag{1}$$

In (1) E is an element and $\Pi_1 \dots \Pi_m$ are attributes of E. When the set $\Pi$ is empty, it refers to the element itself.

A *relationship proposition* of L is an expression of one of the following three forms:

$$E < E_1, \tag{2}$$

$$E \ll E_1, \tag{3}$$

*Figure 2. XML document tree structure*

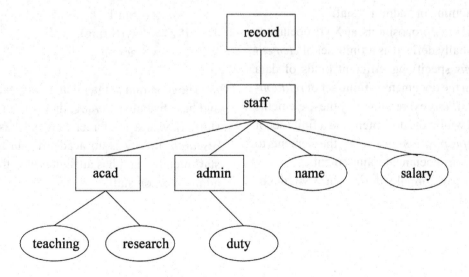

$$E \in E_1, \tag{4}$$

where E and $E_1$ are elements from the document, i.e., E and $E_1$ may be element constants or variables. Clearly, relationship propositions (2), (3) and (4) explicitly represent the hierarchy relations between two elements.

A *constraint proposition* is an expression of the form:

$$\varphi \text{ if } \varphi_1 \ldots, \varphi_\kappa \tag{5}$$

where $\varphi, \varphi_1 \ldots, \varphi_\kappa$ are element propositions. It specifies that $\varphi$ is a derived element from elements $\varphi_1 \ldots, \varphi_\kappa$. When the details of an element proposition are not interested in the context, we usually use the notation $\varphi$ to denote it. A constraint proposition represents some relationship among different elements.

We use the *element proposition* to represent elements and their attributes; the *relationship proposition* to capture the hierarchical structure and membership feature of XML document; and the *constraint proposition* to represent different restrictions on different elements or attributes of an element. A proposition without variables is called a ground proposition.

For instance, the hierarchical structure and membership feature of an XML document can be represented by a *relationship proposition* such as: "Mary ∈ admin" or "admin < staff".

With the three propositions, an XML document can be formally defined as a finite set of *element propositions* specifying different kinds of data elements in the document, a finite set of *relationship propositions* expressing how these elements are related within the document and a finite set of *constraint propositions* restricting the elements to satisfy various document requirements.

We can now formally define our XML document as follows.

**Definition 1.** An *XML document* D is a triplet $(\alpha, \beta, \gamma)$, where $\alpha$ is a finite set of ground element propositions, $\beta$ is a finite set of ground relationship propositions, and $\gamma$ is a finite set of constraint propositions.

For instance, for the document frame in Figure 1, if we have "John is an academic staff; Mary is an admin staff". Using the definition, we have:

1. The set of ground element propositions $\alpha$ consists of:
   staff ⇒ name(String),
   ⇒ salary(Integer), (6)
   acad ⇒ teaching(String),
   ⇒ research(String), (7)
   admin ⇒ duty(String), (8)

2. The set of ground relationship propositions $\beta$ consists of:
   John ∈ acad, (9)
   Mary ∈ admin, (10)
   acad < staff, (11)
   admin < staff, (12)

3. The set of constraint propositions $\gamma$ consists of:
   x ∈ Staff
   **if** x ⇒ teaching(String),
   x ∈ acad, (13)
   y ∈ Staff
   **if** y ⇒ research(String),
   y ∈ acad, (14)
   z ∈ Staff

4. **if** z ⇒ duty(String),
   z ∈ admin (15)

The constraints states that if x is a staff member and has attribute *teaching*, then x is an academic staff; if y is a staff member and has attribute *research*, then y is an academic staff; if z is a staff member and has attribute *duty*, then z is an administration staff.

## Semantics of Language L

In this subsection, we define the semantics of language L by following a classical logic definition. First, we define the structure of L.

**Definition 2:** A *structure* of L is a tuple $S = (U, F_s, <_u, <<_u, \in_u)$ where

1. U is a nonempty set called the *domain* S which represents the set of all *actual* element and attributes in the XML document.
2. $F_s$ is a set of functions, for each function symbol $f \in F_s$, f maps an element to its corresponding set of attributes.
3. $<_u$ and $<<_u$ are partial orderings on U and $\in_u$ is a binary relation on U. We require that if $a \in_u b$ and $b <_u c$, then $a \in_u c$; if $a \in_u b$ and $b <<_u c$, then $a \in_u c$; if $a <_u b$ and $b <<_u c$, then $a <<_u c$.

The above definition states that in a structure S, U represents all the possible *actual* elements in the document domain. That is, each item in U is a real object in our world. A function symbol f in $F_s$ is corresponding to $\Rightarrow$ which is defined in L and maps an element to its set of attributes. The functions of ordering $<_u$ and $<<_u$ are to represent the semantics of relationship propositions in L. For example, $a <_u b$ in the structure is the counterpart of proposition $A < B$, while A and B are elements in L and are mapped to a and b, which are the elements of U respectively. The semantics of the relationship propositions $<<$ and $\in$ in L are provided by $<<_u$ and $\in_u$ in S respectively in a similar way.

Now, we define the entailment relation and models of structure S.

**Definition 3:** Let $S = (U, F_s, <_u, <<_u, \in_u)$ be a structure of L. We define *entailment* relation $\models$ as follows.

1. For ground relationship propositions, $S \models E \in E_1$ if $E \in_u E_1$; $S \models E < E_1$ if $E <_u E_1$; and $S \models E << E_1$ if $E <<_u E_1$.
2. For a ground element proposition $S \models f_1 (E) \Rightarrow \Pi_1, ..., f_m (E) \Rightarrow \Pi_m$ if for each $f_m$ where f is in $\{ f_1, ..., f_m \}$, $\{\Pi_1, ..., \Pi_m\}$ are sets of attributes of E.
3. For a ground constraint proposition, $S \models \varphi$ if $\varphi_1 ..., \varphi_k$ if $S \models \varphi_1, ...S \models \varphi_k$ implies $S \models \varphi$.
4. For any proposition $\psi$ including element variables, $S \models \psi$ if for every instance $\varphi$ of $\psi$ (i.e. $\varphi$ is obtained from $\psi$ by substituted each variable in $\psi$ with some Element of U), $S \models \varphi$.

Now we can formally define the model of an XML document D as follows:

**Definition 4:** A structure M of L is a *model* of an XML document $D = (\alpha, \beta, \gamma)$ if

1. For each proposition $\psi$ in $\alpha \cup \beta \cup \gamma$, $M \models \psi$.
2. For each element proposition $\varphi$, if $M \models \varphi$, then $M \models \varphi'$ where $\varphi'$ is obtained from $\varphi$ by omitting some attributes of $\varphi$.
3. For any relationship proposition $E \in E_1$ and element proposition $f (E_1) \Rightarrow \Pi$, $M \models E \in E_1$ and $M \models f (E_1) \Rightarrow \Pi$ imply $M \models f (E) \Rightarrow \Pi$.
4. For any relationship propositions $E < E_1$, and $E_1 < E_2$, $M \models E < E_1$ and $M \models E_1 < E_2$ imply $M \models E << E_2$.

Condition 1 in the above definition is the basic requirement for a model. Condition 2 allows us to partially represent an element with only those attributes that are of interest in a given context. Condition 3 is a restriction to guarantee necessary inheritance of membership, whereas Condition 4 is needed for the purpose of element property and authorization inheritance in case of conflicts. Let $\Sigma$ be an XML document and $\varphi$ be a proposition. If for every model M of $\Sigma$, M $\models \varphi$, we also call that $\varphi$ *is entailed* by $\Sigma$, denoted as $\Sigma \models \varphi$.

## ACCESS CONTROL IN XML DOCUMENT SPECIFICATION: SYNTAX AND SEMANTICS

This section is to extend the XML document specification language L to include authorization rules in order to control access to the document. A specific authorization rule is to define which subject holds what kind of access right for which object. In this context, a subject is either a user or an application; an object is an element or attribute(s) of an element of the document; and an access right is an operation to be performed on the object.

### Syntax of the Extended Language L

The *vocabulary* of the extended L includes the original vocabulary together with the following additions:

1.  A finite set of *subject variables* $SV = \{s, s_1, s_2, ...\}$ and a finite set of *subject constants* $SC = \{S, S_1, S_2, .... \}$. We denote $S = \{SV \bigcup SC\}$.
2.  A finite set of *access-rights variables* $AV = \{r, r_1, r_2, ...\}$ and a finite set of *access-right constants* $AC = \{R, R_1, R_2, ...\}$. We denote $A = AV \bigcup AC$.
3.  A ternary predicate symbol holds taking arguments subject, access-right, and object respectively.
4.  Logic connectives $\wedge$ and $\neg$.

In the extended L, an authorization fact that a subject S has access right R for element E (or its attribute A) is represented using a ground formula holds(S,R,E) (or holds(S,R,E|A)). A ground

formula is a formula free of variables. We use lower case letters for variables and capital letters for constants.

We define an *access fact* to be an atomic formula holds(s, r, o) or its negation. An *access fact expression* is defined as follows:

1.  Each access fact is an access fact expression;
2.  If $\psi$ is an access fact expression and $\varphi$ is an element or relationship proposition, then $\psi \wedge \varphi$ is an access fact expression;
3.  If $\psi$ and $\varphi$ are access fact expressions, then $\psi \wedge \varphi$ is an access fact expression.

From the above definition,

$$holds(S,R,E) \wedge (E << E_1),$$
$$\neg holds(S,R,E|A) \wedge (E \in E_2)$$

are access fact expressions.

Now, we define an *access proposition* of the extended L as:

$$\psi \text{ implies } \varphi \text{ with absence } \gamma \qquad (16)$$

This proposition says that $\varphi$ is true if $\psi$ is true under the condition that $\gamma$ is not presented.

A special form of the above access proposition occurs when $\gamma$ is empty. In this case, we can rewrite it as:

$$\psi \text{ provokes } \varphi \qquad (17)$$

This is viewed as a *causal* or *conditional* relation between $\psi$ and $\varphi$. Furthermore, when $\psi$ is also empty, we rewrite it as:

$$\text{always } \varphi \qquad (18)$$

which specifies a constant condition which $\varphi$ should always be true.

Now we can define an *authorization rule base* to control access to XML document. It is defined as a finite set of data propositions representing various elements and their attributes, and their relationships within the XML document; a finite set of access propositions specifying access permissions to the data elements; and a finite set of constraints propositions being complied by the data elements regulated by users or systems. Formally, it can be defined as:

**Definition 5:** An *XML document with access control rules* in extended L is a pair $\Lambda = (D,A)$, where $D = (\alpha, \beta, \gamma)$, is the XML document as defined in Definition 1, and A is an *authorization description* on D to specify a set of system and user-defined access propositions.

For example, some authorization rules for accessing an XML document can be specified as:

holds(s, r, e) $\wedge$ (e$_1$ < e)

**implies** holds(s, r, e$_1$)

**with absence** $\neg$holds(s, r, e$_1$),　　　　(19)

holds(s, r, e) $\wedge$ (e$_1$ << e)

**implies** holds(s, r, e$_1$)

**with absence** $\neg$holds(s, r, e$_1$),　　　　(20)

and

holds(s, r, e) $\wedge$ (e$_1$ $\in$ e)

**implies** holds(s, r, e$_1$)

**with absence** $\neg$ holds(s, r, e$_1$),　　　　(21)

The above three propositions express the hierarchy and membership authorization inheritance properties within an XML document.

The proposed high level specification language is expressive enough to represent authorizations in XML document environment. Within this specification, constraints, causal and inherited authorizations as well as general default authorizations can be properly justified.

## Semantics of the Extended Language L

Now we consider the semantics of the extended language L. To define a proper semantics of our access proposition (16), we need to employ a *fix-point semantics* that shares the spirit of fix-point semantics used for *extended logic programs* in (Gelfondand Lifschitz 1991).

Formally, a *structure* $S^\Lambda$ of the extended L is a pair $(S^D, S^A)$, where $S^D$ is a structure of L as defined in Definition 2 and $S^A$ is a finite set of ground literals with forms holds(S,R,E), holds(S,R,E|A), $\neg$holds(S,R,E) or $\neg$holds(S,R,E|A).

Now we can define the entailment relation $\models_\lambda$ of the extended L.

**Definition 6:** Let $S^\Lambda = (S^D, S^A)$ be a structure of the extended L. We define the *entailment relation* $\models_\lambda$ of the extended L as follows.

1. For an XML document proposition $\psi$, $S^\Lambda \models_\lambda \psi$ iff $S^D \models \psi$.
2. For a pure ground access fact expression $\psi \equiv F_1 \wedge \ldots \wedge F_k$, where ach $F_i$ is a ground access fact, $S^\Lambda \models_\lambda \psi$ iff for each i, $F_i \in S^A$.
3. For a ground access fact expression $\psi$, $S^\Lambda \models_\lambda \psi$ iff for each relationship or element proposition $\varphi$ occurring in $\psi$, $S^\Lambda \models \varphi$, and for each ground access fact $\varphi'$ occurring in $\psi$, $\varphi' \in S^A$.
4. For an access fact expression $\psi$, $S^\Lambda \models_\lambda \psi$ iff for each ground instance $\psi'$ of $\psi$, $S^\Lambda \models_\lambda \psi'$.

Now, we are in the position to formally define a model of $\Lambda = (D, A)$.

**Definition 7:** Consider an extended database $\Lambda = (D, A)$ and a structure $S^{\Lambda} = (S^D, S^A)$.

Let A' be an authorization description obtained from A in the following way:

1. By deleting each access proposition $\psi$ **implies** $\varphi$ **with absence** $\gamma$ from A if for some $F_i$ in $\gamma$, $F_i \in S^A$;
2. By translating all other access propositions $\psi$ **implies** $\varphi$ **with absence** $\gamma$ to the form $\psi$ **provokes** $\varphi$, or to the form **always** $\psi$ if $\psi$ is empty.

**Definition 8:** Consider an extended XML document $\Lambda = (D, A)$ and a structure $S^{\Lambda} = (S^D, S^A)$. Let A' be an authorization description obtained from A as described in Definition 7.

$S^{\Lambda} = (S^D, S^A)$ is a *model* of $\Lambda = (D, A)$ if and only if

1. $S^D$ is a model of D;
2. $S^A$ is the smallest set satisfying the following conditions:
    a. for each access proposition **always** $\varphi$ in A', $S^{\Lambda} \models \varphi$;
    b. for each access proposition of the form $\psi$ **provokes** $\varphi$ in A', if $S^{\Lambda} \models \psi$, then $S^{\Lambda} \models \varphi$.

## REASONING ABOUT ACCESS CONTROL IN XML DOCUMENT

In this section, we investigate some properties on the inheritance of access control policies on XML document and provide a detailed case study to demonstrate the expressive power of our underlying formal language.

## Inheritance Properties

An extended XML document does not always have one model, and it may also have multiple models. These have a unique model is called *well-specified*. Let $\Lambda$ be a well-specified extended XML document and S, R, E, $E_1$ and $E_2$ are arbitrary subject constant, access right constant and object constants respectively. Then the following results hold.

**Theorem 1:** Authorization on relationship <

1. If $\Lambda \models_{\lambda}$ holds(S,R, $E_1$) $\wedge$ E < $E_1$ and $\Lambda \neg \models_{\lambda}$ $\neg$holds(S,R,E), then $\Lambda \models_{\lambda}$ holds(S,R,E).
2. If $\Lambda \models_{\lambda}$ holds(S,R, $E_1$|a) $\wedge$ E < $E_1$ and $\Lambda \neg \models_{\lambda}$ $\neg$holds(S,R,E|a), then $\Lambda \models_{\lambda}$ holds(S,R,E|a).

**Proof:** Let $\Lambda = (D, A)$ and $S^{\Lambda} = (S^D, S^A)$ be a model of $\Lambda$. Then from the fact $\Lambda \models_{\lambda}$ holds(S,R, $E_1$) $\wedge$ E < $E_1$, we have holds(S,R, $E_1$) $\in S^A$ and $S^D \models$ E < $E_1$. Since $\Lambda \neg \models_{\lambda}$ $\neg$holds(S,R, E), we have holds(S,R, $E_1$)$\notin S^A$. So from Definition 7, the form of proposition

holds(S,R,E) $\wedge$ E < $E_1$
**implies** holds(S,R, $E_1$)
**with absence** $\neg$holds(S,R, E)
is translated into the form
holds(S,R,E) $\wedge$ E < $E_1$
**provokes** holds(S,R, E).

From Definition 8, we know that $S^{\Lambda}$ satisfies the condition: if $S^D \models$ holds(S,R, $E_1$) and $S^D \models$ E < $E_1$ then $S^D \models$ holds(S,R, E). This concludes that $S^D \models$ holds(S,R, E). As $S^D$ is an arbitrary model of $\Lambda = (D, A)$, we then have $\Lambda \models_{\lambda}$ holds(S,R,E).

We can use a similar approach to prove the rest of the theorems.

**Theorem 2:** Authorization on relationship <<

1. If $\Lambda \models_{\lambda}$ holds(S,R, $E_1$) $\wedge$ E << $E_1$ and $\Lambda \neg \models_{\lambda}$ $\neg$holds(S,R,E), then $\Lambda \models_{\lambda}$ holds(S,R,E).

2.  If $\Lambda \models_\lambda holds(S,R, E_1|a) \wedge E << E_1$ and $\Lambda \neg \models_\lambda \neg holds(S,R,E|a)$, then $\Lambda \models_\lambda holds(S,R,E|a)$.

**Theorem 3:** Authorization on relationship $\in$

1.  If $\Lambda \models_\lambda holds(S,R, E_1) \wedge E \in E_1$ and $\Lambda \neg \models_\lambda \neg holds(S,R,E)$, then $\Lambda \models_\lambda holds(S,R,E)$.
2.  If $\Lambda \models_\lambda holds(S,R, E_1|a) \wedge E \in E_1$ and $\Lambda \neg \models_\lambda \neg holds(S,R,E|a)$, then $\Lambda \models_\lambda holds(S,R,E|a)$.

**Theorem 4:** Authorization on relationships $<$ and $<<$

1.  If (If $\Lambda \models_\lambda holds(S,R, E_1) \wedge E < E_1$ and $\Lambda \neg \models_\lambda \neg holds(S,R,E)$) and (If $\Lambda \models_\lambda \neg holds(S,R, E_2) \wedge E << E_2$ and $\Lambda \neg \models_\lambda \neg holds(S,R,E)$) then $\Lambda \models_\lambda holds(S,R,E)$.
2.  If (If $\Lambda \models_\lambda holds(S,R, E_1|a) \wedge E < E_1$ and $\Lambda \neg \models_\lambda \neg holds(S,R,E|a)$) and (If $\Lambda \models_\lambda \neg holds(S,R, E_2|a) \wedge E << E_2$ and $\Lambda \neg \models_\lambda \neg holds(S,R,E|a)$) then $\Lambda \models_\lambda holds(S,R,E|a)$.

## Case Study

We consider a university staff management scenario. John is the director of Human Resources Department, Sue and Jane are two personal assistants of John, where Sue's duty is to assist John to manage all academic staff's annual salary incremental, and Jane's duty is to arrange meetings between John and academic staff. In general, Sue and Jane should not exchange their duties, but there is an exception if Sue or Jane is on leave.

On the other hand, Alice is a lecturer and Bob is a research fellow in the university. For some reasons, Bob did not get his salary incremental last year, therefore, he is requesting a meeting with John. Alice is also requesting a meeting with John to discuss her annual leave in the next semester. Now in order to organize these two meetings, Sue and Jane need to provide necessary information about Alice and Bob to John before the meetings,

for that they have to access Alice and Bob's certain personal records.

Suppose the university staff information is represented as an XML document tree structure as depicted in Figure 2. Now we will use our formal language developed in this paper to represent this scenario.

Sue $\in$ Admin,

Jane $\in$ Admin,

Alice $\in$ Lecturer,

Bob $\in$ Research,

Admin $\in$ Staff,

Acad $\in$ Staff,

Lecturer $\in$ Acad,

Research $\in$ Acad,

Salary_File(X) $\in$ Record(X),

Leave_Record(X) $\in$ Record(X),

X $\in$ Admin $\wedge$ Y $\in$ Acad $\wedge$ holds(X,Read, Record(Y)) **implies**

$\neg$ holds(X,Read,Salary_File(Y))

**with absence** olds(X,Read,Salary_File(Y))

X $\in$ Admin Y $\in$ Acad $\wedge$ holds(X,Read, Record(Y)) **provokes**

holds(X,Read,Leave_Record(Y)),

Y $\in$ Acad **provokes** holds(Sue, Read, Salary_File(Y)),

Y $\in$ Acad **implies** holds(Jane, Read, Salary_File(Y))

**with absence** $\neg$Onleave(Sue).

Let $\Lambda$ be the set of above sentences. Now suppose Sue is on leave, and in order to make the two meetings happen between John and Alice and Bon respectively, Jane has to access both Alice's personal information as well as Bob's salary file. Under our semantics, we have the following results:

$\Lambda \models_\lambda$ holds(Sue, Read, Record(Alice)),

$\Lambda \models_\lambda$ holds(Sue, Read, Record(Bob)),

$\Lambda \models_\lambda$ holds(Jane, Read, Leave_Record(Alice)),

$\Lambda \models_\lambda \neg$holds(Jane, Read, Salary_File(Bob)),

$\Lambda \bigcup$ {Onleave(Sue)} $\Lambda \models_\lambda$ holds(Jane, Read, Salary_File(Bob))

The first two results show that Sue has the rights to access both Alice and Bob's all records, while the third result shows that Jane can access Alice's annual leave record, so that Jane may organize the meeting between John and Alice. The fourth result indicates that Jane cannot access Bob's salary information, but this becomes possible when Sue is on leave as demonstrated by the fifth result above.

## CONCLUSION

In this paper, we have proposed a formal logic approach for XML document security. We started by analysing the properties of the document, then using a high level logic language to describe the document. The syntax and semantics of the language are provided. We further studied the security features associated with the XML document, identified its specific security characteristics and combined the security policy description into the document specification by extending the language proposed. The semantics of the extended language was investigated and defined. A case study of the theoretical application of the framework outlined by the language was discussed.

The aim of this paper is to investigate a formal approach for XML document specification and the authorization rules for administering the access to the document in order to protect it from unauthorized attempt. We use a formal logic approach since it has a clear and precise semantics and powerful

expressiveness. This work is a theoretical investigation on XML document security. Its application on any particular architecture such as service oriented architecture (SOA) is yet to be investigated. In our future work, more detailed study of the element and attribute will be carried out. The inheritance level and delegation chain issues need to be refined and investigated. So far, the formal specification and reasoning of the document and its access control policies have been completed. We are currently investigating the mapping of the authorization rules to logic programs and the implementation of logic programs. Its application on a particular architecture will be investigated and examined.

## REFERENCES

Bai, Y. (2007). On XML document security. In *Proceedings of the International Conference on Software Engineering and Data Engineering* (pp. 39-42).

Bai, Y. (2008). Access control for XML document. In *Proceedings of the International Conference on Industrial, Engineering and Other Applications of Applied Intelligence Systems* (pp. 621-630).

Bai, Y., & Varadharajan, V. (1997). A language for specifying sequences of authorization transformations and its applications. In *Proceedings of the International Conference on Information and Communication Security* (pp. 39-49).

Bertino, E., Buccafurri, F., Ferrari, E., & Rullo, P. (2000). A logic-based approach for enforcing access control. *Computers & Security*, 8(2), 109–140.

Bertino, E., Catania, B., Ferrari, E., & Perlasca, P. (2003). A logical framework for reasoning about access control models. *ACM Transactions on Information and System Security*, 6(1), 71–127. doi:10.1145/605434.605437

Bertino, E., Jajodia, S., & Samarati, P. (1996). Supporting multiple access control policies in database systems. In *Proceedings of the IEEE Symposium on Research in Security and Privacy* (pp. 94-107).

Bettini, C., Jajodia, S., Wang, X. S., & Wijesekera, D. (2002). Provisions and obligations in policy management and security applications. In *Proceedings of the Very Large Database Conference* (pp. 502-513).

Chomicki, J., Lobo, J., & Naqvi, S. (2000). A logical programming approach to conflict resolution in policy management. In *Proceedings of the International Conference on Principles of Knowledge Representation and Reasoning* (pp. 121-132).

Crampton, J., & Khambhammettu, H. (2008). Delegation in role-based access control. *International Journal of Information Security, 7*, 123–136. doi:10.1007/s10207-007-0044-8

Dacier, M., & Deswarte, Y. (1994). Privilege graph: An extension to the typed access matrix model. In *Proceedings of European Symposium on Research in Computer Security* (pp. 319-334).

Damiani, E., Vimercati, S., Paraboschi, S., & Samarati, P. (2002). A fine grained access control system for XML documents. *ACM Transactions on Information and System Security*, 160–202.

Denning, D. E. (1976). A lattice model of secure information flow. *Communications of the ACM, 19*, 236–243. doi:10.1145/360051.360056

Devanbu, P., Gertz, M., Kwong, A., Martel, C., Nuckolls, G., & Stubblebine, S. G. (2001). Flexible authentication of XML documents. In *Proceedings of the ACM Conference on Computer and Communications Security* (pp. 136-145).

Fagin, R., Halpern, J. Y., Moses, Y., & Vardi, M. Y. (1995). *Reasoning about knowledge*. Cambridge, MA: MIT Press.

Fernandez, E. B., France, R. B., & Wei, D. (1995). A formal specification of an authorization model for object-oriented databases. In *Database security IX: Status and prospects* (pp. 95-109).

Fernandez, E. B., Gudes, E., & Song, H. (1989). A security model for object-oriented databases. In *Proceedings of the IEEE Symposium on Research in Security and Privacy* (pp. 110-115).

Gelfond, M. (1994). Logic programming and reasoning with incomplete information. *Annals of Mathematics and Artificial Intelligence, 12*, 98–116. doi:10.1007/BF01530762

Gelfond, M., & Lifschitz, V. (1991). Classical negation in logic programs and disjunctive databases. *New Generation Computing, 9*, 365–385. doi:10.1007/BF03037169

Jajodia, S., Samarati, P., Sapino, M. L., & Subrahmanian, V. S. (2001). Flexible support for multiple access control policies. *ACM Transactions on Database Systems, 29*(2), 214–260. doi:10.1145/383891.383894

Li, N., Grosof, B., & Feigenbaum, J. (2003). Delegation logic: A logic-based approach to distributed authorization. *ACM Transactions on Information and System Security, 6*(1), 128–171. doi:10.1145/605434.605438

Meadows, C. (1991). Policies for dynamic upgrading. *Database security IV: Status and prospects* (pp. 241-250).

Murata, M., Tozawa, A., & Kudo, M. (2003). XML access control using static analysis. In *Proceedings of the ACM Conference on Computer and Communications Security* (pp. 73-84).

Murray, T., & Grove, D. (2008). Non-delegatable authorities in capability systems. *Journal of Computer Security, 16*, 743–759.

Wang, L., Wijesekera, D., & Jajodia, S. (2004). A logic-based framework for attribute based access control. In *Proceedings of the ACM Workshop on Formal Methods in Security Engineering* (pp. 45-55).

Woo, T. Y. C., & Lam, S. S. (1992). Authorization in distributed systems: A formal approach. In *Proceedings of the IEEE Symposium on Research in Security and Privacy* (pp. 33-50).

Zhang, Y. (2007). Epistemic reasoning in logic programs. In *Proceedings of the 20th International Joint Conference on Artificial Intelligence (IJCAI-2007)* (pp. 647-652).

Zhou, J., & Alves-Foss, J. (2008). Security policy refinement and enforcement for the design of multi-level secure systems. *Journal of Computer Security, 16*, 107–131.

*This work was previously published in International Journal of Secure Software Engineering, edited by Khaled M. Khan, pp. 41-53, Volume 1, Issue 1, copyright 2010 by IGI Publishing (an imprint of IGI Global).*

# Section 5
# Tools for Security–Aware Development

# Chapter 14
# A Tool Support for Secure Software Integration

**Khaled M. Khan**
*Qatar University, Qatar*

**Jun Han**
*Swinburne University of Technology, Australia*

## ABSTRACT

*This paper presents a tool for the integration of security-aware services based applications that is constructed on the principles of security characterization of individual software services. The tool uses the technique of reasoning between the ensured security properties of the services and the security requirements of the user's system. Rather than reporting the research outcomes, in this paper the authors describe the architecture and capabilities of the tool for secure software integration. The main objective of this paper is to show that an automatic tool support could assist the process of security-aware service based software integration.*

## INTRODUCTION

In a service oriented system, an application system can be composed of several stand-alone software services developed by third parties. These services are available from Internet based sources. The development paradigm of service oriented applications is appealing to the software engineers as it promises maximum benefits of reusability, productivity, and efficient utilization of Internet. It provides software engineers with an opportunity to compose application systems with pre-fabricated

services which are provided by stand alone software components. This paradigm represents the LEGO block style of software composition which provides quicker plug and play application development. In a service oriented system a service providing software component is usually developed, owned, and managed by third parties.

However, the conformity between service consumers' security requirements and security assurances of services over the Internet has become an important issue. In a highly open Internet environment, service consumers are virtually forced to

DOI: 10.4018/978-1-4666-1580-9.ch014

consume services of which they have only partial or no knowledge about their underlying security properties (Khan & Han, 2003). When services are discovered from the Internet and composed with the application system of the consumer, it is not always possible to verify the conformity of security properties between the application system and the third part services. A service is actually offered by a software component or an entity. For simplicity, in this paper we use component to refer to a service providing software entity. In a service oriented system, we need tools and techniques that assist us to check the security compatibility between the selected services and the security requirements of the consumers' application system.

To illustrate the main focus of this paper, let us consider a fictitious distributed healthcare scenario. A number of individual healthcare components provide independent services. Assume a consumer's system **y** running on a machine at a general practitioner's (GP) office connects with a component **s** that provides specialist prescription based on diagnosis report. The service **s** is selected from many such services running at various service providers machines. Component **y** provides a patient's diagnosis report to **s** to get a prescription. After receiving the prescription from **s**, **y** sends it electronically to another component **p** residing on a pharmacist's system for a price quotation. In this case developers would independently develop many such **p** and **s**, and make them available from their various distributed sources which are potentially able to deliver the services that **y** wants. However, component **y** is not only interested in specific services but also wants to know upfront the security properties that the components **s** and **p** could provide with the services.

In this scenario, two issues need to be addressed: (i) how to know the security assurances provided by a service; and (ii) how to verify that the required security properties of the client of a service are complied with the ensured security provided by the services. For example, a component offering pathological services may ensure confidentiality through secure storage and transmission of diagnosis reports. The component **y** (GP) may require confidentiality provided with specific encryption schemes with specific key size. The pathology component may or may not satisfy the general practitioner's (GP) security requirements, depending on how the confidentiality is realized by the service providing component.

The current practices and research provide limited supports for software components and systems security at the composition level. While the existing security technologies have made some progresses in addressing security issues of services, however, they have primarily been focusing on system security at the software infrastructure level. A key consideration missing from all these is how to reason about the security compatibility between a service and an application system. No matter how advanced the security techniques used at the individual service level, these would remain useless if the security properties are inconsistent with the required security of the client's system.

In order to facilitate the security-aware service composition, an automatic tool support is required. The tool could be used by the software engineers to identify the suitable services along with the security profiles of the providing software components, and reason about their compatibility with the service consumer's application system. Based on our approaches reported in (Khan & Han, 2003; Khan & Han, 2005), we have developed a simple tool to characterize the security properties of the services, and verify the security compliance between the service and the consumer's application system. This paper reports the architecture, capabilities, and limitations of the security characterization tool. This paper is organized as follows. Next section outlines the requirements for an automatic tool to check the conformity of security properties of services. The section also outlines our earlier work on the security characterization which is used in the tool. Then we discuss the architecture of the tool along with a demonstration of its capabilities with an example. We briefly cite the current practices in security-aware component composition. Finally, we conclude with some outlines of future works.

## REQUIREMENTS FOR AUTOMATIC TOOL SUPPORT

An architecture of a complete system for service composition is shown in Figure 1. The figure shows that the tool has six requirements represented as modules. Some of the requirements focus on the functional issue of the tool, whereas others are related to security-aware compositional issue. The next subsections outline the modules of the architecture and our prior work on which this paper is based on.

## Modules of the Tool

The architecture includes all modules some of these are related to the *functional* and some are related to the *security compositional* issues.

- First, the system has a function which is used to locate and select service providing components based on the required services of the enclosing application (module 1, a functional compositional issue).
- Second, the system loads the candidate components into a repository (module 2, a functional compositional issue).
- Third, an automatic process discloses the security properties of the candidate components for automatic inspection (module 3, a security compositional issue). The system could display these properties in readable form. This process requires identifying and loading the security properties of the participating component and the application system.

*Figure 1. An architecture for security-aware service based system composition*

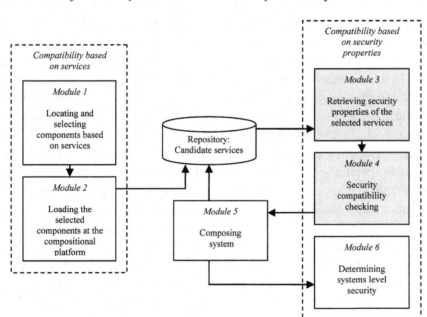

- Fourth, the system is capable of assessing and checking the compatibility of the security properties between the selected component and the application system for a service composition (module 4, a security compositional issue).

- Fifth, a system is composed based on the compliance results in the previous phase (module 5, functional and security composition issues).

- Sixth, a functionality that generates system-level security contract of the entire system based on all services (module 6, a security compositional issue).

Our tool in its current version is capable of delivering the functions of the *third* and *fourth* modules outlined above.

In this paper we focus on two key issues: *retrieving the security properties* of candidate components (module 3, shaded box in the figure), and the *compatibility checking* for a composition (module 4, shaded box in the figure) using characterization framework. Our proposed tool is intended to check the security properties of the individual components and to make compositions between security properties of the components.

## Security Characterization Framework

This section outlines the fundamentals of our security characterization framework (Khan & Han, 2003; Khan & Han, 2005) enabling the readers to familiarize the ideas uses in this paper. The security properties achieved at a service level between two software components are referred to a compositional security contract (CsC). A CsC is basically a conformity between the required security properties of the consumer's application system and the ensured security properties of the service providing by a candidate component. A security conformity or CsC is formed between two participating software entities satisfying each others security requirements.

Our security characterization framework is based on *logic programming*, *common criteria* (Common Criteria, 2005) and *BAN logic* (Burrows et al., 1990). The heart of the framework is a language support in which security properties are represented and expressed in *atoms*. An atom consists of a predicate name usually a security function such as encrypt, decrypt; and a tuple of *variables* or *constants*. Atoms usually express relationships between elements. An atom is of the form *encrypt(file, key$^{bob}$)* where *encrypt* is an n-ary predicate symbol, and *file, key$^{bob}$* are terms (Syrjaanen, 1998). This atom states that the object *file* is encrypted with the *key* owned by an entity *bob*.

A term could be either a variable, a constant value, or a function representing an element such as an entity, data, a password, a key. *Variables* are used to substitute objects such as $X$ and $Y$ for which the inference rules find or substitute an element for each $X$ and $Y$. The predicate name of an atom represents a security property such as *encrypt, own, key_generated, signed* etc. Another example of an atom is *signed(bob,file_x,key$^{bob}$)*. It states that the entity bob digitally signs the object *file_x* with his *key*.

In addition to the representation of security properties as outlined above, inference rules are used to check the conformity of the security properties represented in atoms. A clause is composed of a head and a body. A rule is of the form, signed(file_x,key$^{bob}$):- encrypted(file_y,key$^{alice}$), where *signed(file_x,key$^{bob}$)* is the head of the rule (an atom) and the literals *encrypted(file_y,key$^{alice}$)* constitute the body of the rule. The symbol**:-** is read as "is derived from". The left hand side of **:-** (the head of the rule) represents the ensured security properties. The right hand side of *:-* (the body of the rule) is called the required security properties (Baral, 2003). This rule states that the object *file_x* is digitally signed with the private *key* of *bob* if the object *file_y* is encrypted with the public *key* of *alice*. The second rule just after this like,

```
CsC(alice_system,get_prescription):-
signed(file_x,key^bob)
```

## ARCHITECTURE

The system is developed using a modular approach by separating the whole system into modules. The architectural style used in this system is pipe-and-filter. In this architecture, each module treated as a filter has a set of inputs and a set of outputs. A module reads streams of data about its inputs and produces streams of data about its outputs. We use it because a pipe-and-filter needs little contextual information and retains no state information between instantiations. Our tool with its current features does not need any contextual information. The architecture uses typed pipes which require that the data passed between two modules have a well-defined type. This is necessary because the format of the security properties is well defined. This style also restricts the topologies to a linear sequence of modules that are what we need in this system. This type of architectural style allows the designer to understand the overall input-output behavior of the system.

The pipe-and-filter style supports reuse which means that any two modules can be hooked together provided they agree about the data to be transmitted between them. In our case, it is exactly what we need. The type of data traveling between filters is deterministic and typed. Another reason for choosing this style is that the system is easy to maintain and enhance, and new modules can be added to the existing system. We plan to extend this in the future to add more features such as system-level security characterization (SsC), and possibly, security negotiation capabilities. This style naturally supports a concurrent execution as each module can be implemented as a separate task, and potentially executed parallel to other modules. A high level architecture of the tool is shown in Figure 2.

The figure shows four components in the architecture: *Pre-processor*, *Reasoning engine*, *Output manager*, and *User interface*. Pre-processor receives information about the component identities and the functionality that need to be processed. The user provides this information to the pre-processor. It then locates the appropriate component and retrieves the corresponding files containing the security properties of the participating components. It is the responsibility of the pre-processor to identify and read the correct files containing the security properties from each component participating in a functionality. This processes the files ready for the reasoning engine. The reasoning engine does the actual reasoning

*Figure 2. Pipe-and-filter architecture of the tool*

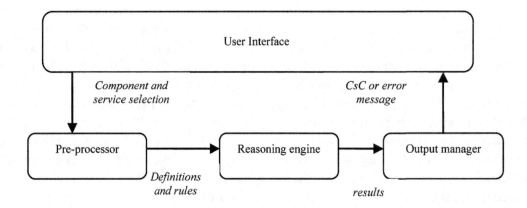

about the security properties and forwards the reasoning result to the output manager. The output manager organizes the result into human readable form and stores it in an internal file before dispatching it to the user. Figure 3 shows a screen layout of the system's *user interface* with the four components currently loaded in it. The components are: GP11 (a consumer's system), SP07 (a specialist service provider), CH03 (a pharmacist) and LB10 (a pathological service provider). It is assumed that the functionality of the selected components is already matched for the application and these four components have been selected to build the application. This tool is intended to check the security properties of the individual components and to make compositions between security properties of the components. In the following subsections we elaborate the functions and the construct of each component of the tool.

## Pre-Processor

The pre-processor identifies the selected components and the common functionality on which a composition is to be established. It aims at handling the files containing the security properties of the enclosing components. Figure 4 shows the internal components of the pre-processor. Each of the four components in the pre-processor is a filter which reads data streams from one of its ports and writes them on its output port. Each connector is considered a pipe which carries a stream of ASCII characters from one filter to another.

The security properties of each component are stored in a file belonging to the respective component. Each file consists of facts (security properties) and inference rules. Each atom represents a security property. Inference rules are used to define the relationship between atoms of different security properties. A component may offer or support more than one functionality, in which case, each functionality has its own security properties.

The two components in Figure 4 are: *File handler for focal component* and *File handler for candidate component*, locate and read the files containing the security properties of the focal component and the candidate components respectively. A *focal* component is the originator of a request for a service --a client of a service; and a *candidate* component is the recipient of a request for a service --a service providing component. The *File merger* merges the security properties available in the files owned by the candidate and the focal components which have a common interest in a particular functionality. The component *Reasoning engine caller* passes the merged file to the next filter, in this case, the *reasoning engine*, for further processing.

The merged file containing the security properties of the focal and candidate components must be compatible with the format that the reasoning engine processes. The merging of the security properties into one file is required for the reasoning engine. Figure 5 displays two example files extracted from the two components in relation to a common functionality. The files show that atoms are predicate symbols starting with lower case letters. The classical negation of an atom is denoted by a *not*. The head of the rule is separated from the tail of the rule by using:- sign. A constant is either a string starting with lower case letters or a numeric number. A numeric constant is an integer.

A variable is a string starting with an upper case letter such as S, K. We can include comments in the file by using the comment character **%**. A comment character is valid for one row. For each row we need to place a comment character in front of the row.

The *pre-processor* locates the security properties of the two participating components related to a specific functionality and merges them into one file. The merged file then contains the security properties of both components. An example of a merged file is shown in Figure 6. The complete merged file is now ready for further processing. The file is then passed to the reasoning engine.

*Figure 3. A screen layout of the Compositional Canvas*

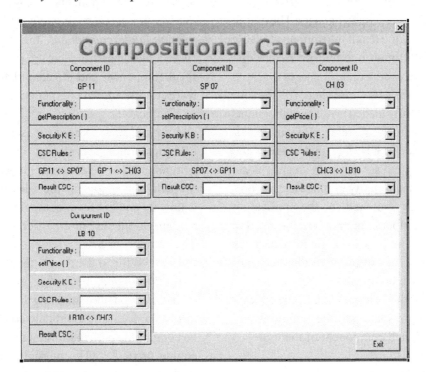

## Reasoning Engine

The main reasoning engine in our tool uses a logic programming tool called SMODELS (Syrjaanen, 2000). The tool is typically used to implement the stable model semantics of logic programs. The reasoning engine has two major processing components: *lparse* and *smodels*. *Lparse* takes care of the syntactical features of the merged file, whereas *smodels* does the actual reasoning about the properties contained in the file. Figure 7 shows the internal components of the reasoning engine.

*Lparse* transforms the complex rules in such a way that it can be accepted by *smodels*. In *lparse*, all the variables in the rules are removed by substituting all the possible values available in the facts (security properties). The process of substituting variables is called *grounding*. This is performed by lparse which simply transforms a normal logic program available in the merged file into an equivalent *ground* logic program.

In the next phase, stable models of the program are computed by the smodels. The representation of the security properties that smodels accepts from lparse is much simpler than the representation created in the initial merged file by the pre-processor. It is a numerical representation of the security properties found in the merged file that smodel processes. A stable model is a set of atoms that satisfies an answer to a problem. That is, it tells which atoms are true. In this case, the rules for making a CsC are stable if every atom in it has some 'reason' to be there. The smodels engine tries to find a solution for the rules with the provided facts specified in the file. Smodels first reads the actual rules, and computes the statement. Consider the following example:

```
signed(amount, tax):- not
encrypted(salary, key) % rule 1.
encrypted(salary, key):-not
signed(amount, tax) % rule 2.
:-encrypted (salary, key).
```

*Figure 4. Pre-processor of the tool*

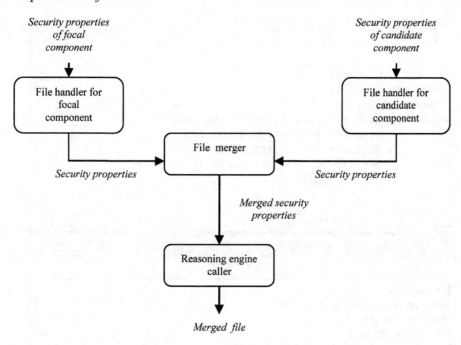

If the first rule is not true, then the second rule must be true and vice versa. Internally, *lprase* transforms these rules into a numeric representation for *smodels*.

More on smodels and lparse can be found in (Syrjaanen, 2000).

## Output Manager

The *Output manager* consists of three internal components, as shown in Figure 8. The component *Deciding output* in Figure 8 sorts out the error message from the successfully generated result file passed by the *reasoning engine*. The error message is handled by the component *Handling error message* and the successful reasoning result is further processed by the component *Displaying reasoning result*. The final reasoning result produced by the reasoning engine for the above example is displayed by the *output manager*, as shown in Figure 9.

The first row of the output displayed in Figure 9 represents the version information of smodels.

The second row confirms that the first model is found. The third row shows the model that satisfies a CsC. The word True in row four indicates that there may be more models in the program, but smodels did not compute them. The remaining rows display some statistics about the program and the processing of smodels. The duration shows the time taken to process this in seconds. In this case, it took 0.023 seconds to complete this reasoning.

The choice points indicate the number of times smodels had to guess a truth value for a ground atom. In this case, it shows that smodels guessed the correct value for each atom because the number of wrong choices is zero, therefore, it did not need to backtrack. The number of total atoms and rules in the grounded program generated by lparse is ten and eight respectively. The complexities of the program can be determined from the number of choice points rather than from the number of atoms or rules in the program (Syrjaanen, 2000). The number of picked atoms represents the number of times heuristic searches smodels has

*Figure 5. Security properties of two components*

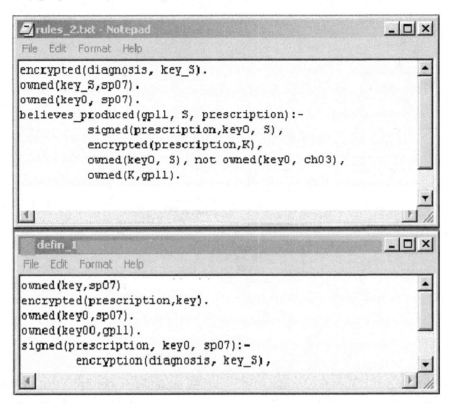

```
rules_2.txt - Notepad
File  Edit  Format  Help

encrypted(diagnosis, key_S).
owned(key_S,sp07).
owned(key0, sp07).
believes_produced(gp11, S, prescription):-
        signed(prescription,key0, S),
        encrypted(prescription,K),
        owned(key0, S), not owned(key0, ch03),
        owned(K,gp11).
```

```
defin_1
File  Edit  Format  Help

owned(key,sp07)
encrypted(prescription,key).
owned(key0,sp07).
owned(key00,gp11).
signed(prescription, key0, sp07):-
        encryption(diagnosis, key_S),
```

*Figure 6. Merged file for security properties of two components*

```
merge.txt - Notepad
File  Edit  Format  Help

encrypted(diagnosis, key_S).
owned(key_S,sp07).

believes_produced(gp11, S, prescription):-
        signed(prescription,key0, S),
        encrypted(prescription,K),
        owned(key0, S), not owned(key0, ch03),
        owned(K,gp11).
csc(gp11,S) :- believes_produced(gp11,S, prescription).

owned(key,gp11).
owned(key_S, sp07).
encrypted(prescription,key).
owned(key0, sp07).
signed(prescription,key0, S):-
        encrypted(diagnosis, key_S),
        owned(key_S,S).
```

256

*Figure 7. Components of the reasoning engine*

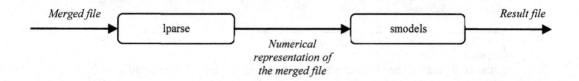

performed to find a truth value in an atom. The number of forced atoms shows how many atoms were added to the model. The number of truth assignments corresponds to the number of times smodels assigned a truth value to an atom. The output of the reasoning is written in a result file, and available for later reference.

## User Interface

The tool provides an easy-to-use user interface which requires a minimum level of training. The *user interface* module contains the classes that implement the system's graphical user interface (GUI). The GUI classes are separated from other modules to allow the system to be easily maintained and updated. All the classes concerned about the GUI are packed in this module. Figure 10 shows the major components of this process.

The components are: *Function selection*, *Component selection* and *CsC selection* receive the respective input from the user. Users can select the focal and candidate components, select the desired functionality on which a compositional reasoning can be performed, and choose a CsC check between the two selected components. The component *Display of security properties* generates the output. We look at more detailed user functions offered by the tool, as shown in Figure 11 which shows eight different features of the user interface.

1. LB10 is the identity of the component. The system displays the identity of each component in the current canvas. This figure shows that, currently, the canvas is loaded with four different components: GP11, SP07, CH07, and LB10. A rectangular area is allocated for each component.

2. If we click on the small arrow of the Functionality, a pull down menu provides the *select functionality* of current interest from

*Figure 8. Components of the output manager*

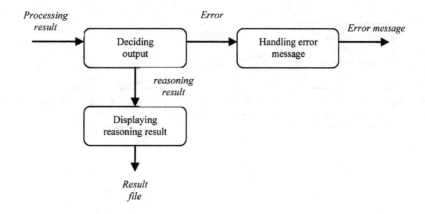

*Figure 9. Example of output*

```
resit_2.txt - Notepad                          _ □ X
File  Edit  Format  Help
smodels version 2.26. Reading...done
Answer: 1
Stable Model: signed(prescription,key0,sp07) owned(key0,sp07)
True
Duration 0.023
Number of choice points: 3
Number of wrong choices: 0
Number of atoms: 10
Number of rules: 8
Number of picked atoms: 1
Number of forced atoms: 0
Number of truth assignments: 8
Size of searchspace (removed): 0 (0)
```

the library of candidate components. After selecting the functionality, the user can see the description of the selected functionality of the component including the *argument types*. All these features are related to the syntactical features of the functionality such as the argument type and the number of arguments.

3. This shows the name of the current functionality of the component. Figure 11 shows that *setPrice()* is the current selected functionality of the component *LB10*. All operations related to the component *LB10* affect this functionality.

4. The right-side bottom corner of the blank area is called the *display area* where the security properties and reasoning results are displayed. The user can choose to display the security properties of the components, and the reasoning result. This area can also be used as an editor with which a systems integrator can directly modify the displayed properties for experimental purposes.

*Figure 10. Components of the user interface*

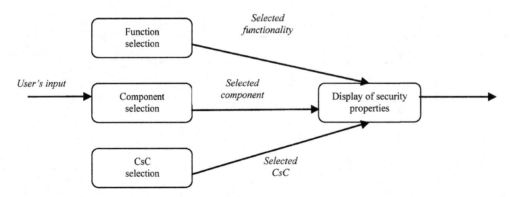

*Figure 11. Component interface supported by the compositional canvas*

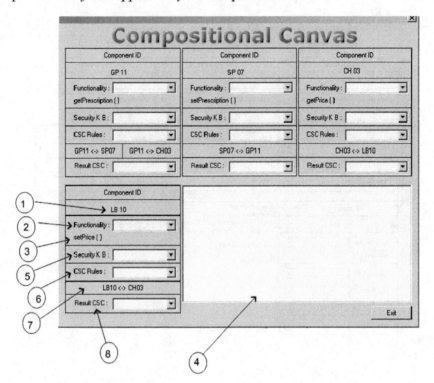

5. The next attribute of the component is *security KB*. Its pull down menu provides two options: *read* or *modify* the static security properties of the candidate component. It allows the user to read the properties. Figure 12 shows the security properties of the candidate component *CH03* in the box located in the right bottom portion of the canvas.

6. The next attribute, *CsC Rules*, displays the rules of both components: focal and candidate. In this case it is for the *LB10*. The properties show all the rules related to the selected functionality of the current selected components for a composition.

7. The button *LB10 <-> CH03* shows that a functional match has already made between components LB10 and *CH03*. This function is used to execute the compositional security check. This means that the security properties of the component *LB10* are reasoned about with the security properties of the component *CH03*. If we click on this button, the process of checking the security compatibility appears as shown in the right bottom box in Figure 13. It displays various information about the security compatibility test result. However, if smodels fails to compute the rules or is unable to conclude 'true' for a CsC, it will not display any such statistics. It simply shows the version of the smodels and leaves a blank screen. This means that there is no satisfying CsC found.

8. The *CsC Result* button displays the compositional security check result previously computed for the current functionality. It keeps the result file updated for each security checking. This only displays the latest CsC checking result between two components related to a particular functionality.

*Figure 12. Security properties of component CH03*

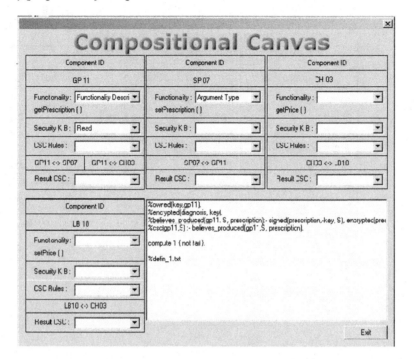

## IMPLEMENTATION

The tool is built on a number of tools and programming languages. The shell of the system is written in programming language C++. The main core processing engine is lparse and smodels. C++ was chosen as the main implementation language for a variety of reasons. The main reason for selecting it as the implementation language is because lparse and smodels are written in C++, which makes it consistent with the tool. The code of the tool is organised into directories. There are currently three directories set up in the tool of the system.

The main directories in the system are *Code, Debugger* and *Res* which, to date, contain the classes that implement the functionality of the current system. Multiple files such as definitions of classes and header files are located under the directory *Code*. The total number of lines of codes developed for the tool is around 4000 excluding the code of SMODELS tools. The size of the entire executable system, including the pre-packaged tools, is about 1MB. We consider this is a light-weight system which is capable of providing the most required functionalities for security characterisation and compositional analysis. Major file definitions and program files that have been written in C++ to implement this tool are briefly described as follows:

### Parser Class: parser.dsp, parser.rc, parser.clw

The parser.dsp file (the project file) contains information about the entire tool. It is used to build a single project. Other users can share this (.*dsp*) file. The *parser.rc* file is a listing all Microsoft Windows resources that the program uses. It includes the icons, bitmaps, and cursors that are stored in the RES subdirectory. The *parser.clw* file contains the information used by ClassWizard to edit existing classes or to add new classes. ClassWizard also uses this file to store the information needed to create and edit message maps, to dialogue data maps, and to create tool member functions.

*Figure 13. Test result of security compatibility between two components*

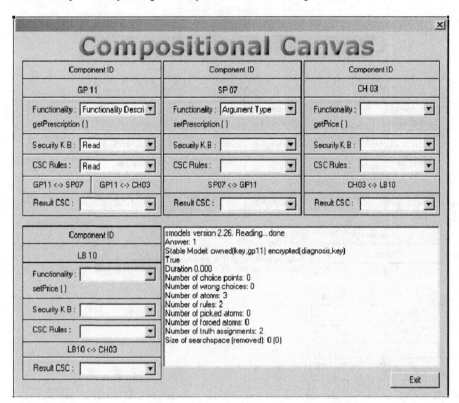

## Header File: parser.h, parser.cpp

The *parser.h* file is the main header file for the application. It includes the declaration of the project-specific headers (including Resource.h). The *parser.cpp* file is the main application source file that contains the application class CParserApp. It defines the class behaviours.

## Dialog Class: parserDlg.h, parserDlg.cpp

These files contain the CParserDlg class which defines the behaviour of the application's main user interfaces.

## An Example

We use a small example to demonstrate the applicability of the proposed tool. As we have seen in Figure 3, four components are currently loaded in the compositional canvas. These are GP11, SP07, CH03, and LB10. Component GP11 represents the focal component **y** running on a machine at a GP's office. Component SP07, loaded in the canvas, represents a specialist component **s**. The chemist's component **p** is represented by CH03. Finally, component LB10 imitates the **patient**. This example is based on a number of assumptions. Security properties of each component are consistent with the actual implemented security of the service. Furthermore, each service ensures the committed security to the composed application. The format used to characterize the security properties is standardized and used by all services. We display the security properties of two participating components before a checking is performed, in order to make a compositional security contract for the functionality getPrescription(). The security properties of GP11 and SP07 are shown in Figures

*Figure 14. Security properties of the component GP11 for getPrescription()*

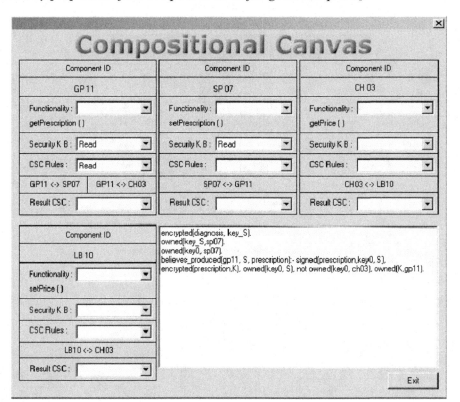

14 and 15 respectively. The security properties of GP11 are shown in Figure 14. To perform the security checks between components, we click on the button GP11◇SP07 as shown with an arrow in the figure.

The output screen displays the reasoning result, as shown in Figure 16. The figure shows that a match has been made between these two components. The processing time, number of matches, number of wrong choices, and so on, is displayed. The figure shows that the system took only 0.041 second to compute this result. It processed 19 atoms, and 20 rules. The system found 9 truth assignments from the security properties of GP11 and SP07. Based on the result, a CsC between these two components is established on the basis of the stable model found.

Component GP11 now makes a composition test with the chemist component CH03 as shown with an arrow in Figure 18. The security proper-

ties of these two for the functionality setPrice() are shown in Figure 17 (a) and (b), respectively.

Note that the security properties of GP11 related to this functionality are quite different from the properties associated with the previous functionality. The security properties of CH03 in Figure 17 (b) show that a CsC between GP11 and SP07 is required in order to satisfy the security requirements of CH03. The result for the compositional test between these two components is shown in Figure 18. The result has proved out to be true.

## RELATED WORK

The major concern of disclosing the security properties of software components has received little attention from the security and software engineering research communities.

*Figure 15. Security properties of the component SP07 for setPrescription()*

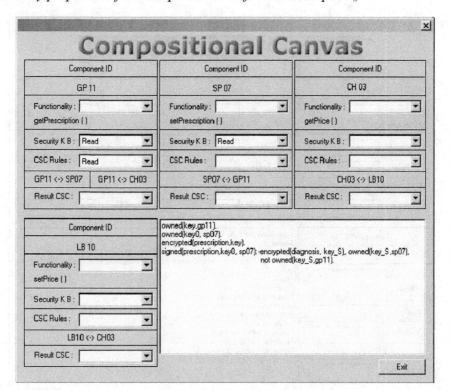

Broadly speaking, software security covers multiple layers of abstractions of the software systems ranging from systems software to application software. The research work and industry practices related to software security could be generally grouped into three abstraction levels of a software system: (i) *software infrastructure* level such as operating systems, security tools, network security; (ii) *middleware* level such as distributed computing framework, web services, security wrappers, testing with fault injection; (iii) *application* level such as security standards, compositional verification, security analysis, and aspect-oriented approach and pattern.

The issue of the characterization of component functionality has already been well studied, but the aspect of the characterization of non-functional attributes such as security, and reliability of components has not yet been adequately addressed. Some of the techniques that are proposed so far to increase the reliability and improve the security

of components include software wrapper (Talbert, 1998; Voas, 1998), operating system support (Zhong & Edward, 1998), built-in-language support (Gong, 1998). There are also other areas related to the security properties of components and their composition such as secure Internet, secure operating systems, secure data transfer protocols and the secure architecture where components are intended to be assembled and used.

A survey on current trends in secure software engineering reported in (Hein & Saiedian, 2009) provides a taxonomy of this topic, on-going challenges, and models for reasoning about threats and vulnerabilities. A thorough evaluation and comparative analysis of various processes for the development of secure software has been conducted recently (Win et al., 2009). It identifies the similarities, differences of various processes to develop secure software systems. The multidimensional Markov process model has been recently applied to develop the security assess-

*Figure 16. Result: security compatibility check*

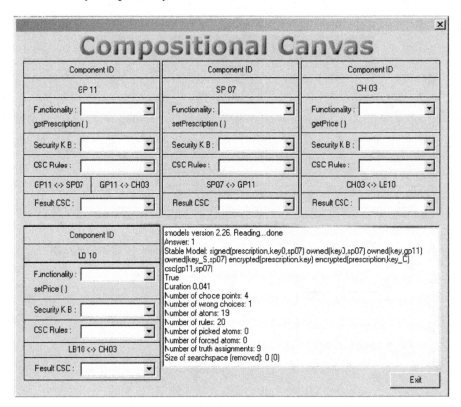

ment model of a software system (Wang et al., 2009). It provides details of the software security assessment for multiple component systems. In another approach in secure software engineering, model based aspect oriented software development technique has been employed to detect intrusion in software systems (Zhu & Zulkernine, 2009). Very few of these actually directly address the issue of characterizing and assessing the security properties of software components and their compositions.

WS-Security addresses Web service security by using existing security standards and specifications. WS-Security is a framework that adds existing mechanisms such as XML

Encryption, XML Signature and XML Canonicalization into a SOAP message. XML Encryption and XML Signature are used to encrypt and sign the contents of XML messages in Web services. XML Canonicalization prepares the XML mes-

sages to be signed and encrypted. In other words, WS-Security is a specification for an XML-based security metadata container (Seely, 2002a). What WS-Security actually does is that it enables security properties to be defined independently in the message in terms of composable message elements to exchange SOAP messages securely.

On another front related to Web-Security, an extension of Microsoft Internet Security and Acceleration (ISA), called ISAPI, has been suggested to secure Web services (Seely, 2002b). The approach offers the traditional way of securing message and communication. Similarly, WS-Trust, WS-SecureConversation, Security Assertion Markup Language (SAML) (OASIS, 1993) are not much different than the WS-Security. The W3C's Web Services Choreography Description Language (WS-CDL) is intended to define peer-to-peer collaboration between Web service participants (Leavitt, 2004). WS-CDL coordinates interactions

*Figure 17. Security properties of GP11 and CH03 for the functionality getPrice()*

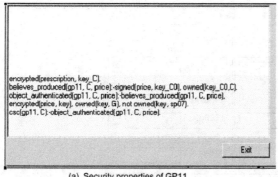

(a) Security properties of GP11

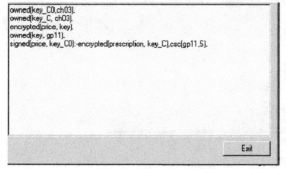

(b) Security properties of CH03

between users and Web services, and is especially critical for enterprises using Web services. Choreography provides a set of rules that describe how different services can work together to form the intended services. All current industry standards and research efforts have led to the development of tools for connecting components and making a Web service more secure based on the traditional security architecture and solutions.

Some classical works on security composition have been reported in (Abadi & Lamport, 1993; Alfaro & Henzinger, 2001) on the composition of specifications, compositional reasoning and the verification of concurrent programs. These papers propose methods for deducing the properties of a system by reasoning about based on assume-guarantee structural properties such as interface compatibility. However, they do not deal with the

non-functional properties such as the security of components. Their reasoning method is primarily based on assume/guarantee specifications similar to the required/ensured pair used in this thesis.

## FUTURE WORK

The current implementation supports a limited number of components at this stage; it does not support the incremental addition and deletion of components in the system. This system is easy to use. It does not require any training to use all the features of the tool. The tool gives software integrators the power to read the actual security properties supported by all candidate components and to reason about their security compatibility for various compositions. The tool also allows integrators to modify the security properties of the component in order to examine the various possibilities for the compositions. It demonstrates that an automated security characterization tool, as shown in this paper, is a quite useful for a viable security-aware composition.

The tool can handle any size of security properties in terms of the number of atoms and the inference rules. Since the data files are in the ASCII format, these are machine as well as human-readable. The performance of the tool is encouraging in the sense that the processing time for a reasoning takes a very negligible amount of CPU power. Since it is considered to be a lightweight tool, it can be used with any application system. The main advantage of this system is that integrators or programmers do not need to worry about the details of low level programming or system information. They simply load the components and check their security compatibility for their application.

One important architectural issue is to be noted in this framework. Instead of giving the reasoning capability to a central server, our framework distributes this capability to the compositional

*Figure 18. Checking security compatibility between two components*

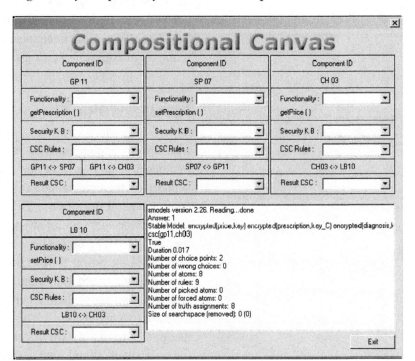

software which has been given sole power to decide the compositional contracts based on the underlying logic in the code. The tool could be further extended with several features. The chosen architectural style is flexible enough to accommodate any number of modules. The feature of system-level security characterization has not been implemented at this stage because the number of components is limited. A separate module computing the SsC could be plugged in with this tool. Such a module needs to include features such as selecting a system-level functionality, identifying the CsCs related to the functionality, extracting the security properties involved in the CsCs, and displaying those properties. It may require human intervention to form a complete SsC.

The suggested features that could be further added to the tool are outlined below:

- The capability of dynamic loading and unloading of the components from the Internet as they are acquired for a particu-

lar application. If a reasoning check of a candidate component does not show the compatibility with the enclosing system, it could be unloaded from the system.

- The Canvas could be expanded further to accommodate more than four components at a time with any number of atoms and rules. It could be achieved with the current architecture without much modification of the codes. Only the presentation layer needs to be changed.

- The security properties are certified by a profession body. The certificate attached with the security properties could be viewed with other information. A certificate carries the proof that the representation of the implemented security of a service is valid.

- The various reports on reasoning failures and successes for all the reasoning attempts could be generated for all the compositions.

• This tool could be integrated on top of most of the existing component platform without much effort.

The security properties built into a component represent the functions already put into place to withstand certain security threats. However, the real protection, along with the committed effort of the component from any security threat, is beyond the control of the component. Whether the available resources disclosed by the component are sufficient to withstand a threat is outside the parameters of our framework. The tool certainly provides a snapshot of how a security characterization and analysis tool could work and the feasibility for such a tool for real application.

The next logical step is to develop a full scale system for real-time systems composition. We extend this tool further for security conflict resolution. The characterization could be flexible enough so that a service could automatically add to or modify its security policies without compromising its security goal to settle a security conflict for a composition. The automatic capability of components for self-modifiable and self-repairable security policies in run-time would provide extra sophistication to the system composition.

The tool could also include automatic negotiation of security properties between agents or between the client and server, integration of the security characterization framework with existing technologies such as Web Services, service oriented computing, Grid services, and mobile networks.

## REFERENCES

Abadi, M., & Lamport, L. (1993). Composing specifications. *ACM Transactions on Programming Languages*, *15*(1), 73–132. doi:10.1145/151646.151649

Alfaro, L., & Henzinger, T. (2001). Interface theories for component-based design. In *Proceedings of the 9th Annual ACM Symposium on Foundation of Software Engineering* (pp. 109-120).

Baral, C. (2003). *Knowledge Representation, Reasoning and Declarative Problem Solving*. Cambridge, UK: Cambridge University Press.

Burrows, M., Abadi, M., & Needham, R. (1990). A Logic of Authentication. *ACM Transactions on Computer Systems*, *8*, 18–36. doi:10.1145/77648.77649

Common Criteria. (2005). *15408. Common Criteria for Information Technology Security Evaluation*. Gaithersburg, MD: NIST. Retrieved from http://csrc.nist.gov/cc/

Gong, L. (1998). *Java security architecture, JDK 1.2 (Tech. Rep.)*. Sun Microsystems Inc.

Hein, D., & Saiedian, H. (2009). Secure Software Engineering: Learning from the Past to Address Future Challenges. *Information Security Journal: A Global Perspective*, *18*(1), 8-25.

Khan, K., & Han, J. (2003). A Security Characterisation Framework for Trustworthy Component Based Software Systems. In *Proceedings of the COMPSAC*, *03*, 164–169.

Khan, K., & Han, J. (2005). Deriving Systems Level Security Properties of Component Based Composite Systems. In *Proceedings of the Conference on Australian Software Engineering Conference*, Brisbane, Australia (pp. 334-343).

Leavitt, N. (2004). Are Web Services finally ready to deliver? *IEEE Computer*, *37*(11), 14–18.

OASIS. (1993). *Security Assertion Markup Language* (Tech. Rep.). Retrieved from http://www.oasis-open.org/committees/security/

Seely, S. (2002a). *Understanding WS-Security (Tech. Rep.)*. Microsoft.

Seely, S. (2002b). *Securing Web Services with ISA Server (Tech. Rep.)*. Microsoft.

Syrjaanen, T. (1998). Implementation of local grounding for logic programs with stable model semantics (Tech. Rep. No. 18). Espoo Finland: Helsinki University of Technology.

Syrjaanen, T. (2000). *Lparse 1.0 User's Manual*. Espoo, Finland: Helsinki University of Technology.

Talbert, N. (1998). The cost of COTS. *IEEE Computer*, *31*(6), 46–52.

Voas, J. (1998). The challenges of using COTS software in component-based development. *IEEE Computer*, *31*(6), 44–45.

Wang, Y., Lively, W. M., & Simmons, D. B. (2009). Software security analysis and assessment model for the web-based applications. *Journal of Computational Methods in Sciences and Engineering, 9*(1,2S2), 179-189.

Win, D. B., Scandariato, R., Buyens, K., Gregoire, J., & Joosen, W. (2009). On the secure software development process: CLASP, SDL and Touchpoints compared. *Information and Software Technology, 51*(7), 1152–1171. doi:10.1016/j.infsof.2008.01.010

Zhong, Q., & Edwards, N. (1998). Security control for COTS. *IEEE Computer*, *31*(6), 67–73.

Zhu, Z. J., & Zulkernine, M. (2009). A model-based aspect-oriented framework for building intrusion-aware software systems. *Journal of Information and Software Technology, 51*(5), 865–875. doi:10.1016/j.infsof.2008.05.007

*This work was previously published in International Journal of Secure Software Engineering, edited by Khaled M. Khan, pp. 35-56, Volume 1, Issue 2, copyright 2010 by IGI Publishing (an imprint of IGI Global).*

# Chapter 15
# Towards Tool–Support for Usable Secure Requirements Engineering with CAIRIS

**Shamal Faily**
*University of Oxford, UK*

**Ivan Fléchais**
*University of Oxford, UK*

## ABSTRACT

*Understanding how to better elicit, specify, and manage requirements for secure and usable software systems is a key challenge in security software engineering, however, there lacks tool-support for specifying and managing the voluminous amounts of data the associated analysis yields. Without these tools, the subjectivity of analysis may increase as design activities progress. This paper describes CAIRIS (Computer Aided Integration of Requirements and Information Security), a step toward tool-support for usable secure requirements engineering. CAIRIS not only manages the elements associated with task, requirements, and risk analysis, it also supports subsequent analysis using novel approaches for analysing and visualising security and usability. The authors illustrate an application of CAIRIS by describing how it was used to support requirements analysis in a critical infrastructure case study.*

## INTRODUCTION

Frequent reports of human and technical security failures in systems highlight the need for designing usable security, but specifying usable and secure systems is easier said than done. Understanding why security controls are unusable means factoring in the characteristics of people using controls, the work they carry out while using controls, and the physical, social, and even cultural contexts within which the controls are used. While it is accepted wisdom that these concerns should be treated as

DOI: 10.4018/978-1-4666-1580-9.ch015

early as possible, eliciting and specifying requirements for secure and usable controls remains a hit-and-miss affair.

Requirements Engineering involves understanding the problem domain within which a system is situated, obtaining data from stakeholders in this domain, analysing this data to elicit a set of requirements, validating these requirements, and managing their evolution. When properly applied, techniques from HCI and Information Security complement these early stages of Requirements Engineering. Techniques used by usability professionals are grounded in observational, performance, and other qualitative and quantitative data. If used properly, this usability data can immerse analysts and stakeholders in the problem domain and help explore assumptions held about threats and vulnerabilities. Similarly, Goal-Oriented Requirements Engineering techniques are not only useful for eliciting requirements from goals, but also threats from anti-goals (Lamsweerde, 2004). Even the traditional workshop setting, where requirements are often elicited and validated, can support the design of usable security; participative approaches to risk analysis, e.g., (Fléchais et al., 2007; Braber et al., 2007) help stakeholders take a situated approach to security by alerting them to threats and vulnerabilities, identifying risks in their environment, and directing mitigating specification and design decisions.

The challenge of specifying usable and secure software systems comes not only from choosing the right combination of techniques, but also from analysing and managing the data arising from them. For non-trivial systems, risk and requirements analysis precipitate voluminous amounts of data. A requirement may be the leaf node of a large goal-tree, the root goal of which may be derived from mitigating a particular risk; this mitigation response may arise as a result of a chain of risk and requirements analysis. Furthermore, empirical usability data needs to contribute to any design decisions; if we mitigate one risk, the resulting usability impact of this design decision

may introduce others. Risk and usability ratings for a system design are also coloured by analyst perceptions; this allows human error to creep into any valuation.

Without tool-support, the security-usability balance can become uneven and overly subjective as risk analysis becomes more advanced. We need tool-support to manage security, usability, and requirements data, automate its analysis, and convey the results to stakeholders. This paper discusses CAIRIS (Computer Aided Integration of Requirements and Risk Analysis): a tool for managing the elements arising from usability, requirements, and risk analysis. This tool supports the elicitation of requirements from goals and tasks, and risks from threats and vulnerabilities. By structuring elicited data according to a meta-model for usable secure requirements engineering (Faily & Fléchais, 2010), meaningful traceability links between different model types can be automatically maintained, allowing data to be quickly analysed and visualised in a participative workshop setting. In the next section, we describe the related work motivating CAIRIS. In the subsequent sections, we introducing the tool, and we describe how CAIRIS was used to elicit requirements in a Critical Infrastructure case study.

## RELATED WORK

We are unaware of any single tool purporting to support the analysis of usability, requirements, and risk analysis. Some coverage is, however, provided by existing tools in each of these areas, and presented in the following sections.

### Conceptual Tools for Usability

Designing usable system requires an early focus on users and their goals (Preece et al., 2007). Although many engineers consider usability as synonymous only with user interface design (Seffah & Metzker, 2004), it is also a quality concerning the people interacting with these interfaces, and how they use them to perform work tasks. Unfortunately, we currently lack tool-support allowing analysts and developers to inform secure system design with usability insights.

Qualitative usability data can be represented as personas: fictitious, specific, concrete representations of target users (Pruitt & Adlin, 2006). By describing how personas carry out these scenarios, we can represent usability data in a meaningful way to stakeholders and inform the subsequent analysis accordingly. A step towards managing personas and the scenarios they participate in involves devising a suitable means of structuring and categorising this interaction. Such categorisations might also help measure the impact to usability of security design decisions, and vice-versa.

## Security Requirements Engineering Tools

Many tools for Security Requirements Engineering are general Requirements Management tools, which have been augmented for security. Such tools are often based on the spreadsheet metaphor, where a table is used to enter the attributes of a natural language requirement. By applying this metaphor, requirement attributes, such as its description, type, and rationale, can be quickly specified. Unfortunately, the generic strength of a Requirements Management tool is also its weakness; the lack of distinct semantics means an analyst must manually maintain traces between requirements and non-requirements artifacts.

Model-based approaches support traceability between different artifacts. If a tool conforms to the requisite meta-model then, as data is entered into the tool, it can be structured in a manner that facilitates automated analysis and visualisation. Tool-support for model-based approaches exist for risk analysis (Braber et al., 2007; Meland et al., 2008) and goal modelling (Respect-IT, 2007), but the task of integrating different model-based approaches for security requirements engineering

is non-trivial. One problem is the diversity of the models to be integrated; tools are often based on different meta-models, making understanding and agreeing interfaces difficult. If we assert that misuse cases <<threaten>> use cases, do we agree what it means for a use case to be threatened? Does a misuse case threaten the work carried out by a use case, or the assets associated with it? Houmb et al. (2009) describes some of the challenges faced when integrating these different techniques.

One strategy for integrating these approaches is to consider how Secure Requirements Engineering and HCISec might complement each other. Thimbleby (2007) argues that usability approaches are necessary, but far from sufficient for critical systems. The sheer size of the state space associated with interactive devices is so big that empirical evaluation on its own is unsustainable. It is, however, possible, to supplement usability analysis with basic technical methods.

## Visualising Secure Systems Design

Before stakeholders can measure the impact of usability of secure system design decisions, they need to understand the rationale underpinning a design. Previous work has illustrated how different visualisation techniques can both explain the results of analysis, and explore the resulting impact. While we are unaware of work purporting to visualise the analysis and resulting impact of usability and security, there has been work on independently visualising analysis in each area.

The canonical visual notation for modelling tasks as scenarios is the UML Use Case Diagram. These diagrams show the relationship between human or non-human actors, represented as stick figures, and coherent units of functionality, represented as ellipses. The diagrams have also been extended to display Misuse Cases, typically represented as black ellipse, and attackers, typically represented as an attacker with a filled black head (Alexander, 2002). Røstad has proposed an extended notation for dealing Misuse Cases, such that threats and vulnerabilities are modelled as separate entities in a Use Case Diagram (Røstad, 2006). With the aid of stereotyped associations and different attacker types, this notation allows more information cogent to a risk analysis to be modelled, and inside and outside attacks to be distinguished.

Techniques from information visualisation have also been used to support risk analysis. Hogganvik (2007) has concluded that colours are a useful means of distinguishing the value of different risks, and Feather et al. has used bar charts to portray information from Defect Detection and Prevention (DDP) models to make problematic areas more evident to stakeholders (Feather et al., 2006).

## CAIRIS

CAIRIS is a step towards tool-support for usable secure requirements engineering. CAIRIS supports the elicitation of usability, requirements, and risk analysis data before and during participative design activities. Data is entered into the CAIRIS front-end, and stored in a back-end database; the constraints in the database are based on the IRIS meta-model (Faily & Fléchais, 2010).

### Requirements Management

A recent survey on techniques for describing security requirements (Tøndel et al., 2008) concluded that there was no consensus on what a security requirement is. We have, therefore, decided to represent all requirements, including security requirements, as natural language text: the lingua franca for requirements specifications in industry. CAIRIS includes an editor for specifying natural language requirements, which is based on the spreadsheet metaphor; the table columns conform to the Volere Requirements Shell (Robertson & Robertson, 2009). Each table of requirements is associated with an asset or an environment. This

enables large specifications to be structured according to the concern most closely related to it.

CAIRIS also supports many of the features found in commercial requirements management tools, such as versioned changes to requirements, forward and backward traceability, and automatic requirements document generation. CAIRIS does not, however, support ad-hoc traceability between all artifacts; almost all traceability links are automatically generated and maintained as part of the modelling process. Manual links can only be created where they are meaningful. For example, it is meaningful to associate a task with a vulnerability; some aspect of a task might be open to exploitation, and it is difficult to cull such a relationship from the textual narrative of the task. However, it is invalid to manually associate a task with a role. Although this relationship may exist implicitly, it is as a corollary of a relationship between tasks and personas. This latter relationship can be generated automatically by CAIRIS when stating a persona participates in a task.

### Task Analysis

Empirical data about how target users plan to use the system-to-be is modelled in CAIRIS using personas (Pruitt & Adlin, 2006) and task based scenarios (Rosson & Carroll, 2002). These personas fulfil one or more roles. Although there is no agreed way of measuring the usability of a task with respect to its participating personas, a number of persona and task attributes match attributes found in the ISO 9241-11 (ISO, 1998) framework. ISO 92411-11 describes how usability goals can be evaluated using the goals of effectiveness, efficiency, and satisfaction. Based on this framework, we have devised a set of task usability properties (Figure 1); these can be used to evaluate how usable a task is to a persona. When defining tasks, these four properties are set for each persona participating in a scenario. Each of these properties map to one of the usability components of ISO 9241-11.

Each property has an associated value *x* which maps to a natural number in the range $0 \leq x \leq 3$; this corresponds to the qualitative values of None, Low, Medium, and High respectively. To ensure equal weighting for all 3 usability components, the usability of a task $U_t$ is computed using the equation

$$U_t = \frac{\overline{a+b}}{2} + \overline{c} + \overline{d} \quad .$$

where $\frac{\overline{a+b}}{2}$ is the mean task efficiency, $\overline{c}$ is the mean task satisfaction, and $\overline{d}$ is the mean task effectiveness. Variables *a*, *b*, *c*, and *d* refer to the task duration, frequency, demands, and goal conflict respectively. The mean value is taken across all personas carrying out the task in question. The higher the value of $U_t$, the less usable a task is for the personas associated with it. More meaningful values must be used for duration and frequency because values like low, medium, and high are

ambiguous. For duration, the qualitative ratings used are *Seconds*, *Minutes*, and *Hours or Longer* are associated with the values 1, 2, and 3 respectively. For frequency, the ratings used are *Monthly or less*, *Daily - Weekly*, and *Hourly or more*.

When mitigating risks, one or more roles are associated with each mitigating countermeasure; these roles will, in some way, be directly affected by the countermeasure being designed. By associating roles with countermeasure within IRIS, candidate personas and their tasks can be identified. For each task-persona pairing, countermeasure usability properties can be specified.

Based on this countermeasure usability data, it is possible to calculate the countermeasure usability factor $TU_t$. The right hand side of the equation computing $TU_t$ is identical to $U_t$, i.e.

$$TU_t = \frac{\overline{a+b}}{2} + \overline{c} + \overline{d}.$$

*Figure 1. Task (left) and countermeasure task (right) usability properties*

| Property | ISO 9241-11 Usability Component | Description | Values |
|---|---|---|---|
| Duration | Efficiency | The time taken by a persona to complete the task. | • None<br>• Seconds<br>• Minutes<br>• Hourly or longer |
| Frequency | Efficiency | The frequency a persona carried out the task. | • None<br>• Hourly or more<br>• Daily - Weekly<br>• Monthly or less |
| Demands | Satisfaction | The mental or physical demands on a persona. | • None<br>• Low<br>• Medium<br>• High |
| Goal Conflict | Effectiveness | The degree to which the task interferes with the persona's work or personal goals. | • None<br>• Low<br>• Medium<br>• High |

| Property | ISO 9241-11 Usability Component | Description | Values |
|---|---|---|---|
| Duration | Efficiency | The degree to which the countermeasure helps or hinders the time taken by a persona to complete the task. | • High Help<br>• Medium Help<br>• Low Help<br>• None<br>• Low Hindrance<br>• Medium Hindrance<br>• High Hindrance |
| Frequency | Efficiency | The degree to which the countermeasure increases or decreases the frequency a persona needs to carry out the task. | • High Help<br>• Medium Help<br>• Low Help<br>• None<br>• Low Hindrance<br>• Medium Hindrance<br>• High Hindrance |
| Demands | Satisfaction | The degree to which the countermeasure increases or decreases the mental or physical demands on a persona while carrying out the task. | • High Help<br>• Medium Help<br>• Low Help<br>• None<br>• Low Hindrance<br>• Medium Hindrance<br>• High Hindrance |
| Goal Conflict | Effectiveness | The degree to which the task helps or hinders the persona's work or personal goals. | • High Help<br>• Medium Help<br>• Low Help<br>• None<br>• Low Hindrance<br>• Medium Hindrance<br>• High Hindrance |

The values are, however, different. $\frac{\overline{a+b}}{2}$ is the mean contribution to task efficiency, $\overline{c}$ is the mean contribution to task satisfaction, and $\overline{d}$ is the mean contribution to task effectiveness. Like $U_t$, the variables $a$, $b$, $c$, and $d$ refer to the task duration, frequency, demands, and goal conflict respectively. The mean contributing value is taken across all countermeasures affecting the task in question. However, unlike $U_t$, each qualitative value $x$ associated with a property maps to an integer in the range $-3 \leq x \leq 3$.

Based on these equations, we compute the task summative usability $SU_t$ to be

$$SU_t = U_t + TU_t$$

like $U_t$, the higher the score, the less usable the task is for the associated personas. After calculating $U_t$ and $SU_t$, the score is normalised to a natural number in the range $0 \leq n \leq 9$. Given the potential of a task to increase or decrease usability, this value remains unchanged irrespective of it being a high positive or negative number.

## Risk Analysis

In CAIRIS, we define a risk as the likelihood of a threat exploiting a vulnerability to cause an impact. Threats are synonymous to attacks, and vulnerabilities are properties of a system making it liable to exploitation.

A risk rating can be assigned based on likelihood and severity tables in IEC 61508 (IEC 1998-2005) (Figure 2). However, this rating does not reflect values held about individual assets or threats. To score risks with respect to the perceived value of the assets threatened, we define a security property as a row vector $\begin{bmatrix} c & i & a & o \end{bmatrix}$, where $c$, $i$, $a$, and $o$ represent the values held for confidentiality, integrity, availability and accountability respectively. Each element $n$ is valued $0 \leq n$

$\leq 3$ based on whether the value held for that element is none, low, medium or high. The likelihood of the threat being realised, $L_r$, is computed using the equation

$$L_r = L_t - \overline{m_t}$$

where $L_t$ is the likelihood of the threat $t$ associated with risk $r$, and $\overline{m_t}$ is the mean likelihood value for the set of countermeasures mitigating the likelihood of $L_t$ occurring. The values of $L_t$ and $\overline{m_t}$ exist within the range $0 \leq n \leq 5$, and map to the likelihood categories in Figure 2. The severity of the vulnerability exposed by risk $r$ is computed using the equation

$$S_r = S_v - \overline{m_s}$$

where $S_v$ is the severity of the vulnerability $v$ associated with risk $r$, and $\overline{m_s}$ is the mean severity for the set of countermeasures mitigating the severity of $S_v$. Like threat severity, vulnerability values exist within the range $0 \leq n \leq 3$ and map to the vulnerability categories in Figure 2.

Risk impact is described by a security property, representing the values held in the assets at risk from risk $r$. Risk impact is computed using the equation

$$P_r = (P_t \times P_a) - \overline{m_p}$$

where $P_t$ is the security property of the threat associated with risk $r$, $P_a$ is the security property of the vulnerable or threatened assets at risk, and $\overline{m_p}$ is the mean security property for the countermeasures targeting the risk's threat or vulnerability.

Finally, the calculation for the Risk Score of risk $r$, $R_r$, is computed, as the product of the threat likelihood, the severity of the vulnerability, and the risk impact to the threatened assets.

*Figure 2. IEC 61508 tables for threat likelihood, vulnerability severity, and risk categorisation*

| Score | Threat Likelihood |
|-------|-------------------|
| 0 | Incredible |
| 1 | Improbable |
| 2 | Remote |
| 3 | Occasional |
| 4 | Probable |
| 5 | Frequent |

| Score | Vulnerability Severity |
|-------|------------------------|
| 0 | Negligible |
| 1 | Marginal |
| 2 | Critical |
| 3 | Catastrophic |

| Score | Risk Rating |
|-------|-------------|
| 1 | Intolerable |
| 2 | Undesirable |
| 3 | Tolerable |
| 4 | Negligible |

| Frequency | Consequence | | | |
|-----------|-------------|---------|----------|------------|
| | Catastrophic | Critical | Marginal | Negligible |
| Frequent | 1 | 1 | 1 | 2 |
| Probable | 1 | 1 | 2 | 3 |
| Occasional | 1 | 2 | 3 | 3 |
| Remote | 2 | 3 | 3 | 4 |
| Improbable | 3 | 3 | 4 | 4 |
| Incredible | 4 | 4 | 4 | 4 |

$$R_r = L_r \times S_r \times P_r.$$

Each element of row vector is added together, and the sum is normalised to an integer between 1 and 9. If, during the above computations, negative numbers are calculated, these values are resolved to 0.

## CAIRIS MODELS

One of the main differences between CAIRIS and related tools for security modelling is the model-driven nature of visualisation; models are automatically generated from specified, declarative data rather than via direct manipulation. This frees analysts from the tedious task of manually maintaining a variety of different models and the traceability relations between them.

Data elicited by CAIRIS is stored in a MySQL database conforming to the IRIS Meta-model (Faily & Fléchais, 2010), a conceptual model for usable secure requirements engineering. Rendering a tabular representation of the model data using the open-source Graphviz framework generates each model view. By using Graphviz's xdot output format, the position of different model elements is retained and, consequently, hit-testing can be supported in CAIRIS model viewer components; this allows analysts to click on nodes in a model viewer to obtain more information about the related model elements.

Several models can be automatically generated by CAIRIS based on elicited data. These are described in the following sections.

## Asset Model

The CAIRIS Asset Model is represented as a UML class model, where assets are represented as classes. If an asset is used within a task then the persona associated with the task is also displayed in the asset model as an actor. Similarly, depending on the level of zoom used in the model, a comment node is also displayed to indicate the traceability origin of the asset and its relationship.

Assets may be generated from countermeasures as part of risk analysis. If this occurs, then an association between the asset at risk and the countermeasure protecting it is generated; this association is labelled with a <<safeguard>> stereotype.

## Task Model

Personas and their task associations are represented using a modified form of UML Use Case diagram, where tasks are modelled as use cases, and personas are modelled as actors. This model also displays Misuse Cases and the attackers who realise them; attackers are displayed as actors wearing a black hat and Misuse Cases are represented as black ellipses with white text. Figure 3 is an example of a CAIRIS task model.

In the same manner that assets are associated with tasks, Misuse Cases are also, albeit indirectly, associated with assets. Each Misuse Case in CAIRIS is associated with a risk and, by exten-

sion, with a single threat and vulnerability. Consequently, if an asset is used by a task and also exposed by a vulnerability or threatened by threat, then we can model this Asset-Misuse Case relationship in CAIRIS. Because these associations potentially add to model clutter in a large task model, these are associations are displayed based on the model's current zoom factor.

## Goal, Obstacle, and Responsibility Models

We adopt a multi-model view of Requirements Engineering based on the goal-oriented KAOS methodology (Lamsweerde, 2009). KAOS defines goals as prescriptive descriptions of system intent, which are used as vehicles for refining requirements. The KAOS modelling notation is compliant with UML and, by extension, compatible with modelling notations commonly used by industry. The polygon KAOS model elements are also comparatively trivial to render visually. This is an important property for tool-support, which needs to rapidly compute and visualise the products of analysis without hindering participative design activities.

High-level goals stipulated by stakeholders at the beginning of a project can be refined by CAIRIS using goal trees; leaf goals can be refined as requirements, which can then be operationalised as tasks. Alternatively, a bottom up approach may

*Figure 3. Task Model example*

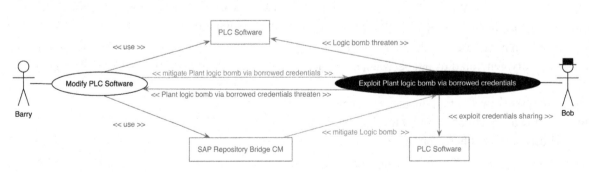

also be taken where goals or requirements are elicited from tasks and retrofitted into the goal tree.

Obstacles can be identified from requirements and goals; these are conditions representing undesired behaviour and prevent an associated goal from being achieved (Lamsweerde & Letier, 2000). By refining obstacles, candidate threats and vulnerabilities may be defined.

Horizontal traceability is implemented using concern links. If assets or asset relationships of concern are identified in goals or tasks, these are automatically generated in the asset model.

## Risk Analysis Model

The Risk Analysis model provides a quick-look view of the current risk analysis. This model only displays the elements of risk analysis, and other non-risk analysis elements associated with them. This view also compresses goal trees arising from risk responses, thereby making it easier to trace risks to mitigating responses, the requirements they treat, and the countermeasures they refine.

Risk Analysis model nodes are both colour coded and encoding with multidimensional data. As Figure 4 illustrates, information about the security properties is coded within asset and threat elements. Histograms indicate whether or not values are held for each property and, if so, whether that property is low, medium, or high. The colours selected for the confidentiality, integrity, availability, and accountability histograms are the 3 primary colours -- red, blue, and green -- together with black; the use of black and primary colours provide the maximum differentiation between property types (Tufte, 1990).

Risk analysis elements are colour coded with information, such as threat likelihood, vulnerability severity, and risk impact. Threats, vulnerabilities, and risks are also coloured based on their criticality: the more critical the element, the deeper the hue of red.

The Risk Analysis model also visualises metrics on requirements quality. These metrics are based on requirements completeness, the presence of an imperative phrase, and ambiguity. These are displayed using cartoon *Chernoff Faces* (Chernoff, 1973), and described in more detail by (Wilson et al., 1996). Eye-brow shape indicates the completeness of a given requirement. If no text is found in certain fields, or phrases like *TBC*, *None*, or *not defined* are present, the completeness score is marked down accordingly, and the eye-brows convey a negative mood. The eye shape indicates whether or not an imperative phrase exists in the requirement description. If such a phrase exists then the eyes becomes vertically elongated. The mouth indicates the presence of weak or fuzzy phrases, such as *mostly*, *appropriate*, *normal*, or *adequate*; the presence of these phrases turn the smile into a frown.

## Clutter Management

With so much information associated with the different model views, visual clutter can become a problem as models grow. Minimal distinctions in colour can be used to reduce visual clutter, and small contrasts enrich the visual signal increasing the number of possible distinctions (Tufte, 1997). To take advantage of this, we map the normalised values for $R_r$ and $SU_t$ to the respective risk (red) and task usability (blue) colour charts. The higher the risk or task usability score, the deeper the hue of red or blue.

Threat likelihood and vulnerability severity scores map to a colour chart similar to that of risk. An example of how these colours are applied to elements on the IRIS risk analysis model is provided in Figure 4.

CAIRIS also uses geometric and semantic zooming to make efficient use of the available viewing area as model data increases. Geometric zooming magnifies detail at the cost of loss of context; semantic zooming conveys additional model information as it is zoomed (Spence, 2007). The risk analysis model supports 3 levels of zooming. At the lowest zoom factor, only

*Figure 4. Risk Analysis model before (left) and after (right) risk mitigation*

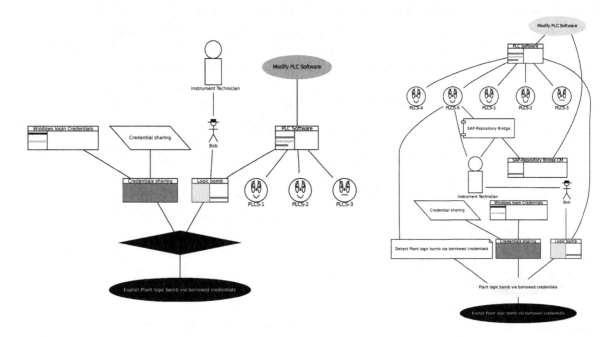

the most salient elements are displayed. As the zoom factor increases, the further elements are displayed, together with the associations between them. At the highest zoom factor, all remaining elements are displayed, together with additional information about assets and threats. At this level of granularity, textual labels are also displayed; at lower levels, such detail would be unreadable and distracting. Zooming is also supported in the task model. Associations between personas and attackers and Tasks and Misuse Cases respectively are displayed at low zoom factors. Associations indicating that a Misuse Case threatens a Task, or a Task mitigates a Misuse Case are displayed at medium zoom factors. Associations indicating assets used by a Task, exploited or threatened by a Misuse Case, or assets mitigating a Misuse Case are displayed at high zoom factors. Figure 3 illustrates a task model at a high zoom factor.

Even with support for zooming, clutter remains a problem in large models when viewed at a high zoom factor. Consequently, filtering is also supported in certain models. Models can be filtered

by task in the task model, and by node name and type, i.e., risk, threat, vulnerability, etc, in the risk analysis model; in these models, only the filtered model node and associated nodes are displayed. In the goal model, filtering is supported by goal name; when the filter is applied, the goal tree is re-displayed such that the filtered node becomes the root node.

## CASE STUDY

In this section, we report on a case study where CAIRIS was used to support the specification of requirements for a central repository for control software; this repository was designed to support the work of instrument technicians at a UK water company.

Water and sewage treatment is controlled by a substantial amount of control software. This software runs on many different devices and locations across wide geographic areas. As part of their responsibility for maintaining the water network, instrument technicians make software modifications to telemetry outstations, PLCs (Programmable Logic Controllers), and SCADA (Supervisory Control and Data Acquisition) workstations. Without a central strategy for controlling such software, water treatment integrity may be compromised if software is lost, or incorrect software is accidentally, or deliberately, installed on critical instrumentation. However, because maintaining the water network can be physically and mentally taxing, any new technology needs to be situated for the contexts within which these technicians work.

Following an initial scoping workshop, empirical data was elicited from 3 contextual interviews (Holtzblatt & Jones, 1993) with instrument technicians, 2 on-site qualitative interviews, and 2 telephone interviews with related stakeholders. Transcripts of these interviews were analysed using qualitative data analysis, the results of which were used to identify the behavioural characteristics of potential users. From these behaviour characteristics, a number of personas were developed. This qualitative data was also used to inform a number of candidate requirements, vulnerabilities, and threats.

Three one-day workshops were held to carry out requirements analysis; participants included instrument technicians, software engineers, IT support staff, and information security officers. Each workshop began by validating the results of previous sessions before undertaking requirements analysis, and supplemental task and risk analysis. CAIRIS was used by a joint facilitator/scribe in each of these workshops to specify the artifacts of task, requirements, and risk analysis, and display different models to facilitate discussion and subsequent analysis activities.

For the purposes of brevity, this section focuses on how CAIRIS was used to elicit and analyse requirements relating to the modification of PLC software.

## Category Definition and Asset Modelling

In the initial workshop, definitions were agreed and candidate assets were elicited. The meanings of Low, Medium, and High values were agreed for security properties, and categorical values for vulnerability severity were agreed and entered into CAIRIS. The IEC and ISO categories for threat likelihood and usability were also discussed with participants.

At this early stage, information about assets of value was also elicited and entered into CAIRIS. For this example, we focus only on two particular assets: PLC control software and repository access credentials. The security properties associated with PLC Software were Integrity (High), Availability (High), and Accountability (Medium). The properties associated with the repository access credentials were Confidentiality (High), and Availability (High).

## Usability Analysis

For reasons of brevity, we focus on the work of Barry, the primary persona in the case study. Barry represented an instrument technician who modifies software as part of his day-to-day work. In several tasks, Barry made infrastructure changes to plant equipment, which led to control software modifications and, consequently, interaction with the software repository. One of these tasks, *Modify PLC Software*, began with Barry examining the details of the task on the SAP-based planning system, determining the required plant changes, and speaking to plant operators about the work. Barry then carried out the necessary modification work and commissioned (tested) the changes. When this task was completed to the satisfaction of the plant operators, Barry closed the job on the planning system, and uploaded the modified programs to the software repository.

Given Barry's profile, this task takes several hours, but only occurs on an infrequent basis. Due to the amount of work involved in this task, coupled with the importance of the task itself, this is a high demand task, which does not interfere with his goals. Based on this information, CAIRIS can compute the usability of this task:

$$U_t = \frac{a \mp b}{2} + \bar{c} + \bar{d}$$
$$= \frac{3+1}{2} + 3 + 1$$
$$= 6.$$

## Goal and Requirement Elicitation

From the scoping workshop, a high-level goal for maintaining control software was elicited; this was broken down to sub-goals for maintaining different classes of software. In this case study, we focus only on the elicitation of security requirements following the analysis of a goal for downloading PLC software.

In this simple example, a number of functional requirements (PLCS-2, PLCS-3, and PLCS-4) were directly elicited from the Download PLC software goal. However, in this context, an instrument technician must be authorised to make any software downloads and potential software modifications. We chose to generate obstacles on each of these goals to explore their consequences. Workshop participants were interested in exploring the unauthorised access of repository login credentials as a cause of unauthorised downloading. While analysing this goal, the assumption that organisational login credentials would be used for accessing the software repository was explicated. This domain assumption was modelled elsewhere in the goal model, and further obstacle refinement proceeded on the basis of this assumption. A number of leaf obstacles, one of which pertained to

login credentials sharing, were identified. Based on this obstacle, a Credentials Sharing vulnerability was specified. Given the resources these credentials facilitate access to this vulnerability was scored as Critical.

The Chernoff Faces for these requirements in Figure 4 suggest quality problems with some of these requirements. In some cases, the eye-brow shape indicates that attributes, such as fit criteria and rationale, are missing in some cases. In the case of PLCS-3, the requirements description ("A user shall be able to download the latest version of the PLC software for a site") is also ambiguous. This is due to the presence of the weak-phrase *be able to*, which is open to multiple interpretations.

## Risk Analysis

Not all threats and vulnerabilities arose from requirements analysis. A *Logic Bomb* threat was defined based on the concern that an inside-attacker instrument technician might intentionally plant malicious code in PLC software to compromise water treatment. An example of such malicious logic involves turning off particular pumps in a water treatment plant at a designated time late one evening; this ensures the malevolent instrument technician receives a financially lucrative call-out to fix the problem. Alternatively, if another instrument technician's credentials are used, the Logic Bomb could undermine the company's confidence in his abilities. In the worst case scenario, turning off critical safety controls can lead to pollution of the water supply or substantial environment damage if raw sewage is released into the surrounding ecosystem. When carrying out this threat, the attacker wishes to hide his Logic Bomb within an innocuous code change carried out by another instrument technician. As such, the attacker looks to target the accountability property of this asset. All participants agreed that, dangerous as this threat is, its likelihood was low.

We defined a *Plant Logic Bomb via borrowed credential risk*. This risk occurs when an attacker carries out a *Logic Bomb* threat by exploiting the *Credentials Sharing* vulnerability. CAIRIS assessed this risk quantitatively by calculating its risk score. The likelihood and severity scores mapped to 1 and 2 respectively. The threat targeted only the accountability property of PLC software. The Windows login credentials, used to access the repository, are exploited by the *Credentials Sharing* vulnerability. Using this information, CAIRIS calculated the risk score $R_r$:

$$L_r = L_t - \overline{m_t}$$
$$= 1 - 0$$
$$= 1$$
$$S_r = S_v - \overline{m_s}$$
$$= 2 - 0$$
$$= 2$$
$$P_r = (P_t \times P_a) - \overline{m_p}$$
$$= ([0\ 0\ 0\ 3] \times [0\ 3\ 3\ 2])$$
$$= [0\ 0\ 0\ 6]$$
$$R_r = L_r \times S_r \times V_r$$
$$= 1 \times 2 \times [0\ 0\ 0\ 6]$$
$$= [0\ 0\ 0\ 12]$$

after rounding $R_r$ down, the normalised score resolved to 9.

This risk was mitigated with a detective mitigation response, such that occurrences of this risk would be detected after the event. A goal was generated to reflect the objective of detecting this risk and, after goal refinement, requirements for peer-reviewing PLC software changes were elicited. One of these requirements stipulated that an instrument technician making a software modification cannot be the technician selected to carry out a peer review. Based on this, a *SAP-Repository bridge* countermeasure was defined. This countermeasure was a software component for cross-checking a peer reviewer with an instrument technician responsible for a modification. This countermeasure is considered reasonably effective at targeting the *Logic Bomb* threat, motivating the value of 2 (Medium) for $\overline{m_t}$. This countermeasure also fosters a high value of accountability, giving rise to a score of $[0\ 0\ 0\ 3]$ for $\overline{m_p}$. Based on this information, the risk score can now be re-evaluated.

$$L_r = L_t - \overline{m_t}$$
$$= 1 - 2$$
$$= -1$$
$$S_r = S_v - \overline{m_s}$$
$$= 2 - 0$$
$$= 2$$
$$P_r = (P_t \times P_a) - \overline{m_p}$$
$$= ([0\ 0\ 0\ 3] \times [0\ 3\ 3\ 2]) - [0\ 0\ 0\ 3]$$
$$= [0\ 0\ 0\ 3]$$
$$R_r = L_r \times S_r \times V_r$$
$$= 0 \times 2 \times [0\ 0\ 0\ 3]$$
$$= [0\ 0\ 0\ 0].$$

These results show that while the accountability security value remains threatened, the likelihood of the threat was rendered inert, thereby reducing the risk score to the lowest possible value. As this countermeasure appeared to be effective, a new asset was defined for this component. The security property of this asset was based on the values placed on the countermeasure.

This countermeasure also positively influenced the task of modifying PLC software. A software component linking the repository with the SAP based work system means that job data can be used to support modification comments and, potentially, the job can be closed off by uploading a modification to the repository; this changes leads to the task being slightly less mentally taxing.

Therefore, the summative task usability can now be re-evaluated.

$$SU_t = U_t + TU_t$$
$$= 6 + \frac{0+0}{2} - 1 + 0$$
$$= 5.$$

The risk analysis model before and after risk mitigation in Figure 4 illustrates how the differences in $R_r$ and $SU_t$ are represented using different colours; the risk node colour has changed from a dark to a light shade of red, while the task node in the mitigated model is now a lighter shade of blue.

## CONCLUSION

Reasoning about security and usability is a challenge during requirements analysis, not least because analyst bias and data explosion can occur as specification and design activities progress. This challenge motivates the need for tool support to manage the results of this analysis, and use these results to further inform security and usability requirements analysis.

This paper has introduced CAIRIS: tool-support for usable secure requirements engineering. Although CAIRIS incorporates much of the functionality found in classic Requirements Management tools, elicited data is structured using a conceptual model for usable security. This allows CAIRIS to analyse risk and task analysis data as it is specified, and automatically generate different views of collected data. Our approach has shown that empirical usability and risk analysis data can be put to good use by applying simple qualitative and quantitative techniques to evaluate risks and tasks. By using this data with simple visualisation techniques, we can validate assumptions underpinning analysis, and explore the impact of certain specification and design designs.

Future work will examine the challenges associated with integrating CAIRIS with other tools, which support downstream secure software engineering activities.

## ACKNOWLEDGMENT

The research described in this paper was funded by EPSRC CASE Studentship R07437/CN001. We are very grateful to QinetiQ Ltd for their sponsorship of this work.

## REFERENCES

Alexander, I. (2002). Initial industrial experience of misuse cases in trade-off analysis. In *Proceedings of Requirements Engineering, IEEE Joint International Conference* (pp. 61-68). Washington, DC: IEEE.

Chernoff, H. (1973). The Use of Faces to Represent Points in K-Dimensional Space Graphically. *Journal of the American Statistical Association, 68*.

den Braber, F., Hogganvik, I., Lund, M. S., Stølen, K., & Vraalsen, F. (2007). Model-based security analysis in seven steps - A guided tour to the CORAS method. *BT Technology Journal, 25*(1), 101–117. doi:10.1007/s10550-007-0013-9

Faily, S., & Fléchais, I. (2010). A Meta-Model for Usable Secure Requirements Engineering. In *Proceedings of the Software Engineering for Secure Systems (SESS '10)*.

Feather, M. S., Cornford, S. L., Kiper, J. D., & Menzies, T. (2006). Experiences using Visualization Techniques to Present Requirements, Risks to Them, and Options for Risk Mitigation. In *Proceedings of Requirements Engineering Visualization (REV '06), the First International Workshop* (p. 10).

Fléchais, I., Mascolo, C., & Sasse, M. A. (2007). Integrating security and usability into the requirements and design process. *International Journal of Electronic Security and Digital Forensics, 1*(1), 12–26. doi:10.1504/IJESDF.2007.013589

Hogganvik, I. (2007). *A graphical approach to security risk analysis.*

Holtzblatt, K., & Jones, S. (1993). *Contextual Inquiry: a participatory technique for systems design* (pp. 177-210).

Houmb, S. H., Islam, S., Knauss, E., Jurjens, J., & Schneider, K. (2009). Eliciting security requirements and tracing them to design: an integration of Common Criteria, heuristics, and UMLsec. *Requirements Engineering*, 1–31.

IEC. (1998-2005). *IEC 61508: Functional safety of electrical/electronic/programmable electronic safety-related systems. Parts 1-7.* Geneva, Switzerland: International Electrotechnical Commission.

ISO. (1998). *ISO 9241-11. Ergonomic requirements for office work with visual display terminals (VDT)s - Part 11 Guidance on usability (Tech. Rep.).* Geneva, Switzerland: ISO.

Lamsweerde, A. v. (2009). *Requirements engineering: from system goals to UML models to software specifications.* Hoboken, NJ: John Wiley.

Meland, P. H., Spampinato, D. G., Hagen, E., Baadshaug, E. T., Krister, K.-M., & Velle, K. S. (2008). SeaMonster: Providing tool support for security modeling. In *Proceedings of NISK 2008.*

Preece, J., Rogers, Y., & Sharp, H. (2007). *Beyond Interaction Design: Beyond Human-Computer Interaction.* New York: John Wiley & Sons, Inc.

Pruitt, J., & Adlin, T. (2006). *The persona life-cycle: keeping people in mind throughout product design.* Amsterdam: Elsevier.

Respect-IT. (2007). *Objectiver.* Retrieved from http://www.objectiver.com

Robertson, J., & Robertson, S. (2009). *Volere Requirements Specification Template: Edition 14 - January 2009.* Retrieved from http://www.volere.co.uk/template.htm

Rosson, M. B., & Carroll, J. M. (2002). *Usability engineering: scenario-based development of human-computer interaction.* San Francisco, CA: Academic Press.

Røstad, L. (2006). An extended misuse case notation: Including vulnerabilities and the insider threat. In *Proceedings of REFSQ, the 12th International Working Conference on Requirements Engineering.*

Seffah, A., & Metzker, E. (2004). The obstacles and myths of usability and software engineering. *Communications of the ACM, 47*(12), 71–76. doi:10.1145/1035134.1035136

Spence, R. (2007). *Information Visualization: Design for Interaction.* Upper Saddle River, NJ: Pearson Prentice Hall.

Thimbleby, H. (2007). *User-centered methods are insufficient for safety critical systems.*

Tøndel, I. A., Jaatun, M. G., & Meland, P. H. (2008). Security Requirements for the Rest of Us: A Survey. *Software, IEEE, 25*(1), 20–27. doi:10.1109/MS.2008.19

Tufte, E. R. (1990). *Envisioning information.* Cheshire, CT: Graphics Press.

Tufte, E. R. (1997). *Visual Explanations: Images and Quantities, Evidence and Narrative*. Cheshire, CT: Graphics Press.

van Lamsweerde, A. (2004). Elaborating Security Requirements by Construction of Intentional Anti-Models. In *Proceedings of the 26th International Conference on Software Engineering (ICSE '04)* (pp. 148-157).

van Lamsweerde, A., & Letier, E. (2000). Handling obstacles in goal-oriented requirements engineering. *Software Engineering, 26*(10), 978–1005. doi:10.1109/32.879820

Wilson, W., Rosenberg, L., & Hyatt, L. (1996). Automated quality analysis of natural language requirement specifications. In *Proceedings of Fourteenth Annual Pacific Northwest Software Quality Conference*.

*This work was previously published in International Journal of Secure Software Engineering, edited by Khaled M. Khan, pp. 56-70, Volume 1, Issue 3, copyright 2010 by IGI Publishing (an imprint of IGI Global).*

# Section 6
# Secure Software
# Education and Training

# Chapter 16
# Secure Software Education:
## A Contextual Model-Based Approach

**J. J. Simpson**
*System Concepts, LLC, USA*

**B. Endicott-Popovsky**
*University of Washington, USA*

**M. J. Simpson**
*System Concepts, LLC, USA*

**V. Popovsky**
*University of Idaho, USA*

## ABSTRACT

*This article establishes a context for secure information systems development as well as a set of models used to develop and apply a secure software production pedagogy. A generic system model is presented to support the system context development, and to provide a framework for discussing security relationships that exist between and among information systems and their applications. An asset protection model is tailored to provide a conceptual ontology for secure information system topics, and a stable logical framework that is independent of specific organizations, technologies, and their associated changes. This asset protection model provides a unique focus for each of the three primary professional communities associated with the development and operation of secure information systems. In this paper, a secure adaptive response model is discussed to provide an analytical tool to assess risk associated with the development and deployment of secure information systems, and to use as a security metric. A pedagogical model for information assurance curriculum development is then established in the context and terms of the developed secure information system models. The relevance of secure coding techniques to the production of secure systems, architectures, and organizational operations is also discussed.*

## INTRODUCTION

Within the software engineering community, there is an increasing recognition that secure coding practices are only a subset of the activities needed to create secure information systems. Information systems, including the software, hardware, and people that contribute to those systems, continue to change and adapt to new technologies and science. This paper is organized around the fundamental ideas that (1) all system and software security exists in an adaptable system context, and (2) a range of conceptual models are necessary to organize, discuss and understand these adaptable

DOI: 10.4018/978-1-4666-1580-9.ch016

security aspects. The practice of secure information systems design, development, deployment and operation is shared by three professional communities, the systems engineering (including software engineering) community, the information assurance community, and the justice and intelligence communities. A generic system model is introduced and combined with a comprehensive, layered asset protection model to establish an abstract set of security concepts that are independent of any specific technology and/or application approach. The generic system model provides a common basis for the communication within the systems/software engineering communities regarding secure information systems. The asset protection model provides a focus point for each of the professional communities, and supports the clear communication of information associated with secure information systems.

As these two models are interrelated and expanded in a combined system security model, operational connections become evident. System operational effectiveness as well as operational suitability are defined, developed and discussed as they relate to security and security education. Potential information system risks need to be understood and addressed. To this end, a system security metric is introduced that enables an analysis of what risks might be present during the development and deployment of secure information systems. This tool also introduces a method to help determine what topics might need to be addressed within secure information systems or secure coding practices curriculum in order to mitigate those risks. This set of security concepts is then integrated with a pedagogical model for information assurance curriculum development. Common system attack patterns, as well as software weaknesses and vulnerabilities, are used as examples to illustrate the processes necessary to increase software quality by improving software security education and development. Standard secure software approaches are mapped over the combined system security model, and discussed

in the proper system context. A rich conceptual topology is developed and used to frame and communicate the many aspects of secure software engineering education. Next the generic system model will be introduced and outlined to support the introduction and discussion of the asset protection model.

## GENERIC SYSTEM MODEL

The practice of systems engineering has produced a number of technical, organizational and process-based approaches to the solution of large-scale, socio-technical engineering and process problems. One of the key aspects associated with systems engineering is the development of system context models and system functional models. The Generic System Model (GSM) is based on the fundamental idea of a system boundary that distinguishes a boundary between inside the system and outside the system. The system context exists outside of the system boundary; the system concept is used to organize the internal system content. The system boundary is composed of an outward-looking portion called the boundary context, and an inward-looking portion called the boundary concept that captures the controlling system values, rule sets, and structural view. As depicted in Figure 1, a specific system is composed of system functions, requirements, architecture and tests (Simpson, 2004).

System functions are the actions or activities that the system is designed to perform. System requirements describe how well the system must do its required functions. In combination, the system functions and the system requirements create the system problem statement. This fact further defines the system concept. The system architecture is the mechanism that performs the system functions as well as stated by the system requirements. Successful system tests indicate that the system architecture performs the functions as well as the requirements stipulate. This Ge-

*Figure 1. Generic System Model (Adapted from Figure 5, Simpson, 2004)*

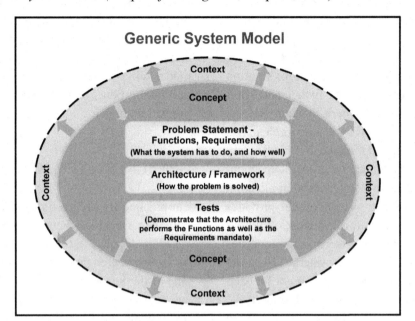

neric System Model is used to develop the structured process and control mechanisms needed to effectively address the many aspects that impact the production and deployment of a secure information system. When a software intensive system is defined at an architectural level, the resulting definition details the functional interactions between the manual-based, hardware-based and software-based processes. Consequently, system security and functional requirements can be allocated and assigned to these respective processes, and documented and recorded at the system level. Then, system security functions and requirements can be evaluated for implementation at (1) a manual, administrative level, (2) a software level, or (3) a hardware level. Using this approach, the system security functions are clearly identified, and assigned to a system architectural element that will perform the system security function. Further, each system component is either assigned a documented role in the system security function, or is documented as having no role in the system security function.

Generally, the practice of system security requirements elicitation is not well integrated into the development of software intensive systems. This is largely the result of environmental and contextual factors that impact the security of a deployed, operational system. These factors are commonly outside the scope and/or control of the software development process. As a consequence, typical security deployment assumptions are not well documented or communicated. The Security Quality Requirements Engineering (SQUARE) process model was developed to address some of the software definition and production issues associated with development of secure software systems (Meade, 2010). However, a large set of issues associated with a more comprehensive specification of the security context and security requirements remain for any given software intensive system. The Generic System Model is applied to help address primary system security context and requirements issues, by defining a general set of systems within which security mechanisms can be applied, maintained, and evaluated.

## GENERIC SYSTEM MODEL AND THREE PRIMARY SYSTEMS

The Generic System Model is used to describe three primary systems: (1) the product system, (2) the process system and (3) the environment system (Mar & Morais, 2002; Simpson, 2002). Based on a very simplified model of industrial production, these three systems are identified and defined by first locating the product system which is the output of the industrial process. The process system is the system that produces the product system. When considering software intensive systems, the environment system contains both the process system that creates the software product, as well as the software product system (see Figure 2). The distinctions between system production, and system operation and maintenance, must be well defined and clearly understood.

The particular type of software product system being developed will determine which software development and deployment processes can be used to increase the security of the deployed software. The process system includes the development and test system used to produce and deploy the software product. An active software security testing and patching process also must be part of any effective, secure software deployment. The process system can be controlled and managed using a wide variety of software development processes and techniques. Within the context of the software product, the environment system contains the hardware and networks that support and enable the execution of the software product. The environment system also contains the organizational and administrative personnel that use and maintain the operational system. System and software security threats also reside in the system environment. Many of the most important system and software security considerations are dependent on factors that exist in the system environment. These external security considerations have a direct impact on, and are reflected in the system architecture.

The dynamic and adaptive nature of the system environment establishes the need for a comprehensive, holistic view of the information system security problem. An expanded information system security model is used to effectively identify and communicate the relationship between the system, threats, and targets that exist in the environmental system.

## INFORMATION ASSET PROTECTION MODEL

An asset protection model (APM) has been developed to organize and communicate the basic aspects and components of overall system security (Simpson & Simpson, 2010). The asset protection model intentionally is designed to be independent of specific organizations and technologies – entities that experience high rates of change over time. As a result, the asset protection model will remain stable for an extended period of time. Two additional features of the APM design establish real value to the secure information systems community; it supports human short-term cognition and methods for computer-enhanced reasoning. Warfield (1990) provides a reasoned basis for the application of behavioral pathology studies related to the span of immediate recall performed by Miller in 1956 at Princeton University, and to the magical number 7 by Herbert Simon in 1974 at Carnegie Mellon University. Warfield goes on to establish a law and its corollary within systems science.

The Law of Triadic Compatibility quantifies the limitations of short-term memory as they related to human decision making. The human mind is compatible with the demand to explore interactions among a set of three elements, because it can recall and operate with seven concepts, these being the three elements and their four combinations; but capacity cannot be presumed for a set that has both four members and for which those members interact.

*Figure 2. Types of systems. (Adapted from Figure 6a, Simpson & Simpson, 2003)*

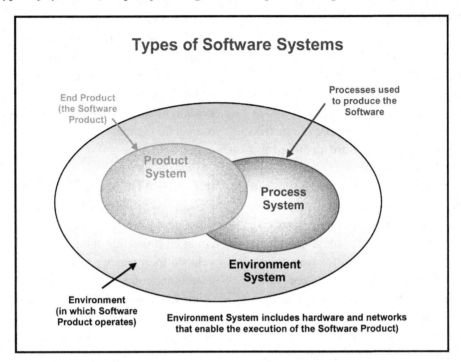

A Corollary to this Law is the Principle of Division by Threes. This principle asserts that: Iterative division of a concept as a means of analysis is mind compatible if each division produces at most three components, thereby creating a tree with one element at the top, at most three elements at the second level, at most nine at the third level, and so on. (Warfield, 1990, p. 45)

As designed, the asset protection model supports recursive definition of levels of abstraction, allowing multiple methods of computer-enhanced reasoning to be applied. These methods include dynamic analysis between interfaces as well as contained and internal controls within any given area of focus.

The asset protection model within this paper is focused on information as its target. With individual nodes patterned after the structure and form of the McCumber Cube, the APM presents a hierarchy of logical abstractions and associated categories designed to decrease the chance of cognitive overload for individuals that must think and

reason about asset protection issues from different points of view. The APM is depicted notionally in Figure 3. The asset protection model is organized in a hierarchy of concepts and logical categories starting with the highest level of abstraction at the top of the hierarchy named APM Level Zero. At Level Zero there is one cube, the asset cube, constructed from the three logical components associated with asset protection: (1) the system, (2) the target, and (3) the threat. These three logical components were selected to represent and focus the attention of the three primary professional communities associated with information asset protection: the systems engineering community (system), the information assurance community (target), and the legal, justice and intelligence community (threat). Each of these components is further elaborated at the next level of abstraction - Level One. At APM Level One, three cubes are used to further define the asset protection model in a more detailed manner: the system cube, the target cube and the threat cube.

*Figure 3. Asset Protection Model. (Adapted from Figure 3 of Simpson & Simpson, 2010)*

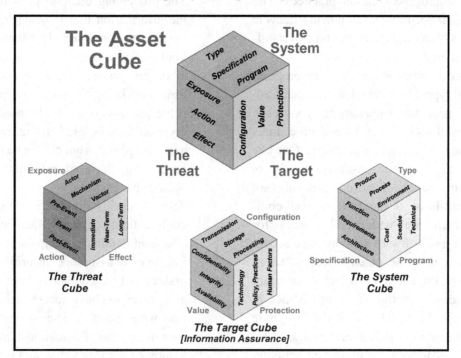

The system cube is developed to address the system type, system specification and system program:

- System type is divided into three systems types: the product system, the production process system, and the environment system. Each of these three system types represent an important system category that must be evaluated during a secure system and software requirements development activity. Many system and software vulnerabilities are found at the interfaces between these system types. These vulnerabilities may provide the foundation for, and support of, a successful breach of the system security. As a result, the definition of each system type as well as the operational role assigned to each system and/or system component is a basic first step in the design and analysis of any given security problem.

- System specification is divided into three specification types: functions, requirements and architecture. Each of these individual system specification types represents an important area of security evaluation during the design, deployment, evaluation and test of a secure software-intensive system. Standard system and software specification practices are used to manage the relationship between and among these system specification types. However, many security vulnerabilities are introduced in deployed systems because of the wide variety of specification, requirement and configuration management systems. These different systems are often organized around (1) the software system, (2) the hardware system, or (3) the integrated deployed system. Incompatibility between system specification management systems is driving the development of system security-based life-cycle practices that are different from the standard specification practices. The Microsoft Security Development Lifecycle process is an example of this type of stand-alone security life-cycle process.

- System program is divided into program control types: cost, schedule and technical. These program management types each have well known metrics and procedures that are used to manage programs. One key aspect of program management that drives the introduction of system and software vulnerabilities is the lack of well-com-municated, well-understood metrics for system and software security. The secure adaptive response potential (SARP) was developed to address this lack of program level security metrics (Simpson, Miller, & Dagli, 2008). SARP can be used to guide programmatic decision and resource al-location. Methods for using and applying SARP will be discussed in more detail later in the paper.

The target cube, at APM Level One, is ex-panded to target configuration, target value, and target protection. The target cube is patterned after McCumber cube, a well-known information assurance security evaluation model (McCumber, 2005). Every one of these target components is the source of essential software security require-ments, and must be considered individually and in combination with the other factors.

- Target configuration is applied to a well-defined information system that has an established boundary and is divided into three configuration types: transmission, storage and processing. The transmission component addresses information that is in the process of being transmitted between or among the other parts of the informa-tion system of interest. The storage com-ponent is designed to identify information that is at rest in the information system.

The processing component is focused on the information that is being transformed by a computer based algorithm, with one kind of information being the input to the algorithm process and a new kind of in-formation being the output from the algo-rithm process. It should be noted that en-cryption may be used in the transmission and storage states but cannot be used in the processing phase of information system operations.

- Target value is divided into three types: confidentiality, integrity, and availability. The confidentiality component is a basic information assurance security value and assures that only authorized agents (people and processes) have access to the informa-tion when needed. The integrity compo-nent is another foundational information assurance security value, and is associated with the fact that information must be ac-curate and maintain a known configura-tion. The availability component addresses the value produced when information can be accessed when needed. A significant system vulnerability exists when any of these foundational information assurance system security values is missing. As in-tegrated operational values, the vulnera-bilities in this area can be introduced from many sectors, including operational policy, system design, system architecture, soft-ware development and software deploy-ment configurations.

- Target protection is divided into three types: technology, policy and human fac-tors. The technology component is the pri-mary protection method used to ensure that the critical information values are main-tained in any information configuration and/or state. The policy component is fo-cused on the use of organizational and sys-tem based policies and practices that are enforced to enable the protection of critical information. The human factors component is focused on security education, training, and awareness activities required for secure operations.

The threat cube, at APM Level One, is defined by the threat exposure, threat action and threat effect. Each of these specific threat areas become key characteristics that drive the design and development of secure systems, software architecture, and software systems.

- Threat exposure is divided into three threat types: actor, mechanism and vector. The actor component addresses the autonomous agent that controls and guides the application of a specific threat. The mechanism component describes the process and equipment that is used to generate and maintain the threat behavior. The vector component identifies the channel and/or pathway used to deliver and/or activate the threat mechanism.
- Threat action is divided into three types: pre-event, event and post-event. The pre-event component is focused on system configuration and behavior prior to the initiation of any threat action. The event component is used to define a specific type of threat action. The post-event component is focused on system configuration and behavior after the threat action has occurred. The pre-event component would address actions necessary to prepare an information system to be "forensic ready." While the post-event component would address the actions necessary to successfully take legal action against a threat actor in a court of law.
- Threat effect is divided into three components: immediate, near-term and long-term. The immediate effect addresses instant impact created by a successful attack on an information system. The near-term

effect is focused on identifying impacts to the organization and/or information system that happen between one and thirty days. The long-term effect is used to analyze and evaluate impacts and changes to the organization and/or information systems that happen after 30 days.

As a focal point for the legal community, the threat cube establishes an area wherein the system requirements needed to support effective legal action against threat actors can be addressed.

The APM provides a rich set of conceptual categories that cover the complete range of information system and software security concerns including aspects of program management, technological, and operational considerations associated with secure system and software development. The secure adaptive response potential (SARP) metric, used to evaluate system and software security, has components that closely correlate with the APM components. System security operations are evaluated using the SARP metric components that generally describe the operation and maintenance profile of the deployed system. SARP's key components are organizational, technical, operational, and context:

- The SARP organizational component includes consideration of security training, policy, resources, culture, values and resource priority.
- The SARP technical component considers cryptographic strength, mean-time-to-attack, attack tree probabilities, intrusion detection, intrusion prevention, and software metrics.
- The SARP operational component evaluates stability, safety, maintainability, reliability, confidentiality, integrity, availability and authentication.
- The SARP context component covers external threat, internal threat, threat monitoring, external stability and internal stability.

Integrating and combining the values associated with each of these SARP components provides useful system security measures that can be used to guide information system and software security decisions.

## APM AND THE SQUARE PROCESS

The conceptual and logical structure provided by the Asset Protection Model provides a well-bounded system security domain that can provide clearly bounded scope for system and software security requirements engineering activities. The SQUARE process, introduced earlier in the paper, has nine basic steps that cover the complete secure software requirements development process. A synopsis of the way in which the APM supports the application of the SQUARE process is presented in Table 1.

The SQUARE process is a valuable tool when it is deployed in an organizational environment that has strong process-based policies and practices (Meade, 2010). The APM works together with the SQUARE process to further define, refine, and structure the software security related activities needed to produce a secure software intensive deployed system.

## ASSET PROTECTION MODEL, LEVEL ONE INTERFACES

The three APM cubes at Level One are designed to create three structured Level One interfaces. Depicted in Figure 4, these structured interfaces are: (1) the Threat-Target Interface, the Target-System Interface, and 3) the System-Threat Interface. These structured interfaces create a conceptual plane upon which the associated professional communities can arrange data and information in a manner that represents the identified items of interest for each type of interface exchange. In

this manner, the structured interfaces support the development of operational security patterns by the professional communities. As noted earlier in the paper, the system cube is used to focus the information and expertise from the systems engineering community. The target cube is used to focus information, expertise, and all related aspects from the IA community. Similarly, the threat cube is designed to have the legal and justice community as its primary controlling group. While there may be strong conceptual overlap and/or conceptual conflicts in many areas of the APM, the model structure and the model interfaces are designed as areas where these conceptual conflicts can be effectively addressed. Operational security patterns associated with the APM interfaces are designed to support the development of suitable software and system security requirements that may be outside the detailed experience of the software developer and/or the system customer. General categories of system deployment patterns and system deployment contexts are used in the education of secure software engineers to identify the controlling contextual security aspects.

Computer forensics is an example of the activity that takes place on the system-threat interface. While no fundamental software security requirements are generated directly from the threat cube, there are a large number of derived system and software security requirements associated with preparing a system to support successful criminal prosecution. The APM can be used to organize and evaluate system and security activities in a systematic fashion. This form of human and computer analysis highlights areas like the threat-system interface wherein an interdisciplinary combination of knowledge, skills, and abilities must be developed and applied. In the area of digital and computer forensics, system and software security topics associated with the development, deployment, and operation of networks, operating systems, file systems, and applications must be addressed. However, law and ethics top-

*Table 1. APM contextual support for SQUARE process*

| SQUARE Process Steps | APM Contextual Support |
|---|---|
| Step 1: Agree on definitions | A. Gross indicates that "All communication takes place in a shared contextual space." (Gross, June 11, 2010). The activity of developing, identifying and gaining agreement on specific system security requirement definitions helps form and structure a shared contextual space for everyone participating in the SQUARE activity. In addition, the APM limits and bounds the valid concepts that can populate the shared contextual space. The APM also develops and reinforces a shared understanding of the secure software system requirements development contextual space. |
| Step 2: Identify security goals | The system security goals must be developed at a typical level of organizational deployment and operation, and/or a range of typical operational deployments. The definition of the deployment and operational environment will begin the process of scoping the operational and application security problem set. The APM assists in the identification of security goals by providing a well understood set of security constructs and concepts that can be used to define and record the needed set of security goals. |
| Step 3: Develop artifacts to support security requirements definition | The APM structure is used to identify, categorize and establish relationships between all requirement artifacts associated with the system development. The system component of the APM provides the framework upon which existing system requirements can be evaluated for system security impacts. The target component of the APM outlines the security configuration, protection and value characteristics that must be considered in the security artifact development and production. The threat component of the APM addresses possible exposure, effect and action that impact security requirements artifacts. |
| Step 4: Perform a risk assessment | The APM supports the activities of performing a risk assessment in a number of fundamental ways. The APM organizes the system information in terms of a system, threat and target. APM target content is based on a well known model for comprehensive system security and risk evaluation, the McCumber Cube (McCumber, 2005). This well known model supports a structured set of risk evaluation techniques and approaches. |
| Step 5: Select elicitation techniques | The well-balanced structure of the APM provides direct support for structured requirements elicitation techniques and processes. |
| Step 6: Elicit security requirements | The APM provides the structure, content organization and artifact framework necessary to support any type of structured security requirements elicitation and development process. |
| Step 7: Categorize requirements into levels (system, software) and type (requirements, constraints) | The APM system specification and program components directly support the evaluation and categorization of system security requirements. In a complete system development, the system software security requirements would be evaluated in the context of all the other system constraints and requirements. |
| Step 8: Prioritize requirements | The complete system scope as well as the attention to value, threat and function in the APM support the activity of requirements prioritization. The structured information and data associated with the APM can be used as direct inputs for formal ranking tools like the analytical hierarchy process (AHP) (Simpson, Miller, & Dagli, June, 2008). |
| Step 9: Inspect requirements | The inspection and evaluation of system and software security requirements is greatly aided using the APM structured framework that is conceptually organized around the fundamental concepts of the system security asset protection domain. |

ics must also be interwoven with the classical system and software topics to address rules of evidence, chain of custody of evidence, process and methods for search and seizure, as well as other items to prepare evidence for presentation in a court of law (Endicott-Popovsky, Popovsky & Frincke. June, 2004).

## ASSET PROTECTION MODEL, LEVEL TWO INTERFACES

At APM Level Two, the system, target and threat components are further delineated into their three essential areas of focus, notionally depicted in Figure 5. Continuing with the systematic decomposition and evaluation of the component interfaces generates a well defined set of localized interac-

*Figure 4. Asset Protection Model (APM) level one interfaces (Adapted from presentation slide 13, Simpson & Endicott-Popovsky, 2010)*

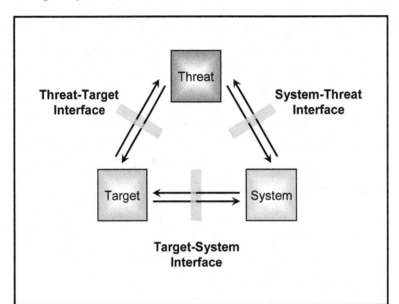

tion areas that must be analyzed and evaluated to enhance the probability that all primary areas of concern have been addressed.

As described in the initial description of the Asset Protection Model, the system type component is expanded to environmental system, process system and product system. The system specification component is expanded into system functions, system requirements and system architectures. The system program component is developed by addressing system cost, system schedule and system technical components. These three system representations at Level Two are designed to create three structured interfaces. These three structured interfaces are: (1) *Type-Specification* Interface, (2) *Program-Type* Interface, and (3) *Specification-Program* Interface. These interfaces are used by the systems engineering community to organize the information exchange between the system representations at APM Level Two. For example, when considering the Type-Specification Interface of the system cube, the content and use of this interface will be greatly impacted by the general system type:

product system, process system, environment system. When the system or software product system is the point of focus, the Type-Specification Interface is highly developed because the product development is controlled by the product system specification. When the product development process system is the point of focus, the Type-Specification Interface is also highly developed because the product quality and configuration depend directly on the product development process. However, when the environment system is the point of focus, the Type-Specification Interface is less well developed because the environmental system is not under the design control of the product developers. It is possible to describe an acceptable product system environment, but the real environment system is always different with varying levels of system threats.

Also in the earlier description of the APM, the target configuration component is expanded into transmission, storage and processing at Level Two. The target value is elaborated to confidentiality, integrity and availability. The target protection component is expanded into technology, policy

*Figure 5. Asset Protection Model (APM) level two interfaces*

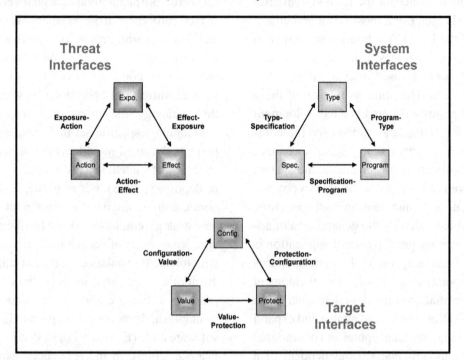

and human factors. These three target representations at Level Two are designed to create three structured interfaces. These three structured interfaces are: (1) *Configuration-Value* Interface, (2) *Protection-Configuration* Interface, and (3) *Value-Protection* Interface. These interfaces are used by the information assurance community to organize the information exchange between the target representations at Level Two. For example, when considering the Protection-Configuration Interface the content of the interface will be determined by the information configuration. Each information configuration category will apply different types of technology, human factors, policies and procedures to the task of providing the required level of information system security and risk reduction. Groups of typical solutions, that address the areas defined by the Protection-Configuration Interface, can be developed into a set of security solution patterns that enhance the ability of educators to clearly communicate these topics among themselves as well as to students.

Again summarizing earlier descriptions from the APM, the threat exposure component is expanded to threat actor, threat mechanism and threat vector at Level Two. The threat action is elaborated to pre-event, event and post-event. The threat effect addresses immediate, near-term and long-term effects. These three threat representations at Level Two are designed to create three structured interfaces: (1) *Exposure-Action* Interface, (2) *Effect-Exposure* Interface, and (3) *Action-Effect* Interface. These interfaces are used by the legal, justice and intelligence community to organize the information exchange between the threat representations at Level Two. The Exposure-Action Interface addresses some of the digital forensic issues discussed earlier. Given the goal of applying legal remedies to computer security breaches, the Exposure-Action Interface can be used to organize and communicate the activities associated with preparing a computer system to collect evidence (pre-event actions) collecting evidence during a security breach (event) and preparing the evidence for the legal system after the security breach event (post-event actions).

Each of the Level Two interfaces, similar to the Level One interfaces, provides a bounded contextual plane that is used to develop operational security patterns. The primary purpose of these operational security patterns is the development of a more formalized mechanism for the communication of security risk in a specific context. While the software engineer and/or the system customer are not expected to be able to provide detailed security requirements in most areas, they should be able to identify the general area of application. Once the general area of application is identified, then the operational security patterns can be incorporated into the software development process. Information content, systems and value to an organization continue to evolve and expand at an increasing rate. Conceptual and operational patterns and models that are independent of a specific technology or specific organization are necessary if they are to remain valuable system security management tools over an extended period of time.

## PEDAGOGICAL MODEL FOR INFORMATION ASSURANCE CURRICULUM DEVELOPMENT

The pedagogical model for information assurance curriculum development (PMIACD) is considered a high-level meta-system model from which a specific Information Assurance Curriculum system may be developed (Endicott-Popovsky, Popovsky, & Frincke, 2005). Secure information systems and software code development is one component of an information assurance (IA) curriculum. The PMIACD is depicted notionally in Figure 6.

The five elements of the PMIACD are composed of two intelligent elements, the instructor and the student, as well as three infrastructure elements that are subject to varying rates of change and adaption. All of the elements of the model function as an interconnected whole. The three infrastructure elements are the goals, content, and didactic processes of the pedagogy. The PMIACD exists in a dynamic professional and social context that includes economic and political environments as well as a constantly evolving set of threats, vulnerabilities and operational systems. Within this pedagogy, the instructor is responsible for developing a specific set of infrastructure components designed to address the needs of a specific type of student in a given context (Popovsky & Popovsky, 2008). For example, given an economic and employment environment wherein a new strategic emphasis is placed on the production and deployment of secure software code, an instructor needs to balance the type of students with economic forces and needs of the employer to produce software engineers that understand the principles and practices of the production of secure software code (Endicott-Popovsky, Popovsky, & Frincke, 2005). In the referenced example, the students were professional software developers that needed to understand the new software coding techniques, and to gain the ability to consistently produce secure software code.

**Goals**: The overall goal was to induce learning within a mature set of students, resulting in a change in behavior. The learning principles and objectives were designed to enhance individual personal and professional growth based on the values expressed, and the expertise demonstrated, by the student. The learning principles helped prioritize the learning objectives, and were based on targeted measurable outcomes. The learning objectives for the secure coding class were based on the information assurance and trustworthy computing best practices. These learning objectives included: understand and iterate information assurance principles and practices, understand and demonstrate threat modeling techniques, implement secure coding techniques, produce systems that protect information.

*Figure 6. Pedagogical model for Information Assurance (IA) curriculum development. (Adapted from Figure 1, Endicott-Popovsky et al., 2005)*

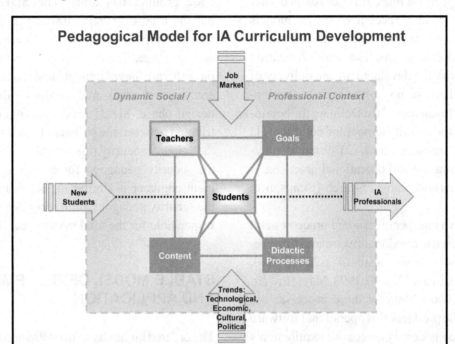

**Content:** Content for a secure software code class is drawn from a large body of knowledge that is based on standards produced by recognized groups and subject matter expert organizations. The specific content for a class must be tailored to the available time and goals of the class. Further, a range of learning levels and acquired skills must be supported by the class content and sequence of presentation. Given the dynamic operational context of current computing systems, the student must learn to analyze new software security problems, develop and adopt new secure software practices and become independent in the practice of secure software development and deployment.

**Didactic Processes:** Didactic processes used to deliver the selected content for the secure software production class are tailored based on a number of environmental factors including class type (class room or online),

student type (beginning or experienced), and learning outcome goals. Secure software techniques can be based on practices for specific types of computer operating systems, kinds of software operations (database), and/or types of system architecture (two tier or three tier). The didactic process is also adjusted to address the unique needs of specific software techniques.

Using the Pedagogical Model for Information Assurance Curriculum Development (PMIACD), the secure software code development (SSCD) curriculum development model retains the same two generic intelligent elements and three generic infrastructure elements as those found in the PMIACD. Instances of PMIACD and the SSCD curriculum development will have different content when different specific types of instructional activity are planned and developed. The primary output from the SSCD curriculum development process is the secure software education system (SSES) that will be more fully developed later in this paper. A set of specialized system models from the systems engineering domain are used to structure and encode processes and information associated with the development and delivery of these specialized secure software code development instructional materials. Defining the boundary between the security impact and control of (1) secure code practices versus (2) system deployment configuration and operational practices, is an area of current active research (Simpson et al, 2010).

There are a number of standard processes and approaches used to develop software and software-intensive systems (IEEE-Std-1471-2000, 2000, October; IEEE/EIA 12207.0, 1998, May; Howard & Lipner, 2006). Many of these processes are focused on the production of operational software that has not considered the security requirements associated with the use of the deployed software. Software development processes that do consider security requirements appear to be constrained to addressing security vulnerabilities that are introduced via software defects and/or system architectural defects. The operational effectiveness and suitability of secure coding practices must be evaluated in terms of the deployed system context. In many cases, the current deployed system configuration and content is the aggregated sum of decisions and actions made by a large group of individuals, many of whom may be unknown to the software and system developers. Specialized system models, like the APM, create a framework that supports the evaluation and documentation of the larger operational system context as well as development of the software system requirements. Such a framework can be used to capture, document and communicate the life-cycle security requirements associated with secure system deployment.

The Microsoft Security Development Life-cycle (SDLC) is an example of a well-defined process used to address the reduction of software defects and security vulnerabilities in software code product baselines. The SDLC process has the following steps: training, requirements, design, implementation, verification, release and response. These process steps are focused on software development, and consider threat analysis and attack analysis during the software design phase. SDLC process activities are distributed between the software product teams and the primary security organization. It is clear that the security pedagogy for a software development engineer is similar to, but different from, the security pedagogy for a security professional responsible for the total system security.

## STABLE MODEL DEVELOPMENT AND APPLICATION

The ordered hierarchy of the APM and the generic system model provide the foundation for long term conceptual stability associated with secure system and software product production, deployment and utilization. The systems engineering community has developed methods and processes that address the total system including software, hardware and personnel. Standard systems engineering analysis techniques are used to create and evaluate a set of system products that are built upon the conceptual foundation established by the APM and GSM. While secure software coding techniques contribute to the total system security evaluation, other system operational aspects must also be considered. Given any system as depicted in Figure 7, the mission function, system function and system architecture comprise system analytical products that can provide insights to topics that need to be addressed, and to scope and identify system risks (Simpson & Simpson, 2006). As earlier defined within the Generic Systems Model, system functions are those actions or activities that the system is designed to perform. The system architecture is the mechanism that performs the system functions as well as stated by the system requirements. Both of these system analytical products – the system function and the system architecture – are part of the concept, or inward-looking, space of a system. A mission function is part of the context, or outward-looking boundary, for any given system. The mission function identifies what actions need to be performed to be successful. A mission often is supported by multiple system functions.

For example, the University of Washington has a Center for Information Assurance and Cybersecurity (CIAC). The primary mission of the CIAC is to identify, address and promote solutions for information assurance and cyber-security problems and issues. Specific CIAC systems, including curricula, are designed to support the fulfillment of specific aspects of the CIAC mission function. Each of these CIAC systems has system functions associated with them. Clearly, secure software coding techniques are only part of the knowledge and skills that must be developed in the students associated with the CIAC. The Secure Software Education System (SSES) within the CIAC is the system that focuses on secure software development, deployment and utilization, and has its own mission function. However, the SSES must reflect and encompass the areas of focus found in the asset protection model – that is, the context of the threat, system and information that are part of the complete deployed system of interest.

It should be noted that Figure 7 also provides some insights to the relationships between mission functions, system functions, and system architectures and the implications therein. Operational effectiveness is considered a property of the system function that determines how well the mission function is performed. Operational suitability and life cycle cost are both properties of the system architecture. Risk, however, is a function of them all – the missions function, the system function, and the system architecture. Mentioned briefly earlier in the paper and in the following pages, the Secure Adaptive Response Potential (SARP) metric was developed in part

to determine where security risks might reside within an overall system, as well as to evaluate operational suitability.

The Secure Software Education System (SSES) is further developed in this paper to demonstrate the structured application of systems engineering techniques. The first step in this structured systems engineering process is to establish the SSES mission function, and its supporting mission sub-functions designed to achieve the mission. The next step is to analyze candidate SSES system functions to determine how each candidate system function supports the SSES mission function. The SSES system functions are based on a generic set of didactic functions associated with a standard educational process. The generic didactic functions are tailored by selecting specific secure software subject content, and complementing the content with applicable methods of demonstration and instruction. Instructional modules are developed to perform each of the selected didactic functions required by the SSES. This process allows for the development and evaluation of a set of alternative instructional and didactic module types. Given a specific educational area, with clearly documented goals and objectives, the instructor can select the modules that best meet the didactic goals and objectives of that specific area, or develop one that is more appropriate.

Considered in this paper are 14 categories of the SSES secure coding system functions that are based on the Common Weakness Enumeration research concept categories (CWE, 2010). These categories are listed and described in Table 2.

A basic course in secure software engineering would introduce the students to each of these categories, but would focus on the most basic and fundamental software security coding techniques. These beginning students would also be introduced to the automated tools, techniques, software languages and architectures that are used to produce a secure software deployed code base. Intermediate and advanced courses in secure software engineering would cover all of the categories, and

*Figure 7. Mission function, system function, and system architecture. (Adapted from Simpson, 2006)*

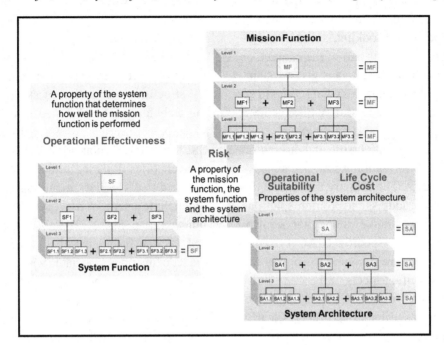

build on the secure coding techniques introduced in the basic class.

The Secure Software Education System (SSES) addresses secure software engineering education using three levels of content difficulty: basic, intermediate and advanced. The SSES basic level educational content includes an introduction to organized responses to software security issues. These sources of publicly available data organize and categorize software security issues, and include the National Vulnerability Database and Common Weakness Enumeration among others. The basic level also includes a strong focus on fundamental software security issues and solutions that address buffer overruns, integer overflows, SQL injection, XML injection, command injection, improper use of cryptography, and failure to protect network traffic. Computer and network architecture security flaws and other issues are introduced at the basic level, but are further developed in the intermediate level didactic material. Computer programmers and beginning software system architects are the primary types of students for the beginning level material.

At the intermediate level of the SSES secure software engineering education, the basic secure coding material is explored in more depth, and provides an additional emphasis on computer, application and network security practices. Also included in the intermediate level content are software security vulnerabilities that are rooted in the application and network architecture, such as cross-site scripting, cross-site request forgery, and HTTP response splitting. Security issues associated with trust boundaries and threat boundaries are emphasized at the intermediate level. Software security development life cycles and specialty security testing methods, like fuzz testing, are included at the intermediate level along with discussions of distributed cryptography system implementation and use. Differences between and among the three most deployed computer operating systems – Microsoft Windows, Mac OS X and Linux – are also discussed in terms of software and architectural deployment patterns, along with an introduction to mobile computing security issues. Lead computer programmers, senior system and software architects and chief information security

*Table 2. Categories of secure coding functions*

| Secure Code Functional Category | Description |
| --- | --- |
| **Category 1:** Functional Effectiveness | Functional effectiveness addresses the programming activities needed to produce software code that provides and/or supports the needed organizational mission function. This category covers what the software must do, without regard to the operational suitability of the software. Code developed using practices in this category is evaluated using techniques contained in the other categories. |
| **Category 2:** Software Engineering Standards | The software engineering standards category addresses the range of existing software engineering standards whose focus is applicable to the current class offering and set of students. The selected standard will be used to assess the correctness of the software architecture and code. |
| **Category 3:** Coding Standards Violations | The coding standards violations category addresses any violations in the selected coding standards and/or well known coding design principles. This category of secure coding practice addresses issues of poor code quality, violation of secure design principles, embedded malicious code, failure to fulfill an API contract, as well as the use of undefined, unspecified or implementation-defined behavior. Software architecture design, code development and system implementation are the most common areas where these software vulnerabilities are introduced. The specific type of system (operating system, network system, three-tier system) chosen for the secure software educational activity will determine the level and applicability of the coding techniques contained in this category. |
| **Category 4:** Exceptional Conditions Handling | The exceptional conditions handling category addresses the handling of exceptional conditions. Some of the specific details of this category are tied directly to the software architecture, and the software language used to implement the secure software system. The improper handling of syntactically invalid structures is an example of an area in this category that is architecture and language dependent. The improper or missing verification of unusual or exceptional conditions, as well as the ineffective handling of exceptions are also included in this category of secure software practices. The primary focus of this area is associated with the careful evaluation and analysis of the programmers assumptions associated with the system configuration and deployment state. |
| **Category 5:** Resources Accessed by Index | The 'resources accessed by index' category addresses the techniques used to manage indexed files, memory locations and other indexical resources. This category includes the classic buffer overflow associated with copying an input buffer to an output buffer without verifying that the size of the input buffer is less than the output buffer. These are language dependent issues associated with structured languages that do not have memory management support. Memory allocation, out-of-bounds read, out-of-bounds write, and pointer value outside of proper range, are all included in this category of secure software techniques. |
| **Category 6:** Resource Lifetime Control | The resource lifetime control category addresses the maintenance of proper resource control over the (creation, use, release) lifetime of the resource. A rich and deep set of software security issues are grouped in this category. This group includes covert channels, uncontrolled resource consumption, improper user authentication, incorrect type conversion, and invalid initialization. Secure software education must highlight the solutions to software security issues contained in this category. |
| **Category 7:** Message or Data Structure Processing | The data structure processing category includes the coding activities that are necessary to properly enforce the structure and content of messages and data structures as they move through the system processing thread of control. Data structure component deletion, improper null termination, and encoding errors are all a part of the secure coding activities included in this category. These issues are primarily language and architecture independent, and are associated with ineffective input and processing control. |
| **Category 8:** Improper Calculation | The improper calculation category is organized around software operations that generate unintended or incorrect calculation results. Due to the ubiquitous use of calculations in every aspect of secure coding activities, the effects of issues in this category may impact resource management, security-critical decisions, privilege assignments, arbitrary code execution, and other security sensitive operations. Software and system design, architecture, and implementation decisions are the main areas that introduce these types of software vulnerabilities that are associated with all types of software languages. |

*continued on following page*

*Table 2. Continued*

| Secure Code Functional Category | Description |
|---|---|
| **Category 9:** Improper Comparison of Security-Relevant Entities | The improper comparison of security-relevant entities category is focused in the area of object comparison. Comparison of object references, instead of object contents, flawed regular expressions, missing default case in a switch statement, partial state distinction and partial comparison are all included in this category of secure coding focus areas. This secure coding area is a basic area of concern, and many other code vulnerabilities may be built on the secure coding flaws in this category. |
| **Category 10:** Thread-of-Control Flow Management | The thread-of-control flow management category is focused in the area of secure software architecture design and implementation. This category includes improper flow control scoping, incorrect iteration control, flawed thread synchronization, multiple types of race conditions, as well as uncontrolled recursion and uncaught exceptions. Secure coding issues associated with this category are fundamental in software and code control, generating significant aberrant behavior if they are introduced into a set of production code. |
| **Category 11:** Error in Interaction | The error in interaction category is focused around the flawed interaction between two software systems that each function correctly when operating independently. This category includes flawed application of memory addressing, compiler modification of security-critical code, as well as improper functional behavior associated with a new version and/or deployment environment. All languages and secure software development process are areas in which these types of secure coding issues may be introduced. |
| **Category 12:** Flawed Protection Mechanisms | The flawed protection mechanisms category is focused on instances of incorrect or missing protection mechanisms in the secure software code. This category focuses on cases where there are known secure software protection mechanisms available, but they are not applied, or are applied incorrectly. Cases of flawed authentication, verification, access control, encryption deployment, and use of untrusted inputs are all included in this category. These issues are applicable to all software language types and secure software development processes. |
| **Category 13:** Improper Application of Pseudorandom Values | The improper application of pseudorandom values category is focused on the use of predictable and insufficiently random values. Improper random seed, hard coded cryptographic key, hard coded credentials, hard coded password and use of cryptographically weak software components are all included in this secure code category. All system development stages and software languages are impacted by issues in this category. |
| **Category 14:** Catch-All | The catch-all category addresses existing and/or emerging security issues that do not fit in the other categories. |

officers (CISO) are the primary types of students for the intermediate level material.

At the advanced level of the SSES, the basic and advanced secure coding material is combined into problem sets and configurations that are commonly found in ongoing commercial, governmental and military practices of secure system and software design, production, deployment and operations. One specific application area may be emphasized more than another depending on the students interest and employment conditions. The primary focus of the advanced level of the SSES material is organizational control of policy, risk, training, and processes that impact the security of operational software intensive systems. Senior

system engineers, software architects and CISO's are primary types of students for the advanced level material.

Specific instances of software security applications and techniques are mapped to a specific operational context, and are evaluated using a secure adaptive response potential (SARP) system security metric, which was introduced earlier in the paper. The SARP security metric was designed to address system security operational suitability throughout the system lifecycle (Simpson, Miller, & Dagli, June, 2008). Specific classes of system operational suitability may be developed and categorized using the SARP metric components that generally describe the operation and maintenance profile of the deployed system. This type of material would be introduced at the SSES intermediate level, and fully developed in the advanced level SSES courses. A typical set of system security metrics is shown in Figure 8.

Once these SARP categories are established, then specific system security architecture cost and risk decisions can be made based on these categories using standard systems engineering analysis techniques. The practice of secure software development can now be organized, discussed and communicated in terms of the Asset Protection Model, the Generic System Model, the Secure Software Education System, and the SARP categories. As shown in Figure 8, the topics in ovals associated with the Microsoft security development lifecycle (Howard & Lipner, 2006) cover only a portion of the SARP areas of interest. The topics associated with writing secure code (Howard & LeBlanc, 2003), shown by the rounded rectangles with dashed lines, cover fewer topics than those covered by the Microsoft security development lifecycle.

The secure software educator is challenged to properly scope, refine and establish context for effective instruction in the practice of secure coding. As security activities are focused on the production of secure code, there is a tendency to focus on only part of the enterprise information assurance problem and context. All of the items listed in Figure 8 are considered in general texts that are focused on information security for the enterprise (Schou & Shoemaker, 2007). As a result, an approach to secure software education that establishes basic, intermediate and advanced sets of knowledge, skills and abilities, as well as restricted system architectures, is used to organize and present the SSES curriculum.

## SYSTEM AND SOFTWARE UTILIZATION CONTEXT

Software is utilized in a number of configurations and deployed system contexts. The basic system types considered in this paper are: (1) a single

*Figure 8. Secure Adaptive Response Potential (SARP), A system security metric (Adapted from Simpson, 2008)*

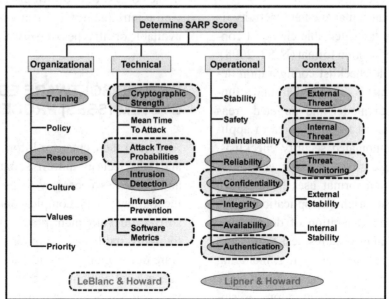

unconnected computing system, (2) an isolated network comprised of host computing systems, and (3) an interconnected group of networks comprised of host computers and associated networks. The terms, concepts and semantics that are contained in the security content automation protocol (SCAP) are also incorporated into the software utilization context (NIST SP 800-126, 2009). The four primary aspects of information technology security that are addressed by the SCAP are: (1) asset management, (2) configuration management, (3) compliance management and (4) vulnerability management.

- The asset management activity is supported by the common platform enumeration which standardizes an information technology system naming structure (DHS-NVD, CPE, 2009). The common platform enumeration is focused on individual platform identification and description.
- The configuration management activity is supported by the common configuration enumeration (DHS-NVD, CCE, 2009). The common configuration enumeration is organized around specific operating system or application recommended product configuration settings.
- The compliance management activity is supported by the extensible checklist configuration description format (NIST, 2008). The extensible checklist configuration description format is organized around a fundamental data model and targeted areas of application. The original area of application was automated security checklists. However, extensible checklist configuration description format uses have grown beyond these original application goals to support the generation of documentation of manual procedures, test results and many other text-based activities, including the production of training materials. The extensible checklist configuration descrip-

tion format has a fundamental data model that is composed of four main object types: (1) benchmark, (2) item, (3) profile and (4) test-result.

- Vulnerability management activities are supported by the common vulnerability enumeration, open vulnerability and assessment language, and the common vulnerability scoring system. The common vulnerability enumeration is an extensive list of publicly known information security vulnerabilities and exposures. The open vulnerability and assessment language standardizes the report and assessment of computer system security states and modes to support the reliable and reproducible automation of security system evaluation. The common vulnerability scoring system is a standardized vulnerability scoring system used for rating, evaluating and communicating system security vulnerabilities.

The secure software production techniques addressed in this document are directly associated with the known system vulnerability type that is being addressed. This direct connection has the benefit of placing the software engineer's activities in the context of a known threat environment as well as introducing the vast amount of information available on all types of software vulnerabilities.

## SECURE SOFTWARE EDUCATION SYSTEM (SSES) PROCESS

As part of the Center for Information Assurance and Cybersecurity, the SSES contains the elements and processes necessary to guide a student on the journey from incomplete and unstable secure software development practices and techniques to highly-stable and comprehensive secure software development practices and techniques. All educational content and components associated with the SSES are delivered using the general process outlined in Figure 9. Educational content and components for each specific subject area are inserted into the general process by the instructor which then creates a specific educational experience for the students learning about that secure software subject.

## SECURE SOFTWARE PRODUCTION EDUCATIONAL FUNCTIONS

The secure software education system functions are designed to support the achievement of the Pedagogical Model for Information Assurance Curriculum Development mission functions by providing the required secure software production educational functions. The functions have been grouped into the following categories: basic software knowledge, advanced software knowledge, basic secure software knowledge, and advanced secure software knowledge. The basic software knowledge category contains secure code software knowledge, practices and techniques that should be known by everyone that produces software for others to use. The basic software knowledge category focuses on host-based systems with a very shallow introduction to network basics and distributed systems. The advanced software

knowledge category covers the area of distributed, networked system code along with associated authentication and access controls.

For effective integration of this approach using these processes, a set of interfaces between the models is essential. Initially, aspects of the Pedagogical Model for Information Assurance Curriculum Development are mapped to the mission function, the system function, and the system architecture. The PMIACD goals – what the system is designed to accomplish – are mapped to the mission function. The PMIACD content are mapped to the system functions, and the PMIACD didactic processes are mapped to the system architecture. As detailed earlier in the paper, the information Asset Protection Model (APM) is a structured model of the information protection domain designed with a clear set of abstraction levels. These abstraction levels are used to identify and organize relevant security concepts in a manner that is accepted by experts in the system and software security field. Once a specific asset protection instance is identified that uses a system architecture, or a software-intensive system architecture, then the specific secure coding techniques can be mapped to the required system specification and threat exposure context. These mappings are shown notionally in Figure 10.

*Figure 9. General educational process steps*

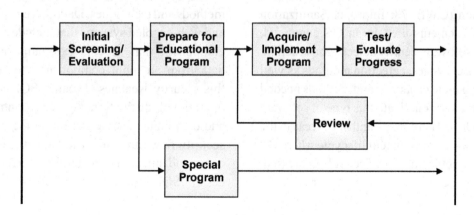

## SPECIFIC SECURE SOFTWARE DEVELOPMENT TECHNIQUES

After the APM has been used to establish the relevant abstraction level, scope and application characteristics associated with a specific secure coding application, standard secure system and software production techniques, and other standard system security practices can be used to generate a system product that provides the required level of risk reduction and information assurance. Administrative, policy, operational, and technical system controls are all evaluated, selected and implemented in a manner that provides the proper level of cost-effective system security in the identified product system context. The following sections outline a proposed set of standard, secure system and software areas that should be included when secure software coding techniques are being taught to students.

## Host Computer Operating System, Operating System (OS) Command Injection

A host computer supports many types of applications and operating system commands. This section of the SSES addresses the use of operating system calls in specific types of applications and application languages. A typical example of OS command injection is recorded in CERT Advisory CA-1996-06 Vulnerability in NCSA/Apache CGI example code. Common Weakness Enumeration (CWE) 78: Improper Sanitization of Special Elements used in an OS command, details this software security defect's construction, typical consequences, detection methods as well as providing code examples and methods needed to mitigate and/or eliminate this type of software security defect. There are a number of areas in the secure software development lifecycle where OS command injection may be effectively addressed. These areas include system architecture and de-

sign development, system implementation and code generation as well as testing and operation (DHS-NVD CWE, 2009).

## Host Computer Operating System, Buffer Overflow

This portion of the SSES covers the security techniques necessary to address buffer overrun. Buffer overflow weaknesses are associated with computer operating systems and applications that are written in languages that do not have automated memory management support, and allow the programmer to directly address, allocate and de-allocate memory registers and computer memory stacks. The consequences of performing an operation outside the bounds of a physical memory buffer vary dramatically depending on the computing language, computing platform and hardware architecture. There is a high potential for vulnerable systems to have their integrity, confidentiality and availability compromised when the buffer overflow weakness is exploited by an attacker (DHS-NVD CWE, 2009).

## Three Tier Database System: Secure Software Access Control

This section of the SSES addresses proper access control and authentication. The access control matrix is introduced and explained using examples. Authentication basics are introduced first, followed by discussion of specific authentication methods and techniques. Data-driven application and web-enabled systems that include a database component that accepts externally-influenced data from an input component, are subject to this security weakness because SQL makes no operational distinction between control input and data input. The net results of these types of security flaws are similar to the net result of OS command injection and buffer overflows. Successful SQL injection attacks are analyzed, and

*Figure 10. Secure software production*

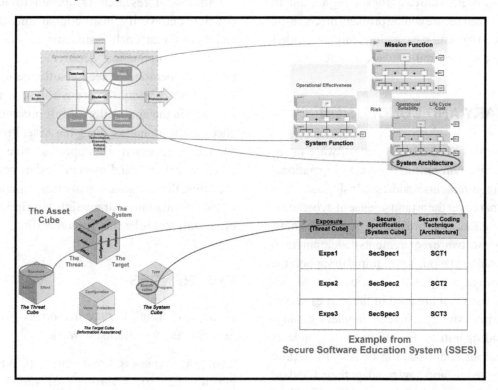

effective secure software development techniques that prevent these types of attacks are identified. Both the attacks and methods of attack are communicated to the students.

### Networked Data Systems: Secure Software Network Security

This section of the SSES addresses secure networking and socket techniques. This instructional unit starts with an overview of policy development, network organization and network security practices. Web applications and data-driven systems that use XML data structuring and accept externally-influenced input data are subject to this weakness, because XML makes no operational distinction between control input and data input. Successful SQL injection attacks can impact system availability, integrity and confidentiality.

### General Secure Coding Techniques and Patterns

This section of the SSES integrates fundamental aspects and procedures contained in all portions of the SSES. These aspects and procedures are packaged as analysis, design and implementation patterns. The patterns from this section are the main educational and technical take-away from the SSES educational activities. These application patterns use the APM to properly scope the type of security problem addressed, as well as to organize the general set of secure coding techniques.

The Secure Software Educational System final project is used to provide the students an opportunity to practice and demonstrate the secure software methods and techniques that they learned in the SSES course of instruction. Secure software modules built during the previous class periods are used as the basis for solving a small- to medium-sized secure coding problem that is based on a three-tier data base architecture or another acceptable system and software architecture.

## SUMMARY AND CONCLUSION

The dynamic nature of deployed software-intensive systems environmental threats and operational security requirements is addressed using a series of models that cover the art and science of cyber security instruction, asset protection, general systems, and secure software requirements development. A targeted range of models is required to support the discussion and analysis of educational techniques and processes that are used in the area of secure software intensive systems development, deployment, and operation. Even entry-level students must gain an understanding of how to acquire new knowledge, and how to adapt their standard software security approaches as a direct result of the fast flux of new technology development and services built on these new technologies.

The Pedagogical Model for Information Assurance Curriculum Development, as deployed at the University of Washington's Center for Information Assurance and Cyber Security, is a dynamic model that provides a focus for the center's operation. The Asset Protection Model is a structured model that focuses on three main aspects of secure systems: the target, the threat and the system. Proposed application processes focus specific professional groups in each of these different areas, and provide a structure through which they can collaborate and define a common view of the security issues. The Generic System Model, combined with other instructional models, is used to analyze and structure material for a specific type of system and a specific type of student.

Additional research is needed to identify, develop and verify instructional and didactic techniques that enable students to effectively address the production, deployment, configuration, and operation of secure software intensive systems in a dynamic threat environment. Further research in the application of information assurance to other domains, using the Asset Protection Model, is expected to support a wide variety of organizational and system design activities, including the development of clear, functionally-based information assurance job descriptions, and organizational roles and responsibilities.\

## REFERENCES

Bishop, M. (2005). *Introduction to Computer Security*. Boston: Addison-Wesley.

Common Weakness Enumeration (CWE) Categories. (2010). *Sponsored by the National Cyber Security Division of the U.S. Department of Homeland Security and hosted by The MITRE Corporation*. Retrieved August 24, 2010, from http://cwe.mitre.org/data/definitions/78.html

Department of Homeland Security, National Cyber Security Division/US-CERT and National Institute of Standards and Technology, National Vulnerability Database. (n.d.). *Common Configuration Enumeration (CCE) Reference Data*. Retrieved August 24, 2010, from http://nvd.nist.gov/cce.cfm

Department of Homeland Security, National Cyber Security Division/US-CERT and National Institute of Standards and Technology, National Vulnerability Database. (n.d.). *Official Common Platform Enumeration (CPE) Dictionary*. Retrieved August 24, 2010, from http://nvd.nist.gov/cpe.cfm

Department of Homeland Security, National Cyber Security Division/US-CERT and National Institute of Standards and Technology, National Vulnerability Database. (n.d.). *Common Weakness Enumeration (CWE)*. Retrieved August 24, 2010, from http://nvd.nist.gov/cwe.cfm

Endicott-Popovsky, B., Popovsky, V., & Frincke, D. (2004, June). *Designing a Computer Forensics Course for an Information Assurance Track.* Paper presented at the 8th Colloquium for Information Systems Security Education, West Point, NY.

Endicott-Popovsky, B., Popovsky, V., & Frincke, D. (2005, June). *Secure Code: The Capstone Class in an Information Assurance Track.* Paper presented at the 2005 Colloquium on Information Systems Security Education (CISSE): Pursuing Quality Solutions—Lessons Learned and Applied.

Gross, A. (June 11, 2010). *Language.* Retrieved August 24, 2010, from http://languag2.home.sprynet.com/f/evishop.htm

Howard, M., & LeBlanc, D. (2003). *Writing Secure Code.* Redmond, WA: Microsoft Press.

Howard, M., & Lipner, S. (2006). *The Security Development Life Cycle.* Redmond, WA: Microsoft Press. IEEE-Std-1471-2000. (2000, October). *Recommended Practice for Architectural Description of Software-Intensive Systems.* Retrieved August 24, 2010, from http://standards.ieee.org/reading/ieee/std_public/description/se/1471-2000_desc.html

IEEE/EIA 12207.0. (1998, May). *Standard for Information Technology – Software Life Cycle Processes.* Washington, DC: IEEE.

Mar, B. W., & Morais, B. G. (2002, August). *FRAT – A Basic Framework for Systems Engineering.* Paper presented at Twelfth Annual International Symposium of INCOSE, Engineering 21st Century Systems: Problem Solving Through Structured Thinking, Las Vegas, NV.

McCumber, J. (2005). *Assessing and Managing Security Risk in IT Systems: A Structured Methodology.* Boca Raton, FL: Auerbach Publications.

Mead, N. R. (2010). Benefits and Challenges in the Use of Case Studies for Security Requirements Engineering Methods. *International Journal of Secure Software Engineering, 1*(1), 74–91.

National Institute of Standards and Technology. (2008, January). *Publication, The eXtensible Configuration Checklist Description Format, Release 1.1.4.* Retrieved August 24, 2010, from http://scap.nist.gov/specifications/xccdf/

National Institute of Standards and Technology. (2009, November). *Publication # NIST SP 800-126, 2009, The Technical Specification for the Security Content Automation Protocol.* National Institute of Standards and Technology.

Popovsky, V., & Popovsky, B. (2008, June). *Integrating Academics, the Community and Industry.* ISBN 978-5-903247-15-8

Schou, C., & Shoemaker, D. (2007). *Information Assurance for the Enterprise: A Roadmap to Information Security.* New York: McGraw-Hill/Irwin.

Simpson, J. J. (2002, August). *Innovation and Technology Management.* Paper presented at the Twelfth Annual International Symposium of INCOSE, Engineering 21st Century Systems: Problem Solving Through Structured Thinking, Las Vegas, NV.

Simpson, J. J. (2004, April). *System Frameworks*. Paper presented at the Second Annual Conference on Systems Engineering Research, Los Angeles.

Simpson, J. J., & Endicott-Popovsky, B. (2010, June 7). *A Systematic Approach to Information Systems Security Education*. Paper presented at the 14th Colloquium for Information Systems Security Education, Baltimore, MD.

Simpson, J. J., Miller, A., & Dagli, C. (2008, June). *Secure Adaptive Response Potential (SARP): A System Security Metric*. Paper presented at the Eighteenth Annual International Symposium of INCOSE, Systems Engineering for the Planet, Utrecht, The Nederlands.

Simpson, J. J., & Simpson, M. J. (2003, July). *Systems and Objects*. Paper presented at the Thirteenth Annual International Symposium of INCOSE, Engineering Tomorrow's World Today, Crystal City, VA.

Simpson, J. J., & Simpson, M. J. (2006, July). *Foundational Systems Engineering (SE) Patterns for a SE Pattern Language*. Paper presented at the Sixteenth Annual International Symposium of INCOSE, Systems Engineering: Shining List on the Tough Issues, Orlando, FL.

Simpson, J. J., & Simpson, M. J. (2010, June 3). Complexity Reduction: A Pragmatic Approach. *Systems Engineering Journal*. DOI:10.1002/sys.20170

Simpson, J. J., Votipka, S., Wang, T., Baklanoff, T., & Sweers, N. (2010, June 2). *Final Project Report, Threat Incident Modeling Team*. Paper presented to IMT 553 – Establishing and Managing Information Assurance Strategies, University of Washington, Seattle, WA.

Warfield, J. N. (1990). *A Science of Generic Design*. Ames, IA: Iowa State University Press.

*This work was previously published in International Journal of Secure Software Engineering, edited by Khaled M. Khan, pp. 35-61, Volume 1, Issue 4, copyright 2010 by IGI Publishing (an imprint of IGI Global).*

# Chapter 17
# Development of a Master of Software Assurance Reference Curriculum

**Nancy R. Mead**
*Carnegie Mellon University, USA*

**Thomas B. Hilburn**
*Embry-Riddle Aeronautical University, USA*

**Julia H. Allen**
*Carnegie Mellon University, USA*

**Andrew J. Kornecki**
*Embry-Riddle Aeronautical University, USA*

**Mark Ardis**
*Stevens Institute of Technology, USA*

**Rick Linger**
*Carnegie Mellon University, USA*

**James McDonald**
*Monmouth University, USA*

## ABSTRACT

*Modern society is deeply and irreversibly dependent on software systems of remarkable scope and complexity in areas that are essential for preserving this way of life. The security and correct functioning of these systems are vital. Recognizing these realities, the U. S. Department of Homeland Security (DHS) National Cyber Security Division (NCSD) enlisted the resources of the Software Engineering Institute at Carnegie Mellon University to develop a curriculum for a Master of Software Assurance degree program and define transition strategies for implementation. In this article, the authors present an overview of the Master of Software Assurance curriculum project, including its history, student prerequisites and outcomes, a core body of knowledge, and curriculum architecture from which to create such a degree program. The authors also provide suggestions for implementing a Master of Software Assurance program.*

DOI: 10.4018/978-1-4666-1580-9.ch017

# INTRODUCTION

Software has become the core component of modern products and services. It has enabled functionality, business operations, and control systems critical to our way of life. However, software's race to ubiquity has outpaced security advances commensurate with software's vital role in our society. Consequently, as our dependence on software and software-intensive systems grows, we find ourselves exposed to an increasing number of risks.

The complexity of software and software-intensive systems, for instance, poses inherent risk. It obscures the essential intent of the software, masks potentially harmful uses, precludes exhaustive testing, and introduces problems in the operation and maintenance of the software. This complexity, combined with the interdependence of the systems we rely on, also creates a weakest link syndrome: attackers need only take down the most vulnerable component to have far-reaching and damaging effects on the larger system. What's more, anywhere-to-anywhere interconnectivity makes the proliferation of malware easy and the identification of its source hard.

The rising number of vulnerabilities compounds risk and—gives attackers even more targets of opportunity—as shown by the rising number of incidents targeting software vulnerabilities (Bosworth, 2002).

In this environment, the threats are large and diverse, ranging from independent, unsophisticated, opportunistic hackers to the very technically competent intruders backed by organized crime (Anderson, 2008). Malicious actors are increasingly acquiring information technology skills that allow them to launch attacks designed to steal information for financial gain, and to disrupt, deny access to, degrade, or destroy critical information and infrastructure systems. Technical sophistication is no longer a necessary requirement: increasingly sophisticated attack methods, thanks to the growing underground trade in productized attack tools, no longer require great technical savvy to execute.

Recognizing these realities, the U. S. Department of Homeland Security (DHS) National Cyber Security Division (NCSD) enlisted the resources of the Software Engineering Institute (SEI) at Carnegie Mellon University to develop a curriculum for a Master of Software Assurance degree program and define transition strategies for future implementation. For the purposes of this curriculum, the discipline of software assurance is targeted specifically to the security and correct functioning of software systems, whatever their origins, application domain, or operational environments.

As noted in our curriculum report, the need for a master's level program in this discipline has been growing for years (Mead, 2010a).

- At the Knowledge Transfer Network Workshop in Paris in March 2009, cyber-security education was recognized as part of the information security, privacy, and assurance roadmap vision. Cyber security education was also identified as one of the workshop's lines of development (LSEC, 2009).

- A study by the nonpartisan Partnership for Public Service points out that "[President Obama's] success in combating these threats [to cyber security] and the safety of the nation will depend on implementing a comprehensive and coordinated strategy—a goal that must include building a vibrant, highly trained and dedicated cyber security workforce in this country." The report found that "The pipeline of new talent [with the skills to ensure the security of software systems] is inadequate.. .. only 40 percent of CIOs [chief information officers], CISOs [chief information security officers] and IT [information technology] hiring managers are satisfied or very satisfied with the quality of applicants applying for federal cyber security jobs, and only 30 percent are satisfied or very satisfied with the number of qualified candidates who are applying (PPS, 2009).

- The need for cyber security education was emphasized by The New York Times in quoting Dr. Nasir Memon, a professor at the Polytechnic Institute on New York University: "There is a huge demand, and a lot more schools have created programs, but to be honest, we're still not producing enough students" (Drew, 2009).

- Carnegie Mellon University and CERT have been active in this area for years, particularly in the Survivability and Information Assurance (SIA) Curriculum and the Scholarship for Service program (CERT, 2007). The SIA Curriculum has been provided to thousands of faculty members and other interested parties. The Federal Cyber Service Scholarship for Service program offers scholarships to applicants who attend an approved institution of higher learning and agree to work for several years in the cyber security area at U.S. government organizations after graduation. The popularity and growth of this program is an indicator of the pressing need for cyber security expertise (OPM, 2010).

- In discussions with industry and government representatives, we have found that the need for more capacity in cyber security continues to grow. Anecdotal feedback from the authors' own students indicates that even a single course with a cyber security focus enhances their positioning in the job market. They felt they were made job offers they would not have received otherwise.

- Another aspect of the need for cyber security education occurs in educational institutions. Based on our collective experience

in software engineering education, we know that it can be very difficult to start a new program or track from scratch, and we want to assist those organizations and faculty members that wish to undertake such an endeavor. Our objective is to support their needs, while recognizing that there are a variety of implementation strategies.

In this article, we will present an overview of the Master of Software Assurance curriculum project (MSwA, 2010), and highlight the *Master of Software Assurance Reference Curriculum* report and its history (Mead et al., 2010a). We define student prerequisites and outcomes, a core body of knowledge, and a curriculum architecture from which to create such a degree program, either as a standalone offering or as a track within existing software engineering and computer science master's degree programs. We also provide suggestions for implementing a Master of Software Assurance program.

## BACKGROUND

As is typical in a project of this nature, a good bit of time is spent deciding how to tackle the project. The team members all had expertise in software engineering. In addition, some had experience in curriculum design, software assurance, or both. However, many decisions had to be made at the outset to get the project off the ground. One of our challenges was to decide how we would operate as a team with members in geographically dispersed locations. Not all of the team members had worked together before, but we quickly coalesced into an effective unit. For the most part, we held weekly telecoms, and occasional face-to-face work sessions when we needed a concentrated block of time. This worked remarkably well.

At the outset, we needed to define *software assurance*, examine recent curriculum and body of knowledge efforts to see which ones would apply, identify the audience for our work, and highlight ways in which our work was unique.

One of our first tasks was to examine existing definitions of software assurance, select a candidate definition from the literature, and assess whether it met our needs. Initially we selected the definition of the Committee on National Security Systems, as this definition was in wide use and used by our Department of Homeland Security sponsor:

Software assurance (SwA) is the level of confidence that software is free from vulnerabilities, either intentionally designed into the software or accidentally inserted at any time during its life cycle, and that the software functions in the intended manner. (Committee on National Security Systems, 2009)

As we got further into the project, we found that the definition needed to be extended slightly for our purposes:

*Software assurance (SwA) is the application of technologies and processes to achieve a required level of confidence that software systems and services function in the intended manner, are free from accidental or intentional vulnerabilities, provide security capabilities appropriate to the threat environment, and recover from intrusions and failures (Mead et al., 2010a).*

The extended definition emphasizes the importance of both technologies and processes in software assurance, notes that computing capabilities may be acquired through services as well as new development, acknowledges the need for correct functionality, recognizes that security capabilities must be appropriate to the threat environment, and identifies recovery from intrusions and failures as an important capability for organizational continuity and survival.

After examining the earlier Master of Software Engineering curriculum documents (Ardis & Ford, 1989; Ford, 1991), we concluded that the *Graduate*

*Software Engineering 2009 (GSwE2009) Curriculum Guidelines for Graduate Degree Programs in Software Engineering* (Pyster, 2009) was the most relevant recent curriculum work to build on. We also drew on work done by Carnegie Mellon University's Software Engineering Institute in support of the U.S. Department of Homeland Security Build Security In website (DHS, 2010a). We found that both the Software Assurance Curriculum Body of Knowledge (SwACBK) (DHS, 2010b) and the SWEBOK (IEEE-CS, 2004) were relevant as well.

We then considered the audience, and quickly concluded that the primary audience for the MSwA2010 curriculum is faculty who are responsible for designing, developing, and maintaining graduate programs that have a focus on software assurance knowledge and practices. However, we expect that the document will be read by other educators and trainers with an interest in this area, as well as industry and government executives and practitioners.

Finally, we identified what was different about this curriculum compared to traditional software engineering and computer science programs. Areas of special emphasis and unique properties that distinguish this curriculum (shown in italics) from others are the following:

- Software *and services*
- Development *and acquisition*
- *Security* and correct functionality
- *Software analytics*
- *System operations*
- *Auditable evidence*
- *Organizational continuity*

We developed the curriculum intending that it would be for practitioners, not for researchers. We also documented some initial thoughts on undergraduate coursework in software assurance in a separate document (Mead et al., 2010b).

We envision that the MSwA2010 curriculum can be offered as an independent master's degree program in software assurance or as a track in a Master of Software Engineering (MSE) or a Master of Computer Science degree program. This article describes how it can be incorporated as a track in an MSE degree program if the software engineering program is based on the GSwE2009 recommendations. The independent master's degree program in software assurance assumes a student enters the program with an undergraduate degree in computer science (ACM & IEEE-CS, 2008), computer engineering (IEEE-CS & ACM, 2004), or software engineering (IEEE-CS & ACM, 2004) and supplements the content of those degrees with appropriate prerequisite materials. For students with other backgrounds, the program incorporates the necessary preparation in computer science and software engineering to allow them to study software assurance.

## Process Used to Develop MSwA2010 Curriculum Content

We started out with a schedule for the MSwA curriculum work and a set of activities to be performed to arrive at the curriculum. Once we decided that the GSwE2009 document would be a primary source, we reviewed it to see what elements could be carried over or modified for the MSwA2010 curriculum, and where we would have to tackle unique aspects. As we proceeded with the work, we realized that we had touched on many different areas that were seemingly unrelated. We therefore decided that it was worthwhile to document the process we had used not only for our own benefit, but also for our readers and others undertaking a similar activity.

We used the following seven-step process to develop the software assurance curriculum topics, practices, knowledge units, outcomes, and core body of knowledge, with course descriptions as an eighth activity (see Table 1).

## PROPOSED OUTCOMES WHEN A STUDENT GRADUATES

We needed to focus on the proposed outcomes in order to drive the program content. The outcomes specify the knowledge, skills, and capabilities that graduates of an MSwA program can expect to have;

*Table 1. Software assurance curriculum development*

| 1. Develop project guidelines | We modified guidelines from the GSwE2009 report for the MSwA2010 curriculum, which significantly influenced the development of outcomes (step 6). |
|---|---|
| 2. Identify and review sources | We reviewed 29 credible and reputable sources of software security practices in industry, government, and academia (at the graduate and undergraduate levels). |
| 3. Define topics | We used the guide in [Allen, 2008] as the organizing structure for our review of sources in Step 2 and supplemented it with our experience. This activity resulted in nine topics. |
| 4. Define SDLC practices and categories | We evaluated sources for the topics listed above to identify practices, which we grouped into four high level categories. |
| 5. Solicit external feedback | We sought input, through a 3-page questionnaire, from representatives of our target audience—managers, practitioners, and educators. |
| 6. Develop outcomes and core Body of Knowledge (BoK) | We identified curriculum outcomes, influenced by GSwE2009 and questionnaire responses. Each outcome is a knowledge area in the BoK. |
| 7. Compare knowledge areas to practices | We performed a cursory gap analysis by comparing the BoK knowledge areas to the SDLC practices and categories |
| 8. Develop course descriptions | We developed course descriptions for the 9 core courses in an MSwA program and the 7 courses that would be added to a GSwE degree program for a software assurance specialization. |

correspondingly, they represent the minimum capabilities that should be expected of a software assurance professional when they complete a master's degree program. Our process was not sequential; rather, we iterated on the outcomes, knowledge areas, and lifecycle practices over the course of the project.

When we solicited external feedback (step 5 in our process), we found that the MSwA2010 curriculum was not necessarily a match for all software assurance positions. Some organizations were more concerned with the qualifications of entry-level programmers who had not completed a master's degree program. Others were concerned with hands-on systems administrators. This curriculum is not a panacea, but it should help to grow the pool of leadership talent in software assurance, in much the same way that graduates of a master of software engineering program can be expected to become leaders in software engineering.

The primary audience for the MSwA2010 project, graduate faculty, should be prepared to teach courses that achieve these outcomes, listed below. Software development and acquisition employers responsible for staffing technical leadership positions in software assurance and developing increased software assurance capabilities of their current employees should expect graduates of an MSwA program to be proficient in capabilities described in these outcomes. The seven outcomes are grouped into two main areas—assurance process and management and assurance product and technology. Their brief descriptions follow (Mead et al., 2010a).

## Assurance Process and Management

### Assurance across Life Cycles

Graduates will have the ability to incorporate assurance technologies and methods into life-cycle processes and development models for new or evolutionary system development, and for system or service acquisition.

### Risk Management

Graduates will have the ability to perform risk analysis, trade-off assessment, and prioritization of security measures.

### Assurance Assessment

Graduates will have the ability to analyze and validate the effectiveness of assurance operations and create auditable evidence of security measures.

### Assurance Management

Graduates will have the ability to make a business case for software assurance, lead assurance efforts, understand standards, comply with regulations, plan for business continuity, and keep current in security technologies.

## Assurance Product and Technology

### System Security Assurance

Graduates will have the ability to incorporate effective security technologies and methods into new and existing systems.

### System Functionality Assurance

Graduates will have the ability to verify new and existing system functionality for conformance to requirements and absence of malicious content.

### System Operational Assurance

Graduates will have the ability to monitor and assess system operational security and respond to new threats.

## CORE BODY OF KNOWLEDGE

The MSwA2010 core body of knowledge (BoK) is characterized by the set of software assurance practices that are required to support the MSwA2010 outcomes. All software assurance professionals must know these practices to perform their jobs effectively. The MSwA2010 BoK is structured into seven knowledge areas (corresponding to the seven outcomes), with each knowledge area subdivided into a set of knowledge units, as shown in Table 2. The information in the table is expanded on in the MSwA2010 document (Mead, 2010a).

The knowledge areas are defined in terms of the Bloom cognitive levels (Bloom, 1956). This taxonomy is often used by educators to set the level of educational and learning objectives required for students engaged in an education unit, course, or program. Bloom's levels used are

- Knowledge (K)
- Comprehension (C)
- Application (AP)
- Analysis (AN)
- Synthesis (S)

Since we were developing a curriculum for a master's degree program, the Bloom's levels ranged from C through AN (Table 2).

## MSwA2010 CURRICULUM ARCHITECTURE

The MSwA2010 specifies an architectural description that provides a framework for organizing and structuring master's programs that focus on software assurance. The curriculum architecture, which was influenced by GSwE2009, contains the following components: preparatory material, core materials, elective materials, and a capstone experience.

Figure 1 depicts the architecture for an MSwA curriculum. The preparatory materials represent the material which students should master before entering the program. Individual programs will determine how to prepare students whose background falls short. The MSwA2010 outcomes and BoK identify the fundamental skills and knowledge that all graduates of a master's program in software assurance must possess. This is captured in the Figure 1 row labeled MSwA Core. Where appropriate, the core curriculum will emphasize the guidelines used to define the MSwA2010 BoK, including its dependencies on related disciplines such as software engineering, testing, and project management. Courses that cover core content should be part of all programs.

Electives accommodate individual students' interests and may cover unique requirements of a program or institution. Students may take electives to gain more depth in a core area (e.g., assurance assessment) or to extend and broaden their knowledge in a particular application domain (e.g., financial systems).

We recommend that students demonstrate their accumulated skills and knowledge in a capstone experience, which engages students in a realistic team project emphasizing software assurance concepts and practices. A capstone project is ideally a practical software assurance undertaking with a real customer, possessing actual software assurance objectives, and using best software assurance practices and tools. Students completing the curriculum must be able to understand and appreciate the skills needed to produce assured software in a typical software development environment. These topics should be integrated into the core materials and perhaps could be reinforced in the elective materials. However, the presence of a capstone project is important, as it offers students the opportunity to tackle a major project that is likely to be more comprehensive in realistic software assurance experience than their prior course projects.

This architecture is not intended to specify course titles, course content, or course sequencing, but rather to indicate the overall content in

*Table 2. MSwA2010 core body of knowledge*

| | Knowledge Area | Bloom Level |
|---|---|---|
| **1. Assurance Across Life Cycles** | 1.1. Software Life-Cycle Processes | |
| | 1.1.1. New development | C |
| | 1.1.2. Integration, assembly, and deployment | C |
| | 1.1.3. Operation and evolution | C |
| | 1.1.4. Acquisition, supply, and service | C |
| | 1.2. Software Assurance Processes and Practices | |
| | 1.2.1. Process and practice assessment | AP |
| | 1.2.2. Software assurance integration into SDLC phases | AP |
| **2. Risk Management** | 2.1. Risk Management Concepts | |
| | 2.1.1. Types and classification | C |
| | 2.1.2. Probability, impact, severity | C |
| | 2.1.3. Models, processes, metrics | C |
| | 2.2. Risk Management Process | |
| | 2.2.1. Identification | AP |
| | 2.2.2. Analysis | AP |
| | 2.2.3. Planning | AP |
| | 2.2.4. Monitoring and management | AP |
| | 2.3. Software Assurance Risk Management | |
| | 2.3.1. Vulnerability and threat identification | AP |
| | 2.3.2. Analysis of software assurance risks | AP |
| | 2.3.3. Software assurance risk mitigation | AP |
| | 2.3.4. Assessment of Software Assurance Processes and Practices | AP |
| **3. Assurance Assessment** | 3.1. Assurance Assessment Concepts | |
| | 3.1.1. Baseline level of assurance; allowable tolerances, if quantitative | AP |
| | 3.1.2. Assessment methods | C |
| | 3.2. Measurement for Assessing Assurance | |
| | 3.2.1. Product and process measures by life-cycle phase | AP |
| | 3.2.2. Other performance indicators that test for the baseline, by life-cycle phase | AP |
| | 3.2.3. Measurement processes and frameworks | C |
| | 3.2.4. Business survivability and operational continuity | AP |
| | 3.3. Assurance Assessment Process (collect and report measures that demonstrate the baseline) | |
| | 3.3.1. Comparison of selected measurements to the established baseline | AP |
| | 3.3.2. Identification of out-of-tolerance variances | AP |

*continued in following column*

*Table 2. Continued*

| | Knowledge Area | Bloom Level |
|---|---|---|
| **4. Assurance Management** | 4.1. Making the Business Case for Assurance | |
| | 4.1.1. Valuation and cost/benefit models, cost and loss avoidance, return on investment | AP |
| | 4.1.2. Risk analysis | C |
| | 4.1.3. Compliance justification | C |
| | 4.1.4. Business impact/needs analysis | C |
| | 4.2. Managing Assurance | |
| | 4.2.1. Project management across the life cycle | C |
| | 4.2.2. Integration of other knowledge units | AN |
| | 4.3. Compliance Considerations for Assurance | |
| | 4.3.1. Laws and regulations | C |
| | 4.3.2. Standards | C |
| | 4.3.3. Policies | C |
| **5. System Security Assurance** | 5.1. For Newly Developed and Acquired Software for Diverse Applications | |
| | 5.1.1. Security and safety aspect of computer-intensive critical infrastructure | K |
| | 5.1.2. Potential attack methods | C |
| | 5.1.3. Analysis of threats to software | AP |
| | 5.1.4. Methods of defense | AP |
| | 5.2. For Diverse Operational (Existing) Systems | |
| | 5.2.1. Historic and potential operational attack methods | C |
| | 5.2.2. Analysis of threats to operational environments | AN |
| | 5.2.3. Designing of and plan for access control, privileges, and authentication | AP |
| | 5.2.4. Security methods for physical and personnel environments | AP |
| | 5.3. Ethics and Integrity in Creation, Acquisition, and Operation of Software Systems | |
| | 5.3.1. Overview of ethics, code of ethics, and legal constraints | C |
| | 5.3.2. Computer attack case studies | C |

*continued on following page*

aggregate. Individual programs may choose the arrangement of courses, topics, and learning activities that best suit the needs and capabilities of their institutions.

Figure 2 illustrates a Master of Software Engineering program with a specialization in Software Assurance. As indicated in the figure, the core BoK

*Table 2. Continued*

| Knowledge Area | | Bloom Level |
|---|---|---|
| | 6.1. Assurance Technology | |
| | 6.1.1. Technology evaluation | AN |
| | 6.1.2. Technology improvement | AP |
| | 6.2. Assured Software Development | |
| | 6.2.1. Development methods | AP |
| | 6.2.2. Quality attributes | C |
| | 6.2.3. Maintenance methods | AP |
| | 6.3. Assured Software Analytics | |
| | 6.3.1. Systems analysis | AP |
| | 6.3.2. Structural analysis | AP |
| 6. System Functionality Assurance | 6.3.3. Functional analysis | AP |
| | 6.3.4. Analysis of methods and tools | C |
| | 6.3.5. Testing for assurance | AN |
| | 6.3.6. Assurance evidence | AP |
| | 6.4. Assurance in Acquisition | |
| | 6.4.1. Assurance of acquired software | AP |
| | 6.4.2. Assurance of software services | AP |
| | 7.1. Operational Procedures | |
| | 7.1.1. Business objectives | C |
| | 7.1.2. Assurance procedures | AP |
| | 7.1.3. Assurance training | C |
| | 7.2. Operational Monitoring | |
| | 7.2.1. Monitoring technology | C |
| 7. System Operational Assurance | 7.2.2. Operational evaluation | AP |
| | 7.2.3. Operational maintenance | AP |
| | 7.2.4. Malware analysis | AP |
| | 7.3. System Control | |
| | 7.3.1. Responses to adverse events | AN |
| | 7.3.2. Business survivability | AP |

includes knowledge areas from both the GSwE core and the MSwA core. Since there is overlap between the two BoKs (e.g., Software Engineering Management and Assurance Management), the required core content would be somewhat less than the sum of the two; however, the program would still be tight and would leave little or no room for electives.

## COURSE DESCRIPTIONS

Once we had the curriculum architecture and the body of knowledge, we were able to develop a sample set of course descriptions for MSwA as a standalone program, as well as courses that could be added to an MSwE program for a software assurance specialization. The knowledge units that each course should cover appear in parentheses by the course name.

### MSwA Standalone Program (nine courses)

- Assurance Management (2.1, 2.2, 2.3, 4.1, 4.2, 4.3)
- Assurance Assessment (3.1, 3.2, 3.3, 6.4)[1]
- System Operational Assurance (7.1, 7.2, 7.3)
- System Security Assurance (5.1, 5.2, 5.3)
- Assured Software Analytics (6.3)
- Assured Software Development 1 (1.1, *1.2*, 6.1, 6.2 [requirements])[2]
- Assured Software Development 2 (6.1, 6.2 [specification, design])
- Assured Software Development 3 (6.2 [code, test, verification, validation])
- Software Assurance Capstone Experience

### MSwA Courses Added to MSwE Program (seven courses)

- Assurance Management (1.2, 2.1, 2.2, 2.3, 4.1, 4.2, 4.3)
- System Operational Assurance (**3.1, 3.2, 3.3, 6.4**, 7.1, 7.2, 7.3)[3]
- System Security Assurance (5.1, 5.2, 5.3)
- Assured Software Analytics (6.3)
- Assured Software Development 1 (1.1, 6.1, 6.2 [requirements, specification, design])
- Assured Software Development 2 (6.2 [code, test, verification, validation])[4]
- Software Assurance Capstone Experience

Figure 1.

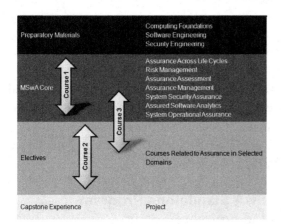

Figure 2.

It is necessary but not sufficient to have a defined set of student prerequisites, established outcomes, a core body of knowledge, a curriculum architecture, and course descriptions. Often the most challenging part of putting a new program or a new track in place is implementation. The next section provides several guidelines and recommendations for faculty members to consider when contemplating such a program.

## IMPLEMENTATION GUIDELINES

We realized that schools choosing to adopt our suggested curriculum would face several challenges besides deciding which topics to teach. In particular, schools would need to address

- Planning and launching a new program
- Recruiting and preparing students
- Finding and training faculty
- Acquiring resources
- Capstone courses

For each of these issues, we offer some discussion of the problems and some advice for addressing those problems, drawing on our experience in starting similar programs. In addition, we found several good suggestions in the Frequently Asked Questions report published with GSwE2009 (Ardis, Lasfer, & Michael, 2009).

## Planning and Launching a New Program

A prerequisite for starting any successful program is a champion who will lead the effort. This might be a faculty member, a department head, a dean, or another member of the academic community dedicated to starting the program. In addition, it helps to have other champions from industry and government who will support the program, perhaps by voicing support to others, hiring graduates, providing resources, and offering projects for the capstone experience. If possible, it is advisable to form an industry advisory board (IAB) early on to help support and shape the program.

The academic champion needs to make a convincing case for the program by preparing a business plan, including a market study. The plan should be used to convince university colleagues and administrators that there will be sufficient interest in the program, and that graduates will be successful in their career plans. Competing programs should be identified, some of which may be on the same campus.

New programs need to be sold at several levels of campus administration, and even at regional levels in some cases. For example, some states require extensive proposals for new academic programs, including details about courses, faculty, and dedicated resources. It is often much easier to get approval to create a new track within an existing program than it is to create a new program.

There are U.S. federal government assistance programs, such as the Scholarship for Service program that may help (U.S. Office of Personnel Management, 2010). These programs provide some financial assistance to students and help justify the need for new academic programs. There are also U.S. federal agencies (for example, the National Science Foundation and the Department of Education) that provide start-up funds for innovative educational programs.

## Recruiting and Preparing Students

If you build it, they may not come. Recruitment of students needs to be a continual process. A good market study should identify the likely areas from which to draw students. An IAB can help keep the study up to date and provide some additional help in recruiting.

Since some of the potential students are already in the workforce, it is helpful to establish relationships with the human resources (HR) departments of likely employers, including those that regularly recruit students from your institution. HR departments administer benefits, such as reimbursement for tuition, and often provide information to employees about educational opportunities. It may be possible to give in-house presentations to local companies, arranged through their HR departments or a member of your IAB.

Local professional organizations may provide opportunities for student recruitment. Trade organizations provide networking for local professionals and many of them have social events sponsored by local companies. There often are opportunities to give a short presentation or set up a booth at some of these meetings.

Most universities have professionals who help recruit students, but these individuals need to be informed about any new program and the types of students who best fit. Developing brochures and a web presence help to inform both internal staff and prospective students.

Some students may need help preparing for graduate study in software assurance. There are usually two kinds of deficiencies to be addressed: knowledge deficiencies and experience deficiencies. Knowledge deficiencies can be addressed by preparatory leveling courses, such as an overview course on software and systems engineering, a survey course in current topics in software engineering, or a survey course on security. Experience deficiencies can be partially overcome by internships in industry and assistantships within the school. Special team projects in various aspects of industrial practice can be offered for cohorts of students who lack sufficient experience (such as a project course on the use of software tools for software development and maintenance, or a project course on procurement, integration, and testing of open source software packages).

## Finding and Training Faculty

There are two sources of faculty to teach in new programs of this type: (1) faculty from related areas who have knowledge and interest in teaching software assurance and (2) experienced practitioners from industry who are interested in teaching. The former often work in computer science academic units, but they may be found in almost any discipline that uses computing. Although they may have good teaching skills, they may need some help adjusting to the professional nature of the program. Some of their students will already have considerable experience and expect to learn about the latest methods and tools. It is important for faculty to stay current in the field. Consulting is one good way to do this.

The second type of faculty candidate (from industry) may need some help making the transition to teaching. If they work part time as adjunct faculty, they will need to balance the demands of two jobs. If they become full-time faculty, there may be some discomfort in taking a salary cut. In either case, it is important to ensure they appreciate the benefits of an academic position.

It is prudent to ramp up faculty at a pace consistent with the growth of the program. This means that some part-time faculty will be needed early on before there is enough demand to justify hiring full-time faculty. Adjunct faculty from industry is often used for this, but also consider faculty from other academic units at your institution.

## Acquiring Resources

Hardware and software may be provided by local companies or members of the IAB. In addition, some vendors have academic alliance programs that provide hardware or software at deep discounts. However, there should be an annual budget allocated to acquiring and maintaining computing systems. A small program should be able to share support staff with other programs.

## Capstone Courses

Capstone courses in software assurance provide their own challenges. Fortunately, there are several models from which to choose. One issue to resolve early on is whether the capstone course(s) will be integrated with other courses in the curriculum. Integrated capstones provide connections to several other courses in the curriculum, offering opportunities for students to practice skills they learn in those courses. Standalone capstones are easier to implement because they do not have to be synchronized with the content of other courses.

To provide a realistic setting for a capstone course, it is helpful to have real clients. Finding clients is another recruiting activity to plan and implement each year. Another alternative is to pursue open source projects. The community of open source developers can play the role of clients, but they usually do not have the same level of commitment as a real client.

For more information about implementation considerations, consult the GSwE2009 FAQ Discussion Forum.[5] The Implementation/Execution forum[6] specifically addresses important issues for faculty members and institutions involved in implementing and executing a graduate program in software engineering. Many of these issues are the same for implementing an MSwA2010 degree program.

## Ways in Which Industry Can Support Software Assurance Education

There are many ways that industry can provide support, from monetary assistance to participation in capstone projects. We describe several of these ideas as suggestions to readers from industry, and as advice to help new programs begin to make connections with potential industry sponsors.

For degree programs targeted toward professionals, such as the MSwA2010, industry support is essential. In addition to participating in industry advisory boards, making donations, or providing discounts on equipment and software, there are a number of other ways in which industry can contribute towards advancing this new discipline. These include

- **Encouraging employees to work with universities as adjunct faculty or guest lecturers:** This can enrich both the industry organization and the university program.
- **Sponsoring and speaking at faculty development workshops:** It's important to provide faculty development workshops for those who wish to teach a new discipline. However, the cost of such workshops can be significant. Industry could assist with the cost, help to shape the material, and provide guest speakers.

- **Providing grants to help develop new degree programs:** implementing new degree programs is very expensive, and assistance with some of the development costs could help get a new program off the ground.

- **Providing scholarships and summer internships to students in these programs:** this is a good way to ensure that graduates can hit the ground running once they complete their degree program.

- **Providing support for realistic capstone projects:** Industry could provide valuable support by proposing capstone problems, acting as a client, reviewing deliverables, and/or furnishing advice about project management, development methods, and technology.

- **Modifying and updating employee position descriptions to raise the bar:** Many industry position descriptions focus on low-level skills, such as ability to code in C or Java and do not highlight the more advanced skills needed to produce assured software, such as background in risk analysis, attack patterns, threat modeling, and secure programming and testing.

- **Creating an endowed chair position in software assurance:** An endowed position would ensure longevity for the program.

## CONCLUSION AND FUTURE PLANS

The work described in this article can serve as a solid foundation for developing a master's degree program in software assurance. But developing the curriculum is just the first step in the set of activities needed to support Master of Software Assurance degree programs and tracks. To be successful, the curriculum model must be available, understood by the targeted academic and industrial communities, viewed as a key reference for software assurance curriculum development, and used to develop and modify software-assurance-focused curricula.

The process that we used worked well, in part because many of us had worked together in previous professional activities. However, there are certainly improvements that could be made. We did not plan as well as we could have for external review of the work. At times we had multiple authors making updates to the material, and coordination was sometimes a challenge. We spent a good bit of time on scope issues because we had not foreseen the need to clearly define the scope at the outset. On the plus side, we found that the diverse backgrounds among the authors allowed us to see different perspectives. We also found that there was benefit to starting outreach activities prior to the publication of the curriculum and presented it at several conferences and workshops.

During the coming year we will be involved in outreach activities. We plan to conduct faculty workshops and work with universities that may wish to adopt aspects of this curriculum. We will also extend our work to include considerations of software assurance specializations within other master's degree programs, such as Information Systems, and will further consider software assurance education needs at undergraduate levels and also in community colleges. We hope that this curriculum will be another step along the path of improving software assurance education and ultimately result in improvements in software systems assurance.

## REFERENCES

ACM & IEEE-CS. (2008). Computer Science Curriculum 2008: An Interim Revision of CS 2001. *Computing Curriculum Series*. Retrieved August 30, 2010, from http://www.acm.org//education/curricula/ComputerScience2008.pdf

Allen, J. H. (2008). *Software security engineering: A guide for project managers*. Reading, MA: Addison-Wesley Professional.

Anderson, R. J. (2008). *Security Engineering: A Guide to Building Dependable Distributed Systems* (2nd ed.). New York: John Wiley.

Ardis, M., & Ford, G. (1989). *1989 SEI Report on Graduate Software Engineering Education* (Tech. Rep. No. CMU/SEI-89-TR-21). Pittsburgh, PA: Carnegie Mellon University, Software Engineering Institute.

Ardis, M., Lasfer, K., & Michael, B. (Eds.). (2009). *Frequently asked questions on implementing GSwE2009*. Hoboken, NJ: Stevens Institute of Technology. Retrieved August 30, 2010, from http://www.gswe2009.org/faq/

Bloom, B. S. (Ed.). (1956). *Taxonomy of educational objectives: The classification of educational goals: Handbook I, cognitive domain*. New York: Longman.

Bosworth, S., & Kabay, M. E. (Eds.). (2002). *Computer Security Handbook*. New York: John Wiley.

CERT. (2007). Survivability and Information Assurance Curriculum. *Software Engineering Institute, Carnegie Mellon University*. Retrieved October 4, 2007, from http://www.cert.org/sia/

Committee on National Security Systems. (2009). *Instruction No. 4009*. National Information Assurance Glossary.

Department of Homeland Security (DHS). (2010a). *Build Security In*. Retrieved August 30, 2010 from https://buildsecurityin.us-cert.gov/bsi/home.html

Department of Homeland Security (DHS). (2010b). Software Assurance (SwA)Workforce Education and Training Working Group. *Software assurance CBK/principles organization*. Retrieved August 30, 2010, from https://buildsecurityin.us-cert.gov/swa/wetwg.html

Drew, C. (n.d.). Wanted: 'Cyber Ninjas.' *New York Times*. Retrieved December 29, 2009, from http://www.nytimes.com/2010/01/03/education/edlife/03cybersecurity.html?emc=eta1

Ford, G. (1991). *1991 SEI Report on Graduate Software Engineering Education* (Tech. Rep. No. CMU/SEI-91-TR-002). Pittsburgh, PA: Carnegie Mellon University, Software Engineering Institute.

IEEE-CS. (2004). IEEE Computer Society. *Software Engineering Body of Knowledge (SWEBOK)*. Retrieved August 30, 2010, from http://www.computer.org/portal/web/swebok

IEEE-CS & ACM. (2004). *Software engineering 2004: Curriculum guidelines for undergraduate degree programs in software engineering. Computing curriculum series*. Retrieved August 30, 2010, from http://sites.computer.org/ccse/SE2004Volume.pdf

Leaders in Security. (2009, March). *Building In ... Information Security, Privacy And Assurance*. Paper presented at the Knowledge Transfer Network Paris Information Security Workshop, Paris.

Mead, N. R., et al. (2010a). *Master of software assurance reference curriculum* (Tech. Rep. No. CMU/SEI-2010-TR-005/ESD-TR-2010-005). Pittsburgh, PA: Carnegie Melon University: Software Engineering Institute.

Mead, N. R., et al. (2010b). *Software Assurance Curriculum Project Volume II: Undergraduate Course Outlines* (Tech. Rep. No. CMU/SEI-2010-TR-019, ESC-TR-2010-019). Pittsburgh, PA: Carnegie Melon, University, Software Engineering Institute.

Partnership for Public Service & Booz Allen Hamilton. (2009). Cyber IN-Security: Strengthening the Federal Cybersecurity Workforce. *Partnership for Public Service*. Retrieved July, 2009, from http://ourpublicservice.org/OPS/publications/viewcontentdetails.php?id=135

Pyster, A. (Ed.). (2009). *Graduate software engineering 2009 (GSwE2009) curriculum guidelines for graduate degree programs in software engineering, version 1.0*. Hoboken, NJ: Stevens Institute of Technology.

## ENDNOTES

[1]  This course is not present in the MSwA Courses Added to the MSwE program.

[2]  The 1.2 knowledge unit, italicized, is different in Assured Development 1 in the standalone program and Assurance Management in the MSwA Courses Added to MSwE program.

[3]  The bolded knowledge units are not covered at the same Bloom's level as in the standalone program.

[4]  Condensed versions of Assured Software Development 1, 2, and 3 from the standalone program are in the MSwE program.

[5]  http://www.gswe2009.org/faq/#cat5

[6]  http://www.gswe2009.org/faq/?tx_mmforum_pi1[action]=list_topic& tx_mmforum_pi1[fid]=8

*This work was previously published in International Journal of Secure Software Engineering, edited by Khaled M. Khan, pp. 18-34, Volume 1, Issue 4, copyright 2010 by IGI Publishing (an imprint of IGI Global).*

# Chapter 18

# A Rigorous Approach to the Definition of an International Vocational Master's Degree in Information Security Management

**Frédéric Girard**
*Henri Tudor Public Research Center, Luxembourg*

**Bertrand Meunier**
*Henri Tudor Public Research Center, Luxembourg*

**Duan Hua**
*Henri Tudor Public Research Center, Luxembourg*

**Eric Dubois**
*Henri Tudor Public Research Center, Luxembourg*

## ABSTRACT

*In Luxembourg, like in many other countries, information security has become a central issue for private companies and public organizations. Today, information is the main asset of a company for its business and, at the same time, regulations are imposing more and more rules regarding its management. As a consequence, in Luxembourg, a clear need has emerged regarding the development of new learning trajectory fulfilling the requirements of the new job profile associated with a Chief Security Officer. This need was relayed by the national professional security association which asked for the development of a new education program targeting professional people engaged in a lifelong learning trajectory. The paper reports on the rigorous and scientific participatory approach for producing the adequate learning program meeting requirements elicited from the professional association members. The authors present the skills card that has been elaborated for capturing these requirements and the program, which has been built together with the University of Luxembourg for matching these requirements. This program proposes a holistic approach to information security management by including organization, human and technical security risks within the context of regulations and norms.*

DOI: 10.4018/978-1-4666-1580-9.ch018

## INTRODUCTION

During the last two decades, the impact of security concerns on the development and exploitation of Information Systems (IS) never ceased to grow, be it in public or private sectors. In this context, information security management has become paramount as demonstrated with the new ISO 2700x series (ISO/IEC 27001, 2005) dedicated to the set-up of Information Security Management System and the existence of over 200 practitioner-oriented security and risk management methods (see Dubois et al., 2010).

Information System Security Management helps companies identify and implement security requirements in a cost-effective manner. Indeed, security threats are so numerous that it is outright impossible to act on all of them, because (1) every technological security solution has a cost, and (2) companies have limited resources. Hence, companies need assurance that they adopt only solutions that will provide significant Return on Investment. This is done by comparing the cost of a solution with the risk of not using it, e.g., the cost of a business disruption due to a successful security attack. In this sense, security management plays an important role in the alignment of a company's business strategy with its Information Technology strategy. Because of this business/IT alignment dimension, the job profile associated this responsibility requires to combine technological competences together with business oriented ones. This twofold orientation makes difficult to find adequate persons, that we will call Chief Security Officer (CSO) in the rest of this paper.

This conclusion applies in Luxembourg where there are many technologically security oriented persons but only a few with the required business and management expertise. Thus a need for a specific education dedicated to CSO was identified. First, we further develop the context regarding the identification for these needs and also the motivation for introducing a university Professional Master programme instead of a pro-

fessional certification. Once this decision taken, the next question was about the content of the programme. This was evident that a multidisciplinary programme is required but its precise content has still to be designed. This is where our Tudor centre, a research public entity dealing with technology transfer and innovation, has been contacted because of its expertise in the design of training content meeting requirements for the development of new competences. For many years, Tudor centre has developed an expertise in previous projects focused on ICT related job profiles evolutions. This expertise is formalized into a rigorous and systematic method supporting the elaboration of a job profile skills card based on a set of iterative processes combining information capture methods such as interviews, focus groups, and information watch techniques. Then, we further detail this method together with its application to the elaboration of the skills card associated with the job of a CSO. Finally, before we conclude, we report on the elaboration of the programme in such a way that each lecture is meeting some of the requirements elicited in skills card and that the complete programme achieves the goal of capturing all of them.

## Luxembourg Context

Luxembourg has a service-intensive economy (over 80% of GNP). The majority of these services use information technology and systems that have been gradually implemented into organizations over a number of years. A large part of the economy depends on financial and insurance related services. In these services, it is clear that aspects related to information security are highly critical. These elements are also subject to international and national regulatory aspects and regulations like the recent ISO 2700x series (ISO/IEC 27001, 2005).

CLUSIL *(Luxembourg Information Security Organisation)* is a professional association that brings together a large number of people working in the security industry, whether as service providers or their clients, in the private and public sectors. An important responsibility of CLUSIL is to initiate national actions that will benefit all professions, such as development methods, support services development, monitoring of certain standards, etc. CLUSIL is also responsible for improving the skills of its members in relation to the various security professions. In this regard, CLUSIL identified a need to strengthen and/or develop the skills needed to be a Chief Security Officer (CSO). The official report revealed that this role did not really exist in many organizations. It found that most often there are security experts for technical and software related aspects in IT departments, but very few people have a role outside the IT department. In particular, they have very little involvement in the business and the importance of aligning technical security solutions with the business requirements related to, among other things, confidentiality, integrity and the availability of information. Moreover, these same people often lack the management skills needed to establish an IT Security Management System.

Based on these reports, CLUSIL created a working group to identify the types of training courses required for the role of CSO. It quickly became apparent that usual certifications in the information security businesses (as for instance ISACA-related certifications) were inadequate because their courses do not cover all the required aspects of the job, with in particular those relating to current European and National privacy laws. Academic qualifications were then considered. In terms of initial education, it was found that many security-related courses either targeted technology or management aspects, but rarely both. Moreover, the complexity of the CSO profession often requires professional experience. It was decided to also look at academic qualifications for working professionals according to the Lifelong Learning formulas. It was again found that there was only a very limited offer that corresponded to the CSO profession that specifically included the technical

skills as well as the soft skills necessary for communication, negotiation or security awareness.

In conclusion, it was decided to create a new professional master's course led by the University of Luxembourg, which already offered an initial education course in technological aspects of security. The diploma with the title "Master in Information System Security Management." is a Master's Degree II (second year master's) available to anyone who already has a Master's Degree I or a bachelor's degree with one year accredited work experience. For practical reasons, this one-year-equivalent course is spread over two years with classes held every second weekend.

It also requires a final thesis to be conducted in the student's place of work and using the lessons from the course to solve a problem in the workplace. This article outlines the content of the new course program, which should be launched in January 2011.

Additionally, as for doctors or architects, CLUSIL encouraged the working group dedicated to the CSO profession to establish a charter for the role of CSO and to establish entry requirements for this profession. These entry requirements are currently being discussed. They obviously include an assessment of professional work experience however the graduate from the new diploma course evidently meets these requirements.

## Continuing Training Context

European higher education for initial or continuing training is changing fundamentally. The Bologna Process, in its aim to create a "European Higher Education Area", requires educational institutions to demonstrate more clearly the value-added nature of their course program for students. This is done most commonly by using a criterion known as "learning outcomes". This criterion will be conveyed to European students and authorities and requires careful consideration as to the relevance of the course program. This new philosophy of educational development empowers educators to impart clearly identifiable knowledge, expertise, and skills.

This position re-emphasises the importance of the theoretical ideal of establishing an educational framework that is based primarily on a professional or skills framework. This seems all the more prudent for specifically job-oriented continuing education programs, such as the Master in Information System Security Management.

Actually setting the "learning outcomes" based on a skills framework will guarantee consistency across a course program. In fact, it will be closer to the reality of the profession in terms of the proposed learning situations.

However, making this transition from a skills framework to an educational framework is a delicate exercise. While in theory, this transformation seems simple, in practice it is highly problematic. Skills framework and educational framework documents are generally not established by the same group of individuals. The first document (skills framework) is particularly useful for human ressources (HR) professionals and others working in the HR field. The second document (educational framework) is primarily useful for educators and educational/training managers.

HR professionals are interested in the professional content, whereas educational professionals are eager to define how to appropriately divide the teaching time for students, in terms of their education and giving them a practical sense of their profession. The specific requirements for each of these are understandably different.

In other words, even if both documents have a greater understanding and analysis of professional practice, they cannot be structured identically.

Moreover, given the participatory method of establishing these documents, their contributor/s and editors will inevitably influence their content. The skills framework provides an outline but does not provide information on how to structure the content of an educational program. At most, it is important to verify that the skills to be acquired or developed for a profession are empirically accessible in a training program. There are therefore two reference documents, established for two different uses with separate information structures, and creating a link between the two is a real challenge; it is time wasting as well as time consuming.

The Tudor centre has previously examined the link between the two documents. This heuristic approach is needed to translate the skills framework into an educational framework.

## Preliminary Requirements and Skills Frameworks Structure

Before explicitly outlining the process and result of this empirical approach, it is important to specify certain preliminary requirements and scientific realities related to this work:

- It is essential to have a job description that is as comprehensive as possible. Comprehensive is understood to mean a vision for the profession or inter-sectoral and inter-organisational operation within a given market.
- The definition should also propose an increasingly refined information structure. This will outline and explain the purpose and activities of a profession in as much detail as possible. Ideally, 80% of the vision for the profession would be explained.
- It is a misapprehension to believe that one can describe an entire profession. It is simply not possible and what is more, it is meaningless. All the activities of a profession cannot be explicitly described. The belief in the logic that 100% can be defined would be to consider the profession as comprised merely of stipulated activities.

However today, very few or no professions can be defined in this way. Professionals now offer a more substantial flexibility to fulfil their responsibilities. They must be skilled and able to adapt to unexpected circumstances.

In order to obtain this representation of a profession, we have structured its contents in the following way. Even if, according to Foucher (2010), anglo-saxon and european approaches differ in the way competences are defined, there is an agreement that the identification of competences is a central issue in the understanding of a job position First of all, following our proposed method, it is important to determine the **"What"** of the profession - i.e. the duties that the professional must perform. These duties appear as several components:

## Activities

Activities are the main areas in which the profession is employed. An activity is the first level of information in other words, the general overview of one component of the profession. Activities help to understand what is generally expected from an employee in a given field. An activity is divided into a set of actions known as "tasks". Generally, four activities are sufficient to characterize a profession. They are expressed by action verbs. The activities do not necessarily need to be defined in a chronological or process type way.

## Tasks

Tasks are work that is "limited" to the context of the activity. Tasks are therefore an action to be performed as part of an activity. They aim to achieve a specific purpose, sometimes in collaboration and/or consultation with a third-party. Tasks are expressed by an infinitive verb. In general, four to six tasks are sufficient enough to form one activity.

## Related Participants

Related participants are anyone who is or will be in regular contact with the employee in a given field in order for them to fulfil their responsibilities.

Subsequently, the skills framework focuses on "what to implement" to achieve the "what".

There are two broad categories for the "what to implement": Technical and behavioural skills.

## Technical Skills

Technical skills are the body of knowledge and know-how related to the technical side of a profession. This is what allows an individual to understand a phenomenon, situation, problem or process (theoretical professional knowledge) and to use the operational capacity to carry out processes, methods, procedures, tools, and instruments for the job. They are necessary to perform tasks associated with activities. Technical competence is expressed using an infinitive verb. Only the most important technical skills for each activity are provided.

## Behavioural Skills

Behavioural skills are the body of know-how and professional attitude required to perform the job. This facilitates effective cooperation and communication with colleagues and clients, particularly to perform the required work. Only the most important behavioural skills for the activity are provided.

It is now important to understand how we obtained the result, before providing you with the process for translating the skills framework into the educational framework.

From 2003 to present, the Tudor centre has worked with a range of partners from the educational sector (professional, entry-level, and vocational training) to define, test, and validate the skills framework model (www.abilitic.eu). More than 20 professions have been the subject of this exercise, from sectors as varied as knowledge management, IT, insurance, logistics, and finance. The professions involved have validated this method in terms of its construction and content. In fact, this notion of skills used in our approach, and by extension, the notion we have of the skills framework, is a social construct (Le Boterf, 1998; Gilbert, 2005) developed and evaluated by many different parties. Therefore, developing a framework is about shaping a project and making it visible. In this regard, we are looking to be able use the skills framework based on a joint regulation (Havard & Krohmer, 2008).

The skills framework is therefore the result of back-and-forth consultation between various stakeholders, practicing professionals, clients, and even managers from the profession. A common language is consequently developed - identical ways to define the skills. A group dynamic is created by assembling different professionals who are hierarchically and typically not inclined to actually meet and exchange ideas. In this regard, the skills framework therefore includes a compromised vision of the profession shared between these different participants.

Then how do we collect the data required to establish this framework? The skills are established in the action, i.e., in real-life work situations faced by those working in the field. It is therefore necessary to look at all this data and the procedures in order to identify the skills.

## Establishing the Skills Framework

In order to establish the skills framework, we rely on combining all additional information to further identify the skills involved.

A preliminary survey of this information establishes an initial representation of the situational context for the profession being analysed. This initial representation identifies the potential activities of the profession and, if possible, associates them with their corresponding tasks. At this point suggestions are merely considered which will subsequently be submitted to experts in the field. The skills framework will therefore initially be established by collecting information on the position being analysed. Those involved in the exercise, i.e. those working in the given profession and their direct supervisors, will of course be required for interviews and working groups. In this regard, the work seeks to always be iterative.

Individual interviews (5 to 10 interviews are required depending on the complexity of the profession) are a preferred first step before forming working groups. According to experimentations reported in Beatty (1996) and Fletcher et al. (1993), a group of 10 persons is enough to build the skills framework for a profession. If used at the beginning of the framework development process, working groups lead to implicit negotiations between participants as to whether or not to accept an activity or whether to include one formulation over another. However, the benefit gained from participation often leads to a loss of accuracy and relevance. In contrast, while establishing the skills framework, we recommend using the working group to validate a framework based on the interviews.

The working group can then modify the formulations so they are understandable and can be used by all involved in the framework. This validation exercise is for security as well as a moment for those involved to own the content and quality of activity descriptions, and the tasks and skills that are associated with the profession. Different target sectors will be required during interviews to give an overall vision of the profession:

- Interact with sponsors of the study,
- Approach direct superiors, clients, and suppliers for the chosen profession to understand the organizational requirements that may be required by the profession.
- Appeal to individuals directly related to the profession. For this final category of participants, it is important to realize that

it is not easy to interpret activities. For the professionals being interviewed, an objective opinion may be insufficient to describe/verbalize the knowledge used in their everyday activity.

It is possible to develop an awareness, however it requires special conditions and methods to articulate "what we do not know we know", or "what we know without ever having acknowledged it" (Teiger, 1987, 1993a; Teiger & Laville, 1989). It is also necessary to pair the individual in question directly with that profession, to allow them to have a reflective view of their activities and to understand the description of the action.

This overcomes the semiotic deficit (Desjours, 2003); the great difficulty in putting work into words to classify the knowledge being used.

Certain methods allow this awareness and the individual or collective expression of this knowledge (among others, refer to Cru, 1992; Boutet et al., 1992; Daniellou & Garrigou, 1993; Hoc, 1984; Teiger, 1993a; Vermersch, 1993) and we prefer this in our interviews or working groups to establish the skills framework.

It should be noted that there are several advantages to developing a skills framework of this kind. The first is on an individual level: by gaining this ability to reflect and by performing this work remotely, the professional involved in our study masters his or her own activity – a self-knowledge in the action which is similar to a form of individual progress.

The second is on a more collective level: the understanding of their own work and the construction of meta-knowledge can allow every individual and the group to work better in terms of effectiveness, efficiency, and reliability. The organizing team allowed for five to eight days to establish the skills framework depending on the complexity of the profession, and the availability of the experts involved. This work may take place over a four- to six-week period.

## TRANSITION TO THE EDUCATIONAL FRAMEWORK

Following the establishment process for the skills framework, it is now possible to specify how we envisage translating this into an educational framework. First of all, it is important to interact in a cooperative and participatory manner with the professional experts, the same as when establishing the skills framework. However, they are not sufficient during this phase. We need to incorporate educational representatives: educators for the training/diploma selected, training managers, and ideally, past students from the educational program who are still practising professionals in the field.

Why is it necessary to expand the profiles of those involved to establish an educational framework from a skills framework?

Tudor Centre and various partners, educational development specialists, are trying to answer this question by taking into account the range of individuals in the learning process and the various documents each of them will use.

The aim is to eliminate the problems of ownership for the document arising from the educational participants. They will not see the document as legitimate, both in substance and in form, if they have not been involved in this translation process or if they find that no representatives from their sector have contributed to establishing the educational framework. It therefore seems imperative to integrate them with collaborative reflections and proposed participation. Their presence early on in this phase will impact the reflective content and pre-adapt it to the end-user: the educators of the intended diploma or training.

How can we effectively accomplish this translation?

The work is done using the skills framework. All the experts involved (practicing professionals, managers in the profession, clients/suppliers, trainers, etc.) meet for the working group. One activity (brainstorming exercise) is proposed during each working group. One or two tasks from the skills framework are considered. We ask participating experts to provide a factual account of their practices, tools, processes, challenges, and risks in their daily work and all the actions they implement to carry out tasks. In order to describe these elements, they have the opportunity to add the skills associated with each task. This ensures that the collected evidence is always consistent and contextualized with the task being studied.

Once all tasks being studied are complete, the data is collected by the organizing team at the Tudor centre. This consolidation of results provides a particular perspective: obtaining a policy framework within the educational framework.

The policy framework is established from the collected observations. It is the future thread that students can follow when they are required to follow the proposed syllabus.

It also provides educators with a reference document; it provides a level of structure for the content of their own educational module. In fact, the proposed policy framework encourages them to integrate their educational module into an overall framework for learning. This framework gives meaning to the act of learning for educators and students. Furthermore it ensures that the educational framework stems from the skills framework.

It is the responsibility of the organizing team at the Tudor centre to provide an analytic proposition to structure the policy framework for the educational program of the diploma in question, which in our case is the Master in Information System Security Management. In this analytic proposition, the idea is to link the learning levels being studied with the diploma's educational faculty. These levels provide a quick understanding of the key learning areas that the student must pass through to complete the diploma. Each of these levels breaks down the content into subjects of learning. These elements may be related to the training modules. With the first two levels of information, it is therefore possible to understand the scope of knowledge, skills and practices to be acquired through the training/qualification.

Guidance or learning objectives are proposed for each subject. They are what were previously known as "learning outcomes". The educator(s) responsible for a training module then have a road map to establish the educational content. They see what skills or abilities should be transferred to students. This information is also useful for the students, as they then know what skills they will have upon graduation as a result of the training modules. The organising team at the Tudor centre also outlines what the student will acquire if they can link the various learning programs available. It refers to the concept of "indirect benefits", which should be highlighted by the diploma's educational faculty.

This information emphasises dynamic learning for the training modules. It facilitates an understanding of the links between these modules and reinforces their usefulness and respective presence in the training. The elements contained in the educational framework are therefore not inconsistent or static. In fact, they are interrelated and dependent on one another. This road map is more understandable and accepted once it is established in part with representatives from the "educational world."

The organising team at the Tudor centre recommends working hypotheses for the educational approach in order to enrich the analytical work. At minimum this should fuel a debate within the educational faculty to determine how best to translate the educational guidelines/objectives into tangible elements for students. There are no specific requirements. The educators should use this to build educational exercises that are as close as possible to the actual profession.

There is one final element needed to complete this road map: the levelling of evaluative exercises to be given to students for each subject. The educators will be able to determine what level of expertise to teach using this method. A traditional measurement scale was used, based on a simplification of Bloom's taxonomy with only three levels instead of six. For the purposes of this study, the

Tudor centre merged levels 1 and 2, levels 3 and 4, and levels 5 and 6 of Bloom's taxonomy. In the new classification, level 1 focuses on assessing a students' ability to understand, learn, and memorize the concepts and practices conveyed in the training modules. In other words, it will ask the student to know basic vocabulary, to have an operational knowledge, and a level of simple comprehension of written procedures and manuals.

The new level 2 will highlight the students' ability to identify, organize, and transfer a practice/concept for use in another application context. At this level, the student is expected to have mastered complex situations using a set of techniques, procedures or specific methods, and not to be unnerved when facing new situations. The final level (level 3) corresponds to a high level of expertise. This translates into a student's ability to be able to take separate elements to form a whole and to make value judgments. In theory, at this stage the student is able to both teach and model complex situations to improve the effectiveness of techniques and to research, initiate, and propose a standardization and establishment of reference procedures.

Once this framework is established and the entire educational team has the overall road map for the training program to be established, one additional step is recommended: to create an ideal fusion between the learning path for subjects identified at each level. In this case, and depending on the extent of education, the student who follows this path will be able to measure his or her progress and the level of technology that is acquired with each step. The educational team will therefore be able to work collectively on the development of student skills training. This will give even more meaning to the educational activities of each educator.

## The Chief Security Officer (CSO) Skills Framework

In this sub-section we first report on the application of our proposed method to the definition of the skills framework associated with the CSO professions.

The following elements provided inputs for this work: the existing skills and educational frameworks, recommendations made by our HR specialists and educational curriculum analysts, an existing prototytpe of a current course program launched three years ago, the audit of this current course program as well as a satisfaction survey of all those involved in this program (including support and coordination services for the Master's Degree), opinions collected from sme well known professionals in the field, and opinions from national and international regulatory and state professionals and organizations. Finally, we also considered the recommendations on European higher education made in Bologna, June 1999 (http://www.bologna-bergen2005.no/EN/BASIC/Pros-descr.HTM, ECTS Users' Guide (2005) Brussels: Directorate-General for Education and Culture), following their recommendations made in Berlin (http://www.bologna-bergen2005.no) and the famous Learning Outcomes (Kennedy, Hyland, Ryan, "Writing and Using Learning Outcomes: a Practical Guide").

After collecting all this work and various sources we have created a group of experts. According to our proposed method, the role of these experts is significant. They should have the skills to understand and produce meaningful analysis on the fundamental knowledge to the profession. This analysis appears even more delicate since the profession itself experiments difficulties to define the perimeter of this job. Therefore we have approached the local network of professionals in information security, the CLUSIL. This network was already very active in terms of the definition of the know-how required fom CSO. However their approach was very pragmatic and seeked for a methodology to structure and manage the work. It was natural to combine our efforts and we were supported in this initiative by the Board of CLUSIL and its President. The CLUSIL quickly realized the usefulness of our approach and its added-value for professionals.

The CLUSIL provided us with names of professionals working and motivated by this work. The selection was made based on the work already done within the CLUSIL by the candidate. Another criterion for selection was to only consider persons professionally active in the CSO scope and exercising responsibility around information security. This responsibility can take various forms. This diversity permits conflicting points of view. This forced us to carry forward work definition and analysis. We made a special significance in the fact of having practitioners within the group. For reasons of availability more than ten people were contacted for a half in the presence in each working groups. The documents have been regularly updated and discussed through the use of the CLUSIL web collaborative platform (www.clusil.lu). This platform enabled us to centralize and accelerate documentation exchanges and contributions outside of the working groups. This is a quality criteria as it allows to maintain a certain amount of tension in the reflective work.

Throughout different working groups, the experts thus identified and analyzed, the outcomes of the preliminary inquiry with the potential of business activities. The enrichment and the proposed clarifications helped to formalize a joint paper for the the entire panel of experts.

The validation was conducted in two stages. The first stage of validation was performed by a focus group of experts who proposed the reformulation and clarified the final details of the repository. Finally an overview of the document was produced for the attention of the members of CLUSIL. Based on their comments, a final document was formalized in terms of a skill card.

This skill acrd document is now considered by the profession as a local reference. It is used by some companies to define internally such job profiles or skills of the associated with CSO.

Below, we present a small fragment of the skill card document:

"The framework of competencies achieved with the CSO presents four dimensions to be mastered by the CSO:

- **Strategic:** Organize and optimize information security within their organization.
- **Tactics:** Ensure the strategic policy of information security within the organization.
- **Operational:** Implement the security policy information.
- **Functional:** Communicate, educate and train the security issues."

These four dimensions identified by the expert members of CLUSIL highlight the responsibility of the CSO in the organization in terms of information security management (including the protection of information). Depending on the size of the structure and positioning the CSO can be involved or not in the operational implementation of security measures.

The complete document (in french) can be found on the CLUSIL web site: http://www.clusil. lu/tiki-download_file.php?fileId=50

## THE CSO DEGREE STRUCTURE

The degree structure has two main components. They reflect the need to combine scientific and professional aspects within the same course program. Therefore there is both an academic and professional component. Equal importance will be given to these two components. This establishes a link and balance between the theoretical education and its application to a real case scenario within a company. For the record, this is in fact a professional course that aims for students to immediately start work in their profession. This is reinforced by those selected to undertake the course. Only candidates with, at minimum, experience in a company and prior management of IT and IT security will be admitted. However, this equivalence does not exist in terms of the number of teaching hours, as the theoretical section, or more precisely, the academic section, occupies three quarters of the teaching time. There is indeed the resolve to assert the scientific influence. The professional section occupies only a quarter of the educational time but has a strong presence. Moreover, this section is continuously and transversely part of the course, since the academic aspects are systematically reinforced by evidence showing their application or use in the workplace.

The academic component covers all the elements necessary to understand, manage and establish information security in the organisation. The elements have been grouped into five separate modules. The modules are divided to more or less meet the Bologna requirements, that is to say, to demonstrate the ECTS (European Credit Transfer and Accumulation System) blocks. The subjects are regrouped into the blocks and the levels of acquired knowledge are achieved using the blocks. This also responds to the need to, if possible, modularize lessons and promote equivalent mechanisms. These five modules are:

- Understanding of Organizations and Management
- Policy Frameworks
- Information Security Management
- Technical (Software, networks, cryptography, PKI, cyphering, etc) Aspects
- Human Aspects

The vocational component focuses on two aspects: working in the field is demonstrated by the professional themselves, applying the academic experience and good practices as demonstrated through a professional project.

This project is carried out in the student's company of choice and based on information security solutions required by the company. This component differs from the previous one because it is carried out without academic classes. It aims for field experience and interactions with professionals in an organization responsible for IT and its security. It also aims to empower the students and offer them the opportunity to apply their acquired skills in a real life environment under business constraints, while still benefiting from the course. It also provides the benefit of ongoing academic and professional mentoring and a tutor while in the work place. This coaching helps to put into practice, in a pilot project situation, all the techniques, knowledge and know-how taught in the course. This provides effective support for decisions during the project with professional coaching and time to reflect on the chosen directions and pursued goals. This is particularly important because expert opinions are part of this profession and can result in a good or bad solution for the company. The modes of decision making and choice are a matter where the professional component relies on the ongoing academic component. This component consists of two modules which are:

- The Role of the Information Security Manager
- The Professional Project and Application of the Thesis

Cross-disciplinary approaches to education should be added to both academic and professional components. There are essentially two new aspects to our course, or at least two that we would like to emphasise: soft skills and a common thread running through the course. These lessons are implicitly transmitted through the course as suggested recommendations or educational advice from the teaching and guidance staff for this

Master's Degree. They are therefore inserted into the background of the educational thread using concrete and situational examples

The first aspect relates to soft skills. Indeed the centre of education has shifted sharply from knowledge to know-how. However this is currently no longer sufficient because implementing solutions and projects in companies, and even more so in information security, involves human interactions and large-scale issues. This particular context, with large constraints, requires managers to be able to communicate complex concepts and sometimes unpleasant messages so that they have an impact on the company business and management.

It is also necessary to more accurately anticipate and interpret potential obstacles and implement appropriate behaviour in situations when necessary in order to obtain the most appropriate outcomes. Soft skills are being identified as an important part of the course for these very reasons. We have provided this in an intersecting form so the technical and management aspects remain at the forefront.

The second aspect is the common thread running through this course. What is it? The subject being studied, information security, is only remotely linked to business. It is not so easy to practice security and skills in just one way within a company. Often the link between the technologies being studied and real-life usability is difficult. In such a course, the consistency between subjects, their aim and purpose may disappear over time. The link with knowledge can remain incomprehensible or unclear which is detrimental during the implementation phase, i.e. when constructing security solutions. In order to ensure students maintain a strong consistency between technical and scientific aspects on the one hand and the responsibility for IT on the other, particular attention is given to always provide academic knowledge within the overall context of the course. The idea is to encourage students to have a back and forth between a local and an

expert view on a particular point (the technical solution for information security) and an overall and contextualized view for their company (the security solution in line with the job). This approach also aims to gradually make the student aware of the implications and responsibility for information security.

## Educational Content

Each educational module includes a series of courses, which are each divided into a series of sessions. We considered the session, that is to say, a half-day or four-hour block of theoretical instruction, to be the secondary part of the course.

The lessons and classes can cover familiar or more or less standard descriptions. In fact, these classes cover subjects outlined in related areas but contextualize them in the field, and with important and useful aspects, of information security. Therefore all lessons are systematically related to the central course area, especially if they stray from this area, as is the case for aspects of communications. In this case, for example, an effort is made to tailor the teaching of communications to the problems and solutions that are specific situations which the future professionals may come across in their field and in their company. This example is valid for all classes.

The following elements are listed for the academic component:

## Understanding Organizations and Management

This module aims to empower the professional to integrate elements of the organization, i.e. its internal context, which may inhibit or promote the establishment of information security. The very popular link between business and IT will be covered here on solid (and often lacking) academic foundations. The two theory courses on organisations and company structure address these, among other issues. This link between business, IT and information security will be outlined, reinforced and strengthened by three courses – Financial Management, Project Management and IT Service Management.

This module is composed of the following courses:

- Organizational Theory
- Structure and Company Strategy
- Financial Management
- Project Management
- IT Service Management

This module introduces the course and, using the Policy framework, will provide solid foundations to study the management of information security module.

## Security Policy Frameworks

This module aims to provide participants with the policy framework and tools to define a policy framework in their own organization. This is the perimeter of the external environment, that is to say a company's external relationships. This has become indispensable in Europe and internationally, in terms of regulating business activities to protect individuals and property. Law is now a factor that affects technical aspects and the CSO becomes a company representative for these points, even above the internal legal department. This module provides the skills to take on this responsibility.

This module is composed of the following courses:

- Legal and Regulatory Aspects
- Application of Legal Provisions
- Sectoral Aspects

This module complements the module on organisations and provides all the elements to address information security management – the next module.

## Information Security Management

This module provides the skills to manage and implement information security management systems. It may be even more critical, in terms of information security, not to implement a system without management for this system. That is the purpose of this module – to provide a hierarchy where management is established before the security itself. Without being exclusive, this module uses the standards of ISO/IEC 27000. These concepts are supplemented with other standards and best practices. Comparative studies and alternative approaches are also offered in order to keep the student objective with regards to the proposed tools and paradigms.

This module is composed of the following courses:

- Information Security Management System (ISMS)
- Analysis and Risk Management
- Security Policy
- Compliance Assurance
- Continuity Management

This module is central to the course and demonstrates the importance of technical aspects. These can then be discussed in depth. They indeed offer an organizational base that ensures effective use of an equipped environment and justifies the investment for implementation. In any case, this is the idea that the course hopes to instil in future professionals.

In a second step, the mastered management aspects also account for the human aspects in a specific module.

## Technical Aspects

This module provides the basic technical skills for information security. In accordance with the student's commitment and experience, the course provides all the skills required to understand security points when seeking a security solution. However an advanced student could develop entire safety solutions even if this is not the purpose of the course. This is what eliminates the course from being a high level technical course in advanced security information. The course provides everything required for students to increase their knowledge in a particular topic.

This module is composed of the following courses:

- Security Technologies (network and tele-communication security, software systems and applications security, secure archietctures, etc.)
- Information Communication, Processing and Persistence
- Threats, Attacks and Computer Security Counter Measures

This module and the information security management module are the core modules for the course. However the objective in the program is not that the the CSO be an expert all these domains but can communicate with such experts and apprehend risk issues asscoaited with technologies.

## Human Aspects

This module is in a sense complemented by the technical module. It concentrates on the elements of information security that have become increasingly present in companies – the human factor and its effect: communication.

This module is composed of the following courses:

- Human Risk
- Human Communication

This module shows a change in a traditional, exclusively technical, and isolated field within the company. This need and strong demand from professionals in the field is taken into account, and led us to integrate these courses that are highly adapted to the target audience and the issues they face in business.

As a conclusion for this section, one can read that the proposed content program is consistent with recommendations like those provided in the [Department of Homeland Security (2008]. Still our porposed program is focusing on the role of a so-called Chief Security Officer which is close to the roles of Chief Information Officer and IT Security Professional referred in the report. Those are more focusing on security management and awareness aspects.

## RESULTS AND CONCLUSION

The developmental work for the new program definitely benefited from all the input that was collected for its establishment. The quantity and diversity of the input has not hampered the creation of a new and original program. This program provides training for senior professionals who are able to assume the responsibility required to grow and develop critically because IT has become the number one priority for companies and their ability to conduct business.

This course is also directly and permanently in tune with current events in international organizations and business. The clarification of guiding criteria and the information structuring that the skills frameworks provided and implemented helped to guide which elements should be retained or discarded.

This no doubt helped to ease the debates between stakeholders from different backgrounds, including the University, research and development and the private sector. The natural consensus, which was gradually established amongst the members of the team who established the program, also provided an in-depth, comprehensive and coordinated project while remaining within the set time-frame.

The leaders of the Master's Degree have profited from the elements and preparatory work carried out to achieve the skills and educational frameworks. The leaders are in charge of the program, the educational strategy, and the Master's Degree. They have been able to evolve from their previous thinking and establish a new vision for their course. They were able to naturally incorporate new and beneficial cross-curricular elements to a course – and a field, which is just as important. The work carried out for the frameworks in fact provided such an abundant amount of material that only part of it could be used immediately. It is indeed necessary to take into account the limited capacity for absorption and application of changes by organizations and individuals. The work is not lost, as, even though the program is finalized, it allows work to begin on continually developing and improving our course. This places the educational team in a proactive position that is highly beneficial for the entire course.

These elements are not the only elements necessary to establish the program. This establishment is still a big jump to take from an educational framework. However the availability of this true reference point allows us to make rapid progress and evolve using a framework that can be shaped and used as a benchmark. This reference point provides both a fresh approach to establishing a course and interdisciplinary elements which are strongly linked with the need to interconnect professions, people and different issues in companies, today, but especially, tomorrow.

The future will tell if implementing security information to directly benefit the business using this type of course will provide a return on investment in information security that all companies will seek. This would paradoxically be the least likely to surprise us.

## REFERENCES

*Abilitic*. (n.d.). Retrieved from www.abilitic.eu

ANACT. (2005). *Elaborer des référentiels de compétences, principes et méthodes – Chapitre: Compétences, de la Définition à l'utilisation CEN*. Bruxelles, Belgium: Workshop ICT Skills Meta Framework.

Beatty, G. O. (1996). Job analysis sample size: how small is large enough? In *Meeting of the Society for Industrial and Organizational Psychology*, San Diego.

*Bikigba-Bergen*. (n.d.). Retrieved from www.bologna-bergen2005.no/EN/BASIC/Pros-descr.HTM

*Bologna-Bergen*. (n.d.). Retrieved from www.bologna-bergen2005.no

*Bologna-Bergen* (n.d.). Retrieved from www.bologna-bergen2005.no/EN/BASIC/Pros-descr.HTM

Boterf, L. (1995). *De la compétence, essai sur un attracteur étrange*. Paris: Editions d'organisation.

Boterf, L. (1998). *Compétence et navigation professionnelle*. Paris: Editions d'organisation.

Boutet, D. Dejours, & Teiger. (1992). *Une approche interdisciplinaire des interactions langagières dans la travail*. Paper presented at the Communication au XXVII ème congrès de la Société d'Ergonomie de Langue Française, Lille, France.

*Chairemm*. (n.d.). Retrieved from www.chairemm.polymtl.ca/cdparentsv2.0/Carriere_files/RIASEC.html

Daniellou, G. (1993). L'ergonome, l'activité, et la parole des travailleurs. In Weill-Fassina, A., Rabardel, P., & Dubois, D. (Eds.), *Représentations pour l'action* (pp. 73–92). Toulouse, France: Octarès.

Dejours. (2003). *L'évaluation du travail à l'épreuve du réel. Critique des fondements de l'évaluation*. Paris: INRA.

Department Of Homeland Security. (2008). *Information Technology (IT) Security Essential Body of Knowledge (EBK): A Competency and Functional Framework for IT Security Workforce Development*. Washington, DC: Office of Cybersecurity and Communications National Cyber Security Division.

Dubois, H., & Mayer, M. (2010). A Systematic Approach to Define the Domain of Information System Security Risk Management. In Nurcan, S. (Eds.), *Intentional Perspectives on Information Systems Engineering*. Berlin: Springer Verlag.

Durand, Barbolosi, Baudet, Hua, Labarrade, Magnin, & Meunier. (2006). *Guide d'utilisateur de la démarche d'anticipation des compétences*. Luxembourg: Centre de Recherche Public Henri Tudor.

ECTS Users' Guide. (2005). *Proceedings of Directorate-General for Education and Culture*, Brussels, Belgium.

Fletcher, J., Friedman, L., Mccarthy, P., Mcintyre, C., O'learly, B., & Rheinstein, J. (1993). Sample sizes required to attain stable job analysis inventory profiles. In *Proceedings of the 8th meeting of the Society for Industrial and Organizational Psychology*, San Francisco.

Foucher, R., Saint-Onge, S., & Haines, V. (2010). *Gestion des performances au travail*. Bruxelles, Belgium: De Boeck.

Gilbert. (2005). La gestion prévisionnelle des RH. In D. Weiss (Ed.), *Ressources Humaines* (5th ed.). Paris: Editions d'Organisation.

Havard & Krohmer. *(2008)*. Création et articulation des règles dans le cadre d'un management des compétences. *In* Proceedings of the Revue de Gestion des Ressources Humaines.

ISO/IEC 27001. (2005). *Information technology – security techniques – information security management systems – requirements*. Geneva, Switzerland: International Organization for Standardization (IOS).

Kennedy, Hyland, & Ryan. (2007). *Writing and Using Learning Outcomes: a Practical Guide*. Cork, UK: University College Cork.

Teiger. (1993a). *Représentations du travail, travail de la Représentation*. In A. Weill-Fassina, P. Rabardel, & D. Dubois (Eds.), *Représentations pour l'action*. Toulouse, France: Octarès.

Teiger. (1995). *Parler quand même! Les fonctions des activités langagières non fonctionnelles*. In J. Boutet (Ed.), *Paroles au travail* (p. 45-72). Paris: L'Harmattan.

Unige. (n.d.). Retrieved from www.unige.ch/fapse/SSE/teaching/tc101/competence_concept.html

Vermersch. (1993). *L'entretien d'explication*. Paris: Edition ESF.

*This work was previously published in International Journal of Secure Software Engineering, edited by Khaled M. Khan, pp. 1-17, Volume 1, Issue 4, copyright 2010 by IGI Publishing (an imprint of IGI Global).*

# Compilation of References

Abadi, M., Budiu, M., Erlingsson, U., & Ligatti, J. (2005, November). Control-flow integrity. In *Proceedings of the 12th acm conference on computer and communications security*, Alexandria, VA (p. 340-353).

Abadi, M., & Lamport, L. (1993). Composing specifications. *ACM Transactions on Programming Languages, 15*(1), 73–132. doi:doi:10.1145/151646.151649

*Abilitic*. (n.d.). Retrieved from www.abilitic.eu

ACM & IEEE-CS. (2008). Computer Science Curriculum 2008: An Interim Revision of CS 2001. *Computing Curriculum Series*. Retrieved August 30, 2010, from http://www.acm.org//education/curricula/Computer-Science2008.pdf

Adams, C., & Barbieri, K. (2006). Privacy Enforcement in E-Services Environments. In Yee, G. (Ed.), *Privacy Protection for E-Services*. Hershey, PA: IGI Global.

Aggarwal, A., & Jalote, P. (2006). Monitoring the Security Health of Software Systems. In *Proceedings of the 17ᵗʰ International Symposium on Software Reliability Engineering*, NC (pp. 146-158).

Aleph One. (1996). Smashing the stack for fun and profit. *Phrack, 49*.

Alexander, I. (2002). Initial industrial experience of misuse cases in trade-off analysis. In *Proceedings of Requirements Engineering, IEEE Joint International Conference* (pp. 61-68). Washington, DC: IEEE.

Alexander, S. (2005, June). Defeating compiler-level buffer overflow protection. *;login: The USENIX Magazine, 30*(3). anonymous. (2001). Once upon a free. *Phrack, 57*.

Alexander, I. (2003). Misuse cases: Use cases with hostile intent. *IEEE Software, 20*(1), 58–66. doi:doi:10.1109/MS.2003.1159030

Alfaro, L., & Henzinger, T. (2001). Interface theories for component-based design. In *Proceedings of the 9th Annual ACM Symposium on Foundation of Software Engineering* (pp. 109-120).

Alghathbar, K., & Wijesekera, D. (2003a). AuthUML: A three-phased framework to model secure use cases. In *Proceedings of the Workshop on Formal Methods in Security Engineering: From Specifications to Code* (pp. 77-87).

Alghathbar, K., & Wijesekera, D. (2003b). Consistent and complete access control policies in use cases. In *"UML" 2003 - The Unified Modeling Language* (LNCS 2863, pp. 373-387).

Allen, J. H. (2008). *Software security engineering: A guide for project managers*. Reading, MA: Addison-Wesley Professional.

Allen, J. H., Barnum, S., Ellison, R. J., McGraw, G., & Mead, N. R. (2008). *Software security engineering: A guide for project managers* (1st ed.). Boston: Addison-Wesley Professional.

Allen, J. H., Ellison, R. J., Mead, N. R., Barnum, S., & McGraw, G. (2010). *A Look at Software Security Engineering: A Guide for Project Managers*. CrossTalk Journal of Defense Software Engineering.

Altarum Institute. (2004). *Does Eveyrone Struggle As Much As We Do? The Role of the Integrated Acquisition Life Cycle in Program Success*. The Hidden Principles of Program Success.

ANACT. (2005). *Elaborer des référentiels de compétences, principes et méthodes – Chapitre: Compétences, de la Définition à l'utilisation CEN*. Bruxelles, Belgium: Workshop ICT Skills Meta Framework.

Anderson, R. J. (2008). *Security Engineering: A Guide to Building Dependable Distributed Systems* (2nd ed.). New York: John Wiley.

Anley, C. (2002). *Advanced SQL injection in SQL server application* (Tech. Rep., NGSSoftware Insight Security Research). Retrieved from http://www.nextgenss.com/papers/advanced_sql_injection.pdf

Antón, A. I., & Potts, C. (2001). Functional paleontology: System evolution as the user sees it. In *Proceedings of the 23rd International Conference on Software Engineering* (ICSE'01).

Anton, A. I., & Potts, C. (2003). Functional paleontology: The evolution of user-visible system services. *IEEE Transactions on Software Engineering, 29*(2), 151–166. doi:doi:10.1109/TSE.2003.1178053

Antonellis, P., Antoniou, D., Kanellopoulos, Y., Makris, C., Theodoridis, E., Tjortjis, C., & Tsirakis, N. (2009). Clustering for monitoring software systems maintainability evolution. *Electronic Notes in Theoretical Computer Science, 233*, 43–57. doi:doi:10.1016/j.entcs.2009.02.060

Antoni, L., Leveugle, R., & Feher, B. (2003). Using run-time reconfiguration for fault injection applications. *IEEE Transactions on Instrumentation and Measurement, 52*(5). doi:doi:10.1109/TIM.2003.817144

Apache Software Foundation. (2007). *Apache JMeter*. Retrieved from http://jakarta.apache.org/jmeter/

AQTRONIX. (2007). *WebKnight*. Retrieved from http://www.aqtronix.com/?PageID=99

Ardis, M., & Ford, G. (1989). *1989 SEI Report on Graduate Software Engineering Education* (Tech. Rep. No. CMU/SEI-89-TR-21). Pittsburgh, PA: Carnegie Mellon University, Software Engineering Institute.

Ardis, M., Lasfer, K., & Michael, B. (Eds.). (2009). *Frequently asked questions on implementing GSwE2009*. Hoboken, NJ: Stevens Institute of Technology. Retrieved August 30, 2010, from http://www.gswe2009.org/faq/

Arnold, J., & Kaashoek, M. F. (2009). Automatic Rebootless Kernel Updates. In *Proceedings of EuroSys*. Ksplice.

Atluri, V., & Huang, W. (1996). An Extended Petri Net Model for Supporting Workflows in a Multilevel Secure Environment. In *Proceedings of DBSec 1996*, Como, Italy (pp. 240-258).

Austin, T. M., Breach, S. E., & Sohi, G. S. (1994, June). Efficient detection of all pointer and array access errors. In *Proceedings of the acm sigplan '94 conference on programming language design and implementation*, Orlando, FL (pp. 290-301).

Avijit, K., Gupta, P., & Gupta, D. (2004, August). Tied, libsafeplus: Tools for runtime buffer overflow protection. In *Proceedings of the 13th usenix security symposium*, San Diego, CA.

Backes, M., Pfitzmann, B., & Waidner, M. (2003). Security in Business Process Engineering. In *Proceedings of 2003 International Conference on Business Process Management* (LNCS 2678, pp. 168-183). New York: Springer.

Backhouse, J., & Dhillon, G. (1996). Structures of responsibility and security of information systems. *European Journal of Information Systems, 5*, 2–9. doi:doi:10.1057/ejis.1996.7

Bai, Y. (2007). On XML document security. In *Proceedings of the International Conference on Software Engineering and Data Engineering* (pp. 39-42).

Bai, Y. (2008). Access control for XML document. In *Proceedings of the International Conference on Industrial, Engineering and Other Applications of Applied Intelligence Systems* (pp. 621-630).

Bai, Y., & Varadharajan, V. (1997). A language for specifying sequences of authorization transformations and its applications. In *Proceedings of the International Conference on Information and Communication Security* (pp. 39-49).

Bai, Y. (2008). Reasoning for Incomplete Authorizations. *KES, 1*, 278–285.

Bandhakavi, S., Bisht, P., Madhusudan, P., & Venkatakrishnan, V. N. (2007, October). CANDID: Preventing SQL injection attacks using dynamic candidate evaluations. In *Proceedings of the 14th ACM Conference on Computer and Communications Security (CCS)* (pp. 12–24). Alexandria, Virginia, USA.

Baral, C. (2003). *Knowledge Representation, Reasoning and Declarative Problem Solving*. Cambridge, UK: Cambridge University Press.

Baratloo, A., Singh, N., & Tsai, T. (2000, June). Transparent run-time defense against stack smashing attacks. In *Usenix 2000 annual technical conference proceedings*, San Diego, CA (pp. 251-262).

Barjis, J. (2009). Collaborative, Participative and Interactive Enterprise Modeling. In J. Filipe & J. (Eds.), *Enterprise Information Systems* (LNBIP 24). Berlin: Springer Verlag.

Barjis, J. (2007). Automatic Business Process Analysis and Simulation Based on DEMO. *Journal of Enterprise Information Systems*, *1*(4), 365–381. doi:d oi:10.1080/17517570701646590

Barjis, J. (2008). The Importance of Business Process Modeling in Software Systems Design. *Journal of the Science of Computer Programming*, *71*(1), 73–87.

Barrantes, E. G., Ackley, D. H., Forrest, S., Palmer, T. S., Stefanović, D., & Zovi, D. D. (2003, October). Randomized instruction set emulation to disrupt binary code injection attacks. In *Proceedings of the 10th acm conference on computer and communications security (ccs2003)*, Washington, DC (pp. 281-289).

Barry, E. J., Kemerer, C. F., & Slaughter, S. A. (2007). How software process automation affects software evolution: a longitudinal empirical analysis. *Journal of Software Maintenance and Evolution. Research and Practice*, *19*(1), 1–31.

Bartoletti, M., Degano, P., & Ferrari, G. L. (2005). Enforcing secure service composition. In *Proceedings of the 18th IEEE Workshop Computer Security Foundations*.

Bartoletti, M., Degano, P., Ferrari, G. L., & Zunino, R. (2008). Semantics-Based design for secure Web services. *IEEE Transactions on Software Engineering*, *34*(1), 33–49. doi:doi:10.1109/TSE.2007.70740

Basin, D. (2006). Model driven security: From UML models to access control infrastructures. *ACM Transactions on Software Engineering and Methodology*, *15*(1), 39–91. doi:10.1145/1125808.1125810

Basin, D. (2009). Automated analysis of security-design models. *Journal of Information and Software Technology*, *51*(5), 815–831. doi:10.1016/j.infsof.2008.05.011

Basin, D. A., Doser, J., & Lodderstedt, T. (2003). Model driven security for process-oriented systems. In *Proceedings of SACMAT, 2003*, 100–109.

Baskerville, R. (1988). *Designing Information Systems Security*. New York: John Wiley & Sons.

Bauer, M. (2002). Practical Threat Analysis and Risk Management. *Linux Journal, 9*(93).

Baumann, A., Appavoo, J., Wisniewski, R. W., Silva, D. D., Krieger, O., & Heiser, G. (2007). Reboots Are for Hardware: Challenges and Solutions to Updating an Operating System on the Fly. In *Proceedings of the USENIX Annual Technical Conference*.

Baumann, A., Heiser, G., Appovoo, J., Silva, D. D., Krieger, O., Wisniewski, R., & Kerr, J. (2005). Providing Dynamic Update in an Operating System. In *Proceedings of the USENIX Annual Technical Conference* (pp. 279-291).

BBP. (2003, May). *BSD heap smashing*. Retrieved from http://www.security-protocols.com/modules.php?name=News&file=article&sid=1586.

Beatty, G. O. (1996). Job analysis sample size: how small is large enough? In *Meeting of the Society for Industrial and Organizational Psychology*, San Diego.

Bell, D., & LaPadula, L. (1975). *Secure computer systems: mathematical foundations model* (Tech. Rep. M74-244). Bedford, MA: Mitre.

Bellard, F. (2003). *TCC: Tiny C Compiler*. Retrieved March 16, 2010, from www.tinycc.org

Berger, E. D., & Zorn, B. G. (2006, June). Probabilistic memory safety for unsafe languages. In *Acm sigplan 2006 conference on programming language design and implementation (pldi 2006)*. Ottawa, Canada: Diehard.

Berger, E. D., Zorn, B. G., & McKinley, K. S. (2001, June). Composing high-performance memory allocators. In *Proceedings of the acm sigplan 2001conference on programming language design and implementation (pldi)*, Snowbird, UT (pp. 114-124).

Berger, E. D., Zorn, B. G., & McKinley, K. S. (2002, Nov). Reconsidering custom memory allocation. In *Proceedings of the 2002 acm sigplan conference on object-oriented programming systems, languages and applications (oopsla)*, Seattle, WA (pp. 1-12). New York: ACM Press.

Berger, E., & Zorn, B. (2006). DieHard: Probabilistic Memory Safety for Unsafe Languages. In *Proceedings of the Conference on Programming Language Design and Implementation*, Ottawa, Canada (pp. 158-168).

Berinato, S. (2002, April 8). Finally, a real return on security spending. *CIO*. Retrieved June 23, 2009, from http://www.cio.com.au/index.php/id;557330171;fp;fpid;pf;1

Bertino, E., Jajodia, S., & Samarati, P. (1996). Supporting multiple access control policies in database systems. In *Proceedings of the IEEE Symposium on Research in Security and Privacy* (pp. 94-107).

Bertino, E. (2000). Temporal authorization bases: From specification to integration. *Journal of Computer Security*, *8*(4), 309–353.

Bertino, E., Buccafurri, F., Ferrari, E., & Rullo, P. (2000). A logic-based approach for enforcing access control. *Computers & Security*, *8*(2), 109–140.

Bertino, E., Catania, B., Ferrari, E., & Perlasca, P. (2003). A logical framework for reasoning about access control models. *ACM Transactions on Information and System Security*, *6*(1), 71–127. doi:doi:10.1145/605434.605437

Bettini, C., Jajodia, S., Wang, X. S., & Wijesekera, D. (2002). Provisions and obligations in policy management and security applications. In *Proceedings of the Very Large Database Conference* (pp. 502-513).

Beznosov, K. (2003). *eXtreme Security Engineering: On Employing XP Practices to Achieve "Good Enough Security" without Defining It.* Paper presented at the First ACM Workshop on Business Driven Security Engineering (BizSec).

Beznosov, K., & Kruchten, P. (2004). *Towards Agile Security Assurance.* Paper presented at the New Security Paradigms Workshop, Nova Scotia, Canada.

Bhatkar, S., DuVarney, D. C., & Sekar, R. (2003, August). Address obfuscation: An efficient approach to combat a broad range of memory error exploits. In *Proceedings of the 12th usenix security symposium*, Washington, DC (pp. 105-120).

Biba, K. (1977). *Integrity considerations for secure computer systems* (Tech. Rep. TR-3153). Bedford, MA: Mitre.

*Bikigba-Bergen*. (n.d.). Retrieved from www.bologna-bergen2005.no/EN/BASIC/Pros-descr.HTM

Bishop, M., & Davis, U. C. (2006). *Foundations of Computer and Information Security – Requirements* (Lecture No. 26).

Bishop, M. (2005). *Introduction to Computer Security*. Boston: Addison-Wesley.

Bishop, P., Bloomfield, R., & Guerra, S. (2004). *The Future of Goal-Based Assurance Cases*. Ontario, Canada: Adelard and City University.

Biskup, J. (2009). *Security in computing systems challenges, approaches, and solutions*. New York: Springer-Verlag.

Bloom, B. S. (Ed.). (1956). *Taxonomy of educational objectives: The classification of educational goals: Handbook I, cognitive domain*. New York: Longman.

Boehm, H. (n. d.). *A garbage collector for c and c++*. Retrieved from http://www.hpl.hp.com/personal/Hans_Boehm/gc/

Boehm, H. (n. d.). *Conservative gc algroithmic overview*. Retrieved from http://www.hpl.hp.com/personal/Hans_Boehm/gc/gcdescr.html

Boehm, B., & Basili, V. R. (2001). Top 10 list *Computer*, *34*(1), 135–137. doi:10.1109/2.962984

Boehm, B., & Papaccio, P. N. (1988). Understanding and controlling software costs. *IEEE Transactions on Software Engineering*, *14*(10), 1462–1477. doi:doi:10.1109/32.6191

Boehm, H., & Weiser, M. (1988, September). Garbage collection in an uncooperative environment. *Software, Practice & Experience, 18*(9), 807–820. doi:10.1002/spe.4380180902

Bohner, S. A. (2002). Software change impacts-an evolving perspective. In *Proceedings of International Conference on Software Maintenance.*

*Bologna-Bergen* (n.d.). Retrieved from www.bologna-bergen2005.no/EN/BASIC/Pros-descr.HTM

Bond, G. W., Cheung, E., Purdy, K. H., Zave, P., & Ramming, C. (2004). An open architecture for next-generation telecommunication services. *ACM Transactions on Internet Technology, 4*(1), 83–123. doi:doi:10.1145/967030.967034

Booch, G., et al. (1999). *The Unified Modeling Language user guide.* Reading, MA: Addison Wesley Professional.

Borland. (2009). *Borland Together Architect.* Retrieved from http://www.borland.com/us/products/together/index.html

Boström, G., Wäyrynen, J., Bodén, M., Beznosov, K., & Kruchten, P. (2006). *Extending XP practices to support security requirements engineering.* Paper presented at the Proceedings of the 2006 international workshop on Software engineering for secure systems (SESS '06).

Bosworth, S., & Kabay, M. E. (Eds.). (2002). *Computer Security Handbook.* New York: John Wiley.

Boterf, L. (1995). *De la compétence, essai sur un attracteur étrange.* Paris: Editions d'organisation.

Boterf, L. (1998). *Compétence et navigation professionnelle.* Paris: Editions d'organisation.

Boutet, D. Dejours, & Teiger. (1992). *Une approche interdisciplinaire des interactions langagières dans la travail.* Paper presented at the Communication au XXVII ème congrès de la Société d'Ergonomie de Langue Française, Lille, France.

Boyd, S. W., & Keromytis, A. D. (2004, June). SQLrand: Preventing SQL injection attacks. In *Proceedings of the second International Conference On Applied Cryptography And Network Security (ACNS)* (pp. 292–302).

Breach Security Inc. (2007). *ModSecurity.* Available from: http://www.modsecurity.org/.

Breaux, T. D., & Anton, A. I. (2008). Analyzing regulatory rules for privacy and security requirements. *IEEE Transactions on Software Engineering, 34*(1), 5–20. doi:doi:10.1109/TSE.2007.70746

Brier, J., Rapanotti, L., & Hall, J. G. (2006). Problem-based analysis of organisational change: A real-world example. In *Proceedings of the 2006 International Workshop on Advances and Applications of Problem Frames,* Shanghai, China, ACM.

Brown, A., & Patterson, D. A. (2002). Rewind, Repair, Replay: Three R's to dependability. In *Proceedings of the ACM SIGOPS European Workshop,* Saint-Emilion, France.

Brown, K. (1999, January). Building a lightweight COM interception framework part 1: The universal delegator. *Microsoft Systems Journal.*

Buehrer, G. T., Weide, B. W., & Sivilotti, P. A. G. (2005, September). SQLGuard: Using parse tree validation to prevent SQL injection attacks. In *Proceedings of the 5th International Workshop on Software Engineering and Middleware* (pp. 106–113). Lisbon, Portugal.

Bulba, & Kil3r. (2000). Bypassing Stackguard and stackshield. *Phrack, 56.*

Burrows, M., Abadi, M., & Needham, R. (1990). A Logic of Authentication. *ACM Transactions on Computer Systems, 8,* 18–36. doi:doi:10.1145/77648.77649

Butler, S. (2002, May). *Security attribute evaluation method: A cost-benefit approach.* Paper presented at the 24th International Conference on Software Engineering, Orlando, FL.

Calder, M., Kolberg, M., Magill, E., & Reiff-Marganiec, S. (2003). Feature interaction: A critical review and considered forecast. *Computer Networks, 41*(1), 115–141. doi:doi:10.1016/S1389-1286(02)00352-3

Calder, M., & Miller, A. (2006). Feature interaction detection by pairwise analysis of LTL properties: a case study. *Formal Methods in System Design, 28*(3), 213–261. doi:doi:10.1007/s10703-006-0002-5

Candea, G., & Fox, A. (2003). Crash-Only Software. In *Proceedings of the Workshop on Hot Topics in Operating Systems (HOTOS-IX)*.

Caulkins, J., Hough, E., Mead, N. R., & Osman, H. (2007). Optimizing investments in security countermeasures: A practical tool for fixed budgets. *IEEE Security & Privacy*, 5(5), 24–27. doi:doi:10.1109/MSP.2007.117

CERT. (2007). Survivability and Information Assurance Curriculum. *Software Engineering Institute, Carnegie Mellon University*. Retrieved October 4, 2007, from http://www.cert.org/sia/

Cesare, S. (1998). *Runtime Kernel kmem Patching*. Retrieved from http://vx.netlux.org/lib/vsc07.html

*Chairemm*. (n.d.). Retrieved from www.chairemm. polymtl.ca/cdparentsv2.0/Carriere_files/RIASEC.html

Chandra, P. (2010). Open Web Application Security Project (OWASP*). Software Assurance Maturity Model: A Guide to Building Security into Software Development v1*. Retrieved from http://www.opensamm.org/downloads/SAMM-1.0.pdf

Charrette, R. N. (2005). Why software fails. *IEEE Spectrum*, 42(9). doi:doi:10.1109/MSPEC.2005.1502528

Checkland, P. (1990). *Soft system methodology in action*. Toronto, Ontario, Canada: John Wiley & Sons.

Chen, H., Yu, J., Chen, R., Zang, B., & Yew, P.-C. (2007). Polus: A powerful live updating system. In *Proceedings of the 29th international conference on Software Engineering (ICSE '07)* (pp. 271-281). Washington, DC: IEEE Computer Society.

Chen, P., Dean, M., Ojoko-Adams, D., Osman, H., Lopez, L., & Xie, N. (2004). *Systems Quality Requirements Engineering (SQUARE) methodology: Case study on asset management system (Special Rep. No. CMU/SEI-2004-SR-015)*. Pittsburgh, PA: Carnegie Mellon University, Software Engineering Institute.

Chernoff, H. (1973). The Use of Faces to Represent Points in K-Dimensional Space Graphically. *Journal of the American Statistical Association, 68*.

Cheswick, B. (1990). *The Design of a Secure Internet Gateway*. Paper presented at the USENIX Conference.

Chien, E., & Szor, P. (2002). Blended Attacks Exploits, Vulnerabilities, and Buffer Overflow Techniques in Computer Viruses. In *Proceedings of the Virus Bulletin Conference*, New Orleans, LA.

Chiueh, T., & Hsu, F. (2006). RAD: A Compile-Time Solution to Buffer Overflow Attacks. In *Proceedings of the 21ˢᵗ International Conference on Distributed Computing Systems, AZ* (pp. 409-417).

Chomicki, J., Lobo, J., & Naqvi, S. (2000). A logical programming approach to conflict resolution in policy management. In *Proceedings of the International Conference on Principles of Knowledge Representation and Reasoning* (pp. 121-132).

Christel, M. G., & Kang, K. C. (1992). *Issues in requirements elicitation* (Tech. Rep. No. CMU/SEI-92-TR-012). Pittsburgh, PA: Carnegie Mellon University, Software Engineering Institute.

Chu, M., Murphy, C., & Kaiser, G. (2008). Distributed in vivo testing of software applications. In *Proceedings of the First International Conference on Software Testing, Verification and Validation* (pp. 509-512).

Chung, L., Hung, F., Hough, E., & Ojoko-Adams, D. (2006). *Security Quality Requirements Engineering (SQUARE): Case study phase III (Special Rep. No. CMU/SEI-2006-SR-003)*. Pittsburgh, PA: Carnegie Mellon University, Software Engineering Institute.

Chung, L., & Subramanian, N. (2003). Architecture-based semantic evolution of embedded remotely controlled systems. *Journal of Software Maintenance and Evolution: Research and Practice*, 15(3), 145–190. doi:doi:10.1002/smr.273

Clark, D., & Wilson, D. (1987). A comparison of commercial and military computer security policies. In *Proceedings of IEEE Symposium on Security and Privacy* (pp. 184-194).

Clarke, T. (2009). *Fuzzing for software vulnerability discovery* (Tech. Rep. No. RHUL-MA-2009-4). London: University of London, Department of Mathematics.

Clause, J., Li, W., & Orso, A. (2007). Dytan: A Generic Dynamic Taint Analysis Framework. In *Proceedings of the International Symposium on Software Testing and Analysis*, London (pp. 196-206).

Committee on National Security Systems. (2009). *Instruction No. 4009*. National Information Assurance Glossary.

Common Criteria. (2005). *15408. Common Criteria for Information Technology Security Evaluation*. Gaithersburg, MD: NIST. Retrieved from http://csrc.nist.gov/cc/

Common Weakness Enumeration (CWE) Categories. (2010). *Sponsored by the National Cyber Security Division of the U.S. Department of Homeland Security and hosted by The MITRE Corporation*. Retrieved August 24, 2010, from http://cwe.mitre.org/data/definitions/78.html

Common Weakness Enumeration (CWE). (n.d.). *Community list. MITRE*. Retrieved http://cwe.mitre.org/

Condit, J., Harren, M., McPeak, S., Necula, G. C., & Weimer, W. (2003). CCured in the real world. In *Proceedings of the acm sigplan 2003 conference on programming language design and implementation*, San Diego, CA (pp. 232-244).

Cook, S., Harrison, R., Lehman, M. M., & Wernick, P. (2006). Evolution in software systems: foundations of the SPE classification scheme. *Journal of Software Maintenance and Evolution: Research and Practice*, *18*(1), 1–35. doi:doi:10.1002/smr.314

Cornford, S. L., Feather, M. S., & Hicks, K. A. (2001). *DDP – a tool for life-cycle risk management*. Retrieved June 23, 2009, from http://ddptool.jpl.nasa.gov/docs/f344d-slc.pdf

Cowan, C., Beattie, S., Johansen, J., & Wagle, P. (2003, Aug). PointGuard: protecting pointers from buffer overflow vulnerabilities. In *Proceedings of the 12th usenix security symposium*, Washington, DC (pp. 91-104).

Cowan, C., Pu, C., Maier, D., Hinton, H., Walpole, J., & Bakke, P. (1998, January). StackGuard: Automatic adaptive detection and prevention of buffer-overflow attacks. In *Proceedings of the 7th usenix security symposium*, San Antonio, TX (pp. 63-78).

Cowan, C., Pu, C., Maier, D., Hinton, H., Walpole, J., Bakke, P., et al. (1998). Automatic Adaptive Detection and Prevention of Buffer Overflow Attacks. In *Proceedings of the 7ᵗʰ USENIX Security Conference*, San Antonio, TX.

Crampton, J., & Khambhammettu, H. (2008). Delegation in role-based access control. *International Journal of Information Security*, *7*, 123–136. doi:doi:10.1007/s10207-007-0044-8

*CSA*. (n.d.). *Principles in Summary. Canadian Standards Association*. Retrieved August 13, 2009, from http://www.csa.ca/cm?c=CSA_Content&childpagename=CSA%2FLayout&cid=1239124803011&p=1239124810319&packedargs=locale%3D1238188967079&pagename=CSA%2FRenderPage

da Silva, B. C., Figueiredo, E., Garcia, A., & Nunes, D. (2009). Refactoring of crosscutting concerns with metaphor-based heuristics. *Electronic Notes in Theoretical Computer Science*, *233*, 105–125. doi:doi:10.1016/j.entcs.2009.02.064

Dacier, M., & Deswarte, Y. (1994). Privilege graph: An extension to the typed access matrix model. In *Proceedings of European Symposium on Research in Computer Security* (pp. 319-334).

Dahn, C., & Mancoridis, S. (2003). Using Program Transformation to Secure C Programs Against Buffer Overflows. In *Proceedings of the 10ᵗʰ Working Conference on Reverse Engineering*, Canada (pp. 323-332).

Dalton, M., Kannan, H., & Kozyrakis, C. (2007). Raksha: A Flexible Information Flow Architecture for Software Security. In *Proceedings of the 34ᵗʰ Annual International Symposium on Computer Architecture*, San Diego, CA (pp. 482-493).

Damiani, E., Vimercati, S., Paraboschi, S., & Samarati, P. (2002). A fine grained access control system for XML documents. *ACM Transactions on Information and System Security*, 160–202.

Daniellou, G. (1993). L'ergonome, l'activité, et la parole des travailleurs. In Weill-Fassina, A., Rabardel, P., & Dubois, D. (Eds.), *Représentations pour l'action* (pp. 73–92). Toulouse, France: Octarès.

D'Aubeterre1, F., Singh, R., & Iyer, L. (2008). Secure activity resource coordination: empirical evidence of enhanced security awareness in designing secure business processes. *European Journal of Information Systems*, *17*, 528-542.

d'Avila Garcez, A. S., Russo, A., Nuseibeh, B., & Kramer, J. (2003). Combining abductive reasoning and inductive learning to evolve requirements specifications. *IEEE Proceedings Software*, *150*(1), 25–38. doi:doi:10.1049/ip-sen:20030207

de Landtsheer, R., & van Lamsweerde, A. (2005). Reasoning about confidentiality at requirements engineering time. Proceedings of the 10ᵗʰ European Software Engineering Conference, (pp. 41-49), Lisbon, Portugal, ACM.

Dejours. (2003). *L'évaluation du travail à l'épreuve du réel. Critique des fondements de l'évaluation.* Paris: INRA.

Del Rosso, C. (2006). Continuous evolution through software architecture evaluation: a case study. *Journal of Software Maintenance and Evolution: Research and Practice*, *18*(5), 351–383. doi:doi:10.1002/smr.337

Demurjian, S., et al. (2001). A user role-based security model for a distributed environment. In B. Thuraisingham, R. van de Riet, K. Dittrich, & Z. Tari (Eds.), *Data and applications security: Developments and directions* (LNCS 73, pp. 259-270).

Demurjian, S., et al. (2004). Concepts and capabilities of middleware security. In Q. Mohammed (Ed.), *Middleware for communications* (pp. 211-236). New York: John-Wiley & Sons.

den Braber, F., Hogganvik, I., Lund, M. S., Stølen, K., & Vraalsen, F. (2007). Model-based security analysis in seven steps - A guided tour to the CORAS method. *BT Technology Journal*, *25*(1), 101–117. doi:10.1007/s10550-007-0013-9

Denning, D. E. (1976). A lattice model of secure information flow. *Communications of the ACM*, *19*, 236–243. doi:doi:10.1145/360051.360056

Department of Defense (DoD). (1997). *DoD Information Technology Security Certification and Accreditation Process (DITSCAP)*. Washington, DC: DoD.

Department of Homeland Security (DHS). (2010a). *Build Security In*. Retrieved August 30, 2010 from https://buildsecurityin.us-cert.gov/bsi/home.html

Department of Homeland Security (DHS). (2010b). Software Assurance (SwA) Workforce Education and Training Working Group. *Software assurance CBK/principles organization*. Retrieved August 30, 2010, from https://buildsecurityin.us-cert.gov/swa/wetwg.html

Department of Homeland Security, National Cyber Security Division/US-CERT and National Institute of Standards and Technology, National Vulnerability Database. (n.d.). *Common Configuration Enumeration (CCE) Reference Data*. Retrieved August 24, 2010, from http://nvd.nist.gov/cce.cfm

Department of Homeland Security, National Cyber Security Division/US-CERT and National Institute of Standards and Technology, National Vulnerability Database. (n.d.). *Common Weakness Enumeration (CWE)*. Retrieved August 24, 2010, from http://nvd.nist.gov/cwe.cfm

Department of Homeland Security, National Cyber Security Division/US-CERT and National Institute of Standards and Technology, National Vulnerability Database. (n.d.). *Official Common Platform Enumeration (CPE) Dictionary*. Retrieved August 24, 2010, from http://nvd.nist.gov/cpe.cfm

Department Of Homeland Security. (2008). *Information Technology (IT) Security Essential Body of Knowledge (EBK): A Competency and Functional Framework for IT Security Workforce Development*. Washington, DC: Office of Cybersecurity and Communications National Cyber Security Division.

Devanbu, P., Gertz, M., Kwong, A., Martel, C., Nuckolls, G., & Stubblebine, S. G. (2001). Flexible authentication of XML documents. In *Proceedings of the ACM Conference on Computer and Communications Security* (pp. 136-145).

Dhurjati, D., Kowshik, S., Adve, V., & Lattner, C. (2003, June). Memory safety without runtime checks or garbage collection. In *Proceedings of the 2003 acm sigplan conference on language, compiler, and tool support for embedded systems*, San Diego, CA (pp. 69-80).

Dietz, J. L. G. (2006). *Enterprise Ontology –Theory and Methodology*. New York: Springer.

*Directive 95/94/EC of the European Parliament and of the Council of 24 October 1995 on the protection of individuals with regard to the processing of personal data and on the free movement of such data.* (1995). Retrieved October 6, 2008, from http://eur-lex.europa. eu/LexUriServ/LexUriServ.do?uri=CELEX:31995L00 46:EN:HTML

Doan, T. (2008). *A framework for software security in UML with assurance.* Unpublished doctoral dissertation, Department of Computer Science and Engineering, University of Connecticut.

Doan, T., et al. (2004a). RBAC/MAC security for UML. In C. Farkas & P. Samarati (Eds.), *Research directions in data and applications security XVIII* (LNCS 144, pp. 189-204).

Doan, T., et al. (2004b). MAC and UML for secure software design. In *Specifications to Code: Proceedings of the 2nd ACM Workshop on Formal Methods in Security Engineering* (pp. 75-85). ACM Publishing.

Dobrovitski, I. (2003, February). *Exploit for CVS double free() for linux pserver.* Retrieved from http://seclists.org/ lists/bugtraq/2003/Feb/0042.html

Drew, C. (n.d.). Wanted: 'Cyber Ninjas.' *New York Times.* Retrieved December 29, 2009, from http://www.nytimes. com/2010/01/03/education/edlife/03cybersecurity. html?emc=eta1

Du, W., & Mathur, A. P. (2000). Testing for software vulnerability using environment perturbation. In *Proceedings of the International Conference on Dependable Systems and Networks* (p. 603).

Dubois, H., & Mayer, M. (2010). A Systematic Approach to Define the Domain of Information System Security Risk Management. In Nurcan, S. (Eds.), *Intentional Perspectives on Information Systems Engineering.* Berlin: Springer Verlag.

Durand, Barbolosi, Baudet, Hua, Labarrade, Magnin, & Meunier. (2006). *Guide d'utilisateur de la démarche d'anticipation des compétences.* Luxembourg: Centre de Recherche Public Henri Tudor.

ECTS Users' Guide. (2005). *Proceedings of Directorate-General for Education and Culture,* Brussels, Belgium.

Elahi, G., & Yu, E. (2007). A Goal Oriented Approach for Modeling and Analyzing Security Trade-Offs. In C. Parent, K.-D. Schewe, V. C. Storey, & B. Thalheim (Eds.), *Proceedings of ER 2007* (LNCS 4801, pp. 87-101). Berlin: Springer.

Ellison, R. J. (2006). *Security and Project Management.* Pittsburgh, PA: Carnegie Mellon University.

Endicott-Popovsky, B., Popovsky, V., & Frincke, D. (2004, June). *Designing a Computer Forensics Course for an Information Assurance Track.* Paper presented at the 8th Colloquium for Information Systems Security Education, West Point, NY.

Endicott-Popovsky, B., Popovsky, V., & Frincke, D. (2005, June). *Secure Code: The Capstone Class in an Information Assurance Track.* Paper presented at the 2005 Colloquium on Information Systems Security Education (CISSE): Pursuing Quality Solutions—Lessons Learned and Applied.

Enright, K. P. (n.d.). *Privacy Audit Checklist.* Retrieved May 6, 2006, from http://cyber.law.harvard.edu/clinical/ privacyaudit.html

Epstein, P., & Sandhu, R. (1999). Towards a UML based approach to role engineering. In *Proceedings of the 4th ACM workshop on Role-based Access Control* (pp. 75-85). ACM Publishing.

EPTA. (2006). *ICT and Privacy in Europe, Experiences from technology assessment of ICT and Privacy in seven different European countries.* Retrieved September 23, 2008, from http://epub.oeaw.ac.at/ita/ita-projektberichte/ e2-2a44.pdf

Erlingsson, U. (2007). *Low-level Software Security: Attacks and Defenses* (Tech. Rep. MSR-TR-07-153). Microsoft Research, Redmond, WA.

Etoh, H. (2005). *GCC Extension for Protecting Applications from Stack-smashing Attacks.* Retrieved March 16, 2010, from http://www.trl.ibm.com/projects/security/ssp

Fabbrini, F., Fusani, M., Gnesi, S., & Lami, G. (2007). Controlling requirements evolution: A formal concept analysis-based approach. *International Conference on Software Engineering Advances.*

Fagan, M. E. (1999). Design and code inspections to reduce errors in program development. *IBM Systems Journal, 38*(2-3).

Fagin, R., Halpern, J. Y., Moses, Y., & Vardi, M. Y. (1995). *Reasoning about knowledge.* Cambridge, MA: MIT Press.

Failure Causes Statistics. (1995). *The Bull Survey (1998), KPMG Canada Survey (1997), and Chaos Report (1995).* Retrieved from http://www.it-cortex.com/Stat_Failure_Cause.htm

Faily, S., & Fléchais, I. (2010). A Meta-Model for Usable Secure Requirements Engineering. In *Proceedings of the Software Engineering for Secure Systems (SESS '10).*

Feather, M. S., Cornford, S. L., Kiper, J. D., & Menzies, T. (2006). Experiences using Visualization Techniques to Present Requirements, Risks to Them, and Options for Risk Mitigation. In *Proceedings of Requirements Engineering Visualization (REV '06), the First International Workshop* (p. 10).

Felty, A. P., & Namjoshi, K. S. (2003). Feature specification and automated conflict detection. *ACM Transactions on Software Engineering and Methodology, 12*(1), 3–27. doi:doi:10.1145/839268.839270

Fernandez, E. B., France, R. B., & Wei, D. (1995). A formal specification of an authorization model for object-oriented databases. In *Database security IX: Status and prospects* (pp. 95-109).

Fernandez, E. B., Gudes, E., & Song, H. (1989). A security model for object-oriented databases. In *Proceedings of the IEEE Symposium on Research in Security and Privacy* (pp. 110-115).

Fernández-Medina, E., Jurjens, J., Trujillo, J., & Jajodia, S. (2009). Model-driven development for secure information systems. *Information and Software Technology, 51*(5), 809–814. doi:doi:10.1016/j.infsof.2008.05.010

Ferraiolo, D. F. (2001). Proposed NIST standard for role-based access control. *ACM Transactions on Information and System Security, 4*(3), 224–274. doi:10.1145/501978.501980

Fetzer, C., & Xiao, Z. (2001). Detecting Heap Smashing Attacks through Fault Containment Wrappers. In *Proceedings of the 20th Symposium on Reliable Distributed Systems*, New Orleans, LA (pp. 80-89).

Firesmith, D. (2003). Security Use Case. *Journal of Object Technology, 2*(3), 53–64.

Firesmith, D. (2004). Specifying reusable security requirements. *Journal of Object Technology, 3*(1), 61–75.

Fischer, M., & Gall, H. (2004). Visualizing feature evolution of large-scale software based on problem and modification report data. *Journal of Software Maintenance and Evolution: Research and Practice, 16*(6), 385–403. doi:doi:10.1002/smr.302

Fléchais, I., Mascolo, C., & Sasse, M. A. (2007). Integrating security and usability into the requirements and design process. *International Journal of Electronic Security and Digital Forensics, 1*(1), 12–26. doi:10.1504/IJESDF.2007.013589

Fletcher, J., Friedman, L., Mccarthy, P., Mcintyre, C., O'learly, B., & Rheinstein, J. (1993). Sample sizes required to attain stable job analysis inventory profiles. In *Proceedings of the 8th meeting of the Society for Industrial and Organizational Psychology*, San Francisco.

Focardi, R., & Gorrieri, R. (1997). The compositional security checker: A tool for the verification of information flow security properties. *IEEE Transactions on Software Engineering, 23*(9), 550–571. doi:doi:10.1109/32.629493

Ford, G. (1991). *1991 SEI Report on Graduate Software Engineering Education* (Tech. Rep. No. CMU/SEI-91-TR-002). Pittsburgh, PA: Carnegie Mellon University, Software Engineering Institute.

Fouché, S., Cohen, M. B., & Porter, A. (2009). Incremental covering array failure characterization in large configuration spaces. In *Proceedings of the Eighteenth International Symposium on Software Testing and Analysis (ISSTA '09)* (pp. 177-188). New York: ACM.

Foucher, R., Saint-Onge, S., & Haines, V. (2010). *Gestion des performances au travail.* Bruxelles, Belgium: De Boeck.

Francesco, N. D., & Lettieri, G. (2003). Checking security properties by model checking. *Software Testing. Verification and Reliability, 13*(3), 181–196. doi:doi:10.1002/stvr.272

Free Software Foundation. (n. d.). *The gnu c library.* Retrieved from http://http://www.gnu.org/software/libc.

Gall, H., Jazayeri, M., & Riva, C. (1999). Visualizing software release histories: The use of color and third dimension. In *Proceedings of the IEEE International Conference on Software Maintenance*, IEEE Computer Society Washington, DC, USA.

Ganesh, V., Leek, T., & Rinard, M. (2009). Taint-based directed whitebox fuzzing. In *Proceedings of the 2009 IEEE 31st International Conference on Software Engineering (ICSE '09)* (pp. 474-484). Washington, DC: IEEE Computer Society.

Gayash, A., Viswanathan, V., Padmanabhan, D., & Mead, N. R. (2008). *SQUARE-Lite: Case study on VADSoft project (Special Rep. No. CMU/SEI-2008-SR-017)*. Pittsburgh, PA: Carnegie Mellon University, Software Engineering Institute.

Gelfond, M. (1994). Logic programming and reasoning with incomplete information. *Annals of Mathematics and Artificial Intelligence*, *12*, 98–116. doi:doi:10.1007/BF01530762

Gelfond, M., & Lifschitz, V. (1991). Classical negation in logic programs and disjunctive databases. *New Generation Computing*, *9*, 365–385. doi:doi:10.1007/BF03037169

Georg, G., Ray, I., Anastasakis, K., Bordbar, B., Toahchoodee, M., & Houmb, S. H. (2009). An aspect-oriented methodology for designing secure applications. *Information and Software Technology*, *51*(5), 846–864. doi:doi:10.1016/j.infsof.2008.05.004

Gerdes, J. (2009). User interface migration of Microsoft Windows applications. *Journal of Software Maintenance and Evolution: Research and Practice*, *9999*(9999).

German, D. M. (2004). Using software trails to reconstruct the evolution of software. *Journal of Software Maintenance and Evolution: Research and Practice*, *16*(6), 367–384. doi:doi:10.1002/smr.301

Ghose, A. K. (1999). A formal basis for consistency, evolution and rationale management in requirements engineering. In *Proceedings of the 11th IEEE International Conference on Tools with Artificial Intelligence*.

Ghose, A. K. (2000). Formal tools for managing inconsistency and change in RE. In *Proceedings of the 10th International Workshop on Software Specification and Design*.

Giannakopoulou, D., & Magee, J. (2003). Fluent model checking for event-based systems. In *Proceedings of the 9th European Software Engineering Conference*, (pp. 257-266) Helsinki, Finland: ACM Press.

Gibson, J. J. (1977). The Theory of Affordances. In Shaw, R., & Bransford, J. (Eds.), *Perceiving*. Acting, and Knowing.

Gilbert. (2005). La gestion prévisionnelle des RH. In D. Weiss (Ed.), *Ressources Humaines* (5th ed.). Paris: Editions d'Organisation.

Giorgini, P., Massacci, F., Mylopoulos, J., & Zannone, N. (2005). Modeling security requirements through ownership, permission and delegation. In *Proceedings of 13th IEEE International Conference on Requirements Engineering*, Paris, France.

Gîrba, T., & Ducasse, S. (2006). Modeling history to analyze software evolution. *Journal of Software Maintenance and Evolution: Research and Practice*, *18*(3), 207–236. doi:doi:10.1002/smr.325

Glaume, V., & Fayolle, P. (2002). *A Buffer Overflow Study: Attacks & Defenses (Tech. Rep.)*. Talence, France: ENSEIRB, Network and Distributed Systems.

Gloger, W. (n. d.). *ptmalloc*. Retrieved from http://www.malloc.de/en/.

Glorie, M., Zaidman, A., Deursen, A. v., & Hofland, L. (2009). Splitting a large software repository for easing future software evolution - an industrial experience report. *Journal of Software Maintenance and Evolution: Research and Practice*, *21*(2), 113–141. doi:doi:10.1002/smr.401

Godefroid, P., Levin, M. Y., & Molnar, D. A. (2008). Automated whitebox fuzz testing. In *Proceedings of the Network Distributed Security Symposium (NDSS)*.

Goertzel, K., Winograd, T., McKinley, H. L., Oh, L., Colon, M., & McGibbon, T. (2007). *Software Security Assurance: A State-of-the-Art Report*. Fort Belvior, VA: DTIC-I.

Goldberg, I., Wagner, D., & Brewer, E. (1997). Privacy-Enhancing Technologies for the Internet. In. *Proceedings of the IEEE COMPCON*, *97*, 103–109.

Gong, L. (1998). *Java security architecture, JDK 1.2 (Tech. Rep.)*. Sun Microsystems Inc.

Goodenough, J., Lipson, H., & Weinstock, C. (2008). *Arguing Security – Creating Security Assurance Cases.* Pittsburgh, PA: Carnegie Mellon University. Retrieved from https://buildsecurityin.us-cert.gov/daisy/bsi/articles/knowledge/assurance/643-BSI.html

Gordon, D., Stehney, T., Wattas, N., Yu, E., & Mead, N. R. (2005). *System Quality Requirements Engineering (SQUARE): Case study on asset management system, phase II (Special Rep. No. CMU/SEI-2005-SR-005).* Pittsburgh, PA: Carnegie Mellon University, Software Engineering Institute.

Greevy, O., & Ducasse, S. and Tudor Gîrba. (2006). Analyzing software evolution through feature views. *Journal of Software Maintenance and Evolution: Research and Practice, 18*(6), 425–456. doi:doi:10.1002/smr.340

Gross, A. (June 11, 2010). *Language.* Retrieved August 24, 2010, from http://languag2.home.sprynet.com/f/evishop.htm

Gross, K. C., Urmanov, A., Votta, L. G., McMaster, S., & Porter, A. (2006). Towards dependability in everyday software using software telemetry. In *Proceedings of the Third IEEE International Workshop on Engineering of Autonomic & Autonomous Systems (EASE '06)* (pp. 9-18). Washington, DC: IEEE Computer Society.

Grossman, D., Morrisett, G., Jim, T., Hicks, M., Wang, Y., & Cheney, J. (2002, June). Region-based memory management in cyclone. In *Proceedings of the 2002 acm sigplan conference on programming language design and implementation*, Berlin (pp. 282-293).

Grunwald, D., Zorn, B., & Henderson, R. (1993, June). Improving the cache locality of memory allocation. In *Proceedings of the acm sigplan 1993 conference on programming language design and implementation (pldi)*, New York (pp. 177-186).

Gupta, S., Pratap, P., Saran, H., & Kumar, A. (2006). Dynamic Code Instrumentation to Detect and Recover from Return Address Corruption. In *Proceedings of the International Workshop on Dynamic Systems Analysis*, Shanghai, China (pp. 65-72).

Hackett, B., Das, M., Wang, D., & Yang, Z. (2006). Modular Checking for Buffer Overflows in the Large. In *Proceedings of the 28th International Conference on Software Engineering*, Shanghai, China (pp. 232-241).

Haimes, Y. Y. (2004). *Risk modeling, assessment, and management* (2nd ed.). Hoboken, NJ: John Wiley and Sons, Inc.

Haley, C. B., Laney, R. C., Moffett, J. D., & Nuseibeh, B. (2004). The effect of trust assumptions on the elaboration of security requirements. In *Proceedings of the 12th IEEE International Requirements Engineering Conference.*

Haley, C. B., Laney, R., Moffett, J. D., & Nuseibeh, B. (2008). Security requirements engineering: A framework for representation and analysis. *IEEE Transactions on Software Engineering, 34*(1), 133–153. doi:doi:10.1109/TSE.2007.70754

Halfond, W. G. J., Orso, A., & Manolios, P. (2006). Using positive tainting and syntax-aware evaluation to counter SQL injection attacks. In *Proceedings of the 14th ACM SIGSOFT International Symposium on Foundations of Software Engineering* (pp. 175–185). Portland, Oregon, USA.

Halfond, W. G., & Orso, A. (2005). AMNESIA: Analysis and monitoring for neutralizing SQL injection attacks. In *Proceedings of the 20th IEEE/ACM international conference on automated software engineering* (pp. 174–183). Long Beach, CA, USA.

Halfond, W. G., Viegas, J., & Orso, A. (2006). A classification of SQL injection attacks and countermeasures. In *IEEE International Symposium On Secure Software Engineering.*

Hall, J. G., Rapanotti, L., & Jackson, M. (2007). Problem oriented software engineering: A design-theoretic framework for software engineering. In *Proceedings of the 5th IEEE International Conference on Software Engineering and Formal Methods.*

Hall, J. G., Rapanotti, L., & Jackson, M. A. (2008). Problem oriented software engineering: Solving the package router control problem. *IEEE Transactions on Software Engineering, 34*(2), 226–241. doi:doi:10.1109/TSE.2007.70769

Hall, R. J. (2000). Feature combination and interaction detection via foreground/background models. *Journal of Computer Networks, 32*(4), 449–469. doi:doi:10.1016/S1389-1286(00)00010-4

Hangal, S., & Lam, M. S. (2002). Tracking down software bugs using automatic anomaly detection. In *Proceedings of the 2002 International Conference on Software Engineering* (pp. 291-301).

Hartman, A. (2005). *Graph Theory, Combinatorics and Algorithms* (*Vol. 34*, pp. 237–266). New York: Springer.

Hassine, J., Rilling, J., Hewitt, J., & Dssouli, R. (2005). Change impact analysis for requirement evolution using use case maps. In *Proceedings of the 8ᵗʰ International Workshop on Principles of Software Evolution.*

Hastings, R., & Joyce, B. (1992). Purify: Fast Detection of Memory Leaks and Access Errors. In *Proceedings of the USENIX Winter Conference*, San Francisco, CA (pp. 125-138).

Havard & Krohmer. *(2008).* Création et articulation des règles dans le cadre d'un management des compétences. *In* Proceedings of the Revue de Gestion des Ressources Humaines.

Hayhurst, K. J., Veerhusen, D. S., Chilenski, J. J., & Rierson, L. K. (2001). *A practical tutorial on modified condition/decision coverage* (Tech. Rep. No. NASA/TM-2001-210876). Houston, TX: NASA.

Hein, D., & Saiedian, H. (2009). Secure Software Engineering: Learning from the Past to Address Future Challenges. *Information Security Journal: A Global Perspective, 18*(1), 8-25.

Henning, J. L. (2000, July). Spec cpu2000: Measuring cpu performance in the new millennium. *Computer, 33*(7), 28–35. doi:10.1109/2.869367

Herrmann, G., & Pernul, G. (1999). Viewing business-process security from different perspectives. *International Journal of Electronic Commerce, 3*(3), 89–103.

Herrmann, P., & Herrmann, G. (2006). Security requirement analysis of business processes. *Electronic Commerce Research, 6*(3-4), 305–335. doi:doi:10.1007/s10660-006-8677-7

HIPAA. (n.d.). *Health Insurance Portability and Accountability Act of 1996 (HIPAA) Privacy Rule.* Retrieved August 13, 2009, from http://www.hhs.gov/ocr/privacy/index.html

His, I., & Potts, C. (2000). Studying the Evolution and enhancement of software features. In *Proceedings of the International Conference on Software Maintenance*, (p. 143), IEEE Computer Society.

Hogganvik, I. (2007). *A graphical approach to security risk analysis.*

Holtzblatt, K., & Jones, S. (1993). *Contextual Inquiry: a participatory technique for systems design* (pp. 177-210).

Hong, J. I., Ng, J. D., Lederer, S., & Landay, J. A. (2004). Privacy Risk Models for Designing Privacy-Sensitive Ubiquitous Computing Systems. In *Proceedings of the 2004 Conference on Designing Interactive Systems: Processes, Practices, Methods, and Techniques*, Cambridge, MA (pp. 91-100).

Hope, P., McGraw, G., & Anton, A. (2004). Misuse and Abuse Cases: Getting Past the Positive. *IEEE Building Security in Security & Privacy Magazine, 2*(3), 32–34.

Horvath, V., & Dörges, T. (2008). From security patterns to implementation using Petri nets. In. *Proceedings of SESS, 2008*, 17–24.

Hough, E., & Mead, N. R. (2006). *Security requirements engineering for software systems: Case studies in support of software engineering education.* Paper presented at the 19ᵗʰ Conference on Software Engineering Education & Training, Turtle Bay, Hawaii.

Houmb, S. H., Islam, S., Knauss, E., Jurjens, J., & Schneider, K. (2009). Eliciting security requirements and tracing them to design: an integration of Common Criteria, heuristics, and UMLsec. *Requirements Engineering*, 1–31.

Howard, M., & LeBlanc, D. (2003). *Writing secure code* (2nd Ed.). Redmond, Washington: Microsoft Press.

Howard, M., & Lipner, S. (2006). *The Security Development Life Cycle.* Redmond, WA: Microsoft Press. IEEE-Std-1471-2000. (2000, October). *Recommended Practice for Architectural Description of Software-Intensive Systems.* Retrieved August 24, 2010, from http://standards.ieee.org/reading/ieee/std_public/description/se/1471-2000_desc.html

Howard, M., & LeBlanc, D. (2003). *Writing Secure Code.* Redmond, WA: Microsoft Press.

Hsi, I., & Potts, C. (2000). Studying the evolution and enhancement of software features. In *Proceedings of the 16th IEEE International Conference on Software Maintenance* (ICSM'00), San Jose, California, USA.

Hsueh, M.-C., Tsai, T. K., & Iyer, R. K. (1997). Fault injection techniques and tools. *Computer*, *30*(4), 75–82. doi:doi:10.1109/2.585157

Huang, Y.-W., Yu, F., Hang, C., Tsai, C.-H., Lee, D. T., & Kuo, S.-Y. (2004). Securing Web application code by static analysis and runtime protection. In *Proceedings of the 13th International Conference on World Wide Web* (pp. 40–52).

Hubbard, R., Mead, N. R., & Schroeder, C. (2000). *An assessment of the relative efficiency of a facilitator-driven requirements collection process with respect to the conventional interview method.* Paper presented at the International Conference on Requirements Engineering.

Ibrahim, N., Wan Kadir, W. M. N., & Deris, S. (2008). Comparative evaluation of change propagation approaches towards resilient software evolution. In *Proceedings of the 3rd International Conference on Software Engineering Advances.*

IEC. (1998-2005). *IEC 61508: Functional safety of electrical/electronic/programmable electronic safety-related systems. Parts 1-7.* Geneva, Switzerland: International Electrotechnical Commission.

IEEE/EIA 12207.0. (1998, May). *Standard for Information Technology – Software Life Cycle Processes.* Washington, DC: IEEE.

IEEE-CS & ACM. (2004). *Software engineering 2004: Curriculum guidelines for undergraduate degree programs in software engineering. Computing curriculum series.* Retrieved August 30, 2010, from http://sites.computer.org/ccse/SE2004Volume.pdf

IEEE-CS. (2004). IEEE Computer Society. *Software Engineering Body of Knowledge (SWEBOK).* Retrieved August 30, 2010, from http://www.computer.org/portal/web/swebok

Ikebe, T., & Kawarasaki, Y. (2006). Retrieved from http://pannus.sourceforge.net/

Ilioudis, C., & Pangalos, G. (2001). A framework for an institutional high level security policy for the processing of medical data and their transmission through the Internet. *Journal of Medical Internet Research*, ▪▪▪, 3.

Institute, Q. F. D. (2005). *Frequently asked questions about QFD.* Retrieved June 23, 2009, from http://www.qfdi.org/what_is_qfd/faqs_about_qfd.htm

ISO. (1998). *ISO 9241-11. Ergonomic requirements for office work with visual display terminals (VDT)s - Part 11 Guidance on usability (Tech. Rep.).* Geneva, Switzerland: ISO.

ISO. (2005). *Evaluation criteria for IT security Part 1: Introduction and general model* (Tech. Rep. No. 15408-1). Geneva, Switzerland: ISO/IEC.

ISO/IEC 27001. (2005). *Information technology – security techniques – information security management systems – requirements.* Geneva, Switzerland: International Organization for Standardization (IOS).

Iyengar, V. S. (2002). Transforming Data to Satisfy Privacy Constraints. In *Proceedings of SIGKDD'02*, Edmonton, Alberta.

Jackson, M. (1995). *Software requirements and specifications: A lexicon of practice, principles and prejudices.* London: Addison-Wesley.

Jackson, M. (2001). *Problem frames: Analysing and structuring software development problems.* Harlow: Addison-Wesley.

Jackson, M., & Zave, P. (1998). Distributed feature composition: A Virtual architecture for telecommunications services. *IEEE Transactions on Software Engineering*, *24*(10), 831–847. doi:doi:10.1109/32.729683

Jacobson, I. (1992). *Object oriented software engineering: A use case driven approach.* Addison-Wesley Professional.

Jajodia, S. (2001). Flexible support for multiple access control policies. *ACM Transactions on Database Systems*, *26*(2), 214–260. doi:10.1145/383891.383894

Jajodia, S., Samarati, P., Sapino, M. L., & Subrahmanian, V. S. (2001). Flexible support for multiple access control policies. *ACM Transactions on Database Systems*, *29*(2), 214–260. doi:doi:10.1145/383891.383894

Jarzombek, J. (2006). A Strategic Initiative of the U.S. Department of Homeland Security to Promote Integrity, Security, and Reliability in Software. In *Considerations in Advancing the National Strategy to Secure Cyberspace*. Software Assurance.

Jarzombek, J. (2007). Software Assurance: A Strategic Initiative of the U.S. Department of Homeland Security to Promote Integrity, Security, and Reliability in Software. In *Proceedings of the Enabling Role and a Broader Perspective for Measurement*.

Jim, T., Morrisett, G., Grossman, D., Hicks, M., Cheney, J., & Wang, Y. (2002, June). A safe dialect of C. In *Usenix annual technical conference* (pp. 275 288). Monterey, CA: Cyclone.

Johnstone, M. S., & Wilson, P. R. (1998, Oct). The memory fragmentation problem: Solved? In *Proceedings of the 1st acm sigplan international symposium on memory management*, Vancouver, Canada (pp. 26-36). New York: ACM.

Joint Holders in Australia/New Zealand, Canada, France, Germany, Japan, Netherlands, Spain, United Kingdom and United States. (2006). *Common Criteria for Information Technology Security Evaluation, Version 3.1, Revision 1.*

Joint Task Force Transformation Initiative. (2009). *National Institute of Standards and Technology (NIST) Special Publication 800-53 revision 3*. Recommended Security Controls for Federal Information Systems and Organizations.

Jones, R. W. M., & Kelly, P. H. J. (1997). Backwards-compatible bounds checking for arrays and pointers in C programs. In *Proceedings of the 3rd international workshop on automatic debugging* (pp. 13-26). Linköping, Sweden: Linköping University Electronic Press.

Jones, R., & Kelly, P. (1997). Backwards-compatible Bounds Checking for Arrays and Pointers in C Programs. In *Proceedings of Automated and Algorithmic Debugging*, Linköping, Sweden (pp. 13-26).

Jones, C. (Ed.). (1986). *Tutorial: Programming productivity: Issues for the eighties* (2nd ed.). Los Angeles: IEEE Computer Society Press.

Jovanovic, N., Kruegel, C., & Kirda, E. (2006, May). Pixy: A static analysis tool for detecting Web application vulnerabilities (short paper). In *Proceedings of the 2006 IEEE Symposium on Security and Privacy.*

Juergens, J., et al. (2008). Automated analysis of permission-based security using UMLsec. In *Fundamental approaches to software engineering* (LNCS 4961, pp. 292-295).

Julisch, K., & Darcier, M. (2002). Mining intrusion detection alarms for actionable knowledge. In *Proceedings of the 8th ACM International Conference on Knowledge Discovery and Data Mining* (pp. 366-375).

Jurani, L. (2006). *Using fuzzing to detect security vulnerabilities* (Tech. Rep. NO. INFIGO-TD-01-04-2006). Richmond, BC, Canada: INFIGO.

Jürjens, J. (2001). Towards Development of Secure Systems using UMLsec. In *Proceedings of the Fundamental Approaches to Software Engineering (FASE/ETAPS) 2001, International Conference*. Berlin: Springer Verlag.

Jurjens, J. (2002). UMLsec: Extending UML for Secure systems development. In *Proceedings of the 5th International Conference on The Unified Modeling Language*, Springer-Verlag.

Jurjens, J. (2002a). *Principles for secure systems design*. Unpublished doctoral dissertation, Oxford University Computing Laboratory, Oxford University.

Jurjens, J. (2002b). UMLsec: Extending UML for secure systems development. *Proceedings of UML* (LNCS 2460, pp. 1-9).

Jürjens, J. (2003). Critical Systems Development with UML. In *Proceedings of the 21st IASTED International Multi-Conference Applied Informatics, International Conference on Software Engineering*.

Jürjens, J. (2005, May 15-21). *Sound Methods and Effective Tools for Model-based Security Engineering with UML*. Paper presented at the International Conference on Software Engineering (ICSE'05), St. Louis, MO.

Jurjens, J. (2004). *Secure systems development with UML*. Heidelberg, Germany: Springer-Verlag.

Kaempf, M. (2001). Vudo - an object superstitiously believed to embody magical powers. *Phrack, 57.*

Kaempf, M. M. (n. d.). *Sudo < 1.6.3p7-2 exploit.* Retrieved from http://packetstormsecurity.org/0211-exploits/hudo.c

Kaindl, H., Brinkkemper, S., Bubenko, J. Jr, Farbey, B., Greenspan, S., & Heitmeyer, C. (2002). Requirements engineering and technology transfer: Obstacles, incentives and improvement agenda. *Requirements Engineering Journal, 7*(3), 113–123. doi:doi:10.1007/s007660200008

Kang, K., Cohen, S., Hess, J., Novak, W., & Peterson, A. S. (1990). *Feature-Oriented Domain Analysis (FODA) feasibility study* (Tech. Rep. No. CMU/SEI-90-TR-021). Pittsburgh, PA: Carnegie Mellon University, Software Engineering Institute.

Karger, P. A. (2006). Privacy and Security Threat Analysis of the Federal Employee Personal Identity Verification (PIV) Program. In *Proceedings of the Second Symposium on Usable Privacy and Security*, Pittsburgh, PA (pp. 114-121).

Karlsson, J., & Ryan, K. (1997). A cost-value approach for prioritizing requirements. *IEEE Software, 14*(5). doi:doi:10.1109/52.605933

Kass, M. (2005). A Taxonomy of Software Assurance Tools and the Security Bugs they Catch. In *Proceedings of the OWASP AppSec DC.*

Kc, G. S., Keromytis, A. D., & Prevelakis, V. (2003, October). Countering code-injection attacks with instruction-set randomization. In *Proceedings of the 10th acm conference on computer and communications security (ccs2003),* Washington, DC (pp. 272-280).

Kc, G., Keromytis, A., & Prevelakis, V. (2003). Countering Code-injection Attacks with Instruction-set Randomization. In *Proceedings of the 10ᵗʰ ACM Conference on Computer and Communications Security*, Washington, DC (pp. 272-280).

Keck, D. O., & Kuehn, P. J. (1998). The feature and service interaction problem in telecommunications systems: A survey. *IEEE Transactions on Software Engineering, 24*(10), 779–796. doi:doi:10.1109/32.729680

Keizer, G. (2008, April). Huge Web hack attack infects 500,000 pages. *Computerworld.* Retrieved from http://www.computerworld.com/action/article.do?command=viewArticleBasic &articleId=9080580

Kemerer, C. F., & Slaughter, S. (1999). An empirical approach to studying software evolution. *IEEE Transactions on Software Engineering, 25*(4), 493–509. doi:doi:10.1109/32.799945

Kennedy, Hyland, & Ryan. (2007). *Writing and Using Learning Outcomes: a Practical Guide.* Cork, UK: University College Cork.

Kenny, S., & Korba, L. (2002). Adapting Digital Rights Management to Privacy Rights Management. *Computers & Security, 21*(7), 648–664. doi:doi:10.1016/S0167-4048(02)01117-3

Keramati, H., & Mirian-Hosseinabadi, S. H. (2008). *Integrating software development security activities with agile methodologies.*

Khan, K. M., Kapurubandara, M., & Chadha, U. (2004). Incorporating Business Requirements and Constraints in Database Conceptual Model. In *Proceedings of APCCM* (pp. 59-64).

Khan, K., & Han, J. (2005). Deriving Systems Level Security Properties of Component Based Composite Systems. In *Proceedings of the Conference on Australian Software Engineering Conference*, Brisbane, Australia (pp. 334-343).

Khan, K., & Han, J. (2003). A Security Characterisation Framework for Trustworthy Component Based Software Systems. In *Proceedings of the COMPSAC, 03,* 164–169.

Kiriansky, V., Bruening, D., & Amarasinghe, S. (2002). Secure Execution via Program Shepherding. In *Proceedings of the 11ᵗʰ USENIX Security Symposium*, San Francisco, CA (pp. 191-206).

Kobsa, A., & Schreck, J. (2003). Privacy Through Pseudonymity in User-Adaptive Systems. *ACM Transactions on Internet Technology, 3*(2), 149–183. doi:doi:10.1145/767193.767196

Kosker, Y., Turhan, B., & Bener, A. (in press). Corrected Proof). An expert system for determining candidate software classes for refactoring. *Expert Systems with Applications.*

Kowshik, S., Dhurjati, D., & Adve, V. (2002, October). Ensuring code safety without runtime checks for real-time control systems. In *Proceedings of the international conference on compilers architecture and synthesis for embedded systems*, Grenoble, France (pp. 288-297). Retrieved from http://llvm.cs.uiuc.edu/pubs/2002-08-08-CASES02-ControlC.html

Koziol, J., Litchfield, D., Aitel, D., Anley, C., Eren, S., & Mehta, N. (2004). *The shellcoder's handbook: Discovering and exploiting security holes*. New York: John Wiley & Sons.

Kozlov, D., Koskinen, J., Sakkinen, M., & Markkula, J. (2008). Assessing maintainability change over multiple software releases. *Journal of Software Maintenance and Evolution: Research and Practice, 20*(1), 31–58. doi:doi:10.1002/smr.361

Kratkiewicz, K., & Lippmann, R. (2005). Using a Diagnostic Corpus of C Programs to Evaluate Buffer Overflow Detection by Static Analysis Tools. In *Proceedings of the Workshop on the Evaluation of Software Defect Detection Tools*, Chicago.

Krennmair, A. (2003, Novomber). *ContraPolice: a libc extension for protecting applications from heap-smashing attacks.* Retrieved from http://www.synflood.at/contrapolice/.

Krügel, C., Toth, T., & Kirda, E. (2002). Service specific anomaly detection for network intrusion detection. In *Proceedings of the 2002 ACM Symposium on Applied Computing (SAC '02)* (pp. 201-208). New York: ACM.

Kunz, W., & Rittel, H. (1970). *Issues as elements of information systems* (Working Paper No. 131). Berkeley, CA: University of California, Institute of Urban & Regional Development.

Lam, W., & Loomes, M. (1998). Requirements evolution in the midst of environmental change: A managed approach. In *Proceedings of the 2nd Euromicro Conference on Software Maintenance and Reengineering*.

LaMantia, M. J., Cai, Y., MacCormack, A., & Rusnak, J. (2008). Analyzing the evolution of large-scale software systems using design structure matrices and design rule theory: Two exploratory cases. In *Proceedings of the Seventh Working IEEE/IFIP Conference on Software Architecture* (WICSA 2008), IEEE Computer Society, (pp. 83-92).

Lamsweerde, A. v. (2009). *Requirements engineering: from system goals to UML models to software specifications*. Hoboken, NJ: John Wiley.

Larus, J. R., Ball, T., Das, M., DeLine, R., Fähndrich, M., & Pincus, J. (2004, May/Jun). Righting software. *IEEE Software, 21*(3), 92–100. doi:10.1109/MS.2004.1293079

Leaders in Security. (2009, March). *Building In... Information Security, Privacy And Assurance*. Paper presented at the Knowledge Transfer Network Paris Information Security Workshop, Paris.

Leah, D. (2000). *A Memory Allocator*. Retrieved March 16, 2010, from http://g.oswego.edu/dl/html/malloc.html

Leavitt, N. (2004). Are Web Services finally ready to deliver? *IEEE Computer, 37*(11), 14–18.

Lee, S. W., & Gandhi, R. (2006). *Requirements as Enables for Software Assurance*. CrossTalk Journal of Defense Software Engineering.

Lehman, M. M., & Ramil, J. F. (2001). Evolution in software and related areas. In *Proceedings of the 4th International Workshop on Principles of Software Evolution*, (pp. 1-16), Vienna, Austria. ACM.

Lehman, M. M., Kahen, G., & Ramil, J. F. (2002). Behavioural modelling of long-lived evolution processes - Some issues and an example. *Journal of Software Maintenance and Evolution: Research and Practice, 14*(5), 335–351. doi:doi:10.1002/smr.259

Lehman, M. M., & Ramil, J. F. (2003). Software evolution: background, theory, practice. *Information Processing Letters, 88*(1-2), 33–44. doi:doi:10.1016/S0020-0190(03)00382-X

Letier, E., Kramer, J., Magee, J., & Uchitel, S. (2005). Fluent temporal logic for discrete-time event-based models. S*IGSOFT Softw. Eng. Notes, 30*(5), 70–79. doi: doi:10.1145/1095430.1081719

Lhee, K., & Chapin, S. (2002). Type-Assisted Dynamic Buffer Overflow Detection. In *Proceedings of the 11ᵗʰ USENIX Security Symposium*, San Francisco, CA (pp. 81-88).

Lin, L., Nuseibeh, B., Ince, D., & Jackson, M. (2004). Using abuse frames to bound the scope of security problems. In *Proceedings of 12ᵗʰ IEEE International Requirements Engineering Conference*.

Lin, L., Nuseibeh, B., Ince, D., Jackson, M., & Moffett, J. (2003). Introducing abuse frames for analysing security requirements. In *Proceedings of 11ᵗʰ IEEE International Requirements Engineering Conference*.

Li, N., Grosof, B., & Feigenbaum, J. (2003). Delegation logic: A logic-based approach to distributed authorization. *ACM Transactions on Information and System Security*, 6(1), 128–171. doi:doi:10.1145/605434.605438

Linger, R. C., Mead, N. R., & Lipson, H. F. (1998). *Requirements definition for survivable systems*. Paper presented at the Third International Conference on Requirements Engineering.

Lin, L., Prowell, S. J., & Poore, J. H. (2009). The impact of requirements changes on specifications and state machines. *Software, Practice & Experience*, 39(6), 573–610. doi:doi:10.1002/spe.907

Lipner, S., & Howard, M. (2005). *The Trustworthy Computing Security Development Lifecycle*. Retrieved from http://msdn2.microsoft.com/en-us/library/ms995349. aspx

Lipson, H. F., Mead, N. R., & Moore, A. P. (2001). *A risk-management approach to the design of survivable COTS-based systems*. Pittsburgh, PA: Software Engineering Institute.

Lipson, H., & Weinstock, C. (2008). *Evidence of Assurance: Laying the Foundation for a Credible Security Case*. Pittsburgh, PA: Carnegie Mellon University.

Liu, K. (2000). *Semiotics in Information Systems Engineering*. Cambridge, UK: Cambridge University Press. ISBN 0521 593352

Liu, L., Yu, E., & Mylopoulos, J. (2003). Security and privacy requirements analysis within a social setting. In *Proceedings of the 11ᵗʰ IEEE International Requirements Engineering Conference*.

Livshits, V. B., & Lam, M. S. (2005, August). Finding security vulnerabilities in Java applications with static analysis. In *Proceedings of the 14ᵗʰ USENIX Security Symposium* (pp. 271-286).

Locasto, M. E., Sidiroglou, S., & Keromytis, A. D. (2006). Software self-healing using collaborative application communities. In *Proceedings of the Internet Society (ISOC) Symposium on Network and Distributed Systems Security (NDSS 2006)* (pp. 95-106).

Locasto, M. E., Stavrou, A., Cretu, G. F., & Keromytis, A. D. (2007). From STEM to SEAD: Speculative Execution for Automatic Defense. In *Proceedings of the USENIX Annual Technical Conference* (pp. 219-232).

Lodderstedt, T., Basin, D., & Doser, J. (2002). SecureUML: A UML-Based Modeling Language for Model-Driven Security. In *Proceedings of the UML 2002* (pp. 426-441).

Lodderstedt, T., Basin, D., & Doser, J. (2002). SecureUML: A UML-Based modeling language for model-driven security. *Lecture Notes in Computer Science*, (2460): 426–441. doi:doi:10.1007/3-540-45800-X_33

Lopez, J., Montenegro, J. A., Vivas, J. L., Okamato, E., & Dawson, E. (2005). Specification and design of advanced authentication and authorization services. *Computer Standards & Interfaces*, 27(5), 467–478. doi:doi:10.1016/j.csi.2005.01.005

Lutz, R. R., & Mikulski, I. C. (2003). Operational anomalies as a cause of safety-critical requirements evolution. *Journal of Systems and Software*, 65(2), 155–161.

Madan, B., Phoha, S., & Trivedi, K. (2005). StackOFFence: A Technique for Defending Against Buffer Overflow Attacks. In *Proceedings of the International Conference on Information Technology: Coding and Computing*, Las Vegas, NV (pp. 656-661).

Mana, A., Montenegro, J. A., Rudolph, C., & Vivas, J. L. (2003). A business process-driven approach to security engineering. In *Proceedings of the 14th International Workshop on Database and Expert Systems Applications*, Prague (pp. 477-481).

Mancoridis, S. (2008). *Software Vulnerabilities: Definition, Classification, and Prevention*. Philadelphia: Drexel University, Reverse Engineering Software Security Course Materials.

Mantel, H. (2001). Preserving information flow properties under refinement. *IEEE Symposium on Security and Privacy*.

Mantel, H. (2002). On the composition of secure systems. *IEEE Symposium on Security and Privacy.*

Maor, O., & Shulman, A. (2005). *SQL injection signatures evasion*. Retrieved from http://www.imperva.com/application_defense_center/white_papers/ sql_injection_signatures_evasion.html.

Mar, B. W., & Morais, B. G. (2002, August). *FRAT – A Basic Framework for Systems Engineering.* Paper presented at Twelfth Annual International Symposium of INCOSE, Engineering 21st Century Systems: Problem Solving Through Structured Thinking, Las Vegas, NV.

Martin, A., Goke, J., Arvesen, A., & Quatro, F. (2003). *P6Spy open source software.* Retrieved from http://www.p6spy.com/

Martin, R. C. (Ed.). (2008). *Clean Code: A Handbook of Agile Software Craftsmanship*. Upper Saddle River, NJ: Prentice Hall.

Matulevicius, R., Mayer, N., Mouratidis, H., Dubois, E., Heymans, P., & Genon, N. (2008). Adapting Secure Tropos for Security Risk Management in the Early Phases of Information Systems Development. In. *Proceedings of CAiSE, 2008*, 541–555.

Mavridis, I., Georgiadis, C., Pangalos, G., & Khair, M. (2001). Access Control based on Attribute Certificates for Medical Intranet Applications. *Journal of Medical Internet Research*, *3*(1). doi:10.2196/jmir.3.1.e9

McConnell, S. (2001). From the editor - an ounce of prevention. *IEEE Software*, *18*(3), 5–7. doi:doi:10.1109/MS.2001.922718

McCumber, J. (2005). *Assessing and Managing Security Risk in IT Systems: A Structured Methodology*. Boca Raton, FL: Auerbach Publications.

McGraw, G. (2005). The 7 Touchpoints of Secure Software. *Dr. Dobb's*. Retrieved August 15, 2009, from http://www.ddj.com/security/184415391

McGraw, G. (2002). Building Secure Software: Better than Protecting Bad Software. *IEEE Software*, *19*(6), 57–58. doi:doi:10.1109/MS.2002.1049391

McGraw, G. (2006). *Software Security: Building Security*. Reading, MA: Addison-Wesley.

McGraw, G. E. (2005). *Risk Management Framework*. Cigital, Inc.

Mead, N. R. (2008a). Requirements elicitation case studies using IBIS, JAD, and ARM. *Build Security In*. Retrieved June 23, 2009, from https://buildsecurityin.us-cert.gov/daisy/bsi/articles/best-practices/requirements/532-BSI.html

Mead, N. R. (2008b). Security requirements engineering. *Build Security In*. Retrieved June 23, 2009, from https://buildsecurityin.us-cert.gov/daisy/bsi/articles/best-practices/requirements/243-BSI.html

Mead, N. R. (2008c). *SQUARE: Requirements engineering for improved system security*. Retrieved June 23, 2009, from http://www.cert.org/sse/square.html

Mead, N. R., Ellison, R. J., Linger, R. C., Longstaff, T., & McHugh, J. (2000). *Survivable systems analysis method* (Tech. Rep. No. CMU/SEI-2000-TR-013). Pittsburgh, PA: Carnegie Mellon University, Software Engineering Institute.

Mead, N. R., et al. (2010a). *Master of software assurance reference curriculum* (Tech. Rep. No. CMU/SEI-2010-TR-005/ESD-TR-2010-005). Pittsburgh, PA: Carnegie Melon University: Software Engineering Institute.

Mead, N. R., et al. (2010b). *Software Assurance Curriculum Project Volume II: Undergraduate Course Outlines* (Tech. Rep. No. CMU/SEI-2010-TR-019, ESC-TR-2010-019). Pittsburgh, PA: Carnegie Melon, University, Software Engineering Institute.

Mead, N. R., Hough, E. D., & Stehney, T., II. (2005). *Security quality requirements engineering* (Tech. Rep. No. CMU/SEI-2005-TR-009). Pittsburgh, PA: Carnegie Mellon University, Software Engineering Institute.

Mead, N. R. (2010). Benefits and Challenges in the Use of Case Studies for Security Requirements Engineering Methods. *International Journal of Secure Software Engineering*, *1*(1), 74–91.

Mead, N. R., & Shoemaker, D. (2008). Novel methods of incorporating security requirements engineering into software engineering courses and curricula. In Ellis, H. J. C., Demurjian, S. A., & Naveda, J. F. (Eds.), *Software engineering: Effective teaching and learning approaches and practices* (pp. 98–113). Hershey, PA: IGI Global.

Mead, N. R., & Stehney, T. (2005). Security quality requirements engineering (SQUARE) methodology. *SIGSOFT Software Engineering Notes, 30*(4), 1–7. doi:doi:10.1145/1082983.1083214

Meadows, C. (1991). Policies for dynamic upgrading. *Database security IV: Status and prospects* (pp. 241-250).

Meland, P. H., Spampinato, D. G., Hagen, E., Baadshaug, E. T., Krister, K.-M., & Velle, K. S. (2008). SeaMonster: Providing tool support for security modeling. In *Proceedings of NISK 2008.*

Memon, A., et al. (2004). Skoll: distributed continuous quality assurance. In *Proceedings of the 26th International Conference on Software Engineering (ICSE)* (pp. 459-468).

Mens, K., Mens, T., & Wermelinger, M. (2002). Supporting software evolution with intentional software views. In *Proceedings of the International Workshop on Principles of Software Evolution,* (pp. 138-142), Orlando, Florida, ACM.

Mens, T., Wermelinger, M., Ducasse, S., Demeyer, S., Hirschfeld, R., & Jazayeri, M. (2005). Challenges in software evolution. In *Proceedings of the 8ᵗʰ International Workshop on Principles of Software Evolution.*

Mens, T., Ramil, J. F., & Godfrey, M. W. (2004). Analyzing the evolution of large-scale software. *Journal of Software Maintenance and Evolution: Research and Practice, 16*(6), 363–365. doi:doi:10.1002/smr.300

Microsoft. (2007). *Microsoft Threat Analysis and Modeling v2.1.2.* Retrieved August 15, 2009, from http://www.microsoft.com/downloads/details.aspx?FamilyId=59888078-9DAF-4E96-B7D1-944703479451&displaylang=en

Microsoft. (n.d.). *Windows Azure Platform.* Retrieved February 19, 2010, from http://www.microsoft.com/windowsazure/

Mikolajczak, B., & Gami, N. (2008). Design and Verification of Loosely Coupled Inter-Organizational Workflows with Multi-Level Security. *JCP, 3*(1), 63–78. doi:doi:10.4304/jcp.3.1.63-78

Mikunov, A. (2003, September). Rewrite MSIL code on the fly with the .NET framework profiling API. *Microsoft MSDN Magazine.* Retrieved from http://msdn.microsoft.com/en-us/magazine/cc188743.aspx

Miyazaki, S., Mead, N. R., & Zhan, J. (2008, December). *Computer-aided privacy requirements elicitation technique.* Paper presented at the 2008 IEEE Asia-Pacific Services Computing Conference.

Mouratidis, H., Giorgini, P., & Manson, G. (2003). Modelling secure multiagent systems. In *Proceedings of the 2ⁿᵈ international joint conference on Autonomous agents and multiagent systems,* (pp. 859-866), Melbourne, Australia, ACM.

Mouratidis, H., J. Jurjens and J. Fox (2006). Towards a comprehensive framework for secure systems development. *Advanced Information Systems Engineering,* 48-62.

Mouratidis, H., & Giorgini, P. (2006). *Integrating security and software engineering: Advances and future visions.* London: Idea Group Publishing.

Mouratidis, H., Giorgini, P., & Manson, G. (2005). When security meets software engineering: A case of modelling secure information systems. *Information Systems, 30*(8), 609–629. doi:doi:10.1016/j.is.2004.06.002

Murata, M., Tozawa, A., & Kudo, M. (2003). XML access control using static analysis. In *Proceedings of the ACM Conference on Computer and Communications Security* (pp. 73-84).

Murphy, C., Kaiser, G., Vo, I., & Chu, M. (2009). Quality assurance of software applications using the in vivo testing approach. In *Proceedings of the Second IEEE International Conference on Software Testing, Verification and Validation (ICST)* (pp. 111-120).

Murray, T., & Grove, D. (2008). Non-delegatable authorities in capability systems. *Journal of Computer Security, 16,* 743–759.

Nagaratnam, N., Nadalin, A., Hondo, M., McIntosh, M., & Austel, P. (2005). Business-driven application security: From modeling to managing secure applications. *IBM Systems Journal, 44*(4). doi:doi:10.1147/sj.444.0847

Narraine, R. (2006). *Hacker Discovers Adobe PDF Back Doors*. Retrieved from http://www.eweek.com/c/a/Security/Hacker-Discovers-Adobe-PDF-Back-Doors/

National Institute of Standards and Technology. (2002). *Software errors cost U.S. economy $59.5 billion annually* (Rep. No. NIST 2002-10). Retrieved June 23, 2009, from http://www.nist.gov/public_affairs/releases/n02-10.htm

National Institute of Standards and Technology. (2008, January). *Publication, The eXtensible Configuration Checklist Description Format, Release 1.1.4*. Retrieved August 24, 2010, from http://scap.nist.gov/specifications/xccdf/

National Institute of Standards and Technology. (2009, November). *Publication # NIST SP 800-126, 2009, The Technical Specification for the Security Content Automation Protocol*. National Institute of Standards and Technology.

National Security Agency. (2004). *INFOSEC assessment methodology*. Retrieved June 19, 2009, from http://www.iatrp.com/iam.cfm

Neamtiu, I. (2009). *Ginseng user's guide*. Retrieved from http://www.cs.umd.edu/projects/PL/dsu/software.shtml

Neamtiu, I., Hicks, M., & Stoyle, G. (2006). Practical dynamic software updating for c. In *Proceedings of the ACM Conference on Programming Languages Design and Implementation* (pp. 72-83).

Necula, G., McPeak, S., & Weimer, W. (2002). CCured: Type-safe Retrofitting of Legacy Code. In *Proceedings of the Symposium on Princliples of Programming Languages*, Portland, OR (pp. 128-139).

Neubauer, T., Klemen, M., & Biffl, S. (2006). Secure business process management: a roadmap. In *Proceedings of the First International Conference on Availability, Reliability and Security (ARES 2006)* (pp. 457-464).

Neumann, P. G. (1994). *Computer-Related Risks*. Reading, MA: Addison-Wesley Professional.

Newsome, J., & Song, D. (2005). Dynamic Taint Analysis for Automatic Detection, Analysis, and Signature Generation of Exploits on Commodity Software. In *Proceedings of the Network and Distributed System Security Symposium*, San Diego, CA.

Nguyen-Tuong, A., Guarnieri, S., Greene, D., Shirley, J., & Evans, D. (2005, May 30-June 1). Automatically hardening Web applications using precise tainting. In *Proceedings of the 20th IFIP International Information Security Conference*, Chiba, Japan (pp. 296-307).

Nhlabatsi, A., R. Laney and B. Nuseibeh (2008). Feature interaction: The security threat from within software systems. *Progress in Informatics* (5), 75-89.

Novark, G., Berger, E. D., & Zorn, B. G. (2008). Exterminator: Automatically correcting memory errors with high probability. *Communications of the ACM, 51*(12), 87–95. doi:10.1145/1409360.1409382

Nuseibeh, B., Easterbrook, S., & Russo, A. (2000). Leveraging Inconsistency in software development. *Computer, 33*(4), 24–29. doi:doi:10.1109/2.839317

O'Neill, M., Hallam-Baker, P., MacCann, S., Shema, M., Simon, E., Watters, P. A., & White, A. (2003). *Web Services Security*. New York: McGraw-Hill/Osborne.

Oar, G. L., & Jackson, R. H. (1998). *The Benefits of Applying the DoD Information Technology Security Certification and Accreditation Process to Commercial Systems and Applications*. Manassas, VA: SphereCom Enterprises Inc.

OASIS. (1993). *Security Assertion Markup Language* (Tech. Rep.). Retrieved from http://www.oasis-open.org/committees/security/

OMG. (2009). *Superstructure, V2.1.2*. Retrieved from http://www.omg.org/spec/UML/2.1.2/Superstructure/PDF

One, A. (1996). Smashing the Stack for Fun and Profit. *Phrack Magazine, 7*(49). Retrieved March 16, 2010, from insecure.org/stf/smashstack.html

Open Vulnerability and Assessment Language (OVAL). (n.d.). *Community list. MITRE*. Retrieved from http://oval.mitre.org/

O'Reilly, C., Morrow, P., & Bustard, D. (2003). Lightweight prevention of architectural erosion. In *Proceedings of 6ᵗʰ International Workshop on Principles of Software Evolution.*

Osborn, S. (2000). Configuring role-based access control to enforce mandatory and discretionary access control policies. *ACM Transactions on Information and System Security, 3*(2), 85–106. doi:10.1145/354876.354878

Osman, S., Subhraveti, D., Su, G., & Nieh, J. (2002). The design and implementation of Zap: A system for migrating computing environments. In *Proceedings of the Fifth Symposium on Operating Systems Design and Implementation (OSDI)* (pp. 361-376).

Osterweil, L. (1996). Perpetually testing software. In *Proceedings of the Ninth International Software Quality Week.*

OWASP. (2007). *Top 10 2007*. Retrieved July 10, 2008, from http://www.owasp.org/index.php/Top_10_2007

OWASP. (2008). *Open Web application security project (OWASP) top ten project.* Retrieved from http://www. owasp.org/index.php/Category:OWASP_Top_Ten_Project

*Parasoft*. (n.d.). Retrieved March 16, 2010, from www. parasoft.com/jsp/home.jsp

Parsons, D., Rashid, A., Telea, A., & Speck, A. (2006). An architectural pattern for designing component-based application frameworks. *Software, Practice & Experience, 36*(2), 157–190. doi:doi:10.1002/spe.694

Partnership for Public Service & Booz Allen Hamilton. (2009). Cyber IN-Security: Strengthening the Federal Cybersecurity Workforce. *Partnership for Public Service.* Retrieved July, 2009, from http://ourpublicservice.org/OPS/publications/viewcontentdetails.php?id=135

Pavlich-Mariscal, J. A., et al. (2008). A framework for component-based enforcement for access control. In *Proceedings of the XXVII International Conference of Chilean Computer Science Society* (pp. 13-22). Washington, DC: IEEE Computer Society.

*PaX Project*. (2003). Retrieved March 16, 2010, from http://pax.grsecurity.net/docs/pax.txt

Peeters, J. (2005). *Agile Security Requirements Engineering*. Paper presented at the Symposium on Requirements Engineering for Information Security.

Pena, J., Hinchey, M. G., Resinas, M., Sterritt, R., & Rash, J. L. (2007). Designing and managing evolving systems using a MAS product line approach. *Science of Computer Programming, 66*(1), 71–86. doi:doi:10.1016/j. scico.2006.10.007

Perens, B. (n. d.). *Electric fence 2.0.5*. Retrieved from http://perens.com/FreeSoftware/

Pfleeger, S. L., & Atlee, J. (2005). *Software Engineering Theory and Practice* (3rd ed.). Upper Saddle River, NJ: Pearon Prentice Hall.

Phantasmagoria, P. (n. d.). *The malloc maleficarum.* Retrieved from http://lists.grok.org.uk/pipermail/full-disclosure/2005-October/037905.html

Phillips, C., et al. (2002a). Security engineering for roles and resources in a distributed environment. In *Proceedings of 3rd ISSEA Conference*. Kluwer Academic Publishers.

Phillips, C., et al. (2002b). Towards information assurance in dynamic coalitions. In *Proceedings of the 2002 IEEE Information Assurance Workshop*. Washington, DC: IEEE Computer Society.

Pietraszek, T., & Berghe, C. V. (2005). Defending against injection attacks through context-sensitive string evaluation. In *Proceedings of the 8ᵗʰ International Symposium on Recent Advances in Intrusion Detection* (pp. 124-145).

Pietrek, M. (2001, December). The. NET profiling API and the DNProfiler tool. *Microsoft MSDN Magazine.* Retrieved from http://msdn.microsoft.com/en-us/magazine/cc301725.aspx

Popovsky, V., & Popovsky, B. (2008, June). *Integrating Academics, the Community and Industry.* ISBN 978-5-903247-15-8

Poppendieck, M., & Morsicato, R. (2002, September). XP in a Safety-Critical Environment. *Cutter IT Journal, 15*, 12–16.

*Poseidon for UML by GentleWare*. (n.d.). Retrieved from http://www.gentleware.com/

Prasad, M., & Chiueh, T. (2003). A Binary Rewriting Defense against Stack based Buffer Overflow Attacks. In *Proceedings of USENIX Annual Conference*, TX (pp. 211-224).

Preece, J., Rogers, Y., & Sharp, H. (2007). *Beyond Interaction Design: Beyond Human-Computer Interaction*. New York: John Wiley & Sons, Inc.

Provos, N., Mavrommatis, P., Rajab, M. A., & Monrose, F. (2008, June 22-27). *All your iFRAMEs point to us*. Paper presented at the 17th USENIX Security Symposium, Boston.

Pruitt, J., & Adlin, T. (2006). *The persona lifecycle: keeping people in mind throughout product design*. Amsterdam: Elsevier.

Pyo, C., Bae, B., Kim, T., & Lee, G. (2004). Run-time Detection of Buffer Overflow Attacks without Explicit Sensor Data Objects. In *Proceedings of the International Conference on Information Technology: Coding and Computing* (pp. 50). Nevada, USA.

Pyster, A. (Ed.). (2009). *Graduate software engineering 2009 (GSwE2009) curriculum guidelines for graduate degree programs in software engineering, version 1.0*. Hoboken, NJ: Stevens Institute of Technology.

Qin, F., Tucek, J., Sundaresan, J., & Zhou, Y. (2005). Rx: Treating Bugs as Allergies – A Safe Method to Survive Software Failures. In *Proceedings of the Symposium on Systems and Operating Systems Principles (SOSP)*.

Ramakrishnan, C., & Sekar, R. (2002). Model-based analysis of configuration vulnerabilities. *Journal of Computer Security*, *10*, 189–209.

Ramil, J. F. (2002). *Laws of software evolution and their empirical support*. International Conference on Software Maintenance.

Ramil, J. F., & Smith, N. (2002). Qualitative simulation of models of software evolution. *Software Process Improvement and Practice*, *7*(3-4), 95–112. doi:doi:10.1002/spip.158

Ravichandar, R., Arthur, J. D., Bohner, S. A., & Tegarden, D. P. (2008). Improving change tolerance through Capabilities-based design: an empirical analysis. *Journal of Software Maintenance and Evolution: Research and Practice*, *20*(2), 135–170. doi:doi:10.1002/smr.367

Ray, I., et al. (2003). Using parameterized UML to specify and compose access control models. In *Proceedings of the 6th IFIP Working Conference on Integrity and Internal Control in Information Systems* (pp. 115-124). ACM Publishing.

Redwine, S. (2007). Introduction to Assurance Cases. In *Proceedings of the OMG Software Assurance Workshop*.

Ren, X., Chesley, O. C., & Ryder, B. G. (2006). Identifying failure causes in Java programs: An application of change impact analysis. *IEEE Transactions on Software Engineering*, *32*(9), 718–732. doi:doi:10.1109/TSE.2006.90

Respect-IT. (2007). *Objectiver*. Retrieved from http://www.objectiver.com

Rinard, M., Cadar, C., Dumitran, D., Roy, D., & Leu, T. (2004). A Dynamic Technique for Eliminating Buffer Overflow Vulnerabilities (and Other Memory Errors). In *Proceedings of the 20th Annual Computer Security Applications Conference*, Tucson, AZ (pp. 82-90).

Rinard, M., Cadar, C., Dumitran, D., Roy, D., Leu, T., & Beebee, W. J. (2004). Enhancing Server Availability and Security Through Failure-Oblivious Computing. In *Proceedings Symposium on Operating Systems Design and Implementation (OSDI)*. sd and devik (2001). *Linux on-the-fly Kernel Patching Without LKM*. Retrieved from http://doc.bughunter.net/rootkit-backdoor/kernel-patching.html

Rinard, M. C. (2008). Technical perspective patching program errors. *Communications of the ACM*, *51*(12), 86–86. doi:10.1145/1409360.1409381

Rippon, W. J. (2006, April). Threat assessment of IP based voice systems. In *Proceedings of the 1st IEEE Workshop on VoIP Management and Security 2006*, Vancouver, B.C., Canada (pp. 19-28).

Robertson, J., & Robertson, S. (2009). *Volere Requirements Specification Template: Edition 14 - January 2009*. Retrieved from http://www.volere.co.uk/template.htm

Robertson, W., Kruegel, C., Mutz, D., & Valeur, F. (2003, October). Run-time detection of heap-based overflows. In *Proceedings of the 17th large installation systems administrators conference*, San Diego, CA (pp. 51-60).

Rodríguez, A., & de Guzman, I. G.-R. (2007). Obtaining Use Case and Security Use Cases from Secure Business Process through the MDA Approach. In *Proceedings of WOSIS 2007*.

Rodríguez, A., Fernández-Medina, E., & Piattini, M. (2006). Towards a UML 2.0 Extension for the Modeling of Security Requirements in Business Processes. *Trust and Privacy in Digital Business* (LNCS 4083, pp. 51-61). Berlin: Springer.

Rodríguez, A., Fernández-Medina, E., & Piattini, M. (2007). A BPMN Extension for the Modeling of Security Requirements in Business Processes. *IEICE - Transactions on Information and Systems. E (Norwalk, Conn.), 90-D*(4), 745–752.

Rosencrance, L. (2007). *Survey: Poor Communication Causes Most IT Project Failures*. Computerworld Electronic Journal.

Roshandel, R., Hoek, A. V. D., Mikic-Rakic, M., & Medvidovic, N. (2004). Mae - A system model and environment for managing architectural evolution. *ACM Transactions on Software Engineering and Methodology, 13*(2), 240–276. doi:doi:10.1145/1018210.1018213

Rosson, M. B., & Carroll, J. M. (2002). *Usability engineering: scenario-based development of human-computer interaction*. San Francisco, CA: Academic Press.

Ross, R., Katzke, S., Johnson, A., Katzke, S., Toth, P., Stoneburner, G., & Rogers, G. (2007). *NIST Special Publication 800-53A*. Guide for Assessing the Security Controls in Federal Information Systems.

Ross, R., Katzke, S., Johnson, A., Swanson, M., Stoneburner, M., & Rogers, G. (2004). *NIST Special Publication 800-37*. Guide for the Security Certification and Accreditation of Federal Information Systems.

Røstad, L. (2006). An extended misuse case notation: Including vulnerabilities and the insider threat. In *Proceedings of REFSQ, the 12th International Working Conference on Requirements Engineering*.

Rubenstein, D., Osterweil, L., & Zilberstein, S. (1997). An anytime approach to analyzing software systems. In *Proceedings of the 10th FLAIRS* (pp. 386-391).

Russo, A., Nuseibeh, B., & Kramer, J. (1998). Restructuring requirements specifications for managing inconsistency and change: A case study. In *Proc. of 3rd International Conference on Requirements Engineering* (ICRE `98), Colorado Springs, USA.

Russo, A., Nuseibeh, B., & Kramer, J. (1999). Restructuring requirements specifications. *IEEE Proceedings Software, 146*(1), 44–53. doi:doi:10.1049/ip-sen:19990156

Ruwase, O., & Lam, M. (2004). A Practical Dynamic Buffer Overflow Detector. In *Proceedings of Network and Distributed System Security Symposium*, San Diego, CA (pp. 159-169).

Ruwase, O., & Lam, M. S. (2004, February). A practical dynamic buffer overflow detector. In *Proceedings of the 11th annual network and distributed system security symposium*, San Diego, CA.

Rysselberghe, F. V., & Demeyer, S. (2004). Studying Software evolution information by visualizing the change history. In *Proceedings of the 20th IEEE International Conference on Software Maintenance* (ICSM'04).

SAFECode. (2008). *Software Assurance: An Overview of Current Industry Best Practices. Software Assurance Forum for Excellence in Code (SAFECode)*. Retrieved from http://www.safecode.org/publications/SAFECode_BestPractices0208.pdf

Salamat, B., Gal, A., Jackson, T., Manivannan, K., Wagner, G., & Franz, M. (2008). Multi-variant Program Execution: Using Multi-core Systems to Defuse Buffer-Overflow Vulnerabilities. In *Proceedings of the International Conference on Complex, Intelligent and Software Intensive Systems*, Barcelona, Spain (pp. 843-848).

Salifu, M., Yu, Y., & Nuseibeh, B. (2007). Specifying monitoring and switching problems in context. In *Proceedings of the 15th IEEE International Conference in Requirements Engineering* (RE '07), New Delhi, India.

Salter, C., Saydjari, O. S., Schneier, B., & Wallner, J. (1998, September). Towards a Secure System Engineering Methodology. In *Proceedings of New Security Paradigms Workshop*.

Sandhu, R., & Munawer, Q. (1998). How to do discretionary access control using roles. In *Proceedings of the Third ACM Workshop on Role-Based Access Control* (pp. 47-54). ACM Publishing.

Sandhu, R. (1996). Role-based access control models. *IEEE Computer, 29*(2), 38–47.

Sassoon, R., Jaatun, M. G., & Jensen, J. (2010). *The road to Hell is covered with good intentions: A story of (in) secure software engineering*. Paper presented at the 4th International Workshop of Secure Software Engineering (SecSE 2010).

Schiffrin, D. (1994). *Approaches to discourse*. Oxford, UK: Blackwell.

Schou, C., & Shoemaker, D. (2007). *Information Assurance for the Enterprise: A Roadmap to Information Security*. New York: McGraw-Hill/Irwin.

Scott, D., & Sharp, R. (2002, May). Abstracting application-level Web security. In *Proceedings of the 11th International Conference on the World Wide Web,* Honolulu, Hawaii (pp. 396-407).

Scrum Alliance, I. (2009). *What is Scrum?* Retrieved March 23, 2010, from http://www.scrumalliance.org/learn_about_scrum

Seely, S. (2002a). *Understanding WS-Security (Tech. Rep.)*. Microsoft.

Seely, S. (2002b). *Securing Web Services with ISA Server (Tech. Rep.)*. Microsoft.

Seffah, A., & Metzker, E. (2004). The obstacles and myths of usability and software engineering. *Communications of the ACM, 47*(12), 71–76. doi:10.1145/1035134.1035136

Sekar, R. (2009, February 8-11). *An efficient black-box technique for defeating Web application attacks*. Paper presented at the 16th Annual Network and Distributed System Security Symposium NDSS'09, San Diego, CA.

Seybold, C., Meier, S., & Glinz, M. (2004). Evolution of requirements models by simulation. In *Proceedings of 7th International Workshop on Principles of Software Evolution.*

Shabalin, P. (2004). *Model Checking UMLsec*. München, Germany: University of München.

Shacham, H., Page, M., Pfaff, B., Goh, E. J., Modadugu, N., & Boneh, D. (2004, October). On the Effectiveness of Address-Space Randomization. In *Proceedings of the 11th acm conference on computer and communications security*, Washington, DC (p. 298-307). New York: ACM Press.

Shahriar, H., & Zulkernine, M. (2010). Classification of Buffer Overflow Vulnerability Monitors. In *Proceedings of the 4th International Workshop on Secure Software Engineering*, Krakow, Poland (pp. 519-524).

Shin, M., & Ahn, G. (2000). UML-based representation of role-based access control. In *Proceedings of the 9th International Workshop on Enabling Technologies: Infrastructure for Collaborative Enterprises* (pp. 195-200). Washington, DC: IEEE Computer Society.

Shin, M. E., & Gomaa, H. (2007). Software requirements and architecture modeling for evolving non-secure applications into secure applications. *Science of Computer Programming, 66*(1), 60–70. doi:doi:10.1016/j.scico.2006.10.009

Sidiroglou, S., Locasto, M. E., Boyd, S. W., & Keromytis, A. D. (2005). Building a Reactive Immune System for Software Services. In *Proceedings of the USENIX Annual Technical Conference* (pp. 149-161).

Simpson, J. J. (2002, August). *Innovation and Technology Management*. Paper presented at the Twelfth Annual International Symposium of INCOSE, Engineering 21st Century Systems: Problem Solving Through Structured Thinking, Las Vegas, NV.

Simpson, J. J. (2004, April). *System Frameworks*. Paper presented at the Second Annual Conference on Systems Engineering Research, Los Angeles.

Simpson, J. J., & Endicott-Popovsky, B. (2010, June 7). *A Systematic Approach to Information Systems Security Education*. Paper presented at the 14th Colloquium for Information Systems Security Education, Baltimore, MD.

Simpson, J. J., & Simpson, M. J. (2003, July). *Systems and Objects*. Paper presented at the Thirteenth Annual International Symposium of INCOSE, Engineering Tomorrow's World Today, Crystal City, VA.

Simpson, J. J., & Simpson, M. J. (2006, July). *Foundational Systems Engineering (SE) Patterns for a SE Pattern Language*. Paper presented at the Sixteenth Annual International Symposium of INCOSE, Systems Engineering: Shining List on the Tough Issues, Orlando, FL.

Simpson, J. J., & Simpson, M. J. (2010, June 3). Complexity Reduction: A Pragmatic Approach. *Systems Engineering Journal*. DOI:10.1002/sys.20170

Simpson, J. J., Miller, A., & Dagli, C. (2008, June). *Secure Adaptive Response Potential (SARP): A System Security Metric*. Paper presented at the Eighteenth Annual International Symposium of INCOSE, Systems Engineering for the Planet, Utrecht, The Nederlands.

Simpson, J. J., Votipka, S., Wang, T., Baklanoff, T., & Sweers, N. (2010, June 2). *Final Project Report, Threat Incident Modeling Team*. Paper presented to IMT 553 – Establishing and Managing Information Assurance Strategies, University of Washington, Seattle, WA.

Sinclair, D. (2005). *Introduction to Assurance*. Dublin, Ireland: School of Computing.

Sindre, G. (2007). Mal-activity Diagrams for Capturing Attacks on Business Processes. In P. Sawyer, B. Paech, & P. Heymans (Eds.), *Proceedings of REFSQ 2007* (LNCS 4542, pp. 355-366). Berlin: Springer.

Sindre, G., & Opdahl, A. L. (2000). *Eliciting security requirements by misuse cases*. Paper presented at the 37th International Conference on Technology of Object-Oriented Languages (Tools 37–Pacific 2000).

Siponen, M., Baskerville, R., & Kuivalainen, T. (2005). *Integrating Security into Agile Development Methods*. Paper presented at the Hawaii International Conference on System Sciences, HI.

Siponen, M. T., Baskerville, R., & Heikka, J. (2006). A design theory for secure information systems design methods. *Journal of the Association for Information Systems*, *7*(8), 568–592.

Smirnov, A., & Chiueh, T. (2005). DIRA: Automatic Detection, Identification, and Repair of Control-Hijacking Attacks. In *Proceedings of the Symposium on Network and Distributed System Security (NDSS)*.

Smith, G. W. (1991). Modeling security relevant data semantics. *IEEE Transactions on Software Engineering*, *17*(11), 1195–1203. doi:10.1109/32.106974

Smith, G., & McComb, T. (2008). Refactoring real-time specifications. *Electronic Notes in Theoretical Computer Science*, *214*, 359–380. doi:doi:10.1016/j.entcs.2008.06.016

Soffer, P. (2005). Scope analysis: identifying the impact of changes in business process models. *Software Process Improvement and Practice*, *10*(4), 393–402. doi:doi:10.1002/spip.242

Sohr, K. (2008). Analyzing and managing role-based access control policies. *IEEE Transactions on Knowledge and Data Engineering*, *20*(7), 924–939. doi:10.1109/TKDE.2008.28

Solar Designer. (2000, July). *JPEG COM marker processing vulnerability in netscape browsers*. Retrieved from http://www.openwall.com/advisories/OW-002-netscape-jpeg.txt.

Solar Designer. (n. d.). *Non-executable stack patch*. Retrieved from http://www.openwall.com

Song, R., Korba, L., & Yee, G. (2006). Pseudonym Technology for E-Services. In Yee, G. (Ed.), *Privacy Protection for E-Services*. Hershey, PA: IGI Global.

Soules, C. A. N., Appavoo, J., Hui, K., Wisniewski, R. W., da Silva, D., Ganger, G. R., et al. (2003). System Support for Online Reconfiguration. In *Proceedings of the USENIX Annual Technical Conference* (pp. 141-154).

Sovarel, N., Evans, D., & Paul, N. (2005, August). Where's the FEEB? the effectiveness of instruction set randomization. In *Proceedings of the 14th usenix security symposium*, Baltimore, MD.

Spence, R. (2007). *Information Visualization: Design for Interaction*. Upper Saddle River, NJ: Pearson Prentice Hall.

Stack Shield. (2001). *A "stack smashing" technique protection tool for Linux*. Retrieved March 16, 2010, from www.angelfire.com/sk/stackshield

Stamper, R. K. (1994). Social Norms in Requirement Analysis – an outline of MEASUR. In Jirotka, M., & Gorguen, J. (Eds.), *Requirements Engineering: Social and Technical Issues*. London: Academic Press Ltd.

Stamper, R. K. (1997). Organizational Semiotics. In Mingers, J., & Stowell, F. (Eds.), *Information Systems: An Emerging Discipline*. London: McGraw Hill.

Stamper, R. K., Liu, K., Hafkamp, M., & Ades, Y. (2000). Understanding the Role of Signs and Norms in Organisations, - a semiotic approach to information systems design. *Journal of Behaviour and Information Technology, 19*(1), 15–27. doi:doi:10.1080/014492900118768

Stefano, A. D., Pappalardo, G., & Tramontana, E. (2004). An infrastructure for runtime evolution of software systems. In. *Proceedings of the IEEE Symposium on Computers and Communications, 2*, 1129–1135.

Stevens, W. R. (1993). *Advanced programming in the unix enironment*. Reading, MA: Addison-Wesley.

Stoneburner, G., Goguen, A., & Feringa, A. (2002). *Risk management guide for information technology systems (Special Publication 800-30)*. Gaithersburg, MD: National Institute of Standards and Technology.

Strunk, E. A., & Knight, J. C. (2006). *The Essential Synthesis of Problem Frames and Assurance Cases*. Charlottesville, VA: University of Virginia, Department of Computer Science.

Su, Z., & Wassermann, G. (2006, January). The essence of command injection attacks in Web applications. In *Proceedings of the 33rd Annual ACM SIGPLAN - SIGACT Symposium on Principles of Programming Languages, Charleston, SC* (pp. 372-382).

Suh, G., Lee, J., Zhang, D., & Devadas, S. (2006). Secure Program Execution via Dynamic Information Flow Tracking. In *Proceedings of the 11th International Conference on Architectural Support for Programming Languages and Operating Systems, CA* (pp. 85-96).

Sullivan, B. (2008). Agile SDL: Streamline Security Practices for Agile Development. *msdn Magazine*. Retrieved from http://msdn.microsoft.com/en-us/magazine/dd153756.aspx van der Haak, M., Wolff, A. C., Brandner, R., Drings, P., Wannenmacher, M., & Wetter, T. (2003). Data security and protection in cross-institutional electronic patient records. *International Journal of Medical Informatics, 70*(2/3), 117-130.

Sun, S.-T., & Beznosov, K. (2009, March 30). *SQL-Prevent: Effective dynamic detection and prevention of SQL injection* (Tech. Rep. No. LERSSE-TR-2009-032). Vancouver, British Columbia, Canada: Laboratory for Education and Research in Secure Systems Engineering, University of British Columbia. Retrieved from http://lersse-dl.ece.ubc.ca

Sutton, M., Greene, A., & Amini, P. (2007). *Fuzzing: Brute Force Vulnerability Discovery* (1st ed.). Reading, MA: Addison-Wesley.

Syrjaanen, T. (1998). Implementation of local grounding for logic programs with stable model semantics (Tech. Rep. No. 18). Espoo Finland: Helsinki University of Technology.

Syrjaanen, T. (2000). *Lparse 1.0 User's Manual*. Espoo, Finland: Helsinki University of Technology.

Talbert, N. (1998). The cost of COTS. *IEEE Computer, 31*(6), 46–52.

Tan, Y., Zheng, J., Cao, Y., & Zhang, X. (2005). Buffer Overflow Protection Based on Adjusting Code Segment Limit. In *Proceedings of the IEEE International Symposium on Communications and Information Technology, Beijing, China* (pp. 947-950).

Teiger. (1993a). *Représentations du travail, travail de la Représentation*. In A. Weill-Fassina, P. Rabardel, & D. Dubois (Eds.), *Représentations pour l'action*. Toulouse, France: Octarès.

Teiger. (1995). *Parler quand même! Les fonctions des activités langagières non fonctionnelles*. In J. Boutet (Ed.), *Paroles au travail* (p. 45-72). Paris: L'Harmattan.

The ELF shell crew. (2005). Embedded elf debugging: the middle head of cerberus. *Phrack Magazine, 11*(63).

The PaX Team. (n. d.). *Documentation for the PaX project*. Retrieved from http://pageexec.virtualave.net/docs/

Thimbleby, H. (2007). *User-centered methods are insufficient for safety critical systems.*

Thompson, H. H., Whittaker, J. A., & Mottay, F. E. (2002). Software security vulnerability testing in hostile environments. In *Proceedings of the 2002 ACM Symposium on Applied Computing* (pp. 260-264). New York: ACM.

Ting, T. C. (1988). A user-role based data security approach. In C. Landwehr (Ed.), *Database security: Status and prospects* (pp. 187-208). Amsterdam: North-Holland.

Tøndel, I. A., Jaatun, M. G., & Meland, P. H. (2008). Security Requirements for the Rest of Us: A Survey. *Software, IEEE, 25*(1), 20–27. doi:10.1109/MS.2008.19

Treasury Board of Canada. (n.d.). *The Privacy Impact Assessment Guidelines: A Framework to Manage Privacy Risk.* Retrieved May 6, 2006, from http://www.tbs-sct.gc.ca/pgol-pged/piatp-pfefvp/course1/mod2/mod2-5_e.asp

Tsai, T., & Singh, N. (2002). Libsafe: Transparent System-wide Protection Against Buffer Overflow Attacks. In *Proceedings of the International Conference on Dependable Systems and Networks*, Bethesda, MD (pp. 541-541).

Tufte, E. R. (1990). *Envisioning information.* Cheshire, CT: Graphics Press.

Tufte, E. R. (1997). *Visual Explanations: Images and Quantities, Evidence and Narrative.* Cheshire, CT: Graphics Press.

Turner, C. R., Fuggetta, A., Lavazza, L., & Wolf, A. L. (1999). A conceptual basis for feature engineering. *Journal of Systems and Software, 49*(1), 3–15. doi:doi:10.1016/S0164-1212(99)00062-X

Turner, K. J. (1997). An architectural foundation for relating features. In *Proc. Feature Interactions in Telecommunication Networks IV.* Amsterdam: IOS Press.

U. S. General Accounting Office. (1999). *Information security risk assessment: Practices of leading organizations - a supplement to GAO's May 1998 executive guide on information security management.* Washington, DC: Author.

Ukai, F. (2004). Retrieved from http://ukai.jp/Software/livepatch/

Unige. (n.d.). Retrieved from www.unige.ch/fapse/SSE/teaching/tc101/competence_concept.html

Valeur, F., Mutz, D., & Vigna, G. (2005). A learning-based approach to the detection of SQL attacks. In *Proceedings of the Conference on Detection of Intrusions and Malware & Vulnerability Assessment (DIMVA 2005)* (pp. 123-140).

*Valgrind.* (2009). Retrieved March 16, 2010, from http://valgrind.org/docs

van der Pas, R. (2002, November). *Memory hierarchy in cache-based systems* (Tech. Rep. No. 817-0742-10). Santa Clara, CA: Sun Microsystems.

van Lamsweerde, A. (2004). Elaborating security requirements by construction of intentional anti-models. In *Proceedings of the 26ᵗʰ International Conference on Software Engineering.*

van Lamsweerde, A., Darimont, R., & Letier, E. (1998). Managing conflicts in goal-driven requirements engineering. *IEEE Transactions on Software Engineering, 24*(11), 908–926. doi:doi:10.1109/32.730542

van Lamsweerde, A., & Letier, E. (2000). Handling obstacles in goal-oriented requirements engineering. *Software Engineering, 26*(10), 978–1005. doi:10.1109/32.879820

Vanegue, J., de Medeiros, J. A., Bisolfati, E., Desnos, A., Figueredo, T., Garnier, T., et al. (2009). *The eresi reverse engineering software interface.* Retrieved from http://www.eresi-project.org/

Velthuijsen, H. (1995). Issues of non-monotonicity in feature interaction detection. In Cheng, K. E., & Ohta, T. (Eds.), *Feature Interactions in Telecommunication Systems III* (pp. 31–42). Amsterdam: IOS Press.

Vermersch. (1993). *L'entretien d'explication.* Paris: Edition ESF.

Villarroel, R., Fernández-Medina, E., & Piattini, M. (2005). Secure information systems development - A survey and comparison. *Computers & Security, 24*(4), 308–321. doi:doi:10.1016/j.cose.2004.09.011

Voas, J. (1998). The challenges of using COTS software in component-based development. *IEEE Computer, 31*(6), 44–45.

Wall, L. (2007). *perlsec - perl security* (Library No. v.5.10). Retrieved from http://perldoc.perl.org/perlsec.html

Wang, L., Wijesekera, D., & Jajodia, S. (2004). A logic-based framework for attribute based access control. In *Proceedings of the ACM Workshop on Formal Methods in Security Engineering* (pp. 45-55).

Wang, Y., Lively, W. M., & Simmons, D. B. (2009). Software security analysis and assessment model for the web-based applications. *Journal of Computational Methods in Sciences and Engineering, 9*(1,2S2), 179-189.

Wang, Q., Shen, J., Wang, X., & Mei, H. (2006). A component-based approach to online software evolution. *Journal of Software Maintenance and Evolution: Research and Practice, 18*(3), 181–205. doi:doi:10.1002/smr.324

Warfield, J. N. (1990). *A Science of Generic Design*. Ames, IA: Iowa State University Press.

Wäyrynen, J., Boden, M., & Boström, G. (2004). Security engineering and eXtreme programming: An impossible marriage? In *Proceedings of the Extreme Programming and Agile Methods - Xp/ Agile Universe 2004* (Vol. 3134, pp. 117-128). Berlin: Springer Verlag.

Weimer, W., Nguyen, T., Goues, C. L., & Forrest, S. (2009). Automatically Finding Patches Using Genetic Programming. In *Proceedings of the International Conference on Software Engineering (ICSE)*.

Welke, S. (2004). *Security Certification & Accreditation: DITSCAP vs. DCID 6/3*. Herndon, VA: Trusted Computer Solutions, Inc.

Werlinger, R., Hawkey, K., Muldner, K., Jaferian, P., & Beznosov, K. (2008, July 23-25). The challenges of using an intrusion detection system: Is it worth the effort? In *Proceedings of the 4th Symposium on Usable Privacy and Security (SOUPS)*, Pittsburgh, PA (pp. 107-116).

Weyuker, E. J. (1982). On testing non-testable programs. *The Computer Journal, 25*(4), 465–470.

Wheeler, D. (n.d.). *Flawfinder*. Retrieved from http://www.dwheeler.com/flawfinder/

Wheeler, D. (2003). *Secure Programmer: Developing Secure Programs*. Alexandria, VA: Institute for Defense Analyses.

Wiegers, K. E. (2003). *Software requirements*. Redmond, WA: Microsoft Press.

*Wikipedia*. (n.d.). Retrieved February 15, 2009, from http://en.wikipedia.org/wiki/Transport_Layer_Security

Wilander, J., & Kamkar, M. (2003). A Comparison of Publicly Available Tools for Dynamic Buffer Overflow Prevention. In *Proceedings of the 10th Network and Distributed System Security Symposium*, San Diego, CA (pp. 149-162).

Wilson, W., Rosenberg, L., & Hyatt, L. (1996). Automated quality analysis of natural language requirement specifications. In *Proceedings of Fourteenth Annual Pacific Northwest Software Quality Conference*.

Win, D. B., Scandariato, R., Buyens, K., Gregoire, J., & Joosen, W. (2009). On the secure software development process: CLASP, SDL and Touchpoints compared. *Information and Software Technology, 51*(7), 1152–1171. doi:doi:10.1016/j.infsof.2008.01.010

Wojtczuk, R. (1998). *Defeating Solar Designer's Non-executable Stack Patch*. Retrieved from http://www.insecure.org/sploits/non-executable.stack.problems.html

Woo, T. Y. C., & Lam, S. S. (1992). Authorization in distributed systems: A formal approach. In *Proceedings of the IEEE Symposium on Research in Security and Privacy* (pp. 33-50).

Wood, J., & Silver, D. (1995). *Joint application development* (2nd ed.). New York: John Wiley & Sons.

Wu, J., Holt, R. C., & Hassan, A. E. (2004). Exploring software evolution using spectrographs. In *Proceedings of the 11th Working Conference on Reverse Engineering* (WCRE'04), 80-89.

Xie, Y., & Aiken, A. (2006, August). Static detection of security vulnerabilities in scripting languages. In *Proceedings of the 15th USENIX Security Symposium* (pp. 179-192).

Xie, N. N., Mead, N. R., Chen, P., Dean, M., Lopez, L., & Ojoko-Adams, D. (2004). *SQUARE project: Cost/ benefit analysis framework for information security improvement projects in small companies (Tech. Note No. CMU/SEI-2004-TN-045)*. Pittsburgh, PA: Carnegie Mellon University, Software Engineering Institute.

Xu, D., & Nygard, K. (2005, November 7-11). A Threat-Driven Approach to Modeling and Verifying Secure Software. In *Proceedings of the 20ᵗʰ IEEE/ACM International Conference on Automated Software Engineering (ASE '05)*, Long Beach, CA.

Xu, R., Godefroid, P., & Majumdar, R. (2008). Testing for Buffer Overflows with Length Abstraction. In *Proceedings of the International Symposium on Software Testing and Analysis*, Seattle, WA (pp. 27-38).

Xu, W., DuVarney, D. C., & Sekar, R. (2004, October-November). An Efficient and Backwards-Compatible Transformation to Ensure Memory Safety of C Programs. In *Proceedings of the 12th acm sigsoft international symposium on foundations of software engineering*, Newport Beach, CA (pp. 117-126). New York: ACM Press.

Yamato, K., & Abe, T. (2009). A Runtime Code Modification Method for Application Programs. In *Proceedings of the Ottawa Linux Symposium*.

Yee, G. (2007, July 9-13). Visual Analysis of Privacy Risks in Web Services. In *Proceedings of the 2007 IEEE International Conference on Web Services (ICWS 2007)*, Salt Lake City, UT.

Yee, G., & Korba, L. (2003a, May 18-21). The Negotiation of Privacy Policies in Distance Education. In *Proceedings of the 14th IRMA International Conference*, Philadelphia, PA.

Yee, G., & Korba, L. (2003b, January 27-31). Bilateral E-services Negotiation Under Uncertainty. In *Proceedings of the 2003 International Symposium on Applications and the Internet (SAINT2003)*, Orlando, FL.

Yee, G., & Korba, L. (2004, July 6-9). Privacy Policy Compliance for Web Services. In *Proceedings of the 2004 IEEE International Conference on Web Services (ICWS 2004)*, San Diego, CA.

Yee, G., & Korba, L. (2005). Semi-Automatic Derivation and Use of Personal Privacy Policies in E-Business. *International Journal of E-Business Research, 1*(1), 54–69.

Yee, G., Korba, L., & Song, R. (2006). Legislative Bases for Personal Privacy Policy Specification. In Yee, G. (Ed.), *Privacy Protection for E-Services*. Hershey, PA: IGI Global.

Yong, S. H., & Horwitz, S. (2003, September). Protecting C programs from attacks via invalid pointer dereferences. In *Proceedings of the 9th european software engineering conference held jointly with 10th acm sigsoft international symposium on foundations of software engineering* (pp. 307-316). New York: ACM Press.

Yoon, I.-C., Sussman, A., Memon, A., & Porter, A. (2008). Effective and scalable software compatibility testing. In *Proceedings of the 2008 International Symposium on Software Testing and Analysis (ISSTA '08)* (pp. 63-74). New York: ACM.

Younan, Y. (2003). *An overview of common programming security vulnerabilities and possible solutions.* Unpublished master's thesis, Vrije Universiteit Brussel.

Younan, Y. (2005). *Dnmalloc 1.0.* Retrieved from http://www.fort-knox.org

Younan, Y., Joosen, W., & Piessens, F. (2004, July). *Code injection in C and C++: A survey of vulnerabilities and countermeasures* (Tech. Rep. No. CW386). Leuven, Belgium: Departement Computerwetenschappen, Katholieke Universiteit Leuven.

Younan, Y., Joosen, W., & Piessens, F. (2006, December). Efficient protection against heap-based buffer overflows without resorting to magic. In *Proceedings of the international conference on information and communication security (icics 2006)*, Raleigh, NC.

Younan, Y., Joosen, W., Piessens, F., & den Eynden, H. V. (2005, July). *Security of memory allocators for C and C++* (Tech. Rep. No. CW419). Leuven, Belgium: Departement Computerwetenschappen, Katholieke Universiteit Leuven.

Younan, Y., Joosen, W., & Piessens, F. (2004). *Code Injection in C and C++: A Survey of Vulnerabilities and Countermeasures (Tech. Rep. No. CW 386)*. Leuven, Belgium: Katholiek Universiteit Leuven.

Zave, P. (2001). Requirements for evolving systems: A telecommunications perspective. In *Proceedings of 5ᵗʰ IEEE International Symposium on Requirements Engineering (RE'01)*, Toronto, Canada, IEEE Computer Society.

Zave, P. (2003). An experiment in feature engineering. *Programming methodology:Monographs In Computer Science*, (pp. 353 - 377).

Zave, P., & Jackson, M. (1997). Four dark corners of requirements engineering. *ACM Transactions on Software Engineering and Methodology*, *6*(1), 1–30. doi:doi:10.1145/237432.237434

Zenger, M. (2005). KERIS: evolving software with extensible modules. *Journal of Software Maintenance and Evolution: Research and Practice*, *17*(5), 333–362. doi:doi:10.1002/smr.320

Zen-parse. (n. d.). *Wu-ftpd 2.6.1 exploit.* Retrieved from http://www.derkeiler.com/Mailing-Lists/securityfocus/vuln-dev/2001-12/0160.html

Zetter, K. (2009, March 24). 'The analyzer' hack probe widens; $10 million allegedly stolen from U.S. banks. *Wired Magazine*. Retrieved from http://blog.wired.com/27bstroke6/2009/03/the-analyzer-ha.html

Zhang, Y. (2007). Epistemic reasoning in logic programs. In *Proceedings of the 20th International Joint Conference on Artificial Intelligence (IJCAI-2007)* (pp. 647-652).

Zhivich, M., Leek, T., & Lippmann, R. (2005). Dynamic Buffer Overflow Detection. In *Proceedings of the Workshop on the Evaluation of Software Defect Detection Tools*, Chicago.

Zhong, Q., & Edwards, N. (1998). Security control for COTS. *IEEE Computer*, *31*(6), 67–73.

Zhou, P., Liu, W., Fei, L., Lu, S., Qin, F., Zhou, Y., et al. (2004). AccMon: Automatically Detecting Memory-related Bugs via Program Counter-based Invariants. In *Proceedings of 37th International Symposium on Micro-architecture*, OR (pp. 269-280).

Zhou, Y., Marinov, D., Sanders, W., Zilles, C., d'Amorim, M., Lauterburg, S., et al. (2007). Delta Execution for Software Reliability. In *Proceedings of the Third Workshop on Hot Topics in System Dependability (HotDep'07)*.

Zhou, J., & Alves-Foss, J. (2008). Security policy refinement and enforcement for the design of multi-level secure systems. *Journal of Computer Security*, *16*, 107–131.

Zhu, G., & Tyagi, A. (2004). Protection against Indirect Overflow Attacks on Pointers. In *Proceedings of the 2nd International Information Assurance Workshop*, NC (pp. 97-106).

Zhu, H., Hall, P. A. V., & May, J. H. R. (1997). Software unit test coverage and adequacy. *ACM Computing Surveys*, *29*(4), 366–427. doi:doi:10.1145/267580.267590

Zhu, Z. J., & Zulkernine, M. (2009). A model-based aspect-oriented framework for building intrusion-aware software systems. *Journal of Information and Software Technology*, *51*(5), 865–875. doi:doi:10.1016/j.infsof.2008.05.007

Zowghi, D., & Offen, R. *(1997). A logical framework for modeling and reasoning about the evolution of requirements. In* Proceedings of the 3rd IEEE International Symposium on Requirements Engineering.

# About the Contributors

**Khaled M. Khan** is an assistant professor and the Graduate Program Coordinator in the department of Computer Science and Engineering at Qatar University. Prior to these, Khaled also served the University of Western Sydney as Head of postgraduate programs in computing. His research interests include secure software engineering, cloud computing, measuring security, trust in computer software, and software evolution. He has taught computing more than twenty years at various universities in Asia, Europe, Africa, and Australia. Khaled received his BS and MS in computer science and informatics from the Norwegian University of Science and Technology. He received his PhD in computing from Monash University, Australia. He also holds a second bachelor's degree from the University of Dhaka (Bangladesh). He's the Editor in Chief of the International Journal of Secure Software Engineering. Khaled has published more than sixty technical papers, and edited two books.

\* \* \*

**Aderemi Adeniji** is presently an Applications Systems Engineer at Wells Fargo, Inc. She earned summa cum laude honors while obtaining her MSc in software engineering from the University of North Carolina Charlotte (2008) as a part time graduate student. She also received her BSc in computer engineering from the University of North Carolina at Charlotte (2002). Remi served on the Knowledge Intensive Software Engineering research group at UNCC with special interests including software engineering, software assurance and certification & accreditation.

**Julia Allen** is a senior researcher within the CERT® Program at the Software Engineering Institute (SEI), a unit of Carnegie Mellon University in Pittsburgh, PA. Allen's areas of interest include operational resilience, software security and assurance, and measurement and analysis. Allen is the author of *The CERT Guide to System and Network Security Practices* (Addison-Wesley 2001) and moderator for the CERT Podcast Series: Security for Business Leaders. She is a co-author of *Software Security Engineering: A Guide for Project Managers* (Addison-Wesley 2008) and a contributing author to CERT's Resilience Management Model.

**Mark Ardis** is a Distinguished Service Professor in the School of Systems and Enterprises at Stevens Institute of Technology. He is interested in the professionalization of software engineering, especially through teaching and technology transfer. In his career Mark has helped create academic programs in software engineering at 5 schools. He received a PhD in computer science from the University of Maryland and is a member of the ACM and the IEEE Computer Society. Mark may be reached at mark.ardis@stevens.edu.

**Yun Bai** received her PhD in computer science from University of Western Sydney Nepean in 2000. Currently she is a senior lecturer in the School of Computing and Mathematics at University of Western Sydney. Her research areas include information security, database security, formal specification and logic reasoning. She is interested in providing a formal specification and reasoning for security policies and rules to protect the information systems. She has published dozens of international conference papers and journal papers and has been served as a program committee member for international conferences such as International Conference on Security and Cryptography, Australasian Joint Conference on Artificial Intelligence, International Conference on Industrial, Engineering and Other Applications of Applied Intelligence Systems.

**Joseph Barjis** is an Associate Professor of Systems Engineering and Modeling & Simulation at Delft University of Technology (The Netherlands). He received his PhD from Moscow Technical University of Communications & Informatics. He did a 4-years post doctorate research at Delft University of Technology. Dr. Barjis research interests are focused on business process modeling and simulation, healthcare processes modeling and simulation, security driven software engineering, enterprise engineering, information systems design, system analysis and design, collaborative, participative, and interactive modeling (CPI Modeling).Dr. Barjis is founder and current chair of the Association for Information Systems Special Interest Group on Modeling and Simulation – SIGMAS (http://www.AIS-SIGMAS. org/); founder of the International Workshop on Enterprise & Organizational Modeling and Simulation (http://www.EOMAS.org/); member of several international professional organizations; member of Program Committee and Editorial Board in several international conferences and journals; frequently invited guest editor for International Journals. Dr. Barjis published over 8 edited conference/scientific books, 12 book chapters, 10 journal articles, 7 special issues guest editor, and dozens of fully peer refereed international conference papers. For further information, refer to Barjis' personal webpage: http://www.JosephBarjis.com.

**Solomon Berhe** is a doctoral student in Computer Science & Engineering at the University of Connecticut working with Dr. Demurjian. His current research focuses mainly on fine-grained Role-Based Access Control (RBAC) in Wikis. S. Berhe's most recent research interests include investigating collaborative access control issues in the health care domain. S. Berhe has published 1 journal article, 2 book chapters, and 3 refereed conference/workshop articles.

**Konstantin (Kosta) Beznosov** is an Assistant Professor at the Department of Electrical and Computer Engineering, University of British Columbia, Vancouver, Canada. He founded and leads the Laboratory for Education and Research in Secure Systems Engineering (LERSSE). Prior that, Dr. Beznosov was a Security Architect with Hitachi Computer Products (America), Inc (HICAM), where he designed and developed products for security integration of enterprise applications. Before HICAM, he consulted large telecommunication and banking companies on the architecture of security solutions for distributed enterprise applications, as a Security Architect at Concept Five Technologies. He graduated from Florida International University in 2000 with a Ph.D. in Computer Science on engineering access control for distributed enterprise applications. He is a co-author of "Enterprise Security with EJB and CORBA" and "Mastering Web Services Security" by Wiley Computer Publishing, and a contributor to "Securing Web Services: Practical Usage of Standards and Specifications" by Idea Group and the "Handbook of Software Engineering and Knowledge Engineering" by World Scientific Publishing. Kosta has published in major academic venues on the topics of access control, distributed systems security, and usable security.

**Sergey Bratus** is a Research Assistant Professor at Dartmouth College, affiliated with the Institute for Security, Technology, and Society (ISTS). Dr. Bratus is interested in a broad range of practical operating systems and network security topics, and frequents hacker conferences.

**Huning Dai** is a PhD Candidate in the Computer Science department also a member of the Programming System Lab at Columbia University. His research focuses on security testing, vulnerability detection and security in software engineering. He received his MS in Computer Science from Columbia University in 2010 and his BE in information Engineering from Beijing University of Posts and Telecommunications in 2008.

**Steven Demurjian** is a Full Professor of Computer Science & Engineering at the University of Connecticut with research interests of: secure-software engineering, security for collaborative web portals with biomedical applications, and security-web architectures. Dr. Demurjian has over 130 archival publications, in the following categories: 1 book, 2 edited collections, 41 journal articles and book chapters, and 87 refereed conference/workshop articles.

**Thuong Doan** is a researcher at Northside, Inc., which conducts research on natural language processing and applies said artificial intelligence to computer gaming. He completed his Ph.D. in computer science & engineering at the University of Connecticut with an emphasis on a framework for software security in UML with assurance. Dr. Doan has published 1 journal article, 3 book chapters, and 6 refereed conference/workshop articles.

**Eric Dubois** received the M.S. degree in computer science from the University of Namur, Belgium, in 1981 and the degree of 'Docteur-Ingenieur en Informatique' from the Institut National Polytechnique de Lorraine, Nancy, France, in 1984. Since 2000, in Luxembourg he works at the Public Research Centre Henri Tudor as the managing director of the "Service Science and Innovation" department. Besides management activities, Dr. E. Dubois is active in the software engineering and information system fields for about 25 years. His specific focus is on the requirements engineering (RE) topic where he published over 100 papers with specific interests in business services and security requirements engineering. Recent interests are in the new discipline of "Service Science". Eric Dubois is member of the ERCIM (European Research Consortium in Informatics and Mathematics) board of directors. He is visiting professor at the Universities of Namur and Luxembourg.

**Barbara Endicott-Popovsky**, Ph.D., is the Director for the Center of Information Assurance and Cybersecurity at the University of Washington, designated by the NSA as a Center for Academic Excellence in Information Assurance Education and Research. She holds a faculty appointment as Res. Asso. Professor with the Information School and is Interim Director for the Strategic Planning for Critical Infrastructure Program within the School of Architecture, following a 20-year industry career marked by executive and consulting positions in IT architecture and project management. Her research interests include enterprise-wide information systems security and compliance management, forensic-ready networks, the science of digital forensics and secure coding practices. Barbara earned her Ph.D. in Computer Science/Computer Security from the University of Idaho (2007), and holds a Masters of Science in Information Systems Engineering from Seattle Pacific University (1987), a Masters in Business Administration from the University of Washington (1985) and a Bachelor of Arts from the University of Pittsburgh (1967).

**Shamal Faily** is a doctoral student at the Computing Laboratory at the University of Oxford. His doctoral research involves understanding how factors relating to 'context of use' impact security, and how these factors can be applied to secure systems design. Shamal graduated with a BSc in Business Computing Systems from City University, and spent nearly 10 years as a software engineer at Logica UK.

**Ivan Flechais** is a Departmental Lecturer in the Software Engineering Programme at Oxford University and his main lecturing and research interests are in the area of computer security. In particular, given that people are the weakest link in the security chain, this involves researching how secure systems can be designed, implemented and tested to take human needs into account. Prior to this, he graduated with a BSc in Computer Science from University College London and then stayed on at UCL to achieve a PhD researching how to design secure and usable systems which resulted in the creation of the AEGIS secure system design methodology.

**Frédéric Girard** has received a Master in computer science, networks and information security. He is senior project leader at the Public Research Centre Henri Tudor where he is actively contributing to the development of various methodologies and tools in the area of information security, process assessment and management. He is also deeply involved in the local information security association (CLUSIL Luxembourg) to develop neutral approaches around information security, skills card for professionals and research and development in methodologies. He currently develops and promotes a Master degree in information security and management in collaboration with the Luxembourg University and the CLUSIL. He is in charge of technology transfer activities related to the methodology and of its supporting tools inside various types of companies, organizations and experimental contexts.

**Jun Han** received his B.Eng.and M.Eng. degrees in computer science and engineering from the University of Science and Technology of Beijing, China, in 1982 and 1986 respectively, and his Ph.D. degree in computer science from the University of Queensland, Australia, in 1992. He has previously held research and academic positions at the University of Queensland and Monash University, Australia. He is currently a professor of software engineering at Swinburne University of Technology, Australia, where he directs research into component-based engineering of software and enterprise systems. He is also a research leader with Australia's Cooperative Research Centre in Advanced Automotive Technology (AutoCRC) and Cooperative Research Centrein Smart Services (Smart Services CRC). He has published over 130 articles in refereed international journals and conferences, including 8 best paper awards at leading international conferences. His research has been supported by the Australian Research Council, other government departments and industry organizations. His current research interests include software architecture design, adaptive software systems, software security engineering, software performance engineering, system integration and interoperability, and services engineering.

**Thomas B. Hilburn** is a Professor Emeritus of Software Engineering at Embry-Riddle Aeronautical University, in Daytona Beach, Florida. His current interests include software processes, object-oriented development, and software engineering education. He is an IEEE Certified Software Developer and was co-editor for the ACM/IEEE-CS Computing Curriculum- Software Engineering 2004 project. He is a member of the ACM and the IEEE-CS and currently chairs the Curriculum Committee for the IEEE-CS Educational Activities Board and the Planning Committee for the IEEE-CS Professional Activities Board.

**Duan Hua** has received a Master in Social and Economic Foresight and a Master in Human Resources Management. He is R&D Engineer at the Public Research Centre Henri Tudor where he is actively contributing to the development of a methodology associated with the competences foresight and with the development of associated trainings. Since 2005, this methodology has been improved and enriched through the foresight and analysis of about 15 job profiles (information systems, security in the finance sector, insurance, quality, logistics, etc.). He is in charge of technology transfer activities related to the methodology and of its supporting tools. Through an INTERREG trans-regional project, he is contributing to the integration of the innovative competences foresight services into a number of training centres located in Luxembourg, France and Belgium.

**Martin Gilje Jaatun** graduated from the Norwegian Institute of Technology (NTH) in 1992, and has been employed as a research scientist at SINTEF ICT in Trondheim since 2004. His research interests include software security "for the rest of us", information security in process control environments, and security in Cloud Computing.

**Martin Gilje Jaatun** graduated from the Norwegian Institute of Technology in 1992, and has been employed as a research scientist at SINTEF ICT in Trondheim since 2004. His research interests include software security "for the rest of us", information security in process control environments, and security in Cloud Computing.

**Wouter Joosen** received the PhD degree in distributed and parallel systems from the Katholieke Universiteit Leuven, Belgium. He is a professor in the Department of Computer Science at the Katholieke Universiteit Leuven. He is also a member of the DistriNet Research Group, which aims at developing open, distributed object support platforms for advanced applications, with a focus on industrial applications. His research interests include distributed and secure software.

**Gail Kaiser** is a Professor of Computer Science and the Director of the Programming Systems Laboratory in the Computer Science Department at Columbia University. She was named an NSF Presidential Young Investigator in Software Engineering and Software Systems in 1988, and has published over 150 refereed papers in a range of software areas. Prof. Kaiser received her PhD and MS from CMU and her SB from MIT.

**Andrew J. Kornecki** is a Professor of Software Engineering at Embry-Riddle Aeronautical University, in Daytona Beach, Florida. His interests include Real-Time Software Development, Real-Time Safety Critical System Testing, Verification and Validation, Aviation Software Certification, Modeling and Computer Simulation for Decision Support, Performance Analysis, and Expert Systems Software. He has led several research projects funded by the FAA, the Guidant Corporation, Lockheed-Martin, and Motorola, and software curriculum efforts funded by the FIPSE Atlantis program. He is a member of IFAC, the IEEE, and the National Academies of Sciences.

**Seok-Won Lee** is currently a visiting professor at the University of Nebraska-Lincoln. He was an assistant professor of software engineering at the University of North Carolina Charlotte (2003-2010) and founded the Knowledge-intensive Software Engineering (NiSE) research group. Prior to joining to the UNCC, he was affiliated with Science Applications International Corporation (SAIC) and IBM T.J. Watson Research Center as senior research scientists. He received his M.Sc. in Computer Science from University of Pittsburgh, and Ph.D. in Information Technology from George Mason University. His areas of specialization include software engineering with specific expertise in ontological requirements engineering and domain modeling, and knowledge engineering with specific expertise in knowledge acquisition, machine learning and knowledge-based systems. He serves as chairs, organizers, editors and the program committee members for numerous journals, conferences, and workshops in software requirements engineering, secure software engineering and other related areas such as critical infra-structure protection, service-oriented computing, visual analytics and self-adaptive software systems. He has published more than 90 refereed articles. He is a professional member of IEEE, ACM and AAAI.

**Maria Bartnes Line** received her MSc degree from the Norwegian University of Science and Tech-nology in 2002, and has since been employed as a research scientist at SINTEF ICT in Trondheim. Her research interests include software security, privacy, intrusion detection and incident response. She is the manager of the information security research group.

**Richard Linger** is manager of the CERT Secure Systems Analysis Group at the Software Engineering Institute, Carnegie Mellon University. He directs research and development on Function Extraction (FX) technology for software behavior computation, with focus on malware analysis and software test and evaluation. He also serves as an adjunct faculty member at the CMU Heinz School of Public Policy and Management. At IBM, he co-developed Cleanroom Software Engineering technology for development of high reliability software systems, including box-structure specification, function-theoretic design and correctness verification, and statistical usage-based testing for certification of software fitness for use. He has extensive experience in project management; software specification, design, verification, testing, and certification; software re-engineering and reverse engineering; and technology transfer and educa-tion. He has published three software engineering textbooks, 12 book chapters, and over 60 papers and journal articles. He is a member of the AIAA and ACM, and a senior member of the IEEE.

**Michael E. Locasto** is a Visiting Professor at George Mason University, where he was an I3P (Insti-tute for Information Infrastructure Protection) Fellow during the 2008-2009 academic year. Dr. Locasto holds an M.Sc., M.Phil., and PhD (all in Computer Science) from Columbia University, He seeks to understand why it seems difficult to build secure systems and how we can get better at it.

**James McDonald,** Associate Professor of Software Engineering at Monmouth University, earned a bachelor's degree from New Jersey Institute of Technology, an MSEE degree from Massachusetts In-stitute of Technology and a PhD from New York University. Dr. McDonald has an extensive industrial background in electrical, computer and software engineering. He served as chair of Monmouth Univer-sity's Department of Software and Electrical Engineering from 1999 through 2008. Prior to joining the Monmouth University faculty he worked at AT&T, Bell Laboratories and Lucent Technologies. He has been responsible for development of a variety of telecommunications products, research in the areas of mathematical programming, statistics and queuing theory, corporate planning, quality engineering and the development of information systems and embedded software. He is a senior life member of the IEEE, and a member the IEEE Computer Society, ACM and ASEE. He teaches courses on Software Project Management, a Software Engineering Practicum, Information Technology and other software engineering topics. He was a recipient of the NATO System Science Prize.

**Nancy R. Mead** is a senior member of the technical staff in the CERT Program at the Software Engineering Institute (SEI). Mead is also a faculty member in the Master of Software Engineering and Master of Information Systems Management programs at Carnegie Mellon University. Her research interests are in the areas of information security, software requirements engineering, and software architectures. Mead has more than 150 publications and invited presentations. She is a Fellow of the Institute of Electrical and Electronic Engineers, Inc. (IEEE) and a Distinguished Member of the Association for Computing Machinery (ACM). Dr. Mead received her PhD in mathematics from the Polytechnic Institute of New York, and received a BA and an MS in mathematics from New York University.

**Nancy R. Mead** is a senior member of the technical staff in the CERT Program at the Software Engineering Institute (SEI). Mead is also a faculty member in the Master of Software Engineering and Master of Information Systems Management programs at Carnegie Mellon University. Her research interests are in the areas of information security, software requirements engineering, and software architectures. Mead has more than 100 publications and invited presentations. She is a Fellow of the Institute of Electrical and Electronic Engineers, Inc. (IEEE) and is also a member of the Association for Computing Machinery (ACM). Dr. Mead received her PhD in mathematics from the Polytechnic Institute of New York, and received a BA and an MS in mathematics from New York University.

**Per Håkon Meland** graduated from NTNU in 2002, and has since been employed as a research scientist at SINTEF ICT in Trondheim. His research interests include software security and service engineering within domains such as healthcare and telecom, and with a special focus on early security awareness and improvements during the software development lifecycle.

**Bertrand Meunier** has received a Master in Social and Economic Foresight and a Master in Human Resources Management. He is R&D Engineer at the Public Research Centre Henri Tudor where he is actively contributing to the development of a methodology associated with the competences foresight and with the development of associated trainings. Since 2005, this methodology has been improved and enriched through the foresight and analysis of about 15 job profiles (information systems, security in the finance sector, insurance, quality, logistics, etc.). He is in charge of technology transfer activities related to the methodology and of its supporting tools. Through an INTERREG trans-regional project, he is contributing to the integration of the innovative competences foresight services into a number of training centres located in Luxembourg, France and Belgium.

**Laurent Michel** is an Associate Professor of Computer Science & Engineering at the University of Connecticut with research interests of: combinatorial optimization, constraint programming, local search, programming languages, and artificial intelligence. Dr. Michel has over 65 archival publications, in the following categories: 2 books, 22 journal articles and book chapters, and 41 refereed conference/workshop articles.

**Christian Murphy** is a PhD Candidate in the Computer Science department at Columbia University. He is a member of the Programming Systems Lab, and his research focuses on software testing, computer science education, and computer-supported cooperative work. He earned a BS (summa cum laude) in Computer Engineering from Boston University in 1995, and an MS in Computer Science from Columbia University in 2006.

**Armstrong Nhlabatsi** is a postdoctoral research associate at the Computing Research Centre in the Open University. His PhD, completed in 2009, focussed on initialisation problems in feature composition. His research interests include feature composition, software evolution, and security requirements engineering. He holds an MSc in Software Engineering from the University of the West of England (2005) and a B. Eng in Electronic Engineering from the University of Swaziland (2000).

**Torstein Nicolaysen** is an MSc student in Computer Science at the Norwegian University of Science and Technology (NTNU). After the completion of his MSc thesis, he will start working for BEKK Consulting. His research interests include making software security more agile, software security in general, Agile methodologies, software development and craftsmanship.

**Bashar Nuseibeh** is Professor of Computing at The Open University, and a Visiting Professor at Imperial College London and the National Institute of Informatics, Japan. He received his PhD degree in Software Engineering from Imperial College London in 1994. His research interests are in software requirements engineering and design, particularly applied to the development of dependable, mission-critical systems. Professor Nuseibeh is formerly Editor-in-Chief of the Automated Software Engineering Journal and Chair of the Steering Committee of the International Conference on Software Engineering. He is currently Chair of IFIP Working Group 2.9 on Requirements Engineering, and is forthcoming Editor-in-Chief of IEEE Transactions on Software Engineering. He received a number of research and service awards, and is an Automated Software Engineering Fellow, a Fellow of the British Computer Society and the Institution of Engineering and Technology, and is a Chartered Engineer.

**James Oakley**, originally a Massachusetts native, is a third-year undergraduate Computer Science student at Dartmouth College. Having come to computer programming by way of microcontroller programming, he enjoys hands-on work with low level systems. His interests include computer graphics (especially culling systems), digital electronics, security, and operating systems. In his unprofessional time he enjoys backpacking, science fiction, and designing games.

**Frank Piessens** is a professor in the Department of Computer Science at the Katholieke Universiteit Leuven, Belgium. His research interests are in software security, including security in operating systems and middleware, architectures, applications, Java, and .NET, and software interfaces to security technologies. He is an active participant in both fundamental research and industrial application-driven projects, provides consulting to industry on distributed system security, and serves on program committees for various security-related international scientific conferences.

**Viatcheslav M. Popovsky**, Ph.D., is an Affiliate Professor at the University of Idaho, where he is responsible for the development of international exchange (Russian/American) for increasing the professional knowledge of educators in the fields of sport, physical education and recreation. He received his Doctor of Philosophy (Kandidat Nauk) of Pedagogical Science from the Lesgaft University in former Leningrad, Soviet Union, where he received his Diploma of Associate Professor from the Ministry for Advanced and Secondary Specialized Education in Moscow, USSR (1987). While an Associate Professor at Lesgaft, Dr. Popovsky created innovative pedagogical programs implemented within the University, locally and nationwide—focusing student/athletes and coaches on achieving their best. He also advised and mentored many doctoral candidates in the successful achievement of their doctoral theses. He has published 60 books and articles in several countries—a prolific author in the field of physical culture. In addition, he has achieved various awards and recognition throughout his academic career.

**Hossain Shahriar** is currently a PhD student in the School of Computing, Queen's University, Canada, where he is a member of the Queen's Reliable Software Technology (QRST) research group. Mr. Shahriar is an expert on software security testing and monitoring with extensive publications and industry experience in the area of software and security engineering. He obtained his MSc degree in Computer Science from Queen's University, Canada, while his MSc thesis research on security testing received the IEEE Kingston Section Research Excellence award. Mr. Shahriar also has been awarded the prestigious Natural Sciences and Engineering Research Council (NSERC) and Ontario Graduate Scholarships for his PhD study. He is a student member of the IEEE and the ACM. More information about his research and publications can be obtained from http://cs.queensu.ca/~shahriar.

**Ashwin Ramaswamy** studied Operating Systems security as a Masters student at Dartmouth College, and graduated in 2009 under Prof. Sean Smith and Prof. Sergey Bratus. He now works at a financial firm.

**Richard Sassoon** recently completed his MSc in Information Security as part of the Erasmus Mundus NordSecMob programme at NTNU and the University of Tartu. His interests include software engineering, software testing (including security testing), and software security with focus on web security. He is currently employed as a software developer at MVisjon AS.

**Joseph J. Simpson** is a Principal with System Concepts, LLC. His experience and interests are focused in the area of complex systems, system science, systems thinking and systems management. Joseph has professional experience in domain areas including environmental restoration, information systems, systems security, aerospace and defense. He was educated at the University of Washington, where he received the B.S. (1988), and the M.S. (1990) in Civil Engineering. He also attended the Missouri University of Science and Technology where he received the M.S. (2004) in Systems Engineering. Joseph is a current Member of INCOSE, and a Sr. Member of IEEE. Joseph's current activities are associated with complex systems modeling, evolutionary programming, the development of a systems engineering language, and organizational assessment and improvement.

**Mary J. Simpson** is a Research Analyst with System Concepts, LLC. Her experience and research interests focus on cognitive support and decision-making systems, integration and complexity reduction, threat and vulnerability analysis, systems sciences and systems engineering. Mary applies systems solutions to complex problems encountered in organizations, processes, and systems interactions ranging from strategic to tactical levels in fields including aerospace, security, information systems, and defense systems. She was educated at the University of Washington, where she received the B.A. (1969) in English, and the B.S. (1990) in Electrical Engineering. Mary is a current Member of INCOSE and of IEEE. Mary's current activities are associated with the formulation and communication of systems concepts and patterns regarding discovery, analysis, optimization, design, verification, validation and testing of systems, and systems of systems, including system attributes of maintainability, supportability, testability, safety, and security.

**Sean Smith** has been working in information security---attacks and defenses---since before there was a Web. He worked for Los Alamos National Lab and IBM Watson before joining the Dartmouth faculty at the turn of the century.

**San-Tsai Sun** is a PhD student in the Electrical and Computer Engineering department (ECE) at the University of British Columbia (UBC). He works in the the Laboratory for Education and Research in Secure Systems Engineering (LERSSE) under the supervision of Professor Konstantin Beznosov. His research interests include Web application security, Web 2.0 security and privacy, and distributed access control architectures. His research focuses on improving the usability of access controls in Web-related systems. Before joining UBC, he was a Information Technology Director at the UCOM Training Center in the Systex Corporation, Taiwan. He obtained his Master degree in Computer Science from Fairleigh Dickinson University (FDU) in 1994.

**Hans Van den Eynden** worked on the research reported in this paper as a master student in computer science & engineering at the Katholieke Universiteit Leuven. His master thesis research focused mainly on Security in Dynamic Memory Allocators. Since 2006 he works for KBC, a Belgian bank, as business analyst risk management.

**George Yee** is an Adjunct Research Professor at Carleton University, Ottawa, Canada, and consults as opportunities arise. He was previously a Senior Research Officer for seven and a half years in the Information Security Group, Institute for Information Technology, National Research Council Canada (NRC). Prior to the NRC, he spent eighteen years as a member of scientific staff and manager at Bell-Northern Research and Nortel Networks. George received his Ph.D. in Electrical Engineering from Carleton University and is a member of Professional Engineers Ontario. In addition, he is a Certified Information Systems Security Professional (CISSP), a Senior Member of IEEE, and a member of ACM. George's research interests include security and privacy for electronic services, privacy assurance for enterprise computing systems, and software engineering for security, privacy, reliability, and performance. A list of his publications may be found at: http://georgeyee.ca.

**Yves Younan** received a Master in Computer Science from the Vrije Universiteit Brussel and a PhD in Engineering: Computer Science from the Katholieke Universiteit Leuven. His PhD focused on efficient countermeasures against code injection attacks on programs written in C and C++. He is currently a post-doctoral researcher at the DistriNet research group, which is part of the Department of Computer Science of the Katholieke Universiteit Leuven, where he continues the research in the area of systems security that was started in his PhD. This research has led to several actual countermeasures being designed and publicly released. Publications are available at http://www.fort-knox.org.

**Yijun Yu** graduated from the Department of Computer Science at Fudan University (B.Sc. 1992, M.Sc. 1995, Ph.D. 1998). He was a postdoc. research fellow at the Department of Electrical Engineering in Ghent University (1999-2002), then he worked as a research associate at the Knowledge Management lab of the Department of Computer Science in University of Toronto (2003-2006). Since October 2006, he has become a Senior Lecturer at the Department of Computing in The Open University. He is a member of the IEEE Computer Society and the British Computer Society. His research interests are mainly in Automated Software Engineering and Requirements Engineering.

**Mohammad Zulkernine** is an Associate Professor in the School of Computing of Queen's University, Canada, where he leads the Queen's Reliable Software Technology (QRST) research group. Currently, he is a Visiting Professor in the Dept. of Information Engg. & Computer Science of the University of Trento, Italy. Dr. Zulkernine received his BSc from Bangladesh University of Engineering and Technology and MEng from Muroran Institute of Technology, Japan. He received his PhD from the University of Waterloo, Canada, where he belonged to the university's Bell Canada Software Reliability Laboratory. Dr. Zulkernine's current research focuses on software reliability and security. His research projects are funded by a number of provincial and federal research organizations of Canada, while he is having industry research partnerships with Bell Canada and Cloakware Corporation. Dr. Zulkernine is a senior member of the IEEE, a member of the ACM, and a licensed professional engineer of the province of Ontario, Canada. More information about his research can be found at http://cs.queensu.ca/~mzulker.

# Index